Media Violence
and Children

Media Violence and Children

A COMPLETE GUIDE FOR PARENTS AND PROFESSIONALS, SECOND EDITION

Douglas A. Gentile, Editor
Foreword by Michael Rich, MD, MPH

 PRAEGER

AN IMPRINT OF ABC-CLIO, LLC
Santa Barbara, California • Denver, Colorado • Oxford, England

Copyright © 2014 by Douglas A. Gentile

Library of Congress Cataloging-in-Publication Data

Media violence and children : a complete guide for parents and professionals /
   Douglas A. Gentile, editor ; foreword by Michael Rich, MD, MPH.—Second edition.
      pages cm
   Includes index.
      ISBN 978–1–4408–3017–4 (alk. paper)—ISBN 978–1–4408–3018–1 (ebook)   1. Children and violence.   2. Violence in mass media.   I. Gentile, Douglas A., 1964–
HQ784.V55M43   2014
303.6083—dc23   2014016047

ISBN: 978–1–4408–3017–4
EISBN: 978–1–4408–3018–1

18 17 16 15 14   1 2 3 4 5

This book is also available on the World Wide Web as an eBook.
Visit www.abc-clio.com for details.

Praeger
An Imprint of ABC-CLIO, LLC

ABC-CLIO, LLC
130 Cremona Drive, P.O. Box 1911
Santa Barbara, California 93116-1911

This book is printed on acid-free paper ∞

Manufactured in the United States of America

The truth knocks on the door and you say,
"Go away, I'm looking for the truth," and so it goes away. Puzzling.

—Robert M. Pirsig, *Zen and the Art of Motorcycle Maintenance*

Contents

Foreword

Violence is exciting! Your eyes and mind are focused. Your heart is in your throat. You fear, you struggle, then you prevail in an explosion of triumph and relief.

We are today what we have always been—hunter-gatherers, evolutionarily programmed to win conflicts in order to survive. We are predators and potential prey—eat or be eaten, kill or be killed. When threatened, we feel the *frisson* of excitement as epinephrine is released. We go on high alert; our heart rates jump, our blood pressure surges, and reflexively we fight or flee. If we successfully kill or escape our opponent, our pleasure centers are flooded with dopamine, powerful reward for behaviors that keep us in the gene pool.

Today, we no longer venture warily out of the cave to seek sustenance. For most of us, daily life is distanced from the primal conflicts of our ancestors. Brain has long ago superseded brawn in the competition for survival. Few of us even break a sweat to earn our daily bread, let alone take our lives in our hands or take the lives of others. We have devised safety devices that protect us in our automobiles and our children on the playgrounds. We have realized a level of human and technological evolution that futurist H. G. Wells anticipated more than a century ago when he wrote,

In these plethoric times, when there is too much coarse stuff for everybody and the struggle for life takes the form of a competitive advertisement and the effort to fill your neighbor's eye, there is no urgent demand either for personal courage, sound nerves or stark beauty, we find ourselves by accident . . . never really hungry nor frightened nor passionately stirred, your highest moment a mere sentimental orgasm, and your first real contact with primary and elemental necessities the sweat of your death bed. (*Tono-Bungay*, 1909)

Because of the absence of "elemental necessities" in our daily lives, we now seek out experiences that give us those rushes of epinephrine and dopamine. Some take real risks, with football, fighting, or extreme sports, but most of us pursue vicarious risk, through a character with whom we identify in a movie or whom we inhabit in a video game. Worldwide, the indirect experience of violence—evading violence, perpetrating violence, and just watching violence—is the most universal and popular form of entertainment. This was brought home to me in a very visceral way when I was traveling in the developing world a few years ago. After struggling through language and cultural barriers to order a meal in rural Indonesia, I looked up at the sound of blood-curdling screams to see a group of local farmers tightly clustered around the restaurant television, watching *Friday the 13th*. Entertainment is America's greatest export; for these men, as for many, our movies, television, and video games are what define the people, lifestyle, and culture of the United States.

Violence works in any language and in any culture because it resonates with our deeper, more primal selves. Since it triggers a reliable reflexive response, violent media content is less expensive to make and much easier to export, a more attractive business investment than entertainment that requires dialogue and cultural understanding to develop characters and complex relationships. From a desperado firing his six-shooter directly at the audience in *The Great Train Robbery* (1903) to the latest version of first-person shooter video games, each of which tops the last in first-day earnings, violent media blockbusters make audiences gasp, thrill with victory, and empty their wallets for more. As attractive as potential profits may be in the short term, we must consider the long-term costs of violent media to individuals and to society.

Because of the potential for windfall profits, violent media will always be made, but the marketplace is crowded. In order to get noticed, a product needs to be different—more unexpected, scarier, and "edgier," that is, more violent. So the first problem that media producers must overcome is the most consistent human response to viewing violent media—desensitization. Media producers and researchers alike have known for years that what scares and excites audiences today will not work tomorrow. Humans are adaptable organisms. Our ability to learn and manage threats has always been critical to our survival. We respond to violence viscerally the first time we experience it, but we anticipate and prepare for it the second time. It is then "old news," fully integrated into our library of experience by the third or fourth exposure. This presents a problem for media producers. They must constantly be topping their previous efforts. The problem that desensitization presents to parents, teachers, psychologists, and society is less immediate and concrete than drop-offs in box office receipts but, as work in this book reveals, no less real and measurable. Desensitization allows one to face violence without flinching, but it also requires one to expect and accept violence in one's world and to be inured to the human suffering that results. The question is whether we want our children and the world they will create to be desensitized by their entertainment.

Although the cliché that children are our future is true, what is more important to realize is that they are our society's potential. A child is constantly observing the world and building her library of human experience. For her, every moment is a "teachable moment" as she learns about herself and others, and the way to interact in successful and healthy ways. Entertainment media made by adults for adults often portray what George Gerbner called a "mean world," a world in which the innocent are victimized and the strongest and meanest prevail. Developmental psychology has demonstrated that children are unable to reliably distinguish fantasy from reality under the age of eight. The adult minds of media producers and consumers, which experience the world through a filter of life experience, including virtual experience through media, are able to see violence as make-believe and distance themselves from the human reality of what they are witnessing. We entertain ourselves with television depicting bullets slicing through brains in slow motion. We divert ourselves from the boredom of daily life by killing as many enemies as we can before they corner us. Some adults see media as a safe way to "toughen up" children for the rigors of adult competition. We may forget, however, that a child's brain is not the same as an adult brain. It is still developing, not only learning about the world but actually making synaptic connections that are reinforced by use or pruned away in disuse. Humans ended up with the most sophisticated brains in the animal kingdom in part because we built them in response to the environment and its challenges. If children grow up witnessing violence, their brains will be built so that they accept violence and learn to live with it.

While there is little point in challenging the oft-stated assertion that entertainment media simply reflect the reality of the world's violence rather than creating violent content, what this argument ignores is the basic fact that media are constructed. Media select what to show and not show and media establish relationships between what is shown. From John Wayne to John Price, media violence, especially the "justified violence" of American cultural legend, focuses on the success of the strong rather than the suffering of the victims. Children aspire to prevail. The lesson they learn is to emulate the victor and to ignore and never become the victim.

This collection of work by researchers in psychology, medicine, communication, and media studies examines the effects of violent media on children and adolescents—how they are actually changed when they witness and perpetrate virtual violence. Drawing together a rich diversity of disciplines and perspectives, the theory and research presented here refocus a public discourse that has become polarized, politicized, and infantilized. While academics debate and policymakers stalemate, families have struggled to make the best choices, losing in the noisy academic argument the important information they need to make thoughtful decisions about how to raise happy, healthy, and successful children in the digital age.

As a pediatrician, as an educator, and most importantly, as a parent, I have been frustrated by the values-driven debate that has probably been occurring since we began telling stories around the cave fire, but that has accelerated with the rapid adoption of television in American homes. Congressional hearings convened in the early and mid-1950s to discuss whether television contributed to juvenile delinquency called on experts from psychology to television. Ultimately, the conclusion drawn was that, indeed, television was a powerful medium and that it was important to our youth and our future to portray the right content. The broadcast industry vowed to do so. In 1968, when the winds of social change led to the lifting of government censorship, the movie industry established a rating system through which they committed to inform the viewing public and protect young people from exposure to age-inappropriate material. Politicians and the public were assuaged and media producers followed market demand. When concerns were raised by parents, teachers, pediatricians, and child advocates, they were brushed aside as "moral panic" generated by narrow-thinking people whose values did not agree with those of the media producers and, presumably, their audience. Because this debate was framed from the beginning as "good vs. bad" and "right vs. wrong," it has been dealt with as a First Amendment issue, a debate over freedom of expression, rather than the healthy development of children. Children and adults alike enjoy and benefit from our hard-won constitutional rights. Ultimately, however, this debate is misdirection from a critical issue on which we need to focus—our responsibility to the well-being of our youngest and most vulnerable citizens, who deserve another of Norman Rockwell's iconic "Four Freedoms": freedom from fear.

In an era when children spend more waking time with media than in any other activity and schools are increasingly teaching with interactive screens, the media children use is no longer just an issue of personal values, but of determining measurable outcomes and choosing the ways children are changed by the media they consume. In our diverse country, there are many different value systems, built on a wide array of cultures, religions, and family traditions. Parents can form and promote their own values in raising their children. They can and do make decisions about raising their children based on their hopes for what their children will become, but they should be able to consider unbiased scientific evidence in making parenting decisions. Just as parents can weigh both their values and scientific findings in considering controversial and value-laden child-rearing decisions from circumcision to immunizations to education, they can and deserve to be aware of what is known about how media can influence their children. What we feed a child's mind is as important as what we feed her body, and we should apply as much attention and care to children's media use as we do to their nutrition.

As you will see from the scientific findings presented in this book, and as many parents, teachers, and pediatricians have observed, children exposed to violent media can exhibit behavior changes ranging from sleep disturbances, academic struggles, and poor socialization to increases in anxiety, depression, and violent behavior. Historically, however, the only times that concern about media violence has risen above the level of parental annoyance into public discourse have been after tragedies like the school shootings at Columbine and Sandy Hook. In the chaos and terror surrounding such horrific events, we seek answers in our attempts to regain control. We point to the violent video games the young shooters played as the explanation, the "cause" of their violent behavior. But, as the media producers and their apologists point out, millions of young people play these games and very few perpetrate school shootings. And they are right—to argue this point actually weakens the case for concern about media violence. The increases in aggressive thoughts and behaviors associated with exposure to media violence are most commonly incremental, much more likely to result in mean behavior, verbal abuse, bullying, or punches thrown earlier in interpersonal conflicts than in extreme violence, which is rare and requires the confluence of mental health problems, access to weapons, and often other issues to occur. By allowing the debate to be narrowed to whether media violence causes school shootings, we have missed the larger issue of how our children are affected.

As you will see in the work presented here, researchers have found wide-ranging influences of exposure to media violence on the psychological and social well-being of young people and the adults they will become. The popular press, in earnest attempts to practice balanced journalism, seeks out opposing opinions on any issue. This strategy, which works so well in public policy, serves science poorly. With the best of intentions, the popular press has found minority opinions, often only a single person who disagrees with and seeks to "debunk" the scientific evidence, and presented these opinions with the same weight as the science he or she opposes. As a result, public perception can be that scientific opinion is split—but what the public does not know is that the split is closer to 99/1 than 50/50.

The confusion among the general public is not solely due to media producers seeking to protect their investments and balanced journalism gone awry. The scientific community can do better at communicating research to the public. How findings are described by researchers can be interpreted variably by laypeople—leading to public misunderstanding and vulnerability to criticism. Specifically, the word "causal" is often interpreted to mean "A causes B, therefore every time A occurs, B will necessarily follow." This is obviously not true in the case of media violence and violent behavior, but criticism of this popular interpretation of the science has led to dismissal of the evidence by the public and even the U.S. Supreme Court. Perhaps the public would be better served by reframing the issue of media violence in terms of public health, where we seldom speak of causality (even with smoking and lung cancer) because of the variability among individuals and the nature of their exposures, but rather of alterations in "relative risk." If the public and the Court were to understand that, like smoking, exposure to media violence can increase the risk of anxiety, depression, desensitization, and, in some cases, violent behavior, they would understand it better and respond with more reasoned and compassionate decisions for their children and for society.

Ultimately, it comes down to what we do, as individuals and as a society, in response to the scientific research presented here. A Luddite approach of limiting devices or arbitrarily restricting content or screen time is unrealistic, unwise, and as likely to backfire as Prohibition. Neither can we continue to increase digital content consumption unthinkingly. The media industry's double standard of seeking to introduce digital devices and content into schools as powerful educational tools while disputing that children learn from or are changed by entertainment media: does not square with logic. Children and adolescents live and breathe media: engaging, connecting, learning, and changing in response to what they experience through media. We can no longer afford to convince ourselves that our children "know it's only make-believe" and expose them to ever more "edgy" entertainment, risking poorer physical, mental, and social health outcomes in the long term for what H. G. Wells called a "sentimental orgasm." We must read, learn, and make difficult decisions about how we will raise, teach, and care for today's digital natives. The health of our children and the future they will create is too important to do any less.

Michael Rich, MD, MPH

Introduction

The first edition of this volume was released just over a decade ago. At that time, it was clear that media violence was one of the most-studied phenomena in all of psychology. It was also clear that youth aggression is a complex phenomenon with multiple risk factors that can influence it, media violence being just one among many. Nonetheless, there was strong consensus among public health professionals, medical organizations, and psychological researchers that media violence was an important one. For example, the American Medical Association, the American Academy of Pediatrics, the American Psychological Association, the National Institute of Mental Health, the American Academy of Child and Adolescent Psychiatry, and two U.S. Surgeon Generals had each reviewed the accumulated research and concluded that media violence is a causal risk factor for aggression. In the past decade, there have been several surprising new developments.

First, as video games moved from being a niche product to being mainstream, the research increased dramatically. There were dozens of published studies about the effects of video games in 2003, and now there are hundreds.

Second, although there had been hundreds of studies examining the psychological and behavioral effects of media violence, we had almost no studies on the neural effects. Our ability to measure the effects at a neural level has increased with improvements in electroencephalography (EEG) and functional magnetic resonance imaging (fMRI) techniques.

Third, media continue to change dramatically. If we look all the way back to 1973, there were three major television stations in the United States, no home computers, no home video game systems, no cell phones, and so on. You watched whatever happened to be on. By 1993 there were hundreds of stations on cable TV, many homes had computers, the Internet was just beginning, and video game systems were starting to become popular. Currently, television is often watched on handheld devices such as iPads, or streamed over computers or Blu-ray players. Most children now have cell phones, handheld video game players, video game consoles, digital video recorders, and so on. This personalization of media has dramatically changed the landscape, allowing children to see things without their parents knowing about it. The Internet also allows for a much wider range of things to see.

Fourth, partly because of these changes in media, children now have far greater access to media and spend far more time with them than ever before in human history. This makes the question about the benefits and risks of media exposure more important. It also has allowed new venues for some old behaviors. For example, although there have always been children who are willing to be mean to other children, this used to be limited by physical proximity and physical ability. Now that children have access to text messaging, social media, and the Internet, they also have new opportunities to perpetrate aggression and to be victimized.

The final surprise of the past decade is that there has been a strong backlash against the science on media violence. Several new strident voices have come to the fore, making strong claims (with no evidence that I can find) that media violence researchers are biased, doing "junk" science, and fomenting a "moral panic." This anti-science backlash has also been seen in the climate change "debate" and the evolution "debate," and is reminiscent of the debates over smoking and lung cancer. What is surprising to me is not that there are people who have opinions that are at odds with the research—that will always be the case. What surprises is the vitriolic tone that the dissenters (and some of the proponents) have taken. Everyone has opinions. The "magic" of science is that it helps us to separate out which opinions have substance behind them. The data are what they are . . . so it surprises me how emotional people get when discussing them.

In this context, it seemed appropriate to ask several of the most respected researchers to write new or updated chapters for this second edition. After 50 years of high-quality research on media violence, one might be forgiven for expecting that we have all of the answers. Again, however, the magic of science is that every question answered leads to more interesting questions.

This scientific curiosity is represented well by the chapters in this book. Much is known and there are still several interesting questions to be answered, and the chapter authors provide measured, expert discussion of each topic.

Finally, I will relate this personal anecdote. As one might imagine, I am very strict with what my children may watch, and they grew up actively discussing the meaning of content and why we choose to watch what we watch. When my older daughter turned 10, I was finally willing (and eager) to let her see the original *Star Wars* movie. This was an important film for me, given that it came out when I was a 12-year-old boy.

She refused to see it.

Her reason? "It's all about people fighting with each other. Why do I want to watch that?" My begging fell on deaf ears. Sometimes when we get what we want, we don't get what we want.

This paradox fits the research. Aggression is partly (many would say largely) a set of learned behaviors. Media violence research has shown us that when we watch, we learn. This answer isn't what any of us would want, but it makes sense. Humans can learn just by seeing something once. We learn it really well if we see it repeatedly. And if we see it repeatedly in multiple contexts, we can more easily use what we learned out in the "real" world. Even this, however, is far too simplistic an explanation. The chapters in this book provide many of the details that allow us to go beyond simple explanations. I am deeply grateful to the authors, each of whom is a true expert in his or her discipline. I am also grateful to my daughters and wife for their support.

Douglas A. Gentile, PhD

CHAPTER 1

The Proliferation of Media Violence and Its Economic Underpinnings

James J. Lindsay, Karen E. Dill-Shackleford, Kathryn B. Anderson, and Bruce D. Bartholow

Violence in entertainment is as old as civilization itself. The Romans delighted in watching gladiators fight for survival. Dramatic theater—from the ancient Greeks to Shakespeare to Andrew Lloyd Webber—has always been thick with jealousy, retribution, and violence. However, it was not until the mass media explosion of the twentieth century that heavy doses of violence were made available to everyone, every day. Over the past hundred years, as media have become more available, they have also become infused with more violent content (e.g., Bushman & Anderson, 2001). This chapter reviews the amount of media consumed by American youth, the amount of violence in the media, and the economic mechanisms that perpetuate media violence. We also analyze two common arguments offered by media executives for continuing to create violent products: "media content reflects real life" and "violence sells."

RECENT CHANGES IN MASS MEDIA CONSUMPTION

media [mee-dee-*uh*] *noun* 1. a plural of medium [one of the means or channels of general communication, information, or entertainment in society, as newspapers, radio, or television]. 2. (*usually used with a plural verb*) the means of communication, as radio and television, newspapers, and magazines, that reach or influence people widely. 3. *adjective* pertaining to or concerned with such means. . . .

—Dictionary.com (2013)

Throughout the majority of the twentieth century, media consumption aligned with the definition above. That is, people obtained their news and much of their entertainment through distinct modes of communication: print (e.g., books, newspapers); television; audio (radio, compact discs, MP3s); motion pictures; and video games. Dramatic changes to media consumption have occurred since 1990. These changes are due largely to advances in Internet functionality and availability. What they mean for consumers, especially youth, is that where and how we access media has changed. Those changes, especially as they relate to the economics of media and media violence, are documented here.

SHIFTS IN TECHNOLOGY

As first observed by Intel executives in the 1960s, the performance of integrated circuits in computers doubles every 18 months (Moore, 1965; *The Economist*, 2005). This principle—sometimes referred to as Moore's law—holds true for other digital and electronic devices as well (e.g., digital audio devices, video cameras). By the late 1990s and early 2000s, advancements in computer circuits and associated software, and in the breadth and speed of Internet connectivity, made it possible for people to create, share, and consume new media-transmitted content.

For many people with access to technology, the Internet also has become a sole source for media. People can download movies, music, television, radio, and video games with nothing more than a computer, smartphone, or tablet, and a connection to the Internet (and sometimes a credit card). News is similarly accessed via the Internet "24/7." These devices also serve as the main conduit for interpersonal communications. Through the Internet or cellular technology, people can send texts, e-mail, and pictures, stay connected with friends through social media, have face-to-face conversations with people, and conduct meetings with others located around the world, even with live video feeds.

Thus, the Internet has revolutionized how people in economically developed countries interact. Recent data indicate that 56 percent of adult Americans own a device capable of retrieving multiple media (smartphone, tablet) (Smith, 2013), while 37 percent of teens own a smartphone and 25 percent own a tablet (Madden, Lenhart, Duggan, Cortesi, & Gasser, 2013). Moreover, 70 percent of children under 12 living in the homes of adult tablet owners use them for games, educational applications, or communication with family or friends (Nielsen, 2013).

YOUTH MEDIA HABITS

In 2009 the Kaiser Family Foundation surveyed youth ages 8 to 18 about their use of media and had some of these young people keep diaries of their media use. The researchers found that in addition to using mobile devices for texting and calling friends, American youth consumed 20 percent of media

Figure 1.1
Hours of Media Consumption per Day among American Youth (ages 8 to 18) from 1999–2009

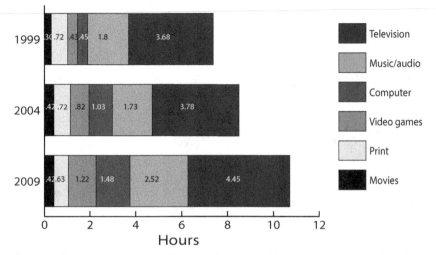

Note: Numbers in bars represent hours and percent of hours. Time spent multitasking is counted double.
Source: Kaiser Family Foundation: Rideout, Foehr, & Roberts (2010).

using a mobile device (Rideout, Foehr, & Roberts, 2010). According to the authors: "Try waking a teenager in the morning, and the odds are good that you'll find a cell phone tucked under their pillow—the last thing they touch before falling asleep and the first thing they reach for upon waking" (Rideout et al., 2010, p. 2).

It should come as little surprise that the overall media consumption among American youth ages 8 to 18 has increased. The Kaiser studies also revealed that between 1999 and 2009, the average media consumption among American youth increased by 20 percent, from 6 hours, 19 seconds to 7 hours, 38 seconds per day. Nearly all of that increase occurred between 2004 and 2009 (Rideout et al., 2010).

However, these time estimates tell only part of the story. American youth often use multiple media simultaneously (i.e., multitasking), such as listening to their iPods while doing homework on the computer, or texting on their smartphones while watching television with the family. Multitasking has become much easier due to the proliferation of mobile media devices. When the researchers counted independently the times during which youth were consuming two types of media simultaneously, the numbers become even more startling. As seen in Figure 1.1, media *exposure* increased from 7 hours, 29 minutes in 1999 to 10 hours, 45 minutes *per day* in 2009 (Rideout et al., 2010).

The Kaiser report suggests that increased accessibility to media content through the Internet and mobile devices is likely responsible for the recent increases in television viewing, listening to music, computer use, and video games. The only media platforms that have not benefitted from the Internet and cellular devices are print media (i.e., newspapers and books) and motion pictures (Rideout et al., 2010).

MEDIA GENRES AND YOUTH

Television

The average time spent watching television among 8- to 18-year-olds increased only slightly between 1999 and 2004 (four minutes); however, during the next five years (2004–2009), television watching jumped an average of 38 minutes. To explain the increase, the researchers suggest that the Internet has made it much easier to watch programs that are missed. They estimated that 41 percent of the consumption of television programming by youth is either "time shifted" (i.e., watched at times other than the scheduled broadcast time) or viewed via a platform other than a television set (Rideout et al., 2010). Smartphones and tablets also make it possible to consume television content anywhere within range of an Internet link or cellular tower. The end result is that children ages 2–11 years will watch an average of at least 1,350 hours of television programming a year, while those ages 12–17 years will watch 1,280 hours per year (Nielsen, 2013). Note that the average number of hours in an American school year is 1,195 (U.S. Department of Education, n.d.). By age 65, Americans will have spent nine years watching television.

Music

Ownership of MP3 players and iPods among children ages 8–18 years has exploded as well. In 2004 only 18 percent of children owned these devices. By 2009 this number jumped to 76 percent. These devices, combined with easy access to MP3 files on the Internet, have led to a 40 percent increase in consumption of music and other audio content between 1999 and 2009. One hour and 44 seconds per day were spent by American youth listening to music or other audio in 1999. Ten years later, this number had jumped to two-and-a-half hours. The Kaiser poll also indicated that in 2009 American youth's preferred platform for music was the iPod/MP3 player (41 minutes), followed by radio and computer (32 minutes for each), and CD and cell phone, accounting for 17 minutes each (Rideout et al., 2010). Moreover, audio is often one of the tasks involved in multitasking. When the Kaiser researchers asked their survey respondents how often they listened to music while doing other activities (e.g., using a computer, watching TV, reading), 43 percent responded "most of the time," 30 percent responded "some of the time," 14 percent responded "a little," and 10 percent responded "never." The numbers of those who responded "most of the time" had jumped 10 percent since 2003–2004.

Computers

Between 1999 and 2009 laptop ownership increased 17 percent in the United States. Computer usage consequently has increased by a full hour per day on average, from 27 minutes to 1 hour, 29 minutes. Home Internet access almost doubled, from 47 percent of American youth with home Internet access in 1999 to 84 percent in 2009. Computers plus Internet service enable youth to access other types of media content, from streaming video, watching previously aired television programs, and downloading music and video games. They can even obtain print material online, such as books, but the Kaiser report notes that young people have less interest in print than they had in 1999. Computers that access the Internet also have become a primary means of communication (i.e., e-mail, Skype), obtaining goods (e.g., through Amazon, eBay), and performing research. It is not surprising, then, that computer use among youth tripled between 1999 and 2009 (Rideout et al., 2010).

Video Games

The quality and realism of video games have made game play more appealing to youth and adults alike. Video game play has become part of what it means to be a youth in the United States. As of 2009 children between the ages of 8 and 18 spent an average of 1 hour and 13 minutes per day playing console or handheld video games (excluding computer games), an increase of 47 minutes since 1999. Video game consoles are common in the homes of American youth, with 87 percent having such devices. If a child is unable to use a particular game console (e.g., a Playstation), they can use a secondary device (e.g., a Wii or an iPad), if available. In 2009 the average child's home had 2.3 video game devices that children could choose from (Rideout et al., 2010).

The most recent nationally representative data on children's video game preferences come from a Pew Internet and American Life survey of 1,102 teens conducted in 2008 (Lenhart et al., 2008). The survey indicated that nearly all children play video games. When asked to list the games they have played, they mentioned a large variety of specific games (2,618 games in all). The games fall into 14 different genres (in order of frequency of naming): racing, puzzle, sport, action, adventure, rhythm, strategy, simulations, fighting, first-person shooter, role playing, survival/horror, multiplayer online games, and virtual world games (Lenhart et al., 2008).

Motion Pictures

In the 2009 Kaiser survey, the researchers defined "movies" as watching films at a movie theater. Viewing movies on the computer or television (via Blu-Ray, DVD, or streaming) was counted as time spent on the computer and watching television, respectively. On average, young Americans spent about 25 minutes per day at the movies, which equates to one two-and-a-half-hour feature film (plus previews) every seven days. It may be that young people still watch movies but prefer to get them in "time shifted" form (i.e., DVD, Internet, streaming), rather than pay for the big-screen experience.

Print Media

Young people in 2009 spent an average of only 17 minutes per day reading newspapers, magazines, and books. This estimate is five minutes less per day than that for respondents in the 1999 study (Rideout et. al., 2010). Given the decline of the newspaper and magazine industries during this 10-year period, a corresponding decrease in reading these types of print material is not surprising. Several large-city newspapers have stopped publishing newspapers, while others have declared bankruptcy (e.g., *Chicago Sun-Times*, *Denver Post*, *Minneapolis Star-Tribune*, *Philadelphia Enquirer*, *Arizona Republic*). Several, such as the *Detroit Free Press*, have moved some or all of their editions to online only (Grabowitz, 2013). The financial hard times of newspapers and magazines probably reflect the decrease in readership among the older groups of readers. Thus, the decrease in reading among youth may partly be a product of this decreased supply, rather than the source of the decreasing demand. In fact, another study conducted by the Pew Internet and American Life Project indicates that the age group that has grown up with digital media (aged 16–29 years) values paper books and e-books, considers libraries to be very important, and has used libraries to sit and read, study, or watch or listen to media (Zickuhr, Rainie, & Purcell, 2013).

HOW MUCH VIOLENCE IS IN THE MEDIA?

The rise in media consumption has important implications for society. Cultural norms and values are reflected in (and partly determined by) the media. Thus, it is important to measure the amount of violence that is present in media to consider the impact on society. Given the dominance of television and video games in children's lives, it is appropriate that most of the media violence research has focused on these two forms of media (Lu, Waterman, & Yan, 2005; Jolin & Weller, 2011). Assessing the amount of violence in films is more challenging given the vague rating system devised by the Motion Picture Association of America (MPAA). Before discussing the violence levels found in media in detail, it is important to describe how researchers define media violence.

DEFINING MEDIA VIOLENCE

The National Television Violence Study (NTVS) was a three-year research program conducted between 1995 and 1998 and funded by the National Cable Television Association. The research program involved several studies that measured the amount of violent content found in television programming. For these studies, the researchers defined media violence as:

Any overt depiction of a credible threat of physical force or the actual use of such force intended to physically harm an animate being or group of beings. Violence also includes certain depictions of physically harmful consequences against an animate being or group that occurs as a result of unseen violent means. Thus there are three primary types of violent depictions: credible threats, behavioral acts, and harmful consequences. (National Television Violence Study, 1998, p. 41)

Although other definitions differ slightly (e.g., Center for Media and Public Affairs, 1999), most scholars generally agree with the definition provided in the NTVS. The director general of the European Institute for the Media concludes that over a broad range of research methodologies (e.g., content analyses, behavioral research, cultural studies) and settings (e.g., North American, Western European, Asian, African), the terms "aggression" and "violence" in the media are defined generally as "behavior that leads to harm of another person" (Groebel, 2001).

Potter (1999) analyzed how theorists, content analysts, and the public define violence and aggression. Starting with a scholarly definition that focuses on causing harm to another, he notes that scientists disagree over specifics such as whether intent matters, whether both physical and verbal aggression should be included, and whether nonhuman targets and off-screen events should be included (also see the chapter by Potter, this volume). Such differences may affect the outcomes of content analyses, and, as such, reports can vary in their conclusions concerning the amount of violence on television and in other media. Potter also found what he called a "profound" difference between what the public considers violent and how scientists conceptualize violence. For example, the public does not consider cartoons to be violent, although scientists note that cartoons feature some of the highest rates of violence found in the media. Parents become concerned when they are shocked or offended by what they see; hence, the graphicness of media violence is the most important factor for many. Critics, then, conclude that scientists use poor definitions of media violence. However, Potter contends that the scientists' definitions are not poor but rather reflect different concerns: the public are concerned with being shocked by what they watch, and scientists are concerned with the potential for harm from the depiction, whether or not it is perceived as shocking.

VIOLENCE ON TELEVISION

As television became more widely consumed over the past half-century, it also became increasingly violent, a fact that has raised concerns among many policymakers. Over 40 years ago, consensus was already building as to the dangers of violence on American television, as indicated by the National Commission on the Causes and Prevention of Violence in 1969: "The preponderance of the available evidence strongly suggests that violence in television programs can and does have adverse effects upon audiences" (cited in Berkowitz, 1993, p. 199). Entertainment industry officials have been reluctant to embrace this conclusion. Still, following a 1972 report by the surgeon general of the United States, which concluded that "there is a causative relationship between televised violence and subsequent antisocial behavior," some industry executives appeared convinced of the evidence and pledged to "manage program planning accordingly" (Communications Subcommittee, 1972). In a policy statement, the National Cable Television Association (1993) condemned the "gratuitous use of violence depicted as an easy and convenient solution to human problems" and vowed to "strive to reduce the frequency of such exploitative uses of violence" (p. 1). The Network Television Association (1992) made similar promises.

In contrast to what was promised, however, violent programming has steadily increased over the past 30 years. Research reports published in the early 1970s indicated that by age 14, the average child had witnessed more than 11,000 murders on television (Looney, 1971). This figure has increased dramatically, with more recent reports indicating that the average American child now witnesses more than 10,000 violent crimes (e.g., murder, rape, and assault) each year on television—about 200,000 total violent crimes by the time they are in their teens (Signorielli, Gerbner, & Morgan, 1995). The NTVS (1998) reported that 61 percent of television programs contain violence, and only 3 percent of them have an anti-violence theme. Other reports contend that the figure for prime-time network programs—those that young people are most likely to watch—is more than 70 percent (Gerbner, Gross, Morgan, & Signorielli, 1994). Is that amount of violence too much? The public thought so. A national survey conducted by the Pew Research Center in 1999 indicated that 70 percent of parents thought that there was too much violence on television (Kohut, Parker, Sonner, Flemming, Nolde, & Donovan, 1999). The authors also stated that the 70 percent figure had remained fairly constant since 1971.

Data from more recent analyses of television content indicate that the amount of violence during prime time has been increasing since 1998. The Parents' Television Council, a nonprofit, nonpartisan parent advocacy orga-

Figure 1.2
Number of Violent Incidents per Hour on Prime-Time Network Programs

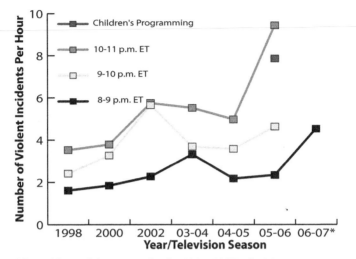

Note: * = This additional data point for the 2006–2007 television season was available only for the 8:00 to 9:00 p.m. time slot. The lone square on this figure represents a content analysis of children's programming in summer of 2005.
Source: Parents' Television Council, 2006, 2007a, 2007b.

nization, analyzed the violent incidents portrayed in network television pro-gramming during primetime (Monday–Friday, 8:00 p.m. Eastern time to 11:00 p.m. Eastern time). Their findings are portrayed in Figure 1.2. Between 1998 and the 2005–2006 television season, the numbers of violent incidents increased in all three time slots (Parents' Television Council, 2007a, 2007b).

The Parents' Television Council performed a separate content analysis on just children's programming during the summer of 2005. The shows con-sisted of network programs occurring during hours when children are home from school and any programming on cable stations whose main audience is children (e.g., the Disney Channel, Nickelodeon). The number of violent incidents per hour (7.86) rivaled that of the 10:00–11:00 p.m. time slot during the 2005–2006 season (9.43). The report also stated that the number of inci-dents during children's viewing time remained relatively high (6.30) even when the unrealistic "cartoony" incidents are removed (e.g., piano falling on Popeye's head; Parents' Television Council, 2006).

VIOLENCE IN VIDEO GAMES

Gamers have a wide range of games to choose from, ranging from the be-nign (Solitaire or Tetris) to the extremely violent and realistic first person

Table 1.1
Records for Opening Day Sales for Video Games

Name of Video Game	Year of Release	Genre	Sales during First 24 Hours
Grand Theft Auto V	2013	Action/adventure	$800 million
Call of Duty: Black Ops 2	2012	First-Person Shooter	$500 million
Call of Duty: Modern Warfare 3	2011	First-Person Shooter	$400 million
Call of Duty: Black Ops	2010	First-Person Shooter	$360 million
Call of Duty: Modern Warfare 2	2009	First-Person Shooter	$310 million

Note: All five of these games received Commonsense.org's highest rating for violence.
Sources: Nayak (2013); Morris (2012).

Figure 1.3
Popularity of Games of Different Genres as Function of Violence Rating

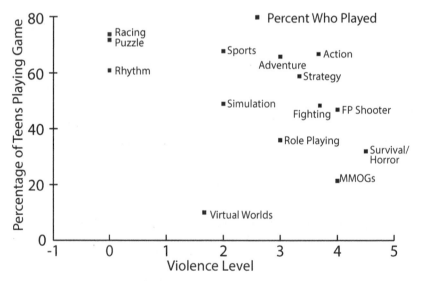

Note: MMOG = massive multiplayer online games. Violence levels represent average of the ratings for most frequently listed games for each genre in Lenhart et al. (2008).
Sources: Percent of teens who play games of different genres taken from 2008 Pew Internet and American Life Survey (Lenhart, Kahne, Middaugh, Rankin-MacGill, Evans, & Vitak, 2008); violence ratings obtained from Commonsense.org.

Figure 1.4
Proportion of Male and Female Video Game Players That Play Games in Different Genres, by Violence Ratings of Games within the Genres

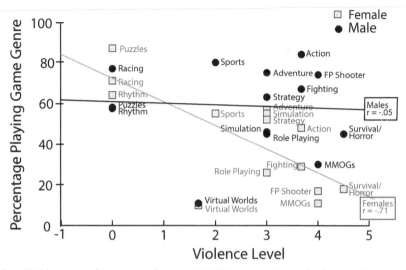

Note: FP Shooter = first person shooter; MMOG = massive multiplayer online game. Violence levels represent average of the ratings for most frequently listed games for each genre in Lenhart et al. (2008).

Sources: Percent of teens who play games of different genres taken from 2008 Pew Internet and American Life Survey (Lenhart et al., 2008); Violence ratings obtained from Commonsensemedia.org.

shooter games such as those in the *Call of Duty* or *Halo* series. Recent video game sales records suggest that there is very strong demand among the public for video games that have realistic graphics, interesting plots, and violence (see Table 1.1). These five games also received Commonsense.org's highest rating for violence.

Lenhart and colleagues' (2008) survey of teen gamers suggests that the record sales numbers may not reflect teens' games of choice. Contrary to conventional wisdom, their survey data suggest that violent video games are not the most frequently played (see Figure 1.3).

But Lenhart and colleagues' Pew survey also found big differences between boys and girls in the games they tend to play. As illustrated in Figure 1.4, as the violence levels of games increases, the percentage of females who play those games tends to decrease. There was no relation between game violence and the percentage of males who play, however.[1] Moreover, the more violent the games, the larger the sex difference for teens who play games in that genre.

In summary, video games can have plots and perspectives that require violent responses on the part of players, but they also can be nonviolent. Whereas it appears that demand is high for violent games among the general public, the most recent data on the playing habits of American youth suggest that they tend to play games in all genres. Girls appear to steer away from games within the more violent genres, but the violence of the games makes little difference for boys.

VIOLENCE IN FILMS

How violent are motion pictures? How can parents determine whether the amount of violence is inappropriate for their children? To date, parents have relied on the well-known ratings provided by the MPAA (G, PG, PG-13, R, NC-17) to determine whether a film was suitable for their children. The rating system has been in existence since 1968, with the current rating symbols in place since 1991.[2] However, parents and social scientists alike have criticized the MPAA's system for numerous reasons, including:

- **Changing standards.** Research has documented "ratings creep," or the trend for MPAA ratings to be less stringent over time. Movies that would previously have been rated R would now receive a PG-13 rating (Bushman, Jamieson, Weitz, & Romer, 2013; Palsson, Price, & Shores, 2013; Thompson & Yokota, 2004).
- **Lack of consideration for contextual factors.** Wilson (1993) suggests that the ratings are based on numbers of behaviors seen in films but ignore contextual information. For example, a traffic fatality that is shown to be caused intentionally (i.e., murder) would receive equal consideration as a traffic fatality that is accidental.
- **Lack of detailed information**. The ratings used by MPAA is an amalgamation of six different film features (theme, language, nudity, sex, drug use, and violence), preventing parents from making more informed decisions about a film's appropriateness given the values of the family.
- **Emphasis on wrong features**. Wilson (1993) and Palsson et al., (2013) note that certain movie features tend to be weighted more than others, and they dispute the emphasis placed on those features. For example, a film will receive more restrictive ratings if three "F-words" are present than if three acts of gory violence are shown.

Thus, one is unable to determine how much violence exists in motion pictures from the MPAA rating alone. Given the lack of substantive change in the MPAA rating system, several parent advocacy organizations have taken it upon themselves to provide parents with more detailed and objective information on multiple factors within films (see Table 1.2). Kids-in-mind.com, for example, provides ratings ranging from 0 to 10 for sex/nudity, violence/gore, and profanity. The organization claims to have used an objective process to rate movies since 1992.

Table 1.2
Alternatives to Industry Ratings for Information about the Amount of Violence in Media

Name of Organization	Organization Type	Media Rated	Features Rated	Scale	Fee
Common Sense Media www.commonsensemedia.com	Non-profit	apps books movies music television video games websites	1. positive messages 2. positive role models 3. violence 4. sex 5. language 6. consumerism 7. drinking/drugs/ smoking	0–5 (Appropriate – Inappropriate)	None, donations accepted
The Dove Foundation www.dove.org	Non-profit	books movies television movies music CDs	1. sex 2. language 3. violence 4. drug/alcohol use 5. nudity 6. other	0–5 (Appropriate – Inappropriate; based on Judeo-Christian values)	None
Kids In Mind www.kids-in-mind.com	For-profit	movies	1. sex/nudity 2. violence/gore 3. profanity	1–10 (Appropriate – Inappropriate)	No, but $25 per year for no ads

(Continued)

Table 1.2
(continued)

Name of Organization	Organization Type	Media Rated	Features Rated	Scale	Fee
Screen It, Inc. www.screenit.com	for-profit	movies	1. alcohol/drugs 2. blood/gross stuff 3. disrespectful/bad attitude 4. frightening/tense scenes 5. guns/weapons 6. imitative behavior 7. jump scenes 8. music (scary/tense) 9. music (appropriate) 10. profanity 11. sex/nudity 12. smoking 13. tense family scenes 14. topics to talk about 15. violence	none minor mild moderate heavy extreme	$47 per year

Note: These are examples of alternative ratings systems for media. The authors have no vested interest in any of these websites or the organizations that run them.

Figure 1.5
Trends in Violence, Sex/Nudity, and Profanity in Films, 1992–2013

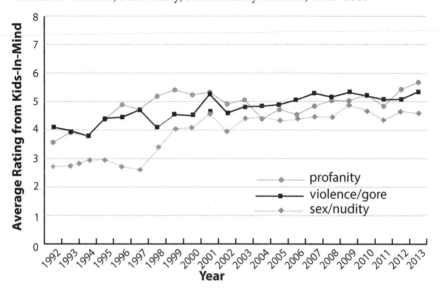

Note: Kids-in-mind ratings are made on a 0 to 10 scale, with higher ratings representing more profanity, sex/nudity, and violence.
Source: Data points represent average kids-in-mind.com ratings for films released each year.

Examination of Kids-in-Mind ratings of movies over time indicates that movies are showing more violence and gore (as well as more sex/nudity and profanity) now than when Kids-in-Mind began in 1991 (see Figure 1.5). The average rating for violent content in films in 1992 was 4.10. Twenty-one years later, Kids-in-Mind's average rating for movie violence was 5.36 (see http://www.kids-in-mind.com).

AGGRESSION IN NEWER FORMS OF MEDIA

Based on a national random survey conducted in 2007 on over 1,000 parents and subsequent focus groups, the Kaiser Family Foundation reported that over 80 percent of parents surveyed believed that media violence contributes to violent behavior in children "somewhat" or "a lot." The media of most concern were television (32%) and the Internet (21%). Most parents felt that the Internet was more of a good influence than a bad one, although some reported that they and their children had seen or experienced "bad things" on social networking sites, leading these children to stay away from those sites (Rideout, 2007).

According to a recent public opinion poll, a third of Americans are "tuning out" of social networking sites; 39 percent of those tuning out cite rude behavior in social networks as the culprit (Weber Shandwick, 2010). Forty-five percent of Americans report that they have unfriended someone or blocked them due to rude behavior. These participants rated blogs as the most uncivil spaces online and politics as the most uncivil facet of daily life.

Online incivility includes trolling and flaming. Urbandictionary.com defines trolling as "being a prick on the internet because, hey, you can," and flaming as "an online argument that becomes nasty or derisive, where insulting a party to the discussion takes precedence over the objective merits of one side or another." One of the issues with online incivility is how to balance free public discourse with enough civility so that the discourse does not break down. One technique practiced by bloggers to combat online incivility is "disemvoweling," or removing the vowels from trolling comments so as to render them unreadable (Caplan et al., 2008).

Incivility also interrupts professional discourse that takes place online. Insulting comments have become a problem for scientists who write blogs. Anderson, Brossard, Scheufele, and Xenos (2014) found that (1) uncivil comments on blogs are common, (2) these comments stifle public participation on these forums, and (3) online incivility tarnishes the reputation of the blog source.

WHY IS THERE SO MUCH VIOLENCE IN THE MEDIA?

> We live in a violent society. Art imitates the modes of life, not the other way around: It would be better to clean up society than to clean up the reflection of that society.
> —Zev Braun, CBS television executive

> The television industry is merely holding a mirror to American society.
> —Howard Stringer, CBS television executive

Media executives publicly claim that the reason for violence in the media is that society is filled with violence, and that the media, in their products, have a responsibility to accurately depict society. But content analyses comparing the level of violence portrayed in media depictions of society and the actual level of violence in society do not support this claim. For instance, Surette (2011) compared rates of violent crime (murder and aggravated assault) occurring in prime-time television programs with actual FBI crime statistics and found that whereas around 30 percent of televised crimes are violent (with murder accounting for two-thirds of those crimes), fewer than 1 percent of crimes committed in the United States are violent. Furthermore, whereas the television murder rate is around 3 percent (i.e., 3% of television characters are murdered in an average evening), the rate of murders per 100,000 inhabitants in the United States is 0.0005 percent (Federal Bureau of Investigation, 2012). In other words, the murder rate portrayed on television is roughly *600 times higher* than the murder rate in society. Clearly, televised portrayals of violence are far from an accurate reflection of reality, and therefore the argument that media content is violent merely because society is violent is not only hollow, but deceitful. Here, we offer what we believe to be the real underlying reasons, based on economic realities of the media industry, for the unrealistic levels of violence depicted in television, movies, video games, and other media.

MEDIA MARKETING: ECONOMIC REASONS FOR VIOLENCE IN MEDIA

If the average person were asked, "What is the purpose of the media?" chances are the response would be something like, "to inform and entertain the public." Indeed, broadcasting licenses are awarded (at essentially no cost) to television networks on the understanding that they broadcast in "the public interest, convenience, and necessity" (Hamilton, 1998, p. 33). From this perspective, it would appear that networks determine what to broadcast based on what the public appears to want. Beth Waxman Bressan, vice president at CBS/Broadcast Group, expressed this sentiment when accounting for the presence of violence on television to a U.S. Senate panel: "TV looks like it does because we try to respond to the wants of viewers" (Violence bill debated in Washington, 1990, p. 78). However, the true purpose of television is not so much to inform and entertain as to provide an audience for product advertisements. The most obvious example of this fact is the daytime drama, or "soap opera." The first televised soap opera (*Search for Tomorrow*) aired on CBS in 1951, though the concept was actually borrowed from radio programs dating back many years. As implied by their name, soap operas were invented as a vehicle for marketing cleaning products, and they aired during the daytime hours when men were presumed to be at work, while most women—those presumed most likely to care about and buy cleaning products—stayed home. To this day, advertisements accompanying programs that air during the daytime hours are primarily for household products, and they are primarily aimed at women. Thus, from the start, media and marketing executives have been targeting specific audiences with the types of programs they are assumed to like in order to sell specific kinds of products.

It is an understatement to note that advertising is a huge business. In 2012, $139.5 billion was spent in the United States for advertising, and $17 billion of that was targeted specifically at children (Kantar Media, 2013; Rhodes, 2013). The most recent development in advertising is digital advertising, which involves placing ads on popular websites for viewing, and tailoring ads that users see based on recent websites visited and their "likes" on Facebook. The advertising industry estimates that in 2012, one in five advertising dollars were spent on digital advertisements, and the share of advertising dollars that go into digital advertising is expected to continue to grow (eMarketer,

2013). In 2012, $102 billion was spent worldwide in advertising in digital media (including online and cell phone formats), and $118.4 billion was projected for 2013. The greatest amount of digital advertising currently occurs in North America (39% in 2012). Western Europe, Asia, and Latin America also significantly contribute to the digital advertising market. Experts anticipate that each Internet user in North America will be exposed to $168 worth of advertisements in 2013. And ads are not only directed toward adults; young users of the Internet will see ads tailored just for them.

Children represent an especially captive audience for TV ads because research shows that children (especially those younger than five years) are unable to discriminate between programs and advertisements (e.g., Levin, Petros, & Petrella, 1982; Ward, Reale, & Levinson, 1972). Even somewhat older children who can discriminate between programs and ads at a perceptual level often do not recognize the persuasive intent of those ads (see Kunkel, 2001). Findings such as these prompted the Federal Communications Commission (FCC) in 1978 to attempt (unsuccessfully) to ban all advertising aimed at children (Fox, 2002).

Hamilton (1998) provides a detailed analysis of the use of violence on television as a marketing strategy to ensure a viewing audience. He explains, "The portrayal of violence is used as a competitive tool in both entertainment and news shows to attract particular viewing audiences" (p. 3); these audiences are chosen based on the kinds of products and services they are likely to purchase. This, then, determines what kinds of ads will be shown during particular time slots, and what prices will be charged by the networks for showing these ads. Demographic characteristics of those who appear to prefer violent programs are thus very important to television executives. There are some data to suggest that a large audience of young men and women—the demographic groups considered most attractive by advertisers—watches violent programs. Hamilton (1998) reports a large survey in which adults in three age categories (18–34, 35–50, and 50 and over) were asked about their viewing habits. Results showed that 73 percent of men in the 18–34 group were heavy consumers of violent programming, and that overall, men in this age category answered yes to an average of almost 5 out of 10 questions related to viewing violent shows. The next-highest violence-viewing group was women in the 18–34 age group, 60 percent of whom were considered heavy consumers of televised violence.

GOVERNMENTAL REGULATION VERSUS INDUSTRY SELF-REGULATION

Congress has held hearings in response to concerns about the effects of children's exposure to violent media since the 1950s (Potter, 1999; Timmer, 2013). The result of these hearings favored not legislation but industry self-regulation, which has been widely criticized as not doing enough (Potter,

2003; Timmer, 2013). For example, the Television Program Improvement Act of 1990 encouraged the industry to develop standards regarding the presentation of television violence. However, these changes were not mandated, and the industry was essentially allowed to police itself. In the late 1990s, Congress deemed that violence on television was detrimental to children, and it passed the Parental Choice in Television Programming Act (Timmer, 2013), the legislation that implemented the V-chip to help parents block violence and other objectionable content. Again, the industry was asked to create a rating system that could be used with the V-chip, which many criticized as inadequate, complaining that this was, again, a case of the fox guarding the henhouse. In other words, it is problematic to expect an industry that profits from selling violent media to discourage consumption of its products (Timmer, 2013). Another outcome of the Senate hearings of the 1990s was the strong encouragement from both the Senate panel and several media experts who testified for industry officials to institute a voluntary, industry-wide cap on the level of violence in video games. Just as television executives have done for decades, leaders in the video game industry ignored this advice (Timmer, 2013). A content analysis of top-selling video games for personal computers (PCs) found that 60 percent of the games contained a main theme of violence, with 17 percent of those depicting sexualized violence (Dill, Gentile, Richter, & Dill, 2005). Believing that realistic depictions of violence are theoretically more likely to incite aggression in the player, Dill et al. (2005) rated the realism of game content, finding that two-thirds of the violent games portrayed realistic (defined as existing or able to exist in the real world) targets, and that 92 percent portrayed realistic weapons. Dietz (1998) analyzed the content of top-selling console video games and found that 79 percent of the games included aggression and that 21 percent of the games depicted violence toward women.

WHY DO WE WATCH? PSYCHOLOGICAL MECHANISMS

> Perhaps the most ironic aspect of the struggle for survival is how easily organisms can be harmed by that which they desire. The trout is caught by the fisherman's lure, the mouse by cheese. Realizing when a diversion has gotten out of control is one of the great challenges of life.
> —R. Kubey and M. Csikszentmihalyi

It is safe to conclude that media consumption is the primary free-time activity of most Americans. The question remains, Why do we watch so much? The simple answer: because media producers are experts at getting our attention. Similarly, the high accessibility of video and music, as well as phone calls, texts, and social media on mobile devices, keeps us in a chronic state of alert.

Kubey and Csikszentmihalyi (2002) explain that TV repeatedly triggers our orienting response—the instinctive reaction to pay attention to any sudden, changing, or novel stimulus. This orienting response evolved in the species because it helps us identify potential threats and react to them. Media producers use features such as edits, cuts, zooms, pans, and sudden noises to continually trigger our orienting response. In short, they exploit basic psychological and biological mechanisms to get and keep our attention. In ads, action sequences, and music videos, the orienting response is triggered at an average rate of once per second (Kubey & Csikszentmihalyi, 2002); essentially, this amounts to a continuous cueing of attention. Aggressive forms of media that involve threats and that surprise the audience with violent acts therefore demand significant attention, as well as cognitive and emotional engagement.

Walsh described "jolts and tricks" within the media (Walsh, 2001). Jolts are devices used by the media that are designed to engage our emotions. The most common emotional jolts are appeals to sex, violence, humor, and belonging needs. Tricks are technical features designed to grab our attention, including those triggering the orienting response. Common tricks used to grab our attention include special effects, edits, pacing, music, camera angles, graphics, color, volume, lighting, makeup, and animation (Walsh, 2001). It is not only the content of programs that attracts attention but also the way in which that content is presented. Media producers know that when an audience's emotions are engaged, that audience is more vulnerable to suggestion (e.g., Cialdini, 2001). In this case, the suggestion may take the form of advertised products. In short, media producers believe that grabbing our attention eventually translates into selling products. As elucidated in the next section, ironically, research has shown that our memory of advertisements that are shown during violent (and sexual) movies may actually be weaker than during nonviolent movies.

So what might be wrong with allowing the media to grab our attention? After all, as Kubey and Csikszentmihalyi (2002) point out, sometimes television is enjoyable and can offer an outlet for fun and relaxation. When, then, does it become a problem? Kubey and Csikszentmihalyi report that 2 out of 5 adults and 7 out of 10 children say that they watch too much TV. Also, viewers often feel that they can't stop watching TV. Furthermore, while people report increased good moods after activities such as sports and hobbies, they report being in the same mood or in a worse mood after watching TV (Kubey & Csikszentmihalyi, 2002). Research also shows that children who habitually view highly attention-grabbing media are more likely to have later attention and impulse-control problems, both of which are related to aggression and school performance (e.g., Swing, Gentile, Anderson, & Walsh, 2010; Gentile, Swing, Lim, & Khoo, 2012; Christakis, Zimmerman, DiGiuseppe, & McCarty, 2004).

THE ECONOMICS OF VIOLENT MEDIA

On the face of it, the economics of violent media appears simple: (1) broadcast television networks, cable networks, video game developers, publishing houses, and many website developers are driven to earn as much profit as possible, and they do so by selling more airtime to advertisers, obtaining more subscribers, and selling more copies of their products; (2) people enjoy being exposed to violent depictions; (3) therefore, providing violent media allows broadcast television producers to charge advertisers more for airtime or exposure to users, allows premium cable networks to charge cable companies more, and allows media producers to sell more units at a higher price.[3] It is classic supply and demand: big media companies supply the violent programming (and may profit from it), people consume what is offered, and everyone is happy. The problem in this reasoning is that there is at least one hole in this chain of logic that invalidates the whole argument. In the following sections, we examine this reasoning in more detail within the medium of broadcast television.

Premise 1: Media and the Bottom Line

The first premise is true. The profit motive is strong among producers of media content. Television networks make their profits by maximizing the appeal of their televised content, minimizing their costs of production (or the cost of a particular program/movie if they did not create it) with the goal of attracting as many viewers as possible in each time slot. When a network obtains a bigger audience in a particular time slot than rival networks, it can charge more for advertising time, assuming that those who view the programming in that slot match the demographic for their products. For cable movie networks (e.g., Cinemax, HBO), the route to profit is different. Cable movie networks compete against each other for the total viewers, not necessarily during particular time slots. The more viewers a cable movie network can attract through its programming, the more it can charge cable providers for its signal. The financial costs are then borne by the consumer: the cable user. Public television is also motivated to reach the most viewers possible. By creating attractive programming and airing those programs during pledge drives, public television networks can generate more underwriting support from corporations, foundations, and public pledges.[4]

The premise is true with other media as well: video game developers, movie studios, and publishers attain revenue as a function of number of units (video games, movie tickets, DVDs or downloads, or books sold) times price per unit. For media companies (indeed, for any companies), profit is made when revenues exceed the costs of production and marketing.

Premise 2: People Want Violent Content

Conventional wisdom suggests that people are drawn to violent media. That is, people believe that violent content is most appealing to the highly sought-after 18- to 49-year-old demographic of television viewers and adolescent males (Groebel, 2001). This perspective is overly simplistic in that producers of television content also have to consider the costs to produce or purchase programs in different genres. However, Hamilton's economic analysis of the incentives for producers to create violent programming suggests that the cost to viewer ratio favors violent programs. According to economics, then, programs with violent content are more appealing to the most desired American audience. Violent action-adventure films and television programs also have less dialogue requiring translation, making them more appealing to international distributors as well (Hamilton, 1998). Groebel (2001) cites many factors that explain why violence is an effective marketing tool. He explains that violent media are successful in part because violence attracts the attention of male adolescents, a highly sought-after demographic for marketers (Hamilton, 1998; Strasburger & Wilson, 2002).

Hamilton's conclusions are not universally accepted. Hamilton's research indicates that programs involving violence tended to get higher Nielsen ratings, even after statistically controlling for a number of factors (Hamilton, 1998). One drawback of his analysis is that it failed to control for other emotion-related characteristics of television programs. A number of studies have attempted to correct this shortcoming by having research participants randomly assigned to watch either a movie with violence or the same movie with the violence edited out. Collectively, these studies found that either participants enjoyed the nonviolent version more (female participants in Berry, Gray, & Donnerstein, 1999; Weaver & Wilson, 2009), or they liked the two versions equally (male participants from Berry et al., 1999; Sparks, Sherry, & Lubsen, 2005). More recent studies suggest that for young males, at least, it is the *action* within programming that draws their attention, rather than the violence (Weaver, Jensen, Martins, Hurley, & Wilson, 2011).

Another view on this premise is that the relationship between the public's viewing preferences and violence is cyclical (Potter, 2003). In his review of various studies on the issue, Potter found that the studies appeared to be equivocal on the issue. That is, some studies found statistically significant relationships between violence and television viewership, while others found that the public preferred nonviolent shows. An analysis of television viewing between the 1950s and 1960s might provide an explanation for the apparent equivocal findings: television producers attempt to create spin-offs and shows that are similar to the successful programs (Clark & Blankenburg, 1972). But most of the similar shows perform poorly, suggesting that the public do not like shows of that kind at all (Potter, 2003). As an example, consider the show *The West Wing*, which was a successful drama about the presidency that ran between 1999 and 2006. From the show's success, one would believe that viewers were drawn to stories about government and politics. So networks began producing political serial dramas like *Mister Sterling*, about a U.S. senator; *The Court*, about the Supreme Court; and *Commander in Chief*, about a female president, each hoping to cash in on the popularity of *The West Wing*.

These three shows were short-lived, however, thus suggesting that the public does not like political serial dramas after all. The same type of "success breeds failure" pattern may happen with violent television programming as well.

Given the findings that television viewers enjoy violent and nonviolent programs equally (or enjoy nonviolent more than violent), how is it that media executives still follow the mantra "violence sells"? The answer: because *violence brings a larger viewership*. The research question for the just-described studies was, "Does the level of violence affect *people's enjoyment* of the movie or television program?" They did not ask about whether people naturally *choose to watch* violent movies or programs over nonviolent programs. Weaver and Kobach (2012) ran a study to examine both research questions. They created descriptions of four prime-time dramas: a description of the dramas as violent or a similar description of the dramas without violence. Research participants were given the choice of watching either a violent program or nonviolent program. Regardless of their choice, the researchers randomly assigned the participants to view a violent or nonviolent film. Weaver and Kobach found that participants tended to choose the violent versions of the television programs. However, participants who actually saw the nonviolent program (regardless of their selection at the beginning of the study) rated it as more enjoyable than participants who saw the violent program. Thus, Weaver and Kobach (2012) make the important distinction between "selecting" a program to watch and actually enjoying the program that one watches. The propensity of research participants to choose violent programs suggests that people *are* drawn to view violent programs. However, in the end, those choosing violent programs may end up not enjoying them.

Research suggests that the same patterns are true for violent video games and films as well. Teenage boys do tend to be more drawn to games in violent and nonviolent game genres about equally, while teen girls actually show a preference for nonviolent games. Likewise, research indicates that movie earnings at the box office and overall are inversely related to MPAA ratings. That is, movies with a G rating earn more at the box office than PG-rated movies, which earn more than PG-13–rated movies, which earn more than R-rated movies. This is true with both box office sales (e.g., Palsson, Price, & Shores, 2013) and total revenue from all the post-theatrical sales (Dove Foundation, 2005, 2012).

Premise 3: Violent Content Allows Broadcast Networks to Charge More

Premise 3 is *not* true; that is, if broadcast networks want to bring in revenue, it is ratings rather than violence that sells. The question of whether people like violent content is not the same as questioning whether advertisers are willing to pay more for violence. Weaver and Kobach's (2012) research on viewers' attraction to violent television or movie content and their enjoyment

Figure 1.6
Ratings and Price per 30-Second Spot, as Function of Violence Rating

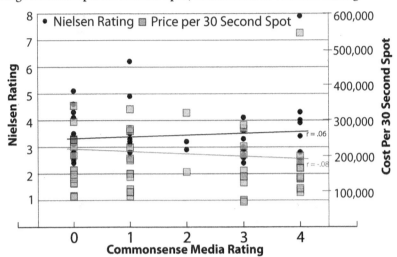

Source: Authors' analysis using Nielsen ratings from deadline.com (http://www.deadline
.com/2013/05/tv-season-series-rankings-2013-full-list/), Commonsense Media violence
ratings from (http://www.commonsensemedia.org/), and price per spot from Adage.com
(http://adage.com/article/media/tv-ad-prices-idol-match-football/237874/).

of such content occurred in a controlled setting, with carefully crafted viewing materials, scripted procedures, and formal questionnaires.

Another way to test whether violent television programming "sells" is to
look at the relationships between violence in television shows, the number of
people who watch the shows, and the costs to advertisers for airing their
30-second ads during shows. The ratings on violence come from Common
Sense Media, which uses a 0–4 scale (with 4 signifying extreme violence).[5] The
viewership ratings come from survey and viewership log data published by the
Nielsen Company (as quoted by Patten, 2013).[6] The price for television spots
comes from *Advertising Age*, a trade publication for advertisers that is now
online (Adage.com). Adage posted the average "upfront" costs to run an ad
during the prime-time programs for the 2012–2013 network television season
(Steinberg, 2012; see http://adage.com/article/media/tv-ad-prices-idol-match
-football/237874/). The relations are portrayed in the scatterplot in Figure 1.6.
As the scatterplot indicates, there is no significant correlation between violence
rating and cost for 30 seconds of airtime to run a commercial.[7]

Conclusion: Violence Does Not Necessarily Sell

Figure 1.7 shows the relation between advertising costs and numbers of
people who are watching the programs. The correlation between ad costs and

Figure 1.7
Price per 30-Second Spot and Nielsen Ratings

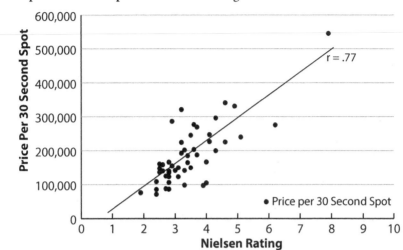

Source: Nielsen ratings from deadline.com (http://www.deadline.com/2013/05 /tv-season-series-rankings-2013-full-list/); Commonsense media ratings from http:// www.commonsensemedia.org/); price per spot from Adage.com (http://adage.com /article/media/tv-ad-prices-idol-match-football/237874/).

viewership is strongly positive and statistically significant.[8] Taken together, these data indicate that for broadcast television, viewership sells, but violence does not.[9] This finding seems to defy logic. If people tend to choose violent over nonviolent programs, then why do we not see a larger viewership for violent shows over nonviolent shows? Why do advertisers pay *less* to run their commercials during violent programs?[10]

There are at least three possible interconnected reasons. First, advertisers might be "placing their bets" on programs that people end up *enjoying* in the long run, rather than going with viewers' initial program choices. This possibility would be consistent with the previously described research on the genres of television and films that people *enjoy*. A second possible reason is that advertisers do not wish for their products or brands to be associated in viewers' minds with violent televised content. The third possible reason is that advertisers might know that violent content impairs viewers' memory of products, compared to nonviolent content. This contention is supported by a series of studies conducted by Bushman and his colleagues. Their research team created versions of film clips that differed only in whether there was violence in the film clip. Bushman and colleagues then had participants complete a memory test for the advertised products. Bushman found that violent content in the film clips actually *impaired* participants' memories of the products (Bushman, 1998). In a second study, Bushman and Bonacci (2002) had community members view one of three television programs: a violent program, a sexually explicit program, or a neutral program. Commercials for nine commonplace products were embedded in the programs, just as normal commercials are. Following the program, participants completed two memory tests—one immediately after the program and a second one over the phone a day later. Participants were asked to recall the brands advertised during the 30-second commercials. The findings showed that those who had watched neutral programs remembered the advertised brands more than the participants who had watched either the violent or sexually explicit programs.

For video games, the best indicator of whether a game is in demand is its price. If the public really wants the game, then game publishers can increase the price and earn more revenue. Networks do the opposite when there is low demand: they reduce the price so as to entice people to purchase the products. We calculated the relations between games' violent content ratings and games' weeks on the market, and their prices.[11] As with television, there is no relation between a game's violence level and the price, once weeks on market were controlled statistically.[12]

WHAT ABOUT CHILDREN?

The discussion up to this point has focused on prime-time television (defined as the period between 8:00 p.m. and 11:00 p.m. Eastern time), a time during which broadcasters and advertisers focus on adult viewers between 18 and 49 years of age. How does this discussion relate to children? First, many children watch prime-time broadcast television and become exposed to that type of content. According to the Parents Television Council and the Nielsen Company, in 2008, 28 percent of children ages 2–11 watched television between the hours of 8:00 p.m. and 6:00 a.m. (programs watched live or through DVR playback), with the total number of children watching during prime-time hours estimated to be about 10 million (Bowling, 2007; McDonough, 2009). In 2007 programs televised during what was once considered "the family hour" (8:00–9:00 p.m. Eastern time, the traditional time when families could watch television together with little concern of inappropriate content), contained 4.19 acts of violence per hour, which was a 52.4 percent increase from 2000. Second, as far as children's programming goes, the same principles apply: children enjoy nonviolent children's shows but will choose to watch the violent action-filled shows (with or without violence) if given the choice (Weaver et al., 2011). Our analysis of violence rankings of children's programs on the broadcast networks and cable (ABC, CBS, FOX, NBC, Nickelodeon, the Cartoon Channel, Disney)[13] and children's viewership showed no relationship.[14] Although no recent data were available for costs for advertising time during these children's shows, we would expect that the demand for advertising space during different shows is based not on how violent a program is, but rather on the number of children watching the program, just as with adults (Hamilton, 1998).

The Broad Economic View of Violent Media

While media corporations may incur financial gains (profit) or losses on any given show, it can be argued that the constant broadcasting of violence in the media produces economic and other costs to society for which media corporations are not held responsible. Media corporations profit from sponsorship of their programs with little regard for how their products affect viewers. Hamilton (1998) has argued that this phenomenon—products or byproducts resulting in costs to those who don't profit from the products—is similar to the health and monetary costs incurred by the public through industrial pollution. Just as an industrial process can produce wastes that pollute the local air and groundwater (resulting in acute and chronic health problems to local inhabitants) while generating commercial products, so too do television networks, film production companies, and video game makers reap the immediate costs and benefits while ignoring the costs to individual viewers and society as a whole. Hamilton has labeled this phenomenon the *theory of negative externalities.*

According to Hamilton (1998), television and cable networks operate according to a relatively simple formula involving the number of viewers for a given program (within a given demographic), the number of competing networks offering a similar type of program, the amount that advertisers or cable subscribers are willing to pay for a program, and the costs involved in producing or acquiring a program. What these economic formulas miss are the costs borne by viewers. For one, television generally increases passivity among viewers, leading to less exercise, increased food intake (generally of high-calorie snack foods), and ultimately a less healthy populace. The link between television viewing, decreased physical activity, and obesity (particularly in children) is well documented (e.g., Andersen, Crespo, Bartlett, Cheskin, & Pratt, 1998; Dennison & Edmunds, 2008; Dietz & Gortmaker, 1985; Govindan et al., 2013; Grontved & Hu, 2011). Studies also have demonstrated that randomly assigning children to watch less television resulted in less weight gain and decreased aggression over seven months in those children compared to weight change and aggression levels of children whose television viewing was not altered (Robinson, 1999, 2001).

Other costs associated with media violence, particularly those related to increased societal violence, are reviewed elsewhere in this book (e.g., Anderson & Gentile, chapter 8; Strasburger & Wilson, chapter 5). However, the tools that economists, accountants, and public health officials use to determine health risks associated with hazardous wastes (e.g., animal testing and lifetime excess cancer risk calculations) cannot be used by researchers to determine risks associated with violent television programs, video games, and other media. Although many of the elements are present to estimate such risks, social scientists' attempts to reveal risks posed by media are hampered by (1) the lack of documentation on the amount and type and severity of violent content, (2) the difficulty showing the long-term effects of repeated exposure of violent media except through correlational models (i.e., research designs that are unable to verify causal impacts), (3) the lack of evidence of physiological changes that link chronic exposure to violent media and behavior, and (4) the inability to predict *violent* behavior (i.e., more extreme aggressive behaviors that can potentially produce serious or lethal harm) with precision.

Hamilton (1998) states that estimates by the Environmental Protection Agency regarding "lifetime excess cancer risk" due to exposure to a particular hazardous waste site are fraught with controversy. Estimates of risks associated with a given television program, video game, or music lyrics may be even more controversial due to sparse or nonexistent data on long-term effects of specific programs, and consumers' general belief that they are immune to such effects (as discussed in the next section). Producers of violent media capitalize on this missing element in the research.

In summary, research suggests that the notion that "violence sells" is erroneous for televised media for adults during prime time, for children during prime time, for children watching children's programming, and for video games. Research suggests that placing a television ad during a violent program may be counterproductive in that the violence impairs memory for commercials and ads. Media corporations do not need to make violent television programs, motion pictures, or video games to turn a profit. Doing so brings them no more profit, yet may produce collective costs to peoples' health and likely puts people at greater risk for becoming aggressive themselves. We suspect that to the degree that the risks and costs associated with violent content of a television show, movie, video game, or song lyric remain uncertain, those in the media industry will continue to make products containing violent content on the basis of this disproven myth. It will be the consumers (and ultimately society at large) who will pay the costs of violent content in the media.

CIRCUMSTANCES UNDER WHICH VIOLENCE *DOES* SELL

Despite the disproven myth that violence sells, violent programming may produce greater profits in post-theatrical sales, where many movie producers are able to turn financial losses into profits (Dove Foundation, 2012). One reason for this is that films with violent content have less dialogue, thereby requiring less translation to sell in other countries (Gerbner, 1994b, 1999; Groebel, 2001; see also Jhally, 1994). In contrast, even though humor is a very popular and proven way to gain attention in the media, what is funny is often culturally specific and can be difficult to translate. Aggressive behavior is also commonly used in slapstick physical comedy (e.g., *The Three Stooges*) as well as when the aggression is presented as justified by the protagonist (e.g., *Home Alone*).

Post-theatrical sales also include sales of DVDs, in-home downloads, and video streaming, another large source of revenue for studios. Blockbuster films with special effects are in the highest demand among at-home audiences, and such films often include violence (National Public Radio, 2013).

Hoad (2013) states that the film industry prefers known ideas and brands for new movies because they require less marketing to gain the public's interest (that is, the public has "preawareness" of the title). This includes movies made from books or video games and that are sequels to previous films. For instance, films based on *Marvel Comics* superheroes have become successful and profitable franchises. Violent blockbusters are typically developed and marketed to encourage male audiences to see films because women tend to see more films than do men. As a result, ironically, women continue to be underrepresented in film (Smith, Chouieti, Scofield, & Pieper, 2013).

Lu and colleagues (2005) argue that there are two reasons why the most popular films are becoming increasingly violent over time. One is the aforementioned globalization of media and the resulting reliance on violent action-adventure films that "travel well" in that they don't need translation to be understood. The other reason is the increase in special effects and other film technologies that lend themselves to more violent genres of film. Lu and colleagues argue that both factors play a role, but that the latter—the technological strides in the film industry—probably accounts for more of the increase in films in what they call "violence-prone" genres.

Why do advances in technology result in more of the top films being violent? One reason is that the films produced with high-tech features are attractive to audiences because they have a high-quality appearance (Lu et al., 2005). High-tech special effects can add credence and believability to the film. Furthermore, using special effects lowers some costs of film production, such as replacing live extras with computer-generated ones (Lu et al., 2005).

Taking all of the theatrical and post-theatrical sales into consideration, what types of movies are most profitable? The answer: those that have less violence/gore, profanity, sex, and drug use. This evidence comes from the film profitability study commissioned by the Dove Foundation (Dove Foundation, 2012). Its data indicate that film profitability is inversely related to the suitability of the movie for general audiences. For each year from 2005 to 2009, movies rated G were more profitable than those rated PG, PG-13, or R. Returns on investment for movies were 61 percent, 40 percent, 47 percent, and 3 percent for films rated G, PG, PG-13, and R, respectively. Although these data do not disentangle the violence from the sexual, profane, and drug use elements of movies, it does suggest that movie studios do not need to make violent movies in order to turn a profit.

EFFECTS OF VIOLENCE IN THE MEDIA ON SOCIETY

Whether it is violence in the entertainment media or violence in the world, communicated to us through the news media, by the time children reach age 18, they will have seen 200,000 acts of violence on television (KidsHealth.org, 2012). The majority of economists, researchers of mass media communications, physicians, and psychologists are reaching a consensus on the immediate impacts of exposure to violent media and aggressive behavior. The research shows that when children and young adults are exposed to violent films, television, or video games, and then given the opportunity to retaliate immediately to some provocation, they display more aggression toward others than those who did not view the violent media (e.g., Anderson & Bushman, 2001; Bushman & Huesmann, 2006; Anderson et al., 2010; Ferguson & Kilburn, 2010; Bushman, Rothstein, & Anderson, 2010). This body of research shows how exposure to media violence can affect individuals in everyday situations.

However, this body of research does not tell the whole story. It is likely that frequent exposure to violent media also may have *long-term*, collective effects that change the way in which society operates as a whole. Violence in the media likely affects how people see the world, determine appropriate reactions to daily encounters, view others' intentions, and make predictions about future events. Media violence also affects people's emotional reactions to real violence that they may encounter.

The Cultivation of a Hostile Worldview

Most theoretical models of aggression indicate that aggressive behavior is produced through a combination of person and situational factors (e.g., Anderson, Anderson, Dill, & Deuser, 1998; Anderson & Carnagey, this volume; Berkowitz, 1993; Finkel et al., 2012; Geen, 1990; Zillmann, 1983). That is, individuals do not enter into situations containing aggression-eliciting stimuli as blank slates, but rather they enter the situations with their own experience-based thoughts and feelings about the world and proper reactions to situations, and well-learned reflexive responses to provocations.

Seldom do social psychological models pay much attention to the development of these interconnected thoughts, feelings, and behavioral associations. Almost from birth, individuals observe the world around them and make associations about how people interact with one another, what types of behaviors get punished and rewarded, and how to respond in certain situations (e.g., Anderson, Spiro, & Anderson, 1978; Bandura & Walters, 1963; Brewer, 2000). As children grow older, the associations—or schemas—become aligned with their observations in their environment, with what they see on television, with the messages conveyed in books they read, with the lyrics in their music, and with behavioral scripts they develop during video game play.

Given that television watching is the preferred leisurely activity among youth (Bureau of Labor Statistics, 2013; Rideout et al., 2010), and that by age 18, young people will see over 200,000 acts of violence and 16,000 depictions of murder on television, it stands to reason that violence in the media influences children's worldview. Put another way, violent media "cultivate" children's beliefs that the world is a mean place, with people constantly trying to harm them (Gerbner, Gross, Morgan, Signorielli, & Shanahan, 2002). This viewpoint posits that the schemas carry on into adulthood and may affect how people interpret the behavior of others and react to provocations, frustrating situations, stress, or discomfort. Thus, in theory, children who are exposed to violent media over time should be more likely to display aggressive behavior throughout their lifetimes (Anderson & Huesmann, 2003). However, it is impossible to directly test this perspective of the development of violence-laden schema. To do so, newborn infants would have to be randomly assigned to a "long-term exposure to media violence" condition or a "no exposure to media violence" condition. Obviously, ethical considerations prohibit such a study.

There are several findings from longitudinal research that support the cognitive/schema developmental position. The Columbia County Longitudinal Study tracked a group of 856 nine-year-old children between 1960 and 2000. The investigators collected data from this group of individuals about every 10 years. At the 10-year mark, the investigators found considerable continuity in the group's aggression levels: those that were prone to aggression at age nine also tended to be aggressive at age 19. However, they also found that boys who had seen more violence on television were more aggressive and had more antisocial beliefs, even after controlling for other potential causal factors statistically (Eron, Huesmann, Lefkowitz, & Walder, 1972; Lefkowitz, Eron, Walder, & Huesmann, 1977). Data from additional follow-up data collections continuously have shown that early levels of viewing television violence were positively related to adult aggressiveness and criminality, even after controlling for early levels of aggressiveness and other potential causal factors (Huesmann, Dubow, Eron, & Boxer, 2006). These positive long-term relations between early levels of watching televised violence and subsequent aggressiveness are consistent across countries in boys *and* girls (Hopf, Huber, & Weib, 2008; Huesmann, 1999; Krahé & Möller, 2010; Stavrinides, Tsivitanou, Nikiforou, Hawa, & Tsolia, 2013) and among samples of children who have been assessed more recently (Gentile, Coyne, & Walsh, 2010; Johnson, Cohen, Smailes, Kasen, & Brook, 2002). It stands to reason, then, that given the amounts of violence in media and the amount of media that children consume into adulthood, the hostile worldview is probably held by many, likely making individuals quicker to perceive slights and more likely to retaliate against those slights through aggression.

Desensitization

Beyond shaping the beliefs underlying our worldview, media violence also has the potential to distort our emotional reactions to fearful and dangerous situations, a process that likely develops over many years and with repeated exposures to violence. Studies indicate that children's initial emotional reaction to seeing a violent scene is fear (Cantor, Byrne, Moyer-Guse, & Riddle, 2010; Cantor & Riddle, this volume; Harrison & Cantor, 1999). If fear becomes associated with violent media, then how is it that adults no longer feel frightened when viewing violent media? The answer appears to involve *desensitization*, a protective psychological mechanism meant to dampen negative feelings and physiological arousal in times of acute stress—for example, in emergencies involving serious injuries—to keep people from panicking or passing out and allow them to take necessary action (e.g., to provide assistance to an injured person). This reduced emotional and physiological responding is crucial in some situations, such as when the soldier must persevere on the battlefield or the physician must attend to grievous wounds in the hospital trauma center. But desensitization can be detrimental in most other situations, such as when deciding whether an environment has become dangerous or whether a stranger needs assistance.

Given their significance in signaling potential danger, the sight of blood and gore generally triggers a cascade of physiological and cognitive responses meant to prepare the body for action—the so-called "fight or flight" response (Cannon, 1929). According to desensitization theory, repeated exposure to violence and its gory aftermath, whether in the media or in life (e.g., in war), results in habituation of the initially negative cognitive, emotional, and physiological responses people experience when they see blood and gore (Brockmyer, 2013; Funk, Bechtoldt-Baldacci, Pasold, & Baumgartner, 2004; Rule & Ferguson, 1986), which in theory can produce more calloused attitudes toward violence and, ultimately, increased aggression.

Numerous studies have provided evidence for the basic premise that media violence can produce desensitization to violence. Individuals exposed to violent media content are less physiologically aroused by subsequent depictions of actual violence (Lazarus, Speisman, Mordkov, & Davison, 1962; Cline, Croft, & Courier, 1973; Thomas, Horton, Lippincott, & Drabman, 1977; Thomas, 1982; Linz, Donnerstein, & Adams, 1989; Carnagey, Anderson, & Bushman, 2007), and are less empathic toward the pain and suffering of others (Bushman & Anderson, 2009) than are individuals initially exposed to nonviolent media.

Recent research by Bartholow and colleagues has tested whether exposure to violence in video games is associated with desensitization as reflected in brain responses to violence, and whether these brain responses predict aggressive behavior (Bartholow, Bushman, & Sestir, 2006; Engelhardt, Bartholow, Kerr, & Bushman, 2011; Bartholow & Hummer, this volume).

Normally, when people are exposed to situations involving potential danger (such as scenes of violence), a brain structure called the locus coeruleus (a part of the brain stem) increases secretion of the neurotransmitter norepinephrine, which in turn will alter cognitive function (i.e., attention to and appraisal of the potential threat), increase motivation (i.e., to defend oneself or escape), and increase blood flow to the major muscle groups in preparation for action. In their research, Bartholow and colleagues measured the magnitude of an electrical brain signal, the P300 (or P3) event-related potential, which is known to index the extent to which the locus-coeruleus norepinephrine system is activated by emotional stimuli (see Nieuwenhuis, Aston-Jones, & Cohen, 2005).

In an initial study, Bartholow et al. (2006) measured the P3 elicited by neutral pictures (e.g., a towel laying on a table), negative nonviolent pictures (e.g., a child with a facial disfigurement), and violent pictures (e.g., a man holding a gun in another man's mouth) in young men who varied in their previous exposure to violent video games. Results showed that young men with a history of violent video game exposure showed much smaller P3 responses to violent pictures compared to their peers who had little violent game exposure. Previous game exposure had no effect on brain responses to negative nonviolent or neutral pictures, however. These data suggest that playing violent video games is associated with desensitization to violence, as indicated by a neural measure of the fight-or-flight system.

Although suggestive of a link between violent media and desensitization, findings from Bartholow et al. (2006) were only correlational in nature. That is, the causal direction could go the other way—maybe individuals with muted brain responses to violence are simply attracted to violent media. To address the question about directionality, Engelhardt et al. (2011) randomly assigned participants to play a violent or nonviolent game in the laboratory (for 25 minutes) prior to completing the picture-viewing task used in Bartholow et al. Results showed that among participants who typically do *not* play violent games, playing a violent game in the lab caused a significant reduction in the size of the P3 elicited by violent pictures. Among participants who typically do play a lot of violent games, the type of game played in the lab didn't matter—their brain responses to violent pictures were reduced, confirming what Bartholow et al. had reported. Moreover, the size of the P3 response to violent pictures significantly mediated the effect of game condition (violent or nonviolent) on a measure of aggressive behavior. In other words, these findings suggest that acute exposure to a violent video game, even for less than 30 minutes, causes acute desensitization to violence, which then increases the tendency to behave aggressively. The larger implication of such findings is that becoming desensitized to violence, whether through repeated media violence exposure or some other means, has the potential to reduce empathy and helping (Funk et al., 2004), and causes people to react to everyday annoyances with increased aggression.

In sum, long-term exposure to violent media creates in us a more hostile worldview and takes away some of the negative feelings that are naturally triggered in violent encounters. The collective consequences of these two longer-term processes are a world populated with people who likely see hostile intent behind everyday interactions, who feel less empathy and less inclination to help those in need and a greater inclination to react to everyday stressors and frustrations with violence.

WHY DO WE REJECT MEDIA VIOLENCE RESEARCH FINDINGS?

Despite the evidence reviewed in this book that there is a link between media violence and antisocial outcomes, many people from the public to politicians and business people reject the research evidence. Strasburger, Wilson, and Jordan note, "Some of the most vocal opponents [of media violence effects on aggression] are those who work in the industry" (2013, p. 171) and therefore have a vested interest in quieting consumers' concerns over negative effects. Huesmann, DuBow, and Yang (2013) note that factors that discourage belief in media violence effects include reactance (feeling that our freedom of choice is threatened), the "third-person effect" (believing that others are influenced by media more than you are), cognitive consistency (the desire to feel that one's decisions are good and sensible), and desensitization (becoming numb to violence through exposure).

CONCLUSION

As media play more prominent roles in our lives over the coming decades, history shows that we can expect the violent content of media to increase as well. The most important challenges for parents in such an environment will revolve around how to model and enforce responsible media consumption, with special emphasis on helping children avoid unnecessary exposure to violent programs and games. Media professionals and policymakers also must begin to recognize the impact of increasingly violent content on the public (see also Bushman & Anderson, 2001), and take responsibility for how violence is portrayed in programming. Likewise, we, the public, should recognize and overcome our own resistance to accepting media violence research. Ultimately, media choices boil down to economics. A media industry powered by profits will produce whatever it believes to be most profitable. As indicated by recent research, the apparent belief among media corporations that "violence sells" may be largely unfounded (e.g., Bushman, 1998; Bushman & Phillips, 2001; Gerbner, 1994a). Perhaps if more research were dedicated to illustrating the economic costs, as well as societal costs, of media violence, eventually media executives would take notice and begin to change programming accordingly. Media will always be aimed at turning children (as well as adults) into consumers above all else. We might hope, however, that in the process children are not also turned on to violence.

NOTES

1. The correlation between violence ratings of genres and girls' self-reported playing of the games in those genres was $r = -.71$, ($p < .01$). For boys, the relationship was calculated to be $r = -.06$, not significant.

2. Wilson (1993) gives a good summary of how MPAA ratings are made.

3. Social media (Facebook, Twitter) does not follow the same advertising model. Social media presumably make their revenue by charging advertising space and allowing advertisers to target their messages to users who have "liked" particular products (Facebook) or follow particular people or who use specific words in their tweets. For Facebook, the advertising appears on a panel next to the person's private content. For Twitter, advertisers are able to send tweets to their targeted users.

4. Public television stations also acquire an average of 18 percent of their revenue from the federal government through the Corporation for Public Broadcasting. The amount of federal support has been decreasing over the years, putting pressure on PBS to allow some toned-down advertising on their networks (Corporation for Public Broadcasting, 2012).

5. Commonsensemedia.org does not have a rating for Sunday Night Football. To be conservative, we rated it a 4 for violence, although most media researchers would not consider it to be violent at all because the goals of the action are not to harm the other players and significant care is taken to reduce the risk of injury.

6. The Nielsen Company publishes two types of numbers that show the popularity of programs. The first is *the rating*, which indicates the percentage of all televisions within the United States that are tuned in to a program at a given time. The other number is *the share*, which represents the percentage of people who are watching television at a particular time who watched a particular program. The numbers that went into our analysis and presented in Figures 1.6 and 1.7 represent Nielsen ratings, not shares.

7. The Pearson correlation coefficient, r, equals $-.04$.

8. The Pearson correlation coefficient, r, equals $.76$, $p < .001$.

9. Because the cost amounts are "up-front" costs (amount that advertisers are willing to spend to advertise during a particular show based on their previewing the programs for the upcoming season), technically one cannot infer that advertisers pay for programs with large numbers of viewers. Rather, one can infer that advertisers are paying little attention to the violence in programs. It is *expected viewership*, not *actual* viewership, that sells.

10. We performed similar analyses looking at ratings, violent ratings, and costs for ad space for the 2010–2011 and 2011–2012 television seasons as well, with similar results.

11. This analysis used video game pricing data from pricecharting.com, which provides daily averages of prices listed on eBay, Amazon, and Half.com. (see http://videogames.pricecharting.com/). Violence ratings come from Common Sense Media (commonsensemedia.org).

12. $\beta = -.187$; $p = .11$, based on an analysis of 76 games.

13. Rankings of children's programs come from TV.com. Nielsen ratings and costs for advertising airtime were not publicly available.

14. Spearman $\rho = -.09$, based on 60 cases.

REFERENCES

Andersen, R. E., Crespo, C. J., Bartlett, S. J., Cheskin, L. J., & Pratt M. (1998). Relationship of physical activity and television watching with body weight and level of fatness among children: Results from the Third National Health and Nutrition Examination Survey. *Journal of the American Medical Association, 279*(12), 938–942.

Anderson, A. A., Brossard, D., Scheufele, D. A., & Xenos, M. A. (2012). Online talk: How exposure to disagreement in online comments affects beliefs in the promise of controversial science. In L. Phillips, A. Carvalho, & J. Doyle (Eds.), *Citizen voices: Performing public participation in science and environment communication* (pp. 119–135). Intellect Books: Bristol, UK.

Anderson, C. A., & Bushman, B. J. (2001). Effects of violent video games on aggressive behavior, aggressive cognition, aggressive affect, physiological arousal, and prosocial behavior: A meta-analytic review of the scientific literature. *Psychological Science, 12*, 353–359.

Anderson, C. A., & Huesmann, L. R. (2003). Human aggression: A social-cognitive view. In M. A. Hogg & J. Cooper (Eds.), *The Sage handbook on social psychology,* pp. 296–323. Thousand Oaks, CA: Sage.

Anderson, C. A., Shibuya, A., Ihori, N., Swing, E. L., Bushman, B. J., Sakamoto, A., Rothstein, H. R., & Saleem, M. (2010). Violent video game effects on aggression, empathy, and prosocial behavior in Eastern and Western countries. *Psychological Bulletin, 136*, 151–173.

Anderson, K. B., Anderson, C. A., Dill, K. E., & Deuser, W. E. (1998). The interactive relations between trait hostility, pain, and aggressive thoughts. *Aggressive Behavior, 24*, 161–171.

Anderson, R. C., Spiro, R. J., & Anderson, M. J. (1978). Schemata as scaffolding for the representation of information in connected discourse. *American Educational Research Journal, 15*(3), 433–440.

Bandura, A., & Walters, R. H. (1963). *Social learning and personality development.* New York, NY: Holt, Rinehart and Winston.

Bartholow, B. D., Bushman, B. J., & Sestir, M. A. (2006). Chronic violent video game exposure and desensitization to violence: Behavioral and event-related brain potential data. *Journal of Experimental Social Psychology, 42*, 532–539.

Berkowitz, L. (1993) *Aggression: Its causes, consequences, and control.* New York, NY: McGraw Hill.

Berry, M., Gray, T., & Donnerstein, E. (1999). Cutting film violence: Effects on perceptions, enjoyment and arousal. *Journal of Social Psychology, 139*, 567–582.

Bowling, A. (2007). *The alarming family hour: No place for children.* Los Angeles, CA: Parents' Television Council.

Brewer, W. F. (2000). Bartlett's concept of the schema and its impact on theories of knowledge representation in contemporary cognitive psychology. In A. Saito (Ed.), *Bartlett, culture and cognition* (pp. 69–89). New York, NY: Psychology Press.

Brockmyer, J. F. (2013). Media violence, desensitization, and psychological engagement. In K. E. Dill (Ed.), *The Oxford handbook of media psychology* (pp. 212–222). New York, NY: Oxford University Press.

Bureau of Labor Statistics. (2013). *American time use survey: 2012 results.* Washington, DC: U.S. Bureau of Labor Statistics.

Bushman, B. J. (1998). Effects of television violence on memory for commercial messages. *Journal of Experimental Psychology: Applied, 4*(4), 291–307.

Bushman, B. J., & Anderson, C. A. (2001). Media violence and the American public: Scientific facts versus media misinformation. *American Psychologist, 56*, 477–489.

Bushman, B. J., & Anderson, C. A. (2009). Comfortably numb: Desensitizing effects of violent media on helping others. *Psychological Science, 20*, 273–277.

Bushman, B. J., & Bonacci, A. M. (2002). Violence and sex impair memory for television ads. *Journal of Applied Psychology, 87*(3), 557–564.

Bushman, B. J., & Huesmann, L. R. (2006). Short-term and long-term effects of violent media on aggression in children and adults. *Archives of Pediatric Adolescent Medicine, 160*, 348–352.

Bushman, B. J., Jamieson, P. E., Weitz, I., & Romer, D. (2013). Gun violence trends in movies. *Pediatrics, 132*(6), 1014–1018.

Bushman, B. J., & Phillips, C. M. (2001). If the television program bleeds, memory for the advertisement recedes. *Current Directions in Psychological Science, 10*, 44–47.

Bushman, B. J., Rothstein, H. R., & Anderson, C. A. (2010). Much ado about something: Violent video game effects and a school of red herring: Reply to Ferguson and Kilburn. *Psychological Bulletin, 136*, 182–187.

Cannon, W. B. (1929). *Bodily changes in pain, hunger, fear and rage: An account of recent research into the function of emotional excitement* (2nd ed.). New York, NY: Appleton-Century-Crofts.

Cantor, J., Byrne, S., Moyer-Gusé, E., & Riddle, K. (2010). Descriptions of media-induced fright reactions in a sample of U.S. elementary school children. *Journal of Children and Media, 4*(1), 1–17.

Caplan, J., Dell, K., Dorfman, A., Fitzpatrick, L., Fox, J., & Gregory, S., et al. (2008, October 30). The best inventions of 2008: 42. Disemvoweling. *Time.com.* Retrieved from http://content.time.com/time/specials/packages/article/0,28804, 1852747_1854195_1854185,00.html

Carnagey, N. L., Anderson, C. A., & Bushman, B. J. (2007). The effect of video game violence on physiological desensitization to real-life violence. *Journal of Experimental Social Psychology, 43*, 489–496.

Center for Media and Public Affairs (1999, June). *Merchandising mayhem: Violence in popular entertainment.* Arlington, VA: Author.

Christakis, D. A., Zimmerman, F. J., DiGiuseppe, D. L., & McCarty, C. A. (2004). Early television exposure and subsequent attentional problems in children. *Pediatrics, 113*(4), 708–713.

Cialdini, R. B. (2001). *Influence: Science and practice* (4th ed.). Boston, MA: Allyn & Bacon.

Clark, D. G., & Blankenburg, W. B. (1972). Trends in violent content in selected mass media. In G. Comstock & E. Rubinstein (Eds.), *Media content and control* (Television and Social Behavior, Vol. 1., pp. 188–243). Washington, DC: Government Printing Office.

Cline, V. B., Croft, R. G., & Courier, S. (1973). Desensitization of children to television violence. *Journal of Personality and Social Psychology, 27*, 360–365.

Communications Subcommittee. (1972). *Hearings on the surgeon general's report by the Scientific Advisory Committee on Television and Social Behavior.* Serial No. 92–52. Washington, DC: U.S. Government Printing Office.

Corporation for Public Broadcasting. (2012). *Alternative sources of funding for public broadcasting stations.* Washington, DC: Author. Retrieved from http://www.cpb. org/aboutcpb/Alternative_Sources_of_Funding_for_Public_Broadcasting_ Stations.pdf

Dennison, B. A., & Edmunds, L. S. (2008). The role of television in childhood obesity. *Progress in Pediatric Cardiology, 25*(2), 191–197.

Dictionary.com. (2013). *Media.* Retrieved from http://dictionary.reference.com /browse/media?s=t

Dietz, T. L. (1998). An examination of violence and gender role portrayals in video games: Implications for gender socialization and aggressive behavior. *Sex Roles, 38*, 807–812.

Dietz, W. H., Jr., & Gortmaker, S. L. (1985). Do we fatten our children at the television set? Obesity and television viewing in children and adolescents. *Pediatrics, 75*(5), 807–812.

Dill, K. E., Gentile, D. A., Richter, W. A., & Dill, J. C. (2005). Violence, sex, race and age in popular video games: A content analysis. In E. Cole and J. Henderson Daniel (Eds.), *Featuring females: Feminist analyses of the media* (pp. 115–130). Washington, DC: American Psychological Association.

Dove Foundation. (2005). *Profitability study of MPAA-rated movies.* Grand Rapids, MI: Author. Retrieved from http://www.dove.org/research/DoveFoundationROI-Study2005.pdf

Dove Foundation. (2012). *Film profitability study 2012.* Grand Rapids, MI: Author. Retrieved from http://www.dove.org/reports/roi/Dove-Profitability-Study-2012-LR.pdf

The Economist. (2005). *Moore's law at 40: Happy birthday; The tale of a frivolous rule of thumb.* New York: Author. Retrieved from: http://news.cnet.com/New-life -for-Moores-Law/2009-1006_3-5672485.html

eMarketer (2013, January 9). *Digital to account for one in five ad dollars.* Retrieved from http://www.emarketer.com/Article/Digital-Account-One-Five-Ad-Dollars /1009592

Engelhardt, C. R., Bartholow, B. D., Kerr, G. T., & Bushman, B. J. (2011). This is your brain on violent video games: Neural desensitization to violence predicts increased aggression following violent video game exposure. *Journal of Experimental Social Psychology, 47*, 1033–1036.

Eron, L. D., Huesmann, L. R., Lefkowitz, M. M., & Walder, L. O. (1972). Does television violence cause aggression? *American Psychologist, 27*, 253–263.

Federal Bureau of Investigation. (2012). *Uniform crime reports: Crime in the United States.* Washington, DC: Criminal Justice Information Services Division.

Ferguson, C. J., & Kilburn, J. (2010). The public health risks of media violence: A meta-analytic review. *Journal of Pediatrics, 154*(5), 759–763.

Finkel, E. J., DeWall, C., Slotter, E. B., McNulty, J. K., Pond, J. S., & Atkins, D. C. (2012). Using I3 theory to clarify when dispositional aggressiveness predicts intimate partner violence perpetration. *Journal of Personality & Social Psychology, 102*(3), 533–549.

Fox, R. F. (2002, Summer). Hucksters hook captive youngsters. *Mizzou: The Magazine of the MU Alumni Association, 90*, 22–27.

Funk, J. B., Bechtoldt-Baldacci, H., Pasold, T., & Baumgartner, J. (2004). Violence exposure in real-life, video games, television, movies, and the Internet: Is there desensitization? *Journal of Adolescence, 27*, 23–39.

Geen, R. G. (1990). *Human aggression.* Pacific Grove, CA: Brooks/Cole.

Gentile, D. A., Coyne, S., & Walsh, D. A. (2010). Media violence, physical aggression, and relational aggression in school age children: A short-term longitudinal study. *Aggressive Behavior, 37*(2), 193–206.

Gentile, D. A., Swing, E. L., Lim, C. G., & Khoo, A. (2012). Video game playing, attention problems, and impulsiveness: Evidence of bi-directional causality. *Psychology of Popular Media Culture, 1,* 62–70.

Gerbner, G. (1994a, January 27). *Highlights of the Television Violence Profile No. 16.* Remarks prepared for the National Association of Television Executives Annual Conference, Miami Beach, FL.

Gerbner, G. (1994b). Making a killing. *Psychology Today, 27,* 18.

Gerbner, G. (1999). The stories we tell. *Peace Review, 11,* 9–16.

Gerbner, G., Gross, L., Morgan, M., & Signorielli, N. (1994). Growing up with television: The cultivation perspective. In J. Bryant & D. Zillman (Eds.), *Media effects: Advances in theory and research* (pp. 17–41). Hillsdale, NJ: Lawrence Erlbaum Associates.

Gerbner, G., Gross, L., Morgan, M., Signorielli, N., & Shanahan, J. (2002). Growing up with television: The cultivation process. In J. Bryant & D. Zillmann, *Media effects: Advances in theory and research* (pp. 43–68). Mahweh, NJ: Lawrence Erlbaum Associates.

Govindan, M., Gurm, R., Mohan, S., Kline-Rogers, E., Corriveau, N., Goldberg, C., DuRussel-Weston, J., Eagle, K. A., & Jackson, E. A. (2013). Gender differences in physiologic markers and health behaviors associated with childhood obesity. *Pediatrics 132*(3), 368–474.

Grabowitz, P. (2013, August 4). *The transition to digital journalism.* Berkeley, CA: University of California, Berkeley School of Journalism. Retrieved from http://multimedia.journalism.berkeley.edu/tutorials/digital-transform/print -editions-decline/

Groebel, J. (2001). Media violence in cross-cultural perspective: A global study on children's media behavior and some educational implications. In D. G. Singer & J. L. Singer (Eds.), *Handbook of children and the media* (pp. 255–268). Thousand Oaks, CA: Sage.

Grontved, A., & Hu, F. B. (2011). Television viewing and risk of type 2 diabetes, cardiovascular disease, and all-cause mortality: A meta-analysis. *Journal of the American Medical Association, 305,* 2448–2455.

Hamilton, J. T. (1998). *Channeling violence: The economic market for violent television programming.* Princeton, NJ: Princeton University Press.

Harrison, K. S., & Cantor, J. (1999). Tales from the screen: Enduring fright reactions to scary media. *Media Psychology, 1*(2), 97–116.

Hoad, P. (2013, October 31). Hollywood and the "new abnormal": Why the industry is scared of risk. *The Guardian.* Retrieved from http://www.theguardian.com /film/2013/oct/31/hollywood-new-abnormal-lynda-obst-scared-risk

Hopf, W. H., Huber, G. L., & Weib, R. H. (2008). Media violence and youth violence: A 2-year longitudinal study. *Journal of Media Psychology, 20*(3), 79–96.

Huesmann, L. R. (1999). The effects of childhood aggression and exposure to media violence on adult behaviors, attitudes, and mood: Evidence from a 15-year cross-national longitudinal study. *Aggressive Behavior, 25,* 18–21.

Huesmann, L. R., Dubow, E. F., Eron, L. D., & Boxer, P. (2006). Middle childhood family-contextual and personal factors as predictors of adult outcomes. In

A. C. Huston & M. N. Ripke (Eds.), *Developmental contexts in middle childhood: Bridges to adolescence and adulthood* (pp. 62–86). New York, NY: Cambridge University Press.

Huesmann, L. R., Dubow, E. F., & Yang, G. (2013). Why it is hard to believe that media violence causes aggression. In K. E. Dill (Ed.), *The Oxford handbook of media psychology* (pp. 159–171). New York, NY: Oxford University Press.

Jhally, S. (Executive Producer/Director). (1994). *The killing screens: Media and the culture of violence* [Video recording]. Northampton, MA: Media Education Foundation.

Johnson, J. G., Cohen, P., Smailes, E. M., Kasen, S., & Brook, J. S. (2002). Television viewing and aggressive behavior during adolescence and adulthood. *Science, 295*, 2468–2471.

Jolin, E. M., & Weller, R. A. (2011). Television viewing and its impact on childhood behaviors. *Current Psychiatry Reports, 13*(2), 122–128.

Kantar Media. (2013, March 11). Kantar Media reports U.S. advertising expenditures increased 3 percent in 2012. New York, NY: Kantar Media. Retrieved from http://kantarmediana.com/intelligence/press/us-advertising-expenditures-increased-3-percent-2012?destination=node%2F24%2Fpress

KidsHealth.org. (2012). *How TV affects your child.* Wilmington, DE: Nemours Foundation. Retrieved from http://kidshealth.org/parent/positive/family/tv_affects_child.html#

Kohut, A., Parker, K., Sonner, S., Flemming, G., Nolde, S., & Donovan, B. (1999). *Teens and traffic top community concerns: Bradley boxes out political center.* New York, NY: Pew Research Center for the People & the Press. Retrieved from http://www.people-press.org/files/legacy-pdf/61.pdf

Krahé, B., & Möller, I. (2010). Longitudinal effects of media violence on aggression and empathy among German adolescents. *Journal of Applied Developmental Psychology, 31*(5), 401–409.

Kubey, R., & Csikszentmihalyi, M. (2002). Television addiction is no mere metaphor. *Scientific American, 286*, 74–83.

Kunkel, D. (2001). Children and television advertising. In D. G. Singer & J. L. Singer (Eds.), *Handbook of children and the media* (pp. 375–393). Thousand Oaks, CA: Sage.

Lazarus, R. S., Speisman, M., Mordkoff, A. M., & Davison, L. A. (1962). A laboratory study of psychological stress produced by a motion picture film. *Psychological Monographs: General and Applied, 76*(34), 1–35.

Lefkowitz, M. M., Eron, L. D., Walder, L. O., & Huesmann, L. R. (1977). *Growing up to be violent: A longitudinal study of the development of aggression.* Oxford, UK: Pergamon.

Lenhart, A., Kahne, J., Middaugh, E., Rankin-MacGill, A., Evans, C., & Vitak J. (2008). *Teens, video games, and civics: Teens' gaming experiences are diverse, and include significant social interaction and civic engagement.* Washington, DC: Pew Internet & American Life Project. Retrieved from http://www.pewinternet.org/~/media//Files/Reports/2008/PIP_Teens_Games_and_Civics_Report_FINAL.pdf.

Levin, S., Petros, T., & Petrella, F. (1982). Preschoolers' awareness of television advertising. *Child Development, 53*, 933–937.

Linz, D., Donnerstein, E., & Adams, S. M. (1989). Physiological desensitization and judgments about female victims of violence. *Human Communication Research, 15*, 509–522.

Looney, G. (1971, October). *Television and the child: What can be done*. Paper presented at the meeting of the American Academy of Pediatrics, Chicago, IL.

Lu, W., Waterman, D., & Yan, M. Z. (2005). *Changing markets, new technology, and violent content: An economic study of motion picture genre trends*. Paper presented at the 33rd annual TPRC conference, Washington, DC, September 23–25.

Madden, M., Lenhart, A., Duggan, M., Cortesi, S., & Gasser, U. (2013). *Teens and technology 2013*. Washington, DC: Pew Research Center. Retrieved from http://www.pewinternet.org/Reports/2013/Teens-and-Tech.aspx

McDonough, P. (2009). *Television and beyond from a kid's-eye view*. New York, NY: The Nielson Company. Retrieved from http://www.nielsen.com/us/en/newswire/2009/television-and-beyond-a-kids-eye-view.html

Moore, G. (1965). Cramming more components onto integrated circuits. *Electronics*, *38*(4), 4. Retrieved from http://download.intel.com/museum/Moores_Law/Articles-Press_Releases/Gordon_Moore_1965_Article.pdf

Morris C. (2012, November 21) The 10 biggest game openings of all time. Yahoo.com: Plugged in [web log]. Retrieved from:https://games.yahoo.com/blogs/plugged-in/10-biggest-game-openings-time-204020614.html;_ylt=AwrBJR8dsdtTyj YAaxvUwOZ_

National Cable Television Association (1993, January). *Industry policy statement regarding violence*. Washington, DC: Author.

National Public Radio (2013, June 30). Casting call: Hollywood needs more women. *All Things Considered*. Summary retrieved from http://www.npr.org/2013/06/30/197390707/casting-call-hollywood-needs-more-women

Nayak, M. (2013, September 18). Take Two's GTA V starts strong with $800 mln in first-day sales. Reuters.com. Retrieved from: http://www.reuters.com/article/email/idUSBRE98H0Z720130918.

National Television Violence Study. (1998). *National Television Violence Study: Vol. 3*. Santa Barbara, CA: University of California Santa Barbara, Center for Communication and Social Policy.

Network Television Association (1992, December). *Standards for depiction of violence in television programs*. New York, NY: Author.

Nielsen. (2013). *A look across screens: The cross platform report*. New York, NY: Author. Retrieved from http://www.nielsen.com/us/en/reports/2013/the-cross-platform-report-a-look-across-screens.html

Nieuwenhuis, S., Aston-Jones, G., & Cohen, J. D. (2005). Decision making, the P3, and the locus coeruleus-norepinephrine system. *Psychological Bulletin*, *131*, 510–532.

Palsson, C., Price, J., & Shores, J. (2013). Ratings and revenues: Evidence from movie ratings. *Contemporary Economic Policy*, *31*(1), 13–21.

Parents' Television Council. (2006). *Wolf in sheep's clothing: A content analysis of children's programming*. Los Angeles, CA: Author.

Parents' Television Council. (2007a). *Dying to entertain: Violence on primetime broadcast television 1998–2006*. Los Angeles, CA: Author.

Parents' Television Council. (2007b). *The alarming family hour: No place for children*. Los Angeles, CA: Author.

Patten, D. (2013, May 23). Full 2012–2013 TV series ratings. *Deadline.com*. Retrieved from http://www.deadline.com/2013/05/tv-season-series-rankings-2013-full-list/

Potter, W. J. (1999). *On media violence*. Thousand Oaks, CA: Sage.

Potter, W. J. (2003). *The 11 myths of media violence*. Thousand Oaks, CA: Sage.

Rhodes, A. (2013, June 4). *Exploiting children one commercial at a time*. Boston, MA: Campaign for a Commercial-Free Childhood. Retrieved from http://www .commercialfreechildhood.org/blog/exploiting-children-one-commercial

Rideout, V. A. (2007). *Parents, children and media: A Kaiser Family Foundation survey*. Menlow Park, CA: Kaiser Family Foundation. Retrieved from http:// kaiserfamilyfoundation.files.wordpress.com/2013/01/7638.pdf

Rideout, V. A., Foehr, U. G., & Roberts, D. M. (2010). *Generation M2: Media in the lives of 8 to 18 year olds*. Menlow Park, CA: Kaiser Family Foundation. Retrieved from kff.org/other/poll-finding/report-generation-m2-media-in-the-lives/

Robinson, T. N. (1999). Reducing children's television viewing to prevent obesity: A randomized controlled trial. *Journal of the American Medical Association, 282*(16), 1561–1567.

Robinson, T. N. (2001). Television viewing and childhood obesity. *Pediatric Clinics of North America, 48*(4), 1017–1025.

Rule, B. K., & Ferguson, T. J. (1986). The effects of media violence on attitudes, emotions, and cognitions. *Journal of Social Issues, 42*, 29–50.

Signorielli, N., Gerbner, G., & Morgan, M. (1995). Violence on television: The cultural indicators project. *Journal of Broadcasting and Electronic Media, 39*, 278–283.

Smith, A. (2013). Smartphone ownership, 2013. New York, NY: Pew Internet and American Life Study. Retrieved from http://pewinternet.org/Reports/2013 /Smartphone-Ownership-2013/Findings/Smartphone-ownership-update.aspx

Smith, S., Chouieti, M., Scofield, E., & Pieper, K. (2013). *Gender inequality in popular films: Examining on screen portrayals and behind-the-scenes employment patterns in motion pictures released between 2007–2012*. Unpublished manuscript, Annenberg School for Communication & Journalism, University of Southern California. Retrieved from http://annenberg.usc.edu/Faculty/Communication%20and%20 Journalism/~/media/5DB47326757B416FBE2CB5E6F1B5CBE4.ashx

Sparks, G. G., Sherry, J., & Lubsen, G. (2005). The appeal of media violence in a full-length motion picture: An experimental investigation. *Communication Reports, 18*(1), 21–30.

Stavrinides, P., Tsivitanou, A., Nikiforou, M., Hawa, V., & Tsolia, V. (2013). Longitudinal associations between bullying and children's preference for television violence. *International Journal of Criminology and Sociology, 2*, 72–78.

Steinberg, B. (2012, October 21). TV ad prices: "Idol" no match for football. *Ad Age .com*. Retrieved from http://adage.com/article/media/tv-ad-prices-idol-match -football/237874/

Strasburger, V. C., & Wilson, B. J. (2002). *Children, adolescents, and the media*. Thousand Oaks, CA: Sage.

Strasburger, V. C., Wilson, B. J., & Jordan, A. B. (2013). *Children, adolescents, and the media* (3rd ed.). Thousand Oaks, CA: Sage.

Surette, R. (2011). *Media, crime, and criminal justice: Images, realities, and policies*. Belmont, CA: Thomson-Wadsworth.

Swing, E. L., Gentile, D. A., Anderson, C. A., & Walsh, D. A. (2010). Television and video game exposure and the development of attention problems. *Pediatrics, 126*(2), 214–221.

Thomas, M. H. (1982). Physiological arousal, exposure to a relatively lengthy aggressive film, and aggressive behavior. *Journal of Research in Personality, 16*, 72–81.

Thomas, M. H., Horton, R. W., Lippincott, E. C., & Drabman, R. S. (1977). Desensitization to portrayals of real life aggression as a function of television violence. *Journal of Personality and Social Psychology, 35*, 450–458.

Thompson, K. M., & Yokota, F. (2004). Violence, sex, and profanity in films: Correlation of movie ratings with content. *Medscape General Medicine, 6*(3). Retrieved from http://www.medscape.com/viewarticle/480900

Timmer, J. (2013). Television violence and industry self-regulation: The V-chip, television program ratings, and the TV parental guidelines oversight monitoring board. *Communication Law and Policy, 18*(3), 265–307.

U.S. Department of Education. (N.d.). Average number of hours in the school day and average number of days in the school year for public schools, by state: 2007–08. Available from http://nces.ed.gov/surveys/sass/tables/sass0708_035_s1s.asp

Violence bill debated in Washington. (1990, February 5). *Broadcasting, 118*(6), 77–78.

Walsh, D. A. (2001). *Doctor Dave's cyberhood.* New York, NY: Simon & Schuster.

Ward, S., Reale, G., & Levenson, D. (1972). Children's perceptions, explanations, and judgments of television advertising: A further exploration. In G. Comstock & E. Rubinstein (Eds.), *Television and social behavior: Vol. 4.* (pp. 468–490). Washington, DC: U.S. Government Printing Office.

Weaver, A. J., Jensen, J. D., Martins, N., Hurley, R. J., & Wilson, B. J. (2011). Liking violence and action: An examination of gender differences in children's processing of animated content. *Media Psychology, 14*(1), 49–70.

Weaver, A. J., & Kobach, M. J. (2012). The relationship between selective exposure and the enjoyment of television violence. *Aggressive Behavior, 38*(2), 175–184.

Weaver, A. J., & Wilson, B. J. (2009). The role of graphic and sanitized violence in the enjoyment of television dramas. *Human Communication Research, 35*, 442–463.

Weber Shandwick. (2010). *Civility in America: A nationwide survey.* Chicago, IL: Author. Retrieved from http://www.webershandwick.com/uploads/news/files/Civility_2010_SocialMediaImplications.pdf

Wilson, B. J. (1993). What's wrong with the ratings? *Media & Values, 63*, 13–15. Retrieved from http://www.medialit.org/reading-room/whats-wrong-ratings

Zickuhr, K., Rainie, L., & Purcell, K. (2013). *Younger Americans' library habits and expectations.* New York, NY: Pew Internet and American Life Study.

Zillmann, D. (1983). Arousal and aggression. In R. G. Geen and E. Donnerstein (Eds.), *Aggression: Theoretical and empirical reviews, Vol. 1: Theoretical and methodological issues* (pp. 75–101). New York, NY: Academic Press.

CHAPTER 2

Why Don't Media Violence Effects Look the Same on Everyone?: Developmental Approaches to Understanding Media Effects

Douglas A. Gentile

When the first edition of this book came out, several violent events had recently occurred that seemed to implicate media violence as a cause. These included a 12-year-old boy brutally killing a 6-year-old girl by imitating professional wrestling moves ("Stiff Sentence," 2001), the Columbine High School massacre, carried out by two adolescents who had practiced their plan by playing violent video games (Gibbs & Roche, 1999), and a 17-year-old setting himself on fire while being videotaped in an attempt to duplicate a stunt called the "human barbecue" from the MTV show *Jackass* (Brachear, 2002). At that time, we argued that these highly publicized stories demonstrated how *not* to think about media effects because they oversimplify complex situations (Gentile & Sesma, 2003). In the past decade, however, the public's understanding of media violence seems to have actually gotten worse. Incidents linking media violence to extreme criminal acts, such as the mass murder at an Aurora, Colorado, movie theater in 2012 (www.cnn.com /SPECIALS/us/colorado-shooting), continue to be reported as if media violence was responsible. These claims understandably beget an equal, but opposite, reaction, with people claiming that they played violent games and haven't shot anyone so therefore they must have no harmful effect, or might even have a helpful effect (e.g., White, 2013). Given the increasing polarization of American society (Dandekar, Goel, & Lee, 2013), perhaps this controversy is to be expected. Nonetheless, even the scientific dialogue appears polarized, with some reviews claiming that the debate should be "over" (Anderson et al., 2003), and others claiming that the researchers are trying to incite a "moral panic" (Ferguson, 2010).

To be able to find the middle ground and to understand media effects on children more fully, it is necessary to dispel some myths. There are many common beliefs about media effects that despite being simple, persuasive, and sometimes partly true, actually hamper comprehension of how media influence youth.

NINE MYTHS ABOUT MEDIA EFFECTS

Myth 1. Media Effects Are Simple and Direct

Examples that appear in the news seem to demonstrate simple and direct effects of children imitating what they have seen. Yet the effects of media are not simple; neither are they usually direct. Most media effects are cumulative and subtle, even when they are specifically designed to influence behavior. This subtlety masks remarkable power and persuasiveness. For example, research on advertisements demonstrates that attitudes and purchasing behavior can be altered by as few as two or three exposures to an advertisement (Woodward & Denton, 2000). Yet, as we watch or drive past advertisements, we don't *feel* our opinions changing. The effects of media usually happen at a level at which we are not consciously aware. We rarely notice that advertisements affect us, partly because ads are generally presented as entertainment, so that viewers are less likely to notice any effect, or to resist their messages. Research suggests that the more one participates in this charade, claiming that advertisements don't affect "me," the *more* likely one is to actually be affected (Greene, 1999).

Thus, to the extent that we expect media effects to be simple and direct, we are probably failing to notice the strongest and most powerful media influences.

Myth 2. The Effects of Media Violence Are Severe

Each of the events mentioned at the beginning of this chapter is extreme, and yet most people who watch media violence never seriously injure other people or themselves. Since media violence does not make them commit the same kind of violence, many people draw the inference that it has no effect on them or on most other people. Potter (1999) noted that there is a flaw in this thinking: "People know that others are committing violent acts, but they also know that they personally have never committed any atrocities. The problem with this reasoning is that people equate [media] effects with atrocities" (p. 122). Watching violent media can have many effects, and we should not expect that exposure to media violence will cause people to begin killing each other. The vast majority of research on media violence demonstrates that it influences aggressive thoughts and behaviors, which in turn increase the odds of an aggressive response when provoked. Nonetheless, this aggressive

Figure 2.1
Incidents of Violent Behaviors in American Schools, 1998

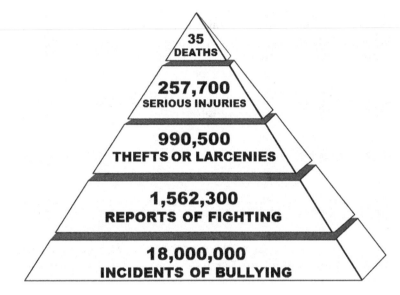

response is most likely to be low-level aggression, such as verbal or relational aggression (see Coyne & Stockdale, this volume). In fact, the largest effect of media violence is probably not illustrated by individual examples of violent behavior, but by the "culture of disrespect" it has fostered and nurtured (Walsh, 2001). Interpersonal violence is just the endpoint on a continuum of disrespectful behavior. As Figure 2.1 shows, for every one example of a school killing, there were over 7,000 serious injuries, 28,000 thefts, 44,000 physical fights, and 500,000 reports of bullying (B. Modzeleski, personal communication, January 9, 2003). Killing someone is just the most visible part of the phenomenon—there is a great deal of aggressive behavior that is not so extreme.

This highlights an important point of agreement within what appears to be disagreement. The critics of media violence research almost always focus on "violence" rather than the less extreme and more inclusive term "aggression." Most of the researchers agree with the critics that there is very little evidence that media violence will cause real world *violence* (defined as physical aggression that would cause severe bodily harm or death). They also agree, however, that there is a lot of evidence that media violence can cause real world *aggression*. This point is often missed in the public dialogue.

Although most of the public concern is about behaviors, violent media affect us much more broadly. Any time that you have laughed, felt excited, become scared or otherwise aroused while watching a violent movie, *you have just been affected.* Positive and negative emotional and physiological reactions to violent media are media effects. Clearly, many people seek out this type of stimulation. After all, who wants to watch a "boring" movie? Violent media have many effects, including emotional, physiological, cognitive, attitudinal, and behavioral effects (see chapters 3, 4, 5, 6, 8, and 11 for more details). To the extent that we expect media effects to be exhibited through atrocities, we are ignoring where the effect really happens.

Myth 3. Media Effects Are Obvious

In each of the examples at the beginning of this chapter it was obvious (often from the perpetrator's own admission) what media product had influenced the subsequent behavior. This leads many to expect that such links should usually be obvious and to take the absence of a direct and obvious link as evidence that no media effects should be implicated. Because the effects of violent media are usually indirect, subtle, and cumulative (and thus not obvious), many people then argue that researchers and policymakers are trying to find an easy "scapegoat" to explain violent behaviors. Indeed, even when the link *is* obvious, many people make this argument; the following anonymous quote was posted in response to the *Jackass* copycat burning: "TV shows are not responsible for copycat attempts of dangerous stunts they portray. . . . Blaming TV shows for the actions of minors is just passing the buck" ("Texas talkback," n.d.).

Humans are not good at detecting small changes across time, which is how the media tend to have their effects. Furthermore, media violence influences psychological variables, such as attitudes, beliefs, feelings, scripts, expectations, biases, and perceptions, none of which are easily visible. Nevertheless, cause-effect relationships need not be obvious to be significant. Most people accept that smoking causes lung cancer, even though the effect is subtle and cumulative (for a description of the many parallels between smoking and media violence, see Bushman & Anderson, 2001). One cigarette does not change a person's health in any particularly noticeable way, but years of smoking can have dire consequences (although not for all people). To the extent that we expect media effects to be exhibited in an obvious manner, we are missing opportunities to see other, less obvious and perhaps more pervasive effects.

Myth 4. Violent Media Affect Everyone in the Same Way

Many people assume that media violence effects must be unidimensional—that is, that everyone must be affected in the same way (by becoming more aggressive). Although that is one of the documented effects, it is not the only one. Meta-analyses (studies that analyze data presented across large numbers of studies) have shown that there are multiple effects. Some of these are at the level of emotions, some at the level of thoughts, some are about attitudes, some are about behavior, and so forth (see Potter, 1999, and this volume, for a listing of about 17 different scientifically documented effects). These multiple effects have been grouped into four, called the *aggressor effect*, the *victim effect*, the *bystander effect*, and the *appetite effect* (Donnerstein, Slaby, & Eron, 1994).

The *aggressor effect* describes how children and adults who watch a lot of violent entertainment tend to become more willing to behave aggressively when provoked, becoming meaner and more aggressive.

The *victim effect* describes how children and adults who watch a lot of violent entertainment tend to see the world as a scarier place, become more scared, and initiate more self-protective behaviors (including going so far as to carry guns to school, which, ironically, *increases* one's odds of being shot).

The *bystander effect* describes how children and adults who watch a lot of violent entertainment tend to habituate to gradually increasing amounts of violence, thereby becoming desensitized, more callous, and less sympathetic to victims of violence (both in the media and in real life).

The *appetite effect* describes how children and adults who watch a lot of violent entertainment tend to want to see more violent entertainment. Simply put, the more one watches, the more one wants to watch.

These effects are well documented in hundreds of studies. What is less well known is which people are more prone to which effects (although these effects are not mutually exclusive). In general, females tend to be more affected by the *victim effect*, whereas males tend to be more affected by the *aggressor*, *bystander*, and *appetite effects*. But it is still unclear how to predict exactly how any given individual will be affected by any given media violence presentation. However, the fact that we cannot yet make this prediction very well should not be taken as evidence that there is no effect. Notice that just because everyone is not affected in the same way does not mean that every viewer is not affected.

To understand where children learn their attitudes, values, and patterns of behavior, we can consider the effects of various proximal and distal sources of influence (see Figure 2.2). The family has the most direct access to the children, and children clearly have their attitudes, values, and behavior patterns shaped and modified by their families. The behaviors defined as "normal" within each family affect the behaviors of the individuals within that family. Beyond the level of the family, the norms of the community affect the norms of the families and individuals within it. Beyond the level of the community, the norms of society affect the norms of the communities, families, and individuals within it. The media operate at this societal level, and media effects can be seen at all levels. Thus, the media can affect us not only one on one when we are watching TV, for example, but they also affect us by affecting the norms, expectations, and patterns of behavior of our families and

Figure 2.2
Multiple Spheres of Influence on Children

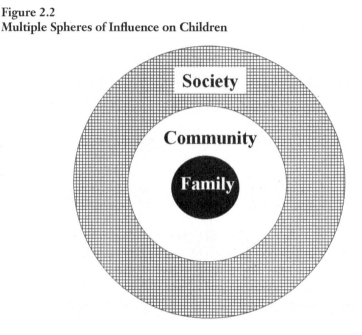

communities. This is another aspect of the media's subtlety—they can affect us from multiple directions at once. Although this makes it likely that everyone will be affected by violent media in some way, it also makes it likely that the effects will not be identical for all people.

Myth 5. Causality Means "Necessary and Sufficient"

Determining if and when something "causes" something else is a problem that has plagued philosophers and scientists for centuries. In the social sciences, it is a surprisingly complex problem to solve. For many people, however, it has become oversimplified—something is a cause if it can be shown to be necessary and/or sufficient as a precursor. This position has been used to argue against the effects of media violence. Ferguson (2002), in a response to Bushman and Anderson's (2001) meta-analyses of media violence and aggression, stated that:

(a) because humans have always been violent, "violent media, then, are not a necessary precursor to violent behavior" (p. 446), and

(b) because many people who are exposed to media violence never commit violent behavior, "violent media, then, are not sufficient to cause violent behavior" (p. 446).

This argument seems, on its surface, to be reasonable. Yet this argument actually betrays a grossly oversimplified idea of causation. Consider, for example, a rock on the side of a hill. Assume that you give the rock a push and it begins rolling down the hill. Did you cause the rock to roll down the hill? Based on the argument laid out above, you did not. Rocks have rolled down hills for eons without someone coming along and pushing them. Therefore pushing it is not necessary. Furthermore, many rocks that are pushed do not roll down hills. Therefore, pushing the rock is not sufficient. Although pushing the rock was neither necessary nor sufficient to make it roll down the hill, that does not mean that pushing was not a cause of the rock's beginning to roll.

Most complex issues of interest (such as aggressive behavior) are multi-causal. In the present example, many other issues interact to determine whether the push you gave to the rock causes it to roll down the hill: the force of gravity, the mass of the rock, the shape of the rock, the friction of the hill surface, the slope of the hill surface, the direction of the push, the force of the push, how deeply the rock is embedded into the ground, and so on, all interact to determine whether your push makes the rock begin to roll or not. Recognition that the issue is multi-causal does *not* mean that your push is not one of the causes; in fact, it may have been a significant determiner or catalyst for the ultimate outcome, without which the other causes would not have been activated or sufficient. Aggressive behavior, too, is multi-causal. Media violence is likely to be one of the pushes that interacts with other forces at work. In most situations, it is neither necessary nor sufficient. However, that does not mean that it is not a cause—it just means that it is *one* of the causes.

When there is a tragedy like a school shooting, we enter what could be called a "culprit mentality," where we seek "the cause" of the tragedy (Gentile & Bushman, 2012). This is akin to the idea of "proximate cause" in law, where the goal is to assign legal responsibility for an action. The proximate cause is the last action to set off a sequence of events that produces an injury. Yet this is an inappropriate way to understand most human behavior. Human behavior is notoriously and amazingly multi-causal; there is almost never one single cause for any behavior, especially aggression. This simplistic approach to thinking about causality is misleading for both scientists and the public. Furthermore, the goal of social science is not the same as in law. Social science is concerned with all of the causes for some behavior, not only necessary, sufficient, the most recent, or the largest causes. Because media violence has been shown to increase the likelihood of aggressive behavior, it is a cause of aggressive behavior, even though it alone is not a necessary or sufficient cause.

Myth 6. Causality Means Immediacy

Many people also expect that causality requires immediacy, as in a fall causing a broken bone. As noted in the smoking and cancer example, however, physical symptoms may become visible only after some threshold of disease process is attained, which may take a long time. With regard to media violence, many people assume that the effects must be seen in the short term in order to be caused by exposure. For example, Ferguson (2002, p. 447) states, "If media violence is a necessary and direct cause of violent behavior, a significant decline in violent crime should not be occurring unless violence in the media is also declining." We have already seen that media violence can be a cause without being a "necessary" cause. The issue of whether it is a "direct" cause seems to be the relationship between the amount of media violence and the incidence of violence in society. From the 1950s until about 1993, both the amount of media violence and the number of aggravated assaults rose in the United States (Grossman, 1996). In the latter half of the 1990s, the aggravated assault rate fell somewhat, while the amount of media violence stayed constant or increased (especially in video games; see chapters 5 and 8). This was taken by many to be "evidence" that media violence does not cause aggressive behavior.

Yet many causes have long-term effects. Consider smoking and lung cancer. Consider water, salt, and your car. Over many years, cars that are repeatedly exposed to salt rust at a higher rate than those that are not. But if you pour salt water on your car, will you see it rust in the next month or even year? No, because it is a long-term effect. Some researchers have presented evidence that the effects of media violence may be long term as well. For example, Centerwall (1989) has documented that the murder rate appears to double about 15 years after the initial introduction of television to communities/ countries. It has been hypothesized that about 15 years must elapse before the full effect is revealed, as that is the amount of time it takes for a generation to grow up with the violent media and to reach prime crime-committing age. If this hypothesis is correct, then we shouldn't expect to see immediate effects. To the extent that we expect causation to appear as immediate or short-term effects, we may miss a number of important long-term effects.

Myth 7. Effects Must Be "Big" to Be Important

Many people have agreed that the accumulated research shows that there is a systematic effect of violent media on aggressive behavior, yet also insisted that it is not a large enough effect to be important. These discussions often include a statistical approach. Meta-analyses document that the amount of variance accounted for by media violence is somewhere between 1 and 10 percent (see Comstock, Scharrer, & Powers, this volume). This means that if we drew a circle representing all the reasons why someone might act violently, media violence would account for between 1 and 10 percent of the pie. (It should be noted that some meta-analyses have reported larger numbers, and that there are a number of methodological reasons why these numbers may be underestimates; see Paik & Comstock, 1994, and Gentile &

Bushman, 2012.) Several critics have argued that these effect sizes are "small and lack practical significance" (e.g., Ferguson, 2002; Freedman, 2002), but it is unclear on what basis it is made. In epidemiological terms, if only 1 percent of the people watching a violent TV show become more aggressive, and one million people watch the program, then 10,000 people were made more aggressive. That does not seem to "lack practical significance." Indeed, many (if not most) medical studies on the effects of drugs or diet are concerned with such small effects. Supplementing one's diet with calcium can increase bone mass, but the effect is "only" about 1 percent (Bushman & Anderson, 2001). Hormone replacement therapy in women may increase the odds of breast cancer, but across the whole population, the effect is probably less than a 1 percent effect. A daily aspirin may reduce the risk of heart attacks, but again, the effect is probably less than 1 percent. The medical profession regards these small effects as clearly important with a great deal of practical significance.

In fact, there are probably hundreds of reasons for any aggressive act (e.g., abuse, poverty, provocation, gang membership, broken home, drug use, etc.). If there are hundreds of reasons, then any single one of them should not account for much variance. That media violence consistently appears to account for at least 1 to 10 percent of the effect strikes me as surprisingly large. The U.S. Surgeon General's report on youth violence places exposure to TV violence as just as strong a risk factor for aggressive behavior as low IQ, and more important than coming from a broken home or having abusive parents (U.S. Surgeon General, 2001). These risk factors also do not have immediate or necessarily extreme effects on aggression, but that does not render them unimportant.

Myth 8. My Child Knows the Difference between Fantasy and Reality

As noted later in the developmental tasks section, young children have a very different understanding of real and pretend than adults do. Your four-year-old may be able to say to you that "monsters aren't real," but she still worries that they will "get" her. This is developmentally accurate up until about age 7, after which children's conception of fantasy and reality becomes similar to adults'. This developmental truth has led many people to believe that therefore media violence only influences people who can't tell the difference between fantasy and reality. Unfortunately, this is not correct. I am certain that all of the children and college students who participate in media violence studies know that the violence they are seeing in the TV show or video game is not real. Nonetheless, they tend to behave more aggressively after seeing it. Similarly, adults know that advertising is fake. Nonetheless, it still works on us. Knowing that media violence is not "real" does not inoculate viewers from the effects.

Myth 9. Media Violence Helps People to Be Less Aggressive Because It Allows Them to Blow off Steam

Hundreds of studies and multiple meta-analyses (cf., chapter 13, this volume; Allen, D'Alessio, and Brezgel, 1995; Anderson, 2004; Anderson & Bushman, 2001; Anderson et al., 2003; Anderson et al., 2010; Andison, 1977; Bushman & Anderson, 2001; Bushman & Huesmann, 2006; Ferguson, 2007a; Ferguson, 2007b; Ferguson and Kilburn, 2009; Hearold, 1986; Hogben, 1998; Paik and Comstock, 1994; Savage and Yancey, 2008; Sherry, 2001; Wood, Wong, and Chachere, 1991) have consistently demonstrated that media violence exposure increases the risk of aggression. This consistency has led several prominent public health organizations (e.g., the American Medical Association, the American Academy of Pediatrics, two U.S. Surgeons General, the American Psychological Association, among others) to conclude that media violence is one causal risk factor for aggression. Despite this apparent consistency, there is still a common belief that playing a violent video game or watching a violent movie can lower the risk of future aggression by allowing the viewer to "vent" their aggression in a socially acceptable way (known as the aggression catharsis hypothesis).

Although it is an elegant idea that feels right, particularly after we have just finished playing that violent game, there are several serious problems with the catharsis hypothesis (for a detailed discussion, see Gentile, 2013). First, the concept is based on a hydraulic drive metaphor, where the pressure builds and builds and needs to "vent" or "blow off steam" in order to keep the system from exploding. Humans do have these types of drives, such as hunger and thirst, where the pressure to eat gets greater and greater and if not reduced by eating, then the system explodes (i.e., you die). Aggression is not like that. We do not become more and more aggressive and need to let it out or else we will die from not aggressing. Second, as demonstrated in most of the chapters of this book and the public health consensus above, the scientific evidence actually points in the opposite direction. Third, and most damning for the catharsis argument, it isn't how the brain works. Every repetition of something helps us learn it better—it doesn't remove it from the brain. Therefore, practicing aggressive thoughts and scripts by watching media violence can only *increase* how accessible and acceptable they are, not decrease them.

SUMMARY

These persistent myths underscore the importance of thinking carefully about what the effects of media violence on individuals may be. We must understand that everyone may be affected, yet not in the same way. We must recognize that most children may be affected, although we may only notice the effects in extreme cases. Two developmental theoretical approaches show a great deal of promise for helping researchers to understand the effects of media violence on children: the developmental tasks approach, and the risk and resilience approach. Each is described below, with emphasis on how they relate to media violence.

DEVELOPMENTAL TASKS APPROACH

Overview

Most children learn to talk. Most children become attached to a primary caregiver. Most children develop relationships with peers. Each of these capacities—language acquisition, development of attachment relationships, and the formation of peer relationships—is a *developmental task*—a capacity or skill that is important for concurrent and future adaptation (Sroufe, 1979). Masten and Braswell (1991, p. 13) defined developmental tasks in the following manner:

In developmental psychopathology, adaptation is often defined in terms of developmental tasks. . . . The basic idea is that in order for a person to adapt, there are developmental challenges that must be met. Some arise through biological maturation, others are imposed by families and society, while others arise from the developing self.

All children of a particular society are presumed to face these tasks at some point in development; thus, these tasks serve as a barometer from which to infer competence (Masten & Coatsworth, 1998). The developmental task approach also provides researchers and practitioners with a framework for understanding how development unfolds over the course of childhood.

There is a hierarchy to these tasks (Sroufe, 1979; 1995). Different issues rise in importance depending on the developmental level of the child. Thus, for infants, the most important task that must be negotiated is developing a trusting relationship with a primary caregiver. As can be seen in Table 2.1, this task recedes in importance as other tasks arise.

This does not mean, however, that early tasks are irrelevant at later stages; to the contrary, later tasks are *contingent* on the success with which earlier tasks were negotiated. That is, any measure of competence is implicitly measuring the totality of adaptation that occurred prior to that measurement. This idea—that development is cumulative and builds on prior adaptation—can also be seen in Table 2.1. Here, the degree to which a child is able to form a trusting relationship with a primary caregiver has direct implications for how she negotiates the next tasks, such as active exploration of her environment. If a child has established a healthy sense of trust and this helped her to actively explore her environment, then the child is in a good position to deal with issues of self-regulation, which are typically encountered in the preschool period. Development proceeds in this way, building on past resolutions and negotiations.

Table 2.1
Examples of Developmental Tasks

Key Developmental Tasks of Infancy (~0 to 12 Months)

- Attachment to caregiver(s)

- Regularity of patterns

- Transition from reflex to voluntary behavior

Key Developmental Tasks of Toddlerhood (~1 to 2½ Years)

- Curiosity, exploration, and mastery

- Differentiation of self from world

- Independence of actions, such as self-care and feeding

- Learning of language

Key Developmental Tasks of Early Childhood (~2½ to 5 Years)

- Learning behavioral self-control and compliance with external rules

- Learning emotional self-control

- Learning gender roles and stereotypes

Key Developmental Tasks of Middle Childhood (~6 to 12 Years)

- Learning how to build loyal friendships and to be accepted by peers

- Learning social rules and norms

- Adjusting to school

- Learning the importance of academic achievement and real-world competence

- Moral development

- Consolidating self-concept (in terms of the peer group)

Key Developmental Tasks of Adolescence (~13 to 18 Years)

- Learning to build intimate and committed friendships/relationships

- Adjustment to pubertal changes

- Transition to secondary schooling

- Develop strong and coherent personal identity

Source: Adapted from Aber & Jones (1997), Masten & Braswell (1991), Sroufe, Cooper, & DeHart (1996), Sroufe, Egeland, & Carlson (1999).

The successful negotiation of earlier tasks sets the child on probabilistic pathways for future competence, and these can change depending on the severity of contemporaneous circumstances (e.g., parental death; Cicchetti & Toth, 1998). The implication of this is that it is erroneous to think of adaptation (or maladaptation) as something a child "has." Instead, adaptation is a dynamic process, predicated both on past history and current context. Although change is possible, it is constrained by prior adaptation (Erikson, 1963; Sroufe, 1997). The longer a child is on an adaptive pathway (i.e., successful negotiation of prior developmental issues), the less likely it is that dire current circumstances can bump the child onto a maladaptive pathway.

Summary of Major Developmental Tasks

The effects that violent (or other) media may have on children and youth may be very different depending on the age of the child in question. As children face different developmental tasks, media are likely to have a greater or lesser effect depending on the specific issues the children are facing at that time. A brief summary of the key developmental tasks at each of five ages is presented below. These are adapted from Masten & Braswell (1991), Sroufe, Cooper, & DeHart (1996), Sroufe, Egeland, & Carlson (1999), and Aber & Jones (1997).

Infancy (approximately birth to 12 months)

During infancy, developing a trusting relationship with a caregiver is the key developmental task for healthy development. In physical development, the brain is undergoing a tremendous amount of neural network development. In cognitive development, infants exhibit learning by habituation, discrimination, classical conditioning, operant conditioning, and imitative learning. The expression of emotions begins to develop, and we see the beginnings of emotional regulation.

Toddlerhood (approximately 1 to 2½ years)

During toddlerhood, children develop a number of capacities that could be affected by media. In cognitive development, children at this age develop the capacity for symbolic representation, including language. Children also grow in their ability to use language in a competent communicative manner to conduct conversations in a socially appropriate and culturally specific manner. Social gestures begin to emerge, including conventional social gestures and symbolic gestures. Children also begin to understand themselves as distinct from others. However, children's cognition is still constrained by limited memory abilities, a lack of logic, and a difficulty distinguishing what is real and what is fantasy.

In social development, children's independence of action and feelings of competence is particularly important during toddlerhood. This is also the period where children begin to be expected to learn to regulate and control their behaviors and expressions of emotions. Toddlers begin to acquire the rules, norms, and values of society through socialization processes. Children begin to look to others for cues about how to act in new or ambiguous situations, and begin to internalize the rules and values.

In emotional development, the so-called "self-conscious" emotions such as shame, guilt, and pride emerge. Early attachment relations and the further development of those attachment relations continue to be important.

Early childhood (approximately 2½ to 5 years)

In cognitive development, children at this age begin to learn to classify things by shared characteristics, such as color, size, and shape (classification). They also begin to be able to organize things along a particular dimension, such as size or height (seriation). Learning to deploy attention with intention begins at this age, although "the tasks of selecting information to attend to, staying focused on it, and ignoring irrelevant stimuli all pose challenges to preschoolers" (Sroufe et al., 1996, p. 348). Children at this age continue to have difficulty solving appearance-reality problems, and reality is usually defined by the surface appearances of things. In addition, children at this age tend to only be able to focus on one piece of information at a time.

In social development, children of this age begin to develop what has been called a theory of mind. The idea is that preschoolers begin to understand that some things happen that cannot be directly observed, such as the idea that other people can make errors. However, preschoolers continue to have difficulty differentiating their own point of view from that of others.

Children at this age begin to learn "scripts" for types of behaviors, such as what happens in restaurants or what happens to get ready for bed. Similarly, preschoolers also begin acquiring a gender-role concept and to conform to sex-typed behavior. Related to this, preschoolers begin to explore adult roles in their play, including identifying with adults and mimicking adult attitudes and behaviors.

However, probably the most important developmental task for early childhood is learning self-control and self-regulation, including reflecting on one's actions, delaying gratification, tolerating frustration, and adjusting or inhibiting one's behaviors to suit the particular situational demands. These actions are part of the preschooler's growing social competence, where children begin to be able to coordinate and sustain interactions with individuals and groups of peers.

In emotional development, preschoolers begin to regulate their own emotions, including learning to be aware of the standards for behavior and using those standards to guide their words and actions. This internalization of standards is a critical part of learning to be able to feel genuine guilt or pride. True empathy and aggression begin at this age, by which we mean actions that have no other purpose than to commiserate with another person or to cause the other person harm or distress.

In moral development, children enter Kohlberg's stage 1 of preconventional moral reasoning, in which "good" behavior is based on a desire to avoid punishments from external authorities.

Middle childhood (approximately 6 to 12 years)

In cognitive development, children at this age begin to understand the distinction between appearance and reality and to look at more than one aspect of things at the same time. They also gain a sense of industry, which Sroufe et al. (1996) defined as a basic belief in one's competence, coupled with a tendency to initiate activities, seek out learning experiences, and work hard to accomplish goals. Ideally these would lead to a sense of personal effectiveness.

In social development, learning how to form friendships is probably the main developmental task of middle childhood. This includes learning how to be part of a peer group and how to learn and adhere to the group norms. These foster the development of the self concept, in which one's sense of self is defined in part by the context of the peer group to which one belongs.

These peer relations are also important for moral development, in that the peer groups help to impart cultural norms and values. They also provide opportunities for children to see other points of view and to grow in understanding of emotion and empathy for others. Children continue to develop through Kohlberg's preconventional moral reasoning (stage 2, in which actions are motivated by desires for rewards more than desires to avoid punishment) and begin conventional moral reasoning (stage 3, in which the child's goal is to act in ways others will approve of and will avoid disapproval). Although the peer group is important as part of the engine of moral development, it is important to remember that peer groups exist within cultures and usually reflect those cultures. In fact, Sroufe et al. (1996, p. 472) have stated clearly that "the particular moral principles that children adopt are largely a product of their culture."

Adolescence (approximately 13 to 18 years)

In cognitive development, adolescents gain the ability to think about abstract concepts and relationships among abstract concepts. Attention skills also make major gains during adolescence.

In social development, the main developmental task is probably learning how to achieve deep levels of trust and closeness with both same-sex and opposite-sex peers. At home, adolescents gain more autonomy and responsibility for homework, finances, jobs, and choices affecting their futures.

Personal identity makes additional gains during adolescence, in which adolescents begin to find a fit for themselves within the larger social context as well as defining themselves as unique and independent of their peer groups. Body image also begins to become important as children adjust to pubertal changes.

In moral development, adolescents continue through Kohlberg's conventional moral reasoning (stage 4, in which actions are defined as good to the extent that they perform one's duties as prescribed by the laws of society), and may begin to develop into Kohlberg's postconventional moral reasoning stages.

Media violence and developmental tasks example

Using a developmental tasks approach can help guide research and theories about media effects in a number of ways. When asking the question, "How will this show/game/movie affect children?" it becomes clear that the answer is not unidimensional. The effects are likely to differ greatly depending on the age of the child. Consider the following example taken from a nationally broadcast episode of professional wrestling (*WWF Smackdown*, Oct 7, 1999). Wrestling was selected as an example of media violence here because it is highly watched by children (it has historically been the highest rated show on cable; Keller, 2002).

A male wrestler, Jeff Jarrett, is angry at his wrestler girlfriend, Miss Kitty, because she lost a wrestling match the previous week. In order to "get back on [his] good side," he requires Miss Kitty to participate in a mud wrestling match. He asks the reigning ladies' champion, Ivory, to stand near the ring to watch. He then announces that the goal of the match is to remove the opponent's shirt and bra in order to win. He then throws Ivory into the mud, to her apparent surprise. Miss Kitty immediately attacks Ivory, removing Ivory's dress. Meanwhile, Jarrett makes comments about women being the lowest form of life and the announcers make lascivious comments about the women's bodies. Ivory eventually removes Miss Kitty's bikini top, "winning" the match. Incensed older women wrestlers arrive to confront Jarrett, who promptly throws them into the mud, while making comments about them being fat old sows. Ultimately, another lady wrestler, Chyna, sneaks up behind Jarrett, and pushes him into the mud. How would children who watch shows like this be affected? The developmental tasks approach provides a framework to understand how children may be affected at different ages.

For infants, it is unlikely to have much effect, unless the parents watch programs like this so much that it interferes with their ability to care for the infant or disrupts the infant's ability to set regular patterns. For toddlers, who are beginning to use language, there were a number of derogatory terms used that children might learn. However, children at this age are just beginning to acquire the standards and values of society through the socialization process. This type of program shows violence as the solution to interpersonal conflict, as well as the "normality" of verbal and physical abuse toward women (especially scantily clad or nude women). Habituation and desensitization processes have begun.

In early childhood, where the main developmental tasks are about behavioral self-control, emotional self-control, and gender roles, this type of program may have a number of negative effects. Very little self-control is displayed. Words are not used to resolve problems but only to enhance the problems. In this specific example, the male was the one with all the power: he set the rules for the engagement, and even though Ivory was "tricked" into the ring, there was no reason she needed to comply with Jarrett's rules—yet she did. The entire episode was derogatory toward women, and even though some might say that the women won in the end, they did it on his terms, not theirs. Children at this age may begin to see women as needing to do whatever men say they should to gain the approval of men and that such behaviors are normal or natural.

In middle childhood, social rules and norms take on increased importance, and they are likely to learn lessons about the importance of physical domination and humiliation of others as an acceptable method of conflict resolution—that is, if they have not already habituated to this level of physical and verbal abuse and therefore do not see it at all. Furthermore, in this example, competence was defined only in terms of ability to fight (although there is also a subtext of sexuality as competence).

In adolescence, the major developmental task is learning how to have intimate and committed relationships. This type of show portrays the relationships between men and women very stereotypically, where the male has the power and the females are submissive. Furthermore, it portrays physical aggression between the sexes as acceptable (and sexual). By this developmental stage, physical and verbal violence in the media will likely appear unremarkable—a natural part of our culture and only a mirror of our society.

We do not mean to suggest that watching one episode of any program is likely to have a large, immediate effect. But any immediate effects as well long-term effects are likely to be different based on the age of the child, and the developmental tasks approach provides a framework for designing and testing hypotheses about the types of effects we might expect at different ages. This approach demonstrates why expecting media violence to affect everyone the same way (myth 4 above) is inappropriate—media violence *shouldn't* affect children of different ages the same way.

A RISK AND RESILIENCE APPROACH TO DEVELOPMENT

The developmental tasks approach focuses on normative development; that is, every child will go through these phases with varying degrees of ease. In contrast, the risk and resilience approach (also called a risk and protective factor approach) focuses on the unique pattern or risk and protective factors for each individual child (see reviews by Glantz & Johnson, 1999; Masten & Coatsworth, 1998; Prot & Gentile, 2014). Risk factors are those that put a child at risk for maladaptive development and poor outcomes, whereas protective factors are those that help to limit the risk or maintain resilience to risk factors. These risk and protective factors can exist at many different levels, including genetic, personality traits, prior trauma, attitudes, family variables, peer support, neighborhood context, cultural context, economics, etc. With regard to aggression, the U.S. Surgeon General's report on youth violence (2001) defines risk factors as "personal characteristics or environmental conditions that predict the onset, continuity, or escalation of violence" (p. 58).

This approach helps to explain why we see greater effects of media violence on some children than on others. Exposure to media violence is likely to be a risk factor for all children, increasing the risk for aggressive behaviors. However, some children have additional risk factors that enhance the effects of media violence exposure, while other children may have protective factors that attenuate the risk of aggressive behavior. This could make it look like only some children are affected by media violence, when in fact they all are affected; it's just much easier to notice the effect in some children.

In the decade since the first edition of this book, much progress has been made in risk and protective factor models, and researchers are beginning to use them to predict aggression. Four primary types of models have been identified: cascade effects, dose-response gradients, pathway models, and turning-point models. (Due to space limitations, these are described only briefly; see Prot & Gentile [2014] for more detail and examples of studies.)

Cascade effects are where small changes in one area of life can "snowball" to spread across areas, across time, across people, and even across generations (Masten & Narayan, 2012). Disruptions in adaptive behavior can spread and have negative consequences in multiple domains, whereas competence can act as scaffolding on which competence in other domains develops (Masten, Burt, & Coatsworth, 2006). For example, Slater, Henry, Swaim, & Anderson (2003) measured students in 20 middle schools four times over two years. They found that aggressive children seek out media violence, but that media violence exposure predicted becoming more aggressive, which further made children seek out more media violence, etc., in a "downward spiral," each influencing the other across development.

Dose-response gradients demonstrate that as the level of risk rises, the likelihood for problems also rises. This may not always happen in a linear fashion, but can also include thresholds, asymptotic patterns, or inverted-U models (Luthar, Cicchetti, & Becker, 2000; Masten, 2012). For example, Gentile and Bushman (2012) examined the cumulative effects of six different risk and protective factors on children's aggressive behavior over a six-month period. Predictors included media violence exposure, physical victimization, participant sex, hostile attribution bias, parental monitoring, and prior aggressive

Figure 2.3
Predicted Likelihood of Time 2 Fights from Number of Risk Factors Present at Time 1, Demonstrating Nonlinear Cumulative Risk

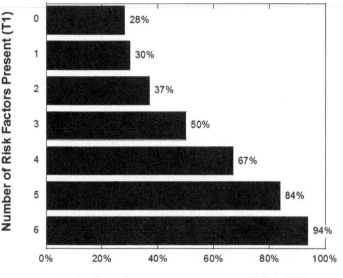

Likelihood of Involvement in a Fight (T2)

Source: Gentile & Bushman, 2012.

behavior. Each risk factor at Time 1 predicted an increased risk of physical aggression at Time 2, whereas each protective factor predicted a decreased risk of physical aggression at Time 2. The combination of risk factors, however, was a better predictor than any individual risk factor (Figure 2.3). Importantly, they found both linear and multiplicative effects of multiple risk factors.

Pathway models describe potential patterns of functioning before, during, and after exposure to some adverse event (Masten, 2011). For example, Krahé, Busching, and Möller (2012) studied 1,715 middle school students and found that across a two-year period there were three types of students: those who consistently did not consume much media violence, those who consistently watched a lot, and those who started high but decreased their media violence exposure. These three trajectories also predicted the trajectory of physical aggression. Stable low media violence exposure predicted stable low aggression. Stable high media violence exposure predicted a small increase in aggression. Decreasing media violence exposure predicted a decrease in aggressive behavior.

Turning point models attempt to explain why some people may seemingly suddenly shift from a bad trajectory to a positive one. Late adolescence/emerging adulthood has been found to be a transitional time during which such cases are more likely, because this period of development provides new opportunities, motivations, and impulse control (Burt & Masten, 2010; Burt & Paysnick, 2012; Masten & Tellegen, 2012). Furthermore, adolescents are more willing to take risks due to changes the adolescent brain is undergoing (Spear, 2000). No media violence studies have yet focused specifically on this approach, although the group described above who stopped viewing media violence and consequently reduced their aggression may be such an example (Krahé et al., 2012).

With regard to media violence, exposure to entertainment media violence acts like a risk factor for aggressive behavior and other negative outcomes. The presence of this single risk factor is not sufficient to cause children to hit someone, and certainly not sufficient to cause someone to pick up a gun and begin shooting. However, each additional risk factor children have for aggressive behavior (e.g., being male, having been bullied, low parental monitoring, poverty, gang membership, drug use, history of being abused, access to guns, etc.) increases the risk of that child acting aggressively. In contrast, each additional protective factor children have (e.g., stable family environment, good school performance, open communication with parents, etc.) decreases the risk of aggressive behavior.

The risk and resilience approach helps to answer the comment most people make about media violence: "I watched a lot of media violence as a kid, and I never shot anyone." We need to remember that "shooting someone" is a highly extreme behavior. Most people will never engage in such an extreme behavior, and exposure to media violence is not such a powerful effect as to be able to make such extreme changes in people. One possible metaphor for this process is to consider the thermometer shown in Figure 2.4.[1] At the lowest end, a child's behavior is routinely respectful and polite. At the highest end, a child engages in the ultimate disrespectful behavior of shooting someone. It is likely that regular exposure to media violence might be able to shift someone about two or three spots on the thermometer. It certainly isn't a strong enough effect to shift someone from routinely respectful behavior to shooting someone, but it might change someone such that he or she begins showing rude and verbally aggressive behavior. If, however, an individual starts out with other risk factors for violent behavior, and is already at the verbally aggressive spot on the thermometer, regular exposure to media violence may just add enough additional risk to get him to start pushing and shoving others around. The child may also have additional protective factors that help to keep the level lower.

We have described a number of commonly held beliefs about media effects, and how those beliefs can hamper the ability to accurately predict and interpret the effects of violent media portrayals on children. These myths include the beliefs that media effects must be simple, direct, obvious, severe, and affect everyone the same way. They also include errors in the idea of what a "cause" must be, or how large an affect must be to be important. Although

Figure 2.4
The Metaphorical Aggression Thermometer

- Potentially lethal violence
- Physical fighting
- Threatening violence
- Pushing and shoving
- Occasional violent thoughts/fantasies
- Relationally aggressive behavior
- Verbally aggressive behavior
- Occasional aggressive thoughts
- Occasional rude behavior
- Always respectful and polite

Source: Gentile & Bushman, 2012.

the research is clear that media violence can have a negative impact on children, it has been less clear why some children may show a larger effect than others, or why some children may be affected in different ways. The persistence of the myths has made it difficult to understand why we should not expect children to be affected identically. The developmental tasks approach helps to describe why children at different developmental "stages" would be expected to be influenced differently. The risk and resilience approach helps to describe why children at any given age could be affected the same way, but one child would show the effects behaviorally and another might not. These two developmental approaches have great promise for the field of media effects research, as they help us to understand why children may be affected differently by exposure to media violence, and also why even though most children will not become seriously violent from exposure to media violence, they may nonetheless be affected in an important manner.

NOTE

1. This metaphor is used in the understanding that it is imperfect. For example, it is not clear that relational aggression is less aggressive than physical aggression, as the consequences are sometimes worse (see Coyne & Stockdale, this volume). It is intended solely to help describe how different risk factors can increase the likelihood of more severe aggressive behaviors, and how protective factors can decrease the likelihood of aggressive behaviors.

REFERENCES

Aber, J. L., & Jones, S. J. (1997). Indicators of positive development in early childhood: Improving concepts and measures. In R. M. Hauser, B. V. Brown, & W. R. Prosser (Eds.), *Indicators of children's well-being* (pp. 395–408). New York, NY: Sage Foundation.

Allen, M., D'Alessio, D., & Brezgel, K. (1995). A meta-analysis summarizing the effects of pornography II: Aggression after exposure. *Human Communication Research*, *22*, 258–283.

Anderson, C. A. (2004). An update on the effects of playing violent video games. *Journal of Adolescence*, *27*, 113–122.

Anderson, C. A., Berkowitz, L., Donnerstein, E., Huesmann, L. R., Johnson, J. D., Linz, D., et al., (2003). The influence of media violence on youth. *Psychological Science in the Public Interest*, *4*, 81–110.

Anderson, C. A., Shibuya, A., Ihori, N., Swing, E. L., Bushman, B. J., Sakamoto, A., et al., (2010). Violent video game effects on aggression, empathy, and prosocial behavior in Eastern and Western countries: A meta-analytic review. *Psychological Bulletin*, *136*(2), 151–173. doi:10.1037/a0018251

Andison, F. S. (1977). TV violence and viewer aggression: A cumulation of study results. *Public Opinion Quarterly*, *41*, 314–331.

Brachear, M. (2002, July 19). Copycat stunt injures youth. *Dallas Morning News.* http://www.dallasnews.com/latestnews/stories/071902dntexstunt.811a0.html

Burt, K. B., & Masten, A. S. (2010). Development in the transition to adulthood: Vulnerabilities and opportunities. In J. E. Grant & M. N. Potenza (Eds.), *Young adult mental health* (pp. 5–18). New York, NY: Oxford University Press.

Burt, K. B., & Paysnick, A. A. (2012). Resilience in the transition to adulthood. *Development and Psychopathology*, *24*(2), 493–505.

Bushman, B. J., & Anderson, C. A. (2001). Media violence and the American public. *American Psychologist*, *56*, 477–489.

Bushman, B. J., & Huesmann, L. R. (2006). Short-term and long-term effects of violent media on aggression in children and adults. *Arch Pediatr Adolesc Med*, *160*(4), 348–352.

Centerwall, B. S. (1989). Exposure to television as a risk factor for violence. *American Journal of Epidemiology*, *129*, 643–652.

Cicchetti, D., & Toth, S. L. (1998). The development of depression in children and adolescents. *American Psychologist*, *53*, 221–241.

Complete coverage on theater shooting in Aurora. www.cnn.com/SPECIALS/us/colorado-shooting

Dandekar, P., Goel, A., & Lee, D. T. (2013). Biased assimilation, homophily, and the dynamics of polarization, *Proceedings of the National Academy of Sciences*, *110*(15), 5791–5796. doi:www.pnas.org/cgi/doi/10.1073/pnas.1217220110

Donnerstein, E., Slaby, R. G., & Eron, L. D. (1994). The mass media and youth aggression. In L. D. Eron, J. H. Gentry, & P. Schlegel (Eds.), *Reason to hope: A psychosocial perspective on violence and youth* (pp. 219–250). Washington, DC: American Psychological Association.

Erikson, E. H. (1963). *Childhood and society* (2nd ed.). New York, NY: Norton.

Ferguson, C. J. (2002). Media violence: Miscast causality. *American Psychologist*, *57*, 446–447.

Ferguson, C. J. (2007a). Evidence for publication bias in video game violence effects literature: A meta-analytic review. *Aggression and Violent Behavior, 12*(4), 470–482.

Ferguson, C. J. (2007b). The good, the bad and the ugly: A meta-analytic review of positive and negative effects of violent video games. *Psychiatric Quarterly, 78,* 309–316.

Ferguson, C. J. (2010). Blazing angels or resident evil? Can violent video games be a force for good? *Review of General Psychology, 14,* 68–81.

Ferguson, C. J., & Kilburn, J. (2009). The public health risks of media violence: A meta-analytic review. *The Journal of Pediatrics, 154,* 759–763.

Freedman, J. L. (2002). *Media violence and its effect on aggression.* Toronto, ON: University of Toronto Press.

Gentile, D. A. (2013). Catharsis and media violence: A conceptual analysis. *Societies, 3,* 491–510. doi:10.3390/soc3040491

Gentile, D. A., & Bushman, B. J. (2012). Reassessing media violence effects using a risk and resilience approach to understanding aggression. *Psychology of Popular Media Culture, 1*(3), 138–151.

Gentile, D. A., & Sesma, A. (2003). Developmental approaches to understanding media effects on individuals. In D. A. Gentile (Ed.), *Media violence and children: A complete guide for parents and professionals.* Westport, CT: Praeger.

Gibbs, N., & Roche, T. (1999, December 20). The Columbine tapes. *Time,* 40–50.

Glantz, M. D., & Johnson, J. L. (Eds.). (1999). *Resilience and development: Positive life adaptations.* New York, NY: Kluwer.

Greene, V. S. (1999). *Television viewing, perceptions of advertising's influence and appearance-related concerns.* Unpublished manuscript, University of Massachusetts, Amherst.

Grossman, D. (1996). *On killing.* Boston, MA: Little, Brown & Co.

Hearold, S. (1986). A synthesis of 1043 effects of television on social behavior. In G. Comstock (Ed.), *Public communication and behavior* (Vol. 1, pp. 65–133). New York: Academic Press.

Hogben, M. (1998). Factors moderating the effect of television aggression on viewer behavior. *Communication Research, 25,* 220–247.

Keller, W. (2002, August 10). *Wrestling's state of business is taking more knocks than deserved.* http://www.pwtorch.com/artman/publish/printer_163.shtml

Krahé, B., Busching, R., & Möller, I. (2012). Media violence use and aggression among German adolescents: Associations and trajectories of change in a three-wave longitudinal study. *Psychology of Popular Media Culture, 1,* 152–166.

Luthar, S. S., Cicchetti, D., & Becker, B. (2000). The construct of resilience: A critical evaluation and guidelines for future work. *Child Development, 71,* 543–562.

Masten, A. S. (2011). Resilience in children threatened by extreme adversity: Frameworks for research, practice, and translational synergy. *Development and Psychopathology, 23,* 141–154.

Masten, A. S. (2012). Risk and resilience in the educational success of homeless and highly mobile children: Introduction to the special section. *Educational Researcher, 41,* 363–365.

Masten, A. S., & Braswell, L. (1991). Developmental psychopathology: An integrative framework. In P. R. Martin (Ed.), *Handbook of behavior therapy and psychological science: An integrative approach* (pp. 35–56). New York, NY: Pergamon Press.

Masten, A. S., Burt, K. B., & Coatsworth, J. D. (2006). Competence and psychopathology in development. In D. Cicchetti & D. J. Cohen (Eds.), *Developmental
psychopathology* (Vol. 3, 2nd ed., pp. 696–738). Hoboken, NJ: Wiley.

Masten, A. S., & Coatsworth, J. D. (1998). The development of competence in
favorable and unfavorable environments: Lessons from research on successful
children. *American Psychologist, 53*, 205–220.

Masten, A. S., & Narayan, A. J. (2012). Child development in the context of disaster,
war and terrorism: Pathways of risk and resilience. *Annual Review of Psychology,
63*, 227–257.

Masten, A. S., & Tellegen, A. (2012). Resilience in developmental psychopathology:
Contributions of the Project Competence Longitudinal Study. *Development
and Psychopathology, 24*, 345–361.

Paik, H., & Comstock, G. (1994). The effects of television violence on antisocial behavior: A meta-analysis. *Communication Research, 21*(4), 516–546.

Potter, W. J. (1999). *On media violence*. Thousand Oaks, CA: Sage Publications.

Prot, S., & Gentile, D. A. (2014). Applying risk and resilience models to predicting
the effects of media violence on development. *Advances in Child Development
and Behavior, 46*, 215–244.

Savage, J., & Yancey, C. (2008). The effects of media violence exposure on criminal
aggression: A meta-analysis. *Criminal Justice and Behavior, 35*, 772–791.

Sherry, J. L. (2001). The effects of violent video games on aggression. *Human
Communication Research, 27*, 409–431.

Slater, M. D., Henry, K. L., Swaim, R. C., & Anderson, L. L. (2003). Violent media
content and aggressiveness in adolescents: A downward spiral model. *Communication Research, 30*, 713–736.

Spear, L. P. (2000). The adolescent brain and age-related behavioral manifestations.
Neuroscience and Biobehavioral Reviews, 24, 417–463.

Sroufe, L. A. (1979). The coherence of individual development: Early care, attachment, and subsequent developmental issues. *American Psychologist, 34*,
834–841.

Sroufe, L. A. (1995). *Emotional development: The organization of emotional life in the early
years*. New York, NY: Cambridge Press.

Sroufe, L. A. (1997). Psychopathology as an outcome of development. *Development
and Psychopathology, 9*, 251–268.

Sroufe, L. A., Cooper, R. G., & DeHart, G. B. (1996). *Child development: Its nature and
course* (3rd ed.). New York, NY: McGraw-Hill, Inc.

Sroufe, L. A., Egeland, B., & Carlson, E. A. (1999). One social world: The integrated
development of parent-child and peer relationships. In W. A. Collins & B.
Laursen (Eds.), *Relationships as developmental context: The 30th Minnesota symposium on child psychology*. Hillsdale, NJ: Erlbaum.

Stiff sentence: 14-year-old gets life in prison for wrestling death. (2001, March 9). *ABC News*.
http://abcnews.go.com/sections/us/DailyNews/tate-sentence010309.html

Texas talkback. (N.d.). http://www.txcn.com/cgi-bin/survey.cgi?survey=1104&step=
View%20comments

U.S. Surgeon General. (2001, April 11). *Youth violence: A report of the surgeon general*.
Washington, DC: United States Surgeon General.

Walsh, D. A. (2001). *Dr. Dave's cyberhood*. New York, NY: Fireside.

White, J. (2013, December 16). I have Asperger's, I play violent video games—and I'm not going to shoot you. *CCN.com*. http://www.cnn.com/2013/12/13 /opinion/aspergers-video-games-sandy-hook-irpt/index.html?iref=allsearch

Wood, W., Wong, F., & Chachere, J. (1991). Effects of media violence on viewers' aggression in unconstrained social interaction. *Psychological Bulletin, 109*, 371–383.

Woodward, G. C., & Denton, R. E. (2000). *Persuasion & influence in American life* (4th ed.). Prospect Heights, IL: Waveland Press.

CHAPTER 3

The Broader Effects of Media on Children and Adults: A Natural Experiment[1]

Tannis M. MacBeth[2]

By the 1960s, almost all North American homes had at least one television set, and watching TV had become the preferred leisure activity of children and adults. Despite increasing use of new technologies such as the Internet, at the turn of this century only sleeping, school, and/or work occupy more time than television. What effects, if any, does TV have on viewers' attitudes and behavior? Does it affect reading skills, creativity, vocabulary, aggressive behavior, gender-role attitudes, participation in community activities, or use of other media? These questions prompted our research. An unusual opportunity in the form of a natural experiment enabled us to avoid a major problem faced by researchers interested in the effects of TV: how to determine whether viewers are affected by TV in each of these areas, whether viewers who differ on these dimensions use TV differently, or whether both influences occur in a transactional relationship, as some researchers (Rosengren, Roe, & Sonesson, 1983; Friedrich-Cofer & Huston, 1986) contend. This "chicken and egg" problem prompted the U.S. Surgeon General's Commission (National Institute of Mental Health, 1972) to lament that there was no longer a North American community without TV reception. Such a town would provide a natural experiment in which to study residents before and after they became regular viewers. It would enable researchers to make causal inferences, provided careful consideration was given to other possible influences, including change due to maturation (normal age-related change), history (other important events occurring in the community during the same period), regression toward the mean (high scores are more likely than low scores to decrease, and vice versa), and so on (Cook, Campbell, & Peracchio, 1990; MacBeth, 1998; MacBeth Williams, 1986a).

To my astonishment, shortly after the publication of the Surgeon General's report, I heard about a Canadian town still without TV reception but due to receive it within a year,[3] two months hence in November.

With great effort, we managed to obtain local permission, funding, assemble all the necessary materials and personnel, and collect baseline data before the town's residents celebrated the arrival of both TV reception and the Grey Cup. We in turn celebrated the beginning of an exciting, extensive, and demanding research project.[4] The details of the methodology and results of this research have been published as a book (MacBeth Williams, 1986b); this chapter provides a summary and overview of what we did, why we did it, and what we found. The overall design of the project is described first, followed by the individual studies presented in the following order: creativity, vocabulary and spatial ability, IQ scores, reading skills, participation in other leisure activities, gender-role attitudes and perceptions, aggressive behavior, and use of TV and other media. This is followed by discussion of the processes underlying the effects of TV and then by some general conclusions regarding our study. The chapter ends with a section providing a brief update on related research and conclusions.

DESIGN OF THE STUDY

The name "Notel" was chosen for the town without TV.[5] If only Notel had been studied, however, it would have been impossible to know whether any changes that occurred were due to the effects of TV or to the effects of some other event that occurred simultaneously with the introduction of TV to Notel. At least one comparison or control town was needed. The first comparison community, about an hour's drive away, was suggested by Notel residents. We gave it the name Unitel because it had had one TV channel, CBC English, for seven years. Notel was going to obtain that same (and only) channel. Residents of both Notel and Unitel agreed that the two towns were similar. We wondered whether the effects of TV might vary depending on whether viewers could watch one channel or several, so a second comparison town was selected. Multitel had had four channels for 15 years: one Canadian channel (CBC English) and three major private networks from the United States (ABC, CBS, and NBC).

As far as could be ascertained, using data from Statistics Canada and other sources, the three towns were similar in size, in demographic variables such as socioeconomic status (SES) and cultural backgrounds of the residents, and in the types of industry in the area. Each village, with a population of about 700, served an area about four times as large, in terms of schools, services, and so on.

One important feature of this experiment is that the people without TV in Notel were not self-selected, which allowed us to compare them with Notel nonviewers. Comparisons between those who choose to have or not to have TV are a problem because the two groups also vary considerably on several other dimensions. This study allowed us to make comparisons between viewers and non-viewers on several dimensions.

Notel, like Unitel and Multitel, was not isolated. This is important because the effects of TV in a community accessible only by sea or by air, as is true of many small Canadian communities, may be different from the effects in a nonisolated community. Notel should have had TV, but the transmitter meant to bring TV to both Notel and Unitel wasn't very successful. Notel was located in a valley in such a way that most residents could not pick up the transmitter's signal most of the time. Some residents could pick up a poor signal occasionally, and did so.

We heard amusing stories of people never seeing the puck while watching hockey games apparently played in snowstorms, and of families driving camper trucks just far enough to pick up a clear TV signal. Notel residents knew what TV was and watched it when they were elsewhere, but most could not watch on a regular basis. The median number of hours viewed per week by Notel school children, that is, the number above and below which 50 percent watched, was zero. By comparison, the median for Unitel was 23.5 hours, and for Multitel, 29.3.

That some Notel residents sometimes watched TV made it less likely that there would be differences amongst the towns, so our research provides a conservative test of TV's effects.

All three towns were studied just before Notel obtained TV (phase 1) and again two years later (phase 2). This interval was chosen because it seemed long enough for any TV effects to be clearly evident, but not so long that other major changes of a historical nature were likely to occur or that many residents would have moved. Attrition from phase 1 to 2 was relatively low and did not differ significantly for the three towns (mean = 28.5 percent).

The topics we chose to study had been identified in previous literature as potential effects of TV, either positive or negative. Some of the studies within this project focused on children, elementary, and high school students, and others focused on adults. Unfortunately, our resources did not enable us to study preschool children. Some of the comparisons were cross-sectional, that is, comparisons among the three towns within each phase of the study, and comparisons from phase 1 to phase 2 that involved different people.

Other comparisons were longitudinal—that is, the same students who were studied in phase 1, for example, when they were in Grade 3, were studied again in phase 2, when they were two years older and in Grade 5. We evaluated whether statistically significant differences occurred among the groups within each phase, for each town from phase 1 to phase 2, and whether patterns of similarities and differences varied according to other factors, for example, grade or gender.

The details of these analyses are provided more comprehensively in our book (MacBeth Williams, 1986b); in this chapter only statistically significant results are discussed.

CREATIVITY

When we designed this project, claims that TV has a negative impact on children's imaginations or creative thinking were heard frequently, but the empirical evidence was sparse. A few researchers had found a negative relationship between creativity scores and amount of TV viewing, and offered the interpretation that the more creative students tend to limit their use of TV. But the correlational nature of their data could not rule out the alternative and widely heard hypothesis that creativity is itself affected by TV. This hypothesis is consistent with theorizing about creativity, which tends to emphasize the role of experience in developing fluidity of ideas. For example, Suler (1980) contends that creativity is a cognitive activity shaped by both the immediate environment and the larger cultural and historical context. For these theoretical and empirical reasons, we hypothesized that TV would have a negative effect on creativity.

Creativity is difficult to define and even more difficult to measure, but there is some agreement that it includes ideational fluency (ability to generate ideas that fulfill particular requirements) and originality (ability to generate unique or unusual ideas). We examined these abilities in both children and adults.

CHILDREN

Harrison and I (1986) assessed children's creativity with the alternate uses task. This is considered a good measure of both ideational fluency and originality. A sample item is, "Tell me all the different ways to use a newspaper."

The children were assessed individually, in a relaxed atmosphere, with no time limits. Both the total number of responses and the uniqueness or originality of each response were scored. In phase 1, a total of 160 students in Grades 4 and 7 were assessed. Two years later, in phase 2, 137 of the same students, now in Grades 6 and 9 (the longitudinal sample), were reassessed, along with 147 students who were in Grades 4 and 7 (the cross-sectional sample).

The results were clear. The pattern was similar for number and uniqueness of ideas and for cross-sectional and longitudinal comparisons. Before their town had TV reception, Notel students scored higher on average than the students in Unitel and Multitel. When Notel had had TV for two years, however, the scores of Notel, Unitel, and Multitel students did not differ. From phase 1 to phase 2, only the scores of Notel students changed significantly, and they decreased.

ADULTS

Creative problem solving by adults was assessed by Suedfeld, Little, Rank, Rank, and Ballard (1986) using tasks that require the individual to "break set"—that is, to think of the materials presented to them in a different, unusual way. The adults (60 per town, per phase) were tested individually in their homes, and they were a random, representative sample of their respective communities.

In phase 1, before Notel had TV, the Duncker candle problem was used. Each adult was given a box of tacks, a vertical cardboard surface, a candle, and a book of matches. They were told to "affix the candle to the cardboard wall, using any of the objects on the table, so that it stays there and burns freely without being held." The trick is to think of the tack box as separate from the tacks, and as a potential support for the candle. One merely has to tack the box to the cardboard surface and then stand the candle in the box. The differences among the proportions solving the problem were in the hypothesized direction but not statistically significant: 40 percent in Notel, 25 percent in Unitel, and 30 percent in Multitel. There was a significant difference, however, in the speed with which the problem was solved. Of those who succeeded, Notel adults did so significantly faster (150.6 seconds) than Unitel adults (251.0) and marginally faster than Multitel (263.1) adults.[6] Most people, however, never did solve the problem. Among those who didn't, Notel adults kept trying significantly longer (401.0 seconds) than did the unsuccessful adults in Unitel (279.9) and marginally longer than those in Multitel (332.4). This is an interesting finding because it is the only one we know that indicates a potential long-term effect of TV on persistence at problem solving. Teachers often complain that children aren't able to concentrate or persist as long as they used to do, and attribute this to TV, but there is very little evidence for children concerning long-term effects of TV on persistence (MacBeth, 1996).

In phase 2, the creative problem-solving task was the 9-dot problem, in which people are shown nine dots, three in each of three rows, forming a square.

The goal is to join all the dots, "using no more than four lines without lifting your pen off the paper or retracing any line." The solution requires going outside the square twice in order to connect the nine dots. This problem turned out to be very difficult; only 7 of 180 adults in the three towns actually solved it. It was not possible, therefore, to compare the three towns in terms of success, but it was possible to consider persistence.

Among those who did not solve the problem, Notel adults persisted significantly longer (292.8 seconds) than Unitel adults (263.8) and marginally longer than Multitel adults (277.3). Change in persistence from phase 1 to phase 2 cannot be evaluated statistically because the problem and its difficulty level changed, but in absolute terms the drop in persistence in Notel (108.2 seconds) was noticeably larger than the drop in the other towns (16.1 seconds in Unitel; 55.1 seconds in Multitel).

The first set of hypotheses revolves around the notion that, for at least some children, watching TV displaced other activities that might have facilitated creativity or creative problem solving. In particular, some other activities could provide experiences that would be helpful on these tasks. For example, in the absence of TV, children might play games that facilitate creativity. These might involve thinking about how various things could be used in a way similar to the questions asked on the alternate uses task given in this study. Television also may displace "doing nothing," and the latter may encourage reflection and thinking about ideas more than does TV.

Another possibility is that TV displaces some activities that require deeper information processing than does watching TV. Salomon (1983) has reported some evidence that the *amount of invested mental effort* (AIME) required to watch North American TV is small. Children and adults are aware of this and, according to Salomon, tend to watch TV most of the time in a relatively mindless as opposed to a relatively mindful way (Langer & Piper, 1988). Salomon contends that children learn when very young that TV requires only lower levels of information processing, that is, encoding (taking in information directly) and chunking (parsing or grouping information), but not mental elaboration. In other words, TV does not require working over or transforming information. Children accustomed to using these relatively mindless processing skills with TV also may use them to process information in other situations, even when they are not adequate. For example, the alternate uses task clearly requires mental elaboration, as do the Duncker candle and 9-dot problems. The content of TV also may provide relatively few models of divergent thinking (coming up with many plausible answers or solutions) as opposed to convergent thinking (one correct answer). In short, this set of hypotheses revolves around the notion that North American TV and perhaps North American culture tend to be oriented more toward entertainment than toward reflective thinking and persistence, so TV viewing does not facilitate performance on tasks that require these skills.

Whatever the processes involved, the creativity findings for children indicate that the better performance of Notel students on creativity tasks in the absence of TV was not maintained once TV became available. This finding contrasts with that for fluent reading skill, discussed later in this chapter.

VOCABULARY AND SPATIAL ABILITY

Not all of our hypotheses about the effects of TV were negative. We predicted that TV would have a positive effect on vocabulary (Harrison & MacBeth Williams, 1986), particularly in the early grades for children not yet able to read for pleasure themselves. In phase 1, M. Morrison gave the Peabody picture vocabulary test (PPVT) to 61 children in kindergarten and Grade 1 in Notel and Unitel, and Harrison and I gave the Wechsler intelligence scale for children (WISC) vocabulary test to 160 children in all three towns in Grades 4 and 7. In phase 2, Harrison and I gave the WISC vocabulary test to 284 students in Grades 4, 6, 7, and 9. The results provided no evidence to support the hypothesis that TV has a positive effect on children's vocabulary.

In interpreting the vocabulary findings, it should be noted that our measures also are considered to be good measures of general verbal intelligence. For example, the child was required to give definitions for a series of words. Whereas one would hypothesize a positive effect of TV on vocabulary, as we did, IQ scores tend to be relatively stable across these age ranges, so little change might be expected for a vocabulary measure of IQ. Even for the PPVT measure of receptive vocabulary given in kindergarten and Grade 1, requiring only word comprehension, however, there was no evidence of any effect of TV.

With hindsight, we think that people do learn some vocabulary from TV but that other sources are more important. For example, in the absence of TV, parents and older siblings may read to young children more than they do when TV is available. Children also may experience more social interaction with adults. They probably learn the kinds of vocabulary that vocabulary tests assess from conversation, from being read to, and later on from reading themselves, as much as or more than they learn such vocabulary from TV (Miller & Gildea, 1988). They may also learn some specific vocabulary from TV, but perhaps not the kind assessed by vocabulary tests.

We studied spatial ability (Harrison & MacBeth Williams, 1986), assessed by the WISC block design task requiring the child to arrange a set of blocks so the surface duplicates a series of two-dimensional spatial designs. In becoming TV "literate," viewers learn to decode two-dimensional spatial representations of three-dimensional space. It seemed reasonable, therefore, to hypothesize that TV experience would be positively related to spatial ability, either because children high in this ability are more attracted to TV or because TV facilitates performance on spatial-ability tasks.

In phase 1, spatial ability was assessed for students in Grades 4 and 7, and in phase 2, for students in Grades 4, 6, 7, and 9. We found no evidence for either a positive or negative effect of TV.

IQ SCORES

As mentioned in the previous section, the vocabulary and spatial ability tests we gave in Grades 4 and 7 in phase 1, and in Grades 4, 6, 7 and 9 in phase 2, were the WISC vocabulary and block design IQ tests. In addition, in phase 1 we obtained group test IQ scores from the permanent school records of 631 students across the three towns. IQ scores from individual tests administered by professionals are considered to be more valid and reliable assessments than are scores from group tests, in part because the latter depend on reading ability and because other factors such as fatigue and attention are not part of the assessment. We used the group test IQ scores primarily as a control when assessing the role of TV in relation to other variables potentially related to IQ, but we also conducted some other analyses of the IQ data (MacBeth, 1996; Harrison & MacBeth Williams, 1986; MacBeth Williams & Boyes, 1986).

We found reasonably strong evidence that children's use of television and other media varies with IQ, as measured both individually and by group tests. Lower-IQ students watched more television and used less print than did higher-IQ students. To me, one of our most intriguing sets of findings in the entire project concerned the relations among IQ scores, reading ability, print use, and the availability of TV. Typically in research, as was the case in our towns when TV was available, substantial interrelations are found amongst IQ scores, reading skill, amount of reading, and type of material read. In our study, however, in the absence of television, IQ was more independent of reading skill and print use. In phase 1, Notel students' IQ scores were not related to their print use and were not related to their performance on an individual measure of fluent reading skill (described below in the next section). In addition, although Notel students' IQ scores were significantly related to their phase 1 group reading test scores, they were less strongly related to those scores than was the case for Unitel and Multitel students. As I discuss in the next section, these findings have prompted me to wonder whether one of the effects of television is to produce more reading dropouts than when it is not available.

READING SKILLS

A number of other researchers have found that in the late elementary grades and in high school, students who report watching more TV tend to be poorer readers and to do worse in school than students who watch less TV. Why would reading achievement be negatively related to amount of TV viewing? One possibility is that it interferes with acquisition and/or maintenance of good reading skills. Another possibility is self-selection: poor readers may choose to watch more TV than do good readers.

On average, students who do worse on IQ tests also tend to be poorer readers, to read less, to read different material, to do worse in school, and to watch more TV. Most researchers have found that significant relationships or correlations between reading achievement and TV become insignificant or even drop to zero after the relationship of IQ to both of these variables is removed. The many difficulties in interpreting correlational data regarding TV and school achievement underscore the importance of the opportunity to study students in Notel before and after reception became available.

In the early stages of learning to read (Sternlicht Chall, 1983), children focus on decoding individual letters and words. Later, reading becomes more fluent and automatic; a brief glance is sufficient to process an entire phrase. Corteen and MacBeth Williams (1986) studied the fluent reading or automated reading skills of students in Grades 2, 3, and 8 in phase 1, and in phase 2, students in

Grades 2, 3, 4, 5, 8, and 10. We also assessed Grade 2 students in all three towns two years after phase 2.[7]

Each student was tested individually. The items of a standardized reading test were given in a tachistoscope, a device that controls the amount of time the item is available to be seen, or in this case, to be read. The student had to read a series of items each presented very briefly. Some were words, some phrases, and some nonsense words—that is, words that follow the spelling rules of English but are not true words (e.g., sked). About 500 students were tested. In addition to this individual measure of fluent reading skill, phase 1 students also were tested on a group reading test that assessed both vocabulary and comprehension. Group reading tests were given in all three towns to 813 students in Grades 1 through 7, six months after the arrival of TV in Notel.

The reading results were complicated and varied according to both grade and gender, but the pattern was clearer when the relationship of IQ scores to other variables was controlled. When all of the findings from the individual reading test were considered, the weight of the evidence suggested that TV slows down the acquisition of fluent reading skills in the early elementary grades, but once good reading skills are acquired, they are not lost.

The group test results corroborated these individual results. In particular, Notel students in Grades 2 and 3 obtained higher comprehension and vocabulary scores than did Unitel and Multitel students, who did not differ.

We did not observe directly the relationship between use of TV and acquisition of reading skills, so we can only speculate about the process, but the pattern of results obtained in this and other studies is consistent with the following set of hypotheses. When no TV is available, most children may practice reading enough to become fluent in the early elementary grades. For most children, however, learning to read is difficult. They have to "crack the code," and when they are first reading, they do so only with great difficulty and slowly. At the initial decoding stage, they are unable to read for entertainment or pleasure and still enjoy having adults or older siblings read to them for these purposes. Reading is hard work, and watching TV is probably more fun. Children who have the most difficulty learning to read may find TV most attractive. The brighter children without learning disabilities may obtain sufficient reading practice in school or may read more at home than others, either on their own or with the aid of parents or siblings.

The rewards associated with the process of learning to read probably are greater for those who acquire the skills more quickly. To the extent that parents consider reading to be an important activity or skill, they may provide more encouragement. Or, parents with a greater orientation to print than to other media may more often encourage and provide help with reading. By the later elementary grades, children who are poor readers will obtain little practice in school. The school curriculum focuses on acquisition of reading skills only in the early grades, and these children are likely to read less outside school and to watch more TV. As other researchers have found and as we noted earlier, by this stage use of TV, IQ scores, reading skills, and amount and type of reading are interrelated. In effect we are suggesting that TV may lead to an increase in the proportion of reading dropouts, especially among the less intelligent students in the early grades. Note, however, that this hypothesized influence of TV is indirect; the real cause is insufficient reading practice, so cutting down on time with TV might be necessary but would not be sufficient to produce good readers. In our view, the correlations between reading achievement and use of TV typically found in the later elementary grades and in high school are the outgrowth of a process that began in the early elementary grades, and are not primarily due to the current influence of TV on reading skill. Older students who watch a lot of TV and read relatively little probably do so because they are poor readers, rather than the other way around.

PARTICIPATION IN OTHER LEISURE ACTIVITIES

In addition to habitually being chosen over other in-home activities, TV viewing may also displace a number of activities typically conducted outside the home, either indoors, in other dwellings, or out of doors. MacBeth Williams & Handford (1986) studied participation in other leisure activities by the residents of Notel, Unitel, and Multitel. The main focus was on adolescents (students in Grades 7 to 12) and on adults (categorized as young, middle aged, and older).

A method called ecological psychology (Barker, 1968), or behavior-settings analysis, was particularly well suited for this study. In the 1950s Barker and Wright (1971) did a behavior-settings analysis of a town in the United States they called "Midwest."

They theorized that each unit of the environment, or behavior setting, places limits on the range and types of behavior likely to occur there, sometimes for physical reasons but also because of social and other conventions. Their system provides a method for specifying units of the environment in a way that could be applied to entire communities such as Notel, Unitel, and Multitel, towns of about the same size as Midwest.

The public behavior settings for each community for the previous year were determined in each phase by visiting the town and interviewing several people in each of the following categories: clergy, retailers, town clerks and elected officials, officers of community clubs/organizations, recreation-commission personnel, school teachers, editors of the newspaper, police, and children. In addition, copies of the community newspaper were obtained for the preceding year and items referring to community activities, organizations, meetings, special events, and so on were gleaned.

The list of activities and events unique to each town was organized into the 12 categories that Barker and Wright had used to describe Midwest. These were *Sports*; *Open Areas*, such as parks, playgrounds, swimming holes; *Businesses*, such as stores and offices; *Civic Activities*, such as the post office and town hall; out-of-school *Educational Activities*, such as open houses, music lessons, and adult classes; *Meetings* of clubs and other non-sports organizations for both children and adults; *Medical Activities*, such as visits to the hospital, doctors' offices, and so on; *Dances, Parties, and Suppers*; *Special Days*, such as weddings, funerals, and elections; *Religious Activities* of the churches and Bible camps; *Entertainment*, such as special movies, parades, bingo; and *Other Activities*, which included fundraising events, clean-up campaigns, and so on.

A questionnaire was developed to cover these 12 categories of community activities, with about 275 individual items in total. Another questionnaire assessed participation in 58 private leisure activities (e.g., reading books, bicycling). Whereas separate community-activity/behavior-setting questionnaires were developed for each phase of the study in each town, the same private leisure activity questionnaire was given in all towns in both phases.

Each person indicated whether and how he or she was involved in each activity during the preceding year. All students in Grades 7 through 12 completed questionnaires at school. The adults were surveyed by mail using a random sample from the electoral lists. Phase 1 questionnaires were completed by 1,023 people, and phase 2 questionnaires by 1,369.

Participation in private leisure activities varied considerably by age and gender, but only minimally by town or phase of the study, so there was little evidence of any impact of TV.

The number of community activities did not vary according to whether TV was available, but participation in those activities did vary. When total participation was considered, summing across the 12 activity categories, residents of Notel in phase 1 reported participating in more of their community's activities than did residents of both Unitel and Multitel, and the difference between Unitel and Multitel was also statistically significant. During the second year after the introduction of TV to Notel, total participation by the Notel residents remained greater than that for Unitel, and Unitel participation remained greater than that for Multitel, but the differences were much smaller than in phase 1. From phase 1 to phase 2 total participation by the longitudinal sample (that is, the same) youths (18 and younger) decreased significantly in Notel, but did not change in Unitel or Multitel. For longitudinal-sample adults (19 and over) there was a decrease in total participation in all three towns, but the decrease in Notel was 33 percent greater than in Unitel and 40 percent greater than in Multitel.

The negative effect of TV was especially strong for *Sports* (both active and spectator), but there also was evidence that TV affected attendance at *Dances, Parties, and Suppers*, particularly by youths, as well as attendance at *Meetings* of clubs and other non-sports organizations, particularly by adults. The results for participation in the categories *Special Days* and *Entertainment* were not as clear, but there was some evidence that TV also had a negative effect for these activities. There were no systematic differences among the towns in attendance at *Medical* and *Religious* activities. There were some differences among the towns for *Open Areas, Businesses, Civic, Educational* (nonschool), and *Other* activities, but the pattern of results suggested that TV did not play a role in these differences.

Television's apparent effect on participation in community activities was found for both adolescents and adults, but the effect was particularly strong for the oldest age group (56 and over). Before reception was available in Notel, adults in this group participated in the activities of their community at about the same rate as middle-aged adults (36 to 55 years), but two years after the arrival of TV there had been a dramatic decrease in their relative participation. This occurred for sports as well as for total activities. This decreased participation by the oldest age group (by comparison with adults in the middle years) found in Notel in phase 2 also was evident in Unitel and Multitel in both phases, which would explain the decrease in total participation for the longitudinal sample of adults, but not for youths in Unitel and Multitel from phase 1 to 2. This pattern of findings suggests that one of the effects of TV may be greater age segregation. These age-related results also are provocative because other research indicates that people age more successfully in later life if they are involved in active rather than just passive leisure pursuits.

The finding that participation in total community activities was greater in both phases in Unitel than in Multitel is striking. It was particularly strong for *Sports*, and is one of only a few results in the entire project indicating that, beyond the presence versus absence of TV, the number and/or type of channels available and/or their use makes a difference. One possible explanation is that the mean difference in hours of TV viewing between Unitel and Multitel (about 7 hours per week for youths and 6 hours for adults) accounts for some of the difference in participation in community activities. Another possibility is that decreases in participation in community activities occur gradually following the introduction of TV reception. Such habits may change slowly. In phase 1, Multitel had had TV twice as long (15 years) as Unitel (7 years). This hypothesis is consistent with the finding that, whereas participation by Notel residents dropped significantly from the year preceding the arrival of TV (phase 1) to the second year after its arrival (phase 2), in phase 2 it remained higher than participation in both Unitel and Multitel. The theory of ecological psychology would predict these findings on the basis that behavior settings constrain and influence people's behavior. If the continued existence of a community activity became threatened by a drop-off in participation, formal and informal pressure would be exerted on participants.

GENDER-ROLE ATTITUDES AND PERCEPTIONS

Attitudes and perceptions regarding gender roles may be acquired through observation of real life, the media, or some combination of the two. From the 1950s onward, content analyses have consistently demonstrated that there are two or three times as many male as female characters on TV, and that both females and males typically are portrayed in traditional gender roles—that is, in sex-typed ways. Evidence regarding the effects of such portrayals is more limited than the evidence regarding how the genders are portrayed, and has more often focused on effects of counter-stereotypical than typical content, since the effects of typical content are more difficult to isolate from the influences of other media and real life. The gender-role perceptions of students in Notel, Unitel, and Multitel therefore promised to yield important insights regarding media effects and were studied in this project by Kimball (1986).

Perceptions about appropriate and typical behaviors of girls and boys "your own age" (peer scale) were assessed using the sex-role differentiation scale (SRD) developed by Lambert (1971). Students also were asked to rate how frequently their own mother and father performed certain tasks (parent scale). For each item on the peer scale, the child rated on a seven-point scale how typical a certain behavior, a certain characteristic, or the future suitability of a certain job was for boys their own age. The child then rated how typical the same item was for girls their own age. Their score for each item was the difference between their ratings for boys and girls. This scale measures degree of sex-typing—in other words, the extent to which the students differentiated or sex-typed their peers. For the parent scales, the children rated how often their mothers and their fathers each performed certain tasks, so the difference scores reflected the students' perceptions of their parents' division of activities, discipline, support, and power.

In both phases, all students in Grades 6 and 9 in each of the three towns completed the scales, a total of approximately 150 students. Longitudinal data were not obtained. Data were also analyzed for a group of Grade 5 and Grade 8 children from Vancouver who had completed the scales eight months prior to the phase 1 testing in Notel, Unitel, and Multitel. This was done to determine whether the scores of students in these small communities were similar to or varied significantly from the scores of children growing up in an urban environment.

The bulk of the evidence for the peer scales indicated that TV did affect students' perceptions of gender roles, and that effect was to make perceptions more sex-typed or traditionally stereotyped. Before their town had TV, Notel students held more egalitarian gender-role perceptions of their peers than did students in Unitel and Multitel. Two years after the introduction of TV, Notel students' gender-role perceptions had become more sex-typed. In phase 2, there were no significant differences among the towns. With regard to the students' perceptions of their own parents' behavior, there was no evidence that exposure to TV had any effect; the parent scores did not vary according to the town or phase of the study. The results for both the peer and parent scales for students who had grown up with TV in Vancouver were similar to those for students who had grown up with TV in Unitel and Multitel. This and other evidence that the data from residents of Notel, Unitel, and Multitel were similar to other North American data supports the generalizability of the project's results regarding the effects of TV.

These findings concerning gender-role attitudes are in some ways surprising. They indicate that TV's impact was sufficiently strong to be measurable over and above the impact of many other influences. When the data for this study were collected, most of the gender-related influences from real-life, from TV, and from other media were relatively traditional. Television may be an especially effective teacher of gender roles, since it provides more models than most children encounter in real life, and during the 1970s, when this study was conducted, they were presented similarly and stereotypically in most TV programs and commercials. All theories of gender-role acquisition emphasize the importance of models. Other processes whereby TV may influence gender-role perceptions are discussed later.

The results of this research corroborate findings obtained in other studies indicating that the media play an important role in the development of gender-role attitudes. What has yet to be demonstrated, however, is the extent to which the media influence gender-role behavior (e.g., assertiveness in female-male interactions). This project did not directly address that question but did produce some provocative hints concerning gender-related behavior. In several substudies, there was a stereotypical gender difference in the towns with TV (Unitel and Multitel in both phases, Notel in phase 2), but no gender difference in the absence of TV (Notel in phase 1). This pattern was evident in performance on the spatial-ability task (block design), for fluent or automated reading skill, for participation in community activities, and for gender-role perceptions.

AGGRESSIVE BEHAVIOR

Perhaps the most widely studied effect of TV is its influence on viewers' aggressive behavior. The U.S. Surgeon General's investigation in the early 1970s focused mainly on this issue. The topic continues to be widely discussed and controversial (Freedman, 1984; Friedrich-Cofer & Huston, 1986; Freedman, 1986). Most academic researchers, after reviewing the literature, have concluded that the weight of the evidence from laboratory experiments, field observational studies, field experiments, and natural experiments indicates that exposure to violence in the media can, and for some viewers does, cause an increase in aggressive behavior. Moreover, there is evidence that aggressive behavior is stable from childhood to adulthood, so to the extent that TV has an influence during childhood, this effect is likely to be maintained into adulthood. The American Psychological Association's (APA) Board on Social and Ethical Responsibility for Psychology (1985) reviewed the available research and concluded that repeated observation of real and dramatized violence during childhood is one factor contributing to the development of stable patterns of aggressive and antisocial behavior.

Laboratory studies have the advantage that researchers can control both the filmed or televised aggressive content and some other variables that might interact with or be confounded with that content in influencing aggressive behavior. They have the disadvantage of not being naturalistic. For example, children may have fewer inhibitions about behaving aggressively when they believe they are not being observed by adults. In other words, laboratory studies indicate whether the media in general or TV in particular *can* in a controlled setting cause an increase in aggressive behavior. They do not indicate whether, given the vicissitudes of daily life, social controls regarding aggression, and so on, TV *does* cause an increase in real life. Most of the field observational studies have the advantage of being more naturalistic than the laboratory studies, but they also have the disadvantage that the data are correlational in nature. This raises the question mentioned earlier of whether children who are more aggressive choose to watch more TV aggression and violence, whether TV causes an increase in aggressive behavior, or whether, as some researchers contend, the relationship is transactional—that is, there is influence in both directions. The natural experiment in Notel, Unitel, and Multitel therefore promised to provide an important new kind of information on this controversial topic. Joy, Kimball, and Zabrack (1986) conducted this study.

Children's aggressive behavior was observed during free play on school playgrounds, before school, at recess, at lunchtime, and after school. In phase 1, children in Grades 1, 2, 4, and 5 were observed in all three towns. In phase 2, children in Grades 1, 2, 3, and 4 were observed. This provided before-and-after cross-sectional comparisons between the phases for children in Grades 1 and 2, and provided longitudinal comparisons for the children who were in Grades 1 and 2 in phase 1, and two years later in Grades 3 and 4 in phase 2. In addition, cross-sectional comparisons were made among the four grades within each phase. A total of 120 children from the three towns were observed in each phase, each for 21 minutes. Five girls and five boys were observed in each grade in each town in each phase. The observations were time-sampled across different days of the week and periods during the day, so each child was observed on a number of different occasions, with the order randomly predetermined and not dictated by the action of the moment. Neither the children nor the teachers were told that the observers were interested in aggressive behavior.

The two observers used checklists of 14 physically aggressive behaviors, such as hits, slaps, punches, kicks, bites, pushes, holds, and grabs, and nine verbally aggressive behaviors, such as disparages, mocks, curses, and commands in a loud, angry tone of voice. For each interval, the observer noted the number of times that each physically and each verbally aggressive behavior occurred. Accidental aggression and rough-and-tumble play were not included. Observer reliability was established initially during training in each phase, checked periodically during the observations, and was found to be high in both phases. The phase 2 observers were different from those who observed the children in phase 1.

In addition to the behavioral observations on the school grounds, peer ratings and teacher ratings of aggression were obtained for each child. In individual interviews, each child indicated the three students in his or her class who were the bossiest, fought the most, talked back to the teacher the most, argued and disagreed the most, and pushed, shoved, and poked the most. Each teacher rated each child in her or his class on several seven-point scales ranging from not at all characteristic to very characteristic (of the child being rated). Both positive and negative behaviors were rated and grouped into four composite teaching ratings: (1) aggressive, argumentative, bossy, and hostile; (2) active and loud; (3) competitive and dominant; and (4) friendly and honest.

There were no differences in aggressive behavior related to grade level. The most important question was whether there would be an increase in the aggressive behavior of Notel children following the inception of TV in their community, and there was. Notel children in the longitudinal sample increased from phase 1 to phase 2 in both physical and verbal aggression. This could not be attributed to maturation (being two years older), since there was no evidence of differences in aggressive behavior among the grades in either phase, and since there was no change for longitudinal-sample Unitel or Multitel children, who also were two years older. Twelve cross-sectional comparisons from phase 1 to phase 2 were made in each town (physical aggression: Grades 1 and 2 girls in phase 1 versus Grades 1 and 2 girls in phase 2, the same comparison for boys, the same comparison for the girls and boys combined, a similar set of three comparisons for Grades 3 and 4 versus 4 and 5, and a similar set of six comparisons for verbal aggression). In Notel, 10 of the 12 comparisons revealed a statistically significant increase in aggression; the other two increases were not statistically significant.

None of the 12 Unitel comparisons and only 2 of the Multitel comparisons (for girls, Grades 1 and 2, verbal aggression decreased; for boys and girls combined, Grades 3 and 4, physical aggression increased) were statistically significant. The increases in Notel occurred not only for both physically and verbally aggressive behavior, for both girls and boys, but also for children who were initially low in aggressive behavior as well as those who were initially high. This latter finding is noteworthy because some people have contended that only children initially high in aggression are affected by violence on TV. It makes sense that children with the least inhibitions against behaving aggressively would be most likely initially to imitate aggression, and that may have happened in Notel. These findings indicate, however, that it is not just these children who are influenced in the longer run, in this case over a period of two years.

The catharsis hypothesis would predict a decrease in aggression in Notel following the introduction of TV, due to vicarious release of aggressive impulses while viewing. All other theories (modeling/imitation, disinhibition, desensitization, arousal, and so on) about the effects of media violence on aggression would predict an increase in Notel, but predictions about comparisons among the towns within each phase are less clear. Most groups have dominance hierarchies and methods of controlling aggression among members, but tolerance of aggression varies considerably (motorcycle gangs and nuns might be extreme examples). It would not necessarily be expected, therefore, that the mean levels of aggression for the three towns would form a sensible pattern in relation to the availability of TV. In phase 1, the mean level of verbal aggression in Notel and Unitel was lower than that in Multitel, and there were no phase 1 differences in physical aggression. Two years after the arrival of TV in Notel, the level of verbal aggression was significantly higher than that for both Unitel and Multitel, which did not differ. In phase 2, Notel children were highest in physical aggression, exhibiting more than Unitel children, who were lowest; Multitel children were in between and not significantly different from Notel or Unitel.

The pattern of findings obtained in this study suggests that the social milieu is important. When social controls are adequate, either for individuals or groups, aggressive behaviors acquired from various models, including TV, may not be performed because of the individual's inhibitions against behaving aggressively. When the social controls are disrupted, however (which may have been what happened with the advent of TV in Notel), behaviors learned from all sources may be more likely to be performed. When considering these and other results regarding the influence of TV on aggression, it is important to remember that aggression is a socially disapproved behavior, albeit sometimes associated with mixed messages. Parents, teachers, and others generally try to teach children not to be physically and verbally aggressive. This is sufficiently successful that researchers who wish to study aggression beyond the middle school years have considerable difficulty doing so. Thus, in studies such as this, for an effect to be measurable it has to be sufficiently strong to overcome or go beyond the individual's inhibitions against behaving aggressively.

In general, the peer and teacher ratings of aggression were consistent with the researchers' observations of aggressive behavior on the school playground. This indicates that the observed behaviors had external validity, that is, that the children observed during this study to be relatively aggressive also were considered by the other children and their teachers to be aggressive relative to their peers.

The processes through which TV is theorized to influence aggressive behavior are discussed later, and an "update" is provided in the "Summary and Conclusions" at the end.

USE OF TELEVISION AND OTHER MEDIA

Was Notel really a town without TV in phase 1? Were Unitel and Multitel residents similar to or different from each other in amount of TV viewing? Information about TV use that would answer these and other questions was obtained from 1,168 children and 239 adults in phase 1 and from 1,206 children and 741 adults in phase 2. In phase 1, students from all grades in Notel and Unitel were interviewed individually at school about their TV viewing. In Phase 1 in Multitel, students in Grades 1 to 8 were interviewed individually, and those in Grades 9 to 12 described their TV viewing habits on the questionnaire regarding participation in community activities. In phase 2, information was obtained not only about TV use but also about the use of other media, including radio, magazines, book reading, use of the library, and parental control of children's TV viewing. In phase 1, information about adults' use of TV was obtained via mailed questionnaires, primarily in Unitel and Multitel, and in phase 2, some adults were interviewed in their homes about their use of TV and other media, whereas others provided information via mailed questionnaires. For both children and adults, the interview and questionnaire samples yielded comparable and reliable results.

MacBeth Williams & Boyes (1986) analyzed the media-use data. The evidence obtained via interviews and questionnaires confirmed that, for most residents, Notel was indeed a town without TV in phase 1. Fully 76 percent of the Notel students in Grades 1 through 12 reported watching zero hours of TV per week, by comparison with 8 percent of Unitel and 3 percent of Multitel students. These Unitel and Multitel percentages are very close to the figure of 5 percent reported by Hirsch (1980) for large representative samples of U.S. residents in 1975, 1976, and 1977. Two years later, in phase 2, only 11 percent of Notel students reported watching zero hours per week. The phase 2 figures for Unitel and Multitel were 13.8 percent and 2.8 percent, respectively.

Students in Multitel, where four channels were available, did report watching more hours per week on average than phase 1 students in Unitel and more than both Notel and Unitel students in phase 2, but the differences were not great. In phase 1, Unitel students in Grades 4 through 10 reported watching a mean of 25.4 hours per week by comparison with 33.6 hours for Multitel students in Grades 4 through 10. In phase 2, data were obtained from students in Grades 1 through 12; the mean for Multitel (26.9 hours per week) was significantly greater than the means for both Unitel (21.0) and Notel (20.9), which did not differ. Since the U.S. networks had longer broadcast days than did CBC, TV was available to Multitel children more hours per week. For example, Notel and Unitel children did not have access to TV prior to 9:00 a.m. on weekdays, whereas Multitel children could watch before school. Given that, it is even more surprising that children with one channel of CBC TV watched only 25 percent fewer hours than did children with access to the three privately owned U.S. networks in addition to CBC. The pattern of results for adult TV use was similar. In phase 2, Multitel adults reported watching a mean of 27.6 hours per week, by comparison with 23.8 for Unitel adults and 22.0 for Notel adults.

In phase 2, when data for other media were obtained, radio use was more similar than different across the towns. Multitel adults reported reading fewer books (2.36) per month than did adults in both Notel (4.68) and Unitel (4.39), and the same was true for checking books out of the library for their own use. More Notel (76.3 percent) than Multitel (68.0 percent) children reported ever going to their library; Unitel children (70.4 percent) did not differ from either Notel or Multitel children. Averaging across the towns, children who watched more TV reported reading more comics, fewer books, and listening to the radio less than did those who watched less television. The findings concerning availability of TV, IQ as a measure of intelligence, book reading, use of other media, and amount of TV viewing two years after the arrival of TV in Notel were consistent with the findings described earlier in this chapter for the relations among ability to read, IQ, and TV use. Children varied less, according to IQ, in their use of print (and to some extent radio), when TV was not available than when it was. And when it was available there was some evidence that the students with lower IQ scores tended to drop some activities in favor of TV viewing, especially those requiring the most mental effort, that is, book reading.[8]

In general, these findings regarding media use corroborate the evidence regarding the effects of TV in this project. Presence versus absence of television was more important than the number of channels or the nature of the channels available.

PROCESSES UNDERLYING THE EFFECTS OF TELEVISION

Many discussions of the effects of television have been based on overly simplistic models. In my view, the processes through which TV influences its viewers are complex. At a minimum, the following points need to be considered.

When watching TV, people usually do not behave in a stereotypically passive or mesmerized fashion. There is a good deal of evidence that children as well as adults are actively engaged (Dorr, 1986; Katz, 1998; Huston & Wright, 1996). The effects of TV result from an interaction of the characteristics of the viewer and the characteristics of the medium.

With regard to viewers, the outcome depends in part on whether they approach TV in a relatively mindful or relatively mindless way, and whether their goal is to seek information, entertainment, or some combination of the two. Viewers frequently time-share television with other activities, and sometimes this is appropriate. Ironing or shoe polishing are less onerous if time-shared with TV, but some activities such as playing or practicing a musical instrument are difficult if not impossible to time-share with TV. Doing homework or studying are important examples of activities probably not best time-shared with TV.

In surveys conducted in the United States (Grades 7 to 9) (Patton, Stinard, & Routh, 1983) and in the Netherlands (Grades 8 to 10) (Beentjes, Koolstra, & van der Voort, 1996), students agreed on the negative impact of TV on homework, whereas in research conducted in the United Kingdom, students who studied while watching TV believed that they could do so effectively (Wober, 1992). All three studies focused on use of media while doing homework rather than on the effects of that practice. In other experimental studies conducted with U.S. university students, background TV interfered with performance on difficult cognitive tasks (Armstrong, 1993; Armstrong, Bioarsky & Mares, 1991; Armstrong & Greenberg, 1990). Children and adults vary in their knowledge of their own thinking processes (metacognition), including, perhaps, their knowledge of their ability to time-share one or another kind of activity with TV. Good high school and university students may be aware that it is better not to study while watching TV, whereas students who do less well may not realize that this practice may affect their school achievement (MacBeth, 1996; Beentjes et al., 1996).

The individual's habits regarding TV, amount of TV, and kinds of programming viewed, are relevant when considering effects. It has been found, for example, in longitudinal studies in both Sweden (Rosengren & Windahl, 1989) and the United States (Huston & Wright, 1996) that preschoolers who watch more children's educational TV programming and less fictional programming intended for children (including cartoons) and for adults do better at school entry and beyond than do children with the opposite viewing patterns in the preschool years, even after socioeconomic status (SES) variables are controlled. What the individual would have done in lieu of watching TV is also important. Would the alternative activities have some other potential benefit (e.g., mental stimulation or physical activity) or might they have been detrimental? In addition, the viewer's stable and transient characteristics play a role in the communication outcome. The person's state of arousal, in terms of relative wakefulness or sleepiness, past experience, cultural background, political views, and so on, will influence comprehension and the impact of the content. McLuhan (1964) contended that the medium is the message—that is, that the characteristics of TV itself are important in its influence. These include *formal* characteristics, that is, those of its form, including music, action, camera angle, and type of shot (Huston & Wright, 1983). The content of TV varies both within a culture and between cultures. Moreover, TV content is by no means stable, but is continuously evolving, which makes it difficult to study both its content and its effects (Comstock, 1998). There are also differences among individuals within a culture in the biases and expectations they bring to the TV-viewing situation. In sum, many factors play a role in the influence of television, and simplistic analyses such as an assumption of all-or-nothing effects should be viewed with skepticism.

In hypothesizing about the processes through which the content of TV influences viewers (for example, with regard to gender-role perceptions and aggression), a psychological theory called *schema theory* or *schematic information processing theory* (Taylor & Crocker, 1978) is helpful. A schema is a self-relevant belief or expectation, and a script is a schema for a sequence of events. The closest everyday concept is a stereotype. Schemata, scripts, and stereotypes tend to direct attention, perceptions, and memory. Once established, they are resistant to change. For example, in one study children were shown either a film of a female physician and a male nurse or a film of a male physician and a female nurse (Cordua, McGraw, & Drabman, 1979). The children who saw the male physician and the female nurse all recalled the situation correctly, but only half of those who saw the female physician and the male nurse did so; the other half reversed their roles. The most likely explanation is that the children processed the information via their gender-role schemata, and they either didn't notice the discrepancy when initially watching the film or subsequently altered their memory to be consistent with their gender schemata. This phenomenon is well known with regard to prejudice. People who hold the view that a particular group is lazy, and then encounter a hardworking member of that group, typically do not change their stereotypes on the basis of the contradictory information. They either do not notice that the individual is both hardworking and a member of that group, or they consider that individual an exception. Schemata and stereotypes are formed through both direct experience, for example nurses and physicians encountered in real life, and from indirect experience, for example hearing physicians (of unknown as well as known gender) referred to with male pronouns and nurses referred to with female pronouns, as well as via the media. Since children in North America typically begin watching TV regularly at two to three years of age, its content must play an important role in both the initial formation and the subsequent maintenance of their schemata and stereotypes in a number of areas, including minorities, aggression, and gender roles.

Among the other ways in which TV content has been shown to influence viewers, *observational learning* via *the imitation of models and their behaviors* is one of the most important (Bandura, 1977; Dubow & Miller, 1996; Geen, 1990). Television provides many models, including models of gender-role behavior, aggressive behavior, and pro-social behaviors such as sharing. It is important to recognize that learning consists of two steps, acquisition and performance (Bandura, 1977). Acquisition would include the initial formation of a schema or stereotype. Behaviors acquired through observation may not be performed because of inhibition, or there may be a gap between acquisition and performance of the modeled behavior. Another possibility is that performance does not occur unless there is some cue in the environment that cognitively triggers the acquired behavior and provides a link for the individual from the previously observed model to the current situation (Huesmann, 1982). Moreover, the environmental cue may be linked up through a network of associative pathways with related thoughts and feelings. Activation of any one component spreads along the pathway to activate the others (for example, feeling activated ideas, thought activated feelings). Researchers have shown, for example, connections among violent cues in media, violent thoughts, and hostile feelings (Bushman & Geen, 1990; Dubow & Miller, 1996).

The viewer's state of *arousal* also plays a role in the effects of TV content. This is true not only in terms of physiological arousal such as sleepiness or wakefulness, as mentioned earlier, but also with regard to attentiveness or cognitive arousal. Salomon's concept of amount of invested mental effort, or AIME, is relevant in this regard (Salomon, 1983). As he has found, North American children tend to believe that TV is a relatively easy medium from which to learn, and that they are good at learning from TV, so they watch with relatively little AIME. This will make it difficult for programming intended to be educational or informative to be effective. It also may make it more likely that children will notice, remember, and acquire negative behaviors (e.g., aggression) but not notice the sanctions portrayed for that behavior (e.g., punishment), particularly if they are imposed much later in the film or TV program. By comparison with the amount of mental effort they invest in watching TV, North American children tend to believe that print is a more difficult medium and to report investing more mental effort when processing information from print. Not surprisingly, these same children have been found to remember more from print than from television.

As mentioned in the earlier discussion of the effects of TV on creativity, it may influence the manner in which people *process information*. As Salomon contends (1983), television requires primarily encoding and chunking of information but does not require or encourage mental elaboration. Indeed, TV and visual media in general may interfere with or prohibit mental elaboration. One cannot stop the flow of incoming information to pose critical questions, whereas while reading one can look up from the page and try to think of counter-examples, ponder the evidence, and then continue without losing one's place. Doing the same thing while watching an audiovisual presentation will result in new information being lost.

Another process underlying some effects of television is *desensitization* or habituation (Bandura, 1978; Comstock, 1980; Lefkowitz & Huesmann, 1980). Viewers may become accustomed to certain behaviors or models, even ones they initially found offensive. Habituation or desensitization to media content may in turn result in *disinhibition* or reduction in inhibitions regarding certain attitudes and/or behaviors. Desensitization and disinhibition apply potentially not only to such behaviors as violence but also to sexist and/or racist comments, the portrayal of women or men as sex objects, and so on. There is empirical evidence that viewers become desensitized to media violence through exposure to it.

Finally, as outlined earlier for some of the phenomena we studied, certain effects seem to occur because watching TV is done in lieu of other activities that could have had a different consequence, at least for some people. These effects include direct *displacement* of other activities, such as sports or attending a community meeting. They also include *indirect* displacement, that is, through problem-solving games that might contribute to creativity or problem-solving performance. Another indirect example would be reading or discussing with others either feminist or very traditional views regarding gender roles, as opposed to exposure to the sorts of portrayals shown on television. The issue of *time-sharing* television with appropriate versus inappropriate activities also comes under the rubric of indirect consequences. Finally, as was noted earlier, displacement by TV of doing nothing—that is, boredom—also may be important if during those bored periods the individual is reflecting upon ideas or engaging in some form of mental elaboration. For additional considerations of the psychological processes by which media can influence viewers, see chapters by Gentile and Anderson and Carnagey in this volume.

SUMMARY AND CONCLUSIONS

When we designed this research we hypothesized that television influences its viewers in a number of ways, both positively and negatively, based on previous research and theories. The natural experiment provided by the imminent arrival of TV reception in Notel was a rare opportunity. But, to be frank, we were skeptical that any effects of TV would be measurable over and above the many other influences that operate in a naturalistic setting. They were measurable and can be summarized as follows:

- TV had a negative effect on creativity, as indicated by the number and unusualness of children's ideas and the speed and persistence of adults in a problem-solving task.

- A negative effect on the acquisition of reading skills in the early elementary grades was found for both an individual fluent-reading task and for a group comprehension and vocabulary test.

- TV negatively affected participation in community activities, particularly *Sports, Meetings* of clubs and organizations, and *Dances, Parties, and Suppers,* and to a lesser extent, *Special Days* and *Entertainment.* Participation decreased for both adolescents and adults, including older adults.

- Students' attitudes and perceptions regarding gender roles became more sex-typed as a result of TV, a finding we also interpret as negative.

- The introduction of TV to Notel led to an increase in children's aggressive behavior; this was true of both verbal and physical aggression for both boys and girls, and for children initially low as well as those initially high in aggression.

- For the areas in which we hypothesized that TV would or might have a positive impact, including vocabulary, spatial ability, field independence, and fineness of information processing, there was little, if any, evidence to support those hypotheses, but also no contradictory evidence.[9]

- Some additional areas in which there was no evidence, positive or negative, of effects of TV were participation in private leisure activities and in certain kinds of community activities (e.g., *Religious, Medical*).

- Finally, because of various constraints we were not able to study the impact of TV in all potentially important areas. Among the areas in which it is likely that TV does have an impact are consumer behavior (as a result of the content of both programs and commercials); information and/or general knowledge (especially type of knowledge, e.g., regarding entertainers versus history); physical fitness and obesity; and attitudes regarding racial and/or ethnic groups.

UPDATE

In almost all cases, the academic community's response to the publication of our findings has been positive. For example, the American Psychological Association's (APA) Task Force on Television and Society (Huston et al., 1992) reviewed research on the positive and negative effects of TV advertising and programming, emphasizing research conducted since the early 1980s. They cited our findings for gender-role attitudes (Kimball, 1986) stating that "demonstrating causal influences of television on sex stereotypes is difficult because such stereotypes abound throughout the society, not just on television" (p. 29). Our findings regarding participation in community and other leisure activities (MacBeth Williams & Handford, 1986) were cited as evidence for a modified version of the displacement hypothesis—that is, that "television viewing does displace other activities, but not at random" (p. 86). It displaces "activities that serve functions similar to TV (e.g., entertainment) and those that are incompatible with viewing (e.g., attending a local sports event)" (p. 86). Along with evidence from other studies, our findings (Corteen & MacBeth Williams, 1986) were cited as evidence that reading is the one academic "subject that may be negatively influenced by TV viewing, but the effects are small" (p. 87).

With regard to our analysis of the processes whereby television may influence acquisition of fluent reading skills, Comstock (1989) quoted our hypothesis, and went on to say that the model we proposed also could readily apply to mathematical and writing skills.

With regard to our other major findings, the APA Task Force's report (Huston et al., 1992) did not mention those concerning vocabulary (Harrison & MacBeth Williams, 1986), persistence at problem-solving tasks (Suedfeld et al., 1986), or media use (MacBeth Williams & Boyes, 1986). The only instance in which their conclusions differed from ours was with regard to creativity. In citing our study they noted that "children showed reduced performance on one of two measures of creativity after television was introduced" (p. 90), and, on balance, they agreed with the conclusions reached by Anderson and Collins (1988) that "there is little evidence that television as a medium has any effects on such cognitive processes as attention, creativity, impulsivity, or attention span" (p. 91) (Huston et al., 1992). In my opinion, our finding that prior to the arrival of TV, Notel children scored higher than both Unitel and Multitel children on the ideational fluency Alternate Uses Task (which is acknowledged to be the better measure) (Harrison & MacBeth Williams, 1986), and our findings regarding persistence on problem solving by adults (Suedfeld et al., 1986), are more important than the preceding quote acknowledges.

Indeed, some of those same authors have more recently pursued the issue empirically by analyzing data from two samples that they studied longitudinally (A. C. Huston, personal communication, June 2000, based on an unpublished manuscript by D. R. Anderson, A. C. Huston, K. L. Schmitt, D. L. Linebarger, & J. C. Wright, *Adolescent outcomes associated with early childhood television viewing: The recontact study*). They found that viewing by preschoolers of informative TV programming intended for children (especially *Mister Rogers*) predicted higher creativity scores on the alternate uses ideational fluency task in adolescence, whereas entertainment viewing in the preschool years predicted lower creativity scores in adolescence. Their findings do not permit causal inferences, but are consistent with our conclusions regarding our own results, and call into question Anderson and Collins's conclusions cited earlier.

In the third edition of their textbook, Liebert and Sprafkin (1988) displayed our before-and-after creativity results in a figure and concluded that, when taken together with the findings of other researchers, our data "suggest that heavy exposure to standard commercial television may inhibit children's imaginative and creativity abilities" (p. 15). Citing our results and those of others, Greenfield and her coauthors (1993) concluded that "the majority of the research on television and imagination indicates a detrimental effect of the medium" (p. 55), and Singer (1993) concluded that the evidence for negative effects on creativity appears to be stronger than for positive effects. These differing interpretations of similar evidence provide a good illustration of the importance to readers of evaluating published evidence in its original form for themselves, rather than relying on summaries provided by others.[10]

The topic of violence in the media and its effects on aggressive attitudes and behavior has continued to receive a great deal of attention from both researchers and the public. The consensus in both groups is that viewing violence does lead to aggressive attitudes and behavior, and that this is a problem in North American society. The APA Task Force's report (Huston et al., 1992) cited our study as "one unique source of information" (p. 56) that, along with other kinds of research evidence they reviewed, supports "the conclusion that viewing television violence leads to aggression that becomes a lasting part of individual behavior patterns" (p. 56).

Since the publication of our study, a number of researchers have demonstrated in both laboratory and field experiments (Bjorkvist, 1985; Bushman, 1995; Bushman & Geen, 1990; Josephson, 1987) that violence viewing causes children as well as adults to have emotional responses and violent thoughts as well as to behave more aggressively toward other humans, not just inanimate objects. Several of these studies included random assignment of individuals to experimental conditions, so causal inferences can be made. In other longitudinal field observational studies it has been demonstrated that viewing TV violence in childhood predicts later aggressive and antisocial behavior, even after early aggressive behavior is statistically controlled (Botha & Mels, 1990; Huesmann & Eron, 1986; Lefkowitz et al., 1977; Weigman, Kuttschreuter, & Baarda, 1986). Researchers who have reviewed the research on media (TV and film) and aggression using the technique called meta-analysis to statistically evaluate the entire body of evidence have concluded that exposure significantly enhances aggressive behavior (Paik & Comstock, 1994; Wood, Wong, & Chachere, 1991) (see chapter 13). For more on meta-analytic studies of media violence, see the chapter by Comstock, Scharrer, & Powers, this volume.

Information-processing theories have been used to develop models for understanding *how* TV exposure influences aggressive behavior, including the roles of individual characteristics and situational influences (Berkowitz & Heimer, 1989; Huesmann, 1988). As Dubow and Miller pointed out, most researchers (Huston et al., 1992; Liebert & Sprafkin, 1988) who have considered the body of evidence "acknowledge that television violence viewing is only one of many causes of aggression (other causes include family environment characteristics) but conclude that it is nevertheless of social significance" (Dubow & Miller, 1996).

In both Canada and the United States, public concern about violence on television has become increasingly evident. The 1992 Larivière petition, begun by a teenager in Quebec who blamed TV violence for her sister's rape and murder, was signed by over one million people. In response to government warnings, the Canadian Association of Broadcasters (CAB) developed a self-regulatory code for private broadcasters that was approved by the CRTC in October 1993. The CRTC has requested that the public networks (including CBC), cable, pay TV, and specialty services also develop self-regulatory standards. Also in October 1993, the U.S. Attorney General Janet Reno warned media executives during a Senate Commerce Committee hearing that if immediate steps were not taken to reduce violent content and deadlines were not established, the government should respond. Such events led some prominent researchers to conclude that the 1992–1993 television season was a turning point from research on television violence to widespread agreement about the need for action to create a cultural environment that is free, diverse, fair, and not threatening to human potentials (Gerbner, Morgan, & Signorielli, 1994). Ratings for violent content in network and cable programs have since been developed for both Canadian and U.S. television programs. Nonetheless, the research on the effectiveness of ratings shows serious problems (see Gentile & Murray, this volume).

In sum, the empirical evidence and theorizing in recent years in the area of media violence and aggressive behavior has been consistent with and has extended our findings and conclusions, and the public has expressed increasing rather than decreasing concern about violence in the media.

Our research findings have been carefully reviewed[11] and widely cited.[12] Almost all of these responses have been positive and have concurred with our interpretations. More recent research has tended to support rather than contradict our findings and conclusions.

No single study can be definitive. Laboratory studies, field experiments, field observational studies, and natural experiments such as our Notel, Unitel, and Multitel study provide different and complementary kinds of evidence concerning the effects of television and other media on human behavior. The results of our research, when added to the converging evidence that has accumulated from other research over the years, indicate that TV does affect its viewers. The hypothesis of no effects, once popular, is no longer tenable. This is certainly not to argue that television is the only or most important influence, but to state that over and above the myriad other influences on human behavior, television plays a role that is measurable on average, despite the many individual differences among viewers.[13]

NOTES

1. This chapter was originally published as an entry in Jeffrey Jensen Arnett, *Encyclopedia of children, adolescents, and the media*, *V2*. New York, NY: Sage Publications, 2007.

2. In previous editions of *Communications in Canadian Society*, and in some other descriptions of this research, I wrote under my former name, Tannis MacBeth Williams. I have since reverted to Tannis M. MacBeth.

3. I would like to express my gratitude to Mary Morrison, a Vancouver psychologist who brought this town without TV to my attention.

4. We are grateful to the Canada Council (later the Social Sciences and Humanities Research Council of Canada) for funding both this research and sabbatical leave fellowships that enabled me to complete the data analyses and writing.

5. Pseudonyms are used for all three towns to protect the anonymity ethically required and promised to the individuals and communities studied.

6. The reason that the difference between 150.6 and 251.0 is statistically significant ($p < .05$), but the difference between 150.6 and 263.1 is only marginally significant ($p < .10$), has to do with controlling the alpha (type I) error level according to the number of comparisons made (three in this case), and in particular, the distance between comparisons.

7. We decided to collect phase 3 data from Grade 2 students because Unitel students in Grade 2 obtained very low phase 2 scores. This is the only instance in the project in which phase 3 data were obtained.

8. In phase 1, data were obtained from students in all grades in each town, but comparisons in hours of TV viewing were made only for Grades 4 through 10. This was because we were not confident in the reports of children in the early grades and because the Unitel high school ended with Grade 10 (Grade 11 and 12 students went elsewhere, including some to Notel). In phase 2, improved interview methods gave us more confidence in the younger children's reports, and the schools in all three towns went to Grade 12.

9. Findings on field independence and fineness of information processing have not been discussed in this chapter; details can be found in Suedfeld et al., Television and adults: Thinking, personality, and attitudes. In T. MacBeth Williams (Ed.), *The impact of television: A natural experiment in three communities* (pp. 361–393). New York, NY: Academic Press.

10. For my own relatively recent review of the literature on creativity, imagination, persistence, IQ, school achievement, participation in other activities, and television, see T. M. MacBeth (1996), Indirect effects of television. In T. M. MacBeth (Ed.), *Tuning in to young viewers: Social science perspectives on television* (pp. 149–219). Thousand Oaks, CA: Sage.

11. In, for example, (1986) *Journal of Communication, 36*(4), 140–144; (1987) *Contemporary Psychology, 32*(4), 309–310; *Contemporary Psychology, 44*(2), 201–204; (1987) *Canadian Psychology, 28*(3), 298–299; (1987, November 13), *Die Zeit*; (1987, Winter) *Journalism Quarterly*; (1987) *New Zealand Journal of Educational Studies, 22,* 131–134; (1987) *Contemporary Sociology,* 553–554; (1990) *Communication Research Trend, 10*(3).

12. For example: Berry & Asamen, *Children and television: Images in a changing sociocultural world*; Murray, Studying television violence: A research agenda for the 21st century, in Asamen & Berry (Eds.), *Research paradigms, television, and social behavior*; Rosengren & Windahl, *Media matter: TV use in childhood and adolescence*; Strasburger, Adolescents and the media: Media and psychological impact, *Developmental Clinical Psychology and Psychiatry, 33.* See also Huston et al., *Big world, small screen*; Comstock, *The evolution of American television*; Liebert & Sprafkin, *The early window.*

13. I would like to express my gratitude to Janet Werker for her very helpful comments on an earlier draft of this chapter.

REFERENCES

American Psychological Association. (1985). *Violence on TV.* A social issue release from the Board of Social and Ethical Responsibility for Psychology. Washington, DC: Author.

Anderson, D. R., & Collins, P. S. (1988). *The impact on children's education: Television's influence on cognitive development.* Washington, DC: U.S. Department of Education.

Armstrong, B. G. (1990). Background TV as an inhibitor of cognitive processing. *Human Communication Research, 16,* 335–386.

Armstrong, B. G. (1993). Cognitive interference from background TV: Structural effects on verbal and spatial processing. *Communication Studies, 44,* 56–70.

Armstrong, B. G., Bioarsky, G. A., & Mares, M. L. L. (1991). Background TV and reading performance. *Communication Monographs, 58,* 235–253.

Armstrong, B. G., & Greenberg, B. S. (1990). Background TV as an inhibitor of cognitive processing. *Human Communication Research, 16,* 335–386.

Bandura, A. (1977). *Social learning theory.* Englewood Cliffs, NJ: Prentice Hall.

Bandura, A. (1978). Social learning of aggression. *Journal of Communication, 28*(3), 12–29.

Barker, R. G. (1968). *Ecological psychology: Concepts and methods for studying the environment of human behavior.* Stanford, CA: Stanford University Press.

Barker, R. G., & Wright, H. R. (1971, originally published 1955). *Midwest and its children.* Hamden, CT: Archon Books.

Beentjes, J. W. J., Koolstra, C. M., & van der Voort, T. H. A. (1996). Combining background media with doing homework: Incidence of background media use and perceived effects. *Communication Education, 45,* 59–72.

Berkowitz, L., & Heimer, K. (1989). On the construction of the anger experience: Aversive events and negative priming in the formation of feelings. *Advances in Experimental Social Psychology, 22,* 1–37.

Bjorkvist, K. (1985). *Violent films, anxiety, and aggression.* Helsinki, FI: Finnish Society of Sciences and Letters.

Botha, M., & Mels, G. (1990). Stability of aggression among adolescents over time: A South African study. *Aggressive Behavior, 16,* 361–380.

Bushman, B. J. (1995). Moderating role of trait aggressiveness in the effects of violent media on aggression. *Journal of Personality and Social Psychology, 69,* 950–960.

Bushman, B. J., & Geen, R. G. (1990). Role of cognitive-emotional mediators and individual differences in the effects of media violence on aggression. *Journal of Personality and Social Psychology, 58,* 156–163.

Comstock, G. (1980). New emphases in research on the effects of television and film violence. In E. L. Palmer & A. Dorr (Eds.), *Children and the faces of television* (pp. 129–148). New York, NY: Academic Press.

Comstock, G. (1989). *The evolution of American television.* Newbury Park, CA: Sage.

Comstock, G. (1998). Television research: Past problems and present issues. In J. K. Asamen & G. L. Berry (Eds.), *Research paradigms, television, and social behaviors* (pp. 11–36). Thousand Oaks, CA: Sage.

Cook, T. D., Campbell, D. T., & Peracchio, L. (1990). Quasiexperimentation. In M. D. Dunnette & L. M. Hough, (Eds.), *Handbook of industrial and organizational psychology* (Vol. 1, 2nd ed.) (pp. 491–576). Chicago, IL: Rand McNally.

Cordua, G. D., McGraw, K. O., & Drabman, R. S. (1979). Doctor or nurse: Children's perceptions of sex-typed occupations. *Child Development, 50,* 590–593.

Corteen, R. S., & MacBeth Williams, T. (1986). Television and reading skills. In T. MacBeth Williams (Ed.), *The impact of television: A natural experiment in three communities* (pp. 39–86). New York, NY: Academic Press.

Dorr, A. (1986). *Television and children: A special medium for a special audience.* Beverly Hills, CA: Sage.

Dubow, E. F., & Miller, L. S. (1996). Television violence viewing and aggressive behavior. In T. M. MacBeth (Ed.), *Tuning in to young viewers* (pp. 117–147). Thousand Oaks, CA: Sage.

Freedman, J. L. (1984). Effect of television violence on aggressiveness. *Psychological Bulletin, 96,* 227–246.

Freedman, J. L. (1986). Television violence and aggression: A rejoinder. *Psychological Bulletin, 100,* 372–378.

Friedrich-Cofer, L., & Huston, A. C. (1986). Television violence and aggression: The debate continues. *Psychological Bulletin 100*, 364–371.

Geen, R. G. (1990). The influence of the mass media. In R. G. Geen (Ed.), *Human aggression* (pp. 83–112). Pacific Grove, CA: Brooks Cole.

Gerbner, G., Morgan, M., & Signorielli, N. (1994). *Television violence profile no. 16: The turning point from research to action.* Philadelphia, PA: The University of Pennsylvania, Annenberg School of Communication.

Greenfield, P. M., Yut, E., Chung, M., Land, D., Kreider, H., Pantoja, M., & Horsley, K. (1993). The program-length commercial: A study of the effects of television/toy tie-ins on imaginative play. In G. L. Berry & J. K. Asamen (Eds.), *Children and television: Images in a changing sociocultural world* (pp. 53–73). Newbury Park, CA: Sage.

Harrison, L. F., & MacBeth Williams, T. (1986). Television and cognitive development. In T. MacBeth Williams (Ed.), *The impact of television: A natural experiment in three communities* (pp. 87–142). New York, NY: Academic Press.

Hirsch, P. (1980). The "scary world" of the non-viewer and other anomalies: A re-analysis of Gerbner et al.'s findings of Cultivational Analysis. *Communication Research*, 7, 403–456.

Huesmann, L. R. (1982). Television violence and aggressive behavior. In D. Pearl, L. Bouthilet, & J. Lazar (Eds.), *Television and behavior: Ten years of scientific progress and implications for the 80s, Vol. 2* (pp. 126–137). Rockville, MD: National Institute of Mental Health.

Huesmann, L. R. (1988). An information processing model for the development of aggression. *Aggressive Behavior, 14*, 13–24.

Huesmann, L. R., & Eron, L. D. (1986). *Television and the aggressive child: A cross-national comparison.* Hillside, NJ: Erlbaum.

Huston, A. C., Donnerstein, E., Fairchild, H., Feshbach, N. D., Katz, P. A., Murray, J. P., Rubenstein, E. A., Wilcox, B. L., & Zuckerman, D. (1992). *Big world, small screen: The role of television in American society.* Lincoln, NE: University of Nebraska Press.

Huston, A. C., & Wright, J. C. (1983). Children's processing of television: The informative functions of formal features. In J. Bryant & D. R. Anderson (Eds.), *Children's understanding of television: Research on attention and comprehension* (pp. 35–68). New York, NY: Academic Press.

Huston, A. C., & Wright, J. C. (1996). Television and socialization of young children. In T. M. MacBeth (Ed.), *Tuning in to young viewers: Social science perspectives on television* (pp. 37–60). Thousand Oaks, CA: Sage.

Josephson, W. L. (1987). Television violence and children's aggression: Testing the priming, social script, and disinhibition predictions. *Journal of Personality and Social Psychology, 53*, 882–890.

Joy, L. A., Kimball, M. M., & Zabrack, M. L. (1986). Television and children's aggressive behavior. In T. MacBeth Williams (Ed.), *The impact of television: A natural experiment in three communities* (pp. 303–360). New York, NY: Academic Press.

Katz, E. (1988). On conceptualizing media effects: Another look. In S. Oskamp (Ed.), *Applied Social Psychology Annual: Television as a social issue* (Vol. 8, pp. 361–374). Beverly Hills, CA: Sage.

Kimball, M. M. (1986). Television and sex-role attitudes. In T. MacBeth Williams (Ed.), *The impact of television: A natural experiment in three communities* (pp. 265–301). New York, NY: Academic Press.

Lambert, R. D. (1971). Sex role imagery in children: Social origins of the mind. *Studies of the Royal Commission on the Status of Women in Canada, no. 6.* Ottawa, ON: Information Canada.

Langer, E. J., & Piper, A. (1988). Television from a mindful/mindless perspective. In S. Oskamp (Ed.), *Applied Social Psychology Annual: Television as a social issue* (Vol. 8, pp. 247–260). Beverly Hills, CA: Sage.

Lefkowitz, M. M., Eron, L. D., Walder, L. O., & Huesmann, L. R. (1977). *Growing up to be violent.* New York, NY: Pergamon.

Lefkowitz, M. M., & Huesmann, L. R. (1980). Concomitants of television violence viewing in children. In E. L. Palmer & A. Dorr (Eds.), *Children and the faces of television.* New York, NY: Academic Press.

Liebert, R. M., & Sprafkin, J. (1988). *The early window* (3rd ed.). Toronto, ON: Pergamon.

MacBeth, T. M. (1996). Indirect effects of television: Creativity, persistence, school achievement, and participation in other activities. In T. M. MacBeth (Ed.), *Tuning in to young viewers: Social science perspectives on television* (pp. 149–219). Thousand Oaks, CA: Sage.

MacBeth, T. M. (1998). Quasiexperimental research on television and behavior. In J. K. Asamen & G. L. Berry (Eds.), *Research paradigms, television, and social behavior* (pp. 109–151). Thousand Oaks, CA: Sage.

MacBeth Williams, T. (1986a). Background and overview. In T. MacBeth Williams (Ed.), *The impact of television: A natural experiment in three communities* (p. 1–38). New York, NY: Academic Press.

MacBeth Williams, T. (Ed.). (1986b). *The impact of television: A natural experiment in three communities.* New York, NY: Academic Press.

MacBeth Williams, T., & Boyes, M. C. (1986). Television viewing patterns and use of other media. In T. MacBeth Williams (Ed.), *The impact of television: A natural experiment in three communities* (pp. 215–263). New York, NY: Academic Press.

MacBeth Williams, T., & Handford, G. C. (1986). Television and other leisure activities. In T. MacBeth Williams (Ed.), *The impact of television: A natural experiment in three communities* (pp. 143–213). New York, NY: Academic Press.

McLuhan, M. (1964). *Understanding Median: The Extension of Man.* New York, NY: McGraw-Hill.

Miller, G. A., & Gildea, P. M. (1988). How children learn words. *Scientific American, 259*(2), 94–99.

National Institute of Mental Health. (1972). *Report of the Surgeon General's Scientific Advisory Committee on television and social behavior.* Rockville, MD: Author.

Paik, H., & Comstock, G. (1994). The effects of television violence on antisocial behavior: A meta-analysis. *Communication Research, 21,* 516–546.

Patton, J. E., Stinard, T. A., & Routh, D. K. (1983). Where do children study? *Journal of Educational Research, 76,* 280–286.

Rosengren, K. E., Roe, K., & Sonesson, I. (1983, May). Finality and causality in adolescents: Mass media use. Paper presented at the meeting of the International Communication Association, Dallas, TX.

Rosengren, K. E., & Windahl, S. (1989). *Media matter: TV use in childhood and adolescence.* Norwood, NJ: Ablex.

Salomon, G. (1983). Television watching and mental effort: A social psychological view. In J. Bryant & D. R. Anderson (Eds.), *Children's understanding of television:*

Research on attention and comprehension (pp. 181–198). New York, NY: Academic Press.

Singer, D. S. (1993). Creativity of children in a television world. In G. L. Berry & J. K. Asamen (Eds.), *Children and television: Images in a changing sociocultural world* (pp. 73–88). Newbury Park, CA: Sage.

Sternlicht Chall, J. (1983). *Stages of reading development*. New York, NY: McGraw-Hill.

Suedfeld, P., Little, B. R., Rank, A. D., Rank, E., & Ballard, E. J. (1986). Television and adults: Thinking, personality, and attitudes. In T. MacBeth Williams (Ed.), *The impact of television: A natural experiment in three communities* (pp. 361–393). New York, NY: Academic Press.

Suler, J. R. (1980). Primary process thinking and creativity. *Psychological Bulletin, 88*, 144–165.

Taylor, S. E., & Crocker, J. (1978). Schematic bases of social information processing. In E. T. Higgins, C. P. Herman, & M. P. Zanna (Eds.), *Social cognition: The Ontario symposium in personality and social psychology* (pp. 89–135). Hillside, NJ: Erlbaum.

Weigman, O., Kuttschreuter, M., & Baarda, B. (1986). *Television viewing related to aggressive and prosocial behavior*. The Hague, NL: Stitching voor Onderzoek van het Onderwijs.

Wober, J. M. (1992). Text in a texture of television: Children's homework experience. *Journal of Educational Television, 18*(1), 23–24.

Wood, W., Wong, F. Y., & Chachere, J. G. (1991). Effects of media violence on viewer's aggression in unconstrained social interaction. *Psychological Bulletin, 109*, 371–383.

CHAPTER 4

The Role of Theory in the Study of Media Violence: The General Aggression Model

Craig A. Anderson and Nicholas L. Carnagey

Much of this book reviews empirical research on the effects of media violence. Researchers have used many tools in this effort to understand the phenomenon of media violence. Creative lab designs and advancement of technology have allowed laboratory researchers to manipulate exposure to media violence and view the short-term results of brief exposure. Cross-sectional and longitudinal studies have allowed the research world to document the "real life" consequences of repeated exposure to large amounts of media violence. Although these empirical research tools have resulted in great advances in understanding by media violence researchers, it is important to remember that the theories guiding and being revised by such research are as important to the scientific enterprise as the data they generate.

THEORY

Theory is typically defined as an organized set of hypotheses that allows a scientist to understand, explain, and predict a wide variety of phenomena (Shaw & Costanzo, 1982). Theory serves the scientist in a number of ways. For example, theory organizes a researcher's thoughts, hypotheses, and existing knowledge. Such organization has many benefits, such as making the researcher more efficient in developing a strategic plan of analysis.

Not only does a good theory help organize concepts but it also indirectly organizes researchers and their products. Think of knowledge as a tower of building blocks, with each block constituting a small piece of empirical knowledge. The more blocks there are, the more is known about a subject.

Without theory to guide them, researchers are forced to individually build their own knowledge about a subject, starting from the ground up. However, with one theory guiding several researchers, they are empowered to build on each other's blocks, with theory establishing the foundation and basic structure for scientific advancement. With scientists able to add blocks to one single tower and indirectly working as a team, the amount of knowledge grows at a greater rate and with greater efficiency than if the scientists were working at individual levels.

In every field of science, including psychology, the purpose of research is to gain an understanding of a particular phenomenon, with the end result being the ability to predict future outcomes involving the phenomenon and to influence those outcomes, depending on how much control exists over particular variables (Shaw & Costanzo, 1982). Theory is useful in this respect because it attaches meaning to the data collected, enabling researchers to look beyond the numbers and understand the phenomenon at a deeper level. This understanding and advancement of knowledge make both prediction and control more accurate and useful.

This is where the scientific meaning of "theory" diverges so greatly from the lay meaning. To many nonscientists (including judges, politicians, and public policy leaders, as well as the general public), "theory" means nothing more than a haphazard guess, or a politically inspired ideological position. This view is one reason why so many attacks on media violence findings (or evolution, global warming, tobacco/cancer, for example) ignore basic theory and tons of empirical findings on which relevant theories are built. Findings on the addictive and cancer-causing properties of substances found in cigarette smoke on lab rats were widely ridiculed by smokers, comedians, and, of course, the tobacco industry for years. Such findings were seen as irrelevant, in part because the lay understanding of "theory" bears little resemblance to the scientific enterprise behind the creation, testing, and modification of good theory. In the media violence domain, this *theory-ignorant* approach to attacks on laboratory studies (as "artificial" or "trivial"), cross-sectional correlational studies ("correlation is not causation"), and longitudinal studies ("what, you didn't use homicide as the outcome variable?") may be motivated by pure ignorance, by threatened self-identity as a gamer or game producer, or by the monetary aspects of the media industries. Regardless of motivation, such attacks are as wrong-headed as joking about how many Marlboro cigarettes a rat has to smoke to get cancer.

As Kurt Lewin noted over 50 years ago, "There is nothing so practical as a good theory" (Lewin, 1951, p. 169). Of course, although a "good" theory is eminently practical, a "bad" theory can lead to major mistakes ranging from poor individual decisions to public policy blunders that affect large populations (e.g., Anderson & Arnoult, 1985; Anderson & Sechler, 1986; Gilovich, 1991; Janis & Mann, 1977). This chapter is not the place for detailed discussion of good theory-building practices, but a key element of a good theory is its ability to account for (and then predict) empirical data obtained from rigorous scientific research.

The purpose of this chapter is to examine the past and current theories in the aggression domain. Particular attention will be paid to the theories that have been used to explain media violence effects, identifying both their strengths and their weaknesses. Finally, the General Aggression Model will be introduced as a comprehensive theory that employs central elements from several of the earlier aggression theories. The chapter concludes with a brief section on applying current theory to public policy discussions.

EARLY AGGRESSION THEORIES

Human aggression was a much-discussed topic throughout the twentieth century, in part because of World Wars I and II. Several broad theories of aggression emerged in the early part of the century, and persisted (especially in the popular mind) despite a lack of scientific support for and considerable scientific evidence against their applicability to human aggression.

Instinct Theories

In his early writings, Freud (e.g., 1909) proposed that all human behavior stems from the life or self-preservation instinct, called eros. "Libido" was defined as the energy of this life-giving instinct. Freud initially did not posit the presence of an independent instinct to explain the darker side of human nature. He wrote: "I cannot bring myself to assume the existence of a special aggressive instinct alongside the familiar instincts of self-preservation and of sex, on an equal footing with them" (Freud, 1909, p. 140). World War I, however, changed his views. By 1920, Freud had again considered the existence of a truly independent death or self-destruction instinct (the "death wish"), called thanatos. This view, which Freud himself did not appear to wholly support, sees aggression as the redirection or displacement of a self-destructive death instinct away from the individual toward others. In a similar vein, Nobel Prize winner Konrad Lorenz (1966) suggested that animals (including people) possess an aggressive or fighting instinct. His evidence came primarily from observation of animal behavior and from evolutionary arguments.

Although the idea of catharsis can be traced to the early Greeks, the modern notion comes from both Freud and Lorenz, particularly their hydraulic metaphors for the necessity of releasing of aggressive energy by aggressing against others. Indeed, the catharsis notion is the only part of these broad models that is relevant to the modern issue of media violence. The main catharsis ideas are that: (1) instinctive self-destructive or aggressive energy is continually added to a closed emotion or energy system; (2) observing, enacting, or releasing aggressive behavior or aggressive emotions against others releases some of this energy, thereby reducing pressure on the system; and that (3) without such releases, the pressure will build until the system explodes, either in self-destructive behavior (e.g., suicide) or extreme violence against others (e.g., homicide, war). Unfortunately, there is no scientific evidence of an instinctual death wish or aggressive energy, of a closed (hydraulic) emotional or motivational pressure system, or of behavioral catharsis (see Anderson, Gentile, & Buckley, 2007, Chapter 9; Bushman, 2002; Geen & Quanty, 1977; Gentile, 2013). Indeed, one major problem with catharsis theory is that its basic tenets are largely empirically untestable, due to the inability to measure or detect variables such as "thanatos" or aggressive "energy." Furthermore, the most important testable aspect of catharsis theory, the idea that either observing or enacting aggressive behavior will reduce later aggression, has been repeatedly disconfirmed (Bushman, 2002; Geen & Quanty, 1977). Nonetheless, this idea persists and has been perhaps one of the most damaging "bad" theoretical ideas in all of psychology. It is still invoked by the purveyors of violent entertainment media and is frequently cited by parents, school officials, and public policymakers as justification for exposing youth to violent media, promoting violent sports, and downplaying the significance of aggressive playground behavior (i.e., bullying).

Frustration

A much more empirically testable approach emerged in the form of the frustration-aggression hypothesis (Dollard, Doob, Miller, Mowrer, & Sears, 1939): (1) "the occurrence of aggressive behavior always presupposes the existence of frustration" (p. 1), and (2) "the existence of frustration always leads to some form of aggression" (p. 1). Miller (1941) revised the second statement to, "Frustration produces instigations to a number of different types of response, one of which is an instigation to some form of aggression" (p. 338). The scientific framing of this theory enabled better empirical testing and subsequent revision than the instinct theories of Freud and Lorenz. It has also fared considerably better over time (Berkowitz, 1989). For instance, Dill and Anderson (1995) demonstrated that even a fully justified frustration can produce an increase in aggressive behavior, as predicted by Berkowitz's reformulated frustration-aggression model (1989). Despite its importance to the understanding of human aggression in general, the frustration-aggression model has little relevance to media violence effects, other than the methodological implication that media violence experiments need to account for potential frustration-inducing properties of their violent and nonviolent stimuli. For example, a frustrating game can increase aggressive tendencies simply because it is frustrating, regardless of violent content. Therefore, to properly test the theoretical hypothesis that violent content can increase aggressive tendencies, one must be sure that the comparison violent and nonviolent games are equated on frustration.

Learning

The extensive literature on learning essentially began in 1898 with E. L. Thorndike's *Animal Intelligence* and continues in various forms to the present day. Here, we confine ourselves to a discussion of the learning theories that emerged from Thorndike's time through B. F. Skinner's. At the risk of over-simplifying, two types of learning were seen as the building blocks of all animal behavior, including human aggression. These two types are respondent (or classical) conditioning and operant (or instrumental) conditioning (see Hilgard & Bower, 1975, for an excellent overview of this work). Classical conditioning consists of pairing an unconditioned stimulus with a conditioned stimulus until the unconditioned response (which is automatically elicited by the unconditioned stimulus) is elicited by the conditioned stimulus. Operant conditioning involves stimulating (or inhibiting) a behavior based on the reward or punishment received after the behavior.

The contributions made by these early theories to understanding human behavior are impressive and important, but they are not comprehensive explanations of human aggression or other forms of human behavior. One problem is that they do not adequately account for the huge effects that the development of language has on human behavior. Nonetheless, they do contribute to our understanding of some of the processes underlying some media violence effects. For example, repeatedly pairing violence with the idea of fun entertainment helps to explain desensitization effects.

RECENT THEORETICAL DEVELOPMENTS

The following sections discuss modern theories of media violence effects. Note that none of these theories were developed to specifically examine media violence effects; however, each has contributed to our understanding of the effects of watching simulated violence in television, movies, and video games.

Social Learning Theory and Social Cognitive Theory

Social learning and social cognitive theories (e.g., Bandura, 1973, 1983; Mischel, 1973; Mischel & Shoda, 1995) contend that children learn behavioral responses by observing others and through direct experience. Furthermore, these approaches emphasize that how a person "construes" (understands) events is also learned and is crucial in determining how that person responds to those events. Children witness social interactions of parents, peers, siblings, and fictional characters on television and in movies. Children also witness the repercussions of these behaviors. Children are more likely to imitate the witnessed behavior if they also witness rewards for the action and less likely to imitate if they witness the action being punished (e.g., Bandura, 1965; Bandura, Ross, & Ross, 1963). Over time, children learn how to perceive and construe events in their social environments and start to assemble a detailed set of rules of behavior. These rules of behavior are then reinforced or inhibited based on the results they encounter in their own social interactions.

The primary strength of social/social cognitive theories is that they account for the acquisition of novel or unusual aggressive behaviors even in the absence of immediate reward. For example, seeing someone else rewarded or punished is sufficient to "learn" the likely consequences of particular behavior (even if the portrayed consequences are inaccurate, as is usually the case with media violence). Another strength is that the theory provides an excellent set of constructs to understand thoughtful behavioral choices. In this sense, it works especially well for instrumental types of aggression (usually defined as thoughtful, planned, or goal-oriented aggression).

Cognitive-Neoassociation Theory

Berkowitz (1989, 1993) proposed that a variety of aversive events (e.g., frustrations, provocations, loud noises, uncomfortable temperatures, unpleasant odors) can lead to negative affect, and subsequently to aggression. Negative affect becomes linked (through learning and conditioning during other life experiences) to a variety of thoughts, memories, expressive motor reactions, and physiological responses. When negative affect becomes linked to these other responses, it automatically activates them whenever negative affect is induced. These responses give rise to two immediate and simultaneous tendencies, fight or flight. The fight associations give rise to rudimentary feelings of anger, whereas the flight associations give rise to rudimentary feelings of fear. If the fight tendency is the stronger of the two, the individual will most likely aggress. If the flight tendency is stronger, aggression will be inhibited. If flight or escape from the situation is blocked, then the fight tendency may become dominant; if aggressive attempts are blocked or thwarted (e.g., initial attempts to overcome the target), then flight tendency may take over.

Cognitive-neoassociation theory contends that cues present during an initial aversive event become linked with thoughts, memories, and motor reactions through processes like classical conditioning. If these cues are present later in different situations, they may trigger those same thoughts and affect that were present during the initial aversive event. For example, Geen and Berkowitz (1966; also Berkowitz & Geen, 1967) showed that the effect of watching a boxing match on subsequent aggression in a different context was larger when the aggression target in that later context had the same name as the losing boxer in the earlier context. In other words, the boxer's name served as an aggression cue in the later context.

Cognitive neoassociation theory also takes into account higher-order cognitive processes, such as appraisal and attribution processes. If motivation is present, people may use these higher-order cognitive processes to further analyze their situations. For example, they might think about how they feel, make causal attributions for those feelings, and consider the consequences of acting on their feelings. This more deliberate thought produces more clearly differentiated feelings of anger, fear, or both. It also can suppress or enhance the action tendencies associated with these feelings. Though aggression and violence scholars usually associate thoughtful processes with reductions in aggression, theoretically (and empirically) it is clear that thoughtful processes can also increase aggression, as in the case of rumination (e.g., Bushman, 2002; Vasquez et al., 2013).

Script Theory

Borrowing from the cognitive and artificial intelligence literature (e.g., Schank & Abelson, 1977), Huesmann (1986, 1998) proposed that people's behavior is guided by the acquisition, internalization, and application of scripts. Scripts are sets of particularly well-rehearsed, highly associated concepts, often involving causal linkages, goals, and action plans (Abelson, 1981; Anderson, 1983; Anderson, Benjamin, & Bartholow, 1998). Scripts define situations and guide behavior in the following way: the person first selects (usually unconsciously) a script that closely resembles the current situation and then assumes a role in the script. Once a script has been learned, it may be retrieved at a later time as a guide for perception, interpretation, and behavior.

One factor involved in the retrieval and implementation of a script is the similarity of the current situation to the situation in which encoding originally occurred. As a child develops, he or she may observe cases in which aggression has been used as means of resolving interpersonal conflicts. If the child is then presented with his or her own conflicts, an aggressive script may be selected as a guide of an appropriate behavioral response. Retrieval of a particular script depends on the similarity between the cues encoded in the original script and the cues present in the current situation.

Script theory also utilizes some ideas from established cognitive-associative models that describe memory as a network consisting of nodes and links (Anderson et al., 1998; Berkowitz, 1993; Collins & Loftus, 1975). In these network models, it is assumed that each concept in memory has an activation threshold. A concept can be activated by the various sources to which it is linked. When the total activation exceeds the threshold, the concept is activated and used. Concepts with similar meanings (e.g., hurt and harm) and those that frequently are activated simultaneously (e.g., shoot and gun), develop strong associations. When a concept is fully activated, its activation spreads to related concepts, as a function of how strongly they are associated.

When items are so strongly linked that they form a script, they may be thought of as a unitary concept in semantic memory as well. Semantic memory is defined as "general knowledge of facts and concepts that is not linked to any particular time and place" (Schacter, 2000, p. 170). A frequently rehearsed script gains accessibility strength in two ways: increasing the number of paths by which it can be activated and increasing the strength of the links themselves. Thus, a child who has witnessed several thousand TV instances of using a gun to settle a dispute is likely to have a very accessible "conflict→gun→resolve conflict" script, one that has generalized across many situations. In other words, the script becomes chronically accessible.

Research has confirmed several aspects of script theory. The early social learning theory studies of learning aggressive behavior from observation of violent television and movie clips can also readily be reinterpreted in script theory terms (e.g., Huesmann & Miller, 1994). Individual differences can also be interpreted as script-like phenomena. For example, one study (Dill, Anderson, Anderson, and Deuser, 1997) found that aggressive individuals were more likely to complete ambiguous story stems with aggressive content than nonaggressive individuals. Similarly, Bushman and Anderson (2002) found that playing a violent video game increases the amount of aggressive content in this same story completion task. Completing a story stem is essentially a script completion task, and violent media are essentially violent scripts. Still other research has shown how scripts can generate intentions for one's own behavior and expectations about others' behaviors (e.g., Anderson & Godfrey, 1987).

Excitation Transfer Theory

Excitation-transfer theory (Zillmann, 1983) rests on the fact that physiological arousal dissipates slowly. If two arousing events are separated by a short period of time, some of the arousal caused by the first event may transfer to the second event and add to the arousal caused by the second event. When this occurs, arousal from the first event may be misattributed to the second event. If the second event is related to anger, the additional arousal should make the person even angrier. The notion of excitation transfer also suggests that anger may be extended over long periods of time, if the person has attributed his or her heightened arousal to anger. Thus, even after the initial arousal has dissipated, the observer may remain ready to aggress for as long as the self-generated label of anger persists. The relevance to understanding media violence effects derives from the fact that violent entertainment media are generally arousing. Zillmann's work goes further, however, in predicting that nonviolent media may also increase aggression via excitation transfer principles if they increase arousal. Studies have confirmed this prediction (Bryant & Zillmann, 1979). For example, Zillmann (1971) found that arousal from viewing an erotic film can increase provoked aggression.

Cultivation Theory

All of the modern theories discussed so far have been theories of general behavior that have been applied to media violence. Cultivation theory is somewhat different because it has been more specifically developed to examine effects of exposure to media. A central assumption of cultivation theory in its initial development is that the number of different messages produced by the media is a fairly small, consistent set. For example, prime-time dramas display over 10 times as much crime as actually occurs in the real world (Gerbner, Gross, Morgan, & Signorielli, 1982). Police officers, lawyers, and judges are over-represented as occupations on television, while engineers or scientists are rarely shown (Gerbner et al., 1982).

When these messages are presented consistently over long periods of time, viewers can come to believe that the messages they see in the media reflect the real world. Exposure to large amounts of television can lead people to overestimate the amount of crime and victimization that exists and conclude the world is a violent place (e.g., Bryant, Carveth, & Brown, 1981; Gerbner, Gross, Jackson-Beeck, Jeffries-Fox, & Signorielli, 1978).

These distortions of reality can have a variety of effects on the viewer. Potentially, overestimations of the amount of violence in the real world could lead to feelings of fear, anxiety, and suspicion. Combined with inaccurate estimations of violence in society, these feelings of fear and anxiety can have numerous effects on an individual's other beliefs and behaviors. It is reasonable to speculate that people who are overestimating the amount of crime in the world are more likely to behave in a more defensive manner, such as purchasing extra locks or firearms for protection, not traveling to certain areas that they believe are high crime areas, or being more suspicious of strangers. Gerbner, Gross, Morgan, and Signorielli (1980) surveyed television viewers in suburban neighborhoods concerning their media usage and perceptions of danger in their neighborhoods. Results showed that among both low- and high-income groups, people who consistently view larger amounts of television consider their own neighborhoods to be more dangerous than people who view smaller amounts of media. Another study by Gerbner and his associates have shown that heavy television viewers have stronger beliefs than light viewers that more money needs to be spent on fighting crime (Gerbner et al., 1982).

In more recent years, as viewer choices have proliferated via cable TV and the Internet, cultivation theory has also changed. The early finding that most television presented the same basic messages to all viewers is less true today. Now, people tend to select a narrow type of preferred shows and movies, and the preferred types of shows vary from person to person. One may watch only (or primarily) sports shows, another only crime shows, and yet another only news shows. This may even exaggerate the cultivation effect, if one specifically restricts the types of portrayals to just one or two.

Desensitization Theory

Techniques of systematic desensitization have been used in the treatment of anxiety disorders for decades. Wolpe (1958) describes systematic desensitization in two parts: first, relaxing the patient through both physiological and emotional relaxing procedures, and then introducing a weak anxiety-producing stimulus. After several series of exposure, the stimulus loses its anxiety-invoking abilities. After desensitization of the initial stimulus has occurred, relatively stronger anxiety producing stimuli are introduced and also treated in the same manner (Wolpe, 1958). There have been refinements and variations in therapeutic techniques. For example, Bandura emphasized the utility of social modeling and guided participation techniques (e.g., Bandura, 1971, 1973). These techniques have been proven to be effective in reducing (and in many cases eliminating) avoidance behavior of individuals with phobic fears of snakes, spiders, dogs, and flying in airplanes, among others. Without doubt, these techniques are extremely effective.

Similar desensitization processes operate in the media violence context. In this context, desensitization is defined as the process of becoming less physiologically and emotionally aroused to scenes of violence (real or mediated) due to extended exposure (Carnagey, Anderson, & Bushman, 2007). This phenomenon has been demonstrated by finding a relative decrease—during the viewing of violence—in physiological arousal, such as heart rate and skin conductance (e.g., Carnagey et al., 2007; Cline, Croft, & Courrier, 1973; Lazarus, Speisman, Mordkoff, & Davison, 1962; Linz, Donnerstein, & Penrod, 1988; Thomas, 1982; Thomas, Horton, Lippincott, & Drabmann, 1977); emotional responsiveness (e.g., Bartholow, Anderson, Carnagey, & Benjamin, 2005; Funk, Baldacci, Pasold, & Baumgardner, 2004; Sakamoto, Yukawa, Shibuya, & Ihori, 2002; Smith & Donnerstein, 1998); and brain activity assessed by fMRI or EEG (e.g., Bailey, West, & Anderson, 2011; Gentile, Swing, Anderson, Rinker, & Thomas, in press; Hummer et al., 2010; Mathews et al., 2005; Weber, Ritterfeld & Mathiak, 2006).

Although a reduction in anxiety or other negative emotion is a positive outcome in many contexts, such as when a fear of spiders is so extreme as to prevent an individual from taking walks or going on picnics, the reduction that occurs in the media violence context is viewed with concern for at least two reasons. First, in choosing among various behavioral alternatives in a conflict situation, anxiety associated with violent alternatives usually serves to inhibit such behaviors. Therefore, a reduction in that anxiety may well increase aggressive behavior (e.g., Anderson & Huesmann, 2003; Bartholow, Bushman, & Sestir, 2006). Second, such reductions in anxiety reactions to violence creates an emotional blunting that may lead to an underestimation of the seriousness of observed violence, and may therefore reduce the likelihood of coming to the aid of a victim of violence (e.g., Bushman & Anderson, 2009). Other research has shown that after viewing several sexually violent movies, participants rated the last movies in the set as less violent (e.g., Cline et al., 1973; Linz et al., 1988) and showed less sympathy for and attributed more responsibility to a rape victim compared to those who viewed nonviolent movies (Dexter, Penrod, Linz, & Saunders, 1997; Linz et al., 1988).

THE GENERAL AGGRESSION MODEL: AN INTEGRATION

All the recent theories discussed earlier have made important contributions. For example, one strength of social learning theory is that it can account for the acquisition of novel or unusual aggressive behaviors even in the absence of immediate reward. However, each theory focuses on a relatively narrow aspect of aggression. For example, Berkowitz's (e.g., 1993) cognitive neoassociation theory does an excellent job of integrating the large affective aggression literature but has somewhat less to say about instrumental aggression. What was needed was a theory that incorporates the strengths of all the earlier theories and thereby could account for a broader range of aggression. Such a theory must also avoid the pitfalls of the early broad aggression "theories," which were largely not subject to empirical test.

The General Aggression Model (GAM) was developed for that purpose (e.g., Anderson & Bushman, 2002; Anderson & Huesmann, 2003; Anderson & Carnagey, 2004; DeWall, Anderson, & Bushman, 2011). GAM is an integration that combines key ideas from earlier models: social learning and social cognitive theory (e.g., Bandura, 1971, 1973; Bandura, Ross, & Ross, 1961, 1963; Mischel 1973; Mischel & Shoda, 1995), Berkowitz's cognitive neoassociationist model (1984, 1990, 1993), Dodge's social information-processing model (e.g., Crick & Dodge, 1994; Dodge & Crick, 1990), Geen's affective aggression model (1990), Huesmann's script theory (Huesmann, 1986), and Zillmann's excitation transfer model (1983). As a biosocial-cognitive theory, GAM describes a cyclical pattern of interaction between the person and the environment. Three main points compose the cycle: *input variables* of person and situation, *present internal state* of the individual, and *outcomes* resulting from various appraisal and decision processes.

Input Variables

GAM suggests that a person's behavior is based on two main kinds of input variables: the person and the situation (see Figure 4.1). The person variables are composed of all the things a person brings with him or her when entering a particular situation, including genetics, traits, current states, beliefs, attitudes, values, sex, scripts, and aggressive personality. The situation variable is composed of the environment surrounding the individual, including factors

Figure 4.1
The General Aggression Model Episodic Processes

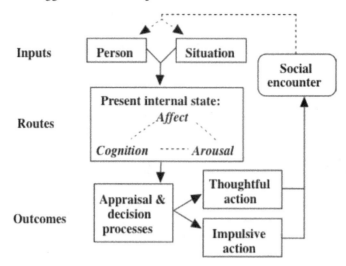

in the environment that could affect the person's actions, like aggressive cues, provocation, pain, rewards, and frustration.

Routes

Input variables, sometimes interactively, affect an individual's appraisal of a situation and ultimately affect the behavior performed in response to that appraisal, primarily by influencing the present internal state of the individual. According to GAM, there are three main routes of impact in which present internal states may be altered: cognition, affect, and arousal.

Cognition

Input variables can influence internal states by making aggressive constructs more readily accessible in memory. Constructs can be either temporarily or chronically accessible (e.g., Bargh, Lombardi, & Higgins, 1988; Sedikides & Skowronski, 1990). As a construct is repeatedly accessed, its activation threshold decreases. This means that the construct requires less energy for activation, making it chronically accessible. A situational input (e.g., a violent film) results in a temporary lowered threshold of activation, making the construct accessible for a short time. This temporary increase in the accessibility of a construct is often called "associative priming."

As script theory has contended, situational variables may also activate aggressive scripts (Huesmann, 1986). As noted earlier, activating aggressive scripts can bias the interpretation of a situation and the possible responses to that situation. Similar to aggressive constructs, repeated access of aggressive scripts makes them more readily accessible and more likely to be activated in future situations.

Affect

Input variables can also influence affect, which in turn can have an impact on later behavior. For example, pain increases state hostility (anger) (K. Anderson, Anderson, Dill, & Deuser, 1998). Uncomfortable temperatures produce a small increase in general negative affect and a larger increase in the more specific affect of state hostility (C. Anderson, Anderson, & Deuser, 1996). Exposure to violent movie clips also increases state hostility (Anderson, 1997; Bushman, 1995; Bushman & Geen, 1990; Hansen & Hansen, 1990). Many personality variables are also related to hostility-related affect. For example, trait hostility as measured by self-report scales is positively related to state hostility (Anderson, 1997; K. Anderson et al., 1998).

Arousal

There are three main ways in which increases in arousal can influence aggressive behavior. First, an increase in arousal can strengthen the already present action tendency, which could be an aggressive tendency. If the person has been provoked or otherwise instigated to aggress at the time this increased activation occurs, aggression will be a likely outcome. Geen and O'Neal (1969) provided an early example of this phenomenon by showing that loud noise increased arousal and aggression. A second possibility was already mentioned when discussing excitation transfer theory. Arousal elicited by other sources (e.g., exercise) may be mislabeled as anger in situations involving provocation, thus producing anger-motivated aggressive behavior. A third, and as yet untested, possibility is that unusually high and low levels of arousal may be aversive and may therefore stimulate aggression in the same way as other aversive or painful stimuli.

Interaction between routes

As mentioned earlier, input variables can influence cognition, affect, and arousal, but these three states may also influence one another. The idea that cognitions and arousal influence affect dates back all the way to William James (1890) and was first popularized among social psychologists by Schachter and Singer (1962). Affect also influences cognition and arousal (Bower, 1981). Research has shown that people often use their affective state to guide inference and judgment processes (Forgas, 1992; Schwarz & Clore, 1996). At a theoretical level, one can view affect as a part of semantic memory that can be primed via spreading activation processes. Thus, hostile cognitions might make hostile feelings more accessible, and vice versa.

Outcomes

Figure 4.2 presents a more detailed look at the appraisal aspects of GAM. Typically, before a behavior is performed the individual will appraise the current situation and then select a behavior appropriate to the situation. Depending on the situational variables present, appraisals may be made hastily and automatically, without much (or any) thought or awareness, resulting in impulsive behavior. However, frequently the individual will have the time and resources to reappraise the situation and perform a more thoughtful action. Of course, impulsive behavior may be aggressive or nonaggressive, just as thoughtful action may be either aggressive or nonaggressive.

Immediate appraisals are automatic, which means that they are spontaneous and relatively effortless, and occur without conscious awareness of the underlying process. As Krull and colleagues have demonstrated, the spontaneous inference process is a flexible one; its outcomes depend largely on the perceptual set of the perceiver (Krull, 1993; Krull & Dill, 1996). Under some circumstances, a behavior of another person is likely to be identified and attributed to that person simultaneously (e.g., Uleman, 1987). For example, if the target person has been thinking aggressive thoughts and is bumped by another person (actor), the target is likely to perceive the bump as an aggressive act by the actor. If the target person has been thinking about how crowded the room is, the same bump is likely to be perceived as an accidental consequence of the crowded situation.

However, what occurs after immediate appraisal depends on the resources available to the individual. If the person has sufficient time and cognitive capacity, and if the immediate appraisal outcome is both important and unsatisfying, then the person will likely engage a more effortful set of reappraisals. If resources are insufficient, or if the outcome of immediate appraisal is unimportant or satisfying, then action will be dictated by the immediate appraisal and the knowledge structure accessed in that appraisal. In essence, this is a type of dual process model, in which relatively effortless automatic processes underlie more effortful controlled processes, but also operate in parallel (Strack & Deutsch, 2004).

Reappraisal consists of searching for additional information in order to view the situation differently. Reappraisal can include a search for relevant information about the cause of the behavior, a search for relevant memories, and a search for features of the present situation. The outcome of reappraisal determines, in part, affective, cognitive, motivational, and behavioral responses. The reappraisal process itself may go through a number of cycles as alternatives are considered and discarded, as long as resources are sufficient and the outcome of each cycle is both important and unsatisfying. At some point, of course, the recycling process ceases, and a thoughtful course of action occurs (including the possibly of "not reacting" to the provocation).

Figure 4.2
The General Aggression Model: Expanded Appraisal and Decision Processes

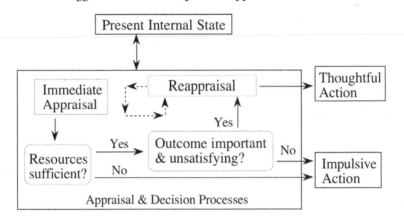

Whether immediate or reappraisal, a decision is made and a behavior follows. This action is then followed by a reaction from the environment, which is typically other people's responses to the action. That environmental reaction may reward the action, for example, by giving the person some sought-after object (e.g., money) or status (e.g., respect). Or, the environmental reaction may be punishing in some way, such as pain encountered by the other person fighting back. This round of the social encounter modifies the situation variables in the present but also influences longer-term person variables (such as expectations, attitudes, scripts) resulting in a reinforcement or inhibition of similar behavior in the future. Thus, both long-term and short-term effects of social encounters are very dynamic, adjusting and changing to situations and to one's life history.

Short-Term vs. Long-Term Effects

Even though GAM has a central focus on the episode, GAM is not restricted to short-term effects. The cyclical process of GAM lends itself to addressing long-term effects of exposure to media violence. With repeated exposure to certain stimuli (e.g., media violence), particular knowledge structures (e.g., aggressive scripts) become more readily accessible. Figure 4.3 displays this process and several common types of long-term changes that may occur. Over time, the individual will employ these knowledge structures and receive environmental reinforcement for their usage. Over time, these knowledge structures become modified, strengthened, and more likely to be used in later situations. Research supports this notion by demonstrating that repeatedly exposing children to media violence produces more aggressive adults (e.g., Huesmann & Miller, 1994). Such long-term effects result from

Figure 4.3
The General Aggression Model: Personality Processes

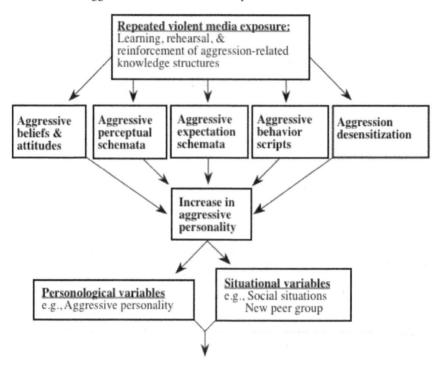

General Aggression Model, as in Figure 4.1

the development, automatization, and reinforcement of aggression-related knowledge structures. In essence, the creation and automatization of these aggression-related knowledge structures and desensitization effects change the individual's personality. Long-term consumers of violent media, for example, can become more aggressive in outlook, perceptual biases, attitudes, beliefs, and behavior than they were before the repeated exposure, or would have become without such exposure.

Recent Advances in GAM

Since the original publication of this volume in 2003, GAM has been expanded and applied in several ways. The utility of GAM has been more clearly illustrated as a way of understanding more extreme forms of physical aggression, namely *violence*. Under this broad heading, GAM has been applied to personality disorders (Gilbert & Daffern, 2011), effects of global warming on violence (Anderson & DeLisi, 2011), war and terrorism (DeWall & Anderson, 2011; DeWall et al., 2011), intimate partner violence and suicide

(DeWall et al., 2011), interventions to reduce aggression (e.g., Barlett & Anderson, 2011), male-on-female aggression and violence (e.g., Anderson & Anderson, 2008), and violence among criminal offenders (DeLisi et al., 2010; DeLisi, Vaughn, Gentile, Anderson, & Shook, 2013; Saleem & Anderson, 2012).

Another type of range expansion has been to more fully delineate the role of biological factors and how they influence aggression, sometimes in interactive ways (e.g., Anderson & DeLisi, 2011; Anderson & Carnagey, 2004; Anderson & Huesmann, 2003). This area needs more work, but there are no known theoretical problems with further integration of biological models with GAM.

A third type of range expansion has to do with underlying processes involved in human aggression, essentially ways that personal and environmental variables combine to lead to aggression. For example, our work on male aggression against women shows that the constellation of variables identified by Malamuth's confluence theory of sexual aggression (Malamuth, Linz, Heavey, Barnes, & Acker, 1995) can be integrated into the GAM framework. Furthermore, doing so results in additional new predictions and confirming results (Anderson & Anderson, 2008). For example, men at high risk for sexual aggression against women are also likely to be relatively more aggressive against women in nonsexual contexts, but are less likely to aggress against other men.

The processes underlying GAM are inherently interactive in several ways (Anderson & Carnagey, 2004). Perhaps most obvious is the fact that person factors, such as personality traits and different life histories, may interact with situational factors to yield different outcomes. For example, Bartholow and colleagues explored the weapons effect (i.e., the finding that people often behave more aggressively in the presence of a gun or other weapon) from GAM's perspective, and found both situational effects (e.g., increases in aggressive thoughts and behavior in the presence of a weapon prime) and more interestingly, interactions between one's life history as a hunter (vs. nonhunters) and type of gun prime. For hunters, photos of hunting weapons led to more positive affect, lower aggressive thought accessibility, and lower aggression than did photos of assault weapons, whereas the opposite pattern occurred for nonhunters (Bartholow et al., 2005).

GAM also views situations as inherently dynamic (interactive) as well. We first illustrated this dynamic process in 2004 (see Figure 4.4), by means of how a social encounter can escalate over a series of actions and reactions (Anderson & Carnagey, 2004). Later, we demonstrated one such escalation cycle in a carefully controlled laboratory study of how highly aggressive people (relative to nonaggressive people) take ambiguous situations and over a series of interactions make them into aggressive encounters (Anderson, Buckley, and Carnagey, 2008). This escalation cycle applies not only to individuals in dyadic interactions but also to variously sized groups of people, including countries, and the instigation of war and terrorism.

Figure 4.4
The Escalation Cycle

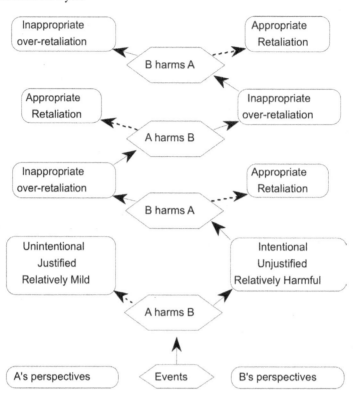

Finally, note that interactions are allowed and expected by GAM between multiple levels of analysis. For example, certain genetic risk factors for violence (biological level) are likely to result in observed high violence rates primarily when certain environmental risk factors (family level) are also present (Caspi et al., 2002).

APPLYING GAM TO MEDIA VIOLENCE

This model can be used to interpret the effects of virtually anything the person comes into contact with in his or her environment, including exposure to violent media. Theoretically, violent media can affect all three components of internal state. The research literature on violent video games has shown that playing them can temporarily increase aggressive thoughts, affect, and arousal (Anderson et al., 2010). For example, Anderson & Dill (2000) showed that playing a violent video game increased the speed with which the person could read aggression-related words (aggressive thoughts). Similarly,

Kirsh (1998) and Bushman & Anderson (2002) found that playing a violent video game subsequently increased hostile interpretations of ambiguous social events (aggressive schemata). And as noted earlier, exposure to violent media can reduce arousal to subsequent depictions of violence. Playing a violent video game can also influence the person's internal state through the affective route by increasing feelings of anger and through the arousal route by increasing heart rate (Anderson et al., 2010; see Anderson & Gentile, this volume, for more details on video game effects).

In sum, GAM can help to explain and predict the wide variety of effects seen in the media violence literature, including both short- and long-term effects on aggressive thoughts, feelings, and behaviors; on desensitization and subsequent declines in prosocial behavior; and on changes in the social environment that occur as the developing child becomes more habitually aggressive. There are two other media violence domains that have not been specifically discussed in past presentations of GAM—the effects of media violence on fear, and broader societal issues concerning the role of violent media in modern society. The former can be easily fit into GAM, although the latter falls outside the intended domain of GAM.

Fear

Exposure to media violence can initially cause sleep disturbances, anxiety, and fear (e.g., Cantor, 1998, 2001; Harrison & Cantor, 1999; Owens et al., 1999; Singer, Slovak, Frierson, & York, 1998). Cantor (1994) has identified several moderating factors (see also Cantor & Riddle, this volume). First, violent media are more likely to evoke fear in viewers if the stimuli are similar to real-life fears. For example, live-action sequences of violence are more likely to produce fear in viewers than animated cartoon violence (Gunter & Furnham, 1984; Osborn & Endsley, 1971; Surbeck, 1975). Second, motivation for viewing potentially frightening scenes of violence also affects whether the stimuli will evoke fear. People who seek out frightening material may voluntarily reduce their own cognitive defenses to enable themselves to be frightened. Those who try to avoid scary scenes may try to discount them when confronted with scenes of violence. A third set of factors concerns other characteristics connected to the presentation, such as stressful music and sound effects (Cantor, 1994). Whereas all of these factors may contribute to an individual being frightened by viewing particular scenes of violence, the most recognized factor is developmental maturity.

As children mature, their fears develop as well, changing from fears of the dark and intangible monsters to fears of personal injury to fears of global and political issues (see Cantor, Wilson, & Hoffner, 1986, for review). Based on her research, Cantor developed some broad generalizations concerning developmental maturity and viewing fear-evoking violence (Cantor, 1994). First, Cantor contends that as a child matures, the importance of perceptible characteristics of media violence decreases. This means that younger children are more likely to become frightened of stimuli that look scary, but could be harmless, whereas older children base their fears on more conceptual information (Cantor & Sparks, 1984; Sparks & Cantor, 1986). As children mature, they develop the ability to distinguish fantasy from reality. Thus, children become more likely to develop realistic fears (e.g., war, kidnappings) at the same time as fantasy fears (e.g., monsters under the bed) diminish (Cantor & Sparks, 1984; Cantor & Wilson, 1984; Sparks & Cantor, 1986). Third, as children mature they become more frightened of abstract concepts portrayed in media, such as nuclear attack and its consequences (Cantor et al., 1986).

All of these fear effects fit neatly into the early stages of GAM. For instance, some of the diminution of fantasy fears likely arises from standard desensitization effects. More broadly, as children develop the knowledge structures they use to perceive and understand media violence, their fears also change and develop in predictable ways.

Broader Issues

There are a host of media violence issues that fall outside of the domain of the General Aggression Model. One set of these issues is nicely described by Potter's lineation theory (1999). Another set more directly involves public policy issues.

Lineation Theory

Lineation theory (Potter, 1999) examines five major facets of the media violence situation: content of media, media industry practices, psychological processing of media violence messages, factors influencing media violence effects, and the effects of viewing media violence. GAM fully addresses the psychological processes underlying media violence effects raised by Potter (1999), and other behavioral science research has examined the content of the U.S. media landscape (e.g., Wilson et al., 1997, 1998). However, behavioral sciences have not thoroughly addressed the practices of the media industry.

It is not clear to us how one should go about an empirical examination of how the media industry decides to include violence in its movies, television programs, and video games. Such an effort falls well outside our range of expertise. However, Potter's book provides some interesting ideas on this topic, and a book by James Steyer (2002) gives an insider's view of the processes, a quite disturbing view indeed. Interested readers should certainly examine these works carefully.

Although empirical examination of the media industry from a behavioral science perspective may not be possible, information from behavioral science may be one way in which social scientists can influence the industries. For example, Bushman and colleagues (Bushman & Bonacci, 2002; Bushman &

Phillips, 2001) have found that violent and sexual content in television shows reduces the viewer's recall of advertisements in that show.

PUBLIC HEALTH AND PUBLIC POLICY

Ideologically Driven Attacks on Research

Scientifically derived findings concerning media violence are relevant to public health issues, and therefore are relevant to public policy. Media violence researchers find themselves drawn into these debates despite a reluctance to participate in them. Such researchers sometimes must defend themselves from well-financed attacks by individuals and groups who have no training or real expertise in conducting media violence research, but who have considerable funding and expertise in influencing public opinion and public policy.

Perhaps even more damaging are those behavioral scientists who have made careers out of attacking media violence research despite having little or no training in such research and never succeeding in publishing an original empirical study of media violence effects in a top-tier scientific journal. Their scholarly credentials (albeit in other domains) make them particularly attractive partners to the media industries that produce and profit from violent media, largely because journalists and the general public can't (or don't) distinguish between them and legitimate experts. For example, one vocal critic (Christopher Ferguson) and the video game industry frequently claim bias by specific research teams (ours and Brad Bushman's), biases both in reporting original research findings and in meta-analytic reviews. Yet those claims are not backed up by evidence of any kind. For instance, if the Anderson and Bushman research groups are engaging in biased data reporting practices, then results of their studies should be systematically larger (i.e., finding more harm) than similar studies conducted by other research teams. A recent meta-analytic study (Greitemeyer & Mügge, 2014) found that the Anderson and Bushman studies of violent video game effects yield results that are almost identical to those found by other researchers around the world; indeed, they are slightly *smaller* (see Table 4.1). Interestingly, it is the research of this critic that appears wildly discrepant with the rest of the research world (Table 4.1).

Concerning meta-analysis bias, the facts are again very different from what the vocal critics would have you believe. The most recent comprehensive meta-analysis of the violent video game literature (Anderson et al., 2010) included 381 effect sizes ("studies") with over 130,000 participants. For the aggressive behavior outcome variable there were 140 independent effect sizes with over 68,000 participants. Meta-analyses by Ferguson and colleagues in 2007 through 2009 report 25 or fewer "relevant" effect sizes with fewer than 4,500 participants. Interestingly, five years earlier we identified 38 independent effect sizes on aggressive behavior with over 7,000 participants (Anderson et al., 2004). It also is interesting that the average effect sizes Ferguson and

Table 4.1
Average Effects of Violent Video Game Exposure on Overall Social Outcome (Combined Behavior, Cognition, Affect, and Arousal) as a Function of Research Group

Author group	N	K	Effect size and 95% CI Point estimate	LL	UL	Test of null (two-tailed) Z	p
Anderson/Bushman	8,595	20	.19	0.14	0.24	7.39	.000
Ferguson	2,444	7	.02	−0.05	0.10	0.61	.540
Others	23,415	58	.20	0.16	0.23	11.50	.000

Note: N = total number of study participants, K = number of independent studies, LL = Lower limit of the 95% confidence interval for the effect size estimate, UL = Upper limit of the 95% confidence interval for the effect size estimate, Z = standardized z-score, p = probability value
Source: From Greitemeyer & Mügge, 2014. Reprinted by permission.

colleagues reported were only slightly smaller than what we reported, at least before he inappropriately applied bias correction procedures that involved adding in hypothetical missing studies. Finally, even when given an opportunity to publicly identify bias in our meta-analytic samples (Ferguson & Kilburn, 2010), the critics were unable to find even one "missing" study that was relevant (Bushman, Rothstein, & Anderson, 2010).

Recently the critics have attacked GAM, social learning theory, and other social cognitive models of aggression and social behavior. Detailing and responding to the many inaccuracies is beyond the scope of this chapter. It should be noted that GAM and other social-cognitive models are dynamic, not static models; they take into account individual differences, and genetic and other biological factors (especially GAM); they have been successfully applied to extreme behaviors, including personality disorders, criminality, and violence; and they are widely accepted as useful tools throughout psychology. Because they are testable and falsifiable, they may also undergo revision as new data become available.

Role of Theory

We believe that it is important for legitimate researchers to remain involved in the public debate. After all, what is the point of doing good research if it is either going to be misrepresented to the general public or is going to be ignored by makers of public policy? This section outlines some of the issues, one of which concerns the role of theory in such debates.

What is the proper role for media violence researchers in such public policy debates? We don't pretend to have an answer for all such researchers. However, we believe that in our role as scientists, it is important to provide an accurate and unbiased assessment of the scientific state of knowledge to any group that requests it, whether it is the local PTA, the state psychological association, child advocacy groups, the U.S. Senate, or even the Entertainment Software Association (though they haven't asked us yet). We also believe that most behavioral scientists (including ourselves) are not very good at this, largely because we often fail to hear the question that is being asked. Here are several things we have learned in such encounters.

First, many participants in public debates about media violence fail to make the crucial distinction between psychological science versus relevant personal values. The result, all too often, is a concerted effort by the media violence industry and its supporters to denigrate the scientific enterprise as well as the scientists involved. Similarly, child advocacy groups occasionally claim that the scientific research itself directly supports certain public policy actions. In fact, such public policy issues revolve around a host of factors, only one of which is the media violence research literature. Thus, media violence researchers should be willing to share their special expertise concerning the scientific issues. However, media violence researchers do not have special expertise concerning legal issues or concerning a host of personal values that are also relevant to making an informed (and personal) decision about appropriate public policy. Reasonable people may well have different personal values relevant to a given issue, and so may come to very different conclusions concerning public policy even if they agree on the scientific conclusions. For example, two people can agree that repeated exposure of children to violent media leads to a significant increase in their propensity to aggress as adults, while simultaneously disagreeing about whether the government should impose restrictions on the kinds of video games youngsters can purchase or rent without parental consent. One person may value children's rights to choose so highly that they are willing to accept higher societal violence rates in order to let children choose their own entertainment. The other may decide that children need protection in this domain, and may be willing to reduce children's rights to choose (and thereby increase parents' rights to control video game access to their children) in order to have a less violent society. Our role as behavioral scientists is to answer the question concerning what the research tells us about violent media effects, but we cannot tell others how highly they should value children's rights versus parents' rights or societal violence rates. For this reason, we try very hard to not make public statements about what politicians or other makers of public policy ought to do, and instead confine our contributions to the scientific ones in our areas of expertise.

Second, the role of theory in such public policy debates is often misrepresented or underutilized. Sometimes this happens for fairly obvious motivational reasons, such as when the 50-plus years of research on TV and movie violence is categorically dismissed by the video game industry as irrelevant to their medium. Good psychological theory about how exposure to media violence influences aggression makes that larger and more developed research literature very relevant. After all, the practicality of a good theory derives from the fact that good decisions in the design of interventions, treatments, or programs—their success in achieving desired results—depends on well-integrated theories whose basic principles generalize.

Third, the entertainment media industries are using essentially the same tactics as the tobacco industry used for many years. One major tactic is to separate each type of video game study from the rest and then attack each type individually. So laboratory experiments are "bad" because they take place in artificial settings; cross-sectional studies are "bad" because they are merely correlational; and longitudinal studies violent video games because homicide rate was not the outcome variable. Similarly, studies with college students are "irrelevant" because they are legally adults and we're really only concerned about kids; studies with children are "irrelevant" because the industry already provides age ratings of video games. This divide and conquer strategy is very effective in misleading an audience about the true overall state of scientific knowledge. What researchers must do, in our view, is not allow such tactics to divert us (or our audiences) from the scientific strategy of looking at the totality of the empirical evidence and the strength (or weakness) of the theory guiding the integration of that evidence.

Good theory generalizes, and therefore should not be ignored. GAM provides one integrative framework for understanding the empirical research on media violence, and for guiding future research and development of intervention strategies. As other chapters in this volume demonstrate, the totality of research and theory on media violence effects is extensive, coherent, and amazingly consistent when one takes the broad view. The public needs to understand this so that the public policy debate can move to legitimate discussions of which public policy options (if any) are appropriate.

REFERENCES

Abelson, R. P. (1981). Psychological status of the script concept. *American Psychologist*, *36*, 715–729.

Anderson, C. A. (1983). Imagination and expectation: The effect of imagining behavioral scripts on personal intentions. *Journal of Personality and Social Psychology*, *45*, 293–305.

Anderson, C. A. (1997). Effects of violent movies and trait irritability on hostile feelings and aggressive thoughts. *Aggressive Behavior*, *23*, 161–178.

Anderson, C. A., & Anderson, K. B. (2008). Men who target women: Specificity of target, generality of aggressive behavior. *Aggressive Behavior*, *34*, 605–622.

Anderson, C. A., Anderson, K. B., & Deuser, W. E. (1996). Examining an affective aggression framework: Weapon and temperature effects on aggressive thoughts, affect, and attitudes. *Personality and Social Psychology Bulletin*, *22*, 366–376.

Anderson, C. A., & Arnoult, L. H. (1985). Attributional models of depression, loneliness, and shyness. In J. Harvey & G. Weary (Eds.), *Attribution: Basic issues and applications* (pp. 235–279). New York, NY: Academic Press.

Anderson, C. A., Benjamin, A. J., & Bartholow, B. D. (1998). Does the gun pull the trigger? Automatic priming effects of weapon pictures and weapon names. *Psychological Science, 9*, 308–314.

Anderson, C. A., Buckley, K. E., & Carnagey, N. L. (2008). Creating your own hostile environment: A laboratory examination of trait aggression and the violence escalation cycle. *Personality and Social Psychology Bulletin, 34*, 462–473.

Anderson, C. A., & Bushman, B. J. (2002). Human aggression. *Annual Review of Psychology, 53*, 27–51.

Anderson, C. A., & Carnagey, N. L. (2004). Violent evil and the general aggression model. In A. Miller (Ed.), *The social psychology of good and evil* (pp. 168–192). New York, NY: Guilford Publications.

Anderson, C. A., Carnagey, N. L., Flanagan, M., Benjamin, A. J., Eubanks, J., & Valentine, J. C. (2004). Violent video games: Specific effects of violent content on aggressive thoughts and behavior. *Advances in Experimental Social Psychology, 36*, 199–249.

Anderson, C. A., & DeLisi, M. (2011). Implications of global climate change for violence in developed and developing countries. In J. Forgas, A. Kruglanski, & K. Williams (Eds.), *The psychology of social conflict and aggression* (pp. 249–265). New York, NY: Psychology Press.

Anderson, C. A., & Dill, K. E. (2000). Video games and aggressive thoughts, feelings, and behavior in the laboratory and in life. *Journal of Personality and Social Psychology, 78*, 772–790.

Anderson, C. A., Gentile, D. A., & Buckley, K. E. (2007). *Violent video game effects on children and adolescents: Theory, research, and public policy.* New York, NY: Oxford University Press.

Anderson, C. A., & Godfrey, S. (1987). Thoughts about actions: The effects of specificity and availability of imagined behavioral scripts on expectations about oneself and others. *Social Cognition, 5*, 238–258.

Anderson, C. A., & Huesmann, L. R. (2003). Human aggression: A social-cognitive view. In M. A. Hogg & J. Cooper (Eds.), *The Sage Handbook of Social Psychology* (pp. 296–323). London, UK: Sage.

Anderson, C. A., & Sechler, E. S. (1986). Effects of explanation and counterexplanation on the development and use of social theories. *Journal of Personality and Social Psychology, 50*, 24–34.

Anderson, C. A., Shibuya, A., Ihori, N., Swing, E. L., Bushman, B. J., Sakamoto, A., Rothstein, H. R., & Saleem, M. (2010). Violent video game effects on aggression, empathy, and prosocial behavior in Eastern and Western countries. *Psychological Bulletin, 136*, 151–173.

Anderson, K. B., Anderson, C. A., Dill, K. E., & Deuser, W. E. (1998). The interactive relations between trait hostility, pain, and aggressive thoughts. *Aggressive Behavior, 24*, 161–171.

Bailey, K., West, R., & Anderson, C. A. (2011). The association between chronic exposure to video game violence and affective picture processing: An ERP study. *Cognitive Affective and Behavioral Neuroscience, 11*, 259–276.

Bandura, A. (1965). Influence of models' reinforcement contingencies on the acquisition of imitative responses. *Journal of Personality and Social Psychology, 6*, 589–595.

Bandura, A. (1971). Psychotherapy based upon modeling principles. In A. E. Bergin and S. L. Garfield (Eds.), *Handbook of psychotherapy and behavior change*. New York, NY: Wiley.

Bandura, A. (1973). *Aggression: A social learning theory analysis*. Englewood Cliffs, NJ: Prentice-Hall.

Bandura, A. (1983). Psychological mechanisms of aggression. In R. G. Geen & E. I. Donnerstein (Eds.), *Aggression: Theoretical and empirical reviews* (Vol. 1, pp. 1–40). New York, NY: Academic Press.

Bandura, A., Ross, D., & Ross, S. A. (1961). Transmission of aggression through imitation of aggressive models. *Journal of Abnormal and Social Psychology, 63*, 575–582.

Bandura, A., Ross, D., & Ross, S. A. (1963). Imitation of film-mediated aggressive models. *Journal of Abnormal and Social Psychology, 66*, 3–11.

Bargh, J. A., Lombardi, W. J., & Higgins, E. T. (1988). Automaticity of chronically accessible constructs in person X situation effects on person perception: It's just a matter of time. *Journal of Personality and Social Psychology, 55*, 599–605.

Barlett, C. P., & Anderson, C. A. (2011). Re-appraising the situation and its impact on aggressive behavior. *Personality and Social Psychology Bulletin, 37*, 1564–1573. doi:10.1177/0146167211423671

Bartholow, B. D., Anderson, C. A., Carnagey, N. L., & Benjamin, A. J. (2005). Interactive effects of life experience and situational cues on aggression: The weapons priming effect in hunters and nonhunters. *Journal of Experimental Social Psychology, 41*, 48–60.

Bartholow, B. D., Bushman, B. J., & Sestir, M. A. (2006). Chronic violent video game exposure and desensitization to violence: Behavioral and event-related brain potential data. *Journal of Experimental Social Psychology, 42*, 532–539.

Berkowitz, L. (1984). Some effects of thoughts on anti- and prosocial influences of media events: A cognitive-neoassociation analysis. *Psychological Bulletin, 95*(3), 410–427.

Berkowitz, L. (1989). Frustration-aggression hypothesis: Examination and reformulation. *Psychological Bulletin, 106*, 59–73.

Berkowitz, L. (1990). On the formation and regulation of anger and aggression: A cognitive-neoassociationistic analysis. *American Psychologist, 45*, 494–503.

Berkowitz, L. (1993). Pain and aggression: Some findings and implications. *Motivation and Emotion, 17*, 277–293.

Berkowitz, L., & Geen, R. G. (1967). Stimulus qualities of the target of aggression: A further study. *Journal of Personality and Social Psychology, 5*, 364–368.

Bower, G. (1981). Mood and memory. *American Psychologist, 36*, 129–48.

Bryant, J., Carveth, R. A., & Brown, D. (1981). Television viewing and anxiety: An experimental examination. *Journal of Communication, 31*, 106–119.

Bryant, J., & Zillmann, D. (1979). Effect of intensification of annoyance through unrelated residual excitation on substantially delayed hostile behavior. *Journal of Experimental Social Psychology, 15*, 470–480.

Bushman, B. J. (1995). Moderating role of trait aggressiveness in the effects of violent media on aggression. *Journal of Personality and Social Psychology, 69*, 950–960.

Bushman, B. J. (2002). Does venting anger feed or extinguish the flame? Catharsis, rumination, distraction, anger, and aggressive responding. *Personality and Social Psychology Bulletin, 28*, 724–731.

Bushman, B. J., & Anderson, C. A. (2002). Violent video games and hostile expectations: A test of the general aggression model. *Personality and Social Psychology Bulletin, 28*, 1679–1686.

Bushman, B. J., & Anderson, C. A. (2009). Comfortably numb: Desensitizing effects of violent media on helping others. *Psychological Science, 20*, 273–277.

Bushman, B. J., & Bonacci, A. M. (2002). Violence and sex impair memory for television ads. *Journal of Applied Psychology, 87*, 557–564.

Bushman, B. J., & Geen, R. G. (1990). Role of cognitive-emotional mediators and individual differences in the effects of media violence on aggression. *Journal of Personality and Social Psychology, 58*, 156–163.

Bushman, B. J., & Phillips, C. M. (2001). If the television program bleeds, memory for the advertisement recedes. *Current Directions in Psychological Science, 10*, 44–47.

Bushman, B. J., Rothstein, H. R., & Anderson, C. A. (2010). Much ado about something: Violent video game effects and a school of red herring: Reply to Ferguson and Kilburn. *Psychological Bulletin, 136*, 182–187.

Cantor, J. (1994). Fright reactions to mass media. In J. Bryant & D. Zillmann (Eds.), *Media effects: Advances in theory and research* (pp. 213–245). Hillsdale, NJ: Erlbaum.

Cantor, J. (1998). *"Mommy, I'm scared": How TV and movies frighten children and what we can do to protect them.* San Diego, CA: Harvest/Harcourt.

Cantor, J. (2001). The media and children's fears, anxieties, and perceptions of danger. In D. G. Singer & J. L. Singer (Eds.), *Handbook of children and the media* (pp. 207–221). Thousand Oaks, CA: Sage.

Cantor, J. & Sparks, G. G. (1984). Children's fear responses to mass media: Testing some Piagetian predictions. *Journal of Communication, 34*, 90–103.

Cantor, J. & Wilson, B. J. (1984). Modifying responses to mass media in preschool and elementary school children. *Journal of Broadcasting, 28*, 431–443.

Cantor, J., Wilson, B. J., & Hoffner, C. (1986). Emotional responses to a televised nuclear holocaust film. *Communication Research, 13*, 257–277.

Carnagey, N. L., Anderson, C. A., & Bushman, B. J. (2007). The effect of video game violence on physiological desensitization to real-life violence. *Journal of Experimental Social Psychology, 43*, 489–496.

Caspi, A., McClay, J, Moffitt, T. E., Mill, J., Martin, J., Craig, I. W., Taylor, A., & Poulton, R. (2002). Role of genotype in the cycle of violence in maltreated children. *Science, 297*, 851–854.

Cline, V. B., Croft, R. G., & Courrier, S. (1973). Desensitization of children to television violence. *Journal of Personality and Social Psychology, 27*, 360–365.

Collins, A. M., & Loftus, E. F. (1975). A spreading activation theory of semantic processing. *Psychological Review, 82*, 407–428.

Crick, N. R., & Dodge, K. A. (1994). A review and reformulation of social information processing mechanisms in children's adjustment. *Psychological Bulletin, 115*, 74–101.

DeLisi, M., Drury, A. J., Kosloski, A. E., Caudill, J. W., Conis, P. J., Anderson, C. A., Vaughn, M. G., & Beaver, K. M. (2010). The cycle of violence behind bars: Traumatization and institutional misconduct among juvenile delinquents in confinement. *Youth Violence and Juvenile Justice, 8*, 107–121.

DeLisi, M., Vaughn, M. G., Gentile, D. A., Anderson, C. A., & Shook, J. (2013). Violent video games, delinquency, and youth violence: New evidence. *Youth Violence and Juvenile Justice, 11*, 132–142. doi:10.1177/1541204012460874

DeWall, C. N., & Anderson, C. A. (2011). The General Aggression Model. In P. Shaver & M. Mikulincer (Eds.), *Human aggression and violence: Causes, manifestations, and consequences* (pp. 15–33). Washington, DC: APA.

DeWall, C. N., Anderson, C. A., & Bushman, B. J. (2011). The General Aggression Model: Theoretical extensions to violence. *Psychology of Violence, 1,* 245–258. doi:10.1037/a0023842

Dexter, H. R., Penrod, S., Linz, D., & Saunders, D. (1997). Attributing responsibility to female victims after exposure to sexually violent films. *Journal of Applied Social Psychology, 27,* 2149–2171.

Dill, J., & Anderson, C. A. (1995). Effects of justified and unjustified frustration on aggression. *Aggressive Behavior, 21,* 359–369.

Dill, K. E., Anderson, C. A., Anderson, K. B., & Deuser, W. E. (1997). Effects of aggressive personality on social expectations and social perceptions. *Journal of Research in Personality, 31,* 272–292.

Dodge, K. A, & Crick, N. R. (1990). Social information-processing bases of aggressive behavior in children. *Personality and Social Psychology Bulletin, 16,* 8–22.

Dollard, J., Doob, L., Miller, N., Mowrer, O., & Sears, R. (1939). *Frustration and aggression.* New Haven, CT: Yale University Press.

Ferguson, C. J., & Kilburn, J. (2010). Much ado about nothing: The misestimation and overinterpretation of violent video game effects in Eastern and Western nations: Comment on Anderson et al. (2010). *Psychological Bulletin, 136,* 174–178.

Forgas, J. P. (1992). Affect in social judgments and decisions: A multiprocess model. *Advances in Experimental Social Psychology, 25,* 227–275.

Freud, S. (1909/1961). *Analysis of a phobia in a five-year-old boy* (standard ed.). London, UK: Norton.

Freud, S. (1920/1961). *Beyond the pleasure principle* (standard ed.). London, UK: Norton.

Funk, J. B., Baldacci, H. B., Pasold, T., & Baumgardner, J. (2004). Violence exposure in real-life, video games, television, movies, and the Internet: Is there desensitization? *Journal of Adolescence, 27,* 23–39.

Geen, R. G. (1990). *Human aggression.* Pacific Grove, CA: McGraw Hill.

Geen, R. G., & Berkowitz, L. (1966). Name-mediated aggressive cue properties. *Journal of Personality, 34,* 456–465.

Geen, R. G., & O'Neal, E. C. (1969). Activation of cue-elicited aggression by general arousal. *Journal of Personality and Social Psychology, 11,* 289–292.

Geen, R. G., & Quanty, M. B. (1977). The catharsis of aggression: An evaluation of a hypothesis. In L. Berkowitz (Ed.), *Advances in Experimental Social Psychology, 10,* 1–37. New York, NY: Academic Press.

Gentile, D. A. (2013). Catharsis and media violence: A conceptual analysis. *Societies, 3,* 491–510. doi:10.3390/soc3040491

Gentile, D. A., Swing, E. L., Anderson, C. A., Rinker, D., & Thomas, K. M. (in press). Differential neural recruitment during violent video game play in violent and nonviolent game players. *Psychology of Popular Media Culture.*

Gerbner, G., Gross, L., Jackson-Beeck, M., Jeffries-Fox, S., & Signorielli, N. (1978). Cultural indicators: Violence profile no. 9. *Journal of Communication, 28,* 176–207.

Gerbner, G., Gross, L., Morgan, M., & Signorielli, N. (1980). The "mainstreaming" of America: Violence profile no. 11. *Journal of Communication, 30,* 10–29.

Gerbner, G., Gross, L., Morgan, M., & Signorielli, N. (1982). Charting the mainstreaming: Television's contributions to political orientations. *Journal of Communication, 32*, 100–127.

Gilbert, F., & Daffern, M. (2011). Illuminating the relationship between personality disorder and violence: Contributions of the General Aggression Model. *Psychology of Violence, 1*, 230–244.

Gilovich, T. (1991). *How we know what isn't so: The fallibility of human reason in everyday life*. New York, NY: The Free Press.

Greitemeyer, T., & Mügge, D. O. (2014). Video games do affect social outcomes: A meta-analytic review of the effects of violent and prosocial video game play. *Personality and Social Psychology Bulletin, 40*, 578–589.

Gunter, B., & Furnham, A. (1984). Perceptions of television violence: Effects of programme genre and type of violence on viewers' judgments of violent portrayals. *British Journal of Social Psychology, 23*, 155–164.

Hansen, C. H., & Hansen, R. D. (1990). The influence of sex and violence on the appeal of rock music videos. *Communication Research, 17*, 212–234.

Harrison, K., & Cantor, J. (1999). Tales from the screen: Enduring fright reactions to scary media. *Media Psychology, 1*(2), 97–116.

Hilgard, E. R., & Bower, G. H. (1975). *Theories of learning*. Englewood Cliffs, NJ: Prentice-Hall.

Huesmann, L. R. (1986). Psychological processes promoting the relation between exposure to media violence and aggressive behavior by the viewer. *Journal of Social Issues, 42*(3), 125–139.

Huesmann, L. R. (1998). The role of social information processing and cognitive schema in the acquisition and maintenance of habitual aggressive behavior. In R. Geen & E. Donnerstein (Eds.), *Human aggression: Theories, research and implications for policy*. (pp. 73–109). New York, NY: Academic Press.

Huesmann, L. R., & Miller, L. S. (1994). Long-term effects of repeated exposure to media violence in childhood. In L. R. Huesmann (Ed), *Aggressive behavior: Current perspectives* (pp. 153–186). New York, NY: Plenum Press.

Hummer, T. A., Wang, Y., Kronenberger, W. G., Mosier, K. M., Kalnin, A. J., Dunn, D. W., & Mathews, V. P. (2010). Short-term violent video game play by adolescents alters prefrontal activity during cognitive inhibition. *Media Psychology, 13*, 136–154.

James, W. (1890). *Principles of psychology*. New York, NY: Holt.

Janis, I. L., & Mann, L. (1977). Decision making: A psychological analysis of conflict, choice, and commitment. New York, NY: The Free Press.

Kirsh, S. J. (1998). Seeing the world through Mortal Kombat–colored glasses: Violent video games and the development of a short-term hostile attribution bias. *Childhood, 5*, 177–184.

Krull, D. S. (1993). Does the grist change the mill?: The effect of perceiver's goal on the process of social inference. *Personality and Social Psychology Bulletin, 19*, 340–348.

Krull, D. S., & Dill, J. C. (1996). On thinking first and responding fast: Flexibility in social inference processes. *Personality and Social Psychology Bulletin, 22*, 949–959.

Lazarus, R. S., Speisman, M., Mordkoff, A. M., & Davison, L. A. (1962). A laboratory study of psychological stress produced by a motion picture film. *Psychological Monographs: General and Applied, 76*(34), 1–35.

Lewin, K. (1951). Problems of research in social psychology. In D. Cartwright (Ed.), *Field Theory in Social Science* (pp. 155–169). New York, NY: Harper & Row.

Linz, D. G., Donnerstein, E., & Penrod, S. (1988). Effects of long-term exposure to violent and sexually degrading depictions of women. *Journal of Personality and Social Psychology, 55*, 758–768.

Lorenz, K. (1966). *On aggression.* New York, NY: Bantam.

Malamuth, N. M., Linz, D., Heavey, C. L., Barnes, G., & Acker, M. (1995). Using the confluence model of sexual aggression to predict men's conflict with women: A 10-year follow-up study. *Journal of Personality & Social Psychology, 69*, 353–369.

Mathews, V. P., Kronenberger, W. G., Wang, Y., Lurito, J. T., Lowe, M. J., & Dunn, D. W. (2005). Media violence exposure and frontal lobe activation measured by functional magnetic resonance imaging in aggressive and nonaggressive adolescents. *Journal of Computer Assisted Tomography, 29*, 287–292.

Miller, N. E. (1941). The frustration-aggression hypothesis. *Psychological Review, 48*, 337–342.

Mischel, W. (1973). Toward a cognitive social learning reconceptualization of personality. *Psychological Review, 80*, 252–283.

Mischel, W., & Shoda, Y. (1995). A cognitive-affective system theory of personality: Reconceptualizing situations, dispositions, dynamics, and invariance in personality structure. *Psychological Review, 102*, 246–268.

Osborn, D. K., & Endsley, R. C. (1971). Emotional reactions of young children to TV violence. *Child Development, 42*, 321–331.

Owens, J., Maxim, R., McGuinn, M., Nobile, C., Msall, M., & Alario, A. (1999). Television-viewing habits and sleep disturbance in school children. *Pediatrics, 104*(3), 552.

Potter, W. J. (1999). *On media violence.* Thousand Oaks, CA: Sage.

Sakamoto, A., Yukawa, S., Shibuya, A., & Ihori, N. (2002). *Seishounen to housou ni kansuru chousa kenkyu: Terebi to terebigemu niokeru bouryoku ga seishounen no kougekisei ni oyobosu eikyou wo chuushin toshite [A survey report about the youth and broadcasting: The influence of television and videogame violence on aggression]* (Unpublished).

Saleem, M., & Anderson, C. A. (2012). The good, the bad, and the ugly of electronic media. In J. Dvoskin, J. L. Skeem, R. W. Novaco, & K. S. Douglas (Eds.), *Applying social science to reduce violent offending* (pp. 83–101). New York, NY: Oxford University Press.

Schacter, D. L. (2000). Memory systems. In A. E. Kazdin (Ed.), *Encyclopedia of Psychology* (Vol. 5, pp. 169–172). New York, NY: Oxford University Press and the American Psychological Association.

Schachter, S., & Singer, J. (1962). Cognitive, social, and physiological determinants of emotional state. *Psychological Review, 69*, 379–399.

Schank, R. C., & Abelson, R. P. (1977). *Scripts, plans, goals and understanding: An inquiry into human knowledge structures.* Hillsdale, NJ: Lawrence Erlbaum.

Schwarz, N., & Clore, G. L. (1996). Feelings and phenomenal experiences. In E. Higgins & A. Kruglanski (Eds.), *Social psychology: Handbook of basic principles* (pp. 433–465). New York, NY: Guilford.

Sedikides, C., & Skowronski, J. J. (1990). Towards reconciling personality and social psychology: A construct accessibility approach. *Journal of Social Behavior and Personality, 5*, 531–546.

Shaw, M. E., & Costanzo, P. R. (1982). *Theories of Social Psychology* (pp. 3–18). New York, NY: McGraw-Hill.

Singer, M. I., Slovak, K., Frierson, T., & York, P. (1998). Viewing preferences, symptoms of psychological trauma, and violent behaviors among children who watch television. *Journal of the American Academy of Child and Adolescent Psychiatry, 37*(10), 1041–1048.

Smith, S. L., & Donnerstein, E. (1998). Harmful effects of exposure to media violence: Learning of aggression, emotional desensitization, and fear. In R. G. Geen & E. Donnerstein (Eds.), *Human aggression: Theories, research, and implications for social policy* (pp. 167–202). New York, NY: Academic Press.

Sparks, G. G., & Cantor, J. (1986). Developmental differences in fright responses to a television program depicting a character transformation. *Journal of Broadcasting and Electronic Media, 30,* 309–323.

Steyer, J. P. (2002). *The other parent: The inside story of the media's effect on our children.* New York, NY: Atria Books.

Strack, F., & Deutsch, R. (2004). Reflective and impulsive determinants of social behavior. *Personality and Social Psychology Review, 8,* 220–247.

Surbeck, E. (1975). Young children's emotional reactions to TV violence: The effect of children's perceptions of reality. *Dissertation Abstracts International, 35,* 5139-A.

Thomas, M. H. (1982). Physiological arousal, exposure to a relatively lengthy aggressive film, and aggressive behavior. *Journal of Research in Personality, 16,* 72–81.

Thomas, M. H., Horton, R. W., Lippincott, E. C., & Drabman, R. S. (1977). Desensitization to portrayals of real life aggression as a function of television violence. *Journal of Personality and Social Psychology, 35,* 450–458.

Thorndike, E. L. (1898). Animal intelligence: An experimental study of the associative processes in animals. *Psychological Review, Monograph Supplements, 2*(8), i-109.

Uleman, J. S. (1987). Consciousness and control: The case of spontaneous trait inferences. *Personality and Social Psychology Bulletin, 13,* 337–354.

Vasquez, E. A., Pedersen, W. C., Bushman, B. J., Kelley, N. J., Demeestere, P., & Miller, N. (2013). Lashing out after stewing over public insults: The effects of public provocation, provocation intensity, and rumination on triggered displaced aggression. *Aggressive Behavior, 39,* 13–29.

Weber, R., Ritterfeld, U., & Mathiak, K. (2006). Does playing violent video games induce aggression? Empirical evidence of a functional magnetic resonance imaging study. *Media Psychology, 8*(1), 39–60.

Wilson, B. J., Kunkel, D., Linz, D., Potter, J., Donnerstein, E., Smith, S. L., Blumenthal, E., & Gray, T. (1997). Violence in television programming overall: University of California, Santa Barbara Study. In M. Seawall (Ed.), *National television violence study* (Vol. 1). Thousand Oaks, CA: Sage.

Wilson, B. J., Kunkel, D., Linz, D., Potter, J., Donnerstein, E., Smith, S. L., Blumenthal, E., & Gray, T. (1998). Violence in television programming overall: University of California, Santa Barbara Study. In M. Seawall (Ed.), *National television violence study* (Vol. 2). Thousand Oaks, CA: Sage.

Wolpe, J. (1958). *Psychotherapy by reciprocal inhibition,* 5-220. Stanford, CA: Stanford University Press.

Zillmann, D. (1971). Excitation transfer in communication-mediated aggressive behavior. *Journal of Experimental Social Psychology, 7,* 419–434.

Zillmann, D. (1983). Arousal and aggression. In R. Geen & E. Donnerstein (Eds.), *Aggression: Theoretical and empirical reviews* (Vol. 1, pp. 75–102). New York, NY: Academic Press.

CHAPTER 5

Television Violence: Sixty Years of Research

Victor C. Strasburger and Barbara J. Wilson

TELEVISION VIOLENCE

The debate about media violence has been raging for 60 years. In 1954 Senator Estes Kefauver, then chairman of the Senate Subcommittee on Juvenile Delinquency, held hearings on whether television violence was contributing to real-life violence in the United States. When questioned, network executives claimed that the available research was not conclusive (Liebert & Sprafkin, 1988). A half-century later, hundreds of research studies and several government reports provide conclusive evidence that media violence can have harmful effects on viewers (e.g., Bushman & Huesmann, 2012; Council on Communications and Media, 2009; Media Violence Commission, 2012; Strasburger, Wilson, & Jordan, 2014). Yet some industry representatives and a few researchers (Ferguson & Kilburn, 2010; Gunter, 2008) continue to argue that television violence is harmless entertainment (see Figure 5.1). How much is actually known about the impact of media violence on children and adolescents, what sorts of studies have been done, and how convincing are the data? Are the media part of the problem of violence in society or, as some TV executives suggest, does television merely reflect the violence that is occurring in society?

VIOLENCE IN AMERICAN SOCIETY

In the debate over television violence and its impact, observers cannot seem to agree on the answer to even this simple question: Is American society becoming more or less violent? According to the Office of Juvenile Justice and

Figure 5.1

Source: Copyright © Sidney Harris; reprinted with permission.

Delinquency Prevention (www.ojjdp.gov), the juvenile arrest rate for murder in 2011 was at its lowest point since 1980, the arrest rate for aggravated assault was at its lowest point since the early 1980s, and the arrest rate for forcible rape in 2010 was one-third of its 1991 peak (U.S. Department of Justice, 2013). The 1.6 million juvenile arrests in 2010 were 21 percent lower than in 2001. Yet the recent mass shootings in Tucson, Aurora, and Newtown have raised new concerns about a culture of violence in the United States. And despite some downward trends in violence, the statistics are still alarming:

- In 2010 there were nearly 1,000 murders in the United States involving known juvenile offenders.
- According to the World Health Organization, the U.S. juvenile murder rate is the third highest in the world and the highest in the Western world (World Health Organization, 2002).
- Homicide is the second leading cause of death among 10- to 24-year-olds in the United States (Centers for Disease Control and Prevention [CDC], 2010).
- In 2010 simple assault arrest rates were almost double those in 1980 for nearly all age groups, but especially for teens and young adults (see Figure 5.2).

Figure 5.2
Rates of Aggravated Assault

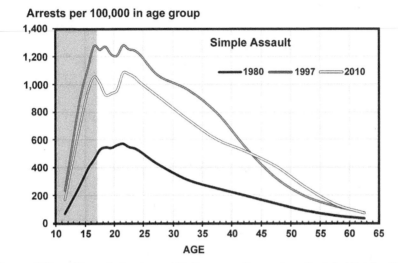

Source: Office of Juvenile Justice and Delinquency Prevention, *Statistical Briefing Book*; available at http://www.ojjdp.gov/ojstatbb/crime/qa05306.asp?qaDate=2010 (released on December 17, 2012).

- According to the 2011 Youth Risk Behavior Survey (YRBS) of 15,425 high school students, 33 percent had been in a fight in the previous year, 5 percent carried a gun to school in the past month, and 20 percent were bullied in school the previous year (Centers for Disease Control and Prevention, 2012).

Although short-term trends in violence may be debatable, what is clear is that violent crime has increased dramatically since the advent of television 50 years ago. From 1960 through 1991, the U.S. population increased by 40 percent but the violent crime rate increased by 500 percent (Grossman & DeGaetano, 1999). Moreover, homicide rates may not be the best indicator of whether violence is increasing. For one thing, murder is the least frequently committed crime. For another, people are now able to survive being shot because of extraordinary advances in medical care (Grossman & DeGaetano, 1999). Some experts contend that levels of *aggravated assault*—interpersonal violence—provide a far more appropriate index of how violent society has become (Grossman & DeGaetano, 1999), and these have risen dramatically during the past 50 years (see Figure 5.3). Perhaps more importantly, most of the real-world aggression that children will experience personally is bullying, relational aggression, and cyberbullying. Although these types of aggression are clearly harmful, they do not show up in national crime statistics. Levels of in-person bullying and cyberbullying vary widely,

Figure 5.3
Violent Crimes in America: A Comparison of Murder, Assault, and Imprisonment Rates, 1957–2005

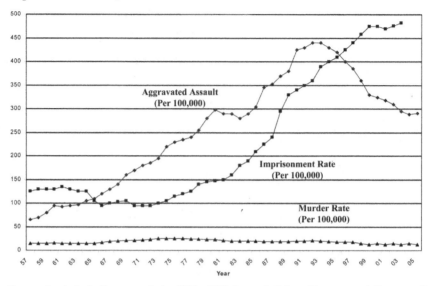

Source: Statistical Abstract of the U.S., FBI Annual Crime Report, and Bureau of Justice Statistics Prison Statistics Report. Killology.com.

from 9 to 35 percent, depending on the age group and time frame studied (Strasburger, Jordan, & Donnerstein, 2012).

In some provocative research, Centerwall (1992) argued that historical changes in violent crime can be tied to television violence. In a 1992 study, he examined white homicide rates in South Africa, Canada, and the United States and found that in the latter two countries 10 to 15 years elapsed between the introduction of television and a subsequent doubling of the homicide rate—exactly what one would expect if TV violence primarily affects young children (see Figure 5.4).

As Centerwall predicted, urban homicide rates rose before rural rates (television was first introduced into urban areas), rates rose first among affluent whites (minorities could not afford early TV sets), and rates increased earlier in those geographical areas where TV was first introduced. South Africa was used as a "control" nation because it closely resembles Western countries, yet it did not have any television until 1973. Predictably, homicide rates in South Africa have now begun to climb as well (Thomson, 2004). Based on his statistical analyses, Centerwall (1992) asserted that long-term exposure to TV violence is a causal factor in approximately half of all homicides in the United States and that 10,000 homicides could be prevented annually if television were less violent. These are intriguing arguments based on data that go well

Figure 5.4
Television Ownership and Homicide Rates in the United States, Compared to Homicide Rates in South Africa

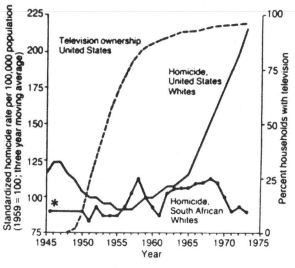

Source: JAMA.

beyond typical correlational analyses. Still, the findings do not meet stringent cause-and-effect criteria and thus are open to alternative explanations.

HOW VIOLENT IS AMERICAN TV?

American television is arguably one of the most violent media landscapes in the world. Early estimates indicated that the average American child or teenager viewed 1,000 murders, rapes, and aggravated assaults per year on television alone (Rothenberg, 1975). A later review by the American Psychological Association puts this figure at 10,000 per year—or approximately 200,000 by the time a child graduates from high school (Huston et al., 1992).

In the largest assessment, researchers at four universities collaborated on the National Television Violence Study (NTVS), which represents the most comprehensive content analysis ever attempted of American television. From 1994 to 1997, over 2,500 hours of content were assessed each year across 23 different channels, including the broadcast networks, independent broadcast, public broadcasting, basic cable, and premium cable (Smith et al., 1998b; Wilson et al., 1997, 1998). Over the three years of the study, a steady 61 percent of programs contained some violence. However, the prevalence of violence varied considerably by channel type. More than 80 percent of programs featured on premium cable contained violence, whereas fewer than 20 percent of programs on public broadcasting did (see Figure 5.5).

Figure 5.5
National Television Violence Study

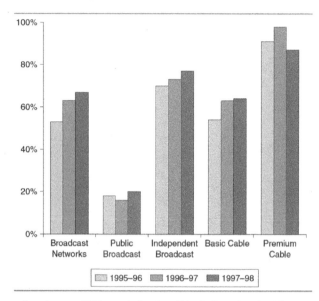

Source: From Strasburger, Wilson, & Jordan (2014). Reprinted with permission.

The researchers also examined *how* violence is portrayed on television. As it turns out, contextual features such as whether a perpetrator is attractive and whether the violence is punished are more important than the sheer amount of aggression in trying to understand the potential harm a portrayal might pose for viewers (for a review, see Wilson et al., 1997). Several conclusions were drawn from the three-year content analysis:

- *Violence on television is frequently glamorized.* Nearly 40 percent of the violent incidents were perpetrated by "good" characters who could potentially serve as role models for young viewers. In addition, a full 71 percent of violent scenes included no remorse, criticism, or penalty for violence at the time that it occurred.
- *Violence on television is frequently sanitized.* Nearly one half of the violent incidents failed to show physical harm or pain to the victim, and fewer than 20 percent of the violent programs portrayed any long-term negative consequences of violence to the victim or the victim's family.
- *Violence on television is often trivialized.* More than half of the violent incidents featured physical aggression that would be fatal if it were to occur in real life. Yet 40 percent of the violent scenes included some form of humor.
- *Very few programs emphasize an anti-violence theme.* Across the three years of the study, fewer than 5 percent of violent programs featured an anti-violence message. In other words, almost all TV violence is glamorized or celebrated in the storyline.

Although televised violence could be shown for educational or prosocial purposes (that is, to teach the true horror that violence begets), it typically is designed for entertainment purposes and to bring in the largest number of viewers (see chapter 1, this volume, for more on the economics of media violence).

More recent studies confirm the findings of the NTVS (Glascock, 2008; Linder & Lyle, 2011). Although violence on television is pervasive, it is even more common in shows targeted specifically to children. Nearly 70 percent of children's shows contain some violence, whereas 57 percent of non-children's shows do (Wilson et al., 2002). Furthermore, a typical hour of children's programming contains 14 different violent incidents, compared with 6 per hour in all other programming. The context of violence is also different in children's programs. For example, children's shows are even less likely than other types of shows to depict the serious consequences of violence. Children's programs are also more likely to portray violence as humorous. Of course, most of the programs targeted to children are animated cartoons.

IS TV STILL IMPORTANT?

With all of the new technology that has been developed in the past two decades (e.g., the Internet, cell phones, smartphones, iPads), many people now seemingly ignore the impact of "old media" (TV, movies, videos) on children and adolescents. That is a serious mistake. Young people spend more than seven hours a day with a variety of different media, but despite all of these new media, TV predominates, even for teenagers (see Figure 5.6) (Rideout, Foehr, & Roberts, 2010). And the presence of a bedroom TV increases the average number of hours of media use to more than 11 hours per day (Rideout et al., 2010). What has changed is that TV is not necessarily viewed on the TV set in the living room anymore—increasingly, older children and teens are downloading shows to their computers, smartphones, iPads, and cell phones. In one national survey, about 60 percent of young people's TV viewing is done live via a TV set, but the other 40 percent is now either time-shifted or viewed online or on mobile devices (Rideout et al., 2010). In another more recent survey, 74 percent of respondents report watching video via the Internet and more than half say they watch video on a mobile phone at least once a month, and 28 percent at least once a day (Nielsen, 2012).

THE IMPACT OF TV VIOLENCE ON VIEWER AGGRESSION

No single factor propels a child or a teenager to act aggressively. Instead, the causes of such antisocial behavior are complex and multifaceted. Hormonal and neurological disorders, impulsivity, and child temperament have been identified as risk factors (Garbarino, 2001; Losel & Farrington, 2012; Ramirez, 2003), as have environmental forces such as poverty, drug use,

Figure 5.6
Media Use, by Age

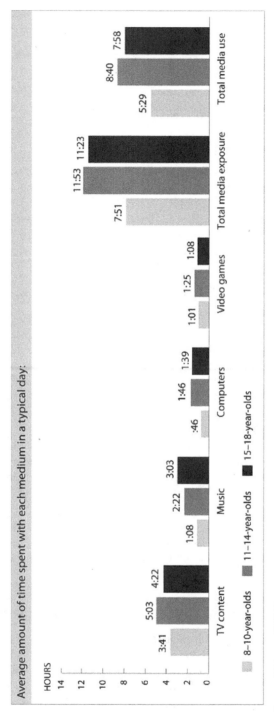

Average amount of time spent with each medium in a typical day:

HOURS

	TV content	Music	Computers	Video games	Total media exposure	Total media use
8–10-year-olds	3:41	1:08	:46	1:01	7:51	5:29
11–14-year-olds	5:03	2:22	1:46	1:25	11:53	8:40
15–18-year-olds	4:22	3:03	1:39	1:08	11:23	7:58

■ 8–10-year-olds ■ 11–14-year-olds ■ 15–18-year-olds

Source: Rideout (2010).

and lack of parental affection (Duke, Pettingell, McMorris, & Borowsky, 2010; Lee et al., 2012). But because the expression of aggression is a *learned* behavior (Eron, 1997), the media too have been identified as a risk factor (see chapter 2, this volume; Bushman & Huesmann, 2012; Comstock & Powers, 2012; Gentile & Bushman, 2012). Several methodologies have been used to study the effects of TV violence on aggression. Experiments are controlled studies in which people are randomly assigned to receive a treatment (e.g., watch something violent on television) or to serve in a control group, and afterward their responses are measured. Experiments can be conducted in a laboratory or in a more naturalistic field setting. Because all other variables are held constant and only the treatment is manipulated, experiments are the best method for establishing cause-and-effect relationships. However, experiments can be criticized for being artificial and for focusing on short-term effects only. Correlational studies typically involve large-scale surveys that ask people about their media habits and about their aggressive behavior. The samples are commonly more representative than those used in experiments, and the results reflect more natural, ongoing behaviors in the real world. Yet it is difficult to ascertain causality when variables are simply correlated or shown to relate to one another at a single point in time: Do media habits influence aggression or do aggressive people seek out violent media? To address this issue, longitudinal studies follow the same sample of individuals over time. This approach allows for the testing of long-term effects and for ascertaining whether early media habits predict subsequent behavior or vice versa.

Given that each method has particular strengths but also certain limitations, no single approach can definitely address the problem. However, by aggregating research across the different methods, we can draw certain conclusions about the impact of media violence (Bushman & Huesmann, 2012). Using each of the methods as a framework, we provide an overview of the evidence below.

Experimental Studies

Some of the earliest research on television violence was conducted in the 1960s by Albert Bandura and his colleagues. In a series of classic experiments (Bandura, Ross, & Ross, 1961; 1963a, 1963b), Bandura observed the behavior of nursery school children in a playroom that was filled with toys, among them a Bobo doll (a punching bag with a sand-filled base and a red nose that squeaked). The purpose of the experiments was to investigate the circumstances under which children would learn and imitate new aggressive behaviors. To test imitation, children typically watched the following filmed sequence on a TV set before being allowed to play:

The film began with a scene in which [an adult male] model walked up to an adult-size Bobo doll and ordered him to clear the way. After glaring for a moment at the noncompliant antagonist the model exhibited four novel aggressive responses, each accompanied by a distinctive verbalization. First, the model laid the Bobo doll on its side, sat on it, and punched it in the nose while remarking, "Pow, right in the nose, boom, boom." The model then raised the doll and pummeled it on the head with a mallet. Each response was accompanied by the verbalization, "Sockeroo . . . stay down." Following the mallet aggression, the model kicked the doll about the room, and these responses were interspersed with the comment, "Fly away." Finally, the model threw rubber balls at the Bobo doll, each strike punctuated with "Bang." This sequence of physically and verbally aggressive behavior was repeated twice. (Bandura, 1965, pp. 590–591)

Bandura and his colleagues varied the endings to this film across different experiments. In one study (Bandura, 1965), for example, children were randomly assigned to one of three conditions: (1) a model-rewarded condition, in which the model was called a "champion" and was treated with a soft drink and an assortment of candies; (2) a model-punished condition, in which the model was severely scolded and called a "bully"; or (3) a neutral condition in which the model received no rewards or punishments for his behavior. Afterward, each child was escorted to the playroom that contained the plastic Bobo doll, along with three balls, a mallet, a dollhouse, and assorted other toys. The results revealed that children in the model-rewarded and neutral groups displayed significantly more imitative aggression than did children in the model-punished group. The fact that the no-consequences condition resulted in just as much aggression as the reward-condition did suggests that so long as no punishments occur, children are likely to imitate a model's behavior.

Other research by Bandura et al. (1963a) found that children could learn new aggressive behaviors as easily from a cartoon-like figure as from a human adult, a result that clearly implicates animated TV shows as an equally unhealthy teacher of aggression. Although Bandura's experiments have been criticized as artificial because children were merely hitting an inflated punching bag, other laboratory research has shown that young children will aggress against a human being dressed as a clown just as readily as they will against a Bobo doll (Hanratty, O'Neal, & Sulzer, 1972). Furthermore, field experiments that have been conducted in more naturalistic settings indicate that aggression can be targeted to peers as well. In one study, preschoolers who watched ordinary violent TV programs during breaks at school displayed more aggressiveness on the playground than did children who viewed nonviolent programs over the same 11-day period (Steuer, Applefield, & Smith, 1971). Two decades later, elementary school children exposed to a single episode of *The Mighty Morphin' Power Rangers* displayed more verbal and physical aggression in the classroom than did children in a no-exposure control group (Boyatzis, Matillo, & Nesbitt, 1995). In fact, the treatment group committed seven times the number of aggressive acts, including hitting, kicking, shoving, and insulting fellow students, than did the control group.

In summary, a large number of well-controlled experiments dating back to the 1960s demonstrate that television violence can *cause* short-term

Table 5.1
Risky versus Educational Depictions of Violence in the Media

Media themes that *encourage* the learning of aggression
    "Good guys" or superheroes as perpetrators
    Violence that is celebrated or rewarded
    Violence that goes unpunished
    Violence that is portrayed as defensible
    Violence that results in no serious harm to the victim
    Violence that is made to look funny

Media themes that *discourage* the learning of aggression
    Evil or bad characters as perpetrators
    Violence that is criticized or penalized
    Violence that is portrayed as unfair or morally unjust
    Violence that causes obvious injury and pain to the victim
    Violence that results in anguish and suffering for the victim's loved ones

Source: Strasburger, Wilson, & Jordan (2014). Reprinted with permission.

aggressive behavior in some children. In addition, by carefully manipulating the program content in some of these studies, researchers have found that certain types of portrayals are more likely to encourage the learning of aggression than others are (for review, see Huesmann, 2007, and Wilson et al., 2002). In other words, not all television violence is alike in the risk that it poses to viewers. Table 5.1 summarizes some of the contextual features of violence that encourage the learning of aggression in viewers as well as features that can actually discourage such learning.

A Unique Quasi-Experiment

In 1986 an unusual study was conducted in Canada to assess the effect that the introduction of television would have on a particular community (Williams, 1986; see MacBeth, this volume, for a detailed review). Children in a Canadian town that had no television (labeled "Notel") were compared with children in two nearby communities that had only one station ("Unitel") or multiple channels ("Multitel"). The three communities were similar in size and socio-economic characteristics; the major difference was the presence and amount of television available. However, the study is called a "quasi-experiment" rather than a true experiment because children were not actually randomly assigned to the different communities at the outset.

Data were collected on children in all three communities prior to 1974, when television was first introduced in Notel, and then in a two-year follow-up. In each town, children received scores for aggression based on observations of their play behavior, teacher ratings, and peer ratings. The researchers found that Notel children showed significant increases in physical and verbal

Figure 5.7
Mean Levels of Physical and Verbal Aggression before and after the
Introduction of Television in the Notel Community in Canada

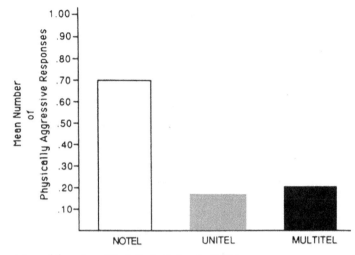

Source: Adapted from Joy, Kimball, & Zobrack, (1986).

aggression after the introduction of television (see Figure 5.7), whereas children in the other two communities showed no significant change in aggression during this same time period (Joy, Kimball, & Zabrack, 1986).

Correlational Studies

In the 1970s many researchers studied large populations of children and teens to determine whether heavy viewers of TV violence were more likely to show aggressive behavior. Such studies were partially a response to criticisms that laboratory experiments might be too artificial, use "play" measures of aggression, actually condone aggression by having adult experimenters encourage violent viewing, and only measure short-term effects (Freedman, 1984, 1986). One critic of the research put it more graphically: "Viewing in the laboratory setting is involuntary, public, choiceless, intense, uncomfortable, and single-minded. . . . Laboratory research has taken the viewing experience and turned it inside out so that the viewer is no longer in charge" (Fowles, 1999, p. 27).

Nevertheless, the correlational studies support the same patterns that have been documented in laboratory experiments. Some of the major early studies include the following:

• **A survey of 2,300 junior and senior high school students in Maryland** (McIntyre & Teevan, 1972). Each student was asked to list four favorite TV programs, which were then analyzed for violent content. Self-reports of aggressive behavior, ranging from fights at school to serious encounters with the law, were obtained. The study found that aggression scores were positively associated with the degree of violent content in favorite programming.

- **A national sample of 1,500 19-year-old males** (Robinson & Bachman, 1972). Those who expressed a preference for violent programming were significantly more aggressive in their self-reported behavior.

- **A study of 850 fourth through sixth graders in Michigan** (Dominick & Greenberg, 1972). The researchers found that the greater the exposure to TV violence, the more the children perceived violence as an effective solution to conflict and a viable option for themselves. The findings held up for both boys and girls.

- **A combined Maryland/Wisconsin study of more than 600 adolescents** (McLeod, Atkin, & Chaffee, 1972). The adolescents were asked how often they viewed 65 prime-time programs that had been rated for violent content by independent coders. The teens were also asked how often they had engaged in various forms of aggressive behavior, as well as how they would likely respond to a series of hypothetical situations. A modest positive correlation was found between violent TV viewing and overall aggressive behavior, even when variables such as IQ, academic performance, and socioeconomic status were statistically controlled.

- **A large-scale study of more than 1,500 English 12- to 17-year-old males** (Belson, 1978). Originally commissioned by the CBS television network, this project involved a representative sample of adolescent males and employed meticulous measures of TV exposure and aggressive behavior. Exposure to TV violence was positively associated with less serious forms of aggression, but the connection to more serious forms of aggression (antisocial and criminal acts) was even stronger. Males who viewed large amounts of violent TV content committed a far greater number of seriously harmful antisocial and criminal acts than did matched peers who were light viewers. More recent studies support these early patterns. One large-scale study of more than 30,000 adolescents from eight different countries found that heavy TV viewing was significantly associated with higher verbal aggression and verbal bullying, even after controlling for gender and age. In the three countries in which teens spent a lot of their weekend time viewing TV (United States, Poland, Portugal), there was also a positive relationship between television exposure and physical bullying (e.g., kicking, shoving) (Kuntsche et al., 2006).

The samples in most of these correlational studies are impressively large and the measures of aggression are presumably more realistic than those collected in lab studies. However, correlational research suffers from the so-called "chicken-and-egg" dilemma: Do aggressive children choose to watch more TV violence, or does TV violence cause aggressive behavior? To help untangle the direction of causality, longitudinal studies are useful because they assess the same sample of children or teens over time.

Longitudinal Studies

Some of the most powerful evidence that television has an impact on young people's behavior comes from longitudinal studies. Several major studies have been conducted by different groups of investigators on different samples of children and teens, and most of them point to a strong connection between early exposure to TV violence and subsequent aggressive behavior.

In one of the earliest studies, Huesmann and his colleagues followed a cohort of children over a 22-year period (Huesmann & Eron, 1986; Huesmann, Lagerspetz, & Eron, 1984; Lefkowitz, Eron, Walder & Huesmann, 1972). The original study began in 1963, with a sample of 875 third graders (age 8) in New York. The researchers were initially interested in the impact of different parenting styles on children's aggressive behavior. As a means for disguising their purposes, the researchers included what they thought were some "innocent" questions about media use in their interviews of parents. But when the data were examined 11 years later, the researchers realized that TV viewing habits seemed to have played a substantial role in the development of aggression. In other words, the findings showed that exposure to TV violence during early childhood was predictive of higher levels of aggressive behavior at age 19 (see Figure 5.8). By contrast, the reverse was not true: being more aggressive at age 8 did *not* predict greater consumption of violent programming at age 19. Consequently, the notion that more aggressive children tend to view more violence on TV was not substantiated. Interestingly, the TV/aggression link held only for boys, not for girls. This may be due to the types of aggression shown on TV and the types measured (physical aggression rather than other forms of aggression). However, the TV/aggression link persisted even when IQ, socioeconomic status, and overall exposure to TV were statistically controlled.

Ten years later, this same cohort was again studied, only this time the data revealed a link between exposure to TV violence at age 8 and self-reported aggression at age 30 among males (Huesmann, 1986; Huesmann & Miller, 1994). In some of the most provocative data reported, childhood TV habits also predicted criminal arrests for violent behavior at age 30 (see Figure 5.9). Based on these longitudinal patterns, Huesmann (1986) argued that:

Aggressive habits seem to be learned early in life, and once established, are resistant to change and predictive of serious adult antisocial behavior. If a child's observation of media violence promotes the learning of aggressive habits, it can have harmful life-long consequences. (p. 129)

In a separate cross-cultural study, Huesmann and Eron (1986) followed more than 1,000 children in the United States, Australia, Finland, Israel, the Netherlands, and Poland over a three-year time period. For every country except Australia, early viewing of TV violence was significantly associated with higher subsequent aggressive behavior, even after controlling for a child's initial level of aggressiveness. This widespread pattern was found despite the fact that crime rates and TV programming differed substantially among the different nations. Furthermore, the pattern was found just as often for girls as

Figure 5.8
TV Violence Watched in 3rd Grade Correlates with Aggressive Behavior at Age 19 for Boys

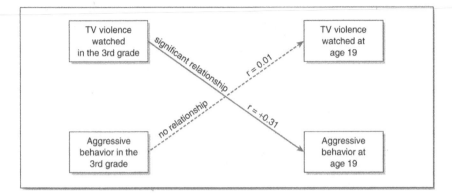

Source: Reproduced from Liebert & Sprafkin (1988).

Figure 5.9
Does Preference for Violent TV at Age 8 Correlate with Criminal Activity at Age 30?

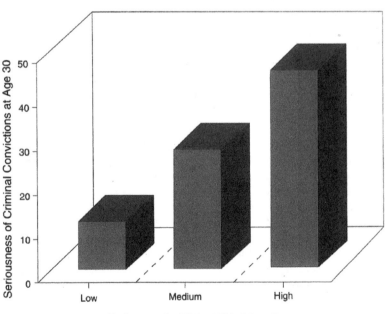

Source: Adapted from Huesmann (1986).

for boys in three of the countries, including the United States. Thus, Huesmann's earlier findings that seemed to pinpoint only boys now could be extended to girls as well. Contradicting the earlier 22-year longitudinal study, there was some evidence in this cross-cultural study that early aggression did predict subsequently higher levels of violent viewing. Huesmann now argues that the relation between TV violence and aggression is probably reciprocal: early viewing of violence stimulates aggression, and behaving aggressively then leads to a heightened interest in violent TV content (Huesmann, Lagerspetz, & Eron, 1984).

In a more recent longitudinal study, Huesmann and his colleagues interviewed over 500 grade school children and then re-surveyed them 15 years later. Again, the researchers found that heavy exposure to TV violence in childhood predicted increased aggressive behavior in adulthood; but now the pattern was the same for both boys and girls (Huesmann, Moise-Titus, Podolski, & Eron, 2003).

Focusing on an even younger age group, Singer and Singer (1981) studied 141 children from nearly 50 different New Haven, Connecticut, kindergartens over a one-year period. The researchers found a significant relation between children's viewing of TV violence (as recorded in daily diaries by parents) and their aggressive behavior as observed in free play at school. The relation held for both sexes and was strongest in those viewing the most violence on TV. In a subsequent five-year study, Singer, Singer, and Rapaczynski (1984) tracked 63 boys and girls from age four to age nine. Again, they found that those who watched the most violent programming as preschoolers displayed the most aggression at age nine, even when controlling for initial levels of childhood aggression.

Additional evidence that early viewing can predict later aggression comes from a 17-year study by Johnson and his colleagues (Johnson, Cohen, Smailes, Kasen, & Brook, 2002). The researchers tracked a random sample of 707 children from two New York counties. The children were between the ages of 1 and 10 at the outset of the study. They were assessed repeatedly, beginning in 1975, with family interviews, personality profiles, individual interviews, and questionnaires. In addition, adult criminal records were obtained from the state and the FBI in 2000. Results revealed that amount of time spent watching TV during early adolescence was associated with a subsequent increase in the likelihood of committing aggressive acts against others, particularly for males (see Figure 5.10). This relation persisted even when other important variables were controlled, such as previous aggressive behavior, childhood neglect, family income, neighborhood violence, parental education, and psychiatric disorders. Notably, the study assessed total TV viewing time rather than viewing of *violent* content, but the results are still quite impressive, especially given that it is the first longitudinal study to link adolescent TV habits to adult aggression (Anderson & Bushman, 2002a, 2002b).

Figure 5.10
Predicting Future Aggression from Early Amount of Television Viewing

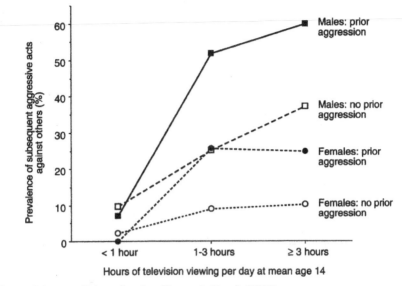

Source: Johnson, Cohen, Smailes, Kasen, & Brook (2002).

The most recent evidence comes from a large-scale study conducted in Dunedin, New Zealand (Robertson, McAnally, & Hancox, 2013). Researchers identified a birth cohort of 1,037 individuals born in 1972–1973, and then tracked them at regular intervals from birth to age 26 years. Results revealed that young adults who had spent more time watching TV between the ages of 5 and 15 were significantly more likely to have a criminal conviction, a diagnosis of antisocial personality disorder, and more aggressive personality traits than were those who had been light TV viewers (Figure 5.11). The association withstood controlling for sex, IQ, socioeconomic status, previous antisocial behavior, and parental control (Robertson et al., 2013).

Meta-Analyses

A meta-analysis is a quantitative review of the research on a given topic, in which the results from a number of separate studies are summarized (see chapter 13 of this volume). Using meta-analytic statistical techniques, a researcher can combine individual studies to yield a picture of the overall pattern across different investigations (O'Keefe, 2002). Meta-analyses result in numerical estimates of the size of an effect across all the studies taken together.

A number of meta-analyses have been conducted on the literature pertaining to the impact of media violence on aggression. *All* of them have found

Figure 5.11
Proportion of Male and Female Adults with a Criminal Conviction as a Function of Their Childhood (between the Ages of 5 and 15 Years) Television Viewing Habits

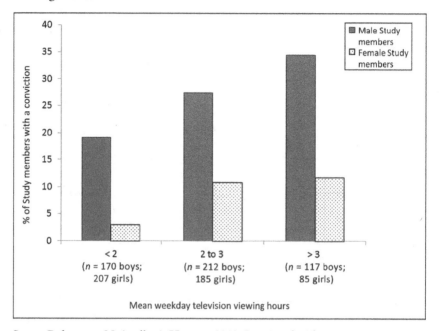

Source: Robertson, McAnally, & Hancox, 2013. Reprinted with permission.

support for the hypothesis that exposure to TV violence increases the likelihood of subsequent aggressive or antisocial behavior. The earliest meta-analysis looked at 67 studies, involving a total of about 300,000 people (Andison, 1977). Cumulatively, the results revealed a weak positive relationship between exposure to TV violence and subsequent aggression.

Roughly 10 years later, Hearold (1986) examined 230 studies, some of which looked at the impact of TV on prosocial behavior and others of which examined the impact on antisocial behavior. Isolating just those involving antisocial behavior, Hearold found an average effect size (analogous to a correlation coefficient) of 0.30 (see Figure 5.12). According to scientific convention, an effect size of 0.10 is considered to be small, 0.30 medium, and 0.5 large. In an update several years later, Paik and Comstock (1994) examined 217 studies and found an almost identical effect size of 0.31.

Two smaller meta-analyses focused only on a subset of the published studies on the impact of TV violence. Wood, Wong, and Chachere (1991) looked at those experiments in which children's aggressive behavior was actually observed in social interactions with peers after exposure to TV violence.

Figure 5.12
A Meta-Analysis of 230 Separate Studies to Examine the Effect Size of Television's Influence on Aggressive Behavior at Different Ages

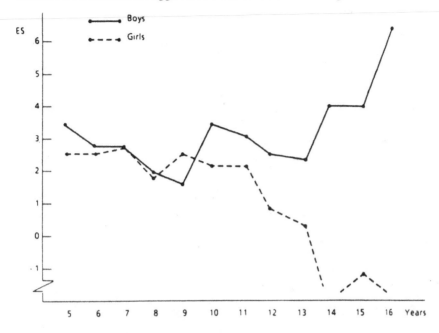

The researchers' goal was to isolate causal studies that employed the most realistic measures of aggression. Once again, across 23 such experiments, there was a significant effect of media violence on aggression. Hogben (1998) examined only those studies that measured naturalistic viewing of TV violence, eliminating any investigation in which viewing was controlled or manipulated. Even with this limited group of studies, he too found a significant relation between viewing of TV violence and aggressive behavior. However, the effect size was smaller than that observed when all types of studies are considered (Hearold, 1986; Paik & Comstock, 1994).

The most recent large-scale meta-analysis by Bushman and Anderson (2001) examined 212 studies of the effects of media violence, looking for patterns over time. The researchers found that since 1975, the size of the effect between media violence and aggressive behavior has steadily increased. There are at least four possible explanations for this trend: people may be spending more time with the media and consequently with violent portrayals; the sheer amount of violence in entertainment programming may be increasing; scientific methods for studying the effects of media violence may be improving; and/or the entertainment industry may be changing the way in which violence is portrayed by making it more graphic or realistic, hence heightening the potential for harmful effects on viewers (Bushman & Anderson, 2001).

In general, all six of the meta-analyses reported here have documented a positive and significant relation between media violence and aggression. The size of the effect varies, although two studies agree that it is roughly around 0.30. Another way to interpret this statistic is that roughly 10 percent of the variance (0.3^2) in aggressive or antisocial behavior can be attributed to exposure to TV violence. If we use this effect size, it means that in the midst of all the complex and multiple causes of violence, television is responsible for roughly 10 percent of the aggression observed in a typical sample of individuals. And this statistic is likely to represent a substantial underestimate for several reasons (Comstock & Strasburger, 1993). First, the unreliability of measurement reduces the degree of association that can be determined. In media research, the measures of behavior and of exposure are far from perfect. Second, there are virtually no control subjects available with truly low or zero exposure to TV. Even low-exposure groups experience some amount of viewing and knowledge about TV violence, thus narrowing the range of associations possible. Third, the standard analytic approaches used in this field appear to be overly conservative because they partial out shared variance among collinear variables (Gentile & Bushman, 2012). Nevertheless, even a 1 percent effect can be significant when considering large populations of child or adolescent viewers.

As it turns out, the link between media violence and aggressive or antisocial behavior is actually stronger than many commonly accepted cause-and-effect associations, such as the relation between calcium intake and bone mass, or between condom use and decreased risk of contracting HIV (Bushman & Huesmann, 2012). And the effect is only slightly smaller than that between smoking and lung cancer, which is nearly 0.40 (see Figure 5.13). Just as not everyone who smokes will develop lung cancer, not everyone who views violence on TV will become violent. But the risk is there and it appears to be quite significant.

Accumulation of Evidence

Collectively, then, there is a great deal of evidence linking media violence to aggression. Experimental studies have established a cause-and-effect relationship in short-term situations; surveys have documented this pattern in large samples of youth; longitudinal studies show that early exposure is predictive of increases in aggression over time; and meta-analyses of all this research show a consistent link between exposure to media violence and aggressive behavior across all types of studies. To be sure, no media researcher today would claim that watching a single violent film or television show directly and immediately *causes* a person to commit aggressive behaviors. Instead, repeated and cumulative exposure to media violence is seen as a risk factor that contributes to the development of aggression over time (see chapter 2 of this volume).

Figure 5.13
A Comparison of the Media Violence-Aggression Link with Other Public
Health Relationships That Have Been Established Scientifically

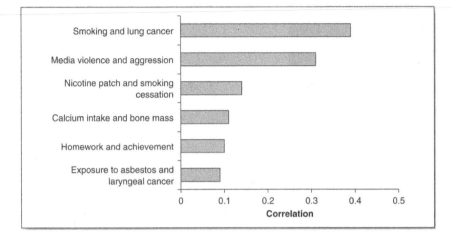

Source: From Strasburger, Wilson, & Jordan (2014). Reprinted with permission.

Despite fairly strong convergence of findings, there are a few researchers who raise doubts about the evidence. Gunter (2008) has highlighted the shortcomings of particular studies and argues that effect sizes are small. Ferguson and Kilburn (2009, 2010) have conducted their own meta-analyses, whereby they include unpublished studies and exclude studies with poor measures of aggression. They find a much smaller effect size (but still significant!), and conclude that there is little evidence that media violence increases aggressive behavior. Ferguson and Kilburn's work has been criticized by some of the most renowned media scholars in the field (Bushman, Rothstein, & Anderson, 2010; Huesmann, 2010; see chapter 12, this volume, for details).

Beyond the research community, several of the major health-related professional associations in the United States (e.g., American Medical Association, American Psychological Association, American Academy of Pediatrics) have each independently reviewed the accumulated evidence from the last 50 years; they all assert that exposure to screen violence increases the risk of aggressive behavior among youth.

WHY DOES TV VIOLENCE ENCOURAGE AGGRESSION?

There are several well-supported theories that help explain how media violence can contribute to aggression (see chapter 4, this volume). Observational or social learning theory is perhaps the oldest and most popular theoretical explanation. According to Bandura (1977), children learn new behaviors by direct experience or by observing and imitating others in their social environment. The rewards or punishments that role models experience are crucial in determining whether certain behaviors will be imitated. As discussed above, children are more likely to imitate a behavior that is rewarded or that goes unpunished (Bandura, 1965). Even Hollywood seems to accept this theory. As a well-known producer once stated:

I'd be lying if I said that people don't imitate what they see on the screen. I would be a moron to say they don't, because look how dress styles change. We have people who want to look like Julia Roberts and Michelle Pfeiffer and Madonna. Of course we imitate. It would be impossible for me to think they would imitate our dress, our music, our look, but not imitate any of our violence or our other actions. (Cited in Auletta, 1993, p. 45)

In the 1980s Bandura (1986) revised his theory to include cognitive processing variables in observational learning. Now called social cognitive theory, the updated version acknowledges that differences in a child's attention to and retention of a model's behavior can help explain imitational responses. This larger framework also allows the theory to extend beyond behavioral outcomes, and to include the learning of aggressive attitudes and normative beliefs from observing a model (Bushman & Huesmann, 2012).

As an extension of social learning, Huesmann (1986, 1988) has proposed a theory involving cognitive scripting. Cognitive scripts are mental routines that are stored in memory and are used to guide behavior (Abelson, 1976). According to Huesmann (1998), violent television programs provide young people with scripts that encourage the use of aggression. Once learned, these scripts can be retrieved from memory at any time, depending on the similarity between the real situation at hand and the fictional event, as well as the circumstances surrounding when the script was first encoded (Huesmann, 1998). When an aggressive script is retrieved, it can be reinforced and broadened to a new set of circumstances (Geen, 1994). In this way, repeated exposure to media violence can encourage a child to develop a set of stable cognitive scripts that emphasize aggression as a typical response to social situations (see Figure 5.14).

Two other theories focus more on how the media might prompt or trigger already learned aggressive behaviors. Zillmann's (1991) excitation transfer theory maintains that media violence can have an impact simply because it is arousing in nature. According to the theory, exposure to TV violence can generate excitement that, because it dissipates slowly, can transfer to other emotional experiences. If a person is already feeling angry or hostile, a stimulating violent TV show can increase the intensity of those feelings and thereby increase the potential for aggressive responding (Zillmann & Johnson, 1973). Because of its arousal properties, even erotic media content can increase aggressive responses in angry or frustrated individuals (Zillmann, 1971).

Berkowitz (1984) proposed a cognitive cueing or priming theory to account for the short-term instigational effects of media violence (also known

Figure 5.14
Use of Scripts in Social Situations

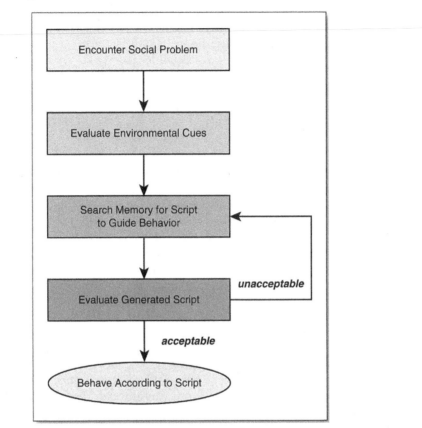

Source: From Strasburger, Wilson, & Jordan (2014). Reprinted with permission.

as cognitive neoassociation theory). According to Berkowitz, a violent television program can activate or "prime" aggressive thoughts in a viewer. Several conditions can encourage these aggressive thoughts to be turned into aggressive action, including intense feelings of negative affect or anger (Berkowitz, 1990), justification for aggressive behavior (Jo & Berkowitz, 1994), and cues in the environment that relate to the program just viewed (Jo & Berkowitz, 1994). In one of the first tests of this theory, Berkowitz and Rawlings (1963) conducted a classic experiment using *Champion*, a boxing film starring Kirk Douglas. One group of college males viewed a scene in which Kirk Douglas is brutally beaten; another group viewed a nonviolent track meet. An experimental assistant—named either "Bob" or "Kirk" Anderson—angered some of the subjects beforehand. The researchers accurately predicted that aggression (as measured by willingness to give electric shocks to the assistant) would be triggered when the subjects were angered, when they saw a violent movie that primed aggressive thoughts, and when there was a "cue" in the environment (i.e., name of the target) that resembled the movie. Dozens of similar experiments have been conducted since, with similar results (Comstock & Strasburger, 1990).

Together these four theories can account for most of the processes by which media violence might contribute to aggression. Social cognitive theory focuses on how particular television programs can teach novel aggressive behaviors to a child, whereas script theory helps explain how cumulative exposure can foster the development of aggressive habits and routines during childhood. In contrast, excitation transfer and cognitive priming are applicable to those situations in which media violence seems to trigger immediate violent responses, particularly among those who are predisposed to act aggressively, as well as those who already have a repertoire of aggressive behaviors at their disposal. More recently, Anderson and Bushman (2002a) developed the General Aggression Model (GAM), which attempts to integrate these smaller theories into one unifying framework. GAM focuses on both individual and situational factors that can influence aggression; it acknowledges that cognitions, emotions, and arousal interact in ways that produce aggression; and it accounts for the initial development as well as the persistence of aggressive behavior (see chapter 4).

THE MYTH OF CATHARSIS

In his *Poetics*, Aristotle suggested that theatergoers could be purged vicariously of their feelings of grief, fear, or pity. The idea that aggression can be "purged" through exposure to fantasy violence is derived from psychoanalytic theories of various "energies" coursing through the body like ancient "humours," just waiting to be drained (although this is an incorrect interpretation of what Aristotle was saying; Gentile, 2013). Obviously, this is an idea that has been quite popular in the Hollywood community (Plagens, Miller, Foote, & Yoffe, 1991) and even among the general public. A few early studies seemed to support the notion of catharsis (Feshbach 1955, 1961), but they had methodological problems (see Liebert & Sprafkin, 1988). Furthermore, the scientific evidence reviewed above overwhelmingly shows that media violence has quite the opposite effect. In other words, in over 40 years of research *there has been no substantiation of the catharsis theory* (Gentile, 2013; Huesmann, Dubow, & Yang, 2013).

Relational or Social Aggression

Aggressive behavior is not always physical in nature. Increasingly, developmental psychologists and pediatricians have come to realize that there are more subtle forms of aggression, such as gossiping, spreading rumors, or engaging in insulting or mean talk (Ostrov & Godleski, 2010). Such relational

Figure 5.15
Types of Verbal and Nonverbal Social Aggression in Programs Popular among Children

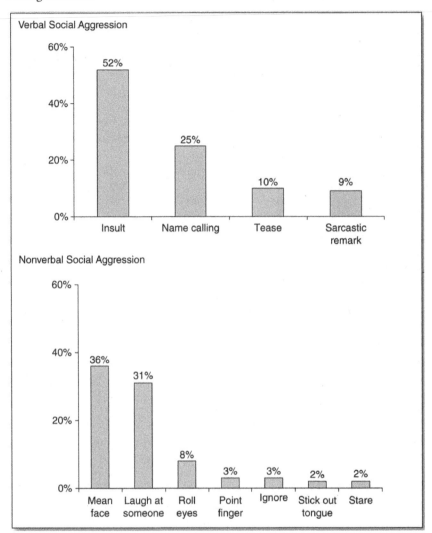

Source: From Strasburger, Wilson, & Jordan (2014). Reprinted with permission.

or social aggression is intended to harm another person emotionally rather than physically. Social aggression seems to be more common among girls than boys (Spieker et al., 2012).

Recent research indicates that social aggression is quite common on television. A content analysis of the 50 most-watched programs among 2- to

11-year-olds found that 92 percent of the shows contained social aggression (Martins & Wilson, 2012a) (see Figure 5.15). Furthermore, a typical hour of such programming featured 14 different incidents of social aggression.

Several studies have assessed whether there is a link between media exposure and relational aggression (see chapter 7, this volume).

- A study of preschoolers found that media exposure was positively associated with physical aggression for boys and relational aggression for girls (Ostrov, Gentile, & Crick, 2006).
- A recent longitudinal study of more than 400 grade school children found that heavy exposure to media violence at the beginning of the school year predicted higher levels of both physical and relational aggression later in the year (Gentile, Coyne, & Walsh, 2011).
- Martins and Wilson (2012b) specifically examined programs high in social aggression and found that among elementary school children exposure to such content was significantly related to greater social aggression for girls but not for boys.

MEDIA VIOLENCE AND FEAR OF VICTIMIZATION

By far, most of the research to date has concentrated on the impact of media violence on aggression. However, in recent years increasing attention has been paid to two other types of effects that can occur as a result of watching violent programs and movies: fear and desensitization (Cantor, 2009; Cantor, Byrne, Moyer-Gusé, & Riddle, 2010; Farr, 2012; Krahe et al., 2011; Potter, 1999; Smith et al., 1998a, 1998b; Wilson et al., 1997).

Experiencing short-term fright reactions to the media is a common occurrence and often is a consequence of viewing material that is violent. According to one study, more than 90 percent of college students could vividly remember a film or TV program that caused them intense fear when they were young (Harrison & Cantor, 1999). TV news stories may be particularly scary for younger children (Riddle, Cantor, Byrne, & Moyer-Gusé, 2012; Otto et al., 2007). Chapter 6 in this volume, by Cantor and Riddle, provides an overview of short-term and even long-term fright reactions to the media, particularly those experienced by children. Such fear, which is intensely emotional and often physiological, can be contrasted with another type of fear that is more cognitive and even attitudinal in nature—fear of victimization (Potter, 1999).

Gerbner and his colleagues have coined the term "mean world syndrome" to explain how heavy viewers of TV develop a greater sense of mistrust and apprehension about the real world (Gerbner, Gross, Morgan, & Signorielli, 1994). According to their theory, television "cultivates" a view of social reality in viewers. Studies of children as well as adults support this; heavy viewers of television routinely perceive the world as a more violent place and give higher estimates of their own risk of being a victim of violence than do light viewers (see Morgan, Shanahan, & Signorielli, 2009). Though most of the evidence to support cultivation theory is correlational in nature, there are a few experiments demonstrating that repeated exposure to television violence can elevate fear and anxiety about real-world violence (Bryant, Carveth, & Brown, 1981; Ogles & Hoffner, 1987). There is also longitudinal research showing that early exposure to adult-oriented violent TV programs is positively correlated with children's beliefs that the world is a fearful and dangerous place (Singer et al., 1984).

Cultivation theory has been critiqued on both methodological and conceptual grounds (Hawkins & Pingree, 1980; Hughes, 1980; Potter, 1993), and in 1980 the theory was refined to acknowledge that the cultivation relationship might vary across different subgroups of individuals (Gerbner, Gross, Morgan, & Signorielli, 1980). More recently, researchers have been testing cognitive processing models to help explain the cultivation effect (Shrum, 2009). In spite of these rigorous challenges to the theory, the data have been remarkably consistent over time (Potter, 1999). Indeed, a meta-analysis of over 20 years of cultivation research found a small but consistent relation between exposure to television and perceptions of violence in the real world (Morgan & Shanahan, 1996). As Shrum (2001) stated, "The notion that the viewing of television program content is related to people's perceptions of reality is virtually undisputed in the social sciences" (p. 94).

MEDIA VIOLENCE AND DESENSITIZATION

Desensitization refers to the idea that repeated exposure to a certain stimulus can lead to reduced emotional and physiological responsiveness to it. In clinical settings, desensitization techniques are used to treat people's phobias. If desensitization to media violence exists, it could explain the public's apparent callousness toward this issue and its acceptance of even more violence in television programming and movies (Comstock & Strasburger, 1993). In their book *High Tech, High Touch: Technology and Our Search for Meaning*, three critics of modern culture (Naisbitt, Naisbitt, & Philips, 1999) write:

In a culture of electronic violence, images that once caused us to empathize with the pain and trauma of another human being excite a momentary adrenaline rush. To be numb to another's pain—to be acculturated to violence—is arguably one of the worst consequences our technological advances have wrought. That indifference transfers from the screen, TV, film, Internet, and electronic games to our everyday lives through seemingly innocuous consumer technologies. (pp. 90–91)

Do studies support the notion of desensitization? The answer is an unqualified yes. Research shows quite clearly that physiological arousal becomes lessened with continued exposure to media violence (Cline, Croft, & Courrier, 1973). Subjects' heart rates and skin conductance decrease over time during

Figure 5.16

Source: By permission of Mike Lukovich and Creators Syndicate, Inc.

prolonged exposure to violence, even within a single program (Lazarus & Alfert, 1964). In one study, both children and adults showed less physiological arousal during a scene of real-life violence after viewing a violent drama on TV (Thomas, Horton, Lippincott, & Drabman, 1977).

A far greater concern, of course, is whether this physiological numbing translates into a callousness or indifference to violence (see Figure 5.16). Numerous experiments suggest that it can. In one early study, children who had been exposed to a violent television show were less ready to intervene when a pair of preschoolers broke into a fight than were children who had seen a nonviolent TV program (Thomas & Drabman, 1975). In fact, many of the children in the violent viewing group never left the room to get help even though they had been instructed to do so. Other studies also have documented a callousness to real-world aggression in children after exposing them to fictional portrayals of violence (Drabman & Thomas, 1974; Molitor & Hirsch, 1994).

Perhaps not surprisingly, adults show the same effect (Bushman & Anderson, 2009). For example, several experiments have shown that exposing college students to a series of slasher films makes them less sympathetic toward an alleged rape victim and more inclined to hold her responsible for her own rape (Donnerstein & Smith, 2001; Linz, Donnerstein, & Penrod, 1984).

Figure 5.17
Perceptions of Domestic Violence Victim Days after Desensitization
to Media Violence

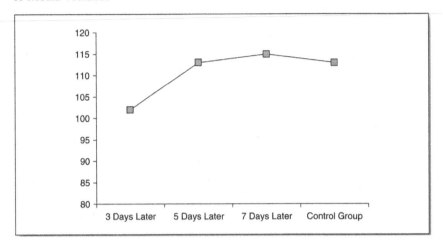

Source: Reprinted from Strasburger, Wilson, & Jordan (2014), with permission.

Clearly, desensitization is not only a real and verifiable process, it also has important implications for society. Have levels of media violence increased because the American population has become desensitized? Have Americans become less empathetic with victims of violence? Are Americans less willing to come to the aid of a victim now than they were 50 years ago? Could desensitization explain some of the recent schoolyard shootings (Strasburger & Grossman, 2001)? Could it also explain why certain elements in society are willing to consider inflicting the death penalty on mentally ill perpetrators or imprisoning 12-year-old juvenile offenders for life? These are all debatable issues that underscore the importance of continuing to examine desensitization as a harmful outcome of repeated exposure to media violence.

One interesting question remains: Is desensitization a transitory or a permanent byproduct of media violence? Can people become *re*sensitized to real-world violence? In a 1995 experiment, male college students were exposed to three slasher films during a six-day period (Mullin & Linz, 1995). In a supposedly unrelated experiment, they were then asked three, five, or seven days later to watch a documentary about domestic abuse. Results revealed that those who had seen the slasher films only three days earlier were less sympathetic to domestic violence victims and rated their injuries as less severe than did a control group (see Figure 5.17). However, those who had viewed the slasher films five and seven days earlier showed levels of sympathy that had "rebounded" to the baseline level of the control group. In other words, desensitization seemed to diminish after a three-day period. Of course, the notion of *re*sensitization requires that a person no longer be exposed to violent media during the "recovery" period, something that is virtually impossible these days if any media are consumed.

One important element of desensitization is that it appears to be a relatively automatic (and autonomic) process. Therefore, people are not aware that they have become desensitized—although they may be perfectly willing to accept that others have been. This tendency is called the "third-person effect," a well-documented phenomenon whereby people assume that others are influenced more by the media than they themselves are (Perloff, 2009). The challenge, then, is to discover ways in which viewers can be made aware of the potential for desensitization to occur, especially among those who consume a great deal of media violence.

CAN TELEVISION VIOLENCE BE PROSOCIAL?

One common technique in many violent programs, especially those targeted at children, is to include a prosocial message or lesson at the end of the plot. Superhero shows such as *Green Lantern* and *Batman: The Animated Series* employ this strategy in nearly every episode. It is tempting to assume that such devices might encourage children to behave in prosocial ways, as is true of many nonviolent programs on television (Mares & Woodard, 2001). However, research cautions against this assumption. In one study, 68 children between the ages of 4 and 10 were exposed to an episode of *Power Rangers* and interviewed about it afterward (McKenna & Ossoff, 1998). When asked about the most important thing they remembered from the show, younger children referred mostly to the fighting sequences. Only the 8- to 10-year-olds referred to the moral theme of the episode—that it is more important to work than to play. When asked directly what the main theme or message of the episode was, once again strong age differences emerged. The oldest children were significantly more likely to recognize the theme than were those under age eight.

Though younger children may misunderstand these messages, even more troubling is the potential impact of "prosocial" violence on viewer aggression. In two experiments, Liss and her colleagues (1983) exposed kindergarten, second-, and fourth-grade children to different versions of a cartoon: (1) a purely prosocial one with no violence in it, (2) a prosocial one with violence in it, and (3) a purely violent one with no prosocial theme in it. After viewing television, children had an opportunity to "help" or "hurt" a peer in a game situation. The researchers found that regardless of age, children had more difficulty comprehending the prosocial message when it was couched in violence than when it was seen with no violence. Consistent with the confusing nature of such messages, the youngest children were more likely to engage in aggression than prosocial helping behavior after viewing the prosocial-violent cartoon. In other words, the superhero's violent behavior was more salient than his prosocial words were. In fact, the prosocial-violent cartoon produced more imitative aggression among kindergartners than did the purely violent cartoon.

These findings suggest that one of the most potent ways to teach aggression to young viewers is to couch the behavior in a moralistic context. Indeed, violence that is depicted as being justified is one of the most strongly reinforcing elements in whether it will be learned or imitated (see Paik & Comstock, 1994). According to Comstock (1991), key factors that determine how violence will be interpreted by viewers include *efficacy*, or whether violence results in the achievement of desired goals, and *normativeness*, or whether the violence is portrayed as socially acceptable. Both of these factors are highlighted in most action-adventure programs that feature superheroes.

Is it possible, then, for violent programming to ever have a positive impact on children and adolescents? One unique study suggests that under certain circumstances, it is possible. In June 1998 Court TV funded a study to assess this issue (Wilson et al., 1999). More than 500 teenagers from three different California middle schools were randomly assigned to receive or not receive the *Choices and Consequences* curriculum in school. The three-week curriculum involved viewing videotaped court cases about real teens who have engaged in risky behavior that resulted in someone dying. For example, in one case a group of teens pushed a young boy off of a railroad trestle and he drowned. Each week, the students watched portions of the trial, discussed the cases, engaged in role-playing, and completed homework based on the cases. Compared with the control group, the teens involved in the curriculum showed significantly reduced verbal aggression and physical aggression. They also had increased empathy. In other words, exposure to programming that emphasizes the lifelong negative consequences of antisocial behavior can have prosocial effects on teens, at least when paired with active discussions of the content.

Huesmann, Eron, Klein, Brice, and Fischer (1983) demonstrated that a slightly different curriculum could work with even younger age groups. In the study, second and fourth graders wrote essays about the unrealistic nature of violent programming as well as the impact of TV violence on young viewers. They were then videotaped reading their essays. Compared with a control group, these children displayed more negative attitudes about TV violence and decreased their aggressive behavior up to four months after the intervention.

Thus, violent programming can be used in structured situations to teach children about the dangers associated with it and with antisocial behavior more generally. In support of this idea, a recent meta-analysis of nine studies found that media literacy programs *can* effectively change how people respond to screen violence (Jeong, Cho, & Hwang, 2012). However, some researchers caution that showing violent video clips, even in the context of media literacy, may inadvertently stimulate aggressive thoughts and attitudes among children (Byrne, Linz, & Potter, 2009).

Rather than relying on formal literacy programs, research suggests that even parents can employ critical viewing strategies that will decrease the impact of media violence on their children (Nathanson, 1999). Some programs may teach these lessons without the need for adult intervention. Hollywood pundits would point to such movies as *Boyz in the Hood*, *Schindler's List*, and *Unforgiven* as being powerfully antiviolent. Although there are no formal studies of the impact of any of these films, all are examples of the fact that sometimes violence needs to be portrayed in order to convey an antiviolence message. Clearly, the *context* that violence is portrayed in is crucial in determining its impact.

CONCLUSIONS

During the 1990s the United States was shocked by an apparent epidemic of schoolyard shootings, ranging from Jonesboro, Arkansas, to Springfield, Oregon, to Littleton, Colorado. In January 2001 a 12-year-old boy was found guilty of murdering a six-year-old girl. He said that he was imitating wrestling moves he had seen on *WWF Smackdown* by Dwayne "The Rock" Johnson. The boy weighed 180 pounds, the girl 48 pounds (Clary, 2001). In 2012 the nation was shaken by mass shootings in Tucson, Aurora, and Newtown. American society seems to still be asking the same question today as Senator Kefauver asked in 1954: Does media violence cause real-life violence?

As we have seen, the scientific literature is robust and consistent in supporting the idea that media violence can contribute to the development of aggressive attitudes and behaviors in childhood and even adulthood. Effect sizes range from small to medium in size, depending on the types of studies involved (see Figure 5.18) (Anderson & Bushman, 2002b; Comstock & Strasburger, 1993).

Certainly other factors are at work too, including poverty, racism, drugs, and unique personality factors. Witnessing violence is important as well (Buka, Stichick, Birdthistle, & Earls, 2001). In one study of 175 9- to 12-year-olds who visited a large urban pediatric primary care clinic, 97 percent reportedly had been exposed to real-life violence (Purugganan, Stein, Silver, & Benenson, 2000). In fact, 31 percent had witnessed someone being shot, stabbed, or killed. Another study found that exposure to real-life violence, along with parental monitoring, television viewing habits, and certain demographic variables, explained nearly half of 2,245 children's self-reported violent behaviors (Singer et al., 1999). If witnessing violence in real life increases the risk of aggressive behavior, it seems reasonable to expect that witnessing it on TV—vicariously—should have an effect as well.

American television not only provides countless ways to witness violence but it also prominently features gun use in this aggression. For example, one fourth of all violent interactions on TV involve guns (Smith, Boyson, Pieper, & Wilson, 2001). Moreover, a typical viewer will witness an average of nearly

Figure 5.18
Average Effect Sizes of Media Violence Studies, Split by Research Method

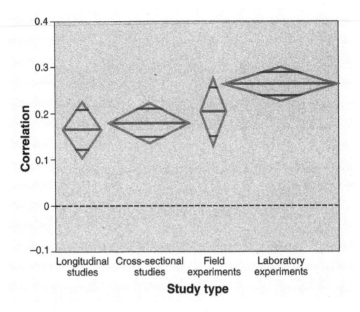

Tops and bottoms of the diamonds show the upper and lower limits of the 99% confidence interval around the average effect size.

two gun-related violent incidents for every hour he or she watches television. Movies also commonly feature guns. A recent study of the 100 top-grossing movies between 1995 and 2004 found that 70 percent contained at least one scene with a firearm (Binswanger & Cowan, 2009). Firearm depictions accounted for 17 percent of the screen time in these movies, and the majority of movies were rated PG-13.

Despite their alignment with entertainment media, guns are serious business in this country. Among U.S. teens and young adults, the death rate due to firearms is 43 times higher than among young people in 23 other industrialized countries *combined* (Children's Defense Fund, 2012). In 2008 and 2009 alone, over 5,000 children and teens died from guns in this country, which translates to one young victim every three hours (Children's Defense Fund, 2012). Although there is no data that directly links the viewing of media gunplay with actual gun-related offenses in real life, a meta-analysis of 56 experiments found that the mere presence of weapons, either in pictures or in the actual environment, significantly enhanced aggressive behavior in angered and nonangered participants (Carlson, Marcus-Newhall, & Miller, 1990).

Obviously, not all children will develop aggressive habits after watching extensive amounts of television violence. But other outcomes such as fear of victimization and desensitization are well documented in the literature and may actually occur more often and among greater numbers of viewers. Donnerstein and his colleagues (1994) offer one way to appreciate how widespread the impact of media violence can be across different types of individuals. After reviewing the scientific literature, they identified the following effects:

- *an aggressor effect* of increased meanness, aggression, and even violence toward others;
- *a victim effect* of increased fearfulness, mistrust, or "mean world syndrome," and self-protective behavior;
- *a bystander effect* of increased desensitization, callousness, and behavioral apathy toward other victims of violence; and
- *an appetite effect* of increased self-initiated behavior to further expose oneself to violent material (p. 240).

To return to the beginning of this chapter, Senator Kefauver's question from 60 years ago seems somewhat narrow today. Yes, there is a correlation between media violence and real-life aggression. But the relationship is certainly complex and probably reciprocal. If the basic question has been answered, then the more critical questions for researchers, parents, and makers of public policy in the twenty-first century are these: What types of violent portrayals pose the greatest risk of viewers learning aggression, becoming frightened, or experiencing desensitization? What types of individuals are most at risk for these effects? What can we do to ameliorate such harmful outcomes?

REFERENCES

Abelson, R. P. (1976). Script processing in attitude formation and decision-making. In J. Carroll & J. Payne (Eds.), *Cognition and social behavior.* Hillsdale, NJ: Lawrence Erlbaum.

Anderson, C. A., & Bushman, B. J. (2002a). Human aggression. *Annual Review of Psychology, 53,* 27–51.

Anderson, C. A., & Bushman, B. J. (2002b). The effects of media violence on society. *Science, 295,* 2377–2378.

Andison, F. S. (1977). TV violence and viewer aggressiveness: A cumulation of study results. *Public Opinion Quarterly, 41,* 314–331.

Auletta, K. (1993, May 17). Annals of communication: What won't they do. *The New Yorker, 69,* 45–53.

Bandura, A. (1965). Influence of models' reinforcement contingencies on the acquisition of imitative response. *Journal of Personality and Social Psychology, 1,* 589–595.

Bandura, A. (1977). *Social learning theory.* New York, NY: Prentice-Hall.

Bandura, A. (1986). *Social foundations of thought and action: A social cognitive theory.* Englewood Cliffs, NJ: Prentice Hall.

Bandura, A., Ross, D., & Ross, S. A. (1961). Transmission of aggression through imitation of aggressive models. *Journal of Abnormal and Social Psychology, 63,* 575–582.

Bandura, A., Ross, D., & Ross, S. A. (1963a). Imitation of film-mediated aggressive models. *Journal of Abnormal and Social Psychology, 66,* 3–11.

Bandura, A., Ross, D., & Ross, S. A. (1963b). Various reinforcement and imitative learning. *Journal of Abnormal and Social Psychology, 67,* 601–607.

Belson, W. A. (1978). *Television violence and the adolescent boy.* Westmead, UK: Teakfield.

Berkowitz, L. (1984). Some effects of thoughts on anti- and prosocial influences of media events: A cognitive-neoassociation analysis. *American Psychologist, 45,* 494–503.

Berkowitz, L. (1990). On the formation and regulation of anger and aggression: A cognitive neoassociationistic analysis. *American Psychologist, 45,* 494–503.

Berkowitz, L., & Rawlings, E. (1963). Effects of film violence on inhibitions against subsequent aggression. *Journal of Abnormal and Social Psychology, 66,* 405–412.

Binswanger, I. A., & Cowan, J. A. (2009). Firearms in major motion pictures, 1995–2004. *Journal of Trauma Injury, Infection, and Critical Care, 66*(3), 906–911.

Boyatzis, J., Matillo, G. M., & Nesbitt, K. M. (1995). Effects of the "Mighty Morphin Power Rangers" on children's aggression with peers. *Child Study Journal, 25,* 45–55.

Bryant, J., Carveth, R. A., & Brown, D. (1981). Television viewing and anxiety: An experimental examination. *Journal of Communication, 31*(1), 106–109.

Buka, S. L., Stichick, T. L., Birdthistle, I., & Earls, F. J. (2001). Youth exposure to violence: Prevalence, risks, and consequences. *American Journal of Orthopsychiatry, 71,* 298–310.

Bushman, B. J., & Anderson, C. A. (2001). Media violence and the American public: Scientific facts versus media misinformation. *American Psychologist, 56,* 477–489.

Bushman, B. J., & Anderson, C. A. (2009). Comfortably numb: Desensitizing effects of violent media on helping others. *Psychological Science, 20,* 273–277.

Bushman, B. J., & Huesmann, L. R. (2012). Effects of violent media on aggression. In D. G. Singer & J. L. Singer (Eds.), *Handbook of children and the media* (2nd ed., pp. 231–248). Thousand Oaks, CA: Sage.

Bushman, B. J., Rothstein, H. R., & Anderson, C. A. (2010). Much ado about something: Violent video game effects and a school of red herring: Reply to Ferguson and Kilburn (2010). *Psychological Bulletin, 136*(2), 182–187.

Byrne, S., Linz, D., & Potter, J. (2009). A test of competing cognitive explanations for the boomerang effect in response to the deliberate disruption of media-induced aggression. *Media Psychology, 12*(3), 227–248.

Cantor, J. (2009). Fright reactions to mass media. In J. Bryant & M. B. Oliver (Eds.), *Media effects: Advances in theory and research* (3rd ed., pp. 287–303). Hillsdale, NJ: Lawrence Erlbaum.

Cantor, J., Byrne, S., Moyer-Gusé, E., & Riddle, K. (2010). Descriptions of media-induced fright reactions in a sample of U.S. elementary school children. *Journal of Children and Media, 4,* 1–17.

Carlson, M., Marcus-Newhall, A., & Miller, N. (1990). Effects of situational aggression cues: A quantitative review. *Journal of Personality & Social Psychology, 58,* 622–633.

Centers for Disease Control and Prevention. (2010). Youth violence. http://www.cdc.gov/violenceprevention/pdf/yv-datasheet-a.pdf

Centers for Disease Control and Prevention. (2012). *Youth Risk Behavior Survey Surveillance: United States, 2012.* MMWR 2012, 61(SS-4), 1–162.

Centerwall, B. S. (1992). Television and violence: The scale of the problem and where to go from here. *Journal of the American Medical Association, 267,* 22–25.

Children's Defense Fund. (2012). *Protect children, not guns 2012.* http://www.childrensdefense.org/child-research-data-publications/data/protect-children-not-guns-2012.pdf

Clary, M. (2001, January 25). Defense pulls pro-wrestling into murder trial: Today a Florida jury begins to consider whether a 12-year-old was simply imitating TV heroes when he killed his playmate, 6; The boy faces life in prison. *Los Angeles Times,* pp. A1, A5.

Cline, V. B., Croft, R. G., & Courrier, S. (1973). Desensitization of children to television violence. *Journal of Personality and Social Psychology, 35,* 450–458.

Comstock, G. (1991). *Television and the American child.* San Diego, CA: Academic Press.

Comstock, G., & Powers, J. (2012). Paths from television violence to aggression: Reinterpreting the evidence. In L. J. Shrum (Ed.), *The psychology of entertainment media: Blurring the lines between entertainment and persuasion* (2nd ed., pp. 305–328). New York, NY: Routledge.

Comstock, G., & Strasburger, V. C. (1990). Deceptive appearances: Television violence and aggressive behavior. *Journal of Adolescent Health Care, 11,* 31–44.

Comstock, G., & Strasburger, V. C. (1993). Media violence: Q & A. *Adolescent Medicine: State of the Art Reviews, 4,* 495–509.

Council on Communications and Media. (2009). Media violence (policy statement). *Pediatrics, 124,* 1495–1503.

Dominick, J. R., & Greenberg, B. S. (1972). Attitudes toward violence: The interaction of television exposure, family attitudes, and social class. In G. A. Comstock & E. A. Rubinstein (Eds.), *Television and social behavior: Television and adolescent aggressiveness* (Vol. 3, pp. 314–335). Washington, DC: Government Printing Office.

Donnerstein, E., Slaby, R. G., & Eron, L. D. (1994). The mass media and youth aggression. In L. D. Eron, J. H. Gentry, & P. Schlegel (Eds.), *A reason to hope: A psychological perspective on youth & violence* (pp. 219–250). Washington, DC: American Psychological Association.

Donnerstein, E., & Smith, S. (2001). Sex in the media. In D. G. Singer & J. L. Singer (Eds.), *Handbook of children and the media* (pp. 289–307). Thousand Oaks, CA: Sage.

Drabman, R. S., & Thomas, M. H. (1974). Does media violence increase children's toleration of real-life aggression? *Developmental Psychology, 10,* 418–421.

Duke, N. N., Pettingell, S. L., McMorris, B. J., & Borowsky, I. W. (2010). Adolescent violence perpetration: Associations with multiple types of adverse childhood experiences. *Pediatrics, 125,* e778–e786.

Eron, L. D. (1997). The development of antisocial behavior from a learning perspective. In D. M. Stoff, J. Breiling, & J. D. Maser (Eds.), *Handbook of antisocial behavior* (pp. 140–147). New York, NY: Wiley & Sons.

Farr, J. (2012, July 21). When movie violence helps inspire real violence, isn't it time to tone it down? *Huffington Post.* http://www.huffingtonpost.com/john-farr/when-movie-violence-inspi_b_1692208.html

Ferguson, C. J., & Kilburn, J. (2009). The public health risks of media violence: A meta-analytic review. *The Journal of Pediatrics, 154*(5), 759–763.

Ferguson, C. J., & Kilburn, J. (2010). Much ado about nothing: The misestimation and overinterpretation of violent video game effects in Eastern and Western nations: Comment on Anderson et al. (2010). *Psychological Bulletin, 136*(2), 174–178.

Feshbach, S. (1955). The drive-reducing function of fantasy behavior. *Journal of Abnormal and Social Psychology, 50*, 3–11.

Feshbach, S. (1961). The stimulating versus cathartic effects of a vicarious aggressive activity. *Journal of Abnormal and Social Psychology, 63*, 381–385.

Fowles, J. (1999). *The case for television violence*. Thousand Oaks, CA: Sage.

Freedman, J. L. (1984). Effect of television violence on aggressiveness. *Psychological Bulletin, 96*, 227–246.

Freedman, J. L. (1986). Television violence and aggression: A rejoinder. *Psychological Bulletin, 100*, 372–373.

Garbarino, J. (2001). Lost boys: Why our sons turn violent and how we can save them. *Smith College Studies in Social Work, 71*, 167–181.

Geen, R. G. (1994). Television and aggression: Recent developments in research and theory. In D. Zillmann, J. Bryant, & A. C. Huston (Eds.), *Media, children, and the family: Social, scientific, psychodynamic, and clinical perspectives* (pp. 151–162). Hillsdale, NJ: Lawrence Erlbaum.

Gentile, D. A. (2013). Catharsis and media violence: A conceptual analysis. *Societies, 3*, 491–510. doi:10.3390/soc3040491

Gentile, D. A., & Bushman, B. J. (2012). Reassessing media violence effects using a risk and resilience approach to understanding aggression. *Psychology of Popular Media Culture, 1*, 138–151.

Gentile, D. A., Coyne, S., & Walsh, D. A. (2011). Media violence, physical aggression, and relational aggression in school age children: A short-term longitudinal study. *Aggressive Behavior, 37*, 193–206.

Gerbner, G., Gross, L., Morgan, M., & Signorielli, N. (1980). The "mainstreaming" of America: Violence profile no. 11. *Journal of Communication, 30*(3), 10–29.

Gerbner, G., Gross, L., Morgan, M., & Signorielli, N. (1994). Growing up with television: The cultivation perspective. In J. Bryant & D. Zillmann (Eds.), *Media effects: Advances in theory and research* (pp. 17–41). Hillsdale, NJ: Lawrence Erlbaum.

Glascock, J. (2008). Direct and indirect aggression on prime-time network television. *Journal of Broadcasting and Electronic Media, 52*, 268–281.

Grossman, D., & DeGaetano, G. (1999). *Stop teaching our kids to kill: A call to action against TV, movie and video game violence*. New York, NY: Crown.

Gunter, B. (2008). Media violence: Is there a case for causality? *American Behavioral Scientist, 51*(8), 1061–1122.

Hanratty, M. A., O'Neal, E., & Sulzer, J. L. (1972). Effect of frustration upon imitation of aggression. *Journal of Personality & Social Psychology, 21*, 30–34.

Harrison, K., & Cantor, J. (1999). Tales from the screen: Enduring fright reactions to scary media. *Media Psychology, 1*, 97–116.

Hawkins, R. P., & Pingree, S. (1980). Some processes in the cultivation effect. *Communication Research, 7*, 193–226.

Hearold, S. (1986). A synthesis of 1045 effects of television on social behavior. In G. Comstock (Ed.), *Public communication and behavior* (Vol. 1, pp. 65–133). New York, NY: Academic Press.

Hogben, M. (1998). Factors moderating the effect of televised aggression on viewer behavior. *Communication Research, 25,* 220–247.

Huesmann, L. R. (1986). Psychological processes promoting the relation between exposure to media violence and aggressive behavior by the viewer. *Journal of Social Issues, 42,* 125–139.

Huesmann, L. R. (1988). An information processing model for the development of aggression. *Aggressive Behavior, 14,* 13–24.

Huesmann, L. R. (1998). The role of social information processing and cognitive schemas in the acquisition and maintenance of habitual aggressive behavior. In R. G. Geen & E. Donnerstein (Eds.), *Human aggression: Theories, research, and implications for social policy* (pp. 1120–1134). San Diego, CA: Academic Press.

Huesmann, L. R. (2007). The impact of electronic media violence: Scientific theory and research. *Journal of Adolescent Health, 41,* S6–S13.

Huesmann, L. R. (2010). Nailing the coffin shut on doubts that violent video games stimulate aggression: Comment on Anderson et al. (2010). *Psychological Bulletin, 136*(2), 179–181.

Huesmann, L. R., Dubow, E. F., & Yang, G. (2013). Why it is hard to believe that media violence causes aggression? In K. E. Dill (Ed.), *The Oxford handbook of media psychology* (pp. 159–171). New York, NY: Oxford University Press.

Huesmann, L. R., & Eron, L. D. (1986). *Television and the aggressive child: A cross national comparison.* Hillsdale, NJ: Lawrence Erlbaum.

Huesmann, L. R., Eron, L. D., Klein, R., Brice, P., & Fischer, P. (1983). Mitigating the imitation of aggressive behaviors by changing children's attitudes about media violence. *Journal of Personality & Social Psychology, 44,* 899–910.

Huesmann, L. R., Lagerspetz, K., & Eron, L. D. (1984). Intervening variables in the TV violence-aggression relation: Evidence from two countries. *Developmental Psychology, 20,* 746–775.

Huesmann, L. R., & Miller, L. S. (1994). Long-term effects of repeated exposure to media violence in childhood. In L. R. Huesmann (Ed.), *Aggressive behavior: Current perspectives.* (pp. 153–186). New York, NY: Plenum Press.

Huesmann, L. R., Moise-Titus, J., Podolski, C., & Eron, L. D. (2003). Longitudinal relations between children's exposure to TV violence and their aggressive and violent behavior in young adulthood: 1977–1992. *Developmental Psychology, 39,* 2001–2021.

Hughes, M. (1980). The fruits of cultivation analysis: A re-examination of television in fear of victimization, alienation, and approval of violence. *Public Opinion Quarterly, 44,* 287–302.

Huston, A. C., Donnerstein, E., Fairchild, H. H., Feshbach, N. D., Katz, P. A., Murray, J. P., Rubinstein, E. A., Wilcox, B. L., & Zuckerman, D. (1992). *Big world, small screen: The role of television in American society.* Lincoln, NE: University of Nebraska Press.

Jeong, S., Cho, H., & Hwang, Y. (2012). Media literacy interventions: A meta-analytic review. *Journal of Communication, 62*(3), 454–472.

Jo, E., & Berkowitz, L. (1994). A priming effect analysis of media influences: An update. In J. Bryant & D. Zillmann (Eds.), *Media effects: Advances in theory and research* (pp. 43–60). Hillsdale, NJ: Lawrence Erlbaum.

Johnson, J. G., Cohen, P., Smailes, E. M., Kasen, S., & Brook, J. S. (2002). Television viewing and aggressive behavior during adolescence and adulthood. *Science, 295*, 2468–2471.

Joy, L. A., Kimball, M. M., & Zabrack, M. L. (1986). Television and children's aggressive behavior. In T. M. Williams (Ed.), *The impact of television: A natural experiment in three communities* (pp. 303–360). New York, NY: Academic Press.

Krahe, B., Moller, I., Huesmann, L. R., Kirwil, L., Felber, J., & Berger, A. (2011). Desensitization to media violence: Links with habitual media violence exposure, aggressive cognitions, and aggressive behavior. *Journal of Personality and Social Psychology, 100*, 630–646.

Kuntsche, E., Pickett, W., Overpeck, M., Craig, W., Boyce, W., & deMatos, M. G. (2006). Television viewing and forms of bullying among adolescents from eight countries. *Journal of Adolescent Health, 39*, 908–915.

Lazarus, R. S., & Alfert, E. (1964). Short-circuiting of threat by experimentally altering cognitive appraisal. *Journal of Abnormal & Social Psychology, 69*, 195–205.

Lee, C., Cronley, C., White, H. R., Mun, E-Y., Stouthamer-Loeber, M., & Loeber R. (2012). Racial differences in the consequences of childhood maltreatment for adolescent and young adult depression, heavy drinking, and violence. *Journal of Adolescent Health, 50*, 443–449.

Lefkowitz, M. M., Eron, L. D., Walder, L. O., & Huesmann, L. R. (1972). Television violence and child aggression: A follow-up study. In G. A. Comstock & E. A. Rubinstein (Eds.), *Television and social behavior: Television and adolescent aggressiveness* (Vol. 3, pp. 33–135). Washington, DC: Government Printing Office.

Liebert, R. M., & Sprafkin, J. (1988). *The early window: Effects of television on children and youth* (3rd ed.). Elmsford, NY: Pergamon Press.

Linder, J., & Lyle, K. (2011). A content analysis of indirect, verbal, and physical aggression in television programs popular among school-aged girls. *American Journal of Media Psychology, 4*, 24–42.

Linz, D., Donnerstein, E., & Penrod, S. (1984). The effects of multiple exposures to filmed violence against women. *Journal of Communication, 34*(3), 130–147.

Liss, M. B., Reinhardt, L. C., & Fredriksen, S. (1983). TV heroes: The impact of rhetoric and deeds. *Journal of Applied Developmental Psychology, 4*, 175–187.

Losel, F., & Farrington, D. P. (2012). Direct protective and buffering protective factors in the development of youth violence. *American Journal of Preventive Medicine, 43*(Suppl. 1), S8–S23.

Mares, M.-L., & Woodard, E. H. (2001). Prosocial effects on children's social interactions. In D. G. Singer & J. L. Singer (Eds.), *Handbook of children and the media* (pp. 183–205). Thousand Oaks, CA: Sage.

Martins, N., & Wilson, B. J. (2012a). Mean on the screen: Social aggression in programs popular with children. *Journal of Communication, 62*, 991–1009.

Martins, N., & Wilson, B. J. (2012b). Social aggression on television and its relationship to children's aggression in the classroom. *Human Communication Research, 38*, 48–71.

McIntyre, J. J., & Teevan, J. J., Jr. (1972). Television violence and deviant behavior. In G. A. Comstock & E. A. Rubinstein (Eds.), *Television and social behavior: Television and adolescent aggressiveness* (Vol. 3, pp. 173–238). Washington, DC: Government Printing Office.

McKenna, M. W., & Ossoff, E. P. (1998). Age differences in children's comprehension of a popular television program. *Child Study Journal, 28*, 53–68.

McLeod, J. M., Atkin, C. K., & Chaffee, S. H. (1972). Adolescents, parents, and television use: Adolescent self-report measures from Maryland and Wisconsin samples. In G. A. Comstock & E. A. Rubinstein (Eds.), *Television and social behavior: Television and adolescent aggressiveness* (Vol. 3, pp. 173–238). Washington, DC: Government Printing Office.

Media Violence Commission, International Society for Research on Aggression (ISRA). (2012). *Aggressive Behavior, 38*, 335–341.

Molitor, F., & Hirsch, K. W. (1994). Children's toleration of real-life aggression after exposure to media violence: A replication of the Drabman and Thomas studies. *Child Study Journal, 24*, 191–207.

Morgan, M., & Shanahan, J. (1996). Two decades of cultivation analysis: An appraisal and a meta-analysis. In B. Burleson (Ed.), *Communication yearbook* (Vol. 20, pp. 1–45). Thousand Oaks, CA: Sage.

Morgan, M., Shanahan, J., & Signorielli, N. (2009). Growing up with television: Cultivation processes. In J. Bryant & M. Oliver (Eds.), *Media effects: Advances in theory and research* (3rd ed., pp. 34–49). Hillsdale, NJ: Erlbaum.

Mullin, C. R., & Linz, D. (1995). Desensitization and resensitization to violence against women: Effects of exposure to sexually violent films on judgments of domestic violence victims. *Journal of Personality & Social Psychology, 69*, 449–459.

Naisbitt, J., Naisbitt, N., & Philips, D. (1999). *High tech, high touch: Technology and our search for meaning.* New York, NY: Broadway.

Nathanson, A. I. (1999). Identifying and explaining the relationship between parental mediation and children's aggression. *Communication Research, 26*, 124–143.

Nielsen Company. (2012). Global report: multi-screen media usage, May 15, 2012. http://blog.nielsen.com/nielsenwire/global/global-report-multi-screen-media-usage/

Ogles, R. M., & Hoffner, C. (1987). Film violence and perceptions of crime: The cultivation effect. In M. L. Mclaughlin (Ed.), *Communication yearbook* (Vol. 10, pp. 384–394). Newbury Park, CA: Sage.

O'Keefe, D. J. (2002). *Persuasion: Theory and research* (2nd ed.). Thousand Oaks, CA: Sage.

Ostrov, J. M., Gentile, D. A., & Crick, N. R. (2006). Media exposure, aggression and prosocial behavior during early childhood: A longitudinal study. *Social Development, 15*, 612–627.

Ostrov, J. M., & Godleski, S. A. (2010). Toward an integrated gender-linked model of aggression subtypes in early and middle childhood. *Psychological Review, 117*(1), 233–242.

Otto, M. W., Henin, A., Hirshfeld-Becker, D. R., Pollack, M. H., Biederman, J., & Rosenbaum, J. F. (2007). Posttraumatic stress disorder symptoms following media exposure to tragic events: Impact of 9/11 on children at risk for anxiety disorders. *Journal of Anxiety Disorders, 21*, 888–902.

Paik, H. J., & Comstock, G. (1994). The effects of television violence on antisocial behavior: A meta-analysis. *Communication Research, 21*, 516–546.

Perloff, R. M. (2009). Mass media, social perception, and the third-person effect. In J. Bryant & M. B. Oliver (Eds.), *Media effects: Advances in theory and research* (pp. 252–268). New York, NY: Routledge.

Plagens, P., Miller, M., Foote, D., & Yoffe, E. (1991, April 1). Violence in our culture. *Newsweek, 117* (U.S. ed.), 46–52.

Potter, W. J. (1993). Cultivation theory and research: A conceptual critique. *Human Communication Research, 19*, 564–601.

Potter, W. J. (1999). *On media violence.* Thousand Oaks, CA: Sage.

Purugganan, O. H., Stein, R. E. K., Silver, E. J., & Benenson, B. S. (2000). Exposure to violence among urban school-aged children: Is it only on television? *Pediatrics, 106*, 949–953.

Ramirez, J. M. (2003). Hormones and aggression in childhood and adolescence. *Aggression and Violent Behavior, 8*, 621–644.

Riddle, K., Cantor, J., Byrne, S., & Moyer-Gusé, E. (2012). "People killing people on the news": Young children's descriptions of frightening television news content. *Communication Quarterly, 60*, 278–294.

Rideout, V. J., Foehr, U. G., & Roberts, D. F. (2010). *Generation M2: Media in the lives of 8- to 18-year-olds.* Menlo Park, CA: Kaiser Family Foundation.

Robertson, L. A., McAnally, H. M., & Hancox, R. J. (2013). Childhood and adolescent television viewing and antisocial behavior in early adulthood. *Pediatrics, 131*, 439–446.

Robinson, J. P., & Bachman, J. G. (1972). Television viewing habits and aggression. In G. A. Comstock & E. A. Rubinstein (Eds.), *Television and social behavior: Television and adolescent aggressiveness* (Vol. 3, pp. 173–238). Washington, DC: Government Printing Office.

Rothenberg, M. B. (1975). Effect of television violence on children and youth. *Journal of the American Medical Association, 234*, 1043–1046.

Shrum, L. J. (2001). Processing strategy moderates the cultivation effect. *Human Communication Research, 27*, 94–120.

Shrum, L. J. (2009). Media consumption and perceptions of social reality: Effects and underlying processes. In J. Bryant & M. Oliver (eds.), *Media effects: Advances in theory and research* (3rd ed., pp. 50–73). Hillsdale, NJ: Erlbaum.

Singer, J. L., & Singer, D. G. (1981). *Television, imagination, and aggression: A study of preschoolers' play.* Hillsdale, NJ: Lawrence Erlbaum.

Singer, J. L., Singer, D. G., & Rapaczynski, W. (1984). Family patterns and television viewing as predictors of children's beliefs and aggression. *Journal of Communication, 34*(2), 73–89.

Singer, M. I., Miller, D. B., Guo, S., Flannery, D. J., Frierson, T., & Slovak, K. (1999). Contributors to violent behavior among elementary and middle school children. *Pediatrics, 104*, 878–884.

Smith, S. L., Boyson, A. R., Pieper, K. M., & Wilson, B. J. (2001, May). Brandishing guns on American television: How often do such weapons appear and in what context? Paper presented at the annual meeting of the International Communication Association, Washington, DC.

Smith, S. L., Wilson, B., Colvin, C., Kunkel, D., Potter, J., Linz. D., & Donnerstein, E. (1998a). Violence in children's television programming: assessing the risks.

Paper presented at the meeting of the International Communication Association, 1998.

Smith, S. L., Wilson, B. J., Kunkel, D., Linz, D., Potter, W. J., Colvin, C., & Donnerstein, E. (1998b). Violence in television programming overall: University of California, Santa Barbara study. In *National television violence study* (Vol. 3, pp. 5–200). Newbury Park, CA: Sage.

Spieker, S. J., Campbell, S. B., Vandergrift, N., Pierce, K. M., Caufmann, E., Susman, E. J., & Roisman, G. I. (2012). Relational aggression in middle childhood: Predictors and adolescent outcomes. *Social Development, 21*(2), 354–375.

Steuer, F. B., Applefield, J. M., & Smith, R. (1971). Televised aggression and interpersonal aggression of preschool children. *Journal of Experimental Child Psychology, 11*, 442–447.

Strasburger, V. C., & Grossman, D. (2001). How many more Columbines? What can pediatricians do about school and media violence? *Pediatric Annals, 30*, 87–94.

Strasburger, V. C., Jordan, A. B., & Donnerstein, E. (2012). Children, adolescents, and the media: health effects. *Pediatric Clinics of North America, 59*, 533–587.

Strasburger, V. C., Wilson, B. J., & Jordan, A. B. (2014). *Children, adolescents, and the media* (3rd ed.). Los Angeles, CA: Sage.

Thomas, M. H., & Drabman, R. S. (1975). Toleration of real-life aggression as a function of exposure to televised violence and age of subject. *Merrill-Palmer Quarterly, 21*, 227–232.

Thomas, M. H., Horton, R. W., Lippincott, E. C., & Drabman, R. S. (1977). Desensitization to portrayals of real-life aggression as a function of exposure to television violence. *Journal of Personality & Social Psychology, 35*, 450–458.

Thomson, J. D. S. (2004). A murderous legacy: Coloured homicide trends in South Africa. *South Africa Crime Quarterly, 7*, 9–14.

U.S. Department of Justice. (2013). *Juvenile arrests 2011*. Available at www.ojjdp.gov

Williams, T. B. (Ed.). (1986). *The impact of television: A natural experiment in three communities*. New York, NY: Academic Press.

Wilson, B. J., Kunkel, D., Linz, D., Potter, W. J., Donnerstein, E., Smith, S. L., Blumenthal, E., & Berry, M. (1998). Violence in television programming overall: University of California, Santa Barbara study. In *National television violence study* (Vol. 2, pp. 3–204). Thousand Oaks, CA: Sage.

Wilson, B. J., Kunkel, D., Linz, D., Potter, W. J., Donnerstein, E., Smith, S. L., Blumenthal, E., & Gray, T. (1997). Violence in television programming overall: University of California, Santa Barbara study. In *National television violence study* (Vol. 1, pp. 3–268). Thousand Oaks, CA: Sage.

Wilson, B. J., Linz, D., Federman, J., Smith, S., Paul, B., Nathanson, A., Donnerstein, E., & Lingsweiler, R. (1999). *The choices and consequences evaluation: A study of Court TV's anti-violence curriculum*. Santa Barbara, CA: Center for Communication and Social Policy, University of California.

Wilson, B. J., Smith, S. L., Potter, W. J., Kunkel, D., Linz, D., Colvin, C. M., & Donnerstein, E. (2002). Violence in children's television programming: Assessing the risks. *Journal of Communication, 52*(1), 5–35.

Wood, W., Wong, F., & Chachere, J. G. (1991). Effects of media violence on viewers' aggression in unconstrained social interaction. *Psychological Bulletin, 109*, 371–383.

World Health Organization. (2002). *World report on violence and health*. Geneva, CH: WHO.

Zillmann, D. (1971). Excitation transfer in communication-mediated aggressive behavior. *Journal of Experimental Social Psychology*, 7, 419–434.

Zillmann, D. (1991). Television viewing and physiological arousal. In J. Bryant & D. Zillmann (Eds.), *Responding to the screen: Reception and reaction processes* (pp. 103–133). Hillsdale, NJ: Lawrence Erlbaum.

Zillmann, D., & Johnson, R. C. (1973). Motivated aggressiveness perpetuated by exposure to aggressive films and reduced by exposure to nonaggressive films. *Journal of Research in Personality*, 7, 261–276.

CHAPTER 6

Media and Fear in Children and Adolescents

Joanne Cantor and Karyn Riddle

When I was seven years old, I watched (although it felt like I witnessed) Friday the Thirteenth, Part 2. My family didn't have cable television or any movie channels but my friend Mark's family did. One day, just he and I watched Jason Voorhees chop up and mutilate a camp full of oversexed teenagers. I hadn't seen an R-rated movie before this gruesome experience. It blew me away. I stayed for the entirety of the film because I didn't want Mark to think I was a "wussy," and I was also morbidly fascinated by something I'd never been exposed to. After viewing the film, I had nightmares for weeks. I would even lie awake at night (with all the lights on) wondering how long it would take Jason and his twenty-inch blade to find me! (Cantor, 1998a, pp. 34–35)

The preceding quote is from a first-person account by a college student,[1] and it is typical of responses that children and adolescents commonly experience from watching media violence. Yet media-induced fear and its attendant lingering effects have not received nearly the public attention that the aggression-promoting effects of media violence have. This is not because it is a newly discovered problem. As early as 1917, the following observations appeared in a report of the Cinema Commission of Inquiry established by the National Council of Public Morals in London, England:

My chief objection to the films is that they make children, whose thoughts should be happy and wholesome, familiar with ideas of death by exhibiting shootings, stabbings, and the like. Nor are these death scenes merely brief incidents in the stories, for where a character is represented to be mortally wounded[;] the story pauses while the children are shown an enlarged view of the victim's features during the death and agony. Owing to this deliberate emphasis of the repulsiveness of such situations, it is difficult to see how the child's nerves can maintain their tone; we should look for a want of balance in children subjected repeatedly to these ordeals, and thence delinquency would not be unlikely. At any rate, such exhibitions are highly objectionable for children, whether they lead to delinquency or not. (Leeson, 1917, p. 187)

By the 1930s in the United States, researchers had begun to look at media-induced fear systematically. Blumer (1933) reported that 93 percent of the children in a study he conducted said they had been frightened or horrified by a motion picture. Other researchers in the 1930s and 1940s also noted the prevalence of children's fright reactions to movies and to radio crime dramas (Eisenberg, 1936; Preston, 1941). But as television took hold in the 1950s and 1960s, more attention was paid to the role this new medium might be playing in the increasing levels of violence in society than to its stimulation of children's fears.

Interest in media and fear reemerged in the 1970s, as highly popular movies were becoming increasingly graphic and full of horror. For example, *The Exorcist* (1973), a supernatural thriller about the demonic possession of a young girl, was reported to be causing *even men*(!) to faint or vomit, and *Jaws* (1975), a blockbuster movie about a killer shark, reportedly ruined many vacations at the seashore. Adults were considered to be on their own, but there was increasing concern about children's responses. In the mid-1980s, the reactions of children (and angry parents) to intense scenes in *Indiana Jones and the Temple of Doom* (1984), a violent action-adventure movie, and *Gremlins* (1984), a comic horror story about adorable pets that transform into vicious killers, led the Motion Picture Association of America to add PG-13 ("Parents Strongly Cautioned") to its rating system (Zoglin, 1984).

Psychiatric case studies of acute and disabling anxiety states precipitated by movies have been reported sporadically over the years (Buzzuto, 1975; Mathai, 1983; Simons & Silveira, 1994), but researchers again began quantitatively studying fright reactions to media in the 1980s. B. R. Johnson (1980) asked a random sample of adults whether they had ever seen a motion picture that had disturbed them "a great deal." Forty percent said they had, and the median length of the reported disturbance was three days. Respondents also reported on the type, intensity, and duration of symptoms such as nervousness, depression, fear of specific things, and recurring thoughts and images. Based on these reports, Johnson judged that 48 percent of these respondents (19% of the total sample) had experienced what he termed a "significant stress reaction" for at least two days as the result of watching a movie. Johnson argued,

It is one thing to walk away from a frightening or disturbing event with mild residue of the images and quite another thing to ruminate about it, feel anxious or depressed for days, and/or to avoid anything that might create the same unpleasant experience. (Johnson, 1980, p. 786)

Research continues to show that media induced fears are a problem for a sizable majority of children. In the mid-1980s, Barbara J. Wilson and her associates (Wilson, Hoffner, & Cantor, 1987) surveyed preschool and elementary school children in Wisconsin and Pennsylvania and noted that 75 percent of the children questioned reported having been scared by something they had seen on TV or in a movie. Gentile and Walsh (2002) conducted the first U.S. random national survey on this topic and noted that 62 percent of parents reported that their child had become scared by something he or she had seen on television or in a movie. Korhonen and Lahikainen (2008) and Paavonen, Pennonen, Roine, Valkonen, and Lahikainen (2006) queried two random samples of parents of children ages five to six years in Finland and reported that 75 to 80 percent of the children had experienced fright reactions from television. When Cantor, Byrne, Moyer-Gusé, and Riddle (2010) interviewed children in two elementary schools in California, 76 percent of the children reported that a television program or movie had frightened them.

Correlational studies have shown that television viewing is related to the occurrence of anxiety and other negative affective states. A survey of elementary and middle school children in Ohio reported that the more television a child watched, the more likely he or she was to report the symptoms of anxiety, depression, and posttraumatic stress (Singer, Slovak, Frierson, & York, 1998). Similarly, Paavonen, Roine, Pennonen, and Lahikainen (2009) also reported that amount of TV viewing was correlated with TV-induced fears.

There is more evidence of a relationship between television viewing and sleep disturbances. A survey of elementary school children in Rhode Island reported that the more television a child watched (especially at bedtime), the higher the rate of reported sleep disturbances, such as nightmares, difficulty falling asleep, and the inability to sleep through the night (Owens, Maxim, McGuinn, Nobile, Msall, & Alario, 1999). In a diary study of a random sample of parents of three- to five-year-olds in Seattle, Garrison, Liekweg, and Christakis (2011) found that TV viewing time, evening viewing, and the viewing of violence all correlated with sleep disturbances. Although the aforementioned correlational studies could not determine cause and effect, Johnson, Cohen, Kasen, First, and Brook (2004) provided evidence that viewing promotes sleep disturbances (rather than the reverse) in a longitudinal design in which they interviewed adolescents and their mothers. In these data, not only was heavy television viewing related to later sleep problems; a reduction in television viewing led to a lessening of these problems over time.

Research involving retrospective reports by college students provides powerful evidence of the prevalence and severity of the problem of media-induced fear. Harrison and Cantor (1999) offered college students at the University of Wisconsin and the University of Michigan extra course credit for filling out a questionnaire. The initial question read as follows: "Have you ever seen a television show or movie that frightened or disturbed you so much that the emotional effect endured after the program or movie was over?" Respondents could reply "yes" or "no." If they said "no," that's all they had to do. But if they said "yes," they were required to write a paper about the experience and to fill out a three-page questionnaire. Either way, respondents received the same amount of extra credit.

In spite of the fact that the procedure made it a great deal easier to say "no" than "yes," 90 percent of the respondents said "yes," and most went on to describe intensely negative emotional experiences, similar to the one described at the beginning of this chapter. More than half of the respondents (52%) reported disturbances in eating or sleeping, 35 percent said they had become anxious about or avoided situations similar to those depicted in the program or movie, and 22 percent reported difficulty getting the images or events they had seen out of their heads. The most striking findings relate to the duration of these responses: 35 percent of the respondents said that these effects had endured a year or more and 26 percent said that these responses were still with them at the time the survey was taken. Given that the average age at exposure was 14 and the average age of the respondents was close to 21, these effects had been lingering for an average of more than 6 years. The following excerpt of one student's account from this study is typical of these enduring responses:

After the movie [Jaws], *I had nightmares for a week straight. Always the same one. I'm in a room filled with water with ducts in the walls. They would suddenly open and dozens of sharks would swim out. I felt trapped with no place to go. I would usually wake up in a sweat. Occasionally I'll still have that exact same dream. The movie didn't just affect me at night. To this day I'm afraid to go into the ocean, sometimes even a lake. I'm afraid there will be a shark even if I know deep down that's impossible.* (Cantor, 1998a, pp. 9–10)

Richard J. Harris and his associates also conducted a series of retrospective studies and reported similar results regarding the prevalence and intensity of media-induced fright reactions (Harris et al., 2000; Hoekstra, Harris, & Helmick, 1999). In these studies, intense reactions and lingering effects, such as general anxiety, "wild imagination," and fear of sleeping alone, were commonly observed. In Cantor et al.'s (2010) interviews with elementary school children, each of the following reactions was reported by more than half of those describing media-induced fears: not wanting to go to sleep, not wanting to sleep alone, having nightmares, worrying about what they saw, and not being able to stop thinking about it.

In summary, research shows that media-induced fright reactions are quite common. A substantial proportion of children experience lingering effects that disturb their sleep and interfere with a variety of normal, healthy activities.

ENTERTAINMENT IMAGES THAT FRIGHTEN

It should come as no surprise that violence or the threat of violence is the most prominent feature of television programs and movies that produce fear. In fact, it is difficult to conceive of a horror movie that does not focus on the threat of violence. As has been argued elsewhere (Cantor, 2009), fear is the natural response to a perceived physical threat, and it is reasonable to expect that viewers respond with fear to threats depicted in the media through a process of stimulus generalization (see Pavlov, 1960). In other words, events that would produce fear if encountered in the real world produce similar, although less intense reactions if encountered in the media. Two categories of real-world stimuli that typically cause fear and that are prominent in fear-evoking media are the display of dangers and injuries and the depiction of fearful or endangered people (see Cantor, 2009, for a more extensive discussion). Violent encounters and other things that are considered dangerous, such as vicious animals, natural disasters, and life-threatening diseases naturally cause fear. The sight of injuries or other people who are in danger or are fearful should also be frightening because the presence of others who are injured or in danger often suggests that those in the vicinity are in danger as well. Even when viewers know they are not in immediate danger, the mediated depiction of these images is often frightening.

A third category of fear-evoking stimuli has been termed *distortions of natural forms* (see Cantor, 2009). These consist of injuries and mutilations as well as bodily distortions that occur in nature, as in dwarves, giants, hunchbacks, and mutants. Injured and deformed realistic characters are prominent in scary movies and television shows, as are weird-looking supernatural and fantasy creatures, like monsters, witches, vampires, and ghosts. Often in television programs and movies, distorted creatures are depicted as evil and violent. However, as will be seen in the next section, even when such creatures are kind and benevolent, they often produce fear anyway, especially in young children. It is possible that certain types of physical distortions implicitly convey a sense of danger or impending threat (Cantor, 1998a).

It should be noted here that the types of images and events that induce fright reactions are in no way limited to horror movies or adult-oriented fare. Violence, conflict, peril, frightened protagonists, and distortions are found in entertainment fare of all kinds. Indeed, in the Cantor et al. (2010) study in which elementary school children were interviewed, 36 percent of the movies cited as causing fear had been given G or PG ratings by the Motion Picture Association of America, suggesting that they were relatively innocuous. A variety of studies have documented that MPAA ratings, and media ratings in general, inadequately warn parents of potentially disturbing or violent content (Cantor, 1998b; Linder & Gentile, 2009; Thompson & Haninger, 2001). Moreover, none of the current rating systems explicitly focuses on scary themes, which, as will be seen in the next section, may or may not include the explicit depiction of violence.

Developmental Differences in Fright Responses to Entertainment

What frightens a particular child is no doubt a function of many individual factors, including temperament, real-world experience, and concurrent events in the child's life. In addition to these idiosyncratic factors, research has determined that a viewer's chronological age is an important determinant of the source and intensity of media-induced fears.

Children of different ages tend to fear different things. According to a variety of studies of fears in general, children up to eight years of age are frightened primarily by animals, the dark, supernatural beings—such as ghosts, monsters, and witches—and by anything that looks strange or moves suddenly. The fears of 9- to 12-year-olds are more often related to personal injury and physical destruction and the injury and death of family members. Adolescents continue to fear personal injury and physical destruction, but school fears and social fears arise at this age, as do fears regarding political, economic, and global issues (see Cantor, Wilson, & Hoffner, 1986, for a review).

A large body of research has examined the types of mass media stimuli and events that frighten children at different ages. Experiments and surveys have been conducted to test expectations based on theories and findings in cognitive development. The experiments have the advantage of testing rigorously controlled variations in program content and viewing conditions, using a combination of self-reports, physiological responses, the coding of facial expressions of emotion, and behavioral measures. For ethical reasons, only small excerpts of relatively mild television shows and movies are used in experiments. In contrast, the surveys investigate the responses of children who have been exposed to a particular mass media offering in their natural environment, without any researcher intervention. Although less tightly controlled, the surveys permit the study of responses to much more intensely frightening media fare and can involve explorations of effects of longer duration.

The findings regarding the media stimuli that frighten children at different ages are consistent with observed changes in children's fears in general. This section summarizes broad generalizations and supportive findings (see Table 6.1).

The Importance of Appearance

Research on cognitive development indicates that, in general, very young children react to stimuli predominantly in terms of their perceptible characteristics, and with increasing maturity they respond more and more to the conceptual aspects of stimuli (see Flavell, 1963; Melkman, Tversky, & Baratz, 1981). Research findings support the generalization that the impact of appearance in frightening media decreases as the child's age increases. In other words, preschool children (up to the age of about 5 years) are more likely to be frightened by something that looks scary but is actually harmless than by something that looks attractive but is actually harmful; for older elementary school children (approximately 9 to 11 years), appearance carries much less weight, relative to the behavior or destructive potential of a character, animal, or object.

Table 6.1
Developmental Differences in the Media Stimuli That Frighten Children

Approximate Age Group Characteristics	Typically Frightening Stimuli
Up to 8 Years: Perceptual dependence; inability to fully grasp fantasy-reality distinction	• Threatening visual images, real or not, including vicious animals, and grotesque, mutilated, or deformed characters (can be cartoon or live-action images) • Physical transformations of characters • Natural disasters, shown vividly • Visual images of devastation or traumatized victims • Sudden loud or eerie noises
8–12 Years: Grasp of fantasy-reality distinction; limited capabilities for abstract thought	• Realistic threats and dangers, especially things that can happen to children • Violence or the threat of violence • Victimization of children
13 Years and Older: Grasp of fantasy-reality distinction and abstract reasoning; awareness of world issues; ambiguity about supernatural forces	• Realistic physical harm or threats of intense harm • Molestation, sexual assault, and stalking • Threats from aliens, demonic possession, or global threats

This generalization is supported by a survey conducted in 1981 (Cantor & Sparks, 1984), in which parents were asked to name the programs and movies that had frightened their children the most. Parents of preschool children most often mentioned offerings with grotesque-looking characters, such as the television series *The Incredible Hulk* and the feature film *The Wizard of Oz*; parents of older elementary school children more often mentioned programs or movies (like *The Amityville Horror*) that involved threats without a strong visual component, and that required imagination to comprehend. Sparks (1986) replicated this study, using children's self-reports rather than parents' observations, and obtained similar findings. Both surveys included controls for possible differences in exposure patterns in the different age groups.

Another study supporting a similar conclusion explored children's reactions to excerpts from *The Incredible Hulk* (Sparks & Cantor, 1986). Although this program, about a man who transforms into a grotesque superhero to perform good deeds, was not intended to be scary, Cantor and Sparks's (1984) survey reported that it was named by 40 percent of the parents of preschoolers as a show that had scared their child. When children were shown a shortened episode of the *Hulk* program and were asked how they had felt during different scenes, preschool children reported the most fear after the attractive, mild-mannered hero had transformed into the monstrous-looking Hulk. Older elementary school children, in contrast, reported the least fear at this time, because they understood that the Hulk was really the benevolent hero in another physical form, and that he was using his superhuman powers to rescue a character who was in danger. Preschool children's unexpectedly intense reactions to this program seem to have been partially due to their over-response to the visual transformation into the Hulk character and to their inability to look beyond his appearance and appreciate his benevolent behavior.

Another study (Hoffner & Cantor, 1985) tested the effect of appearance more directly by creating a story in four versions, so that a major character was either attractive and grandmotherly looking or ugly and grotesque. The character's appearance was factorially varied with her behavior—she was depicted as behaving either kindly or cruelly. Figure 6.1 illustrates this manipulation, using one frame from the same moment in each of the four versions. In judging how nice or mean the character was and in predicting what she would do in the subsequent scene, preschool children were more influenced than older children (6 to 7 and 9 to 10 years) by the character's looks and less influenced by her kind or cruel behavior. As the age of the child increased, the character's looks became less important and her behavior carried increasing weight. A follow-up experiment revealed that in the absence of information about the character's behavior, children in all age groups engaged in physical appearance stereotyping, that is, they thought that the ugly woman would be mean and the attractive woman would be nice.

Harrison and Cantor's (1999) retrospective study of fright responses to media also provided evidence of the diminishing influence of appearance. When students' descriptions of the program or movie that had frightened them were categorized as to whether they involved immediately perceptible stimuli (e.g., monstrous-looking characters, eerie noises), the percentage of respondents whose described scene fell into this category declined as the student's age at the time of the incident increased.

Responses to fantasy content

The data on trends in children's fears in general suggest that very young children are more likely than older children and adolescents to fear things that are not real, in the sense that their occurrence in the real world is impossible (e.g., monsters). The development of more "mature" fears seems to require the acquisition of knowledge regarding the objective dangers posed by different situations. One important component of this knowledge includes an understanding of the distinction between reality and fantasy, a competence that develops only gradually throughout childhood (see Flavell, 1963; Kelly, 1981; Morison & Gardner, 1978).

Research shows that as children mature cognitively, they become less responsive to fantastic dangers and more responsive to realistic threats

Figure 6.1
Illustration of Manipulation of Character's Appearance and Behavior;
Conditions Are (Clockwise from Upper Left): Attractive Kind, Ugly Kind,
Ugly Cruel, Attractive Cruel

Source: Reprinted from C. Hoffner & J. Cantor (1985), Developmental Differences in Responses to a Television Character's Appearance and Behavior, *Developmental Psychology*, 21, 1065–1074; copyright American Psychological Association.

depicted in the media. In Cantor and Sparks's (1984) survey of what had frightened children, the parents' tendency to name fantasy offerings, depicting events that could not possibly occur in the real world, decreased as the child's age increased, and the tendency to mention fictional offerings, depicting events that could possibly occur, increased. Sparks (1986) replicated these findings using children's self-reports. Further support comes from a survey of parents of children in kindergarten and second, fourth, and sixth grades in Wisconsin (Cantor & Nathanson, 1996). This study reported that the percentage of children frightened by fantasy programs decreased as the child's grade increased. Valkenburg, Cantor, and Peeters (2000), in a random survey of children in the Netherlands, also found a decrease between the ages of 7 and 12 in fright responses to fantasy content. The following anecdote is typical of young children's responses to blatantly unrealistic content:

An example that I will never forget is when I watched the movie Pinocchio. *I saw this movie with my mother when I was about four or five years old. I really thought that what was happening in the movie was real. In the movie, if a child misbehaved, he or she was turned into a donkey. Also, if a child lied, their nose would grow. I really believed that this would happen to me if I was bad. I remember being extremely scared even a few weeks after I had seen the movie because I thought that the same thing would happen to me if I misbehaved.* (Cantor, 1998a, p. 89)

Although fright reactions to overtly fantastic content decline with age, retrospective reports reveal that a certain type of fantasy stories—those that involve the supernatural—retain their ability to frighten viewers through the teen years and beyond (see Cantor, 1998a). Supernatural themes occupy an ambiguous border between fantasy and realistic fiction. Even when children mature enough to become aware of the difference between what is real and what is make-believe, they often have ambivalent feelings about the veracity of stories involving demonic possession (e.g., *The Exorcist*) or attacks by alien invaders or individuals with supernatural powers (e.g., *Alien, A Nightmare on Elm Street, The Blair Witch Project*). The mass media often amplify this ambiguity by featuring purportedly true instances of supernatural forces and demonic possession. The following student's experience illustrates this process:

The film I viewed was The Exorcist. *It contained graphic scenes of a young girl possessed by the devil. I was approximately twelve years old at the time and was in a slumber-party situation. I vividly remember the stress this film caused me. I was not only extremely afraid of the devil and evil, but I became obsessed with the possibility of becoming possessed myself. To make matters worse, later on in the same week I came home from school and turned on some afternoon talk show with the subject matter consisting of "real" stories of "real" people who were at one time possessed. That program and the movie were enough to keep me from sleeping for two nights straight and finally when I did fall asleep I had terrible nightmares. I slept with my parents for the next few weeks.* (Cantor, 1998a, pp. 109–110)

Responses to abstract threats

Theories and findings in cognitive development show that the ability to think abstractly emerges relatively late in cognitive development (e.g., Flavell, 1963). This generalization is consistent with the general sources of children's fears, cited earlier. Similarly, as children mature, they become frightened by media depictions involving increasingly abstract concepts.

Data supporting this generalization come from a survey of children's responses to the television movie *The Day After* (Cantor et al., 1986). Although many people were concerned about young children's reactions to this movie, which depicted the devastation of a Kansas community by a nuclear attack (Schofield & Pavelchak, 1985), developmental considerations led to the prediction that the youngest children would be the least affected by it. In a random telephone survey of parents conducted the night after the broadcast of this movie, children under 12 were reportedly much less disturbed by the film than were teenagers, and parents were the most disturbed. The very youngest children were the least frightened. The findings seem to be due to the fact that the emotional impact of the film comes from the contemplation of the potential annihilation of the earth as we know it, an abstract concept that is beyond the grasp of the young child. The visual depictions of injury in the movie were quite mild compared to the enormity of the consequences implied by the plot.

FRIGHT RESPONSES TO NEWS COVERAGE

Although most early studies of media and children's fear focused on entertainment media, studies have increasingly begun to target children's emotional responses to news stories. Children and adolescents do, in fact, see the news, and they often experience fright reactions in response to what they see. Riddle and colleagues (Riddle, Cantor, Byrne, & Moyer-Gusé, 2012), for example, asked elementary school children in California if they "ever see the news on TV." Out of all the children interviewed, 84 percent answered in the affirmative. Furthermore, 42 percent of children who reported watching the news indicated that they had seen something that made them scared. Smith and Moyer-Gusé (2006) surveyed parents in Michigan who had children ages 5 to 17, and 50 percent of them reported that their child had been concerned, frightened, or upset due to news coverage of the second Iraq War. In a survey of Dutch children, 87 percent of 9- to 12-year-olds and 51 percent of 7- to 8-year-olds reported watching the adult news (Walma van der Molen, Valkenburg, & Peeters, 2002). Out of the children who watched the adult news, roughly half (48%) reported having become frightened by something they saw. Thus, there is mounting evidence documenting child and adolescent exposure to the news, as well as the prevalence of fear and anxiety reactions as a result of that exposure (see also Cantor, Mares, & Oliver, 1993; Cantor & Nathanson, 1996; Smith & Wilson, 2002).

Perhaps not surprisingly, heavy news exposure increases the likelihood and intensity of children's fright reactions. In the survey by Smith and Moyer-Gusé (2006), for example, children who watched more news reports of the second Iraq War were more likely to be concerned about their own personal safety. In a study conducted in the Netherlands, the degree to which children (8 to 12 years old) followed the news coverage of the brutal assassination of Theo van Gogh, a prominent activist and film director, positively predicted their feelings of fright, worry, anger, and sadness over his death (Buijzen, Walma van der Molen, & Sondij, 2007). Additional studies of children and adolescents suggest a link between the amount of exposure to news reports and negative emotional reactions, such as fear, worry, and even anger (De Cock, 2012; Wilson, Martins, & Marske, 2005; Walma van der Molen & Konijn, 2007).

Children's fright reactions to some news stories are quite severe, such as the space shuttle Challenger explosion in the 1980s (Terr et al., 1999), the Oklahoma City bombing (Pfefferbaum et al., 2001), and the September 11 terrorist hijacking-murders (Otto et al., 2007; Schuster et al., 2001). For example, in a random survey of parents of children between the ages of 5 and 17 in Michigan during the week following the September 11 attacks, most of the children (87%) were said to have been exposed to news coverage of the events on that day and the days immediately afterward (Smith, Moyer, Boyson, & Pieper, 2002). Moreover, 60 percent of the children were said to have experienced fear, and 25 percent were said to exhibit "behavioral upsets" (sleep disturbances, nightmares, eating difficulties, or anxiety attacks). A study of the longer-term responses of children in New York City schools (Applied Research and Consulting et al., 2002) reported a broad range of mental health problems six months after the September 11 attacks, including agoraphobia (15%), separation anxiety (12%), and post-traumatic stress (11%). A subsequent study also documented PTSD symptoms in children in response to the attacks, especially among those who were heavy viewers of televised news reports (Otto et al., 2007).

Similarly to Harrison and Cantor's (1999) retrospective study documenting enduring fright reactions to fictional media, Riddle (2012) surveyed young adults about frightening news stories they had seen during childhood. Riddle found that 50 percent of young adults could remember a *specific* news story seen during childhood (ages 2 to 10) that had frightened, worried, or upset them. Participants were most likely to mention terrorist attacks, murders/killings, kidnappings, and natural disasters as causing fear. Out of the 50 percent of young adults who could remember a specific news event, only 14 percent reported being frightened for less than a day, whereas 39 percent reported being frightened for a full week after seeing the news report, and 16 percent indicated fear lasting two to four weeks. Furthermore, 7 percent indicated their feelings of fear and worry had continued "to this day." Almost half (48%) reported experiencing at least one kind of enduring effect due to exposure to the news story, such as ongoing concern for personal safety, sleep disturbances, altering behaviors, or obsessive thinking about the event.

Developmental Differences in Fright Reactions to News Coverage

Research shows that exposure to and fear reactions from the news generally increase with age (Cantor & Nathanson, 1996; Riddle et al., 2012; Smith & Wilson, 2002; Smith & Moyer-Gusé, 2006). For young children, who are not adept at distinguishing fantasy from reality, news reports are no more likely to be frightening than reports of things that cannot possibly happen. Young children may be less frequently frightened by the news because news stories are usually not as visually spectacular as fantasy stories. However, certain types of news stories do frighten young children, especially if they vividly display dangers, injuries, and terrorized victims. For example, Cantor and Nathanson's (1996) survey of parents reported that 58 percent of the kindergarteners who were frightened by a news report were scared by coverage of natural disasters. Among sixth graders, this proportion was only 7 percent. A survey of parents conducted by Smith and Moyer-Gusé (2006) during the second Iraq War found that younger children (5 to 8 years old) were more likely than older children (9 to 17 years old) to be frightened by visual images related to the war, such as depictions of weapons and physical harm. In interviews conducted with children themselves (Riddle et al., 2012; Smith & Wilson, 2002), younger children tended to list concrete, visual news stories such as natural disasters and accidents as causing fright reactions more often than older children. These patterns, therefore, mirror those revealed in studies of entertainment media: due to their perceptual dependence and concrete thinking, young children appear to be heavily influenced by appearances. As such, they are especially vulnerable to news reports that show destruction or gory images.

Older children, in contrast, are more likely to be concerned about their own personal safety, and they can process abstract concepts that are not necessarily tied to visual images. For example, a random survey of parents of children in public school in Madison, Wisconsin, was conducted shortly after the first Gulf War (Cantor et al., 1993). The results revealed that parents of older children were more likely than those of younger children to cite abstract, conceptual aspects of the coverage (e.g., the possibility of the conflict spreading) as causing fear reactions. Smith and Moyer-Gusé's (2006) study, conducted during the second Gulf War, revealed similar findings: Parents of children in the middle (9 to 12 years) and older (13 to 17 years) age groups were more likely than parents of younger children (5 to 8 years) to report that their child was frightened by abstract threats, such as a possible war draft and the proliferation of weapons of mass destruction.

These developmental trends extend beyond research conducted during wartime. Although violent crime is usually visual when it happens, when it is reported on television, the actual crime is rarely shown. As a result, news reports of violent crimes tend to affect older children more than younger children. Smith and Wilson's (2002) survey of elementary school–aged children, for example, found that older children (fourth to sixth grade) were more likely than younger children (kindergarten through third grade) to describe news stories about crime and violence as causing fear. Cantor and Nathanson (1996) also found that older children who were frightened by the news were more likely than younger children to be frightened by violent crime. Thus, older children appear to be more concerned than younger children about their own susceptibility to violent acts, especially when these acts are described rather than displayed.

THE ROLE OF PERSONAL RELEVANCE IN RESPONSES TO NEWS COVERAGE

In addition to these robust developmental patterns, some additional factors can contribute to children's fright reactions to the news. Some studies, for example, suggest that children, especially older children, feel more vulnerable when exposed to news stories that they perceive as being personally relevant or proximate. Smith and Wilson (2000), for example, found that older children (ages 10 to 11) were more frightened by news stories depicting local crimes than they were by crime stories that did not occur nearby. For younger children (ages 6 to 7), however, level of proximity did not affect fear reactions. In Riddle and colleagues' (2012) survey of elementary school children, many children spoke about being frightened by news stories of crimes or accidents that took place "near my old house" or "in the local area." In her study exploring young adults' memories for news stories that had disturbed them during childhood, Riddle (2012) found that news stories that were *believed* to be personally relevant were more likely to lead to fright reactions than those perceived as less relevant. The results of that study also suggest, however, that children's perceptions of what is personally relevant may not reflect reality. In open-ended essays, some of the participants admitted that as children, they had interpreted news reports as being more personally relevant or proximate than they really were. For example, one participant wrote about experiencing fear due to the 2002 Washington, D.C., sniper attacks, which were perceived to be occurring close to home. In reality, this participant lived in New York City, far from the events. Another described how news reports about inner city robberies were seen as extremely frightening, even though he lived in the suburbs. He wrote:

I was watching the news with my parents at home, and I distinctly remember being very fearful and worried that the events described on the news would happen to our family. I know that the story was about the inner city, but I do not think I was old enough at the time to acknowledge that I lived in a suburb far from the robbery itself.

Other research suggests that parents and other adults can be important sources of influence when disturbing news events occur. Wilson and colleagues (2005), for example, found that children were more likely to be frightened by kidnapping stories in the news if their parents had also been frightened by kidnapping stories. In a study conducted shortly after the September 11 terrorist attacks, Schuster and colleagues (2001) found that parents who had experienced significant stress reactions to the terrorist attacks were more likely to report that their children (ages 5 to 18) had experienced symptoms of stress. In a survey of parents in New York City with children 4 to 17 years old, Fairbrother and colleagues (Fairbrother, Stuber, Galea, Fleischman, & Pfefferbaum, 2003) found that the children were more likely to experience post-traumatic stress reactions (PTSR) after September 11 if their parents had cried in front of them.

GENDER DIFFERENCES IN FRIGHT RESPONSES TO MEDIA

Research on gender differences has explored whether females are more frightened by media than males in general, independent of the media content. There is a common stereotype that girls are more easily frightened than boys (Birnbaum & Croll, 1984; Cantor, Stutman, & Duran, 1996), and indeed that females in general are more emotional than males (e.g., Fabes & Martin, 1991; Grossman & Wood, 1993). A good deal of research would seem to support this contention with regard to responses to scary media entertainment (e.g., Harris et al, 2000; Nolan & Ryan, 2000) as well as news (e.g., Buijzen et al., 2007; De Cock, 2012; Riddle, 2012; Smith & Moyer-Gusé, 2006), although the gender differences may be weaker than they appear at first glance. Moreover, the observed differences seem to be partially attributable to socialization pressures on girls to express their fears and on boys to inhibit them.

Peck (1999) conducted a meta-analysis of the studies of media-induced fear that were produced between 1987 and 1996. Her analysis, which included 59 studies that permitted a comparison between males and females, reported a moderate gender-difference effect size ($d = 0.41$), with females exhibiting more fear than males. Females' responses were more intense than those of males for all dependent measures. However, the effect sizes were largest for self-report and behavioral measures (those that are arguably under the most conscious control) and smallest for heart rate and facial expressions. In addition, the effect size for gender differences increased with age, in line with the notion that gender-role pressures mount as children get older (e.g., Crouter, Manke, & McHale, 1995).

Peck (1999) also conducted an experiment in which male and female college students were exposed to two movie scenes from the *Nightmare on Elm Street* series, one featuring a male victim and the other featuring a female victim. She found that women's self-reports of fear were more intense than those of males, especially when the victim was female. However, when the victim was male, certain of the physiological responses (pulse amplitude and hemispheric asymmetry) suggested that men may have been experiencing more intense physiological reactions than women.

More research is needed, therefore, to explore the extent of gender differences in media-induced fear and the factors that contribute to them. However, these findings suggest that the size of the gender difference may be partially a function of social pressures to conform to gender-appropriate behavior.

STRATEGIES FOR ALLEVIATING OR PREVENTING MEDIA-INDUCED FEAR

Coping Strategies

No matter how sensitive parents are to the emotional vulnerabilities of their children or how vigilant they are about preventing their exposure to scary content, children are likely to be frightened at one time or another by what they see on television or in a movie. The choice of an effective coping strategy is not always obvious, however. Research shows that there are consistent age and gender differences in the strategies that typically work in alleviating media-induced fear. The next sections summarize the findings of this research.

Developmental Differences in the Use and Effectiveness of Coping Strategies

Developmental differences in children's information-processing abilities yield differences in the effectiveness of strategies to prevent or reduce the severity of their media-induced fears (Cantor & Wilson, 1988). The findings of research on coping strategies can be summarized as follows: in general, preschool children benefit more from "noncognitive" than from "cognitive" strategies; both cognitive and noncognitive strategies may be effective for older children, although this age group tends to prefer cognitive strategies.

Noncognitive strategies

Noncognitive strategies are those that do not involve the processing of verbal information and that appear to be relatively automatic. The most heavily tested noncognitive strategy is desensitization, or gradual exposure to threatening images in a nonthreatening context. This strategy has been shown to be effective for both preschool and older elementary school children. Studies have used prior exposure to filmed snakes, live lizards, still photographs of worms, and rubber replicas of spiders to reduce the emotional impact of frightening movie scenes involving similar creatures (Weiss, Imrich, & Wilson, 1993; Wilson, 1987, 1989a; Wilson & Cantor, 1987). In addition, fear reactions to the Hulk character in *The Incredible Hulk* were shown to be reduced by exposure to footage of Lou Ferrigno, the actor who plays the character, having his make-up applied so that he gradually took on the menacing appearance of the character (Cantor, Sparks, & Hoffner, 1988). None of these experiments revealed developmental differences in the effectiveness of desensitization.

Other noncognitive strategies involve physical activities, such as clinging to a loved one or an attachment object, having something to eat or drink, or leaving the situation and becoming involved in another activity. Although these techniques can be used by viewers of all ages, there is reason to believe they are more effective for younger than for older children. First, it has been argued that the effectiveness of such techniques is likely to diminish as the infant's tendency to grasp and suck objects for comfort decreases (Bowlby, 1973). Second, it seems likely that the effectiveness of such techniques is partially attributable to distraction, and distraction techniques should be more effective in younger children, who have greater difficulty allocating cognitive processing to two simultaneous activities (e.g., Manis, Keating, & Morison, 1980).

Children seem to be intuitively aware that physical techniques work better for younger than for older children. In a study asking children to evaluate the effectiveness of various strategies for coping with media-induced fright, pre-school children's rankings of "holding onto a blanket or a toy" and "getting something to eat or drink" were significantly higher than those of older elementary school children (Wilson, Hoffner, & Cantor, 1987). Similarly, Harrison and Cantor's (1999) retrospective study showed that the percentage of respondents who reported having used a "behavioral" (noncognitive) coping strategy to deal with their media-induced fear declined as the respondent's age at exposure to the frightening fare increased.

Another noncognitive strategy that has been shown to have more appeal and more effectiveness for younger than for older children is covering one's eyes during frightening portions of a presentation. In an experiment by Wilson (1989b), when covering their eyes was suggested as an option, younger children used this strategy more often than older children. Moreover, the suggestion of this option reduced the fear of younger children, but actually increased the fear of older children. Wilson noted that the older children may have recognized the limited effectiveness of covering their eyes (while still being exposed to the audio features of the program) and that they may have reacted by feeling *less* in control, and therefore more vulnerable, when this strategy was offered to them.

Cognitive strategies

In contrast to noncognitive strategies, cognitive strategies involve verbal information that is used to cast the threat in a different light. These strategies involve relatively complex cognitive operations, and research consistently finds such strategies to be more effective for older than for younger children.

When dealing with fantasy depictions, the most typical cognitive strategy seems to be to provide an explanation focusing on the unreality of the situation. This strategy should be especially difficult for preschool children, who do not have a full grasp of the implications of the fantasy-reality distinction. In an experiment by Cantor and Wilson (1984), older elementary school children who were told to remember that what they were seeing in *The Wizard of Oz* was not real showed less fear than their classmates who received no instructions. The same instructions did not help preschoolers, however. A later study (Wilson & Weiss, 1991) showed similar developmental differences in the effectiveness of reality-related strategies.

Children's beliefs about the effectiveness of focusing on the unreality of a media offering have been shown to be consistent with these experimental findings. In the study of perceptions of fear-reducing techniques (Wilson, 1987), preschool children's ranking of the effectiveness of "tell yourself it's not real" was significantly lower than that of older elementary school children. In contrast to both preschool and elementary school children, who apparently view this strategy accurately, parents do not seem to appreciate the inadequacy of this technique for young children. Eighty percent of the parents of both the preschool and elementary school children who participated in another study (Wilson & Cantor, 1987), reported that they employed a "tell them it's not real" coping strategy to reduce their child's media-induced fear. The following anecdote illustrates this misunderstanding and the ineffectiveness of cognitive strategies for young children:

My mom claims that one calm warm summer night, she and my father felt like watching a scary film, Creature from the Black Lagoon. I must have been about four to five years old, and they figured I would have no problem watching because I was with them. Their rationale was, "Hey, he's with us, so we can explain to him that none of this is real." After maybe the first five minutes of the film, when the creature pops out of the pond, I maniacally began to cry my eyes out, and would not stop until my father turned off the television. Mother tells me that no matter how much they tried to explain to me that what was on TV was make-believe, I was still shaking. Her only option was to stay up with me all night, touching me and singing to me softly. (Cantor, 1998a, p. 131)

To reduce fright reactions to media depictions involving realistic threats, the most prevalent cognitive strategy seems to be to provide an explanation that minimizes the perceived probability of the depicted danger's occurring. This type of strategy is not only more effective with older children than with younger ones, in certain situations it has been shown to have a fear-enhancing rather than anxiety-reducing effect with younger children. In an experiment involving the frightening snake-pit scene from *Raiders of the Lost Ark* (Wilson & Cantor, 1987), children were first exposed to an educational film involving the presence or absence of reassuring information about snakes (including, for example, the statement that most snakes are not poisonous). Although this information tended to reduce the fear of older elementary school children while watching the snake-pit scene, kindergarten and first-grade children seem to have only partially understood the information, responding to the word "poisonous" more intensely than to the word "not." For them, negative emotional reactions were more prevalent if they had heard the supposedly reassuring information than if they had not heard it.

Data also indicate that older children use cognitive coping strategies more frequently than preschool children do. In the survey of reactions to *The Day After* (Cantor et al., 1986), parents' reports that their child had discussed the movie with them after viewing it increased with the age of the child. In a laboratory experiment involving exposure to a scary scene (Hoffner & Cantor,

1990), significantly more 9- to 11-year-olds than 5- to 7-year-olds reported that they had spontaneously employed cognitive coping strategies (thinking about the expected happy outcome or thinking about the fact that what was happening was not real). Similarly, Harrison and Cantor's (1999) retrospective study showed that the tendency to employ a cognitive strategy to cope with media-induced fear increased with the respondent's age at the time of the incident.

Studies have also shown that the effectiveness of cognitive strategies for young children can be improved by providing visual demonstrations of verbal explanations (Cantor et al., 1988), and by encouraging repeated rehearsal of simplified, reassuring information (Wilson, 1987). In addition, research has explored some of the specific reasons for the inability of young children to profit from verbal explanations, such as those involving relative quantifiers (e.g., "some are dangerous, but most are not," Badzinski, Cantor, & Hoffner, 1989) and probabilistic terms (e.g., "this probably will not happen to you," Hoffner, Cantor, & Badzinski, 1990; see also Cantor & Hoffner, 1990).

The process of parents attempting to discuss or explain programming with their children has been termed "active mediation" (Nathanson, 1999, 2002). Although the experimental studies discussed above suggest that developmentally appropriate active mediation strategies can reduce media-induced fear, correlational studies of the relationship between active parental mediation and children's fears provide a mixed picture of its effectiveness. A recent survey of parents of five- to six-year-olds (Paavonen et al., 2009), for example, reported that parental co-viewing and discussion of the content were *positively* associated with children's media-induced fears, even when the child's overall media exposure and exposure to adult programs were controlled. It is unclear how to interpret this correlation. It could be that parents who co-view and discuss programs with their children are more aware of any fears that surface. Or, it could be that co-viewing and discussion are the results of children's fears having occurred in the past. It is also possible, however, that parents are saying things they think will be reassuring but that, in fact, increase children's fears (cf. Wilson & Cantor, 1987).

In the news realm, De Cock (2012) asked 11- and 12-year-olds how much their parents co-viewed and talked to them about incidents reported on the news. She found that these active mediation strategies were not related to the children's tendency to experience fright reactions. They did, however, increase the likelihood that the children felt sadness in response to disturbing news reports. As with the Paavonen et al. (2009) study, above, it cannot be determined whether parents enacted active mediation strategies in response to their children's emotional reactions, or if those conversations contributed to the child's emotional reactions.

Other studies of active mediation are more promising. A study conducted by Buijzen and colleagues (Buijzen et al., 2007) found that among younger children (Grades 3 and 4) living in households in which the parents explained the details of a particular disturbing news story, the relationship between news exposure and fear, worry, and anger was reduced. (The same effect was not found, however, among older children [Grades 5 and 6].) Similarly, in a study by Ortiz, Silverman, Jaccard, and La Greca (2011), children in a hurricane-prone region who were exposed to a news story about a Category 5 hurricane were less frightened if they indicated having high levels of social support from parents, teachers, and other people in their lives.

Prevention Efforts

A second type of strategy to reduce media-induced fears is termed *restrictive mediation* (Nathanson, 1999, 2002), which refers to rules or regulations that parents implement in order to prevent children's exposure to media. Much of the research on restrictive mediation has been conducted on violent media and aggressive outcomes, with conflicting findings in terms of success (Nathanson, 1999, 2002).

Although there is not much research on the effects of restricting children's access to scary fictional content, the recent interview study by Cantor et al. (2010) asked children to indicate whether their parents had rules restricting their television use, and specifically, whether they had rules about their viewing of particular shows, whether their viewing was restricted to certain times, and whether the amount of time they could spend watching TV was restricted. None of these restrictions nor the number of rules in place predicted the child's tendency to experience fear from TV or the severity of the fright reactions that did occur (although there is evidence of them decreasing other negative effects, such as sleep disturbances or aggressive behavior; Gentile, Reimer, Nathanson, Walsh, & Eisenmann, 2014).

Several studies regarding the effectiveness of rules restricting children's news viewing have also failed to show that restrictions are effective in preventing fears. The study by Riddle et al. (2012) found that elementary school-aged children in households with strict rules about television use and little access to TV sets were just as likely to have seen scary news stories and to have experienced negative reactions as children with easier access. Moreover, in a study of children 11 to 12 years old, De Cock (2012) found that having restrictive mediation strategies within a household (e.g., not allowing children to view the news with violent images) *positively* predicted the degree to which the children reported being scared and uncomfortable in reaction to news reports. Due to the correlational nature of the data, however, it could be the case that parents had enacted rules and regulations after seeing their children experience negative emotions in response to disturbing news stories. On the other hand, Buijzen and colleagues (2007) have suggested that rules and regulations could possibly *increase* fear and worry on the part of younger children, especially in the case of a high profile news story. Although their study found that *talking* to young children about news stories reduced the relationship between news exposure and negative emotions, they found the opposite effect in families that restricted their children's news exposure. Among the younger children in their sample (Grades 3 and 4), they found that the relationship between exposure to a disturbing news story and fear reactions were stronger among children living in restrictive households (compared to less restrictive households). (The same effect was not found, however, among the older children [Grades 5 and 6]). These authors speculated that in the case of a high profile crime, restricting exposure to the story might increase vigilance and negative expectations on the part of children in this age group, who are likely to be exposed to the story eventually via other sources (e.g., friends, school). Thus, restricting children's exposure to the news may not necessarily prevent them from seeing disturbing news stories, and it may not necessarily eliminate or reduce the degree to which children experience fear and worry in response to the news.

Although parental rules and restrictions may be ineffective or even backfire, a total laissez-faire attitude has its perils as well. In the interview study by Cantor et al. (2010), the only home context variable that had an impact on children's fright reactions to television was having a TV in the child's bedroom: bedroom TV was associated with significantly more severe fright reactions. Obviously, allowing a child access to television in his or her own bedroom leaves the access to TV totally unsupervised during the times when the potentially scariest content is available.

IMPLICATIONS FOR PROMOTING CHILDREN'S MENTAL HEALTH

It is clear that the twenty-first-century media environment is fraught with opportunities for children to encounter media that will scare them. The ready availability of all forms of media content at all times of the day and night make it likely that children will access frightening media even when they are not interested in seeing it. The interview study by Cantor et al. (2010) revealed that only 40 percent of the children who reported a frightening incident had wanted to watch the program that had scared them, 40 percent saw it because someone else was watching it, and 20 percent stumbled on to it by accident. Similarly, in Riddle's (2012) study of young adults' memories for news stories seen during childhood, 65 percent of respondents indicated that their parents had been watching the news report and that they saw it accidentally. Only 15 percent of participants indicated that they had chosen, on their own, to watch the remembered televised news report. Parents should be aware, therefore, that their children may be affected by what other family members (themselves included) are viewing, even if the children don't seem to be paying attention.

The research reported in this chapter reveals that the overwhelming majority of children experience fright reactions to media at some point in their lives and that these reactions can negatively affect their emotional well-being, often for long periods of time. Moreover, these unhealthy effects on a child can be physical as well as emotional, such as when children are suddenly unable to sleep or are reluctant to engage in everyday activities that remind them of the fear-provoking television show or movie (see also Cantor & Omdahl, 1991). These findings highlight the importance of taking the child's media exposure seriously and of trying to prevent severe emotional disturbances to the extent possible.

There are a variety of things we can do to reduce the likelihood that children will experience unduly intense fear responses to media. Parents are the first line of defense. Simply cutting down on the time children spend with media is a good idea for a variety of reasons. For example, research by Barlett, Gentile, Barlett, Eisenmann, and Walsh (2012) has shown that amount of screen time—including television, video games, and computers—is associated with less time sleeping, and that lower levels of sleep mediate several other effects of media exposure, including aggression, attention difficulties, and weight problems.

To further minimize children's likelihood of becoming frightened by media, parents can monitor their children's media exposure and be aware of the content of the television and movies their children see. They can do this by watching programs and movies beforehand and by acquiring whatever information is available from reading reviews and program descriptions on helpful websites (e.g., kids-in-mind.com, commonsensemedia.org, screenit. com). Movie and television ratings are also available, but they should only be a first step since, as reported earlier, their validity in signaling problematic content is inadequate (e.g., Gentile & Walsh, 2002), and many movies and television shows with reassuring ratings have resulted in fright reactions (e.g., Cantor et al., 2010). Because ratings are not provided for televised news reports, and because it is difficult to predict the types of stories likely to appear on the local or national news, parents should take great care with their own exposure to the news when children are present. For example, parents can minimize the degree to which the news is used as "background television" within the household. On the other hand, if parents want their children to view developmentally appropriate news stories for educational reasons, they can screen news stories first, and using technologies such as the DVR (digital video recorder), for example, replay appropriate stories for their children.

An awareness of developmental trends in the media images and events that frighten children can help parents choose programs that are less likely to cause problems (see Table 6.1). Parents should avoid placing a television in children's bedrooms, where it is easy for them to view without parental knowledge and where television viewing at bedtime is likely. It should also be noted that having a TV in a child's bedroom is associated with a variety of other negative outcomes as well, including lower school performance (Gentile

& Walsh, 2002), pathological video-gaming (Choo et al., 2010), and less time spent reading (Rideout, Foehr, & Roberts, 2010).

Despite parents' best efforts at preventing their children from seeing disturbing media content, many young people will experience frightening media at some point in time. The takeaway from research on active mediation and coping strategies is that parents should enact developmentally appropriate approaches when trying to calm children who are frightened. Parents of children younger than eight are most likely to succeed using noncognitive techniques like desensitization, physical comforting, or distraction. Books aimed at young children who are afraid can be helpful in this context (e.g., Cantor, 2004). Older children can benefit from explanations or discussions that emphasize the unreality of fantasy depictions or minimize the perceived threat. All of these remedies may take time to work, however, especially when the media offering is powerful and the child's reaction has been intense. Parents should remember that media-induced fear is a normal reaction, and that patience with lingering fears is often necessary.

Parents should take care to monitor their own reactions to the media, too, especially in the case of disturbing news stories. Children appear to use parental reactions as cues when making sense of disturbing news stories and they may empathize strongly with their parents' emotions. Although it might be difficult for even the most hardened adult to manage emotional reactions to major news crises—examples in 2012–2013 included the Sandy Hook school massacre, the Boston Marathon bombing, and the Aurora theater shooting—it is especially important to do so when children are present. Parents should also be aware that their children (especially boys) may be unwilling to admit their fears, but they may nevertheless be in need of parental reassurance.

Schools, childcare providers, and teachers can also help reduce the risk that children will experience traumatic reactions to media. They can use an understanding of developmental differences to make sound choices of audiovisual stimuli for their classes, as well as the movies they choose for students' entertainment. They can also make sensible, age-appropriate decisions regarding which news stories to bring into the classroom, and they can be prepared to help their students cope with the unsettling issues that confront them in the media. For example, many teachers exposed their students to live news coverage of the September 11 attacks and subsequent events without anticipating the consequences and without being prepared to help their students manage their anxieties. Although it is important for students to be aware of what is going on in the world around them, live television news is often not the age-appropriate way to keep them informed.

The media could make it easier to shield children from content that they are not yet able to handle effectively. This means television programmers could endeavor to make access to frightening content predictable from the viewer's standpoint. Stations and channels should be pressured to refrain from airing ads with scary images and promos for intensely violent and frightening movies during programs with a sizable child audience. They should also be urged to avoid showing threatening visual images in newscasts in the early evening—or to at least to give viewers advance warning that horrific images are upcoming. Finally, media companies should be encouraged to rate and label media offerings in a way that warns parents of potentially threatening and scary content.

Government can play a role, too. If the media industries' rating systems aren't working to inform parents, lawmakers can pressure the media industries to provide a universal, readily understandable rating system that is based on sound criteria that should include an awareness of which stimuli are likely to be harmful. Gentile and others have called for such a rating system for all media, which would have input from child development experts to ensure that the ratings are not based solely on the opinions of the staff of media companies (e.g., Gentile, Humphrey, & Walsh, 2005; see also Gentile & Murray, this volume).

Finally, children's media environment is rapidly expanding, with the Internet and social media becoming ever more dominant in their lives. Future research should focus on the role that these newer tools and entertainment options play in the development, maintenance, and potential moderation of children's fears. As these tools become more individualized, it becomes even harder for parents to monitor their children's access. In the end, media literacy education teaching children how and why to be selective media consumers may be the most effective approach as children mature and become independent of their parents' guidance.

NOTE

1. All of the personal accounts in this chapter (presented in italics) are excerpts of reports by individuals. They are either the questionnaire responses of research participants or papers written by students in classes that had not covered the effects of frightening media. The only modifications from the original texts involve changing names to protect privacy and correcting mistakes in grammar or spelling.

REFERENCES

Applied Research and Consulting, LLC, Columbia University Mailman School of Public Health, & New York State Psychiatric Institute. (2002). *Effects of the World Trade Center attack on NYC public school students*. New York, NY: New York City Board of Education.

Badzinski, D. M., Cantor, J., & Hoffner, C. (1989). Children's understanding of quantifiers. *Child Study Journal, 19,* 241–258.

Barlett, N. D., Gentile, D. A., Barlett, C. P., Eisenmann, J. C., & Walsh, D. A. (2012). Sleep as a mediator of screen time effects on U.S. children's health outcomes. *Journal of Children and Media, 6,* 37–50.

Birnbaum, D. W., & Croll, W. L. (1984). The etiology of children's stereotypes about sex differences in emotionality. *Sex Roles, 10,* 677–691.

Blumer, H. (1933). *Movies and conduct.* New York, NY: Macmillan.

Bowlby, J. (1973). *Separation: Anxiety and anger.* New York, NY: Basic Books.

Buijzen, M., Walma van der Molen, J. H., & Sondij, P. (2007). Parental mediation of children's emotional responses to a violent news event. *Communication Research, 34,* 212–230.

Buzzuto, J. C. (1975). Cinematic neurosis following *The Exorcist. Journal of Nervous and Mental Disease, 161,* 43–48.

Cantor, J. (1998a). *"Mommy, I'm scared": How TV and movies frighten children and what we can do to protect them.* San Diego, CA: Harcourt.

Cantor, J. (1998b). Ratings for program content: The role of research findings. *Annals of the American Academy of Political and Social Science, 558,* 54–69.

Cantor, J. (2004). *Teddy's TV troubles.* Madison, WI: Goblin Fern Press.

Cantor, J. (2009). Fright reactions to mass media. In J. Bryant and M. B. Oliver (Eds.), *Media effects: Advances in theory and research* (3rd. ed., pp. 287–303). New York, NY: Routledge.

Cantor, J., Byrne, S., Moyer-Gusé, E., & Riddle, K. (2010). Descriptions of media-induced fright reactions in a sample of U.S. elementary school children. *Journal of Children and Media, 4,* 1–17.

Cantor, J., & Hoffner, C. (1990). Children's fear reactions to a televised film as a function of perceived immediacy of depicted threat. *Journal of Broadcasting & Electronic Media, 34,* 421–442.

Cantor, J., Mares, M. L., & Oliver, M. B. (1993). Parents' and children's emotional reactions to televised coverage of the Gulf War. In B. Greenberg & W. Gantz (Eds.), *Desert storm and the mass media* (pp. 325–340). Cresskill, NJ: Hampton Press.

Cantor, J., & Nathanson, A. (1996). Children's fright reactions to television news. *Journal of Communication, 46*(4), 139–152.

Cantor, J., & Omdahl, B. (1991). Effects of fictional media depictions of realistic threats on children's emotional responses, expectations, worries, and liking for related activities. *Communication Monographs, 58,* 384–401.

Cantor, J., & Sparks, G. G. (1984). Children's fear responses to mass media: Testing some Piagetian predictions. *Journal of Communication, 34*(2), 90–103.

Cantor, J., Sparks, G. G., & Hoffner, C. (1988). Calming children's television fears: Mr. Rogers vs. the Incredible Hulk. *Journal of Broadcasting & Electronic Media, 32,* 271–188.

Cantor, J., Stutman, S., & Duran, V. (1996). *What parents want in a television rating system: Results of a national survey.* Chicago, IL: National PTA. http://yourmind onmedia.com/wp-content/uploads/parent_survey.pdf

Cantor, J., & Wilson, B. J. (1984). Modifying fear responses to mass media in preschool and elementary school children. *Journal of Broadcasting, 28,* 431–443.

Cantor, J., & Wilson, B. J. (1988). Helping children cope with frightening media presentations. *Current Psychology: Research & Reviews, 7,* 58–75.

Cantor, J., Wilson, B. J., & Hoffner, C. (1986). Emotional responses to a televised nuclear holocaust film. *Communication Research, 13,* 257–277.

Choo, H., Gentile, D. A., Sim, T., Li, D., Khoo, A., & Liau, A. K. (2010). Pathological video-gaming among Singaporean youth. *Annals Academy of Medicine, 39,* 822–829.

Crouter, A. C., Manke, B. A., & McHale, S. M. (1995). The family context of gender intensification in early adolescence. *Child Development, 66,* 317–329.

De Cock, R. (2012). Mediating Flemish children's reactions of fear and sadness to television news and its limitations: Survey and in-depth interview results. *Journal of Children and Media, 6,* 485–501.

Eisenberg, A. L. (1936). *Children and radio programs: A study of more than three thousand children in the New York metropolitan area.* New York, NY: Columbia University Press.

Fabes, R. A., & Martin, C. L. (1991). Gender and age stereotypes of emotionality. *Personality and Social Psychology Bulletin, 17,* 532–540.

Fairbrother, G., Stuber, J., Galea, S., Fleischman, A. R., & Pfefferbaum, B. (2003). Posttraumatic stress reactions in New York City children after the September 11, 2001, terrorist attacks. *Ambulatory Pediatrics, 3,* 304–311.

Flavell, J. (1963). *The developmental psychology of Jean Piaget.* New York, NY: Van Nostrand.

Garrison, M. M., Liekweg, K., & Christakis, D. A. (2011). Media use and child sleep: The impact of content, timing, and environment. *Pediatrics, 128*(1), 29–35.

Gentile, D. A., Humphrey, J., & Walsh, D. A. (2002). Media ratings for movies, music, video games, and television: A review of the research and recommendations for improvements. *Adolescent Medicine Clinics, 16,* 427–446.

Gentile, D. A., Reimer, R. A., Nathanson, A. I., Walsh, D. A., & Eisenmann, J. C. (2014). A prospective study of the protective effects of parental monitoring of children's media use. *JAMA-Pediatrics, 168,* 479–484.

Gentile, D. A., & Walsh, D. A. (2002). A normative study of media habits. *Applied Developmental Psychology, 23,* 157–178.

Grossman, M., & Wood, W. (1993). Sex differences in the intensity of emotional experience: A social role interpretation. *Journal of Personality and Social Psychology, 65,* 1010–1022.

Harris, R. J., Hoekstra, S. J., Scott, C. L., Sanborn, F. W., Karafa, J. A., & Brandenburg, J. D. (2000). Young men's and women's different autobiographical memories of the experience of seeing frightening movies on a date. *Media Psychology, 2,* 245–268.

Harrison, K., & Cantor, J. (1999). Tales from the screen: Enduring fright reactions to scary media. *Media Psychology, 1*(2), 97–116.

Hoekstra, S. J., Harris, R. J., & Helmick, A. L. (1999). Autobiographical memories about the experience of seeing frightening movies in childhood. *Media Psychology, 1*(2), 117–140.

Hoffner, C., & Cantor, J. (1985). Developmental differences in responses to a television character's appearance and behavior. *Developmental Psychology, 21,* 1065–1074.

Hoffner, C., & Cantor, J. (1990). Forewarning of a threat and prior knowledge of outcome: Effects on children's emotional responses to a film sequence. *Human Communication Research, 16,* 323–354.

Hoffner, C., Cantor, J., & Badzinski, D. M. (1990). Children's understanding of adverbs denoting degree of likelihood. *Journal of Child Language, 17,* 217–231.

Johnson, B. R. (1980). General occurrence of stressful reactions to commercial motion pictures and elements in films subjectively identified as stressors. *Psychological Reports, 47,* 775–786.

Johnson, J. G., Cohen, P., Kasen, S., First, M. B., & Brook, J. S. (2004). Association between television viewing and sleep problems during adolescence and early adulthood. *Archives of Pediatrics and Adolescent Medicine, 158*, 562–568.

Kelly, H. (1981). Reasoning about realities: Children's evaluations of television and books. In H. Kelly & H. Gardner (Eds.), *Viewing children through television* (pp. 59–71). San Francisco, CA: Jossey-Bass.

Korhonen, P., & Lahikainen, A. R. (2008). Recent trends in young children's television-induced fears in Finland. *Journal of Children and Media, 2*(2), 147–162.

Leeson, C. (1917). Statement for the report of and chief evidence taken by the Cinema Commission of Inquiry instituted by the National Council of Public Morals. In *The cinema: Its present position and future possibilities*. London, UK: Williams and Norgate.

Linder, J. R., & Gentile, D. A. (2009). Is the television rating system valid? Indirect, verbal, and physical aggression in programs viewed by fifth grade girls and associations with behavior. *Journal of Applied Developmental Psychology, 30*, 286–297.

Manis, F. R., Keating, D. P., & Morison, F. J. (1980). Developmental differences in the allocation of processing capacity. *Journal of Experimental Child Psychology, 29*, 156–169.

Mathai, J. (1983). An acute anxiety state in an adolescent precipitated by viewing a horror movie. *Journal of Adolescence, 6*, 197–200.

Melkman, R., Tversky, B., & Baratz, D. (1981). Developmental trends in the use of perceptual and conceptual attributes in grouping, clustering and retrieval. *Journal of Experimental Child Psychology, 31*, 470–486.

Morison, P., & Gardner, H. (1978). Dragons and dinosaurs: The child's capacity to differentiate fantasy from reality. *Child Development, 49*, 642–648.

Nathanson, A. I. (1999). Identifying and explaining the relationship between parental mediation and children's aggression. *Communication Research, 26*, 124–143.

Nathanson, A. I. (2002). The unintended effects of parental mediation of television on adolescents. *Media Psychology, 4*, 207–230.

Nolan, J. M., & Ryan, G. W. (2000). Fear and loathing at the cineplex: Gender differences in descriptions and perceptions of slasher films. *Sex Roles, 42*, 39–56.

Ortiz, C. D., Silverman, W. K., Jaccard, J., & La Greca, A. M. (2011). Children's state anxiety in reaction to disaster media cues: A preliminary test of a multivariate model. *Psychological Trauma: Theory, Research, Practice, and Policy, 3*, 157–164.

Otto, M. W., Henin, A., Hirshfeld-Becker, D. R., Pollack, M. H., Biederman, J., & Rosenbaum, J. F. (2007). Posttraumatic stress disorder symptoms following media exposure to tragic events: Impact of 9/11 on children at risk for anxiety disorders. *Journal of Anxiety Disorders, 21*, 888–902.

Owens, J., Maxim, R., McGuinn, M., Nobile, C., Msall, M., & Alario, A. (1999). Television-viewing habits and sleep disturbance in school children. *Pediatrics, 104*(3), 552, e27.http://pediatrics.aappublications.org/cgi/content/full/104/3/e27

Paavonen, E. J., Pennonen, M., Roine, M., Valkonen, S., & Lahikainen, A. R. (2006). TV exposure associated with sleep disturbances in 5- to 6-year-olds. *Journal of Sleep Research, 15*, 154–161.

Paavonen, E. J., Roine, M., Pennonen, M., & Lahikainen, A. R. (2009). Do parental co-viewing and discussions mitigate TV-induced fears in young children? *Child: Care, Health and Development, 35*(6), 773–780.

Pavlov, I. P. (1960). *Conditioned reflexes* (G. V. Anrep, Trans.). London, UK: Oxford University Press. (Original work published 1927).

Peck, E. Y. (1999). *Gender differences in film-induced fear as a function of type of emotion measure and stimulus content: A meta-analysis and a laboratory study.* Unpublished doctoral dissertation, University of Wisconsin–Madison.

Pfefferbaum, B., Nixon, S. J., Tivis, R. D., Doughty, D. E., Pynoos, R. S., Gurwitch, R. H., & Foy, D. W. (2001). Television exposure in children after a terrorist incident. *Psychiatry, 64,* 202–211.

Preston, M. I. (1941). Children's reactions to movie horrors and radio crime. *Journal of Pediatrics, 19,* 147–168.

Riddle, K. (2012). Young adults' autobiographical memories of frightening news stories seen during childhood. *Communication Research, 39,* 738–756.

Riddle, K., Cantor, J., Byrne, S., & Moyer-Gusé, E. (2012). "People killing people on the news": Young children's descriptions of frightening news content. *Communication Quarterly, 60,* 278–294.

Rideout, V. J., Foehr, U. G., & Roberts, D. F. (2010). *Generation M²: Media in the lives of 8–18 year olds.* (Publication No. 8010). Kaiser Family Foundation. http://www.kff.org/entmedia/upload/8010.pdf

Schofield, J., & Pavelchak, M. (1985). "The Day After": The impact of a media event. *American Psychologist, 40,* 542–548.

Schuster, M. A., Stein, B. D., Jaycox, L. H., Collins, R. L., Marshall, G. N., Elliott, M. N., Zhou, A. J., Kanouse, D. E., Morrison, J. L., & Berry, S. H. (2001). A national survey of stress reactions after the September 11, 2001, terrorist attacks. *New England Journal of Medicine, 345,* 1507–1512.

Simons, D., & Silveira, W. R. (1994). Post-traumatic stress disorder in children after television programmes. *British Medical Journal, 308,* 389–390.

Singer, M. I., Slovak, K., Frierson, T., & York, P. (1998). Viewing preferences, symptoms of psychological trauma, and violent behaviors among children who watch television. *Journal of the American Academy of Child and Adolescent Psychiatry, 37*(10), 1041–1048.

Smith, S. L., Moyer, E., Boyson, A. R., & Pieper, K. M. (2002). Parents' perceptions of the children's fear reactions to TV news coverage of the terrorists' attacks. In B. Greenberg, (Ed.), *Communication and terrorism.* Cresskill, NJ: Hampton Press.

Smith, S. L., & Moyer-Gusé, E. (2006). Children and the war on Iraq: Developmental differences in fear responses to television news coverage. *Media Psychology, 8,* 213–237.

Smith, S. L., & Wilson, B. J. (2000). Children's reactions to a television news story: The impact of video footage and proximity of the crime. *Communication Research, 27,* 641–673.

Smith, S. L., & Wilson, B. J. (2002). Children's comprehension of and fear reactions to television news. *Media Psychology, 4,* 1–26.

Sparks, G. G. (1986). Developmental differences in children's reports of fear induced by the mass media. *Child Study Journal, 16,* 55–66.

Sparks, G. G., & Cantor, J. (1986). Developmental differences in fright responses to a television program depicting a character transformation. *Journal of Broadcasting and Electronic Media, 30,* 309–323.

Terr, L. C., Bloch, D. A., Michel, B. A., Shi, H., Reinhardt, J. A., & Metayer, S. (1999). Children's symptoms in the wake of Challenger: A field study of distant-traumatic effects and an outline of related conditions. *American Journal of Psychiatry, 156,* 1536–1544.

Thompson, K. M., & Haninger, K. (2001). Violence in E-rated video games. *Journal of the American Medical Association, 286,* 591–598.

Valkenburg, P. M., Cantor, J., & Peeters, A. L. (2000). Fright reactions to television: A child survey. *Communication Research, 27,* 82–99.

Walma van der Molen, J. H., & Konijn, E. A. (2007). Dutch children's emotional reactions to news about the war in Iraq: Influence of media exposure, identification, and empathy. In D. Lemish & M. Gotz (Eds.), *Children and media in times of war and conflict* (pp. 75–97). Cresskill, NJ: Hampton Press.

Walma van der Molen, J. H., Valkenburg, P. M., & Peeters, A. L. (2002). Television news and fear: A child survey. *Communications, 27,* 303–317.

Weiss, A. J., Imrich, D. J., & Wilson, B. J. (1993). Prior exposure to creatures from a horror film: Live versus photographic representations. *Human Communication Research, 20,* 41–66.

Wilson, B. J. (1987). Reducing children's emotional reactions to mass media through rehearsed explanation and exposure to a replica of a fear object. *Human Communication Research, 14,* 3–26.

Wilson, B. J. (1989a). Desensitizing children's emotional reactions to the mass media. *Communication Research, 16,* 723–745.

Wilson, B. J. (1989b). The effects of two control strategies on children's emotional reactions to a frightening movie scene. *Journal of Broadcasting & Electronic Media, 33,* 397–418.

Wilson, B. J., & Cantor, J. (1987). Reducing children's fear reactions to mass media: Effects of visual exposure and verbal explanation. In M. McLaughlin (Ed.), *Communication Yearbook 10* (pp. 553–573). Beverly Hills, CA: Sage.

Wilson, B. J., Hoffner, C., & Cantor, J. (1987). Children's perceptions of the effectiveness of techniques to reduce fear from mass media. *Journal of Applied Developmental Psychology, 8,* 39–52.

Wilson, B. J., & Martins, N., & Marske, A. L. (2005). Children's and parents' fright reactions to kidnapping stories in the news. *Communication Monographs, 72,* 46–70.

Wilson, B. J., & Weiss, A. J. (1991). The effects of two reality explanations on children's reactions to a frightening movie scene. *Communication Monographs, 58,* 307–326.

Zoglin, R. (1984, June 25). Gremlins in the rating system. *Time,* p. 78.

CHAPTER 7

Meanness and Manipulation in the Media: Portrayals and Effects of Viewing Relational Aggression in the Media

Sarah M. Coyne and Laura Stockdale

Researchers, policymakers, parents, and educators have long been concerned about aggression and bullying in schools and communities. This concern has resulted in much research attention to understanding the multiple causes and consequences of aggression, with one focus being on media effects on aggression (e.g., Anderson et al., 2003). However, these researchers have historically focused on traditional forms of physical aggression such as hitting, kicking, punching, and shoving. In more recent years, researchers have begun to examine the development of more subtle, manipulative, and interpersonal forms of aggression. This subtle and socially based aggression has been called a variety of names by researchers, such as relational aggression, indirect aggression, and social aggression. These forms of aggression may have some differences, but the underlying constructs are remarkably similar and the consequences of such aggression seem to be the same (Archer & Coyne, 2005). Thus, for the purposes of this chapter, we will refer to this socially based aggression as *relational aggression*.

As demonstrated by many chapters in this book, hundreds of studies have been conducted on the effects of viewing physical violence in the media. In contrast, the purpose of this chapter is to examine the portrayal of relational aggression in the media and any potential effects on viewers. We begin by briefly discussing the research literature on the development of relational aggression, and show that this form of aggression can be exceptionally harmful. We then discuss content analyses of relational aggression in various types of media, focusing on childhood, adolescence, and adulthood. Next, we discuss the studies that have examined associations between viewing relational aggression in the media and in real life, focusing on specific developmental periods. Finally, we discuss the interventions that have focused on relational aggression, and suggest future areas of study.

UNDERSTANDING RELATIONAL AGGRESSION: DEFINITIONS, GENDER, AND DEVELOPMENT

Relational aggression has been defined as "behaviors that are intended to significantly damage another's friendships or feelings of inclusion by the peer group" (Crick & Grotpeter, 1995, pp. 711). Crick, Casas, and Nelson (2002) expanded this definition by calling relational aggression "events or behaviors in which the perpetrator attempts to harm the victim through the manipulation of relationships, threat of damage, or both" (p. 98). For example, relational aggression can include threatening to not invite a peer to an important social event if the person does not do what the aggressor wants (social exclusion); spreading rumors to damage another's reputation; giving the silent treatment to a peer to force compliance; and telling another's secrets in order to cause embarrassment. Relationally aggressive behaviors change with age and as children develop. For example, young children display relational aggression in the peer group by placing their hands over their ears and refusing to listen to a peer who has made them angry, whereas adolescents may display more subtle forms of relational aggression, such as intentionally stealing a peer's romantic partner (Crick, Casas, & Nelson, 2002). Likewise, adults display relational aggression through behaviors such as withdrawing love and affection from their romantic partners or giving their partners the silent treatment in order to punish or force compliance (Carroll et al., 2010).

Children, adolescents, and young adults who use relational aggression in their peer group tend to be lonelier, more depressed, and feel more isolated (Crick & Grotpeter, 1995); are more rejected by their peers (Crick, 1996; Werner & Crick, 2004); display more antisocial behavior, egocentricity, identity problems, self-harm, decreased life satisfaction, and emotional instability: all symptoms of overall maladjustment (Crick, Casas, & Mosher, 1997). Furthermore, relationally aggressive individuals have less stable relationships (Carroll et al., 2010), more jealously and distrust in their friendships (Grotpeter & Crick, 1996), and friendships that are less fulfilling and supportive (Crick, Casas, & Mosher, 1997; Linder, Crick, & Collins, 2002). These relational disturbances many explain why relationally aggressive adolescents are typically identified as "popular" within their peer group, meaning that they are identified as powerful and well known within the peer group but generally are not well-liked by their peers (Putallaz et al., 2007; Rose, Swenson, & Waller, 2004). Victims of relational aggression may also experience a host of negative outcomes including maladjustment and social withdrawal (Murray-Close, Ostrov, & Crick, 2007) more depression (Putallaz et al., 2007), more internalizing behaviors such as anxiety, and have less positive peer relationships (Crick, Casas, & Ku, 1999). This body of research is similar to studies focusing on physical aggression that also show marked consequences for both perpetrators and victims of physical violence (e.g., Coyne, Nelson, & Underwood, 2010). Regardless of whether a person is a perpetrator or victim of relational aggression, relational aggression appears harmful and detrimental to healthy social and emotional development; accordingly, many schools are implementing intervention strategies specifically aimed at decreasing levels of relational aggression (e.g., Leff, Waasdorp, & Crick, 2010).

While it is clear that relational aggression may be harmful, it is also clear that gender plays an important role in the use of relational aggression. Early studies found that females are more likely to use relational aggression, while males are more likely to use physical aggression (Crick, 1996; Crick & Gropeter, 1995; Crick et al., 2006; Gropeter & Crick, 1996; Werner & Crick, 2004). These gender differences are present in preschool (Bonica, Arnold, Fisher, Zeljo, & Yershova, 2003), adolescence (Rose, Swenson, & Waller, 2004), young adulthood (Linder, Crick, & Collins, 2002), and adulthood (Carroll et al., 2010). Similarly, females who use physical aggression with peers and males who use relational aggression with peers are more rejected and more isolated than peers who use gender "appropriate" forms of aggression, suggesting strong social norms regarding gender and aggression (Crick, 1997). In contrast, the few meta-analyses that have been conducted on gender differences in relational aggression generally either show no differences or a very small difference in the female direction (Card & Hodges, 2006; Card, Stucky, Sawalani, & Little, 2008). Therefore, although gender seems to be important in understanding relational aggression, actual gender differences may be smaller than first believed.

Given the harmful effects of both relational aggression use and victimization, psychologists have studied the developmental course of relational aggression and its causes. Relational aggression is first present in preschool children, who are beginning to experience autonomy from parents and are learning to navigate the social world (Crick, 1996). Relational aggression appears to be relatively stable across time (Crick, 1996; Crick et al., 2006; Kawabata, Crick, & Hamaguchi, 2010; Ostrov, Crick, & Stauffacher, 2006), but increases during the transition to middle school and early adolescence (Werner & Hill, 2010) as peer relationships become more salient. Several factors are important to the development of relational aggression. For example, parents who use relational aggression within their marriages and as a form of discipline (in terms of psychological control) have children who are more relationally aggressive with peers (Casas et al., 2006; Hart, Nelson, Robinson, Olsen, & McNeilly-Choque, 1998; Nelson, Hart, Yang, Olsen, & Jin, 2006). Similarly, peers (Werner & Nixon, 2006) and older siblings (Ostrov, Crick, & Stauffacher, 2006) that use relational aggression and are more supportive of the use of relational aggression create a culture of acceptance of relational aggression that makes it more likely for other members of the social group to use relational aggression. Witnessing others (such as parents, siblings, and peers) use relational aggression can increase its use, and therefore media portrayals also have the potential to influence the use of relational aggression.

CONTENT ANALYSES OF RELATIONAL AGGRESSION

Relational aggression in the media is not a new phenomenon. From Shakespeare's comedies and Greek tragedies to reality television, relational aggression has appeared in various media. Research into media violence reveals that the effects of viewing violence on physical aggression often depend on a number of contextual features (e.g., Anderson et al., 2003). Therefore, before researchers can understand the effects of viewing relational aggression in the media it is important to understand the prevalence of this type of relational aggression, how it is portrayed, characteristics of victims of aggressors, and how these portrayals vary across target audiences.

Childhood

According to a recent study of the 50 most popular television programs for children between the ages of 2 and 11, 92 percent of popular children's television programs contain relational aggression. Furthermore, for every hour of television that a child watches, he or she is exposed to an average of 14 acts of relational aggression (Martins & Wilson, 2012). When television programs popular among fifth grade girls were examined, 77 percent contained relational aggression, and the average viewer was exposed to approximately four acts of relational aggression per hour of viewing (Linder & Lyle, 2011). Relational aggression in children's television programming is often portrayed by attractive (Martins & Wilson, 2012) female characters (Linder & Lyle, 2011) with few negative consequences (Martins & Wilson, 2012). When aggression is portrayed by powerful characters who receive no punishment for their aggressive behavior, it is significantly more likely to be reenacted by viewers (Berkowitz & Green, 1966; Cantor & Wilson, 2003; Leyens & Picus, 1973; Meyer, 1972) and children might be particularly vulnerable to these effects (Gentile, Saleem, & Anderson, 2007; Anderson et al., 2003). In fact, children's television programming contains more justified and rewarded relational aggression than programs designed for general audiences, suggesting that age-based ratings do not adequately take into account relational aggression (Linder & Gentile, 2009). The frequency and content of relational aggression portrayals thus place children at risk for reenacting the aggression they see on television.

In contrast to television, however, children's films portray relational aggression in a more negative light. A content analysis of Disney animated films found that relational aggression was common (100% of films contained relational aggression, with an average of 9.28 acts per hour); characters who used relational aggression were typically portrayed as the "bad guys" and their aggression was not rewarded, hypothetically (Coyne & Whitehead, 2008). Taken together, these studies suggest that children are exposed to a significant amount of relational aggression in the media; that this aggression is sometimes portrayed in ways that make relational aggression look "cool," effective, and associated with increased social power; and that negative messages regarding relational aggression are relatively rare.

Adolescence

Media specifically marketed toward teens portrays relational aggression as a comical and normative part of adolescent female friendships and female empowerment (Cecil, 2008). In fact, teens are exposed to 10 times more relational aggression while watching television than they are exposed to at school (Coyne, Archer, & Eslea, 2006). In movies, a study examining the top 20 teen-marketed films from 1995 to 2002 found that female characters were significantly more likely to be portrayed using relational aggression, rarely received negative consequences for their aggressive behavior, and were often rewarded for using relational aggression (Behm-Morawitz & Mastro, 2008). The portrayal of relational aggression in teen-marketed media as normative, effective for gaining social power, and associated with increased attractiveness and popularity may teach adolescents that relational aggression is an effective strategy for gaining social power and prestige, and that such use is more common and acceptable for females.

Recently, researchers examined the prevalence of relational aggression in adolescent novels. The top 40 best-selling novels for adolescents were examined and were found to contain high levels of relational aggression. According to this study, the average adolescent was exposed to one act of relational aggression for every five pages of a book. Similar to other forms of media, relational aggression was often portrayed as justified, with few negative consequences, by female characters who were powerful and popular (Coyne et al., 2011).

Emerging Adulthood

Researchers examining media popular in emerging adulthood have found similar results. Relational aggression in prime time television programming is pervasive, with 97 percent of television programming between the hours of 8:00 p.m. and 11:00 p.m. containing at least one act of relational aggression (Glascock, 2008). Likewise, reality television, such as ABC's *The Bachelor* and FOX's *American Idol*, contains some of the highest levels of relational aggression of all programming types (Coyne & Archer, 2004; Coyne, Robinson, & Nelson, 2010). In line with children and adolescent media, relational aggression in these programs is most commonly portrayed by female, powerful, and attractive characters, and the aggression is typically justified, rewarded, and portrayed as having few or no consequences (Coyne & Archer, 2004; Coyne, Robinson, & Nelson, 2010; Fernández-Villanueva, Revilla-Castro, Domínguez-Bilbao, Gimeno-Jiménez, & Almagro, 2009; Glascock, 2008).

THEORETICAL FOUNDATION

Though most aggression theories (and the learning theories they are based upon) do not specifically mention relational aggression, many can be applied to suggest mechanisms to explain why relational aggression might influence subsequent behavior and cognitions. From a social learning perspective, individuals might be more likely to imitate relationally aggressive models who are being rewarded for their behavior (Bandura, Ross, & Ross, 1963). As previously discussed, the majority of portrayals of relational aggression show it as either rewarded or as having no negative consequences, perhaps increasing the likelihood that viewers would imitate such behavior in their own lives.

Most published relational aggression research tends to apply the General Aggression Model (GAM: Anderson & Bushman, 2002; chapter 4, this volume) when examining media effects. This theory states that viewing media aggression (and we would include relational aggression) can influence a viewer in both the short and long term. In the short term, viewing relational aggression in the media might influence immediate behavior by activating cognitive scripts relating to aggression, influencing physiological arousal, and altering affect. By activating these three internal routes (cognition, arousal, and affect), the viewer is now primed to act aggressively. Whether aggression occurs is dependent on a host of personality and situational factors. The theory states that the viewer goes through a decision-making process (which can be automatic or thoughtful) before deciding whether relational aggression would be an appropriate response for the particular situation. Then, when the viewer encounters a social situation in which a response could include aggression in any form, these scripts and schemas are more likely to be activated. In the long term, the GAM would suggest that a heavy diet of relational aggression may shape norms and scripts relating to aggressive behavior; help the individual to repeatedly rehearse such scripts; and even influence personality, social groups, and situations, increasing the likelihood of relational aggression in a general setting. This theory (and the social-cognitive theories on which it is based) and its specific predictions have been repeatedly confirmed by research (see chapter 4, this volume).

EFFECTS OF VIEWING RELATIONAL AGGRESSION IN THE MEDIA

A long history of research has revealed that exposure to violence in the media may increase subsequent aggressive behavior and cognitions, while decreasing prosocial behavior and empathy (e.g., see chapters 3, 5, 8, 13 in this volume; Anderson et al., 2003, 2010; Bushman & Huesmann, 2006). A number of studies have found that exposure to relational aggression in the media can also influence aggressive behavior. We will examine these associations according to the developmental level of the viewer.

Childhood

The few existing studies on relational aggression and media in childhood have focused on middle childhood. According to Gentile and Sesma (2003; see also chapter 2, this volume) there are a number of key developmental tasks that relate to the development of relational aggression in this age period. For example, children are learning how to "build loyal friendships and to be accepted by peers," as well as "learning social rules and norms" (p. 29). Additionally, a child's sense of morality really begins to develop during middle childhood. Though relational aggression has existed in the peer group since preschool (Hart et al., 1998), peers become extremely important during this age and relational aggression becomes increasingly sophisticated. Children need to learn the social rules of interacting with peers and typically develop normative beliefs regarding the acceptability of relational aggression during this age (Werner & Hill, 2010). As discussed earlier, relational aggression in the media aimed at children is very common but sends a mixed message, with many media portrayals depicting the behavior as acceptable and having few consequences (e.g., Martins & Wilson, 2012), although sometimes such behavior is portrayed as unacceptable and punished (e.g., see Coyne & Whitehead, 2008). Accordingly, the media may be particularly influential on both the behavior and attitudes regarding relational aggression during middle childhood as compared to older ages, though it may depend on how such aggression is portrayed in children's media.

The studies found that exposure to relational aggression can influence behavior, but results do depend on a number of contextual and individual factors. For example, Linder and Gentile (2009) found that aggressive behavior was only associated with viewing *rewarded* relational aggression (as opposed to punished aggression). According to social learning theory (Bandura et al., 1963), individuals are more likely to imitate behavior that is rewarded. In this case, children who view rewarded relational aggression in the media may learn that relational aggression can be an effective tactic in obtaining what the aggressor wants, whether that be a tangible reward, seeing the victim suffer, or gaining popularity or social status. This is consistent with the broader research on media aggression (e.g., Anderson et al., 2003; Bandura et al., 1963).

Some research has found that the association depends on the sex of the viewer. For example, Martins (2009) found that exposure to "social aggression" (behaviors aimed to damage another's self-esteem) in the media was associated with social aggression in real life, but only for girls in this sample. Though there are fewer sex differences in actual use (Card et al., 2008), beliefs surrounding the appropriateness of relational aggression tend to be more supported in female social groups (Werner & Nixon, 2006). In addition, several studies found that relational aggression tends to be portrayed more frequently by females in the media (e.g., Archer & Coyne, 2005; Linder & Lyle, 2011). Accordingly, it is unsurprising that girls may be particularly influenced by such portrayals. Certainly, other research would suggest that children learn more quickly and are more likely to imitate models they find to be similar in sex, age, and other characteristics (Anderson et al., 2003; Anderson & Bushman, 2002). Future research should continue to examine how sex of viewer influences responses to relational aggression by models of both sexes in the media. Linder and Werner (2012) found that exposure to relational aggression in the media predicted acceptance of relationally aggressive behaviors a year later. The study was limited by a small sample size, but this provides initial evidence of a longer-term effect of viewing relational aggression in the media in children.

Adolescence

During adolescence, the development of intimacy in peer relationships remains important, but key developmental tasks also revolve around the development of an identity and sense of autonomy (Gentile & Sesma, 2003; chapter 2, this volume). Relational aggression is common during adolescence, but the behavior becomes even more subtle and refined (Archer & Coyne, 2004). Normative beliefs regarding relational aggression stem from middle childhood but can still change over the course of adolescence (Werner & Nixon, 2006). For example, as adolescents explore their identities, they might examine the possibility that a core component of their identity would involve the use of relational aggression (e.g., "I have a sarcastic sense of humor"). Adolescents are also particularly attuned to peer social norms and many are focused on what behaviors may increase their likability and popularity within the peer group (Steinberg, 2009).

To our knowledge, there have been only three studies conducted on the effects of viewing relational aggression in the media on adolescents. All were conducted on British teenagers (ages 11 to 14) but represent different methodologies. The first revealed that adolescents report witnessing about 10 times more relational aggression in the media as compared to in real life (Coyne, Archer, & Eslea, 2006). The high frequency of media relational aggression compared to real life suggests that television is not simply a "mirror" reflecting such behavior in the real world. Another study found that adolescents who viewed relational aggression in the media tended to be more relationally aggressive in the real world, but again this was only true for girls (Coyne & Archer, 2005).

In an experimental study (Coyne, Archer, & Eslea, 2004), adolescents were randomly assigned to view a video clip containing either relational, physical, or no aggression. They were later provoked by an obnoxious confederate and then given the opportunity to relationally aggress against him. Both males and females who viewed the relational aggression clip were significantly more relationally aggressive against the confederate than those viewing either the physical aggression or no aggression clip. The experimental nature of this study provides evidence of a causal role of viewing relational aggression on subsequent relational aggression in the short term.

Though these studies provide some indication that relational aggression can influence aggressive behavior during adolescence, all are from the same research group and use similar samples. Accordingly, in order for the results to be generalizable, these studies should be replicated using diverse populations.

Emerging Adulthood

During emerging adulthood, individuals make the transition from adolescence to adulthood. Identity development is still extremely common during this period, with many individuals exploring their identity in terms of politics, religion, employment, romantic relationships, sexuality, and more (Arnett, 2006). On the whole, relational aggression appears to decrease during emerging adulthood (Archer & Coyne, 2005), though there is a marked range, with many individuals maintaining strong normative beliefs regarding relational aggression and using such behavior in both peer and romantic relationships (Nelson, Springer, Nelson, & Bean, 2008). As mentioned earlier, relational aggression in the media is commonly portrayed in adult programming, with messages trending toward supporting the acceptability of such behavior (e.g., Coyne, Robinson, & Nelson, 2010). These strong messages combined with research showing that emerging adults are still susceptible to media messages (Coyne, Padilla-Walker, & Howard, 2013) suggest that relational aggression in the media is likely to have an influence on both attitudes and behaviors during emerging adulthood, though effects may be not be as strong as in earlier ages. As the development of romantic relationships becomes increasingly important (Arnett, 2006), a number of studies have also specifically examined the influence of relational aggression in this context.

Two experimental studies showed that viewing relational aggression in the media increased subsequent aggressive behavior (Coyne et al., 2008) and aggressive cognitions (Coyne, Linder, et al., 2012) specific to relational aggression. However, both studies involved only women. In correlational studies, Coyne, Nelson, Graham-Kevan, et al. (2010, 2011) found that viewing relational aggression in the media was associated with romantic relational aggression for both men and women. Coyne, Busby, et al. (2012) also found that men who played a significant amount of video games and who had high levels of conflict with their romantic partners about the media also tended to use more relational aggression toward their romantic partners. This latter study did not specifically examine relational aggression in video games, but it does support a view that high levels of time spent engaging in media can have a negative impact on romantic relationships, specifically on levels of relational aggression. Additionally, though almost all the studies on relational aggression in the media have been conducted on television or film, Coyne, Callister, et al. (2011) found that reading relational aggression in books was also associated with relational aggression, as measured in an experimental context.

As a whole, these studies show that exposure to relational aggression in various media types (television, film, books) is associated with relationally aggressive behavior and cognitions across development (childhood, adolescence, and emerging adulthood); this has been tested using a number of different methodologies (experimental, cross-sectional, longitudinal) and in at least two different cultures (the United States and England). Though this field is still small (though growing), such studies provide initial evidence that relational aggression in the media may be one socializing factor for the development of relational aggression.

Crossover Effects

Although the bulk of the research has examined the specific effects of viewing relational aggression in the media, a growing body of research reveals a more generalized effect of viewing media aggression, in that viewing one form of aggression can influence other forms. According to the GAM, viewing any type of aggression in the media may influence an individual's cognition, affect, and arousal, increasing the likelihood for subsequent aggressive behavior. However, behavior is both situationally and culturally determined, and certain types of aggressive behavior may not be appropriate for the individual in many circumstances. For example, if an individual views a bloody gunfight in the movie theater, even though the person may be "primed" to act aggressively, he or she is not likely to pick up a gun and shoot someone. Such aggression is culturally unacceptable and would probably land the individual in prison for a very long time. Instead, the individual may choose to use a more socially sanctioned form of aggression, for example, gossiping about someone with whom they are angry.

We see this crossover effect across developmental periods and using different methodologies. In childhood, several cross-sectional (Gentile, Mathieson, & Crick, 2011; Linder & Gentile, 2009) and longitudinal studies, including one spanning 22 years, have found that viewing physical aggression in the media is associated with relationally aggressive behavior (Gentile, Coyne, & Walsh, 2011; Huesmann, Moise-Titus, Podolski, & Eron, 2003; Ostrov, Gentile, & Crick, 2006). However, the evidence seems mixed for adolescent samples. Some studies show that viewing physical aggression in the media is associated with relationally aggressive behaviors (Coyne et al., 2004), while others do not, including two longitudinal studies with German adolescents (Krahé & Möller, 2010; Möller & Krahé, 2009), though it should be noted that these latter studies focused on video games, where relational aggression is much less likely to be portrayed as compared to other media. In emerging adulthood, there are also mixed results. Again, a number of studies (Coyne et al., 2008), including a few focused on comic books (Kirsh & Olczak, 2002a, 2002b) find that exposure to physical aggression in the media is associated with relational aggression in viewers. However, several focusing specifically on romantic relationships do not find a generalized effect (Coyne, Nelson, Graham-Kevan, et al., 2010, 2011).

These studies all focus on associations between media violence and relational aggression, and tend to show a trend toward a generalized effect of viewing media aggression. According to Gentile and Sesma (2003), relational aggression may be considered a less risky and safer form of aggression for individuals to use. Certainly, the vast majority of individuals do not murder (or even hit) someone after viewing a physically aggressive film. However, according to a number of theoretical perspectives (Anderson & Bushman, 2002; Gentile & Sesma, 2003), it may be more likely for an individual to use relational or verbal aggression after witnessing physical aggression in the media if the situation permits. This answers critics' claims of why so many people view aggression in the media but so few commit violent crimes. It may be that aggression in the media is having an effect, but the effect is seen in a type of aggression that is more normative, accepted by society, and less likely to be counted in crime statistics.

Finally, one study tested the opposite effect, whether viewing relational aggression influences subsequent physical aggression. Coyne et al. (2008) showed emerging adult women one of three different movie clips, either portraying relational (*Mean Girls*), physical (*Kill Bill*), or no aggression (*What Lies Beneath*). Participants who viewed the relational or the physical aggression clips were both more likely to be physically aggressive after exposure as measured through administering louder and longer "noise blasts" to a confederate of the study, as compared to participants who viewed the no-aggression clip. Though many situational and personality factors come into play when examining what type of aggression may be more likely after viewing media aggression, this study is the first to show that viewing relational aggression may result in subsequent physical aggression. This study needs to be replicated, and cross-sectional research hasn't yet found a similar association (Coyne, Nelson, Graham-Kevan, et al., 2010, 2011). These results should be considered tentative, but this study provides some initial evidence of a crossover effect of viewing any type of aggression in the media on any type of aggression in real life.

INTERVENTION

A number of studies have found that media literacy or parental monitoring and mediation may be useful in decreasing aggressive behavior following exposure to media violence (e.g., Cantor & Wilson, 2003; Nathanson & Yang, 2003). For relational aggression, some suggest using a feminist counseling perspective (Goldberg, Smith-Adcock, & Dixon, 2011), while others have used more traditional methods. For example, Hammel (2009) found that adolescents who took part in a workshop on recognizing relational aggression in the media and the real life consequences of such behavior tended to be more aware of relational aggression when seen in the media. Linder and Werner (2012) also found that parental mediation tactics, such as discussing media content, reduced the effects of viewing relational aggression in the long term. Finally, Möller, Krahé, Busching, and Krause (2012) designed a school intervention program aimed at reducing use of aggressive media and aggressive behavior, and at promoting critical thinking while viewing. The intervention group reported watching less aggressive media content seven months after the intervention and reported lower levels of physical and relational aggression as compared to those in the control group. Though few in number, these studies reveal that parental mediation and formal intervention can both be effective in helping youth recognize relational aggression in the media and in mitigating some of the harmful effects.

FUTURE RESEARCH

Compared to studies on media violence, research focusing on relational aggression and media are few in number. Accordingly, there is much potential for future research on the topic. In this section, we offer some suggestions for where we feel the field should focus its initial efforts to increase understanding of the relationship between exposure to relational aggression in the media and aggressive behavior.

First, we need much more research on the effects of relational aggression in the media on relationally aggressive behavior across the life course. The bulk of the research has focused on middle childhood, adolescence, and emerging adulthood. However, young children are exposed to media, even as babies. There have been a number of studies involving the effects of physically aggressive media on relational aggression and other behaviors during the preschool years (e.g., Christakis et al., 2013; Ostrov et al., 2006), however, we are unaware of any focusing specifically on relational aggression and media. Ostrov, Gentile, and Mullins (2013) did find a longitudinal association between viewing educational programs and later relational aggression in preschoolers, but this study did not specifically focus on relationally aggressive content. Content analyses show that children's programming (many of which may be deemed "educational") may still contain high levels of relational aggression (Martins & Wilson, 2012). Given the complexity of relational aggression, preschoolers may be unable to understand the "moral message" often given in these types of programs to dissuade such behavior in real life. Though we know a little about relational aggression in preschool media (e.g., Martins & Wilson, 2012), we are unaware of studies specifically focusing on the effects of viewing relational aggression in the media in this age group. It is likely that this age represents a particularly important time in the development of relational aggression. Relational aggression appears for the first time in preschool (Archer & Coyne, 2005; Nelson, Robinson, & Hart, 2005), and individuals begin laying down the foundation for normative beliefs regarding the acceptability of such behavior across the lifespan (Werner & Nixon, 2006). Accordingly, this represents a particularly useful avenue for future research.

Few researchers have examined portrayals of relational aggression in media targeted at adults in middle adulthood and older adulthood. Given that relational aggression is the dominant form of aggression seen in adulthood (Werner & Crick, 1999), and that it is routinely used in adult programming, viewing such behavior may be associated with increased relational aggression.

A truly life-course perspective of the development of aggressive behavior requires investigating the causes, consequences, and contexts of relational aggression in all stages of life. Therefore, future researchers should seek to understand the influence of the media on the use of relational aggression in middle and older adult romantic relationships and peer networks.

Our review also revealed that the vast majority of research on relational aggression in the media involves television or movies. Certainly, this represents a sizable amount of media use by individuals (Kaiser Family Foundation, 2010); however, other forms of media are consistently used and require research attention. For example, video games, social media networks such as Facebook, and YouTube are frequently used by teens and adults and potentially contain relational aggression. Understanding the influence of such forms of media on aggressive behavior will add richness and depth to the existing literature and will provide greater insight into the development of relational aggression.

The majority of research examining the effect of viewing relationally aggressive media on relational aggression has employed the General Aggression Model as a theoretical perspective. This theory suggests that the media influence viewers in various ways. Another leading media theory, the uses and gratifications theory, would suggest that individuals turn to certain types of media in order to satiate wants, desires, or other interpersonal needs (Katz, Blumler, & Gurevitch, 1974). Relational aggression in the media is extremely frequent in television and movies aimed at children, adolescents, and adults (e.g., Coyne & Archer, 2004; Linder & Gentile, 2009; Coyne, Robinson, & Nelson, 2010). However, we have not yet examined the uses and gratifications of viewing relational aggression in the media. This may answer some questions regarding why producers continue to add relational aggression to media storylines and why viewers continue to tune in. It is possible that some viewers seek out media portrayals of relational aggression to confirm and support their own aggressive behavior (e.g., Coyne & Archer, 2005); however, there are likely a host of needs that viewing media relational aggression fulfills in viewers, such as sensation seeking, coping, interpersonal, vengeance, humor, or even voyeuristic needs (Katz et al., 1974). Examining why individuals are drawn to relational aggression in the media will help us understand its portrayal and potential effects on individuals.

Developmental psychologists have long taken a risk/resiliency approach when seeking to understand the development of any behavior (see chapter 2, this volume). This approach takes into account that children can be placed on trajectories or pathways from a very young age that put them at increased or decreased risk for the development of positive or negative behaviors. For example, children born into poverty are known to be placed on a trajectory that puts them at increased risk for academic failure, school dropout, deviant behavior, and poor nutrition, all factors that can have lifelong consequences. In contrast, children who are born into a supportive community are more likely to graduate from high school, have higher self-esteem, and have more positive peer relationships, placing them on a more positive developmental trajectory.

Taking a risk/resiliency approach to the influence of relational aggression in the media on subsequent aggressive behaviors would allow researchers to take into account that children do not develop in isolation. It is important to understand not only how media influence the development of aggression but also how media interact with preexisting developmental trajectories, such as parenting practices, community support, and school and home environment.

As a whole, a small but growing line of research has found that relational aggression is portrayed frequently in media aimed at children, adolescents, and emerging adults, and that exposure to relational aggression in the media can influence both aggressive cognitions and behavior. Such behavior in the real world can result in severe and long-lasting consequences for both perpetrators and victims, yet this message is rarely portrayed in mainstream media. There are many reasons why individuals act aggressively, and the causes behind such behavior are as a varied as they are complex. However, because parents, individuals, and societies have much more control over what they choose to expose themselves and their children to through the media, the media may be one area to focus on as we attempt to understand the many reasons why individuals use relational aggression to manipulate, hurt, and demean each other.

REFERENCES

Anderson, C. A., Berkowitz, L., Donnerstein, E., Huesmann, L. R., Johnson, J. D., Linz, D., Malamuth, N. M., & Wartella, E. (2003). The influence of media violence on youth. *Psychological Science in the Public Interest, 4,* 81–110. doi:10.1111/j.1529-1006.2003.pspi_1433.x

Anderson, C. A., Shibuya, A., Ihori, N., Swing, E. L., Bushman, B. J., Sakamoto, A., et al. (2010). Violent video game effects on aggression, empathy, and prosocial behavior in Eastern and Western countries: A meta-analytic review. *Psychological Bulletin, 136,* 151–173.

Anderson, C. A., & Bushman, B. J. (2002). Human aggression. *Annual Review of Psychology, 53,* 27–51. doi:10.1146/annurev.psych.53.100901.135231

Archer, J., & Coyne, S. M. (2005). An integrated review of indirect, relational, and social aggression. *Personality and Social Psychology Review, 9,* 212–230. doi:10.1207/s15327957pspr0903_2

Arnett, J. J. (2006). Emerging adulthood: Understanding the new way of coming of age. In J. J. Arnett & J. L. Tanner (Eds.), Emerging adults in America: Coming of age in the 21st century (pp. 1–19). Washington, DC: American Psychological Association.

Bandura, A., Ross, D., & Ross, S. A. (1963). Imitation of film-mediated aggressive models. *The Journal of Abnormal and Social Psychology, 66,* 3–11. doi:10.1037/h0048687

Behm-Morawitz, E., & Mastro, D. A. (2008). Mean girls? The influence of gender portrayals in teen movies and emerging adults' gender-based attitudes and beliefs. *Journalism and Mass Communication Quarterly, 85,* 131–146. doi:10.1177/107769900808500109

Berkowitz, L., & Green, R. G. (1966). Film violence and the cue properties of available targets. *Journal of Personality and Social Psychology, 3,* 525–530. doi:10.1037/h0023201

Bonica, C., Arnold, D. H., Fisher, P. H., Zeljo, A., & Yershova, K. (2003). Relational aggression, relational victimization, and language development in preschoolers. *Social Development, 12,* 551–562. doi:10.1111/1467-9507.00248

Bushman, B. J., & Anderson, C. A. (2001). Media violence and the American public: Scientific facts versus media misinformation. *American Psychologist, 56,* 477–489. doi:10.1037/0003-066X.56.6-7.477

Bushman, B. J., & Huesmann, L. R. (2006). Effects of televised violence on aggression. In D. G. Singer & J. L. Singer (Eds.), *Handbook of children and the media* (pp. 223–254). London, UK: Sage.

Cantor, J., & Wilson, B. J. (2003). Media and violence: Intervention strategies for reducing aggression. *Media Psychology, 5,* 363–403. doi:10.1207/S1532785X MWP0504_03

Card, N. A., & Hodges, E. V. E. (2006). Shared targets for aggression by early adolescent friendships. *Developmental Psychology, 42,* 1327–1338. doi:10.1037/0012-1649.42.6.1327

Card, N. A., Stucky, B. D., Sawalani, G. M., & Little, T. D. (2008). Direct and indirect aggression during childhood and adolescence: A meta-analytic review of gender differences, intercorrelations, and relations to maladjustment. *Child Development, 79,* 1185–1229. doi:10.1111/j.1467-8624.2008.01184.x

Carroll, J. S., Nelson, D. A., Yorgason, D. A., Harper, J. M., Ashton, R. H., & Jensen, A. C. (2010). Relational aggression in marriage. *Aggressive Behavior, 36,* 315–329. doi:10.1002/ab.20349

Casas, J. F., Weigel, S. M., Crick, N. R., Ostrov, J. M., Woods, K. E., Jansen Yeh, E. A., & Huddleson-Casas, C. A. (2006). Early parenting and children's relational and physical aggression in the preschool and home contexts. *Journal of Applied Developmental Psychology, 27,* 209–227. doi:10.1016/j.appdev.2006.02.003

Cecil, D. K. (2008). From *Heathers* to *Mean Girls*: An examination of relational aggression in films. *Journal of Criminal Justice and Popular Culture, 15,* 262–276. Retrieved from http://www.albany.edu/scj/jcjpc/jcjpc_home.html

Christakis, D. A., Garrison, M. M., Herrenkohl, T., Haggerty, K., Rivara, F. P., Zhou, C., & Liekweg, K. (2013). Modifying media violence for preschool children: A randomized controlled trial. *Pediatrics, 131*, 431–438. doi:10.1542 /peds.2012-1493

Coyne, S. M., & Archer, J. (2004). Indirect aggression in the media: A content analysis of British television programs. *Aggressive Behavior, 30*, 254–271. doi:10.1002/ ab.20022

Coyne, S. M., & Archer, J. (2005). The relationship between indirect and physical aggression on television and in real life. *Social Development, 14*, 324–338.

Coyne, S. M., Archer, J., & Eslea, M. (2004). Cruel intentions on television and in real life: Can viewing indirect aggression increase viewers' subsequent indirect aggression? *Journal of Experimental Child Psychology, 88*, 234–253.

Coyne, S. M., Archer, J., & Eslea, M. (2006). "We're not friends anymore! Unless . . ." The frequency and harmfulness of indirect, relational, and social aggression. *Aggressive Behavior, 32*, 294–307. doi:10.1002/ab.20126

Coyne, S. M., Busby, D., Bushman, B. J., Gentile, D. A., Ridge, R., & Stockdale, L. (2012). Gaming in the game of love: Effects of video games on conflict in couples. *Family Relations, 61*, 388–396.

Coyne, S. M., Callister, M., Pruett, T., Nelson, D. A., Stockdale, L., & Wells, B. M. (2011). A mean read. *Journal of Children and Media, 5*, 411–425. doi:10.1080/1 7482798.2011.587148

Coyne, S. M., Callister, M., & Robinson, T. (2010). Yes, another teen movie: Three decades of physical violence in films aimed at adolescents. *Journal of Children and Media, 4*, 387–401. doi:10.1080/17482798.2010.510006

Coyne, S. M., Linder, J. R., Nelson, D. A., & Gentile, D. A. (2012). "Frenemies, frai-tors, and mean-em-aitors": Priming effects of viewing physical and relational aggression in the media on women. *Aggressive Behavior, 38*, 141–149. doi:10.1002/ab.2140

Coyne, S. M., Nelson, D. A., Graham-Kevan, N., Keister, E., & Grant, D. M. (2010). Mean on the screen: Psychopathy, relationship aggression, and aggression in the media. *Personality and Individual Differences, 48*, 288–293. doi:10.1016/j .paid.2009.10.018

Coyne, S. M., Nelson, D. A., Graham-Kevan, N., Tew, E., Meng, K. N., & Olsen, J. A. (2011). Media depictions of physical and relational aggression: Connections with aggression in young adults' romantic relationships. *Aggressive Behavior, 37*, 56–62. doi:10.1002/ab.20372

Coyne, S. M., Nelson, D. A., Lawton, F., Haslam, S., Rooney, L., Titterington, L., Trainor, H., Remnant, J., & Ogunlaja, L. (2008). The effects of viewing physical and relational aggression in the media: Evidence for a cross-over effect. *Journal of Experimental Social Psychology, 44*, 1551–1554. doi:10.1016/j .jesp.2008.06.006

Coyne, S. M., Nelson, D. A., & Underwood, M. K. (2010). Aggression in childhood. In P. K. Smith & C. H. Hart (Eds.), *The Wiley-Blackwell handbook of childhood social development* (2nd ed., pp. 491–509). Chichester, UK: Wiley-Blackwell.

Coyne, S. M., Padilla-Walker, L. M., & Howard, E. (2013). Emerging in a digital world: A decade review of media use, effects, and gratifications in emerging adulthood. *Emerging Adulthood, 1*, 125–137. doi:10.1177/2167696813479782

Coyne, S. M., Ridge, R., Stevens, M., Callister, M., & Stockdale, L. (2012). Backbiting and bloodshed in books: Short-term effects of reading physical and relational aggression in literature. *British Journal of Social Psychology*, *51*, 188–196. doi:10.1111/j.2044-8309.2011.02053.x

Coyne, S. M., Robinson, S. L., & Nelson, D. A. (2010). Does reality backbite? Physical, verbal, and relational aggression in reality television programs. *Journal of Broadcasting and Electronic Media*, *54*, 282–298. doi:10.1080/08838151003737931

Coyne, S. M., & Whitehead, E. (2008). Indirect aggression in animated Disney films. *Journal of Communication*, *58*, 382–395. doi:10.1111/l.1460-2466.2008.00390.x

Crick, N. R. (1996). The role of overt aggression, relational aggression, and prosocial behavior in the prediction of children's future social adjustment. *Child Development*, *67*, 2317–2327. doi:0009-3920/96/6705-0019

Crick, N. R. (1997). Engagement in gender normative versus non-normative forms of aggression: Links to social-psychological adjustment. *Developmental Psychology*, *33*, 610–617. doi:10.1037/0012-1649.33.4.610

Crick, N. R., Casas, J. F., & Ku, H. (1999). Relational and physical forms of peer victimization in preschool. *Developmental Psychology*, *35*, 376–385. doi:10.1037/0012-1649.35.2.376

Crick, N. R., Casas, J. F., & Mosher, M. (1997). Relational and overt aggression in pre-school. *Developmental Psychology*, *33*, 579–588. doi:10.1037/0012-1649.33.4.579

Crick, N. R., Casas, J. F., & Nelson, D. A. (2002). Toward a more comprehensive understanding of peer maltreatment: Studies of relational victimization. *Current Directions in Psychological Science*, *11*, 98–101. doi:10.1111/1467-8721.00177

Crick, N. R., & Grotpeter, J. K. (1995). Relational aggression, gender, and social-psychological adjustment. *Child Development*, *66*, 710–722. doi:009-3920/95/6603-0013

Crick, N. R., Ostrov, J. M., Burr, J. E., Cullerton-Sen, C., Jansen-Yeh, E., & Ralston, P. (2006). A longitudinal study of relational and physical aggression in pre-school. *Journal of Applied Developmental Psychology*, *27*, 254–268. doi:10.1016/j.appdev.2006.02.006

Fernández-Villanueva, C., Revilla-Castro, J. C., Domínguez-Bilbao, R., Gimeno-Jiménez, L., & Almagro, A. (2009). Gender difference in the representation of violence on Spanish television: Should women be more violent? *Sex Roles*, *61*, 85–100. doi:10.1007/s11199-009-9613-9

Gentile, D. A., Coyne, S. M., & Walsh, D. A. (2011). Media violence, physical aggression, and relational aggression in school age children: a short-term longitudinal study. *Aggressive Behavior*, *37*, 193–206. doi:10.1002/ab.20380

Gentile, D. A., Mathieson, L. C., & Crick, N. R. (2011). Media violence associations with the form and function of aggression among elementary school children. *Social Development*, *20*, 213–232. doi:10.1111/j.1467-9507.2010.00577

Gentile, D. A., Saleem, M., & Anderson, C. A. (2007). Public policy and the effects of media violence on children. *Social Issues and Policy Review*, *1*, 15–61. doi:10.1111/j.1751-2409.2007.00003.x

Gentile, D. A., & Sesma, A. (2003). Developmental approaches to understanding media effects on individuals. In D. A. Gentile (Ed.), *Media violence and children* (pp. 19–38). Westport, CT: Praeger.

Glascock, J. (2008). Direct and indirect aggression on prime-time network television. *Journal of Broadcasting and Electronic Media*, *52*, 268–281. doi:10.1080/08838150801992078

Goldberg, R. M., Smith-Adcock, S., & Dixon, A. L. (2011). The influence of the mass media on relational aggression among females: A feminist counseling perspective. *Journal of Aggression, Maltreatment & Trauma, 20*, 376–394. doi:10.1080/1 0926771.2011.568995

Grotpeter, J. K., & Crick, N. R. (1996). Relational aggression, overt aggression, and friendship. *Child Development, 67*, 2328–2338. doi:0009-3920/96/6705-0039

Hammel, L. (2009). Media interaction on relationally aggressive behaviors of middle school girls. *Dissertation Abstracts International Section A, 70*, 1–133.

Hart, C. H., Nelson, D. A., Robinson, C. C., Olsen, S. F., & McNeilly-Choque, M. (1998). Overt and relational aggression in Russian nursery-school-age children: Parenting style and marital linkages. *Developmental Psychology, 34*, 687–697. doi:10.1037//0012-1649.34.4.687

Huesmann, L. R., Moise-Titus, J., Podolski, C.-L., & Eron, L. D. (2003). Longitudinal relations between children's exposure to TV violence and their aggressive and violent behavior in young adulthood: 1977–1992. *Developmental Psychology, 39*, 201–221. doi:10.1037/0012-1649.39.2.201

Kaiser Family Foundation. (2010). *Generation M2: Media in the lives of 8- to 18-year olds.* Menlo Park, CA: Kaiser Family Foundation.

Katz, E., Blumler, J. G., & Gurevitch, M. (1974). Utilization of mass communication by the individual. *The uses of mass communications: Current perspectives on gratifications research* (pp. 318–330). Beverly Hills, CA: Sage Publications.

Kawabata, Y., Crick, N. R., & Hamaguchi, Y. (2010). Forms of aggression, social-psychological adjustment, and peer victimization in a Japanese sample: The moderating role of positive and negative friendship quality. *Journal of Abnormal Child Psychology, 38*, 471–484. doi:10.1007/s10802-010-9386-1

Kirsh, S. J., & Olczak, P. V. (2002a). The effects of extremely violent comic books on social information processing. *Journal of Interpersonal Violence, 17*, 1160–1178. doi:10.1177/088626002237400

Kirsh, S. J., & Olczak, P. V. (2002b). Violent comic books and judgments of relational aggression. *Violence and Victims, 17*, 373–380. Retrieved from http://www .springerpub.com/product/08866708#.UYGAmrUp9I4

Krahé, B., & Möller, I. (2010). Longitudinal effects of media violence on aggression and empathy among German adolescents. *Journal of Applied Developmental Psychology, 31*, 401–409. doi:10.1016/j.appdev.2010.07.003

Leff, S. S., Waasdorp, T. V., & Crick, N. R. (2010). A review of existing relational aggression programs: Strengths, limitations, and future directions. *School Psychology Review, 39*, 508–535. Retrieved from http://www.nasponline.org/

Leyens, P., & Picus, S. (1973). Identification with the winner of a fight and name mediation: Their differential effects on subsequent aggressive behavior. *British Journal of Clinical Psychology, 12*, 374–377. doi:10.1111/j.2044-8260.1973 .tb00083

Linder, J. R., Crick, N. R., & Collins, W. A. (2002). Relational aggression and victimization in young adults' romantic relationships: Associations with perceptions of parent, peer, and romantic relationship quality. *Social Development, 11*, 69–86. doi:10.1111/1467-9507.00187

Linder, J. R., & Gentile, D. A. (2009). Is the television rating system valid? Indirect, verbal, and physical aggression in programs viewed by fifth-grade girls and associations with behavior. *Journal of Applied Developmental Psychology, 30,* 286-297. doi:10.1016/j.appdev.2008.12.013

Linder, J. R., & Lyle, K. A. (2011). A content analysis of indirect, verbal, and physical aggression in television programs popular among school-aged girls. *American Journal of Media Psychology, 4,* 24-42. http://www.hogrefe.com/periodicals /journal-of-media-psychology/

Linder, J. R., & Werner, N. E. (2012). Relationally aggressive media exposure and children's normative beliefs: Does parental mediation matter? *Family Relations, 61,* 488-500. doi:10.1111/j.1741-3729.2012.00707.x

Martins, N. (2009). You don't have to get hit to get hurt: Social aggression on television and its relationship to children's aggression in the classroom. *Dissertation Abstracts International Section A, 70,* 1–257.

Martins, N., & Wilson, B. J. (2012). Mean on the screen: Social aggression in programs popular with children. *Journal of Communication, 6,* 991–1009. doi:10.1111/j.1460-2466.2011.01599.x

Meyer, T. P. (1972). Effects of viewing justified and unjustified real film violence on aggressive behavior. *Journal of Personality and Social Psychology, 23,* 21–29. doi:10.1037/h0032868

Möller, I., & Krahé, B. (2009). Exposure to violent video games and aggression in German adolescents: A longitudinal analysis. *Aggressive Behavior, 35,* 75–89. doi:10.1002/ab.20290

Möller, I., Krahé, B., Busching, R., & Krause, C. (2012). Efficacy of an intervention to reduce the use of media violence and aggression: An experimental evaluation with adolescents in Germany. *Journal of Youth and Adolescence, 41,* 105–120. doi:10.1007/s10964-011-9654-6

Murray-Close, D., Ostrov, J. M., & Crick, N. R. (2007). Short-term longitudinal study of growth of relational aggression during middle childhood: Associations with gender, friendship intimacy, and internalizing problems. *Development and Psychopathology, 19,* 187–203. doi:10.1017/S0954579407070101

Nathanson, A. I., & Yang, M.-S. (2003). The effects of mediation content and form on children's responses to violent television. *Human Communication Research, 29,* 111–134. doi:10.1111/j.1468-2958.2003.tb00833.x

Nelson, D. A., Hart, C. H., Yang, C., Olsen, J. A., & Jin, S. (2006). Aversive parenting in China: Associations with child physical and relational aggression. *Child Development, 77,* 554–572. doi:10.1111/j.1467-8624.2006.00890.x

Nelson, D. A., Robinson, C. C., & Hart, C. H. (2005). Relational and physical aggression of preschool-age children: Peer status linkages across informants. *Early Education and Development, 16,* 115–139. doi:10.1207/s15566935eed 1602_2

Nelson, D. A., Springer, M. M., Nelson, L. J., & Bean, N. H. (2008). Normative beliefs regarding aggression in emerging adulthood. *Social Development, 17,* 638–660. doi:10.1111/j.1467-9507.2007.00442.x

Ostrov, J. M., Crick, N. R., & Stauffacher, K. (2006). Relational aggression in sibling and peer relationships during early childhood. *Journal of Applied Developmental Psychology, 27,* 241–253. doi:10.1016/j.appdev.2006.02.005

Ostrov, J. M., Gentile, D. A., & Crick, N. R. (2006). Media exposure, aggression and prosocial behavior during early childhood: A longitudinal study. *Social Development, 15,* 612–627. doi:10.1111/j.1467-9507.2006.00360.x

Ostrov, J. M., Gentile, D. A., & Mullins, A. D. (2013). Evaluating the effect of educational media exposure on aggression in early childhood. *Journal of Applied Developmental Psychology, 34*, 38–44. doi:10.1016/j.appdev.2012.09.005

Putallaz, M., Grimes, C. L., Foster, K. J., Kupersmidt, J. B., Coi, J. D., & Dearing, K. (2007). Overt and relational aggression and victimization: Multiple perspectives within the school setting. *Journal of School Psychology, 45*, 523–547. doi:10.1016/j.jsp.2007.05.003

Rose, A. J., Swenson, L. P., & Waller, E. M. (2004). Overt and relational aggression and perceived popularity: Developmental difference in concurrent and prospective relations. *Developmental Psychology, 40*, 378–387. doi:10.1037/0012-1649 .40.3.378

Steinberg, L. (2009). *Adolescence.* New York, NY: McGraw-Hill.

Werner, N. E., & Crick, N. R. (1999). Relational aggression and social-psychological adjustment in a college sample. *Journal of Abnormal Psychology, 108*, 615–623. doi:10.1037/0021-843X.108.4.615

Werner, N. E., & Crick, N. R. (2004). Maladaptive peer relationships and the development of relational and physical aggression during middle childhood. *Social Development, 13*, 495–514. doi:10.1111/j.1467-9507.2004.00280

Werner, N. E., & Hill, L. G. (2010). Individual and peer group normative beliefs about relational aggression. *Child Development, 81*, 826–836. doi:10.1111/j.1467-8624 .2010.01436.x

Werner, N. E., & Nixon, C. L. (2006). Normative beliefs and relational aggression: An investigation of the cognitive bases of adolescent aggressive behavior. *Journal of Youth and Adolescence, 34*, 229–244. doi:10.1007/s10964-005-4306-3

CHAPTER 8

Violent Video Game Effects on Aggressive Thoughts, Feelings, Physiology, and Behavior

Craig A. Anderson and Douglas A. Gentile

In 1972 a new form of entertainment became commercially available with the release of the video game *Pong*. In *Pong*, two players tried to "hit" an electronic "ball" back and forth. From these humble beginnings, a revolution in the entertainment industry was born. Interactive game revenues are now significantly greater than the domestic film industry ("Industrial Strengths," 2000). In the United States alone, video game sales (including accessories) exceeded $20 billion in 2012 (Entertainment Software Association, 2013). In this chapter, the term "video game" will be used to describe games played on video game consoles (e.g., PlayStation, XBox), computers, hand-held video game devices (e.g., GameBoy), or cell phones.

The last 15 years have yielded a massive increase in studies of video game effects, thereby allowing clearer answers to the more specific questions of violent video game effects on children, adolescents, and young adults. That is the focus of this chapter, though the reader should bear two things in mind: (1) research on other forms of media violence (e.g., TV, films) is also relevant, and the results from that broader body are generally consistent; and (2) there is a growing body of research demonstrating positive effects of video games.

TIME SPENT WITH VIDEO GAMES

Video games have become one of the dominant entertainment media for children in a very short time. In the mid-1980s children averaged about four hours a week playing video games, including time spent playing at home and in arcades (Harris & Williams, 1985). By the early 1990s home video game use had increased and arcade play had decreased. By the mid-1990s home use had increased to 4.5 hours per week for fourth grade girls and to 7.1 hours per week for fourth grade boys (Buchman & Funk, 1996). By the turn of the century, national surveys showed that school-age children (boys and girls combined) devoted an average of about seven hours per week playing video games (Gentile & Walsh, 2002; Woodard & Gridina, 2000). Two national surveys of American youth ages 8 to 18 found that video game play increased from about 26 minutes a day in 1998–1999 (Rideout, Foehr, & Roberts, 2010) to almost 110 minutes a day a mere decade later (Gentile, 2009), an increase of over 400 percent.

Even very young children are playing video games. Woodard & Gridina (2000) found that preschoolers ages two to five average 28 minutes of video game play per day. Surprisingly, the amount of time children watch television has remained remarkably stable even as the amount of time devoted to video and computer games has increased. Thus, total screen time has been increasing steadily, averaging over six hours a day for the average American child (Rideout et al., 2010; see also chapter 1, this volume).

Over the past 20 years, gaming changed from being primarily a children's activity to being something adults also do; the average age of American gamers is 30 (Entertainment Software Association, 2013). A substantial portion of young adults play video games more than 20 hours per week (e.g., 3.8% of college freshman males; see Pryor et al., 2012). It is not difficult to find male college students who play 40 hours or more per week (Bailey, West, & Anderson, 2010). Figure 8.1 displays the increase in the percent of entering college freshmen who reported playing at least 15 (solid lines) or at least 20 hours (dashed lines) per week during the prior year, from 1995 to 2012. Very few females (fewer than 1%) reported playing at such high levels.

Although the research evidence is still limited, amount of video game play has been linked with a number of risk factors for maladaptive development, including smoking (Kasper, Welsh, & Chambliss, 1999), obesity (Berkey et al., 2000; Subrahmanyam, Kraut, Greenfield, & Gross, 2000; Vandewater, Shim, & Caplovitz, 2004), attention problems (Gentile, Swing, Lim, & Khoo, 2012; Swing & Anderson, 2014; Swing, Gentile, Anderson, & Walsh, 2010) and poorer academic performance (e.g., Anderson & Dill, 2000; Anderson, Gentile, & Buckley, 2007; Creasy & Myers, 1986; Harris & Williams, 1985; Lieberman, Chaffee, & Roberts, 1988; Lynch, Gentile, Olson, & van Brederode, 2001; Roberts, Foehr, Rideout, & Brodie, 1999; Van Schie & Wiegman, 1997; Walsh, 2000; Weis & Cerankosky, 2010). All of these results parallel similar findings in the TV/film research domain.

PREFERENCES FOR VIOLENT VIDEO GAMES

Although video games are designed to be entertaining, challenging, and sometimes educational, most include violent content. Content analyses of video games show that as many as 89 percent of games contain some violent

Figure 8.1
Percent of Entering College Freshmen in U.S. Colleges and Universities Who Report Playing Video Games at Least 15 and at Least 20 Hours per Week during the Previous Year, by Sex

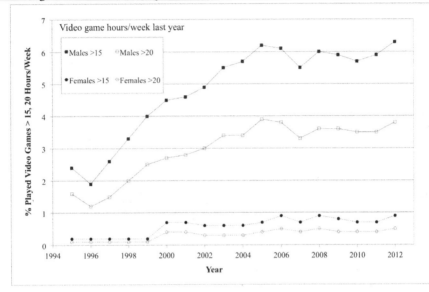

Note: The survey began asking about time on social network sites in 2007.
Source: Data from the American Freshman survey series, 1995–2012.

content (Children Now, 2001), and that about half of the games include violent content toward other game characters that would result in serious injuries or death (Children Now, 2001; Dietz, 1998; Dill, Gentile, Richter, & Dill, 2001). Several studies have shown that the official ratings of video games by the industry-sponsored group Entertainment Software Ratings Board (ESRB) underreport the amount of violence in the games (Haninger & Thompson, 2004; Thompson & Haninger, 2001; Thompson, Tepichin, & Haninger, 2006). Nonetheless, these official ratings still demonstrate that violent content is prevalent in the vast majority of games on the market (Gentile, 2008). For example, 91 percent of games rated as appropriate for "everyone 10 years and older" (E10+) contain an official violence descriptor, slightly higher than the percentage of mature-rated games (for 17 and older, 89%) that have such a descriptor.

Many children prefer to play violent games. Generally, researchers consider as "violent" those games in which the player can harm other characters in the game. In many popular video games, harming other characters is the main activity. (See Appendix A for recent recommendations regarding features of violent video games.)

In studies of fourth- through eighth-grade children, more than half of the children reported preferring games in which the main action is predominantly human violence or fantasy violence (Buchman & Funk, 1996; Funk, 1993). In surveys of children and their parents, about two-thirds of children named violent games as their favorites. Interestingly, only one-third of parents were able to correctly name their child's favorite game; in 70 percent of the incorrect matches, children described their favorite game as violent (Funk, Hagan, & Schimming, 1999). A large nationally representative sample of American children in 2003–2004 found that 38 percent of 8- to 10-year-old boys had played *Grand Theft Auto*, an M-rated ("Mature") game that involves playing the role of a criminal, hiring and killing prostitutes, and killing police and civilians in a wide variety of ways (e.g., clubs, guns, flame throwers, cars, rockets). Seventy-four percent of boys and 60 percent of girls 11 to 14 years old had played that particular violent game series (Rideout et al., 2010).

POTENTIAL FOR EFFECTS OF PLAYING VIOLENT VIDEO GAMES

Over a decade ago, there already had been over 280 independent tests involving over 51,000 participants of the effects of violent media on aggressive behavior (Anderson & Bushman, 2002a). The vast majority of those studies focused on television and movies. Meta-analyses (studies that measure the effects across many studies) have shown four main effects of watching a lot of violent entertainment. These effects have been called the *aggressor effect*, the *victim effect*, the *bystander effect*, and the *appetite effect* (Donnerstein, Slaby, & Eron, 1994; see also Strasburger & Wilson, this volume). These can be summarized as follows.

The *aggressor effect* states that people (both children and adults) exposed to a lot of violent entertainment tend to become meaner, more aggressive, and more violent.

The *victim effect* states that people (both children and adults) exposed to a lot of violent entertainment tend to see the world as a scarier place, become more scared, and initiate more self-protective behaviors (such as carrying guns to school, which, ironically, *increases* one's odds of getting shot).

The *bystander effect* states that people (both children and adults) exposed to a lot of violent entertainment tend to become more desensitized to violence (both in the media and in real life), more callous, and less sympathetic to victims of violence.

The *appetite effect* states that people (both children and adults) exposed to a lot of violent entertainment tend to get an increased appetite for seeing more violent entertainment. Simply put, the more violence one sees, the more violence one wants to see.

The scientific debate over *whether* media violence has an effect has been answered, and the most interesting questions now involve whether some types of people are more likely to be affected and whether some types of media have a more powerful effect.

Why Violent Video Games May Have a *Greater* Effect Than Violent TV/Films

There are at least six reasons why violent video games might have an even greater impact than violent television (Anderson & Dill, 2000; Gentile & Walsh, 2002). These reasons are based on what is known from television and educational literature.

1. **Identification with an aggressor increases imitation of the aggressor.** Children tend to imitate aggressive actions more readily when they identify with an aggressive character in some way. On television, it is hard to predict with which characters, if any, a person will identify. In most violent video games, however, the player necessarily takes the point of view of one particular character.

2. **Active participation increases learning.** This is one reason why computer technology in the classroom is considered to be educationally beneficial. Viewers of violent content on television are passive observers of the aggressive acts, whereas game players are active participants in the violent acts.

3. **Practicing an entire behavioral sequence is more effective than practicing only a part.** It is rare for television shows or movies to display all of these steps necessary to find and kill an enemy. Violent video games regularly require players to practice each of the many steps repeatedly. For example, the popular violent video game series *Rainbow Six* is so good at teaching all of the steps necessary to plan and conduct a successful special operations mission that the U.S. Army has licensed the game engine to train their special operations soldiers (Ubi Soft, 2001). Furthermore, the U.S. Army has created its own violent video game as a recruitment tool (Associated Press, 2002).

4. **Violence is continuous.** Research with violent television and movies has shown that the effects on viewers are greater if the violence is unrelieved and uninterrupted (Comstock & Paik, 1991; Donnerstein, Slaby, & Eron, 1994). However, in both television programs and movies, violent content is rarely sustained for more than a few minutes before changing pace or changing scenes. In contrast, the violence in some violent video games is continuous.

5. **Repetition increases learning.** If one wishes to learn a new phone number by memory, one often will repeat it over and over to aid memory. With few exceptions (e.g., *Blue's Clues*), children rarely see the same television shows over and over. In a violent video game, however, players often spend a great deal of time doing the same aggressive actions (e.g., shooting things) over and over. Furthermore, the games are usually played repeatedly, thus giving a great deal of practice repeating the violent game actions. This increases the odds that not only will children learn from them, but will make these actions habitual to the point of automaticity.

6. **Rewards increase imitation.** There are at least three different reward processes involved. First, rewarding aggressive behavior in a video game (e.g., winning extra

points and lives) increases the frequency of behaving aggressively in that game (see point 5 above; see also Carnagey & Anderson, 2005). Second, rewarding aggressive behavior in a video game teaches more positive attitudes toward the use of force as a means of solving conflicts. Television programs rarely provide a reward structure for the viewer, and it would be rarer still to have those rewards dependent on violent acts. In contrast, video games often reward players for participating. Third, the reward patterns involved in video games increase the player's motivation to persist at the game. Interestingly, all three of these processes help educational games be more effective. The latter process can make the games somewhat addictive.

The very first "violent" video game, *Death Race*, was released in 1976 by Exidy Games. It was a freestanding driving simulator arcade game. In it, one attempted to drive a "car" over little stick figures that ran around. When hit by the car, the stick figures would turn into tiny gravestones with crosses. Over the years, as technology improved, the violence became less abstract, more graphic, more realistic, and more human-centered (see Gentile & Anderson, 2003, for a brief history of violence in games). In the current era of gaming (2005–present), even the smallest of platforms (e.g., cell phones) can have very high-quality images. Computer and console-based games now include photographic quality images. This era also has seen the growth of Internet-based games, some of which are quite simple, with low-quality graphics. Others are quite complex, involving large numbers of other players; some require team-based play. Bandwidth is the key to high-quality graphics and smooth play.

Changes in technology have also produced changes in the nature of empirical studies of violent video game effects across time. Consider early experimental studies, in which participants played either a randomly assigned violent or nonviolent video game and then engage in some task that allows a measure of aggression to be obtained. The difference between the treatment condition (violent game) and the control condition (nonviolent game) was likely to be relatively small in early studies, mainly because the early violent video games were not very violent. Now consider correlational studies, in which video game habits and aggressive behavior habits of participants are simultaneously measured and compared. In early studies of this type, participants who preferred to play violent video games and those who preferred to play nonviolent games likely had fairly similar video game experiences because there weren't any extremely violent games available. Thus, in both types of studies, early studies probably had pretty small differences in the independent variable of interest (i.e., amount of exposure to video game violence) and therefore might have discovered fairly weak effects. Furthermore, in the early years, there were probably social class differences in who could afford home video game systems.

Meta-Analytic Summary of Violent Video Game Effects

Narrative reviews of a research literature, such as that by Dill and Dill (1998), are very useful ways of examining prior studies. Typically, the researchers try to find an organizing scheme that makes sense of the varied results that typically occur in any research domain. However, as useful as such reviews of the literature are, meta-analyses (studies of studies) are a much more powerful technique to find the common effects of violent video games across multiple studies (see chapter 13). Specifically, a meta-analysis uses statistical techniques to combine the results of various studies of the same basic hypothesis, and provides an objective answer to the questions of whether or not the key independent variable has a reliable effect on the key dependent variable, and if so, what the magnitude of that effect is. The most comprehensive meta-analysis to date found that across 136 studies, a consistent pattern of the effects of playing violent games was documented in six areas (Anderson et al., 2010). Figure 8.2 displays these results. It is worth noting that all of the published meta-analyses, *even those conducted by the critics*, find essentially the same results with a significant effect size ranging between about 0.10 and 0.29 (Anderson, 2004; Anderson & Bushman, 2001; Anderson et al., 2010; Anderson, Carnagey, Flanagan, Benjamin, Eubanks, & Valentin, 2004; Bushman & Huesmann, 2006; Ferguson, 2007a, 2007b; Greitemeyer & Mügge, 2014; Sherry, 2001).

1. Playing violent video games increases the odds of aggressive behaviors. Studies measuring aggressive behaviors after playing violent video games have shown that aggressive behaviors are increased compared to playing nonviolent video games (e.g., Anderson, Carnagey, Flanagan, et al., 2004; Irwin & Gross, 1995; Schutte, Malouff, Post-Gorden, & Rodasta, 1988; Silvern & Williamson, 1987). The average effect size across studies between violent game play and aggressive behaviors was 0.24 (Anderson et al., 2010). These effects have been found in children and adults, in males and females, and in experimental and nonexperimental studies. As can be seen in the first three columns in Figure 8.2, the 95 percent confidence interval around this average effect size is quite small and does not come close to including zero. Thus, the results across these 79 independent tests involving over 21,000 participants are quite consistent.

In experimental studies, participants are randomly assigned to play violent or nonviolent games before the outcome variable is measured. For example, in a study of second-grade boys, those who played a violent video game were more likely than those who played a nonviolent game to be both verbally and physically aggressive toward peers in a free-play setting and a structured frustrating task setting (Irwin & Gross, 1995). Neither arousal nor impulsivity moderated the effects.

Other experimental studies have ruled out a host of alternative explanations and have extended the basic violent game effect on aggressive behavior in many ways. For example, Anderson, Carnagey, Flanagan, et al. (2004) controlled for a number of affective and arousal variables and showed that violent game content still increased physically aggressive behavior in college students. This rules out claims that violent games lead to more aggression only

Figure 8.2
Violent Video Game Effects, Best Practices Studies

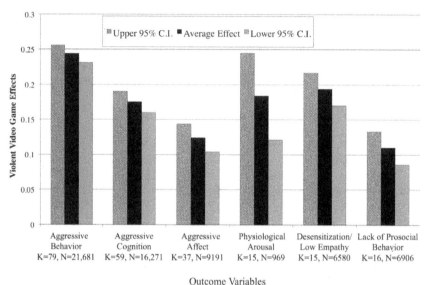

Source: Adapted from Anderson et al., 2010.

because they are more (or less) fun, frustrating, or arousing than the comparison games used in experimental studies, or that only very young children who can't tell the difference between fantasy and reality can be harmed by violent video games. Likewise, although some recent work (e.g., Adachi & Willoughby, 2011) has suggested that some of the results of violent game studies might be due to the competitiveness of the games rather than the violent content, a series of experiments by Carnagey and colleagues has tested this claim and found that it cannot account for the violent game effects (Anderson, & Carnagey, 2009; Carnagey & Anderson, 2005). For example, Anderson and Carnagey (2009) had male and female college students play one of two standard sports games or one of two extra-violent sports games that were matched on specific sport (two football and two baseball games), physiological arousal, enjoyment, excitement, and competitiveness. Also controlled were frustration and perceived difficulty of the games, and trait aggression and sex of the participants. Physical aggression was measured using a standard laboratory task in which participants delivered noxious noise blasts to an opponent. Participants who had just played one of the extra-violent sports games delivered 75 percent more high intensity noise blasts to their opponent than did those who had just played an equally competitive but nonviolent sports game.

Experimental studies from other countries, both Western and Eastern cultures, show that these effects are not limited to the United States or similar

Figure 8.3
Effects of Playing Violent Video Games on Aggressive Behavior

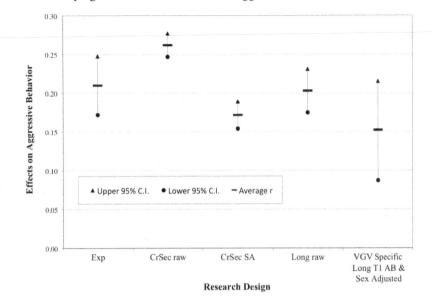

Averages and 95% confidence intervals by research design. Exp = experimental studies (same in best raw and best partials data); CrSec = cross-sectional studies; Raw = data from best raw samples; SA = sex adjusted (data from best partials samples); Long = longitudinal studies; VGV Specific = studies that used the more specific type of video game violence exposure measure; T1 & SA = Time 1 and sex adjusted. *Source:* Adapted from Anderson et al., 2010.

countries (e.g., Konijn, Bijnank, & Bushman, 2007; Sakamoto et al., 2001). On the whole, the average effect size of best practices experimental studies is about 0.21, as shown in Figure 8.3.

Cross-sectional correlation studies are those in which video game habits and an outcome variable (e.g., aggressive behavior in school) are measured at one point in time, often with several other control and explanatory variables. Such correlational studies are not as conclusive as true experiments in terms of establishing causality but are nonetheless very useful in testing causal theories and alternative explanations (Prot & Anderson, 2013). On average, the best estimates of the effect of violent video games on physical aggression in this type of study ranges from about 0.26 to about 0.17 (Figure 8.3), the latter being conservative (Prot & Anderson, 2013). In one such correlational study, young adolescents who played more violent video games were more likely to become involved in physical fights (Gentile, Lynch, Linder, & Walsh, 2004). This effect remained significant even when subject sex, trait hostility, and weekly amount of video game play were statistically controlled, thus simultaneously ruling out several key alternative explanations of the link between violent video game play and physical aggression.

The most significant development in this literature in the last decade is the arrival of several high-quality longitudinal studies. In such studies, the key measures of video game habits and the outcome variables are taken at two or more points in time that are separated by an appropriate time period (i.e., at least several months, often 12 months or longer). One can then test whether violent game exposure at the initial assessment predicts changes in aggressive behavior at later assessments even after controlling (statistically) for aggressiveness at the initial assessment. This allows for stronger causal conclusions because controlling for earlier aggressiveness rules out a large number of the most plausible alternative explanations, such as reverse causality (i.e., being an aggressive person causes one to play more violent video games) and third variable confounds (i.e., having psychopathic genes leads to both high aggression and a preference for violent games) (Prot & Anderson, 2013). Certainly, longitudinal designs are usually not as definitive as experimental ones in establishing causality, but because remaining noncausal alternative explanations must become increasing convoluted, evidence that is consistent with the causal model from well-conducted longitudinal studies greatly increases scientists' confidence in the causal hypothesis.

There is now considerable longitudinal evidence that habitual exposure to violent video games causes an increase in the likelihood of physically aggressive behavior. The 2010 meta-analysis yielded average effect sizes ranging from about 0.20 to 0.15 (Figure 8.3). The first English-language longitudinal study of this type assessed video game habits, physical aggression, and several additional control and mediating variables in elementary school students at two points in time separated by an average of five months (Anderson et al., 2007). One major strength of this study was the use of multiple sources of information on physical aggression: teachers, peers, and self-report. The study yielded a significant long-term effect of early violent game exposure on later physical aggression, even after controlling for early levels of physical aggressiveness, sex, race, total screen time, hostile attribution bias (HAB), and parental involvement in media. Other studies from various countries have confirmed such longitudinal effects (e.g., Gentile, Li, Khoo, Prot, & Anderson, 2014 [Singapore]; Möller & Krahé, 2009 [Germany]; Naito, Kobayashi, & Sakamoto, 1999 [Japan]; Wallenius & Punamaki, 2008 [Finland]).

A recent Canadian longitudinal study tracked high school students over a four-year period and included a huge number of background variables, such as sex, parent SES, academic performance, depression, delay of gratification, peer deviance, sports involvement, friendship quality, parental relationship, and school culture, among others (Willoughby, Adachi, & Good, 2012). This was made statistically feasible by the large sample size (over 1,400). They found a significant longitudinal effect of violent video game exposure even after statistically controlling for this wide array of variables.

Figure 8.4
Comparison of Violent Video Game Effects on Overall Social Outcomes (Combined Behavior, Cognition, Affect, and Arousal) as a Function of Research Group

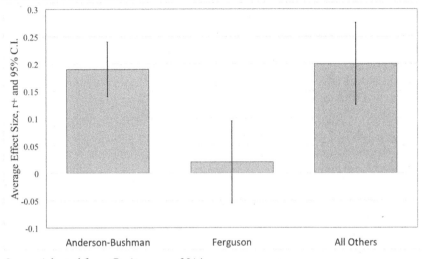

Source: Adapted from Greitemeyer, 2014.

There are, of course, occasional studies that fail to find significant effects. Some of these may be the result of poor methods, small samples, or the normal amount of randomness that is observed in any set of empirical studies. Interestingly, a recent meta-analysis of modern era studies (2009–2013) compared the violent video game effect sizes reported by two different research teams (Anderson and/or Bushman-authored papers, versus Ferguson-authored papers) to effect sizes reported by all other research teams (Greitemeyer & Mügge, 2013). The reason for doing this was to empirically examine Ferguson's frequent claims that the Anderson and Bushman teams' studies are somehow biased and report inflated effect sizes. The fascinating result of this comparison was that the 20 studies (N = 8,595) by the Anderson and the Bushman teams found the same effects (average $r+$ = 0.19) as the rest of world (average $r+$ = 0.20, 58 studies, N = 23,415), whereas Ferguson's 7 studies (N = 2,444) yielded significantly smaller effect sizes (average $r+$ = 0.02) (see Figure 8.4). It is interesting that the researcher who has frequently accused others of bias is the one whose research findings are very discrepant from all the other researchers.

In sum, when all studies are included in appropriate meta-analyses (even those by Ferguson and his colleagues), the picture that emerges is one of consistency across research methods, research team (except Ferguson's), culture, age, and personality type. In sum, the current array of studies on violent video games demonstrates that violent games are a causal risk factor for aggression, both in the short term and across development.

2. Playing violent video games increases aggressive cognitions. Numerous studies have uncovered a strong link between playing violent video games and aggressive thinking. This is true of studies from all gaming eras (e.g., Anderson, Carnagey, Flanagan, et al., 2004; Graybill, Kirsch, & Esselman, 1985; Kirsh, 1998; Saleem & Anderson, 2013). The average effect size across types of studies is about 0.17 to 0.18 (Figure 8.2). These effects have been found in children and adults, in males and females, in experimental and nonexperimental studies, and in Western and Eastern cultures (Anderson et al., 2010).

Aggressive cognitions have been measured in many ways. For example, Anderson & Dill (2000) found that playing a violent game primed aggressive thoughts, as measured by the relative speed with which players could read aggression-related words on a computer screen. Barlett and Rodeheffer (2009) used a word completion task and found that briefly playing a violent video game increased the proportion of word fragments that were completed with aggressive words.

Studies of children's social information processing have shown that playing violent games increase children's hostile attribution biases. Hostile attribution bias (HAB) is important because children who have this social problem-solving deficit are also more likely to act aggressively and are likely to be socially maladjusted (Crick & Dodge, 1994). Kirsh (1998) randomly assigned third and fourth grade children to play either a violent or a nonviolent video game. Children were then presented with stories in which a same-sex peer caused a negative event to occur, but where the peer's intent was ambiguous, and were asked to explain the event. Violent video game–playing children gave responses attributing greater aggressive intent to the peer (i.e., they had greater HAB) than children who played the nonviolent game; they also were more likely to suggest retaliation.

Bushman and Anderson (2002) randomly assigned college student participants to play one of four violent or one of four nonviolent video games for 20 minutes. Next, participants completed three ambiguous story stems (ambiguous as to aggressive content) by indicating what the main character would do or say, think, or feel. Coders blind to experimental condition counted the number of aggressive actions, thoughts, and feelings contained in each story completion. Playing a violent video game increased aggressive story elements by over 40 percent. In a more recent study using the story completion method, Hasan, Begue, and Bushman (2012) replicated this expectation bias and found that it mediated the effect of a violent video game manipulation on later physical aggression.

Uhlmann and Swanson (2004) used the Implicit Attitudes Test procedure to assess self-associations to aggression. They found that playing a violent video game increased such self-associations.

Saleem and Anderson (2013) used implicit and explicit measures of attitudes toward Arab/Muslims. College student participants who had just played a violent terrorism–themed video game displayed more anti-Arab attitudes than those who played a nonviolent game, even when the terrorism game was set in Russia and didn't involve Arab/Muslims. Interestingly, playing a violent game that did not involve a terrorism theme did not produce an increase in anti-Arab attitudes.

Numerous cross-sectional and several longitudinal studies have assessed the effects of violent video game exposure on aggression-related cognitions (e.g., Anderson et al., 2007; Möller and Krahé, 2009). For example, in a longitudinal study of over 3,000 Singaporean children, aggressive cognitions (defined as HAB, normative beliefs about aggression, and aggressive fantasies) mediated the longitudinal effect (Gentile et al., 2014). That is, children who played more violent games began by the next year to have more aggressive thoughts, which predicted more aggressive behaviors the following year.

3. Playing violent video games increases aggressive affect (emotion). Studies measuring emotional responses to playing violent video games have shown that aggressive affect is increased as compared to playing nonviolent video games. The average effect size across 37 studies with over 9,000 participants between violent game play and aggressive affect was 0.12 (Figure 8.2). Interestingly, and as expected theoretically, the long-term effects on aggressive affect are considerably smaller than the immediate short-term effect, as shown by the differences in average effect size by design. The short-term experimental studies yielded an average effect size of 0.29, considerably larger than the cross-sectional studies (0.10) or the longitudinal studies (0.08) (Anderson et al., 2010).

There are fewer aggressive affect studies than aggressive behavior and cognition, in part because it is less interesting theoretically. That is, aggressive feeling can be activated temporarily by nonviolent video games too, especially if they are difficult or frustrating. Another reason that fewer aggressive affect studies meet the "best practices" criteria is that many studies intentionally control for aggressive affect in order to more cleanly test the effects of violent game content on behavior or cognition. Nonetheless, violent video game effects on aggressive affect have been found in children and adults, in males and females, and in Eastern and Western cultures. In the first published experimental study, college student participants reported greater state hostility and anxiety levels after playing a violent game than after playing nonviolent games (Anderson & Ford, 1986). Other experimental studies have found similar effects in subsequent eras (e.g., Arriaga, Esteves, Carneiro, & Monteiro, 2006; Fleming & Rickwood, 2001).

4. Playing violent video games increases physiological arousal. Experimental studies measuring heart rate, skin conductance, and systolic and diastolic blood pressure tend to show larger increases from violent games than from nonviolent video games (e.g., Gwinup, Haw, & Elias, 1983; Murphy, Alpert, & Walker, 1992; Segal & Dietz, 1991). The average effect size across studies between violent game play and physiological arousal was 0.18 (Figure 8.2). For example, Ballard and Wiest (1996) showed that a violent game (*Mortal Kombat* with the blood "turned on") resulted in higher systolic blood pressure responses than either a nonviolent game or a less graphically violent game (*Mortal Kombat* with the blood "turned off").

Other physiological reactions have also been found. Adult males' brains have been shown to release dopamine in response to playing a violent video game (Koepp et al., 1998). In addition, Lynch (1994, 1999) has found that the physiological effects of playing violent video games may be even greater for children who already show more aggressive tendencies. Adolescents who scored in the top quintile for trait hostility, measured by the Cook & Medley (1954) scale, showed greater increases in heart rate, blood pressure, and epinephrine and testosterone levels in the blood. There were also trends for increased levels of norepinephrine and cortisol in the blood for the more hostile children. This interaction with trait hostility suggests that the effects of playing violent games may be even greater for children who are already at higher risk for aggressive behavior.

5. Playing violent video games decreases prosocial behaviors. Studies have shown that playing violent video games decreases prosocial behavior, relative to playing nonviolent video games. This was found in early studies as well as in more recent ones (e.g., Ballard & Lineberger, 1999; Bushman & Anderson, 2009; Chambers & Ascione, 1987; Silvern & Williamson, 1987; Wiegman & Van Schie, 1998). The average effect size at the time of the most recent comprehensive meta-analysis was relatively small ($r+ = -0.11$)* but still significant (Figure 8.2). Furthermore, the average effect was significant for each of the three design types (experimental, cross-sectional, longitudinal).

In a cross-sectional study, Gentile et al. (2009) showed that violent video game play was negatively associated with helpful behavior in a large sample of Singaporean 12- to 14-year-olds, even after controlling for sex, age, total amount of game play per week, and prosocial video game play. They also reported an experimental study with U.S. college student participants in which briefly playing a violent game led to less helpful and more hurtful behavior than playing a neutral or prosocial game. Demonstrating that game content matters, this study also showed that playing a game with prosocial themes (rather than violent ones) increased prosocial behaviors after play.

Bushman and Anderson (2009) randomly assigned college student participants to play either one of four violent video games or one of four nonviolent games for 20 minutes. After game play, while completing a lengthy questionnaire alone, they heard a loud fight apparently taking place in the hallway outside the lab, in which one person was injured. Participants who had played one of the violent games took longer to help the injured victim, rated the fight as less serious, and were less likely to "hear" the fight in comparison to participants who played a nonviolent game.

Anderson et al. (2007), and Yukawa & Sakamoto (2001) reported longitudinal studies showing similar negative effects of violent game habits on prosocial behavior with U.S. elementary students and Japanese high school students, respectively. In a more recent longitudinal study, Prot, Gentile, Anderson et al. (2014) assessed the effects of violent and prosocial video game play of over 3,000 Singaporean 9- to 13-year-olds on prosocial behavior two years later. They found that violent game play led to a decrease in later prosocial behavior even after controlling for initial level of prosocial behavior, empathy, prosocial game use, total game time, and sex (whereas prosocial game play increased prosocial behaviors).

6. Playing violent video games decreases empathy and increases desensitization. The 2010 meta-analysis found too few high-quality studies of empathy and desensitization to warrant separate meta-analyses of these two theoretically linked variables, so they were combined. There was a significant harmful effect of violent video game play: $r+ = -0.19$. Exposure to violent video games led to relatively lower empathy/higher desensitization scores (Figure 8.2).

In the only experimental study, Carnagey, Anderson, and Bushman (2007), showed that playing a randomly assigned violent video game caused a significant reduction in physiological reactivity (cardiovascular function, skin conductance) to later scenes of real violence, relative to playing a nonviolent game. In a correlational study, Funk, Baldacci, Pasold, & Baumgardner (2004) found that in a sample of 8- to 11-year-olds, video game violence exposure was negatively related to trait empathy, even after controlling for sex, and for exposure to real-life, television, movie, and Internet violence. Bartholow, Sestir, and Davis (2005) found that in college students, violent video game exposure was negatively related to trait empathy and that this relationship partially mediated the violent video game effect on aggressive behavior. More recently, a longitudinal study (Prot et al., 2014) found that violent video game exposure in year 1 led to a decline in empathy in later years, and that this decline in empathy partially mediated the harmful longitudinal effect of year 1 violent video game exposure on year 3 prosocial behavior. Figure 8.5 shows the longitudinal results.

MODERATORS OF VIDEO GAME EFFECTS

In the previous edition of this book, we noted that the research literature was too small to allow sensitive tests of potential moderator effects (moderator variables can enhance or diminish other effects). Such effects, essentially interactions between exposure to video game violence and the moderating variable (e.g., sex, age), require very large samples for adequate tests. The

Figure 8.5
Path Model of Prosocial and Violent Video Game Use as Predictors of Empathy and Prosocial Behavior over Time

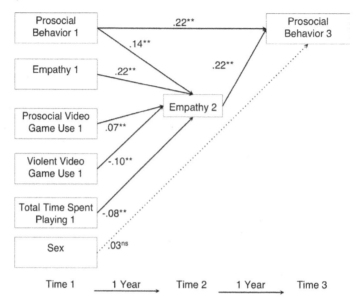

$\chi 2 = 9.05$, df = 5, p > 0.05; TLI = 0.98; CFI = 0.99; RMSEA = 0.02, 90% CI = 0.00 − 0.03. Standardized coefficients are shown; * p < 0.02, ** p < 0.01.
Source: Adapted from Prot et al., 2014.

2010 meta-analysis included such a set of studies but still found very few moderation effects. For example, when physical aggression was the outcome variable, none of the participant characteristics (sex, age, culture) yielded significant moderation—that is, the effects were similar for younger and older ages, for both boys and girls, and for both Eastern and Western cultures.

Nonetheless, there are theoretical, methodological, and empirical reasons to expect some groups to be somewhat more susceptible to violent video game effects than others, though existing theory and evidence does not provide reasons to expect any particular group to be totally immune. Funk and her colleagues (Funk, 2001, 2003; Funk & Buchman, 1996; Funk, Buchman, & Germann, 2000) have described how many of the effects of video game play could be enhanced by other personal characteristics and risk factors. These include player sex, age, status as bullies or victims of bullies, children with poor social problem-solving skills, and children with poor emotion regulation abilities. To this list we would add children who are generally more hostile in personality, who have a history of aggressive behavior, or whose parents do not monitor or limit their video game play. These risk factors will be described briefly below.

Although there is insufficient evidence to make strong claims about certain groups being more vulnerable to violent video game effects, there are a few individual studies that provide some such evidence. For instance, Markey and Scherer (2009) found that the violent video game effect on state hostility and on aggressive cognition was somewhat greater for college student participants who scored high on a psychoticism measure than for those who scored low on psychoticism.

Longitudinal studies have repeatedly demonstrated that the best predictor of future aggressive or violent behavior is past history of aggression and violence (Anderson & Huesmann, 2003; U.S. Surgeon General, 2001). Bushman and Huesmann (2006) conducted a meta-analysis of TV and video game effects as a function of age and type of study (short-term vs. long-term effects). They found some evidence that short-term effects (which rely on priming of well-established knowledge structures about aggression) are larger for older participants than for younger children, whereas long-term effects (which involve change in behavioral tendencies) are larger for children than young adults. Both of these trends make sense theoretically, in that younger children have relatively less well-developed aggression knowledge structures and relatively more malleable behavioral tendencies. However, it also important to note that the few studies that include both children and adults in the same study have not replicated the meta-analysis–based pattern. For example, Anderson et al. (2007, Study 1) experimentally manipulated whether children (9-to 12-years old) and college students played a violent or a nonviolent children's game and later assessed aggressive behavior using a standard laboratory task. In both age groups, the violent video game yielded significantly greater aggression than the nonviolent game. But in contrast to the Bushman and Huesmann (2006) meta-analytic finding, the short-term experimental effect of the video game manipulation was slightly larger for the children than it was for the college students.[1]

Parental monitoring and limiting of children's media use has been found to be an important moderating factor with other media such as television. Limits on the amount of time, coviewing, and mediation (discussion) of television messages have been shown to have beneficial effects (e.g., Austin, 1993; Gadberry, 1980; Robinson, Wilde, Navracruz, Haydel, & Varady, 2001; Strasburger & Donnerstein, 1999). Active parental involvement, such as rules limiting media use and active mediation (both positive encouragement to watch "positive" media and discouragement of "negative" messages) can be effective in influencing children's viewing, understanding, reactions to, and imitation of program content (Dorr & Rabin, 1995; Lin & Atkin, 1989).

In the video game domain, only a few studies have tested parental involvement as a potential moderator, with mixed results. The experimental study in Anderson et al. (2007) described earlier found that participants whose parents were actively involved in their media use were significantly less affected by the experimental manipulation of violent versus nonviolent game play on aggression in the lab task. Also, in a correlational analysis of the children's self-reports of violent behavior history, it was found that parental involvement moderated the effect of media violence habits. That is, children whose parents were uninvolved in their child's media use showed a stronger relationship between exposure to media violence and behaving violently.

The longitudinal study reported in Anderson et al. (2007) also assessed parental involvement in their children's media habits. That study failed to find a significant moderating effect on physical aggression, as did a recent longitudinal study of 3,000 Singaporean youth (Gentile et al., 2014). Thus, as noted earlier, evidence of moderation of media violence effects by personal and family characteristics remains mixed at best. This, of course, contrasts with the generally consistent effects of media violence (and video game violence) on aggressive behavior, affect, and cognition.

When parents are asked if they have rules about the amount of time their children may play video or computer games, 62 percent say "yes," but if one asks the children themselves, that number drops to 32 percent (Gentile, Nathanson, Rasmussen, Reimer, & Walsh, 2012). When asked how often parents use the ratings to choose video games, only 34 percent of parents report using them "every time" or "most of the time" (Gentile, Maier, Hasson, & de Bonetti, 2011). Despite this apparent lack of consistent parental monitoring, parental limits on the time and content of video games are significantly related to lower levels of youth aggressive behavior (e.g., Gentile et al., 2004).

Although there appear to be general effects of playing violent video games on aggression and aggression-related outcomes, we believe that the effects are not likely to be identical for all children. The characteristics that we believe are most likely to emerge as significant risk factors for the negative effects of exposure to violent video games are: younger ages, poor social problem-solving skills, low parental monitoring, gender, hostile personality, and a history of aggression and violence. To date, none of these variables has yielded consistent moderation effects, in either the video game literature or the broader media violence literature. The fact that moderation effects have proven elusive suggests that the major effects of violent media are broad, apply to most people, and are more robust than any true moderation effect that the field has yet to identify.

NEW TRENDS AND CHALLENGES IN VIOLENT VIDEO GAME RESEARCH

New Trends

Although parents tend to be most concerned with potentially harmful effects of games, several new lines of research have documented that game effects are complex and that even violent games can have some benefits. In this section, we briefly highlight some recent trends in violent video game research.

Effects of playing as a criminal

Several recent studies have examined the potential effects of playing violent video games in which the player takes the role of a criminal. The most notorious game series of this type, of course, is the highly popular *Grand Theft Auto* series (*GTA*), though there are other games that allow one to assume the role of an immoral or criminal character. Several experimental studies have found that playing a game as an immoral or criminal character can lead to increases in feelings of guilt (e.g., Hartmann, Toz, & Brandon, 2010). In one study (Gollwitzer & Melzer, 2012), college student participants played either a game that required violence against objects but not humans (*Flat Out 2*, in Demolition Derby mode) or a game that required criminal violence against humans (*GTA*), for about 20 minutes. Later, and supposedly as part of another study, they were shown a table with 10 products, 5 of which were hygiene related (e.g., shower gel), and were asked to indicate four that they would like to take with them. Consistent with the authors' *moral cleansing* hypothesis, those who had just played *GTA* chose significantly more cleansing items than those in the other game condition. This effect was especially pronounced for relatively inexperienced players. Similar results were obtained on a moral distress measure.

. Another experimental study (Lee, Peng, & Klein, 2010) randomly assigned college students to either a no-game control condition or to play *True Crime*, a game in which the main character—a police officer—uses excessive violence to catch lawbreakers and sometimes harms innocent people for fun. Those in the *True Crime* condition played the game for two hours. Later, all participants read four case histories, two real-life crime cases committed by police officers and two by generic criminals. After reading each case, they answered questions on their judgments of the crime and the criminal. Participants who played the violent game were more accepting of crimes and criminals compared to people who did not play the violent game. This effect was especially strong when the real-life criminal actions were perpetrated by police officers (matching the game role participants had played) and if the real criminal actions were similar to the activities they perpetrated during game play.

A fascinating pair of experiments reported by Fischer, Aydin, Kastenmuller, Frey, & Fischer (2012) had participants play either a delinquency-reinforcing video game (e.g., *Burn Out*, *GTA*) or a neutral game (*Tetris*). Experiment 1 found that players of a delinquency-reinforcing driving video game displayed more tolerance for a severe road traffic offense than players of the control game. Experiment 2 found that players of *GTA* were more likely to steal laboratory equipment (pens and candy bars) than players of the control game.

A recent cross-sectional study by Gabbiadini, Andrighetto, and Volpato (2012) investigated the effect of playing *GTA* on moral disengagement, a process in which people shift their moral boundaries, creating a version of reality in which reprehensible conduct becomes morally acceptable (Bandura, Barbaranelli, Caprara, & Pastorelli, 1996). They found that Italian high school students who had played *GTA* scored higher on moral disengagement than those who had not. This effect remained significant even after controlling for sex, age, and overall exposure to video games in general.

Risk glorification effects

A recent review of research on the effects of exposure to media that glorify risk-taking behavior found strong evidence that such media, particularly active participation media (e.g., video games), causes an increase in the likelihood of later risk-taking behavior in the real world (Fischer, Krueger, Greitemeyer, Asal, Aydin, & Vingilis, 2012). For example, playing racing video games that encourage risky driving appears to lead to real riskier driving.

Effects on civic engagement

A recent cross-sectional study examined associations among video game habits, family characteristics, and civic engagement attitudes and behavior (Anderson, 2013). This study was based on a national U.S. sample of teens by the Pew Internet & American Life Project (Lenhart et al., 2008). Path analyses found that violent gaming was negatively associated with attitudes toward civic engagement and with civic engagement behavior, even after controlling for participant gender, age, social connectedness, internet use, parent education, parent involvement in their child's gaming decisions, and parent civic engagement. Prosocial and nonviolent gaming were positively associated with civic attitudes and behavior. Youth civic engagement was also predicted by social connectedness and by parent civic engagement. Parent involvement moderated the violent gaming effects; for both civic attitudes and behavior, parent involvement in youth gaming activities (which included talking about game content and limiting games) significantly moderated the harmful effects of playing violent video games. That is, a high level of parent involvement reduced (but did not eliminate) the negative effects of violent gaming on youth civic attitudes and engagement. Figure 8.6 displays a simplified depiction of the main results.

Effects on attention and spatial cognition

Both positive and negative effects on visual attention have been found in video game studies. For more detailed reviews, see Bailey, West, and Anderson (2011) and Prot, Anderson, Gentile, Brown, and Swing (in press).

Positive effects of violent video game play on visual-spatial skills have been found both in correlational and experimental studies. Gamers have been found to outperform nongamers on a number of visual and spatial tasks, demonstrating faster visual reaction times and improved target localization and mental rotation (Achtman, Green, & Bavelier, 2008; Green & Bavelier, 2003, 2007). Experimental studies have shown that only 10 hours of video

Figure 8.6
Effects of Violent, Nonviolent, and Prosocial Gaming and Parent Involvement on Youth Civic Attitudes and Behavior (Engagement); Full Final Path Analysis Model Showing Only the Key Gaming Variables and Directional Paths

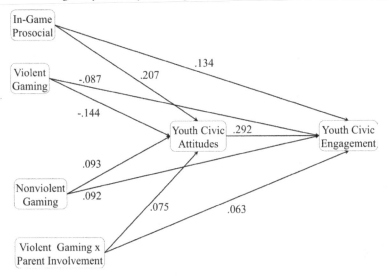

Note: All paths are significant at $p < 0.05$. Standardized betas are shown. N = 821, GFI = 0.99, CFI = 0.99, AGFI = 0.97, NFI = 0.97. Chi-square (38) = 63.71, RMSEA = 0.03.
Source: Adapted from Anderson, 2013.

game play can improve spatial attention and mental rotation (Feng, Spence, & Pratt, 2007; Green & Bavelier, 2003). Of course, improvement of visual-spatial skills can also be made by playing certain types of nonviolent video games (e.g., Okagaki & Frensch, 1994). Two additional issues should be noted, however. First, although these studies often are discussed in terms of improving "attention," what is actually improved is merely the ability to notice things on a screen; it is not the kind of sustained and focused attention that classroom teachers mean when they discuss "attention." Second, these positive effects appear to be narrowly limited to spatial skills very similar to tasks performed in the video games. Other studies suggest that these effects do not generalize easily to real-world navigation performance (Richardson, Powers, & Bousquet, 2011).

Negative effects of video game play on other types of attention-related measures have been reported in recent years. These include problems such as attention deficit disorders, impulsiveness, self-control, school performance, executive functioning, and cognitive control. These effects remain even after controlling for sex, age, race, and socioeconomic status. Violent game playing has been linked with attention problems (e.g., Hastings et al., 2009), and some studies find that the violent content link explains some unique variance beyond the overall hours of video game playing (Gentile et al., 2012). Longitudinal studies have found that overall video game exposure is related to greater subsequent attention problems, even when earlier attention problems are statistically controlled (Gentile et al., 2012; Swing et al., 2010; for a review see Prot et al., in press).

A number of studies have found that violent video game play is associated with poorer executive control (e.g., Hummer et al., 2010; Bailey et al., 2011; Kirsh, Olczak, & Mounts, 2005; Mathews et al., 2005). One particularly disturbing finding comes from brain wave (ERP) research comparing high versus low gamers' brain responses to photos of people in positive, neutral, negative nonviolent (e.g., diseased), and negative violent (e.g., knife to someone's throat) states. One specific contrast suggested that high exposure to video game violence can result in violent and positive images taking on positive affective valence (Bailey et al., 2011).

Swing and Anderson (2012) trained video game novices for 10 weeks on the same fast-paced violent video game (*Unreal Tournament*) that has been shown in prior studies to improve visual/spatial skills. Other participants were randomly assigned to train on a slower-paced nonviolent game (*The Sims*) or were in a no-training control condition. The results mirrored those of Green and colleagues, in that training on the violent game led to more improvement on a visual/spatial skill (Useful Field of View task) than in the two control conditions. What is unique about this study, though, is that proactive and reactive executive control were also assessed (using a Stroop task) (Green & Bavalier, 2007). Even as the violent game improved visual/spatial skill, it also reduced performance on the proactive executive control measure.

A recent cross-sectional study of college students also suggests unique links between violent media exposure (including video games), certain types of attention problems, and impulsive aggression (Swing & Anderson, 2014). As can been seen in Figure 8.7, even after taking into account total time spent on electronic media, violent media exposure was still uniquely and directly associated with attention problems (self-reported ADHD, impulsiveness), and indirectly (through attention problems, aggressive cognitions, and anger/hostility) to impulsive aggression.

Other problems

Two other important issues do not at present seem to be specifically related to the violent content of video games—school performance problems and video game (or Internet) addiction. Several cross-sectional and at least one experimental and one longitudinal study have linked video game use with poor school performance (e.g., Anderson & Dill, 2000; Chan & Rabinowitz, 2006; Cordes & Miller, 2000; Gentile, 2009; Sharif & Sargent, 2006). Similar results have been found for elementary school through college student participants. For example, a recent survey of a large, nationally representative

Figure 8.7
Effects of Total Screen Media Exposure and Violent Media Exposure on Attention Problems, Aggressive Cognition, Anger/Hostility, and Impulsive and Premeditated Aggression

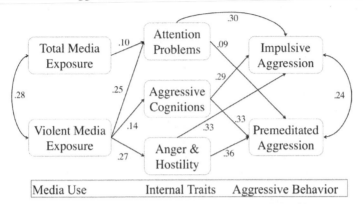

CMIN: 15.37, df = 11, p = 0. 166, GFI: 0.99, AGFI: 0.97, CFI: 0.99, RMSEA: 0.032 (90% CI: 0.000, 0.066). All paths are significant. Sex was included as a covariate, though the paths and coefficients are not displayed. Standardized path coefficients are reported. *Source:* Adapted from Swing & Anderson, 2014.

sample of American children and adolescents found that nearly half (47%) of heavy media users get poor grades, compared to 23 percent of light media users (Rideout et al., 2010).

In a study of eighth and ninth grade students (Gentile et al., 2004), lower grades were associated with both more years of video game play and with more hours played each week (by self-report). Path analyses yielded a significant effect of amount of video game play on school performance but no additional effect of violent game content. However, violent content showed an independent significant effect on aggressive behavior. This analysis lends support for considering amount of game play and content of game play as two independent potential risk factors for children but for different outcome variables (i.e., school performance, aggression; see Gentile, 2011, for discussion of the five dimensions along which games can have unique effects). Other research further supports the idea that video game time displacing academic time is the primary way that video games pose a risk for poorer academic performance. For example, adolescent video gamers have been found to spend 30 percent less time reading and 34 percent less time doing homework than nongamers (Cummings & Vandewater, 2007).

A longitudinal study of elementary school children showed that total screen time significantly predicts poorer grades later in the school year, even while controlling for other relevant covariates (Anderson, Gentile, & Buckley, 2007). An experimental study by Weis and Cerankosky (2010) further confirmed that these effects are causal, in a sample of 6- to 9-year-old boys whose families did not currently have a video game system. First, the researchers did a baseline assessment of boys' academic achievement and parent- and teacher-reported behavior. Next, the boys were randomly assigned to receive PlayStation II video game systems either immediately or after the follow-up assessment four months later. During that four-month interval, boys who received the system immediately spent more time playing video games and less time on after-school academic activities than comparison children. They also had lower reading and writing scores and greater teacher-reported academic problems at the four-month follow-up than comparison children. The amount of video-game play time mediated the relation between video-game ownership and academic outcomes.

The second emerging video game problem that appears to owe more to the amount of time playing games than the violent content is video game (and Internet) addiction, or pathological gaming. Researchers define pathological use of video games in the same way as pathological gambling—focusing on damage to family, social, school, occupational, and psychological functioning (Sim, Gentile, Bricolo, Serpelloni, & Gulamoydeen, 2012). Like gambling, playing video games starts as a form of entertainment. It becomes pathological for some people when video games start producing negative life consequences. This condition (now called Internet gaming disorder) has recently been classified as a medical disorder in the Diagnostic and Statistic Manual of Mental Disorders (DSM-5).

Overall, studies examining pathological video gaming show good reliability and validity (Gentile, Coyne, & Bricolo, 2013). Regarding prevalence, one national study conducted in the United States with a sample of 1,100 youth found that 8.5 percent of youth gamers could be classified as pathological (Gentile, 2009). Similar percentages are found in several other countries, including 8.7 percent in Singapore (Choo et al., 2010), 10.3 percent (Peng & Li, 2009) and 10.8 percent (Lam, Peng, Mai, & Jing, 2009) in China, 8.0 percent in Australia (Porter, Starcevic, Berle, & Fenech, 2010), 11.9 percent in Germany (Grüsser, Thalemann, & Griffiths, 2007), and 7.5 percent in Taiwan (Ko, Yen, Yen, Lin, & Yang, 2007). These studies have not used a common methodology or definition, however, so each estimate of prevalence should be considered to be preliminary (although it is interesting that the percentages are so similar given the differences in methods and populations).

In both of these problems—school performance and pathological gaming—there is not yet adequate research that uniquely implicates violent game content as a causal culprit. Nonviolent games and Internet use can also displace time spent on academic, family, social, school, and occupational activities. Of course, it also is possible that violent action games may be particularly apt to cause such problems because of their ability to attract and maintain users' attention through brain systems involved in reward circuits or fight/flight circuits. More research is needed on these questions.

NEW (AND CONTINUING) CHALLENGES

Any new research domain has strengths and weaknesses. When the new research domain appears to threaten the profits of some large industry, there is a tendency for that industry to deny the threatening research and to mount campaigns designed to highlight the weaknesses, obfuscate the legitimate findings, and cast doubt on the quality of the research and the researchers. The history of the tobacco industry's attempt to ridicule, deny, and obfuscate research linking smoking to lung cancer is the prototype of such efforts. This type of effort has been mounted by the video game industry and its supporters. We do not claim that there are no weaknesses in the video game research literature. Indeed, over recent years we have highlighted some of them and conducted research to address them. In this final section, we focus on two types of challenges, insufficient/invalid ones and remaining legitimate ones.

Insufficient/Invalid Challenges

1. *There are too few studies to warrant any conclusions about possible negative effects.*

This can be a legitimate concern if the small number of studies yields a lack of power to detect small effects. However, it is invalid when used to claim that the current set of video game studies do not warrant serious concern about exposure to violent video games. With over 100 published studies, especially several longitudinal studies, this is no longer a serious criticism.

2. *There are problems with the external validity of lab experiments due to demand characteristics, participant suspicion and compliance problems, trivial measures, artificial settings, and unrepresentative participants.*

These arguments against laboratory studies in the behavioral sciences have been tested many times, in many contexts, and in several different ways. Both logical and empirical analyses of such broad-based attacks on lab experiments have found little cause for concern (Anderson, Lindsay, & Bushman, 1999; Banaji & Crowder, 1989; Kruglanski, 1975; Mook, 1983). Specific examination of these issues in the aggression domain have consistently found evidence of high external validity (Anderson & Bushman, 1997; Berkowitz & Donnerstein, 1982; Carlson, Marcus-Newhall, & Miller, 1989; Giancola & Chermack, 1998). Furthermore, recent meta-analyses have found that the most heavily criticized laboratory procedure, the Competitive Reaction Time (CRT) task, yields essentially the same violent video game effects as other procedures that measure aggressive behavior. In short, studies using the CRT task do not yield biased or inflated effect sizes. Interestingly, a recent experimental study found that lab experiments and measures that do not sufficiently disguise the real intent to study violent video game effects on aggression leads to underestimates of the true effects (Bender, Rothmund, & Gollwitzer, 2013). Specifically, gamers who play lots of violent games intentionally sabotage studies by displaying artificially low levels of aggression when they suspect (correctly) that the study is about video games and aggression. This "anti-demand characteristics" effect may explain why a few studies find weak or no harmful effects; such studies tend to not report cover stories or suspicion checks.

3. *Complete dismissal of correlational studies: "Correlation is not causation."*

This is an overly simplistic view of modern science. Psychology and statistics instructors teach this mantra to introductory students but hope that they will gain a much more sophisticated view of methods and scientific inference by the time they are seniors. Whole fields of science are based on correlational data (e.g., astronomy). Correlational studies are used to test causal theories and thus provide falsification opportunities. A well-conducted correlational design, one that attempts to control for likely "third variable" factors, can provide much useful information. To be sure, correlational studies are usually less informative about causality than experimental ones. What is most important in determining causality is the whole pattern of results across studies that differ in design, procedure, and measures (Prot & Anderson, 2013).

4. *There are no studies linking violent video game play to "serious" or actual aggression.*

Although it is true that most studies focus on subclinical or noncriminal aggression (e.g., threats, verbal aggression, hitting)—the most typical types seen in childhood—numerous correlational studies have linked violent video game exposure to serious aggression. One of the earliest (Anderson & Dill, 2000, Study 1) showed that college student reports of violent video game play in prior years were positively related to aggression that would be considered criminal (e.g., assault, robbery) if known to police. Other cross-sectional and longitudinal studies have included measures of real world aggression and violence, and have found that video game habits do predict serious forms of aggression (e.g., Anderson et al., 2004, 2007; DeLisi, Vaughn, Gentile, Anderson, & Shook, 2013; Gentile et al., 2004; Hopf, Huber, & Weiß, 2008). For example, DeLisi et al. (2013) found a significant violent video game effect on violence by juvenile delinquents even after controlling for the effects of screen time, years playing video games, age, sex, race, delinquency history, and psychopathic personality traits.

5. *Violent media affect only a few who are already disturbed.*

As discussed earlier, there are some reasons (theoretical, empirical) to believe that some populations (e.g., more aggressive) will be more affected than others. No totally "immune" population has ever been identified, however, and some research has found the opposite result—that less-aggressive children are more affected by violent games (e.g., Gentile et al., 2014). It is certainly likely that the effect may be more noticeable for children who are already aggressive, but that is different from stating that they are more influenced (see chapter 2, this volume).

6. *Effects of media violence are trivially small.*

This is ultimately a subjective judgment. It is the case that the effect sizes are in what is considered the "small" to "moderate" range. Violent video game effects are bigger than (1) effects of passive tobacco smoke and lung cancer; (2) exposure to lead and IQ scores in children; and (3) calcium intake and bone mass. Small effect sizes become more socially important when a large proportion of the population is exposed, when the effects accumulate across time, and when the outcomes are serious.

7. There is no consensus on the effects of violent video games.

At least nine meta-analyses of violent video games have been published (Anderson, 2004; Anderson & Bushman, 2001; Anderson et al., 2004; Anderson et al., 2010; Ferguson, 2007a, 2007b; Ferguson & Kilburn, 2010; Greitemeyer & Mügge, 2014; Sherry, 2001). Two interesting things stand out. First, although they vary greatly in terms of how many studies they include, they find almost identical effect sizes for violent video games on aggressive thoughts, feelings, and behaviors (see Table 8.1). Second, although they find almost identical effect sizes, Sherry and Ferguson interpret the effect as unimportant, whereas Anderson and colleagues interpret it as highly important. It is normal for scientists to differ in their interpretations of data. Nonetheless, the numbers are empirically derived, and all of these meta-analyses seem to agree with each other.

It is also interesting that although these authors appear to disagree with regard to how to interpret the link between violent game exposure and aggressive behavior, they do not disagree about the other effects. For example, although Ferguson (2007a, p. 479) feels that the evidence on violent games and aggressive behaviors is not compelling, he believes that the effects on aggressive thoughts, prosocial behaviors, and physiological arousal "appear to be more sound." This seems odd, because thoughts and feelings are related to behaviors—so if the critics agree that violent games can influence thoughts and feelings, why do they conclude that there is no effect on behaviors? It seems, therefore, that the disagreement about the effects of violent video games is much more apparent than real. Meta-analyses agree that there is a non-zero relation between violent gaming and aggressive thoughts, feelings, arousal, and behaviors. It is also clear that the effect is not overwhelming— these are generally small to moderate effect sizes. This also fits well with existing theory and data about aggression: aggression is multi-causal, and therefore no single environmental factor should overwhelm all others (including genetic, personality, and situational factors).

8. Violent crime rates have dropped in recent years, so violent video games can't be a cause of violent behavior.

There are multiple problems with this argument. First, the effect of violent games is expected to be more easily detected in higher-frequency, low-level forms of aggression than in the low-frequency extreme forms such as murder. Second, it assumes that violent video games would exert such a powerful effect that they would totally overwhelm the effects of changes in laws, the economy, the number of police on the streets, improvements in survival rates from violent attacks, an aging population, the percent of young males serving

Table 8.1
Effect Size Findings from Nine Meta-Analytic Reviews of Violent Video Game Effects on Aggression and Related Variables

	Anderson & Bushman (2001)	Sherry (2001)	Anderson (2004)	Anderson et al. (2004)	Ferguson (2007a)	Ferguson (2007b)	Ferguson & Kilburn (2010)	Anderson et al. (2010)	Greitemeyer & Mügge (2014)
Number of independent estimates	54	25	86	55	25	21	27	381	85
Number of participants	4,262	1,716	11,014	15,491	4,205	3,602	12,436	130,295	34,454
Aggressive thoughts	.27	–	.24	.31/.24*	.25	–	–	.16	.25
Physiological arousal	.22	–	.16	.22	.27	–	–	.18	.22
Aggressive feelings	.18	–	.16	.29/.16*	–	–	–	.14	.17
Aggressive behaviors	.19	.16	.20	.23/.28*	.29	.14	.14	.19	.19
Prosocial behaviors	–.16	–	–.21	–.25/–.30*	30	–	–	–.10	–.11

Notes: – = Not provided; * = Studies split into experimental and correlational studies, and no overall estimate was given.

in the military, or any of the approximately 100 other known risk factors for violent crime. For example, recent environmental research suggests that the reduction in blood levels of lead due to the outlawing of leaded gasoline accounts for much of the recent drop in violent crime rates (Mielke & Zahran, 2012). Furthermore, using societal level measures of violence to test psychological-level hypotheses is a statistical fallacy, known as the "ecological fallacy." In short, the whole argument is based on an assumption that is known to be false—that media violence is the *only* factor that causally contributes to violent crime (cf., Anderson & Bushman, 2002b).

9. *Violent video game effects on aggression are the result of competitiveness*.

Although some studies (e.g., Adachi & Willoughby, 2011) suggest that controlling for competitiveness eliminates violent content effects, studies with better controls have found the opposite. For example, Anderson and Carnagey (2009) had college students play a randomly assigned extra-violent or normal-rules sports game. The games were equated on competitiveness and sport. The extra-violent sports games yielded significantly greater levels of aggressive affect, cognition, and behavior, clearly showing that violent content caused an increase independent of competitiveness. This does not mean that competitiveness has no affect on aggression (see Anderson & Morrow, 1995), only that competitiveness can't fully explain short-term violent content effects, and probably can't explain long-term effects at all, although studies designed to test that hypothesis have not been conducted.

10. *Controlling for personality effects wipes out the video game effect*.

This is incorrect in several ways. First, experimental studies automatically control for individual differences, which is why experimental studies allow such strong causal conclusions. Second, longitudinal studies that control for the outcome variable at Time 1 (e.g., aggressive behavior tendency at the beginning of a school year) also control for personality variables. That is, if a child "has" an aggressive personality that is causally linked to aggressive tendencies, controlling for aggressive tendencies at the beginning of a school year also controls (at least partially, if not wholly) for personality effects on end of school year behavior. Third, video game experience is theoretically expected to change personality, so in certain types of studies (especially cross-sectional studies) controlling for aggressive personality (or personality variables known to be correlated with aggression) inappropriately removes a large portion of what is truly part of the violent video game effect (Prot & Anderson, 2013).

11. *The media violence research community is biased*.

Several different versions of this claim are out there, ranging from relatively mild claims that there is publication bias in favor of studies that "work" to outrageous claims that research teams selectively report only data analyses that work or make up their data. These claims ignore the evidence. For example, the 2010 meta-analysis included detailed analyses of selection and publication bias (see the section labeled "Sensitivity Analyses"). The results ruled out this claim.

Interestingly, the most vocal critic of video game studies was given an opportunity to comment on the 2010 meta-analysis article (at the suggestion of Anderson to the editor). Yet as Bushman, Rothstein, and Anderson (2010) noted, Ferguson and Kilburn failed to identify any biased search processes, any biased search outcomes, or any studies that should have been but were not included in our meta-analysis. (See also the commentary by Huesmann, 2010). Furthermore, as discussed earlier, a recent meta-analysis (Greitemeyer & Mügge, 2014) showed that the research performed by this same vocal critic is discrepant from what the other research groups find (Figure 8.4).

LEGITIMATE CHALLENGES

1. Sample sizes tend to be too small in many studies.

Because the average effect size is about $r = 0.20$, the N (number of study participants) should be at least 200 to achieve 0.80 power (the likelihood detecting a true difference between groups). That is, a simple two-group experiment should have 100 participants in the nonviolent game condition and 100 in the violent game condition. If the study is designed to test more than this basic difference, such as looking for interaction effects between game and personality variables, then the sample size will need to be substantially larger. When N is too small, individual studies will *appear* inconsistent even if they all accurately sample the true effect ($r = 0.20$). The best way of summarizing the results of a set of too-small studies is to combine the results via meta-analysis, rather than using the more traditional narrative review that simply counts significant and nonsignificant tests.

This problem continues to crop up in the video game research literature and may worsen as researchers begin to conduct more complicated studies looking for complex interactions, such as whether first-person shooter games have a bigger effect on aggression than third-person shooter games. The sample size problem increases dramatically for these types of studies because the likely effect sizes of such interactions are quite small. For example, a recent highly publicized study claimed that violent games don't produce antisocial behavior (Tear & Nielsen, 2013). The study had four game conditions (antisocial, violent, prosocial, and neutral). The differences between each of these would likely be a small effect size, therefore power analyses dictate a total sample of 1,096 participants. This published study had only 64 participants, which yields a *post-hoc* power of 0.09! It is not surprising they failed to find any statistically significant effects. Similarly, given that the likely effect sizes for certain types of longitudinal studies will be smaller than 0.20, new studies of this type will also need very large samples.

2. What is the proper or best control condition in experimental studies?

There are several important issues here. First, do comparison conditions differ sufficiently on the independent variable of interest? For most studies, this is whether the "violent" game is sufficiently violent and whether the "nonviolent" game is in fact nonviolent. Studies still occasionally fail this minimal requirement. Second, do the comparison conditions differ on other dimensions that might be related to the outcome variable? For example, was a "control" or "nonviolent game" condition more boring, annoying, fun, competitive, or frustrating than the violent game? Third, some dimensions along which video games can differ may be necessarily confounded with the dimension that the researcher wants to isolate. Sometimes, one can overcome this by reprogramming a video game (Carnagey & Anderson, 2005), or by creating one's own video game. Finally, it may be impossible to experimentally control all relevant dimensions, in which case we recommend inclusion of appropriate pilot testing on relevant dimensions, inclusion of dimensional ratings in the main experiment (if feasible), and using appropriate statistical controls (Gentile et al., 2009, Study 3).

3. *More large-scale studies of more extreme forms of violence are needed.*
In light of recent mass shootings by heavy users of violent media and calls by politicians to investigate why such shootings occur, it certainly seems reasonable to call for large-scale studies of extreme forms of violence, including various types of violent crimes such as assault, intimate partner violence, other forms of domestic violence, and even gun-related crimes. At the time of this writing, in the United States it is illegal for the CDC to fund research into gun violence if the findings may lead to gun control advocacy. Assuming that that problem is overcome, what is needed? Sample sizes for studies of more extreme forms of aggression will need to be substantially larger than past studies of media violence, likely in the tens of thousands. There are several reasons for this, including the fact that extreme behavior is rare, numerous risk factors should be assessed, and the unique effect size of each is likely to be very small. Second, new studies need to follow up the participants for many years, from a very young age through the high violence years (e.g., at least age 30). That is because some of the causal risk factors may come into play at a very young age and because the appearance of violent behavior can occur many years later. Third, the new studies need to take a risk and resilience approach (see chapter 2). Extreme acts of violence typically require the convergence of multiple risk factors and a simultaneous lack of resilience factors. If one wants to test whether a heavy media violence diet contributes to extreme acts of violence, it can be adequately tested only if the other main risk factors are also assessed. Playing a lot of violent video games won't turn a normal 14-year-old who has few risk factors into a school shooter or a serial killer or a habitual violent offender. Similarly, no other single known violence risk factor will lead to such extreme forms of behavior. What has never been tested is whether high media violence exposure can increase the likelihood of extremely violent behavior when there are many other known risk factors present. The most relevant

data to date on this question suggest that the answer is "yes" (e.g., Huesmann, Moise-Titus, Podolski, & Eron, 2003).

CONCLUSIONS

Research on violent video game effects has come a long way since the first edition of this book. We now know that violent video games have a host of causal effects on children, adolescents, and young adults, mostly revolving around aggression-related outcomes. A number of new questions have also arisen in recent years, some concerning all video games and others concerning violent games.

Because the focus of this chapter is on violent video games, we have not reviewed the growing literature on positive uses of video games in education, health, and industry. Please keep in mind that we are fans of video games and of their positive uses (e.g., Prot, Anderson, Gentile, et al., in press), and hope that future research will lead to better understanding and use of well-designed games to influence people in positive ways.

APPENDIX A: LETTER TO PARENTS: HOW CAN YOU TELL IF A VIDEO GAME IS POTENTIALLY HARMFUL?

1. Play the game, or have someone else demonstrate it for you.
2. Ask yourself the following six questions:
   - Does the game involve some characters trying to harm others?
   - Does this happen frequently, more than once or twice in 30 minutes?
   - Is the harm rewarded in any way?
   - Is the harm portrayed as humorous?
   - Are nonviolent solutions absent or less "fun" than the violent ones?
   - Are realistic consequences of violence absent from the game?
3. If two or more answers are "yes," think very carefully about the lessons being taught before allowing your child access to the game.

Source: Video Game Suggestions from Dr. Craig A. Anderson, April 23, 2002. Copyright Craig A. Anderson. The entire document can be found at http://www.psychology.iastate.edu/faculty/caa/VG_Recommend.pdf.

NOTE

1. Interestingly, this experimental study also included a measure of media habits. This allowed a test of whether the brief experimental manipulation of violent versus nonviolent video game play had different effects on participants who had a history of prior media violence exposure than on those who had little prior exposure to violent media. There was no significant moderation effect, indicating that participants with

high and low media violence exposure were affected by the brief game play in pretty much the same way.

REFERENCES

Achtman, R. L., Green, C. S., & Bavelier, D. (2008). Video games as a tool to train visual skills. *Restorative Neurology and Neuroscience, 26*(4–5), 435–446.

Adachi, P. J. C., & Willoughby, T. (2011). The effect of violent video games on aggression: Is it more than just the violence? *Aggression and Violent Behavior, 16*, 55–62.

Anderson, C. A. (2004). An update on the effects of violent video games. *Journal of Adolescence, 27*, 113–122.

Anderson, C. A. (2013). Violent, nonviolent, and prosocial gaming effects on teens' civic engagement. In K. Dill (Ed.), *The Oxford handbook of media psychology, electronic edition*. New York, NY: Oxford University Press.

Anderson, C. A., & Bushman, B. J. (1997). External validity of "trivial" experiments: The case of laboratory aggression. *Review of General Psychology, 1*, 19–41.

Anderson, C. A., & Bushman, B. J. (2001). Effects of violent games on aggressive behavior, aggressive cognition, aggressive affect, physiological arousal, and prosocial behavior: A meta-analytic review of the scientific literature. *Psychological Science, 12*, 353–359.

Anderson, C. A., & Bushman, B. J. (2002a). The effects of media violence on society. *Science, 295*, 2377–2378.

Anderson, C. A., & Bushman, B. J. (2002b). Media violence and the American public revisited. *American Psychologist, 57*, 448–450.

Anderson, C. A., & Carnagey, N. L. (2009). Causal effects of violent sports video games on aggression: Is it competitiveness or violent content? *Journal of Experimental Social Psychology, 45*, 731–739.

Anderson, C. A., Carnagey, N. L., Flanagan, M., Benjamin, A. J., Eubanks, J., & Valentine, J. C. (2004). Violent video games: Specific effects of violent content on aggressive thoughts and behavior. *Advances in Experimental Social Psychology, 36*, 199–249.

Anderson, C. A., & Dill, K. E. (2000). Video games and aggressive thoughts, feelings, and behavior in the laboratory and in life. *Journal of Personality and Social Psychology, 78*, 772–790.

Anderson, C. A., & Ford, C. M. (1986). Affect of the game player: Short-term consequences of playing aggressive video games. *Personality and Social Psychology Bulletin, 12*, 390–402.

Anderson, C. A., Gentile, D. A., & Buckley, K. E. (2007). *Violent video game effects on children and adolescents: Theory, research, and public policy*. New York, NY: Oxford University Press.

Anderson, C. A., & Huesmann, L. R. (2003). Human aggression: A social-cognitive view. In M. A. Hogg & J. Cooper (Eds.), *The Sage handbook of social psychology* (pp. 296–323). London, UK: Sage Publications.

Anderson, C. A., Lindsay, J. J., & Bushman, B. J. (1999). Research in the psychological laboratory: Truth or triviality? *Current Directions in Psychological Science, 8*, 3–9.

Anderson, C. A., & Morrow, M. (1995). Competitive aggression without interaction: Effects of competitive versus cooperative instructions on aggressive behavior in video games. *Personality and Social Psychology Bulletin, 21*, 1020–1030.

Anderson, C. A., Shibuya, A., Ihori, N., Swing, E. L., Bushman, B. J., Sakamoto, A., Rothstein, H. R., & Saleem, M. (2010). Violent video game effects on aggression, empathy, and prosocial behavior in Eastern and Western countries. *Psychological Bulletin, 136*, 151–173.

Arriaga, P., Esteves, F., Carneiro, P., & Monteiro, M. B. (2006). Violent computer games and their effects on state hostility and physiological arousal. *Aggressive Behavior, 32*, 358–371.

Associated Press. (2002, July 2). Be all you can be in computer games. Retrieved from http://www.msnbc.com

Austin, E. W. (1993). Exploring the effects of active parental mediation of television content. *Journal of Broadcasting & Electronic Media, 37*, 147–158.

Bailey, K., West, R., & Anderson, C. A. (2010). A negative association between video game experience and proactive cognitive control. *Psychophysiology, 47*, 34–42.

Bailey, K., West. R., & Anderson, C. A. (2011). The influence of video games on social, cognitive, and affective information processing. In J. Decety & J. Cacioppo (Eds.), *Handbook of social neuroscience* (pp. 1001–1011). New York, NY: Oxford University Press.

Ballard, M. E., & Lineberger, R. (1999). Video game violence and confederate gender: Effects on reward and punishment given by college males. *Sex Roles, 41*, 541–558.

Ballard, M. E., & Weist, J. R. (1996). *Mortal Kombat*: The effects of violent video game play on males' hostility and cardiovascular responding. *Journal of Applied Social Psychology, 26*, 717–730.

Banaji, M. R., & Crowder, R. G. (1989). The bankruptcy of everyday memory. *American Psychologist, 44*, 1185–1193.

Bandura, A., Barbaranelli, C., Caprara, G. V., & Pastorelli, C. (1996). Mechanisms of moral disengagement in the exercise of moral agency. *Journal of Personality and Social Psychology, 71*(2), 364–374.

Barlett, C. P., & Rodeheffer, C. (2009). Effects of realism on extended violent and nonviolent video game play on aggressive thoughts, feelings, and physiological arousal. *Aggressive Behavior, 35*, 213–224.

Bartholow, B. D., Sestir, M. A., & Davis, M. D. (2005). Correlates and consequences of exposure to videogame violence: Hostile personality, empathy, and aggressive behavior. *Personality and Social Psychology Bulletin, 31*, 1573–1586.

Bender, J., Rothmund, T., & Gollwitzer, M. (2013). Biased estimation of violent video game effects on aggression: Contributing factors and boundary conditions. *Societies, 3*, 383–398.

Berkey, C. S., Rockett, H. R. H., Field, A. E., Gillman, M. W., Frazier, A. L., Camargo, C. A., et al. (2000). Activity, dietary intake, and weight changes in a longitudinal study of preadolescent and adolescent boys and girls. *Pediatrics, 105*, E56 (9 pages).

Berkowitz, L., & Donnerstein, E. (1982). External validity is more than skin deep: Some answers to criticism of laboratory experiments. *American Psychologist, 37*, 245–257.

Buchman, D. D., & Funk, J. B. (1996). Video and computer games in the '90s: Children's time commitment and game preference. *Children Today, 24*, 12–16.

Bushman, B. J., & Anderson, C. A. (2002). Violent video games and hostile expectations: A test of the general aggression model. *Personality and Social Psychology Bulletin, 28*, 1679–1686.

Bushman, B. J., & Anderson, C. A. (2009). Comfortably numb: Desensitizing effects of violent media on helping others. *Psychological Science, 20*, 273–277.

Bushman, B. J., & Huesmann, L. R. (2006). Short-term and long-term effects of violent media on aggression in children and adults. *Archives of Pediatric and Adolescent Medicine, 160*, 348–352.

Bushman, B. J., Rothstein, H. R., & Anderson, C. A. (2010). Much ado about something: Violent video game effects and a school of red herring; Reply to Ferguson and Kilburn. *Psychological Bulletin, 136*, 182–187.

Carlson, M., Marcus-Newhall, A., & Miller, N. (1989). Evidence for a general construct of aggression. *Personality and Social Psychology Bulletin, 15*, 377–389.

Carnagey, N. L., & Anderson, C. A. (2005). The effects of reward and punishment in violent video games on aggressive affect, cognition, and behavior. *Psychological Science, 16*, 882–889.

Carnagey, N. L., & Anderson, C. A., Bushman, B. J. (2007). The effect of video game violence on physiological desensitization to real-life violence. *Journal of Experimental Social Psychology, 43*, 489–496.

Chambers, J. H., & Ascione, F. R. (1987). The effects of prosocial and aggressive video games on children's donating and helping. *Journal of Genetic Psychology, 148*, 499–505.

Chan, P. A., & Rabinowitz, T. (2006). A cross-sectional analysis of video games and attention deficit hyperactivity disorder symptoms in adolescents. *Annals of General Psychiatry, 5*(16). doi:http://dx.doi.org/10.1186/1744-859X-5-16

Children Now. (2001). *Fair play? Violence, gender and race in video games.* Los Angeles, CA: Children Now.

Choo, H., Gentile, D. A., Sim, T., Li, D., Khoo, A., & Liau, A. K. (2010). Pathological video-gaming among Singaporean youth. *Annals of the Academy of Medicine Singapore, 39*, 822–829.

Comstock, G., & Paik, H. (1991). Television and the American child. New York, NY: Academic Press.

Cook, W. W., & Medley, D. M. (1954). Proposed hostility and parisaic-virtue scales for the MMPI. *Journal of Applied Psychology, 38*, 414–418.

Cordes, C., & Miller, E. (2000). *Fool's gold: A critical look at computers in childhood.* College Park, MD: Alliance for Childhood.

Creasy, G. L., & Myers, B. J. (1986). Video games and children: Effects on leisure activities, schoolwork, and peer involvement. *Merrill-Palmer Quarterly, 32*, 251–262.

Crick, N. R., & Dodge, K. A. (1994). A review and reformulation of social information-processing mechanisms in children's social adjustment. *Psychological Bulletin, 115*, 74–101.

Cummings, H. M. M., & Vandewater, E. A. P. (2007). Relation of adolescent video game play to time spent in other activities. *Archives of Pediatric and Adolescent Medicine, 161*(7), 684–689.

DeLisi, M., Vaughn, M. G., Gentile, D. A., Anderson, C. A., & Shook, J. (2013). Violent video games, delinquency, and youth violence: New evidence. *Youth Violence and Juvenile Justice, 11*, 132–142.

Dietz, T. L. (1998). An examination of violence and gender role portrayals in video games: Implications for gender socialization and aggressive behavior. *Sex Roles, 38*, 425–442.

Dill, K. E., & Dill, J. C. (1998). Video game violence: A review of the empirical literature. *Aggression and Violent Behavior: A Review Journal, 3*, 407–428.

Dill, K. E., Gentile, D. A., Richter, W. A., & Dill, J. C. (2001, August). *Portrayal of women and minorities in video games*. Paper presented at the 109th Annual Conference of the American Psychological Association, San Francisco, CA.

Donnerstein, E., Slaby, R. G., & Eron, L. D. (1994). The mass media and youth aggression. In L. D. Eron, J. H. Gentry, & P. Schlegel (Eds.), *Reason to hope: A psychosocial perspective on violence and youth* (pp. 219–250). Washington, DC: American Psychological Association.

Dorr, A., & Rabin, B. E. (1995). Parents, children, and television. In M. Bornstein (Ed.), *Handbook of parenting* (Vol. 4, pp. 323–351). Mahwah, NJ: Erlbaum.

Entertainment Software Association. (2013). *Essential facts about the computer and video game industry*. Washington, DC: Author. http://www.theesa.com/facts/

Feng, J., Spence, I., & Pratt, J. (2007). Playing an action video game reduces gender differences in spatial cognition. *Psychological Science, 18*, 850–855.

Ferguson, C. J. (2007a). Evidence for publication bias in video game violence effects literature: A meta-analytic review. *Aggression and Violent Behavior, 12*, 470–482.

Ferguson, C. J. (2007b). The good, the bad and the ugly: A meta-analytic review of positive and negative effects of violent video games. *Psychiatric Quarterly, 78*, 309–316.

Ferguson, C. J., & Kilburn, J. (2010). Much ado about nothing: The misestimation and overinterpretation of violent video game effects in Eastern and Western nations: Comment on Anderson et al. (2010). *Psychological Bulletin, 136*, 174–178.

Fischer, J., Aydin, N., Kastenmuller, A., Frey, D., & Fischer, P. (2012). The delinquent media effect: Delinquency-reinforcing video games increase players' attitudinal and behavioral inclination toward delinquent behavior. *Psychology of Popular Media Culture, 1*, 201–205.

Fischer, P., Krueger, J. I., Greitemeyer, T., Asal, K., Aydin, N., & Vingilis, E. (2012). Psychological effects of risk glorification in the media: Towards an integrative view. *European Review of Social Psychology, 23*, 224–257.

Fleming, M. J., & Rickwood, D. J. (2001). Effects of violent versus nonviolent video games on children's arousal, aggressive mood and positive mood. *Journal of Applied Social Psychology, 31*, 2047–2071.

Funk, J. B. (1993). Reevaluating the impact of video games. *Clinical Pediatrics, 32*, 86–90.

Funk, J. B. (2001). *Children and violent video games: Are there "high risk" players?* Paper presented at Playing by the Rules: Video Games and Cultural Policy Conference, Chicago, IL.

Funk, J. B. (2003). Violent video games: Who's at risk? In D. Ravitch and J. P. Viteritti (Eds.), *Kid stuff: Marketing sex and violence to America's children* (pp. 168–192). Baltimore, MD: Johns Hopkins University Press.

Funk, J. B., Baldacci, H. B., Pasold, T., & Baumgardner, J. (2004). Violence exposure in real-life, video games, television, movies, and the Internet: Is there desensitization? *Journal of Adolescence, 27*, 23–39.

Funk, J. B., & Buchman, D. D. (1996). Playing violent video and computer games and adolescent self-concept. *Journal of Communication, 46*, 19–32.

Funk, J. B., Buchman, D. D., & Germann, J. N. (2000). 'Preference for violent electronic games, self-concept, and gender differences in young children. *American Journal of Orthopsychiatry, 70,* 233–241.

Funk, J., Hagan, J., & Schimming, J. (1999). Children and electronic games: A comparison of parents' and children's perceptions of children's habits and preferences in a United States sample. *Psychological Reports, 85,* 883–888.

Gabbiadini, A., Andrighetto, L., & Volpato, C. (2012). Brief report: Does exposure to violent video games increase moral disengagement among adolescents? *Journal of Adolescence, 35*(5), 1403–1406.

Gadberry, S. (1980). Effects of restricting first graders' TV-viewing on leisure time use, IQ change, and cognitive style. *Journal of Applied Developmental Psychology, 1,* 45–57.

Gentile, D. A. (2008). The rating systems for media products. In S. Calvert & B. Wilson (Eds.), *The Handbook of Children, Media and Development* (pp. 527–551). Malden, MA: Blackwell Publishing.

Gentile, D. A. (2009). Pathological video-game use among youth ages 8 to 18: A national study. *Psychological Science, 20,* 594–602.

Gentile, D. A. (2011). Multiple dimensions of video game effects. *Child Development Perspectives, 5,* 75–81.

Gentile, D. A., & Anderson, C. A. (2003). Violent video games: The newest media violence hazard. In D. A. Gentile (Ed.), *Media violence and children* (pp. 131–152). Westport, CT: Praeger.

Gentile, D. A., Anderson, C. A., Yukawa, S., Ihori, N., Saleem, M., Ming, L. K., Shibuya, A., Liau, A. K., Khoo, A., & Sakamoto, A. (2009). The effects of prosocial video games on prosocial behaviors: International evidence from correlational, experimental, and longitudinal studies. *Personality and Social Psychology Bulletin, 35,* 752–763.

Gentile, D. A., Coyne, S. M., & Bricolo, F. (2013). Pathological technology addictions: What is scientifically known and what remains to be learned? In K. Dill (Ed.), *The Oxford handbook of media psychology* (pp. 382–402). New York, NY: Oxford University Press.

Gentile, D. G., Li, D., Khoo, A., Prot, S., & Anderson, C. A. (March 24, 2014). Practice, thinking, and action: Mediators and moderators of long-term violent video game effects on aggressive behavior. *JAMA-Pediatrics,* published online. doi:10.1001/jamapediatrics.2014.63

Gentile, D. A., Lynch, P. J., Linder, J. R., & Walsh, D. A. (2004). The effects of violent video game habits on adolescent hostility, aggressive behaviors, and school performance. *Journal of Adolescence, 27,* 5–22.

Gentile, D. A., Maier, J. A., Hasson, M. R., & de Bonetti, B. L. (2011). Parents' evaluation of media ratings a decade after the television ratings were introduced. *Pediatrics, 128,* 36–44.

Gentile, D. A., Nathanson, A. I., Rasmussen, E. E., Reimer, R. A., Walsh, D. A. (2012). *Family Relations: An Interdisciplinary Journal of Applied Family Studies, 61,* 470–487.

Gentile, D. A., Swing, E. L., Lim, C. G., Khoo, A. (2012). Video game playing, attention problems, and impulsiveness: Evidence of bidirectional causality. *Psychology of Popular Media Culture, 1,* 62–70.

Gentile, D. A., & Walsh, D. A. (2002). A normative study of family media habits. *Journal of Applied Developmental Psychology, 23,* 157–178.

Giancola, P. R., & Chermack, S. T. (1998). Construct validity of laboratory aggression paradigms: A response to Tedeschi and Quigley (1996). *Aggression and Violent Behavior, 3*, 237–253.

Gollwitzer, M., & Melzer, A. (2012). Macbeth and the joystick: Evidence for moral cleansing after playing a violent video game. *Journal of Experimental Social Psychology, 48*(6), 1356–1360.

Graybill, D., Kirsch, J. R., & Esselman, E. D. (1985). Effects of playing violent versus nonviolent video games on the aggressive ideation of aggressive and nonagressive children. *Child Study Journal, 15*, 199–205.

Green, C. S., & Bavelier, D. (2003). Action video game modifies visual selective attention. *Nature, 423*, 534–537.

Green, C. S., & Bavelier, D. (2007). Action video game experience alters the spatial resolution of attention. *Psychological Science, 18*(1), 88–94.

Greitemeyer, T., & Mügge, D. O. (2014). Video games do affect social outcomes: A meta-analytic review of the effects of violent and prosocial video game play. *Personality and Social Psychology Bulletin, 40*, 578–589.

Grüsser, S. M., Thalemann, R., & Griffiths, M. D. (2007). Excessive computer game playing: Evidence for addiction and aggression? *CyberPsychology & Behavior, 10*, 290–292.

Gwinup, G., Haw, T., & Elias, A. (1983). Cardiovascular changes in video-game players: Cause for concern? *Post Graduate Medicine*, 245–248.

Haninger, K., & Thompson, K. M. (2004). Content and ratings of teen-rated video games. *Journal of the American Medical Association, 291*, 856–865.

Harris, M. B., & Williams, R. (1985). Video games and school performance. *Education, 105*(3), 306–309.

Hartmann, T., Toz, E., & Brandon, M. (2010). Just a game? Unjustified virtual violence produces guilt in empathic players. *Media Psychology, 13*, 339–363. doi:10.1080/15213269.2010.524912

Hasan, Y., Begue, L., & Bushman, B. J. (2012). Viewing the world through "blood-red tinted glasses": The hostile expectation bias mediates the link between violent video game exposure and aggression. *Journal of Experimental Social Psychology, 48*(4), 953–956.

Hastings, E. C., Karas, T. L., Winsler, A., Way, E., Madigan, A., & Tyler, S. (2009). Young children's video/computer game use: Relations with school performance and behavior. *Issues in Mental Health Nursing, 30*, 638–649.

Hopf, W. H., Huber, G. L., & Weiß, R. H. (2008). Media violence and youth violence: A 2-year longitudinal study. *Journal of Media Psychology, 20*, 79–96.

Huesmann, L. R. (2010). Nailing the coffin shut on doubts that violent video games stimulate aggression: Comment on Anderson et al. (2010). *Psychological Review, 136*, 179–181.

Huesmann, L. R., Moise-Titus, J., Podolski, C. L., & Eron, L. D. (2003). Longitudinal relations between children's exposure to TV violence and their aggressive and violent behavior in young adulthood: 1977–1992. *Developmental Psychology, 39*, 201–221.

Hummer, T. A., Wang, Y., Kronenberger, W. G., Mosier, K. M., Kalnin, A. J., Dunn, D. W., & Mathews, V. P. (2010). Short-term violent video game play by adolescents alters prefrontal activity during cognitive inhibition, *Media Psychology, 13*, 136–154.

"Industrial strengths: New vs. old economy earnings." (2000, November). *Wired*, p. 122.

Irwin, A. R., & Gross, A. M. (1995). Cognitive tempo, violent video games, and aggressive behavior in young boys. *Journal of Family Violence, 10*, 337–350.

Kasper, D., Welsh, S., & Chambliss, C. (1999). Educating students about the risks of excessive videogame usage. ERIC Document Reproduction Service No. ED426315. Collegeville, PA.

Kirsh, S. J. (1998). Seeing the world through *Mortal Kombat*–colored glasses: Violent video games and the development of a short-term hostile attribution bias. *Childhood, 5*, 177–184.

Kirsch, S. J., Olczak, P. V., & Mounts, J. R. W. (2005). Violent video games induce an affective processing bias. *Media Psychology, 7*, 239–250.

Ko, C. H., Yen, J. Y., Yen, C. F., Lin, H. C., & Yang, M. J. (2007). Factors predictive for incidence and remission of Internet addiction in young adolescents: A prospective study. *Cyberpsychology & Behavior, 10*, 545–551.

Koepp, M. J., Gunn, R. N., Lawrence, A. D., Cunningham, V. J., Dagher, A., Jones, T., Brooks, D. J., Bench, C. J., & Grasby, P. M. (1998). Evidence for striatal dopamine release during a video game. *Nature, 393*, 266–268.

Konijn, E. A., Bijnank, M. N., & Bushman, B. J. (2007). I wish I were a warrior: The role of wishful identification in the effects of violent video games on aggression in adolescent boys. *Developmental Psychology, 43*, 1038–1044.

Kruglanski, A. W. (1975). The human subject in the psychology experiment: Fact and artifact. In L. Berkowitz (Ed.), *Advances in experimental social psychology* (Vol. 8, pp. 101–147). New York, NY: Academic Press.

Lam, L. T., Peng, Z., Mai, J., & Jing, J. (2009). Factors associated with Internet addiction among adolescents. *CyberPsychology & Behavior, 12*(5), 551–555. doi:http://dx.doi.org/10.1089/cpb.2009.0036

Lee, K. M., Peng, W., & Klein, J. (2010). Will the experience of playing a violent role in a video game influence people's judgments of violent crimes? *Computers in Human Behavior, 26*, 1019–1023.

Lenhart, A., Kahne, J., Middaugh, E., Macgill, A. R., Evans, C., & Vitak, J. (2008). *Teens' video games, and civics*. Washington, DC: Pew Internet & American Life Project.

Lieberman, D. A., Chaffee, S. H., & Roberts, D. F. (1988). Computers, mass media, and schooling: Functional equivalence in uses of new media. *Social Science Computer Review, 6*, 224–241.

Lin, C. A., & Atkin, D. J. (1989). Parental mediation and rulemaking for adolescent use of television and VCRs. *Journal of Broadcasting & Electronic Media, 33*, 53–67.

Lynch, P. J. (1994). Type A behavior, hostility, and cardiovascular function at rest and after playing video games in teenagers. *Psychosomatic Medicine, 56*, 152.

Lynch, P. J. (1999). Hostility, Type A behavior, and stress hormones at rest and after playing violent video games in teenagers. *Psychosomatic Medicine, 61*, 113.

Markey, P. M., & Scherer, K. (2009). An examination of psychoticism and motion capture controls as moderators of the effects of violent video games. *Computers in Human Behavior, 25*, 407–411.

Mathews, V. P., Kronenberger, W. G., Wang, Y., Lurito, J. T., Lowe, M. J., & Dunn, D. W. (2005). Media violence exposure and frontal lobe activation measured by functional magnetic resonance imaging in aggressive and nonaggressive adolescents. *Journal of Computer Assisted Tomography, 29*, 287–292.

Mielke, H. W., & Zahran, S. (2012). The urban rise and fall of air lead (Pb) and the latent surge and retreat of societal violence. *Environment International*, *43*, 48–55.

Möller, I., & Krahé, B. (2009). Exposure to violent video games and aggression in German adolescents: A longitudinal analysis. *Aggressive Behavior*, *35*, 75–89.

Mook, D. G. (1983). In defense of external invalidity. *American Psychologist*, *38*, 379–387.

Murphy, J. K., Alpert, B. S., & Walker, S. S. (1992). Ethnicity, pressor reactivity, and children's blood pressure: Five years of observations. *Hypertension*, *20*, 327–332.

Naito, M., Kobayashi, K., & Sakamoto, A. (1999). Terebigemu no shiyou to kougeki-sei no ingakankei no kentou (3): Chugakusei ni taisuru paneru kenkyu [Testing a causal relationship between video game use and aggression: A panel study on junior high school students]. *Proceeding of the 40th Convention of the Japanese Society of Social Psychology*, pp. 288–289.

Okagaki, L., & Frensch, P. A. (1994). Effects of interactive entertainment technologies on development. *Journal of Applied Developmental Psychology*, *15*, 33–58.

Peng, L. H., & Li, X. (2009). A survey of Chinese college students addicted to video games. *China Education Innovation Herald*, *28*, 111–112.

Porter, G., Starcevic, V., Berle, D., & Fenech, P. (2010). Recognizing problem video game use. *Australian and New Zealand Journal of Psychiatry*, *44*, 120–128.

Prot, S., & Anderson, C. A. (2013). Research methods, design, and statistics in media psychology. In K. Dill (Ed.), *The Oxford handbook of media psychology* (109–136). New York, NY: Oxford University Press.

Prot, S., Anderson, C. A., Gentile, D. A., Brown, S. C., & Swing, E. L. (in press). The positive and negative effects of video game play. In A. Jordan & D. Romer (Eds.), *Children and media*. New York, NY: Oxford University Press.

Prot, S., Gentile, D. G., Anderson, C. A., Suzuki, K., Swing, E., Lim, K. M., Horiuchi, Y., Jelic, M., Krahé, B., Liuqing, W., Liau, A., Khoo, A., Petrescu, P. D., Sakamoto, A., Tajima, S., Toma, R. A., Warburton, W. A., Zhang, X., & Lam, C. P. (2014). Long-term relations between prosocial media use, empathy and prosocial behavior. *Psychological Science*, *25*, 358–368. doi:10.1177/09567976 13503854

Pryor, J. H., Eagan, K., Blake, L. P., Hurtado, S., Berdan, J., & Case, M. H. (2012). *The American freshman: National norms fall 2012 expanded edition*. Los Angeles, CA: Higher Education Research Institute, UCLA. http://www.heri.ucla.edu /monographs/TheAmericanFreshman2012-Expanded.pdf

Richardson, A. E., Powers, M. E., & Bousquet, L. G. (2011). Video game experience predicts virtual, but not real navigation performance. *Computers in Human Behavior*, *27*, 552–560. doi:10.1016/j.chb.2010.10.003

Rideout, V. J., Foehr, U. G., & Roberts, D. F. (2010). *Generation M²: Media in the lives of 8- to 18-year-olds*. Menlo Park, CA: Kaiser Family Foundation. http://www .kff.org/entmedia/entmedia012010nr.cfm

Roberts, D. F., Foehr, U. G., Rideout, V. J., & Brodie, M. (1999). *Kids & media @ the new millennium*. Menlo Park, CA: Kaiser Family Foundation.

Robinson, T. N., Wilde, M. L., Navracruz, L. C., Haydel, K. F., & Varady, A. (2001). Effects of reducing children's television and video game use on aggressive behavior: A randomized controlled trial. *Archives of Pediatric Adolescent Medicine*, *155*, 17–23.

Sakamoto, A., Ozaki, M., Narushima, R., Mori, T., Sakamoto, K., Takahira, M., et al. (2001). Terebigemu asobi ga ningen no bouryoku koudou ni oyobosu eikyo to sono katei: Joshidaigakusei ni taisuru 2-tsu no shakaishinrigakuteki jikken [The influence of video game play on human violence and its process: Two social psychological experiments of female university students]. *Studies in Simulation and Gaming, 11*(1), 28–39.

Saleem, M., & Anderson, C. A. (2013). Arabs as terrorists: Effects of stereotypes within violent contexts on attitudes, perceptions and affect. *Psychology of Violence, 3*, 84–99.

Schutte, N. S., Malouff, J. M., Post-Gorden, J. C., & Rodasta, A. L. (1988). Effects of playing video games on children's aggressive and other behaviors. *Journal of Applied Social Psychology, 18*, 454–460.

Segal, K. R., & Dietz, W. H. (1991). Physiologic responses to playing a video game. *American Journal of Diseases of Children, 145*, 1034–1036.

Sharif, I., & Sargent, J. D. (2006). Association between television, movie, and video game exposure and school performance. *Pediatrics, 118*(4), e1061–1070.

Sherry, J. L. (2001). The effects of violent video games on aggression: A meta-analysis. *Human Communication Research, 27*, 409–431.

Silvern, S. B., & Williamson, P. A. (1987). The effects of video game play on young children's aggression, fantasy, and prosocial behaviour. *Journal of Applied Developmental Psychology, 8*, 453–462.

Sim, T., Gentile, D. A., Bricolo, F., Serpelloni, G., & Gulamoydeen, F. (2012). A conceptual review of research on the pathological use of computers, video games, and the Internet. *International Journal of Mental Health and Addiction, 10*(5), 748–769.

Strasburger, V. C., & Donnerstein, E. (1999). Children, adolescents, and the media: Issues and solutions. *Pediatrics, 103*, 129–139.

Subrahmanyam, K., Kraut, R. E., Greenfield, P. M., & Gross, E. F. (2000). The impact of home computer use on children's activities and development. *Future of Children, 10*, 123–144.

Swing, E. L., & Anderson, C. A. (2014). The role of attention problems and impulsiveness in media violence effects on aggression. *Aggressive Behavior, 40*, 197–203. doi:10.1002/ab.21519

Swing, E. L., Gentile, D. A., Anderson, C. A., & Walsh, D. A. (2010). Television and video game exposure and the development of attention problems. *Pediatrics, 126*, 214–221.

Swing., E. S., & Anderson, C. A. (2012). *Video game playing and links to attention problems, proactive cognitive control, and visual attention.* Symposium presentation at the 24th Annual Convention of the Association for Psychological Science, May 24–27, 2012, Chicago, Illinois.

Tear, M. J., & Nielsen, M. (2013). Failure to demonstrate that playing violent video games diminishes prosocial behavior. *PLOS ONE 8*(7): e68382. doi:10.1371 / journal.pone.0068382

Thompson, K. M., & Haninger, K. (2001). Violence in E-rated video games. *Journal of the American Medical Association, 286*, 591–598.

Thompson, K. M., Tepichin, K., & Haninger, K. (2006). Content and ratings of Mature-rated video games. *Archives of Pediatric and Adolescent Medicine, 160*, 402–410.

Ubi Soft. (2001, February 12). *Ubi Soft licenses Tom Clancy's Rainbow Six Rogue Spear game engine to train U.S. soldiers* [webpage]. http://corp.ubisoft.com/pr_release_010829a.htm.

Uhlmann, E., & Swanson, J. (2004). Exposure to violent video games increases implicit aggressiveness. *Journal of Adolescence, 27,* 41–52.

U.S. Surgeon General. (2001). *Youth violence: A report of the Surgeon General.* Rockville, MD: U.S. Department of Health and Human Services.

Vandewater, E. A., Shim, M., & Caplovitz, A. G. (2004). Linking obesity and activity level with children's television and video game use. *Journal of Adolescence, 27,* 71–85.

Van Schie, E. G. M., & Wiegman, O. (1997). Children and videogames: Leisure activities, aggression, social integration, and school performance. *Journal of Applied Social Psychology, 27,* 1175–1194.

Wallenius, M., & Punamaki, R. (2008). Digitial game violence and direct aggression in adolescence: A longitudinal study of the roles of sex, age, and parent-child communication. *Journal of Applied Developmental Psychology, 29,* 286–294.

Walsh, D. (2000). *5th annual video and computer game report card.* Minneapolis, MN: National Institute on Media and the Family.

Weis, R., & Cerankosky, B. C. (2010). Effects of video-game ownership on young boys' academic and behavioral functioning: A randomized, controlled study. *Psychological Science, 21,* 463–470.

Wiegman, O., & van Schie, E. G. M. (1998). Video game playing and its relations with aggressive and prosocial behaviour. *British Journal of Social Psychology, 37,* 367–378.

Willoughby, T., Adachi, P. J. C., & Good, M. (2012). A longitudinal study of the association between violent video game play and aggression among adolescents. *Developmental Psychology, 48,* 1044–1057.

Woodard, E. H., & Gridina, N. (2000). *Media in the home: The fifth annual survey of parents and children.* Philadelphia, PA: The Annenberg Public Policy Center of the University of Pennsylvania.

Yukawa, S., & Sakamoto, A. (2001). Terebi oyobi terebigemu niokeru bouryoku ga seishounen no kougekisei ni oyobosu eikyo: Chugakusei oyobi koukousei wo taisho toshita juudan deta no bunseki [The effects of television and videogame violence on aggression of youth: A longitudinal study of junior high school and high school students]. *Proceeding of the 42nd Convention of the Japanese Society of Social Psychology,* pp. 502–503.

CHAPTER 9

Cyberbullying

*Susan P. Limber, Robin M. Kowalski, and
Patricia W. Agatston*

In recent years, there has been a surge of interest in the topic of bullying
by researchers, legislators, educators, and members of the lay public. Since
1999, the year of the Columbine High School shootings, hundreds of
research articles and books have been published on the topic;[1] 49 states
have passed laws requiring that school districts establish policies about
bullying (U.S. Department of Education, 2011); numerous programs, curricula, and campaigns have been launched in schools and communities to address bullying; and thousands of articles about bullying have appeared in
media outlets.[2] With the increased use of cyber technologies by youth in the
last 10 years (Madden, Lenhart, Duggan, Cortesi, & Gasser, 2013), a new
form of bullying has emerged. Cyberbullying, or electronic bullying, has
raised many questions among researchers and concerns among parents and
educators.

The purpose of this chapter is to explore these questions and concerns.
Specifically, we will (1) examine key definitional and conceptual issues with
regard to cyberbullying (What is it? How is it similar to/different from traditional forms of bullying?); (2) provide an overview of the current research
that is attempting to answer questions about its prevalence: about demographic, personal, and situational factors related to individuals' involvement
in cyberbullying, and about consequences of cyberbullying; (3) highlight
theoretical frameworks that are useful in understanding cyberbullying; (4)
discuss the role of media in perpetuating and addressing cyberbullying; and
(5) highlight roles of parents, educators, and other adults in preventing and
intervening in instances of cyberbullying.

DEFINING CYBERBULLYING

Most researchers agree that bullying is an act of aggression that is typically repeated over time and that occurs between individuals where there is a power imbalance (Gladden, Vivolo-Kantor, Hamburger, & Lumpkin, 2014; Olweus, 2013). This power imbalance can be physical, social, psychological, or, in the case of cyberbullying, may involve technological expertise (Dooley, Pyzalski, & Cross, 2009; Monks & Smith, 2006; Olweus, 2013). Broadly speaking, cyberbullying has been defined as the use of information and communication technologies (ICTs) to bully others. Kowalski, Limber, and Agatston (2012) defined cyberbullying more specifically as "bullying through e-mail, instant messaging (IM), in a chat room, on a website, on an online gaming site, or through digital messages or images sent to a cellular phone" (p. 1).

In the short time that cyberbullying has been a topic of investigation, several important issues have emerged that have made conceptualizing the behavior difficult. First, although most researchers agree with this general perspective on cyberbullying, there remains a lack of agreement regarding the specific parameters by which cyberbullying should be defined (Kowalski, Giumetti, Schroeder, & Lattanner, 2014; Olweus, 2013; Smith, del Barrio, & Tokunaga, 2012; Ybarra, Boyd, Korchmaros, & Oppenheim, 2012). The fact that researchers have used slightly different definitions in their research is important because it means that they have consequently used slightly different means of measuring cyberbullying, leading to widely varying prevalence rates and differential reports in terms of predictors of cyberbullying victimization and perpetration, creating a field with a fair amount of confusion and disparate findings.

Second, a number of different behaviors can be subsumed within the term cyberbullying, making it, at times, difficult to determine when cyberbullying has or has not occurred. To guide our understanding of cyberbullying, Nancy Willard (2007) proposed a typology of cyberbullying, suggesting that the behavior can be broken down into seven different types. Willard's taxonomy includes flaming (i.e., an online fight), harassment (i.e., repetitive, negative messages replayed to the victim by the perpetrator), impersonation (i.e., adopting the victim's online persona and distributing offensive communications online as if they were coming from the victim himself or herself), outing and trickery (i.e., leading the victim to disclose personal information that he/she would not choose to have shared with others and then disseminating that information online), exclusion (i.e., blocking the target from friend and buddy lists), cyberstalking (i.e., stalking someone online by repeatedly sending threatening electronic communications), and sexting (i.e., distributing or threatening to distribute sexual pictures of someone without their consent). Taxonomies such as this are useful in allowing individuals to identify whether or not particular behaviors are, in fact, cyberbullying.

Third, as technology is ever-changing, the venues by which one person can cyberbully another are also changing and varied, as reflected in the definition presented above, which includes cyberbullying through e-mail, instant messages, text messages, on websites, through online gaming, in chat rooms, and on social network sites, to name a few methods (Kowalski, Limber, & Agatston, 2012). At any particular point in time, one venue is likely to emerge as a more popular method for cyberbullying than another. Whereas Katzer, Fetchenhauer, and Belschak (2009) observed that chat rooms were the most common venue for involvement in cyberbullying in a population of fifth to eleventh graders in German schools, Kowalski and Limber (2007) found instant messaging was the most frequent means by which U.S. middle school students both perpetrated and were victims of cyberbullying. Robers, Kemp, and Truman (2013) found that U.S. middle and high school students were most likely to say they were the subject of harassing text messages. With 80 percent of teens using social network sites (Brenner, 2012) and youth sharing more personal information than ever on their profiles (Madden et al., 2013), we suspect that social media, such as Facebook, Twitter, and Instagram may soon emerge as the most common venue for cyberbullying.

Fourth, from a theoretical and empirical perspective, researchers and others have questioned the degree to which cyberbullying is similar to and different from traditional bullying. Cyberbullying shares the three defining features of traditional bullying: it is an act of aggression, it is typically repeated over time, and it occurs among individuals between whom there is a power imbalance (Kowalski, Limber, & Agatston, 2012; see also Gladden et al., 2014; Olweus, 2012, 2013; Smith et al., 2012).

However, there are key ways in which cyberbullying and traditional bullying differ from one another. Perhaps the most salient of these is the perceived anonymity that often accompanies cyberbullying. Although it is possible to bully anonymously through more "traditional" means (e.g., writing mean messages on a bathroom stall), the opportunity is clearly greater in cases of cyberbullying. In a study by Kowalski and Limber (2007), almost 50 percent of the victims indicated that they did not know the identity of the person who perpetrated cyberbullying against them. Although people are never as anonymous online as they think they are, the cloak of anonymity will often lead people to say and do things online that they would never say or do in face-to-face interactions (Diener, 1980). Thus, anonymity opens up the pool of individuals who might be willing to perpetrate cyberbullying. In some cases, this pool has expanded to include the individual himself/herself, as anonymity allows some users to engage in self-cyberbullying, whether to gain attention or to send out a cry for help (Patchin, 2013).

Another difference between cyberbullying and more traditional forms of bullying is that, while most traditional bullying occurs at school during the school day (Nansel et al., 2001), cyberbullying can occur at any time of the day or night. Even if a victim chooses not to view derogatory messages that are being left about him/her on a website, for example, he/she knows that others are likely viewing those messages. The 24/7 accessibility of cyberbullying has the potential of magnifying the effects that accompany cyberbullying relative to traditional bullying.

A third way in which cyberbullying and traditional bullying differ from one another is in the punitive fears that young people report. While bullied youth often do not report involvement in any type of bullying (Limber, Olweus, & Luxenberg, 2013), their reasons differ depending on the type of bullying. Victims of traditional bullying often don't tell parents or other authority figures about their victimization because they fear retaliation on the part of the perpetrator should he/she find out, and they worry that adult intervention may make the situation worse. Targets of cyberbullying may share these concerns, but they may also fail to report their victimization because they fear that their parents will take away their technology (i.e., the means by which they are being victimized) (Kowalski, Limber, & Agatson, 2012).

A fourth way in which cyberbullying may differ from traditional forms of bullying is on the dimension of repetition. As previously noted, bullying typically is repeated over time. The nature of this repetition may be quite different online versus in person, however. For example, a single act (such as a nasty e-mail, text message or web post) may be viewed over time by hundreds or thousands of individuals, including the target, who visit a site or receive and forward the message (Kowalski, Limber, & Agatston, 2012). An individual who is the target of this single act may feel that he or she is being bullied over and over again, as he or she learns or suspects that others are viewing the message over time.

Finally, while many parents of victims themselves had experiences with traditional bullying as victims, perpetrators, or bystanders, the same cannot be said for cyberbullying. Adults today did not grow up with the technology with which their children are so connected, creating a digital divide between the adults (digital immigrants) and youth (digital natives).

In an attempt to address the similarities and differences between traditional bullying and cyberbullying, a number of researchers have empirically tested the relation between involvement in traditional bullying and involvement in cyberbullying. The strongest relations appear to be between traditional bullying victimization and cyberbullying victimization, as well as between traditional bullying perpetration and cyberbullying perpetration (e.g., Gradinger, Strohmeier, & Spiel, 2009; Hinduja & Patchin, 2008; Kowalski et al., 2014; Kowalski, Morgan, & Limber, 2012; Schneider, O'Donnell, Stueve, & Coulter, 2012). In addition, a positive correlation has been observed between involvement in cyberbullying as both victim and perpetrator (Kowalski, Morgan, & Limber, 2012). Although the degree of overlap between traditional bullying and cyberbullying varies by study, a meta-analysis conducted by Kowalski et al. (2014) found a correlation of 0.45 between being a perpetrator of traditional bullying and perpetrating cyberbullying. Similarly, they found a correlation of 0.40 between traditional victimization and cyberbullying victimization. However, some estimates of the degree of overlap between traditional bullying and cyberbullying are much higher. Olweus (2013), for example, reported that only 10 percent of individuals are cyberbullied independently of involvement in traditional bullying, leading him to conclude that "to be cyberbullied or to cyberbully others seems to a large extent to be part of a general pattern of bullying, where the use of the electronic media is only one possible form" (p. 10). More research is needed examining the joint and independent effects of involvement in traditional bullying and cyberbullying on physical, psychological, and behavioral outcomes for those affected.

PREVALENCE OF CYBERBULLYING

Rates of cyberbullying vary substantially among studies, likely reflecting discrepancies in the definition of cyberbullying (or lack thereof) used by researchers; other factors associated with measuring the phenomenon (e.g., the type of instruments used, the time frame assessed); the age and characteristics of the population studied; and the date of the study (Kowalski, Limber, & Agatston, 2012; Kowalski, et al., 2014). For example, in a 2009 survey of 655 teens ages 13 to 18, researchers reported that 19 percent *had ever* been cyberbullied and 10 percent *had ever* cyberbullied others (Cox Communications, 2009). Hinduja and Patchin (2009) surveyed middle school students and reported that 9 percent had been cyberbullied *in the previous 30 days*, and 17 percent had been cyberbullied *in their lifetime*. Eight percent had cyberbullied others *in the previous 30 days*, and 18 percent had done so *in their lifetime*. In another study of middle schoolers, Kowalski and Limber (2007) found that 18 percent had been cyberbullied *at least once in the previous two months*, and 11 percent had cyberbullied others within this period of time. Olweus (2013) examined data from 440,000 students in grades 3 through 12 in the United States between 2007 and 2010 and reported that 4.5 percent had been cyberbullied with some frequency (*two to three times/month or more often*) and 2.8 percent had cyberbullied others (two to three times/month or more).

In a nationally representative sample of 12- to 18-year-old students, 9 percent reported having been cyberbullied *during the 2011 school year* (in or outside of school), compared with 28 percent of students who reported having been traditionally bullied at school during this same period (Robers et al., 2013). Four percent said they had experienced harassing text messages, 4 percent reported that another student had posted hurtful information about them on the Internet, 3 percent said they had experienced harassing instant messaging, and 2 percent had been the subject of harassing e-mails. Smaller percentages of students reported having private information purposely shared on the Internet (1%), being excluded online (1%), and being harassed while playing online games (2%).

Just as there is great variability among studies about the current prevalence of cyberbullying, there also is debate about whether or not cyberbullying has been on the rise in recent years. Data from the first and second Youth Internet Safety Surveys demonstrated that *online harassment* (defined as threats or other offensive behavior other than sexual solicitation that were sent online to a youth or posted online about a youth) increased from 6 percent in 2000 to 9 percent in 2005, and to 11 percent in 2010 (Jones, Mitchell, & Finkelhor, 2012). It is important to note, however, that the largest increase occurred between 2000 and 2005, as many youth became new adopters of social media. The rates of online harassment increased at a slower rate over the next five years. Data from the National Crime Victimization Survey similarly suggest slight increases in the percentage of students who report having been cyberbullied (from 6% in 2009 to 9% in 2011; see Robers et al., 2013; Robers, Zhang, Truman, & Snyder, 2012). On the other hand, citing data from a large-scale study of 440,000 students in the United States in grades 3 through 12, and data from Norwegian schools, Olweus (2013) did not find systematic changes in the prevalence of being cyberbullied or cyberbullying others between 2007 and 2010.

CHARACTERISTICS OF VICTIMS AND PERPETRATORS

Just as there is no profile of an individual who is involved with traditional bullying, so too, there is no single character portrait of the individual who perpetrates or is a victim of cyberbullying. However, research over the last few years has identified some characteristics that are associated with involvement in cyberbullying. Naturally, demographic characteristics (i.e., gender, race, and age) of victims and perpetrators were some of the initial variables examined for their relationship to involvement in cyberbullying.

Gender

Research on aggression has shown that males tend to engage in more direct forms of aggression whereas females tend to engage in more indirect types of aggression (Bjorkqvist, Lagerspetz, & Osterman, 1992). Because cyberbullying is a type of indirect aggression, girls might be expected to engage in cyberbullying to a greater extent than boys. However, research on the relation between gender and cyberbullying has been mixed. In their study with middle school children, Kowalski and Limber (2007) found that girls were more likely to be both victims and perpetrators of cyberbullying than boys (see also Tokunaga, 2010). Sourander et al. (2010), on the other hand, observed that males were more likely to perpetrate cyberbullying whereas females were more likely to be targets of cyberbullying. Still other research has found no significant gender differences in boys' and girls' involvement with cyberbullying (e.g., Hinduja & Patchin, 2008; Williams & Guerra, 2007; Ybarra & Mitchell, 2004).

Additional research revealed no differences between males and females when participants were asked about their overall involvement with cyberbullying but did find differences when participants were asked about the extent to which they have experienced cyberbullying via particular venues (e.g., chat rooms, social media). For example, Hinduja and Patchin (2008) found that males and females did not differ in their overall prevalence rates of cyberbullying but that females reported more cyberbullying victimization via e-mail than did males (see also Smith et al., 2006). Data from the School Crime Supplement to the National Crime Victimization Survey indicated that girls were more likely than boys to experience most forms of cyberbullying (with the exception of being bullied while gaming and being excluded online) (Robers et al., 2013). This national study also reported gender differences in the intensity with which boys and girls are cyberbullied. Among students who reported being cyberbullied, girls were more likely to experience occasional cyberbullying (e.g., once or twice in the school year), whereas boys were more likely to experience frequent cyberbullying. A meta-analysis conducted by Kowalski et al. (2014) suggested that gender is involved in cyberbullying, but as a moderator of the relation between cyberbullying victimization and depression. Specifically, the adverse effects of cyberbullying may be magnified for females relative to males.

Age

Cyberbullying behavior has a decidedly middle school connotation to it. This perception has been exacerbated by the fact that a large percentage of the research on cyberbullying has been conducted using middle school samples. Among these samples, age-related changes have been observed with sixth graders showing less involvement in cyberbullying than seventh or eighth graders (Kowalski & Limber, 2007; see also Hinduja & Patchin, 2008; Williams & Guerra, 2007). Recent research among middle and high school students, however, has noted that a higher percentage of students in tenth grade report being cyberbullied, compared with students in sixth, seventh, eighth, ninth, and twelfth grades (Robers et al., 2013). Other researchers have also observed age-related variations in cyberbullying as a function of the venue being examined. For example, Smith et al. (2008) found that text messaging, instant messaging, and picture bullying were less common among younger than older students.

However, two qualifiers are in order here. First, as younger and younger children use technology, these age-related variations are likely to attenuate. Second, research in the last couple of years has begun to investigate the experience of older samples, namely college students, with cyberbullying (Kowalski, Giumetti, Schroeder, & Reese, 2012; Schenk & Fremouw, 2012). The outcome of this research is that cyberbullying is hardly limited to middle school. Rather, college campuses have had to wrestle with the negative effects stemming from websites such as Juicycampus.com and College ACB, where students can post feeder lines (e.g., "Top 10 Sluts at [College Name]") to which people respond with their personal opinions, to the great detriment of those who are named. Additionally, although more research is needed in this area, evidence suggests that cyberbullying is alive and well in the workplace as well, where the digital age has ushered in a time of online workplace incivility (Giumetti, McKibben, Hatfield, Schroeder, & Kowalski, 2012).

Race/Ethnicity

Research on racial and ethnic influences on cyberbullying has been much more circumscribed, due in large part to the homogeneous nature of the samples used in much of the research. Two studies that are particularly noteworthy, however, did not observe any significant effect of race on cyberbullying victimization or perpetration (Hinduja & Patchin, 2008; Ybarra, Diener-West, & Leaf, 2007). On the other hand, nationally representative data from the School Crime Supplement to the National Crime Victimization Survey showed higher rates of cyber victimization among white middle and high school students (11%) compared to Hispanic (8%) or black (7%) students (Robers et al., 2013). Moreover, Shapka and Law (2013) found evidence for cultural differences in an examination of engagement in cyberbullying among East Asian adolescents and those of European descent. East Asian adolescents were less likely to engage in cyberbullying than adolescents of European descent. Importantly, in the virtual world, an individual's race is not immediately identifiable, so one would not expect it to necessarily play a role in cyberbullying situations, particularly given the umbrella of anonymity under which so much cyberbullying occurs (Kowalski, Limber, & Agatston, 2012).

Urbanicity

A final demographic variable that has received a bit of attention with regard to prevalence of cyberbullying is urbanicity. Robers and colleagues (2013) observed that sixth through twelfth graders living in suburban areas reported experiencing more cyberbullying than those from urban areas (10% and 7%, respectively), although there were no significant differences in rates between rural and urban or rural and suburban students. Additional research is needed in this area.

Personal and Situational Predictors

Beyond demographic variables, a number of personal and situational variables have been identified that are related to cyberbullying victimization and perpetration. In terms of personality variables, social intelligence is negatively related to cybervictimization (Hunt, Peters, & Rapee, 2012), whereas hyperactivity is positively related to cybervictimization (Dooley, Shaw, & Cross, 2012). Individuals who experience cyberbullying also report higher scores on measures of anxiety and depression than individuals not involved in bullying (Kowalski et al., 2014; Ybarra & Mitchell, 2004). However, as will be discussed later, it is difficult to know if this is an antecedent or a consequence of involvement in cyberbullying. Relatedly, victims of cyberbullying show lower levels of self-esteem compared to those not involved with cyberbullying (Kowalski, Limber, & Agatston, 2012). This may stem, in part, from the fact that cyberbullying victims may have fewer friends than those not involved with cyberbullying (O'Brennan, Bradshaw, & Sawyer, 2009). Targets also engage in riskier online behaviors, such as disseminating personal information online (Bauman, 2010; Erdur-Baker, 2010; Görzig & Ólafsson, 2013), and have a higher level of exposure to violent video games (Lam, Cheng, & Liu, 2013) than those individuals who had not been involved with cyberbullying.

Empathy is related to cyberbullying perpetration. Individuals higher in cognitive empathy report engaging in cyberbullying less frequently than those lower in cognitive empathy (Ang & Goh, 2010). Not surprisingly, narcissism also has a positive relationship to cyberbullying perpetration (Ang, Tan, & Mansor, 2011; Fanti, Demetriou, & Hawa, 2012). As with victimization, anxiety, depression, and low self-esteem are associated with cyberbullying perpetration, although the temporal order of this relation is, again, an open question (Didden et al., 2009).

Perpetrating cyberbullying, similar to traditional bullying, has also been linked to a number of academic difficulties. Perpetrators of cyberbullying report problems with concentration (Beran & Li, 2007), lower grades, lower school commitment, and a higher number of school absences (Kowalski & Limber, 2013; Ybarra & Mitchell, 2004). These academic difficulties may be confounded by the fact that perpetrators often display a number of other maladaptive behaviors relative to those not involved in bullying, including alcohol and tobacco use, physical assault, and clashes with law enforcement (Ybarra & Mitchell, 2004).

Compared to those not involved with bullying, perpetrators of cyberbullying also appear to have a different set of attitudes and values than those not involved with bullying that may predispose them to engage in cyberbullying behavior. They display moral approval of bullying (Williams & Guerra, 2007) and a process of moral disengagement whereby they minimize the negative impact of their behavior on the victim(s) (Almeida, Correia, Marinho, & Garcia, 2012; Bandura, 1999; Bauman, 2010; Menesini, Nocentini, & Camodeca, 2013; Pornari & Wood, 2010). Barlett and Gentile (2012) found that positive attitudes toward online anonymity (e.g., "I feel comfortable sending mean messages or e-mails to anybody no matter if I know them or not") and differential power (e.g., acknowledging that it is easy to send mean messages online no matter how big or strong one is) predicted positive attitudes toward cyberbullying (Barlett & Gentile, 2012). When youth had positive attitudes toward cyberbullying, they were more likely to cyberbully others (Barlett & Gentile, 2012; Barlett et al., 2014).

For both victims and perpetrators, support from friends, family, and the school are critical variables in predicting involvement in cyberbullying. Youth who feel that they have a network of supportive friends are less likely to be involved with cyberbullying as either victim (Ubertini, 2011) or perpetrator (Fanti et al., 2012). Youth whose friends are involved in cyberbullying report a higher likelihood of becoming involved in cyberbullying themselves (Hinduja & Patchin, 2013). Poor parental control of technology and poor communication between parents and youth regarding the potential hazards of the Internet have been associated with heightened levels of electronic victimization (Aoyama, Utsumi, & Hasegawa, 2012; Wade & Beran, 2011). Similarly, youth who report poor relationships with their parents report higher levels of perpetrating cyberbullying (Wang, Iannotti, & Nansel, 2009). Youth who are reinforced for cyberbullying by family members or friends are more likely to cyberbully others (Barlett & Gentile, 2012; Barlett et al., 2014). School climate is also involved in affecting involvement in cyberbullying for victims and perpetrators, with students who feel that their school environment is supportive, warm, and trusting reporting less involvement in cyberbullying (Williams & Guerra, 2007).

CONSEQUENCES OF CYBERBULLYING

As the media have sensationalized a number of suicides that have seemingly stemmed from involvement in cyberbullying, researchers have turned their attention to the effects of cyberbullying. Three points are noteworthy. First, the effects of cyberbullying tend to mirror those associated with traditional bullying, including anxiety, depression, low self-esteem, reduced school performance, and suicidal ideation, a point we will return to below (Juvonen & Gross, 2008; Kowalski & Limber, 2013; Patchin & Hinduja, 2010; Ybarra & Mitchell, 2004). Second, because of the overlap between involvement in traditional bullying and cyberbullying, it is difficult to completely separate out the independent contributions of cyberbullying to the negative effects that are observed above and beyond those associated with traditional bullying (see, however, Bonanno & Hymel, 2013). Third, consistent with research on stress and coping (Lazarus & Folkman, 1984), people appraise cyberbullying situations differently, leading to different effects for different people. As implied in Lazarus and Folkman's appraisal model of coping, when confronted with a stressor, such as cyberbullying, people engage in a process of primary appraisal, in which they evaluate the harm, threat, and challenge presented by a particular situation, as well as a process of secondary appraisal, whereby they evaluate their ability to handle the demands of a particular situation.

More attention has been paid to the consequences of cyberbullying for victims than for perpetrators. Unfortunately, because there have been few longitudinal studies on cyberbullying (Barlett & Gentile, 2012; Barlett et al., 2014), the area is plagued with a bit of a chicken-egg problem. As noted earlier, although anxiety, depression, loneliness, and the like may be consequences of cyberbullying, these same variables may also predispose certain individuals to be cyberbullied. For example, people who are socially anxious may find social interactions smoother in the virtual world than in the real world, leading them to spend more time online. However, time spent online is a predictor of cyberbullying victimization (Kowalski et al., 2014). Meta-analytic results revealed that outcomes associated with cyberbullying victimization include suicidal ideation, anxiety, depression, loneliness, low self-esteem, as well as externalizing difficulties (Kowalski et al., 2014; see also Kowalski & Limber, 2013). Additionally, in some instances, perpetrators are putting victims in actual physical danger via their cyberbullying. For example, perpetrators who impersonate their victim and post hate messages in chat rooms along with the victim's identifying information may be setting the victims up for retaliation by members of the chat room who have taken offense at the hate message ostensibly posted by the target.

Involvement in cyberbullying for perpetrators is also associated with a number of negative outcomes, many of which mirror those associated with victimization. Compared to those not involved with cyberbullying, perpetrators report higher levels of depression, anxiety, suicidal ideation, and loneliness (Hinduja & Patchin, 2010). They also show lower levels of self-esteem and poor academic performance (Kowalski et al., 2014; see also Kowalski & Limber, 2013). Additionally, some perpetrators may experience guilt and remorse (Dempsey, Sulkowski, Nichols, & Storch, 2009).

Although there is no research to date on this topic, concern has been raised that social networking sites may trigger a "suicide contagion effect." The idea for this stems from the Werther effect (Becker & Schmidt, 2005), which refers to the increase in suicides by individuals who read in newspapers about suicides of individuals similar to them. Given the popularity of social networking sites, and the fact that not only are memorial pages created but also some people write good-bye posts on their Facebook profiles before they commit suicide, it is not surprising that suicide contagion might occur.

THEORETICAL FRAMEWORKS FOR UNDERSTANDING CYBERBULLYING

Research questions such as those addressed above are best approached within a theoretical framework. Indeed, a theoretical basis is important for uncovering risk and protective factors for involvement in and possible effects of cyberbullying and designing assessment measures and interventions that effectively address cyberbullying (Kowalski et al., 2014). Although it is beyond the scope of this chapter to provide detailed descriptions of the wide range of theories that may be relevant to research on cyberbullying, we will briefly highlight two theories that have been used by researchers to explain the involvement of children and youth in bullying.

Ecological Systems Theory

Many researchers have relied upon Bronfenbrenner's Ecological Systems Theory (Bronfenbrenner, 1979, 2005) to understand the complexity of bullying behavior (see, e.g., Hong & Espelage, 2012; Swearer & Doll, 2001). Bronfenbrenner's perspective recognizes that an individual is an active agent who both influences and is influenced by many environments or systems. He described a series of nested systems that affect an individual—the microsystem (a child's immediate environment of family, peer group, school, etc.), the mesosystem (the connections between structures in a child's microsystem), the exosystem (the social settings beyond a child's immediate environment that influence a child through his or her microsystem), and the macrosystem (the customs, values and laws of a culture). Motivated by Bronfenbrenner's work, researchers have recognized that children's behavior (whether bullying others, being bullied, or reacting as a witness to bullying) is determined by many factors within the family, peer group, school, neighborhood, the broader community, and society.

General Aggression Model

Another theory, which similarly takes into account the complexity of influences on an individual's behavior, is the General Aggression Model (GAM; see Anderson & Carnagey, this volume). The GAM focuses upon *individual inputs* (e.g., gender, age, motives, personality, psychological states, socioeconomic status, technology use) and *situational inputs* (e.g., provocation, perceived support, parental involvement, school climate) that influence an individual's aggressive behavior (Anderson & Bushman, 2002; Kowalski et al., 2014). These inputs affect social, cognitive, emotional, and behavioral outcomes through three direct *routes*—cognition (e.g., aggressive thoughts), affect, and arousal (Anderson & Bushman, 2002). After taking into account personal and situational inputs and these internal cognitive, affective, and arousal states, an individual engages in appraisal and decision-making. Finally, outcomes of the aggression (e.g., psychological and physical health, social functioning, behavioral problems) are examined. Several researchers have relied upon the GAM in their conceptualizations of bullying and cyberbullying behavior (Gullone & Robertson, 2008; Kowalski et al., 2014; Vannucci, Nocentini, Mazzoni, & Menesini, 2012).

THE ROLE OF MEDIA IN PERPETUATING AND ADDRESSING CYBERBULLYING

There has been an onslaught of media attention to issues of electronic aggression, with particular attention to tragic and provocative cases of cyberbullying. The popular media's mentions of cyberbullying increased from fewer than 20 media reports in the global media in 2005 to more than 3,500 media reports across the globe in 2010 (Kowalski, Limber, & Agatston, 2012).

Inaccurate Portrayals by Media

Sensational and exaggerated media reports have helped to create some inaccurate impressions of the nature and prevalence of cyberbullying and the incidence of school violence, more broadly.

Cyberbullying prevalence and its relation to suicide

For example, it is now fairly common to hear cyberbullying described as an "epidemic" by many reporters and media personalities (Sabella, Patchin, & Hinduja, 2013). This terminology suggests that cyberbullying involves large percentages of children and youth in dramatically increasing numbers. In reality, research suggests that rates of cyberbullying are substantially lower than a number of more "traditional" forms of bullying, such as face-to-face verbal bullying or rumor-spreading (Limber et al., 2013; Livingston, Haddon, Gorsig & Olafsson, 2011; Olweus, 2012; Robers et al., 2013). Moreover, as previously noted, researchers do not agree on whether cyberbullying is increasing.

Media reports have not only overemphasized the prevalence of cyberbullying, but, in focusing on the most tragic cases, they have also promoted the belief that being cyberbullied can frequently lead directly to youth suicide (Sabella et al., 2013). The term "bullycide" has been increasingly used to describe cases of suicide that some feel were "caused" by bullying (e.g., Hewitt, 2012; Kessler, 2010). Such assumptions are not supported by research.

Tragically, suicide is all too common among teens and young adults. It is the third leading cause of death among 15- to 24-year-olds. Fifteen percent of high school students seriously considered suicide in the previous 12 months, and 7 percent reported making at least one suicide attempt in the previous year (Centers for Disease Control and Prevention [CDC], 2009). But there is no single cause of suicide. As the CDC (n.d.) highlights, "a combination of individual, relational, community, and societal factors contribute to the risk of suicide," including a family history of suicide or child maltreatment, a history of mental disorders (especially depression) or alcohol and substance abuse, feelings of hopelessness, impulsive or aggressive tendencies, isolation, loss, physical illness, local epidemics of suicide, and easy access to lethal methods. That is, no single risk factor is "the" cause, but each additional risk factor can causally increase the risk (see also chapter 2, this volume).

Although involvement in bullying is related to a greater likelihood of suicidal thoughts and behavior (Annenberg Public Policy Center, 2010; Arseneault, Bowes, & Shakoor, 2010; Hinduja & Patchin, 2010; Kim, Leventhal, Koh, & Boyce, 2009; Klomek, Marrocco, Kleinman, Schoenfeld, & Gould, 2007, 2008;

Pranjic & Bajraktarevic, 2010), these studies have mostly been correlational. Therefore, it is impossible to know how serious a risk factor cyberbullying may be for the average victim (Edgerton & Limber, 2013; Federal Partners in Bullying Prevention, n.d.; Sabella et al., 2013). Other risk factors, such as mental health problems, appear to play a much larger role than bullying in predicting suicidal thoughts and behavior (Hinduja & Patchin, 2010).

Trends in victimization at school

Also lost in the media attention to cyberbullying are the emerging data that indicate that many forms of school victimization are on the decline. New numbers from the National Center for Educational Statistics indicate that total victimization rates for students ages 12 to 18 have decreased between 1992 and 2011, as have thefts, violent victimizations, and serious violent victimizations (Robers et al., 2013). Moreover, the percentages of students who fear being attacked or harmed at school has dropped from 12 percent in 1995 to 4 percent in 2011 (Robers et al., 2013). Thus, although media reporting can be productive in drawing attention to a problem, it is most helpful when it is done objectively and rationally rather than in a sensational manner that overemphasizes negative behavior among youth.

Negative portrayals of youth

Extensive media coverage of youth aggression and violence may, in fact, exacerbate the problem. Research in the area of social norming suggests that youth may be more likely to take part in negative behavior and less likely to stop others acting badly if they perceive that the behavior is common or socially accepted by peers (Perkins, Craig, & Perkins, 2011). On the other hand, research suggests that sharing messages that emphasize that most youth do not support bullying can result in less bullying (Perkins et al., 2011).

Despite the tendency of many media accounts to focus on tragic and sensational cases of bullying, many responsible media organizations are beginning to recognize positive youth bystander behaviors (often referred to as "upstanders") (National School Climate Center, n.d.) that youth engage in and have begun to highlight such actions through news coverage, websites, and social media. The Family Online Institute's "Platform for Good" is an example of a website and social media campaign that highlights the positive actions that are occurring via social media. Many Twitter campaigns have turned from destructive to constructive as youth begin to develop agency and redirect negative threads to positive threads. For example, Trendmicro (n.d.) ("What's Your Story" contest) and Common Sense Media (A Platform for Good, n.d.) have developed video contests and strategies that allow youth to engage in positive media messaging that counters the view that youth are cruel and uncaring. Thus, the use of social media can be a promising tool to combat both online and offline cruelty. The nature of the Internet allows negative messages to spread virally, but it also allows for positive messages to be spread widely. The "net effect," which was originally conceived by danah boyd (2008), refers to the characteristics of replicability, scalability, and invisibility of audiences online. Just as the net effect can rapidly spread negative messages, it can also be harnessed to promote the positive behavior in which youth engage. Thus, harnessing social media for good shows great promise and may help to reduce rates of cyberbullying, in particular.

MEDIA VIOLENCE AS A POSSIBLE RISK FACTOR FOR CYBERBULLYING

To what extent might exposure to violence in the media increase the likelihood that a child is involved in cyberbullying? Several cross-sectional and longitudinal studies have established a relationship between consumption of violent media and aggressive behavior among children (Gentile, Coyne, & Walsh, 2010; Ostrov, Gentile, & Crick, 2006). For example, Gentile et al. (2010) found that, among third to fifth graders, consumption of media violence early in the school year was related to greater verbal, relational, and physical aggression and less prosocial behavior later in the school year. Research has also shown that interventions to reduce exposure to screen violence and increase exposure to prosocial television, video game, and computer use among children can enhance their social and emotional competence (Christakis et al., 2013).

From this line of research, one might hypothesize that consumption of media violence may increase the likelihood of children and youth cyberbullying others. Indeed, Fanti, Demetriou, and Hawa (2012) found that among 11- to 14-year-olds living in Cyprus, media violence exposure was associated with an increase in both cyberbullying and cybervictimization one year later. The authors speculated that there may be different mechanisms at play among these different youth. Those who cyberbully others may perceive the aggressive behavior in media as "appropriate, profitable, or even morally justified" (p. 178), which, in turn, increases their own aggressive behavior. Cyberbullied youth who view media violence, on the other hand, may perceive that the world is a mean and scary place, which may lead to increased fear and a greater likelihood of being bullied by peers. Although this short-term longitudinal study is enlightening, additional research is needed to clarify the relationship between exposure to different forms of media violence and cyberbullying among children and youth.

WHAT CAN PARENTS DO TO PREVENT AND ADDRESS CYBERBULLYING?

Parenting has changed as children increasingly live their lives online, and parents of tweens and teens rely on mobile phones to keep in touch with their children throughout the day. As children increasingly socialize online, some bullying behaviors have also moved online. Many parents appreciate the positive aspects of their children engaging in the participatory online culture, but they wish to have a presence in their children's digital lives. Yet even the most vigilant parents cannot expect to always be present in the online world of their children, and many parents do not want to be constantly hovering over their children, even if they had the time. Although limiting access and filtering content works well with younger children, it is also important for parents to take a developmentally appropriate role in monitoring their older children's use of technology. As youth mature, digital fences can be replaced with conversation, supervised practice, more limited monitoring, and teachable moments. Parents and the community as a whole need to recognize that raising good "digital citizens" fits into the broader goal of raising healthy, responsible, engaged, and caring kids.

Preventing Cyberbullying

Many parents are particularly concerned about bullying and thus will benefit from incorporating discussions about both traditional bullying and cyberbullying with their children at an early age. The following are recommendations to help prevent cyberbullying from occurring in the first place.

Begin by modeling positive behavior

Model civility online and offline by treating others in a respectful manner. Demonstrate being fully present with family and friends by establishing times during which no cellphones or digital devices are used, such as during meal times and other important gatherings.

Discuss desired digital behaviors as well as undesirable behaviors

Online learning, research, collaboration, creativity, connectedness, and group problem solving are all desirable activities and potential positive outcomes from using technology wisely. Yet there are negative behaviors to avoid, such as cyberbullying; inappropriate site, photo, or video sharing; plagiarizing; and cheating. Protecting the privacy of self and others is also an important topic of discussion. Remind youth that anything shared digitally can be potentially public and permanent. Research regarding online aggressive behavior (Ybarra, Mitchell, Finkelhor, & Wolak, 2007) found that engaging in harassment or threats actually doubles the aggressor's risk of being victimized. The result is such that treating others with respect online will help to protect them from online victimization. Thus, how youth behave online is core to their overall well-being, which is an important principle for digital citizens to grasp.

Become educated about appropriate strategies for monitoring a child's digital world, but keep the focus on communication

Monitoring should primarily be used to encourage conversations and "course corrections" when necessary. As teens mature and demonstrate responsibility, conversations should be the primary method of engaging in a youth's digital world. Parents and guardians can ask tweens and teens about favorite social media sites where they engage with their friends, ask them to demonstrate how to set the privacy settings and how they protect themselves and others from cyberbullying or oversharing, and discuss whether the site provides any social reporting tools that can be used in case of cyberbullying or other forms of abuse. Websites such as connectsafely.org provide useful parent guides to many of the popular social media platforms that are popular with youth.

Suggestions for Addressing Cyberbullying among Children

While adults are justifiably concerned when a child experiences or engages in bullying or cyberbullying behavior, it is important to also focus on the role of a child who is an observer of such behavior. Research on bullying has demonstrated that most young people do not find themselves in the role of one who bullies or one who is bullied (Olweus, 1993); rather, the majority of young people are involved in bullying as witnesses. Cyberbullying that occurs through the use of social media is also frequently witnessed online or discussed at school the following day. Thus it is just as important to discuss the bystander role in cyberbullying as the role of aggressor or target.

How to help if youth witness cyberbullying

Adults can help children be part of the solution in cyberbullying situations by discussing various options that might help a peer. Children and youth can provide support to a bullied peer by refusing to join in with the cyberbullying, sending positive messages, and spending time with the one being bullied. Some proactive youth have taken action to change negative conversational threads or hashtags to positive threads that focus on caring messages toward a targeted peer or group rather than negative messages. Youth can also be proactive by using social reporting tools to report negative behavior or by reporting the behavior to an appropriate adult.

What to do if youth engage in cyberbullying

It is difficult to witness or hear that our children have engaged in cyberbullying or any other form of bullying, but it is important to recognize when it occurs that it is a teachable moment. Many children engage in some form of cruel or bullying behavior at some point in their lives (Dreikurs & Soltz, 1991). Although it is useful to empathize with children regarding their mistake, it is also important to hold them accountable for their behavior and have a discussion that encourages empathy for the targeted individuals, logical consequences for the behavior, and restoration of any harm that was done. When possible, try to determine the goal of the behavior (i.e., attention, power, revenge, or excitement) and discuss other ways to meet that goal (Dreikurs, Cassel, & Ferguson, 2004). Appropriate consequences might include increased monitoring and restrictions on social media or mobile phone use. There also may be steps children can take to repair the harm that they caused, such as removing content, correcting false information, and encouraging other peers to avoid engaging in similar behavior. Although forced apologies are rarely helpful, a sincere apology may be appropriate if the targeted individual is willing to receive it. Consultation with a mental health professional may also be warranted.

What to do if youth are targeted by cyberbullying

There are warning signs that may suggest that a child is involved in cyberbullying, such as appearing upset after being online or viewing a text message, withdrawing from social interaction, exhibiting poor academic performance, and being the target of traditional bullying (Kowalski, Limber, & Agatston, 2012). If a parent or guardian discovers that a child has been targeted, there are some steps that can be taken to intervene. It is important to keep in mind that some youth indicate that they are able to handle cyberbullying on their own and are not that bothered by it (Ybarra & Mitchell, 2007). Thus, having a discussion with youth about how distressed they are, the strategies that they have pursued thus far, and whether they have been effective or not is a useful place to start. Although ignoring one or two mean messages or blocking a user or sender may be effective in some instances, in other cases additional steps are necessary. One of the unique features of cyberbullying compared to traditional bullying is that there is often digital evidence of the abuse that can be used to report an aggressor or that can be shared with the parent of the aggressor in an effort to encourage a cessation of the behavior. If the identity of the aggressor is difficult to determine due to fake screen names or accounts, it is important to notify the web or social networking site or the phone company.

In severe cases of cyberbullying, it may be necessary to contact the police or other legal authorities for assistance. Examples of such instances include threats, stalking behavior, sexually explicit content, and blackmail or extortion (Willard, 2007). Law enforcement may be able to trace the aggressor's identity if the behavior is illegal. Attorneys may be able to send a written demand that the behavior cease, or initiate legal action to seek civil remedies in cases of extreme cyberbullying. Some communities are using practices based on restorative justice principles that focus on "repairing the harm" as opposed to punitive responses in an effort to guide, teach, and bring about change in a youthful offender.

Finally, consider mental health services for any individual who is struggling with depression, anxiety, and feelings of hopelessness, low self-esteem, or suicidal ideation. As noted previously, although there are numerous risk factors for suicide, studies show an association between bullying, cyberbullying, and suicide-related behaviors (Hertz, Donato, & Wright, 2013; Hinduja & Patchin, 2010; Kowalski & Limber, 2013).

WHAT CAN EDUCATORS AND OTHER PROFESSIONALS DO TO PREVENT CYBERBULLYING?

With increased attention to cyberbullying among the public, and with the passage of laws in 49 states that require school districts to develop policies and strategies to address bullying (including cyberbullying in many cases) (U.S. Department of Education, 2011), many educators and other professionals are seeking effective strategies to prevent and address cyberbullying (Kowalski, Limber, & Agatston, 2012). Given the newness of the phenomenon of cyberbullying, such strategies have emerged only in the last several years and currently lack rigorous evaluation. The following recommendations of best practice (see also Kowalski, Limber, & Agatston, 2012) have been developed based on research on youth aggression, bullying prevention, and experiences with effective practices in the field.

Incorporate Cyberbullying Prevention into Comprehensive Bullying Prevention Efforts

Many schools have implemented comprehensive bullying prevention programs as a result of conclusions from researchers that schoolwide efforts that focus on changing the norms within the social environment of the school are the most promising. A meta-evaluation by Ttofi and Farrington (2009) concluded that school-based bullying prevention programs could be effective, resulting in a 20 to 23 percent reduction in bullying. Those that embraced a comprehensive approach to bullying prevention were most effective (see also Olweus & Limber, 2010; Federal Partners in Bullying Prevention, n.d., for a discussion of the importance of comprehensive efforts). Cyberbullying, as a form of bullying, should best be addressed within the broader context of the prevention of bullying—not as an add-on issue.

Assess Cyberbullying

Adults cannot assume that they have a good understanding of the nature and frequency of cyberbullying that occurs among students. Therefore, just as it is recommended practice to regularly collect data about the nature and prevalence of bullying among students (Federal Partners in Bullying Prevention, n.d.), it is also important to ensure that these assessments address cyberbullying. This data collection may be formal, involving the completion of anonymous written or online surveys by students, or it may be less formal, involving interviews or focus groups of students, educators, and parents. These data may be used to help plan prevention efforts (e.g., assess the need for training), motivate staff and parents to address the issue, and evaluate the impact of prevention and intervention efforts.

Provide Staff Training

All educators and adults who work with youth can benefit from a general staff training that addresses basic information about the nature and extent of cyberbullying and effective prevention efforts. Approximately half of current anti-bullying laws now require or encourage school districts to provide training for school personnel on bullying prevention (Sacco, Silbaugh, Corredor, Casey, & Dohert, 2012; U.S. Department of Education, 2011), and information on cyberbullying should naturally be included in this training. More in-depth training is recommended for key staff who may be responsible for investigating and addressing specific cases of cyberbullying and should include administrators, media or technology specialists, and school counselors (Kowalski, Limber, & Agatston, 2012).

Develop Rules and Policies about Cyberbullying

As previously noted, under state law, nearly all public school districts are required to develop school policies about bullying, and more than half require that districts include cyberbullying in these policies (Sacco et al., 2012). Even if not required by state law, school personnel and adult leaders of other organizations should incorporate cyberbullying into their bullying prevention policies, after consultation with legal counsel about relevant state and municipal laws. Cyberbullying behavior should be incorporated into schools' policies that address the responsible use of the school's technology (Kowalski, Limber, & Agatston, 2012).

Expectations about cyberbullying should also be made clear in school (or organizational) rules governing student behavior. Many school administrators have found it important to develop clear and widely posted rules about bullying behavior that make clear to students, parents, and educators what is/is not acceptable behavior and how they should behave to prevent and address bullying (Federal Partners in Bullying Prevention, n.d.; Olweus et al., 2007a, 2007b). These rules should apply to all forms of bullying—including cyberbullying.

Encourage Reporting of Cyberbullying

Bullied students often do not notify parents or adults at school when they are bullied (Limber et al., 2013; Robers et al., 2013), and those who experience cyberbullying are particularly reluctant to report their experiences. In a nationally representative survey of sixth through twelfth graders in the United States, Robers and colleagues (2013) found that only one-quarter (26%) of students who had been cyberbullied during the 2011 school year had notified an adult (compared with 40% of students who had been bullied at school in a variety of ways). Given the reluctance of children and youth to report their experiences to adults, in is important to establish easy, comfortable ways (e.g., online report forms) for them to do so, and to prepare adults to receive these reports sensitively and address them competently (Kowalski, Limber, & Agatston, 2012).

Spend Class Time Discussing Cyberbullying

As part of comprehensive school-based bullying prevention efforts, it is recommended that teachers spend regular class time discussing bullying and other social emotional-related issues with students (Federal Partners in Bullying Prevention, n.d.; Olweus et al., 2007a, 2007b). Olweus and colleagues (2007a) have noted that such discussions have several goals, including: (1) to educate students about bullying, its consequences, rules governing bullying at school, and effective ways to help prevent and react to bullying; (2) to enhance students' social and emotional learning (e.g., improve communication among students, increase empathy and perspective taking); (3) to build a sense of community and belonging among students in the class; (4) to help teachers to learn more about the class culture, relationships, and possible power struggles; and (5) to provide a forum for dealing with bullying problems in the class and school. Research also indicates there are greater reductions in bullying in classes that systematically use class meetings than those that do not (Olweus & Kallestad, 2010). The topic of cyberbullying is a natural one for these class meetings. Discussions can focus on defining cyberbullying, school rules and policies about cyberbullying, online "netiquette" and safety, monitoring one's online reputation, and how best to respond to cyberbullying (Kowalski, Limber, & Agatston, 2012; Limber, Kowalski, & Agatston, 2009a, 2009b).

Use Youth as Resources

Although youth may lack the maturity of adults to understand the implications of their online actions (Walsh, 2007), they are often more knowledgeable about the digital world than adults (McAfee, 2013) and, as a result, can be empowered to use their skills to lead class discussions about cyberbullying, teach digital citizenship to younger children, and lead in campaigns to raise awareness about social norms regarding online behavior (Kowalski, Limber, & Agatston, 2012).

Build Strong Parent Partnerships

Many parents may feel at a loss to address cyberbullying due to the digital divide that often exists between adults and children (Kowalski, Limber, & Agatston, 2012; see also Herring, 2008). School or youth organizations can help to bridge this generational divide by hosting parent information nights at which a panel of high school students share tips and trends with parents, sending printed tips and literature home and providing a contact person at the school or organization who can help parents who are concerned about cyberbullying or other harmful online behavior (Kowalski, Limber, & Agatston, 2012).

CONCLUSIONS AND FUTURE DIRECTIONS

Although bullying among children and youth is an age-old phenomenon, cyberbullying is a relatively new concern, having emerged only in the past 10 years, as children's interactions through electronic forms of communication have skyrocketed (Brenner, 2012). Researchers have made important strides to answer basic questions about its nature and prevalence, individual and situational factors related to involvement in it, and its potential costs to those involved.

Nevertheless, numerous challenges and questions remain for researchers to tackle. Some of the most pressing involve understanding the prevalence and effects of various types or forms of cyberbullying, and how these vary according to key individual and situational variables. For example, as most research has focused on middle- and high-school-aged students from urban and suburban communities, we know very little about experiences of younger (elementary-age children) or older individuals (e.g., young adults in college, adults in the workplace) or the experiences of individuals in rural communities with different types of cyberbullying. Research is also scant regarding the relations between individuals' involvement in different forms of media (e.g., exposure to media violence) and their experiences with cyberbullying.

In addition, although researchers have begun to examine the relation between involvement in cyberbullying and more traditional forms of bullying, more research is needed to determine the extent of overlap between them and implications of students experiencing multiple forms of bullying. For example, are negative effects compounded if youth experience face-to-face *and* online bullying? To what extent? What implications are there for prevention and intervention if many youth experience both traditional and electronic forms of bullying?

Other basic questions about cyberbullying prevention and intervention exist. Although research on bullying prevention has shown promise in reducing bullying (e.g., Ttofi & Farrington, 2010) and has informed the development of best practices in cyberbullying prevention and intervention, we lack studies to inform us which strategies are more or less effective in specifically reducing cyberbullying or ameliorating its effects. Also unknown are whether and how the media itself may be used to reduce bulling among children and youth.

Adding to the challenge of this lengthy research agenda is the recognition that researchers and practitioners must be aware of the rapidly evolving forms of technology that may be used to bully. We must be nimble to alter measurement strategies and adjust our prevention and intervention prevention efforts to take into consideration changes in children's use of technology over time.

NOTES

1. A search of PsychINFO for 2012 produced 530 articles and books with a variant of the term "bullying" as a key subject term.

2. According to a search of Lexix/Nexis, in 2012, 917 English-language stories appeared in newspapers, wires and press releases, web publications, and magazines.

REFERENCES

Almeida, A., Correia, I., Marinho, S., & Garcia, D. (2012). Virtual but not less real: A study of cyberbullying and its relations to moral disengagement and empathy. In Q. Li, D. Cross, & P. K. Smith (Eds.), *Cyberbullying in the global playground: Research from international perspectives* (pp. 223–244). Malden, MA: Blackwell.

Anderson, C. A., & Bushman, B. J. (2002). Human aggression. *Annual Review of Psychology, 53*, 27–51. doi: 10.1037/0033-2909.106.1.74

Ang, R. P., & Goh, D. H. (2010). Cyberbullying among adolescents: The role of affective and cognitive empathy, and gender. *Child Psychiatry and Human Development, 41*, 387–397. doi:10.1007/s10578-010-0176-3

Ang, R. P., Tan, K., & Mansor, T. A. (2011). Normative beliefs about aggression as a mediator of narcissistic exploitativeness and cyberbullying. *Journal of Interpersonal Violence, 26*(13), 2619–2634. doi:10.1177/0886260510388286

Annenberg Public Policy Center of the University of Pennsylvania. (2010). *Adolescent and young adult victims of cyberbullying at increased risk of suicide.* Philadelphia, PA: Author. Retrieved from http://www.annenbergpublicpolicycenter.org /Downloads/Releases/ACI/Cyberbullying%20release.pdf

Aoyama, I., Utsumi, S., & Hasegawa, M. (2012). Cyberbullying in Japan: Cases, Government reports, adolescent relational aggression, and parental monitoring roles. In Q. Li, D. Cross, & P. K. Smith (Eds.), *Cyberbullying in the global playground: Research from international perspectives* (pp. 183–201). Malden, MA: Blackwell.

A Platform for Good. (N.d.). Retrieved from http://www.aplatformforgood.org/

Arseneault, L., Bowes, L., & Shakoor, S. (2010). Bullying victimization in youths and mental health problems: "Much ado about nothing"? *Psychological Medicine, 40*, 717–729.

Bandura, A. (1999). Moral disengagement in the perpetration of inhumanities. *Personality and Social Psychology Review, 3*, 193–209. doi:10.1207/s15327957pspr0303_3

Bartlett, C. P., & Gentile, D. A. (2012). Attacking others online: The formation of cyberbullying in late adolescence. *Psychology of Popular Media Culture, 1*, 123–135.

Bartlett, C. P., Gentile, D. A., Anderson, C. A., Suzuki, K., Sakamoto, A., Yamaoka, A., & Katsura, R. (2014). Cross-cultural differences in cyberbullying behavior: A short-term longitudinal study. *Journal of Cross Cultural Psychology, 45*, 300–313.

Bauman, S. (2010). Cyberbullying in a rural intermediate school: An exploratory study. *The Journal of Early Adolescence, 30*(6), 803–833. doi:10.1177/0272431609350927

Becker, K., & Schmidt, M. H. (2005). Internet chat rooms and suicide. *Journal of the American Academy of Child & Adolescent Psychiatry, 43*(3), 246–247.

Beran, T., & Li, Q. (2007). The relationship between cyberbullying and school bullying. *Journal of Student Wellbeing, 1*(2), 15–33.

Bjorkqvist, K., Lagerspetz, K. M. J., & Osterman, K. (1992). The development of direct and indirect aggressive strategies in males and females. In K. Bjorkqvist & P. Nimela (Eds.), *Of mice and women: Aspects of female aggression* (pp. 51–64). San Diego, CA: Academic Press.

Bonanno, R. A., & Hymel, S. (2013). Cyber bullying and internalizing difficulties: Above and beyond the impact of traditional forms of bullying. *Journal of Youth and Adolescence, 42*(5), 685–697.

Boyd, D. (2008). *Taken out of context: American teen sociality in networked publics* (doctoral dissertation, University of California, Berkeley). Retrieved from www.danah.org/papers/TakenOutOfContext.pdf

Brenner, J. (2012). *Pew Internet: Teens.* Retrieved from Pew Research Internet Research Project website: http://pewinternet.org/Commentary/2012/April/Pew-Internet-Teens.aspx

Bronfenbrenner, U. (1979). *The ecology of human development: Experiments by nature and design.* Cambridge, MA: Harvard University Press.

Bronfenbrenner, U. (2005). Ecological systems theory. In U. Bronfenbrenner (Ed.), *Making human beings human: Bioecological perspectives on human development* (pp. 106–173). Thousand Oaks, CA: Sage.

Centers for Disease Control and Prevention. (2009). Suicide: Facts at a glance. Atlanta, GA: Author. Retrieved from http://www.cdc.gov/violenceprevention/pdf/Suicide-DataSheet-a.pdf

Centers for Disease Control and Prevention. (N.d.). Suicide: Risk and protective factors. Retrieved from: http://www.cdc.gov/violenceprevention/suicide/riskprotectivefactors.html

Christakis, D. A., Garrison, M. M., Herrenkohl, T., Haggerty, K., Rivara, F. P., Zhou, C., & Liekweg, K. (2012). Modifying media content for preschool children: A randomized controlled trial. *Pediatrics, 131*, 431–438.

Cox Communications. (2009). Teen online & wireless safety survey: Cyberbullying, sexting, and parental controls. Retrieved from http://ww2.cox.com/wcm/en/aboutus/datasheet/takecharge/2009-teen-survey.pdf?campcode=takecharge research-link_2009-teen-survey_0511

Dempsey, A. G., Sulkowski, M. L., Nichols, R., & Storch, E. A. (2009). Differences between peer victimization in cyber and physical settings and associated psychosocial adjustment in early adolescence. *Psychology in the Schools, 46*(10), 962–972. doi:10.1002/pits.20437

Didden, R., Scholte, R. H. J., Korzilius, H., de Moor, J. M. H., Vermeulen, A., O'Reilly, M., . . . Lancioni, G. E. (2009). Cyberbullying among students with intellectual and developmental disability in special education settings. *Developmental Neurorehabilitation, 12*, 146–151. doi:10.1080/17518420902971356

Diener, E. (1980). *The psychology of group influence*. New York, NY: Erlbaum.

Dooley, J. J., Pyzalski, J., & Cross, D. (2009). Cyberbullying versus face-to-face bullying: A theoretical and conceptual review. *Zeitschrift für Psychologie/Journal of Psychology, 217*, 182–188. doi:10.1027/0044-3409.217.4.182

Dooley, J. J., Shaw, T., & Cross, D. (2012). The association between the mental health and behavioural problems of students and their reactions to cyber-victimization. *European Journal of Developmental Psychology, 9*(2), 275–289. doi:10.1080/17405629.2011.648425

Dreikurs, R., Cassel, P., & Ferguson, E. (2004). *Discipline without tears*. Hoboken, NJ: Wiley & Sons.

Dreikurs, R., & Soltz, V. (1991). *Children: The challenge*. New York, NY: Penguin Press.

Edgerton, E., & Limber, S. (2013, November 27). Research brief: Suicide and bullying. Retrieved from stopbullying.gov website: http://www.stopbullying.gov/blog/2013/02/27/research-brief-suicide-and-bullying

Erdur-Baker, Ö. (2010). Cyberbullying and its correlation to traditional bullying, gender and frequent and risky usage of internet-mediated communication tools. *New Media & Society, 12*(1), 109–125. doi:10.1177/1461444809341260

Fanti, K. A., Demetriou, A. G., & Hawa, V. V. (2012). A longitudinal study of cyberbullying: Examining risk and protective factors. *European Journal of Developmental Psychology, 9*(2), 168–181. doi:10.1080/17405629.2011.643169

Federal Partners in Bullying Prevention. (N.d.). *Bullying prevention & response: Base training module*. Retrieved from stopbullying.gov website: http://www.stopbullying.gov/prevention/in-the-community/community-action-planning/training-module-speaker-notes.pdf

Gentile, D. A., Coyne, S., & Walsh, D. A. (2010). Media violence, physical aggression, and relational aggression in school age children: A short-term longitudinal study. *Aggressive Behavior, 37*, 193–206.

Giumetti, G. W., McKibben, E. S., Hatfield, A. L., Schroeder, A. N., & Kowalski, R. M. (2012). Cyber-incivility @ work: The new age of interpersonal deviance. *Cyberpsychology, Behavior, and Social Networking, 15*, 148–154. doi:10.1089/cyber.2011.0336

Gladden, R. M., Vivolo-Kantor, A. M., Hamburger, M. E., & Lumpkin, C. D. (2014). *Bullying surveillance among youths: Uniform definitions for public health and recommended data elements, version 1.0*. Atlanta, GA: National Center for Injury Prevention and Control, Centers for Disease Control and Prevention and U.S. Department of Education.

Görzig, A., & Ólafsson, K. (2013). What makes a bully a cyberbully? Unravelling the characteristics of cyberbullies across twenty-five European countries. *Journal of Children and Media, 7*(1), 9–27.

Gradinger, P., Strohmeier, D., & Spiel, C. (2009). Traditional bullying and cyberbullying: Identification of risk groups for adjustment problems. *Zeitschrift Für Psychologie/Journal of Psychology, 217*(4), 205–213. doi:10.1027/0044-3409.217.4.205

Gullone, E., & Robertson, N. (2008). The relationship between bullying and animal abuse behaviors in adolescents: The importance of witnessing animal abuse. *Journal of Applied Developmental Psychology, 29*, 371–397.

Herring, S. C. (2008). Questioning the generational divide: Technological exoticism and adult constructions of online youth identity. In D. Buckinham (Ed.), *Youth, Identity, and Digital Media* (pp. 71–92). The John D. and Catherine T.

MacArthur Foundation Series on Digital Media and Learning. Cambridge, MA: The MIT Press. doi:10.1162/dmal.9780262524834.071

Hertz, M. F., Donato, I., & Wright, J. (2013). Bullying and suicide: A public health approach. *Journal of Adolescent Health, 53*(Suppl 1), S1–S3.

Hewitt, B. (2012, October 15). His name was Brian: A 13-year-old victim of bullycide. *Huffington Post.* Retrieved from http://www.huffingtonpost.com/jonathan-hewitt/bullying_b_1968592.html

Hinduja, S., & Patchin, J. W. (2008). Cyberbullying: An exploratory analysis of factors related to offending and victimization. *Deviant Behavior, 29,* 129–156. doi:10.1080/01639620701457816

Hinduja, S., & Patchin, J. W. (2009). *Bullying beyond the schoolyard: Preventing and responding to cyberbullying.* Thousand Oaks, CA: Sage (Corwin Press).

Hinduja, S., & Patchin, J. W. (2010). Bullying, cyberbullying, and suicide. *Archives of Suicide Research, 14*(3), 206–221.

Hinduja, S., & Patchin, J. W. (2013). Social influences on cyberbullying behaviors among middle and high school students. *Journal of Youth and Adolescence, 42*(5), 711–722. doi:10.1007/s10964-012-9902-4

Hong, J. S., & Espelage, D. L. (2012). A review of research on bullying and peer victimization in school: An ecological system analysis. *Aggression and Violent Behavior, 17,* 311–322.

Hunt, C., Peters, L., & Rapee, R. M. (2012). Development of a measure of the experience of being bullied in youth. *Psychological Assessment, 24*(1), 156–165. doi:10.1037/a0025178

Jones, L. M., Mitchell, J. K., & Finkelhor, D. (2012). Trends in youth Internet victimization: Findings from three youth Internet safety surveys 2000–2010. *Journal of Adolescent Health, 50*(2), 179–186.

Juvonen, J., & Gross, E. F. (2008). Extending the school grounds? Bullying experiences in cyberspace. *Journal of School Health, 78,* 496–505. doi:10.1111/j.1746-1561.2008.00335.x

Katzer, C., Fetchenhauer, D., & Belschak, F. (2009). Cyberbullying: Who are the victims? A comparison of victimization in Internet chatrooms and victimization in school. *Journal of Media Psychology, 21,* 25–36. doi:10.1027/1864-1105.21.1.25

Kessler, B. (2010, October 4). *The grief of bullycide.* CNN. Retrieved from http://www.cnn.com/2010/LIVING/10/04/o.grief.of.bullycide/index.html

Kim, Y. S., Leventhal, B. L., Koh, Y., & Boyce, W. T. (2009). Bullying increased suicide risk: Prospective study of Korean adolescents. *Archives of Suicide Research, 13,* 15–30.

Klomek, A. B., Marrocco, F., Kleinman, M., Schonfeld, I. S., & Gould, M. S. (2007). Bullying, depression, and suicidality in adolescents. *Journal of the American Academy of Child and Adolescent Psychiatry, 46,* 40–49.

Klomek, A. B., Marrocco, F., Kleinman, M., Schonfeld, I. S., & Gould, M. S. (2008). Peer victimization, depression, and suicidiality in adolescents. *Suicide and Life-Threatening Behavior, 28,* 166–180.

Kowalski, R. M., Giumetti, G. W., Schroeder, A. N., & Lattanner, M. (2014, February 10). Bullying in the digital age: A critical review and meta-analysis of cyberbullying research among youth. *Psychological Bulletin.* Advance online publication. http://dx.doi.org/10.1037/a0035618

Kowalski, R. M., Giumetti, G. W., Schroeder, A. N., & Reese, H. (2012). Cyberbullying among college students: Evidence from multiple domains of college life. In C. Wankel & L. Wankel (Eds.), *Misbehavior online in higher education* (pp. 293–321). Bingley, UK: Emerald Publishing Group.

Kowalski, R. M., & Limber, S. P. (2007). Electronic bullying among middle school students. *Journal of Adolescent Health, 41*(6, Suppl), S22–S30. doi:10.1016/j.jadohealth.2007.08.017

Kowalski, R. M., & Limber, S. P. (2013). Psychological, physical, and academic correlates of cyberbullying and traditional bullying. *Journal of Adolescent Health, 53*, S13–S20.

Kowalski, R. M., Limber, S. E., & Agatston, P. W. (2012). *Cyberbullying: Bullying in the digital age* (2nd ed.). Malden, MA: Wiley-Blackwell.

Kowalski, R. M., Morgan, C. A., & Limber, S. P. (2012). Traditional bullying as a potential warning sign of cyberbullying. *School Psychology International, 33*, 505–519. doi:10.1177/0143034312445244

Lam, L. T., Cheng, Z., & Liu, X. (2013). Violent online games exposure and cyberbullying/victimization among adolescents. *Cyberpsychology, Behavior, and Social Networking, 16*(3), 159–165. doi:10.1089/cyber.2012.0087

Lazarus, R. S., & Folkman, S. (1984). *Stress, appraisal, and coping*. New York, NY: Springer.

Limber, S. P., Kowalski, R. M., & Agatston, P. W. (2009a). *Cyber bullying: A prevention guide for grades 3–5*. Center City, MN: Hazelden.

Limber, S. P., Kowalski, R. M., & Agatston, P. W. (2009b). *Cyber bullying: A prevention guide for grades 6–12*. Center City, MN: Hazelden.

Limber, S. P., Olweus, D., & Luxenberg, H. (2013). *Bullying in U.S. schools: Status report*. Retreieved from Violence Prevention Works website: http://www.violencepreventionworks.org/public/index.page

Livingston, S., Haddon, L., Gorzig, A., & Olafsson, K. (2011). Risks and safety on the Internet: The perspective of European children: summary. Retrieved from the London School of Economics and Political Science website: http://eprints.lse.ac.uk/33731/8/EU_Kids_Online_Summary_Risks_safety_internet%28lsero%29.pdf

Madden, M., Lenhart, A., Cortesi, S., Gasser, U., Duggan, M., Smith, A., & Beaton, M. (2013). *Teens, social media, and privacy*. Retrieved from the Pew Research Internet Project website: http://pewinternet.org/Reports/2013/Teens-Social-Media-And-Privacy.aspx

Madden, M., Lenhart, A., Duggan, M., Cortesi, & Gasser, U. (2013). *Teens and technology 2013*. Retrieved from the Pew Research Internet Project website: http://www.pewinternet.org/Reports/2013/Teens-and-Tech.aspx

McAfee. (2013). *McAfee digital deception study 2013: Exploring the online disconnect between parents & pre-teens, teens, and young adults*. Retrieved from http://www.mcafee.com/us/resources/reports/rp-digital-deception-survey.pdf

Menesini, E., Nocentini, A., & Camodeca, M. (2013). Morality, values, traditional bullying, and cyberbullying in adolescence. *British Journal of Developmental Psychology, 31*(1), 1–14.

Monks, C. P., & Smith, P. K. (2006). Definitions of bullying: Age differences in understanding of the term, and the role of experience. *British Journal of Developmental Psychology, 24*(4), 801–821. doi:10.1348/026151005X82352

Nansel, T., Overpeck, M., Pilla, R., Ruan, W., Simons-Morton, B., & Scheidt, P. (2001). Bullying behaviors among U.S. youth: Prevalence and association with psychosocial adjustment. *Journal of the American Medical Association, 285*, 2094–2100. doi:10.1001/jama.285.16.2094

National School Climate Center. (N.d.). 10 ways to be an upstander. Retrieved from http://www.schoolclimate.org/bullybust/students/upstander

O'Brennan, L. M., Bradshaw, C. P., & Sawyer, A. L. (2009). Examining developmental differences in the social-emotional problems among frequent bullies, victims, and bully/victims. *Psychology in Schools, 46*, 100–115. doi:10.1002/pits.20357

Olweus, D. (1993). *Bullying at school: What we know and what we can do*. Cambridge, MA: Blackwell.

Olweus, D. (2012). Cyberbullying: An overrated phenomenon? *European Journal of Developmental Psychology, 9*, 520–538. doi:10.1080/17405629.2012.682358

Olweus, D. (2013). School bullying: Development and some important challenges. *Annual Review of Clinical Psychology, 9*, 1–14. doi:10.1146/annurev-clinpsy -050212-185516

Olweus, D., & Kallestad, J. H. (2010). The Olweus bullying prevention program: Effects of classroom components at different grade levels. In K. Osterman (Ed.), *Indirect and direct aggression* (pp. 113–131). New York, NY: Peter Lang.

Olweus, D., & Limber, S. P. (2010). Bullying in school: Evaluation and dissemination of the Olweus Bullying Prevention Program. *American Journal of Orthopsychiatry, 80*, 124–134.

Olweus, D., Limber, S. P., Flerx, V. C., Mullin, N., Riese, J., & Snyder, M. (2007a). *Olweus Bullying Prevention Program schoolwide guide*. Center City, MN: Hazelden.

Olweus, D., Limber, S. P., Flerx, V. C., Mullin, N., Riese, J., & Snyder, M. (2007b). *Olweus Bullying Prevention Program teacher guide*. Center City, MN: Hazelden.

Ostrov, J. M., Gentile, D. A., & Crick, N. R. (2006). Media exposure, aggression, and prosocial behavior during early childhood: A longitudinal study. *Social Development, 15*, 612–627.

Patchin, J. (2013, August 13). *Hannah Smith: Even more tragic than originally thought* [web log message]. Retrieved from http://cyberbullying.us/hannah-smith -even-more-tragic-than-originally-thought/

Patchin, J., & Hinduja, S. (2010). Cyberbullying and self-esteem. *Journal of School Health, 80*(12), 614–621. doi:10.1111/j.1746-1561.2010.00548.x

Perkins, H. W., Craig, D. W., & Perkins, J. M. (2011). Using social norms to reduce bullying: A research intervention in five middle schools. *Group Processes and Intergroup Relations, 14*(5), 703–722.

Pornari, C. D., & Wood, J. (2010). Peer and cyber aggression in secondary school students: The role of moral disengagement, hostile attribution bias, and outcome expectancies. *Aggressive Behavior, 36*, 81–94. doi:10.1002/ab.20336

Pranjic, N., & Bajraktarevic, A. (2010). Depression and suicide ideation among secondary school adolescents involved in school bullying. *Primary Health Care Research & Development, 11*, 349–362.

Robers, S., Kemp, J., & Truman, J. (2012). *Indicators of school crime and safety: 2012* (NCES 2013-036/NCJ241446). Washington, DC: National Center for Education Statistics, U.S. Department of Education, and Bureau of Justice Statistics, Office of Justice Programs.

Sabella, R. A., Patchin, J. W., & Hinduja, S. (2013). Cyberbullying myths and realities. *Computers in Human Behavior, 29*, 2703–2711.

Sacco, D. T., Silbaugh, K., Corredor, F., Casey, J., & Dohert, D. (2012). An overview of state anti-bullying legislation and other related laws. Retrieved from the Berkman Center for Internet and Society website: http://cyber.law.harvard.edu/publications/2012/state_anti_bullying_legislation_overview

Schenk, A. M., & Fremouw, W. J. (2012). Prevalence, psychological impact, and coping of cyberbully victims among college students. *Journal of School Violence, 11*, 21–37. doi:10.1080/15388220.2011.630310

Schneider, S., O'Donnell, L., Stueve, A., & Coulter, R. S. (2012). Cyberbullying, school bullying, and psychological distress: A regional census of high school students. *American Journal of Public Health, 102*, 171–177. doi:10.2105/AJPH.2011.300308

Shapka, J. D., & Law, D. M. (2013). Does one size fit all? Ethnic differences in parenting behaviors and motivations for adolescent engagement in cyberbullying. *Journal of Youth and Adolescence, 42*(5), 723–738.

Smith, P. K., del Barrio, C., & Tokunaga, R. (2012). Definitions of bullying and cyberbullying: How useful are the terms? In S. Bauman, D. Cross, & J. Walker (Eds.), *Principles of cyberbullying research: Definition, measures, and methods* (pp. 29–40). Philadelphia, PA: Routledge.

Smith, P. K., Mahdavi, J., Carvalho, M., & Tippett, N. (2006). *An investigation into cyber bullying, its forms, awareness and impact, and the relationship between age and gender in cyber bullying: A report to the Anti-Bullying Alliance* (Brief No. RBX03-06). Retrieved from the National Archives (UK) website: http://webarchive.nationalarchives.gov.uk/20130401151715/https://www.education.gov.uk/publications/eOrderingDownload/RBX03-06.pdf

Smith, P. K., Mahdavi, J., Carvalho, M., Fisher, S., Russell, S., & Tippett, N. (2008). Cyberbullying: Its nature and impact in secondary school pupils. *Journal of Child Psychology and Psychiatry, 49*(4), 376–385. doi:10.1111/j.1469-7610.2007.01846.x

Sourander, A., Klomek, A. B., Ikonen, M., Lindroos, J., Luntamo, T., Koskelainen, M., Ristkari, T., & Henenius, H. (2010). Psychosocial risk factors associated with cyberbullying among adolescents. *Archives of General Psychiatry, 67*, 720–728. doi:10.1001/archgenpsychiatry.2010.79

Swearer, S. M., & Doll, B. (2001). Bullying in schools: An ecological framework. *Journal of Emotional Abuse, 2*(2–3), 7–23.

Tokunaga, R. S. (2010). Following you home from school: A critical review and synthesis of research on cyber bullying victimization. *Computers in Human Behavior, 26*, 277–287. doi:10.1016/j.chb.2009.11.014

Trend Micro. (N.d.) *What's your story?* Retrieved from http://whatsyourstory.trendmicro.com/

Ttofi, M., & Farrington, D. P. (2009). What works in preventing bullying: Effective elements of anti-bullying programs. *Journal of Aggression, Conflict and Peace Research, 1*, 13–24.

Ubertini, M. (2011). *Cyberbullying may reduce adolescent's well-being: Can life satisfaction and social support protect them?* (doctoral dissertation). Available from Dissertation Abstracts International.

U.S. Department of Education, Office of Planning, Evaluation, and Policy Development, Policy and Program Studies Service. (2011). *Analysis of state bullying laws and policies.* Washington, DC: Author.

Vannucci, M., Nocentini, A., Mazzoni, G., & Menesini, E. (2012). Recalling unpresented hostile words: False memories predictors of traditional and cyberbullying. *European Journal of Developmental Psychology, 9,* 182–194.

Wade, A., & Beran, T. (2011). Cyberbullying: The new era of bullying. *Canadian Journal of School Psychology, 26*(1), 44–61. doi:10.1177/0829573510396318

Walsh, D. (2007). *Why do they act that way?: A survival guide to the adolescent brain for you and your teen.* New York, NY: Free Press.

Wang, J., Iannotti, R. J., & Nansel, T. R. (2009). School bullying among adolescents in the United States: Physical, verbal, relational, and cyber. *Journal of Adolescent Health, 45,* 368–375. doi:10.1016/j.jadohealth.2009.03.021

Willard, N. E. (2007). *Cyberbullying and cyberthreats: Responding to the challenge of online social aggression, threats, and distress.* Champaign, IL: Research Press.

Williams, K. R., & Guerra, N. G. (2007). Prevalence and predictors of Internet bullying. *Journal of Adolescent Health, 41,* 14–21. doi:10.1016/j.jadohealth.2007.08.018

Ybarra, M. L., Boyd, D., Korchmaros, J. D., & Oppenheim, J. (2012). Defining and measuring cyberbullying within the larger context of bullying victimization. *Journal of Adolescent Health, 51,* 53–58. doi:10.1016/j.jadohealth.2011.12.031

Ybarra, M. L., Diener-West, M., & Leaf, P. J. (2007). Examining the overlap in Internet harassment and school bullying: Implications for school intervention. *Journal of Adolescent Health, 41,* 42–50. doi:10.1016/j.jadohealth.2007.09.004

Ybarra, M. L., & Mitchell, K. J. (2004). Online aggressor/targets, aggressors, and targets: A comparison of associated youth characteristics. *Journal of Child Psychology and Psychiatry, 45,* 1308–1316. doi:10.1111/j.1469-7610.2004.00328.x

Ybarra, M. L., Mitchell, J. K., Finkelhor, D., & Wolak, J. (2007). Internet prevention messages: Are we targeting the right online behaviors? *Archives of Pediatrics and Adolescent Medicine, 161,* 138–145.

CHAPTER 10

The Effects of Violent and Antisocial Music on Children and Adolescents

Wayne A. Warburton, Donald F. Roberts, and Peter G. Christenson

"Music can change the world"

—Ludwig Van Beethoven

"All you need is love"

—The Beatles, 1967

"Just bend over and take, it slut"

—Eminem, 2000

Music enriches the lives of most people in the world today. For children, music is linked with popular games, is a pleasurable pastime, and is a part of popular culture around which tastes become a talking point and identities are formed. Children, adolescents, and adults all listen to music because it has a unique power to touch our feelings. Indeed, the world would be an impoverished place without music.

It is important, when setting the stage for this chapter, to keep these thoughts in mind. Even though the latter parts of this chapter will explore the effects of violent and antisocial music, the earlier sections will demonstrate that music has an overwhelmingly positive role in the lives of most children and adolescents. It is also important to remember that popular songs with violent and antisocial themes are a minority. In a content analysis of widely accessed popular music, Christenson, Roberts, and ter Bogt (unpublished) found that in the 2000s, fewer than 10 percent of top 40 songs made reference to violence, fewer than 2 percent referred to hatred, and fewer than 1 percent mentioned suicide. In contrast, almost two-thirds referred to love.

Nonetheless, the Internet has made music with extreme antisocial themes much more accessible (Whelan, 2010). Moreover, some genres of music include far more violent and antisocial content than others. For example, such themes predominate in heavy metal and death metal music. Although these genres do not figure heavily in mainstream music sales, they nevertheless claim many devotees. Rap music also contains a good deal of antisocial content, but unlike heavy/death metal music, has become increasingly popular in mainstream music over the last two decades. Indeed, there is evidence that rap music has driven a steady trend over the last 20 years for themes in popular music, on average, to be increasingly about violence, lifestyle, sex, and material pursuits (Christenson, Roberts, & Bjork, 2012; Christenson et al., unpublished).

But does exposure to such themes change the way our children think, feel, and behave? In this chapter we will argue that they can, but that the influence of music is only one of many influences in a child's life. Serious issues such as violence, suicide, and antisocial behavior implicate multiple risk factors (Gentile & Bushman, 2012; Warburton, 2013). Music is never the only causal factor when such issues arise, and is unlikely to be more important than an array of other factors: family environment, the influence of peers, mental health concerns, and a range of other possible contributors (see chapter 2). Thus, although music sometimes can be a negative influence in children's lives, it is important not to overstate its impact. A balanced approach supported by empirical research is preferable.

THE IMPORTANCE OF MUSIC IN THE LIVES OF CHILDREN AND ADOLESCENTS

Music plays an important role throughout the human lifespan (Rentfrow & Gosling, 2003). Music experienced prenatally influences music preferences for up to a year afterward (Hepper, 1991; Lamont, 2001) and musical interactions between parents and infants are a fundamental means of communication and attunement (e.g., Trehub, Hill, & Kamenetsky, 1997). Across cultures, lullabies are used to help infants and toddlers sleep (Gregory, 1997), and by 8 to 9 months, infants can discriminate between happy and sad music (Flom, Gentile & Pick, 2008). During early childhood, music preferences become more differentiated and music features more in play, games, and social activities. Through the school years, children develop definite music preferences, and those preferences become part of the child's developing identity (Roe, 1996). For teenagers, music themes often resonate with adolescent experience, such as attitudes to authority and intense feelings in relationships (Zillmann & Gan, 1997). Music becomes a point of connection with peers (e.g., ter Bogt, Keijsers, & Meeus, 2013), and the musicians themselves are often loved and admired, thus exerting an influence in their own right (Strasburger, Wilson, & Jordan, 2009).

In adolescence and adulthood, music is linked with such positive experiences as relaxation, enjoyment, confidence, higher morale, absorption, expression of feelings, better mood, and coping with problems (Rana, Tanveer, &

North, 2009; ter Bogt, Mulder, Raaijmakers, & Gabhainn, 2010), experiences that are linked with high levels of dopamine release and pleasure and are thus intrinsically rewarding (Salimpoor, Benovoy, Larcher, Dagher, & Zatorre, 2011). Small wonder, then, that adolescents value music so highly. Indeed, when Roberts and Henrikson (1990) asked high school students what media they would take if stranded on a desert island, music media were preferred over television in all grades, and senior high students ranked music as the most preferred media content by a margin of two to one.

Clearly, music plays an important role throughout development and is literally part of the sound track that accompanies the lives of children and adolescents.

How much music do children and adolescents listen to?

This question is hard to answer, if only because music plays so much in the background of people's day-to-day lives. Studies consistently reveal that, across all ages, music is the second most popular form of media used (behind television), with the most recent U.S. study showing that 8- to 18-year-olds listened to music an average of two-and-a-half hours per day (Rideout, Foehr, & Roberts, 2010). Moreover, studies that try to ascertain total levels of exposure to music find even higher levels. For example, Greenberg, Ku, and Li (1989) found that when music from all sources, including background music, was taken into account, sixth-grade children listened to nearly as much music as they watched television (3.8 vs. 4.1 hours per day on average) and tenth-grade students listened to substantially more music (4.9 vs. 3.9 hours per day on average).

What is particularly interesting about young people's music listening is the pattern of use across age (see Table 10.1). Music use increases steadily from childhood to late adolescence, rising from just over an hour a day at ages 8 to 10 years to over three-and-a-half hours per day at ages 15 to 18. Race and gender differences also emerge. Girls and boys report similar music exposure in grade school (Christenson, DeBenedittis, & Lindlof, 1985), but girls listen to substantially more music than boys by high school (Roberts & Henriksen, 1990; Rideout et al., 2010). Studies also consistently show that African American and Hispanic American adolescents spend more time listening to music than do white adolescents (Brown, Childers, Bauman, & Koch, 1990; Rideout et al., 2010).

Historically, emerging technologies and products have made it increasingly easy to listen to music. From live music to gramophones, then to radios and portable media players, and eventually to miniaturized MP3 devices and Internet players, this pattern continues. For current listeners, online radio from "Grooveshark" and "Jango" allows people to select their own program of music and then listen while working on the computer. Away from the computer, music is available on a wide and increasing range of relatively small portable devices, many of them developed only in the last few years—smartphones,

Table 10.1
Music Use in the United States and Breakdown by Demographics

United States: 8–18 year olds			
Hours spent with music per day	2.31		
Age	**8–10**	**11–14**	**15–18**
Hours per day	1.08	2.36	3.21
Ethnicity	**White**	**Black**	**Hispanic**
Hours per day	1.56	3.00	3.08
Gender	**Male**	**Female**	
Hours per day	2.16	2.45	

Source: Rideout, Foehr & Roberts, 2010.

digital portable music players, and tablet, laptop, and android computers, among others. Moreover, these new sources of music are not replacing the old but rather are supplementing them, thus adding to overall listening time (Roberts & Foehr, 2008).

USES AND BENEFITS

Affective Uses

One defining characteristic of music is its capacity to influence people's feelings, particularly when they are alone (Egerman et al., 2011). Music is commonly used to induce a particular mood in research or therapy (e.g., Kenealy, 1988; Pignatiello, Camp, & Rasar, 1986; Pignatiello, Camp, Elder, & Rasar, 1989), and people often use music as a means of regulating their mood(s).

Mood regulation

For most young people, the primary motivation to listen to music is to regulate mood and enhance emotional states (Bishop, Karageorghis, & Loizou, 2007; Lonsdale & North, 2011; Miranda & Gandreau, 2011; Saarikallio & Erkkila, 2007; Thoma, Scholz, Ehlert, & Nater, 2012). Bruner's (1990) review of the effects of music on mood found that specific types of musical structures could influence tranquillity/peacefulness, excitement, happiness, sadness, and "seriousness," and that music can be used to both amplify a desired mood or state, or to counteract an undesired one. In summarizing the research on adolescent uses of music, Christenson and Roberts (1998) suggested a principle they labeled "primacy of affect." When adolescents want to initiate or maintain a certain mood, when they seek reinforcement for a certain mood, when they feel lonely, or when they seek distraction from their troubles, music tends to be the medium of choice.

There do appear to be gender differences when using music for mood regulation. Women are more likely than men to say they listen to music to lift their spirits when they're sad or lonely, or even to dwell on a sombre mood (Arnett, 1991a; Larson, Kubey, & Colletti, 1989; Roe, 1985; Wells, 1990). Additionally, Nater, Abbruzzese, Krebs, and Ehlert (2006) found that compared to males, females had an elevated physiological response to heavy metal music pre-rated as arousing and inducing negative feelings, and concluded that "women tend to show hypersensitivity to aversive musical stimuli" (p. 300). In contrast, males are more likely than females to use music as a tool to increase their energy level and seek stimulation (to get "pumped up"), although from time to time males also match music with their negative moods.

The "valence" of music is also important in mood regulation. Ali and Peyni (2011) found that song lyrics enhance the impact of sad and angry music but not happy music, and other studies suggest that people who are sad prefer sad music and find more sadness in music (e.g., Hunter, Schellenberg, & Griffith, 2011). Interestingly, it is possible to listen to sad music without displeasure, possibly because listeners become absorbed in the music, reflect on life events, and enjoy the emotional communion or release that they feel (Garrido & Schubert, 2011a, 2011b). There is some evidence that as people age they tend to become less responsive to sad or scary music, but that people maintain their recognition of the positive aspects of music (such as happiness and peacefulness) throughout the lifespan (Lima & Castro, 2011).

Affect and prosocial behavior

If music makes people feel good, does it also help them to do good? Music that induces a good mood in listeners also appears to have a positive effect on behavior. For example, Fried and Berkowitz (1979) found that playing soothing and stimulating music invoked positive moods in subjects while also increasing the likelihood of subsequent helpful behavior, and North, Tarrant, and Hargreaves (2004) found that uplifting music increased the likelihood that gym users would behave prosocially. Music that makes people feel good can also reduce levels of anger, aggressive cognitions, and aggressive behavior following a provocation (Krahé & Bieneck, 2012).

Social Uses

As children move toward their teens, music preferences increasingly converge toward popular music such as rock, pop, hip hop, and rap, with some difference according to cultural origin (e.g., Cremades, Lorenzo, & Herrero, 2010). This convergence in musical taste as children age is linked to the increasing influence of peers and mass media, and the decrease of parental influence. The use of music at this age also ties in with key developmental tasks, such as forming relationships and developing one's identity (Laiho, 2004; see also chapter 2 for more on developmental tasks).

Peer relationships

Although it is far from the only indicator of group membership—school performance, extracurricular interests, social background, clothing, and other elements of personal style are important too—an adolescent's music affiliation says much about his or her social affiliation and can help foster friendships (Selfhout, Branje, ter Bogt, & Meeus, 2009). Music is often a point of conversation and common experience in peer groups, and many youth are loath to confess to musical tastes that differ from their peers (Finnäs, 1989). Indeed, the identity of some peer groups revolves primarily around a preference for a particular music style such as rap or heavy metal (Hansen & Hansen, 1991; Larson, 1995). Music is also used by some young adults to avoid feelings of isolation and loneliness (e.g., Thoma et al., 2012).

Identity development

Because shared music preferences are an important part of the social experience of children and adolescents, they are also an important part of their developing identity (Laiho, 2004; Roe, 1996). Roe notes that "music plays a central role in the process of identity construction of young people. This process includes not only elements of personal identity but also important aspects of national, regional, cultural, ethnic, and gender identity" (p. 85). Music seems to begin making a substantial impact on child identity formation from around eight years of age, a time where fitting in with a peer group becomes increasingly important. Girls tend to differentiate their musical tastes earlier than boys (Roe, 1996).

Apart from influencing one's personal identity, music contributes to parts of one's wider identity, for example, one's religious, cultural, or national affiliation. Singing along to the national anthem is a strong symbol of national identity that begins early in schooling for many Western children (Gregory, 1997). Music is also crucial to the group identity of many indigenous populations, such as Australian Aboriginal peoples, whose links to land and ancestry are expressed and passed on through music and dance (e.g., Magowen, 1994). In addition, cultures from around the world have their own musical identity and many subcultures within those communities identify with a particular musical style or genre. Clearly, for many people, music becomes a part of who one is, and with whom one identifies.

Courting and ceremony

Many courtships occur to the backdrop of music—indeed Gueguen, Jacob, and Lamy (2010) found that the judicious use of music increased the chance of winning over a romantic partner. Music also accompanies a wide range of common social activities, including parties, dances, clubs, celebrations, mourning, worshipping, and being entertained (see Crozier, 1997; Gregory, 1997 for reviews).

Games

Music and play are often inextricably entwined. Gregory (1997) notes that children in all cultures play games, and that these are frequently accompanied by music or songs. Sometimes games are built around songs, and sometimes songs are used by children to learn key knowledge such as the alphabet.

Prosocial behavior

Music lyrics can provide guidance on how to behave morally and socially. One study of high school students found that 16 percent ranked music among the top three sources for moral guidance (alongside such influences as parents, teachers, friends, and church leaders), and 24 percent rated music among the top three sources of information on social behavior (Rouner, 1990). Recent research has shown that exposure to music with prosocial (compared to neutral) lyrics is linked with increases in helping behavior (Greitemeyer, 2009a), and that this is probably facilitated by concomitant increases in empathy (Greitemeyer, 2009b). Prosocial music has also been shown to decrease aggressive thoughts, feelings, and behaviors in university students (Greitemeyer, 2011).

Music and musical artists have also been successfully used to provide pro-social information to youth—for example, information on drug use and safe sex (e.g., Pareles, 1990; Perry, 1995). One notable campaign using rap and hip hop artists to educate African American youth on reducing AIDS risk resulted in 94 percent of the target audience surveyed being aware of the campaign and 83 percent taking their sexual practices more seriously (Kaiser Family Foundation, 2003).

Clinical Uses

Treatment and well-being

There is a long history of music being used as a means of healing and alleviating distress (Bruner, 1990). Music therapy has become recognized and used in medical and psychological treatment (see Bunt, 1997). For example, music therapy has been used with children to increase self-esteem, decrease aggressive and maladaptive behaviors (e.g., Jorgenson, 1974) and enhance attention and educational outcomes (e.g., Roskam, 1979).

Positive music experiences can also elicit a range of responses linked to well-being and pleasure (Rana et al., 2009; Salimpoor et al., 2011). Hays (2005) found that "music provides people with ways of understanding and developing their self-identity and maintaining well-being" and that "music contributes to positive ageing by providing ways for people to maintain positive self-esteem, feel competent and independent, and avoid feelings of isolation and loneliness" (p. 28). In adolescents, music contributes to healthy development and mental wellbeing by fostering relationships, a sense of agency, and identity formation (Laiho, 2004).

Alleviating pain

The use of music to alleviate pain and anxiety, primarily through distraction and emotion regulation, is becoming more common (e.g., see Brown, Chen, & Dworkin, 1989; Savarimuthu, 2004). In 1995 Standley had noted there were at least 125 applications for music in medical and dental practice described in the literature, and there are surely more applications today. Standley found that the benefits were stronger for children than for adults or infants, and for women than for men. The most effective applications were for chronic pain and dental pain and respiratory problems, and for offsetting the need for analgesic medications.

VIOLENT AND ANTISOCIAL MUSIC

Clearly music can have many benefits for listeners. Nevertheless, some musical choices are linked with less desirable outcomes for children and teens. Although many children and adolescents who listen to violent and antisocial music show few ill effects, youths who are "troubled" are more likely to be drawn to such music, and are possibly more influenced by it.

The past three decades have seen a number of studies examining links between music use and various antisocial outcomes: aggression, substance use, premature sexual behaviors, misogynistic attitudes, and suicide. Because two genres of music—heavy metal/death metal and rap—consistently feature antisocial content (for reviews see American Academy of Pediatrics, 1996, 2009), we begin by examining research on these genres, then turn to specific types of antisocial song content.

Heavy Metal and Death Metal

Although heavy metal music (and its subgenre death metal) attracts a devoted following, such music rarely finds its way into the mainstream. This said, fans of such music often incorporate heavy metal culture into their identity and pay closer attention to lyrics than do other teens (Arnett, 1991a, 1998; Greenfield et al., 1987; Roberts, Foehr, & Rideout, 2005). Moreover, heavy metal lyrics frequently focus on such topics as death, murder, suicide, sexual violence, and misogyny. Consider the following list of titles from the well-known death metal band, Cannibal Corpse:

Albums:

Butchered at Birth (1991)

Hammer Smashed Face (1993)

Gallery of Suicide (1998)

Kill (2006)

Evisceration Plague (2009)

Songs:

"Meat Hook Sodomy"

"Entrails Ripped from a Virgin's C—t"

"She Was Asking for It"

"Necropedophile"

"Relentless Beating"

"Murder Worship"

"Five Nails through the Neck"

"Submerged in Boiling Flesh"

"Dismembered and Molested"

"Frantic Disembowelment"

"Hacksaw Decapitation"

Common sense would suggest that frequent immersion into music with such dark themes must have some impact on the listener, and research suggests that a high exposure can be linked to a number of negative outcomes: risk taking (Arnett, 1991a, 1991b); the construction of "macho" identities and low respect for women in males (Adams & Fuller, 2006; Hansen & Hansen, 1991; Rafalovich, 2006); and belief systems that overestimate the societal prevalence of occultism, drug use, and antisocial behaviors (Strasburger et al., 2009). Many studies also find links with mental health issues, including ADHD (Ekinci, Bez, Topcuoglu, & Nurmedow, 2011), depression, particularly in female listeners (Ekinci et al., 2011; Miranda & Claes, 2007, 2009; Mula & Trimble, 2009), family dysfunction and delinquency (Mula & Trimble, 2009; but see Recours, Aussaguel, & Trujillo, 2009, for a null finding).

It is important to remember that most young heavy metal fans are not taking drugs, engaging in antisocial behaviors, and experiencing mental health issues. However, arguing the other way, if we know a youth is white, male, 15 years old, drug involved, and in trouble with the law, then the odds are high that his music of choice will be some form of heavy metal. For this reason, it is important to consider how music with antisocial themes may affect children who are already at risk for antisocial behaviors. Will the music reinforce aggressive and antisocial thoughts and feelings, and thus make those thoughts and feelings more likely to occur in the future? Heavy metal music may be a risk factor that can have a stronger impact on those who are already more at risk.

Rap Music

Rap and hip-hop music have featured more frequently in the music mainstream over the last 20 years; thus children and teenagers likely have more exposure to this genre than to heavy metal and its sub genres (e.g., Christenson et al., in press). As with heavy metal music, preference for rap and hip hop music is fairly stable in devotees (Selfhout, Delsing, ter Bogt, & Meeus, 2008). Rap music often features lyrics with nihilistic, angry, violent, and antisocial themes that seem to reflect the chaotic and often violent lifestyles of high-profile artists such as Snoop Dogg, Tupac Shakur, Dr. Dre, Lil Wayne, and Biggie Smalls (e.g., see Kubrin 2005a, 2005b).

In the year 2000, music journalist Allison Samuels and her colleagues wrote that "hard core rap music [is] now driven almost exclusively by sex, violence and materialism" (2000) and recent content analyses of rap lyrics support this notion (e.g., Conrad, Dixon, & Zhang, 2009; Primack, Dalton, Carroll, Agarwal, & Fine, 2008; Roberts, Foehr, Rideout, & Brodie, 1999). Importantly, Herd (2009) has found a dramatic and sustained increase in the level of violence in rap music, as well as an increase in positive portrayals of violence, as shown by an increased association with glamor, wealth, masculinity, and personal prowess.

Across a range of studies, listening to rap music has been associated with deviant behaviors, misogyny, alcohol use, drug use, aggression, and antisocial attitudes and behaviors (e.g., Chen, Miller, Grube, & Waiters, 2006; Miranda & Claes, 2004; Weitzer & Kubrin, 2009; Wingood et al., 2003).

OUTCOMES OF LISTENING TO MUSIC WITH ANTISOCIAL THEMES

Substance Use

Substance use is one of the most studied aspects of popular music. Several recent analyses of substance references in popular music or music videos show that many popular music lyrics refer to substance use, and that most of those references portray substance use in a positive light (Christenson et al., 2012; Christenson et al., in press; Gruber, Thau, Hill, Fisher, & Grube, 2005; Markert, 2001; Mulder et al., 2009; Primack et al., 2008; Roberts et al., 2005; Sloan, Wilson, & Gunasekara, 2013). Primack and colleagues concluded that "the average [U.S.] adolescent is exposed to approximately 84 references to explicit substance use daily in popular songs" (p. 169). These include references to alcohol, tobacco, and illicit drugs.

Although the most recent content analysis finds that 22.5 percent of top 40 songs in the 2000s had substance references (Christenson et al., in press), it is noteworthy that (1) this had increased from just 8.5 percent in the 1990s and 2.5 percent in the 1980s, and (2) that some genres have far more substance references than others. Rap music, for example, is consistently singled out as having the most references, with content analyses finding prevalence of up to 90 percent (Primack et al., 2008). Roberts et al. (2005) found that 53 percent of the rap songs they examined contained references to both alcohol and marijuana and 37 percent of these songs referenced other illicit drugs. It also appears that the prevalence of drug-related themes in rap music fits with wider societal drug trends and is currently increasing (Diamond, Bermudez, & Schensul, 2006).

Of course hearing about (or viewing portrayals of) substance use is not the same as using them; it is important to ask whether one might influence the other. Correlational studies find a relation between exposure to marijuana references and marijuana use (Primack, Douglas, & Kraemer, 2009), music video watching and alcohol use (Van den Bulck, Beullens, & Mulder, 2006), levels of rap music exposure and alcohol and illicit drug use (Chen et al., 2006; Wingood et al., 2003) and preference for house/trance and techno/hardhouse dance music and substance use (ter Bogt et al., 2012). Interestingly, preferences for mainstream pop music and classical music are negatively correlated with substance use—indeed, ter Bogt and his colleagues (2012) suggest that such genres may even operate as a protective factor.

Research also indicates that links between music exposure and substance use may be facilitated by peer groups. That is, shared music becomes part of the process of being socialized into peer group substance use patterns (see Mulder et al., 2010; Slater & Henry, 2013). Whether the effect is direct or not, it is clear that a lot of exposure to music that approves substance use is a likely risk factor in the initiation and continuation of substance use.

Stereotyping, Prejudice, and Misogyny

Research suggests that "concept"[1] music videos, rap, and heavy metal music disproportionately contain themes around gender stereotypes and misogyny (Adams & Fuller, 2006; Conrad et al., 2009; Frisby & Aubrey, 2012; Weitzer & Kubrin, 2009) and that exposure to such material can influence listeners' beliefs about others in both the short and long term.

Short-term exposure to music containing misogynous themes in experiments can cause increased willingness by males to expose women to assaultive vignettes (Barongen & Hall, 1995), to males being more aggressive toward women (Fischer & Greitemeyer, 2006), and to females being more accepting of date violence perpetrated against other women (Johnson, Adams, Ashburn, & Reed, 1995). In addition, brief exposure to sexually explicit lyrics has been linked with greater objectification and stereotyping of women, as well as increased acceptance of rape (Kistler & Lee, 2009).

Studies of longer-term linkages show heavy metal music preference is related to negative attitudes toward women (Rubin, West, & Mitchell, 2001) and to the construction of stereotypical masculine identities (Rafalovich, 2006). Greater exposure to heavy metal music videos is positively correlated with gender stereotypical attitudes (Ward, Hansbrough, & Walker, 2008) and with adolescent males' acceptance of rape (Kaestle, Tucker-Halpern, & Brown, 2007). As with substance use, these effects may be facilitated to some extent by peers. For example, Beentjes and Konig (2013) found that "time spent watching music videos, peer group discussions about music videos, and perceived realism of music videos are all positively related to the traditional attitudes that men dominate sexual relationships, and that women are sex objects" and thus play a role in the "formation and reinforcement of traditional sexual attitudes" (p. 1).

Sexualized Behavior

Themes around sex rather than romantic love have increased in popular music over the last decade (Christenson et al., in press). This is nowhere more obvious than in recent music video clips and the performance of artists such as Miley Cyrus at the 2013 MTV awards. Sexual content in music and music videos appeals strongly to many children and adolescents (e.g., Zillmann & Mundorf, 1987) and may influence behavior. However, experiments examining the short-term impact of sexualized material on attitudes are sparse, and Sprankle and End (2009) found no such effect at all.

Some evidence indicates that longer-term exposure to sexually explicit music and music videos is associated with more promiscuous attitudes toward sex (Zhang, Miller, & Harrison, 2008), accelerated teen sexual activity, and a doubling of the likelihood of early intercourse (Brown et al., 2006). In a study that took into account a range of factors linked to early sexual activity, Martino and colleagues (2006) found that 12- to 17-year-olds who listened more to music themed around casual sex, or that sexually objectified women, were, *over time*, more likely than teens who listened to music lacking such themes to be having intercourse and to be advanced in sexual activities. In other words, exposure to sexually themed music at Time 1 appeared to be causally related to sexual activity at Time 2.

Antisocial Behavior

An increasing number of studies reveal links between music with antisocial themes and the development of attitudes and behaviors that match. Allen and colleagues (2007) analyzed 23 studies with over 7,000 participants that examined the link between music and a variety of attitudes and behaviors, including those related to violence, aggression, illegal drug use, vandalism, law-breaking, delinquency, racism, rebellion against societal rules, and date rape. They found, on average, a robust positive relationship between exposure to antisocial themes in music and various antisocial actions and beliefs in listeners.

Studies also reveal links between certain musical genres and antisocial behavior. A preference for heavy metal music has been linked to delinquency (Mula & Trimble, 2009), and to higher levels of such reckless behavior as substance use, vandalism, fast driving, shoplifting, and drunk driving (Arnett, 1992). In their study of 2,700 14- to 16-year-old white males in the United States, Klein and colleagues (1993) found that those who reported five or more antisocial behaviors (such as smoking, drinking alcohol, stealing, illegal drug use, promiscuity, cheating at school, and cutting school) were more likely to prefer heavy metal music. Ter Bogt, Keijsers, and Meeus (2013) found that fans of rock, heavy metal, gothic, punk, rhythm and blues, hip-hop, trance, and techno/hardhouse music in early adolescence showed elevated minor delinquency in later adolescence. Another study of African American teenage girls found that those who watched more than 20 hours of rap music videos per week had a substantially higher likelihood of being arrested, assaulting a teacher, acquiring a sexually transmitted disease, or using illegal drugs and alcohol (see Peterson, Wingood, DiClemente, Harrington, & Davies, 2007; Wingood et al., 2003).

Interestingly, music preferences may also be a protective factor for antisocial behavior, with studies finding lower levels among listeners who prefer mainstream pop music (Mulder, ter Bogt, Raaijmakers, & Vollebergh, 2007), classical music and jazz (ter Bogt et al., 2013).

Clinical Problems and Suicide

For some decades now there has been concern about the impact of music with nihilistic and suicide-approving lyrics on teen mental health, and in particular on suicidal thoughts. Heavy metal music, which often has dismal and depressing themes, has attracted the most attention. The evidence suggests links between heavy metal music preference and an increased likelihood of a range of mental health issues, including attention deficit disorders, depression, self-injurious thoughts and behaviors, suicidal thoughts, and other psychopathologies (see Baker & Bor, 2008; Stack, Lester, & Rosenberg, 2012 for reviews; see also Ekinci et al., 2011; Martin, Clarke, & Pearce, 1993; Miranda & Claes, 2007; Mula & Trimble, 2009; North & Hargreaves, 2006; Scheel & Westefield, 1999; Stack, Gundlach, & Reeves, 1994; but see Recours et al., 2009 for a null finding). There may also be links between mental health issues and other subcultures that embrace music with nihilistic themes. For example, Young, Sweeting, and West (2006) found that 19-year-olds who identified with the goth music subculture were over 16 times more likely than non-goths to have attempted suicide. The "emo" subculture is also known to be suicidogenic but has been under-researched to date (Baker & Bor, 2008).

Clearly, links between some music genres and poor mental health are often found in research, but it is important to examine these findings carefully. Members of goth and heavy metal music subcultures range from those who have no mental health issues at all to those who are very troubled. It is more reasonable to suggest that youth who are already depressed, angry, alienated, experiencing suicidal thoughts, having family problems, or having difficulty at school may be more drawn to music genres and subcultures that resonate with their feelings. Music within that subculture may then amplify negative emotions such as depression and anger (e.g., Wells, 1990) and reinforce maladaptive thoughts (e.g., Stack et al., 1994). Music is only one of many risk factors that can contribute to mental illness; its role should be neither under- nor overstated.

OUTCOMES OF LISTENING TO MUSIC WITH VIOLENT AND AGGRESSIVE THEMES

There has been far less research on music with violent content than for other media such as violent television, movies, and video games (Fischer & Greitemeyer, 2006; Warburton, 2012b; Warburton, Gilmore, & Laczkowski, 2008), and findings have been mixed. Some early studies found no link between violent song lyrics and anger (Ballard & Coates, 1995), hostility (Wanamaker & Reznikoff, 1989) and acceptance of violence against women (St. Lawrence & Joyner, 1991). Others found links with desensitization to violence (Peterson & Pfost, 1989), hostility (Rubin, West, & Mitchell, 2001), and acceptance of violence and date violence (Johnson, Adams, et al., 1995; Johnson, Jackson, & Gatto, 1995).

Anderson, Carnagey, and Eubanks (2003) examined the methods used in earlier studies that failed to find an effect of violent music and concluded that their "null-results" may have been due to "methodological problems involving confounds with arousal, or lyrics that were indecipherable" (p. 961). More recent studies have tended to try to avoid these issues with careful methodological design, and typically find that exposure to violent music increases the likelihood of aggressive thoughts, feelings, and behaviors (e.g., Anderson et al., 2003; Brummert-Lennings & Warburton, 2011; Fischer & Greitemeyer, 2006; Mast & McAndrew, 2011).

A study of longer-term effects by Warburton and colleagues (2008) found that greater exposure to music with violent themes or an aggressive tone[2] was correlated with increases in trait aggression and a higher incidence of aggression over the previous two months. Interestingly, whereas exposure to violent media such as television, movies, and video games were linked to increases in physical aggression, exposure to violent music was linked to increases in aggression that involved hurting another indirectly or sabotaging other people's relationships (there were also significant but smaller correlations with recent physical aggression as well; see Table 10.2).

Table 10.2
Correlations between Exposure to Violent Media and Several Types of Aggressive Behavior

Exposure to:	Indirect Aggression	Relational Aggression	Trait Physical Aggression	Recent Physical Aggression
Violent visual media	.20	.18	**.29**	**.26**
Violent music	**.27**	**.25**	.12	**.17**
Violent lyrics	**.26**	**.20**	.07	**.14**
Obtained violent lyrics	**.16**	**.25**	**.16**	.12
Music with angry feel	.08	**.23**	.06	**.14**
Angry musicians	.04	**.20**	**.19**	.12

Bolded correlations are significant at p < .05.
Source: Warburton et al., 2008.

In assessing the impact of violent music, another factor has become important over the last two decades or so—many songs with violent content supplement their lyrics with visual content in music videos.

Music Videos

The launch of MTV in 1981 changed the way many children and teens in Western countries engage with popular music. Although children and teens spend considerably more time simply listening to music, the vast majority also watch music videos (Christenson, 1992), with the amount of time dropping off in late adolescence (Christenson, 1992). About half of the music videos shown are "concept videos" (Strasburger et al., 2009), many of which objectify women (Frisby & Aubrey, 2012; Kistler & Lee, 2009), center on themes around materialism and misogyny (Conrad, Dixon, & Zhang, 2009; Frisby & Aubrey, 2012), and have been linked with gender stereotyping in watchers (Beentjes & Konig, 2013; Ward, Hansbrough, & Walker, 2008). In terms of violence, a content analysis of 518 music concept videos showed that around 15 percent had violent portrayals (DuRant et al., 2011), and an analysis of rap videos found 39 percent had violent content, with 59 percent of these containing frequent talk about guns (Jones, 1997). On MTV, two analyses have found that more than 50 percent of music concept videos contained violent themes (Ashby & Rich, 2005; NTVS, 1998). Ashby and Rich further found that the protagonist (hero) was the aggressor in 90 percent of such videos, with aggression thus being linked with an admired character who was often rewarded for the aggressive actions.

Does this combination of violent lyrics, violent portrayals, and modeling of aggression by central characters lead to such videos being especially effective in eliciting aggressive behavior? Gentile, Linder, and Walsh (2003) found that third- through fifth-grade children who watched MTV regularly were rated as significantly more aggressive by peers and teachers, and self-reported more physical fights than children who watched MTV less often. In another study, Waite, Hillbrand, and Foster (1992) examined the effect of removing MTV from a maximum-security forensic hospital. After measuring the aggression levels of 222 patients for a period of 33 weeks, they removed MTV and then measured aggression for a further 22 weeks. Removal of MTV resulted in a considerable reduction in aggression (see Table 10.3).

Experimental studies have also shown that short-term exposure to violent music videos can lead to increases in aggression, aggressive attitudes, antagonism toward women, and greater acceptance of violence (Brummert-Lennings & Warburton, 2011; Greeson & Williams, 1986; Hansen & Hansen, 1990; Johnson, Jackson, & Gatto, 1995).

The key question, of course, is whether the visual portrayals or the music itself drive these effects on aggressive behavior. To our knowledge, only one study to date has tested this directly (Brummert-Lennings & Warburton, 2011). They found that participants who heard any sort of violence-themed music were more aggressive than participants who didn't, but that adding a violence-themed video clip increased the level of aggression only a little.

Lyrics and Musical Tone

As noted earlier, it is the capacity of music to touch our emotions that is its greatest attraction to children, teens, and adults. People use music to control

Table 10.3
Removing MTV in an Institution—A Summary
of Findings

Type of Aggression	% Reduction
Verbal aggression	32.4
Against objects	51.7
Against others	47.5
Against self	5.5

Source: Waite et al. (1992).

and enhance their emotions and often listen to music that resonates with how they feel. This raises the further question of the impact of music that has an angry or aggressive musical "tone" or "feel" to it. Anderson and Bushman (2002) note that cues in our environment can lead to aggressive behavior by eliciting aggressive emotions, eliciting aggressive thoughts, or raising levels of physiological arousal that can provide an impetus to act on aggressive impulses. It seems reasonable to assume that musical tone would have a greater impact on people's feelings and levels of arousal than on their thoughts. For example, loud harsh music with heavy major chords and a driving beat may cause people to feel "pumped up" (aroused) and emotionally stirred up (irritable/angry). Violent lyrics, on the other hand, seem more likely to bring to mind aggression-related concepts, ideas, and thoughts, although lyrics have also been shown to enhance the emotional content of angry and sad (but not happy) music (Ali & Peynircioğlu, 2006).

There has been some discussion among researchers about which factor is most responsible for the impact of violent music on aggressive behavior. Is it because the musical tone changes the way we feel or "pumps us up," or because the lyrics arouse aggressive concepts in semantic memory? (Or is it both—or something else?)

A number of researchers have indicated that the powerful impact of music on emotions means that musical tone may have a stronger impact on aggressive behavior (e.g., Christenson & Roberts, 1998). It has also been noted that many lyrics are hard to understand, not attended to, or are beyond the capacity of children to understand at some ages (e.g., Greenfield et al., 1987; Prinsky & Rosenbaum, 1987), although this seems less relevant given that teenagers do attend to the lyrics of music they think is salient to them, and that devotees of more controversial music such as heavy metal are also known to pay particular attention to the lyrics. Despite some early null findings for lyrics effects, more recent and better-designed studies typically find an impact of violent lyrics on aggressive behavior (e.g., Anderson et al., 2003; Brummert-Lennings & Warburton, 2011; Fischer & Greitemeyer, 2006; Mast & McAndrews, 2011; Warburton et al., 2008).

Very few studies have directly compared the impact of tone and lyrics; however, in the Brummert-Lennings and Warburton (2011) study, both lyrics and tone seemed to influence aggressive behavior, with lyrics having the strongest impact. Unpublished studies by the first author replicate this finding. Together the findings seem to find a role for both musical tone and lyrics on aggressive behavior, but with lyrics likely having a more powerful effect.

School Shootings and Risk Factors

Can simply listening to music with extreme themes create serial killers or cause acts of mass violence such as school shootings? The answer is an emphatic no. Any act of violence results from the convergence of many risk factors that may include access to weapons, home environment, peer influences, mental health issues, substance use, and social isolation, among many others. Violent media, including music, may be one of those risk factors but is neither sufficient nor necessary for people to commit acts of violence (see chapter 2).

CONCLUSIONS AND SUGGESTIONS FOR PARENTS

Warburton (2012a, 2012b) likens media to food. He notes that the human brain "wires up" every second of every day in response to our experiences, and so the tone of those experiences, both virtual and in the "real" world, set the pattern for future thoughts, feelings, memories, and action tendencies. As with food, we become what we eat—our thoughts, feelings, and expectations align with our experiences in life. And, as with food, principles for a healthy media diet are relatively simple. Have regard for how much (moderation in amount), have regard for what (moderation in regards to certain content), and have regard for what is appropriate at different ages.

This healthy media diet approach seems quite apt for music. Most music contains themes and references that are benign. Music use is linked to a range of positive personal experiences and important social experiences, and generally enriches the lives of children, adolescents, and adults alike. That is, listening to music is a normal part of healthy development. However, if parents are concerned that their children are listening to too much music with extreme themes or antisocial content, they may find value in answering the following questions: Are your child's grades good, or have they been slipping? Is your child's mood generally angry or depressed? Do you like your child's friends? If your child is generally happy, you like your child's friends, and his or her grades are fine, then there's probably little to worry about from the lyric content of the songs he or she likes.

If music seems to be having an adverse impact on a child or adolescent's life, it may be important to take a two-pronged approach. The first would be to identify issues underlying the child's media choices. Why is the child angry? What is the influence of peers? What issues might a child be struggling with at school or in relationships? Once identified, action may be taken to help the child in those areas, and the issues with music may resolve as the underlying issues are themselves resolved.

The second would be to deal with the issue of the music itself. This can be tricky, as musical preference is strongly linked to identity, especially in teenagers. Any perceived "attack" on a teen's music preference may be perceived as an attack on the person. Rather, a more "side door" approach may work best—allowing children to make their own musical choices but helping them to also understand the science behind media impacts (you are what you eat) and subtly increasing their range of music exposure by playing music in the household that has more benign or prosocial themes. Often children and teenagers will sample and adopt music introduced by others if they have enjoyed it. Helping a child to make his or her own healthy choices with music preferences seems to be a good way to assist children and adolescents in getting the most from one of this world's most enjoyable pastimes—listening to music.

ACKNOWLEDGMENTS

We would like to acknowledge and thank Chanelle Tarabay for her outstanding work assisting in the preparation of this manuscript, and Doug Gentile for his support and feedback. Your assistance is greatly valued.

NOTES

1. "Concept music videos" differ from simple music performance videos by including additional material that tells a story about the song. On channels such as MTV, about half of the music videos are of simple performances and about half include conceptual material.

2. This includes music that is only listened to; it does not include music videos.

REFERENCES

Adams, T. M., & Fuller, D. B. (2006). The words have changed but the ideology remains the same: Misogynistic lyrics in rap music. *Journal of Black Studies, 36*, 938–957.

Ali, S. O. & Peynircioğlu, Z. F. (2006). Songs and emotions: Are lyrics and melodies equal partners? *Psychology of Music, 34*, 511-534.

Allen, M., Herrett-Skjellum, J., Jorgensen, J., Ryan, D. J., Kramer, M. R., & Timmerman, L. (2007). Effects of music. In R. W. Preiss, B. M. Gayle, N. Burrell, M. Allen, & J. Bryant (Eds.), *Mass media effects research: Advances through meta-analysis* (pp. 263–279). Mahwah, NJ: Lawrence Erlbaum.

American Academy of Pediatrics. (1996). Policy statement: Impact of music lyrics and music videos on children and youth. *Pediatrics, 98*, 1219–1221.

American Academy of Pediatrics. (2009). Policy statement: Impact of music lyrics and music videos on children and youth. *Pediatrics, 124*, 1488–1494.

Anderson, C. A., & Bushman, B. J. (2002). Human aggression. *Annual Review of Psychology, 53*, 27–51.

Anderson, C. A., Carnagey, N. L., & Eubanks, J. (2003). Exposure to violent media: The effects of songs with violent lyrics on aggressive thoughts and feelings. *Journal of Personality and Social Psychology, 84*, 960–971.

Arnett, J. (1991a). Adolescence and heavy metal music: From the mouths of metalheads. *Youth and Society, 23*(1), 76–98.

Arnett, J. (1991b). Heavy metal music and reckless behavior among adolescents. *Journal of Youth and Adolescence, 20*, 573–592.

Arnett, J. (1992). The soundtrack of recklessness: Musical preferences and reckless behavior among adolescents. *Journal of Adolescent Research, 7*, 313–331.

Arnett, J. J. (1998). Learning to stand alone: The contemporary American transition to adulthood in cultural and historical context. *Human Development, 41,* 295–315.

Ashby, S. L., & Rich, M. (2005). Video killed the radio star: The effects of music videos on adolescent health. *Adolescent Medicine Clinics, 16,* 371–393.

Baker, F., & Bor, W. (2008). Can music preference indicate mental health status in young people? *Australasian Psychiatry, 16,* 284–288.

Ballard, M. E., & Coates, S. (1995). The immediate effects of homicidal, suicidal, and nonviolent heavy metal and rap songs on the mood of college students. *Youth and Society, 27,* 148–169.

Barongen, C., & Hall, G. C. N. (1995). The effect of misogynous rap music on sexual aggression against women. *Psychology of Women Quarterly, 19,* 195–207.

Beentjes, J. W. J., & Konig, R. P. (2013). Does exposure to music videos predict adolescents' sexual attitudes? *European Scientific Journal, 9,* 1–20.

Bishop, D. T., Karageorghis, C. I., & Loizou, G. (2007). A grounded theory of young tennis players' use of music to manipulate emotional state. *Journal of Sport and Exercise Psychology, 29,* 584–607.

Brown, C. J., Chen, A. C. N., & Dworkin, S. F. (1989). Music in the control of human pain. *Music Therapy, 8,* 47–60.

Brown, J. D., Childers, K., Bauman, K., & Koch, G. (1990). The influence of new media and family structure on young adolescents' television and radio use. *Communication Research, 17,* 65–82.

Brown, J. D., L'Engle, K. L., Pardun, C. J., Guo, G., Kenneavy, K., & Jackson, C. (2006). Sexy media matter: Exposure to sexual content in music, movies, television and magazines predicts Black and White adolescents' sexual behaviour. *Pediatrics, 117,* 1017–1027.

Brummert-Lennings, H. I., & Warburton, W. A. (2011). The effect of auditory versus visual violent media exposure on aggressive behaviour: The role of song lyrics, video clips and musical tone. *Journal of Experimental Social Psychology, 47,* 794–799.

Bruner, G. (1990). Music, mood and marketing. *Journal of Marketing, 54,* 94–105.

Bunt, L. (1997). Clinical and therapeutic uses of music. In D. J. Hargreaves & A. C. North (Eds.), *The social psychology of music* (pp. 249–267). Oxford, UK: Oxford University Press.

Chen, M. J., Miller, B., Grube, J. W., & Waiters, E. D. (2006). Music, substance use, and aggression. *Journal of Studies on Alcohol, 67,* 373–381.

Christenson, P. G. (1992). The effects of parental advisory labels on adolescent music preferences. *Journal of Communication, 42,* 106–113.

Christenson, P. G., Debenedittis, P., & Lindlof, T. (1985). Children's use of audio media. *Communication Research, 12,* 327–343.

Christenson, P. G., & Roberts, D. F. (1998). *It's not only rock & roll: Popular music in the lives of adolescents.* Cresskill, NJ: Hampton Press.

Christenson, P. G., Roberts, D. F., & Bjork, N. (2012). Booze, drugs, and pop music: Trends in substance portrayals in the Billboard Top 100: 1968–2008. *Substance Use and Misuse, 47,* 121–129.

Christenson, P. G., Roberts, D. F., & ter Bogt, T. (Unpublished doctoral dissertation). *What has America been singing about? Trends in major themes and references in the U.S. top-40: 1960–2010.* Portland OR: Lewis and Clark College.

Conrad, K., Dixon, T., & Zhang, Y. (2009). Controversial rap themes, gender portrayals and skin tone distortion: A content analysis of rap music videos. *Journal of Broadcasting and Electronic Media, 53*, 134–156.

Cremades, R., Lorenzo, O., & Herrera, L. (2010). Musical tastes of secondary school students with different cultural backgrounds: A study in the Spanish North African city of Melilla. *Musicae Scientiae, 14*, 121–141.

Crozier, W. R. (1997). Music and social influence. In D. J. Hargreaves & A. C. North (Eds.), *The social psychology of music* (pp. 67–83). New York, NY: Oxford University Press.

Diamond, S., Bermudez, R., & Schensul, J. (2006). What's the rap about ecstasy?: Popular music lyrics and drug trends among American youth. *Journal of Adolescent Research, 21*, 269–298.

DuRant, R. H., Rich, M., Emans, S. J., Rome, E. S., Allred, E., & Woods, E. R. (2011). Violence and weapon carrying in music videos. *Archives of Pediatrics and Adolescent Medicine, 151*, 443–448.

Egermann, H., Sutherland, M. E., Grewe, O., Nagel, F., Kopiez, R., & Altenmuller, E. (2011). Does music listening in a social context alter experience? A physiological and psychological perspective on emotion. *Musicae Scientiae, 15*, 307–323.

Ekinci, O., Bez, Y., Topcuoglu, V., & Nurmedow. (2011). Attention deficit hyperactivity disorder and social anxiety in Istanbul heavy metal bar patrons. *Balkan Medical Journal, 28*, 307–312.

Finnäs, L. (1989). A comparison between young people's privately and publicly expressed musical preferences. *Psychology of Music, 17*, 132–145.

Fischer, P., & Greitemeyer, T. (2006). Music and aggression: The impact of sexual-aggressive song lyrics on aggression-related thoughts, emotions, and behavior toward the same and the opposite sex. *Personality and Social Psychology Bulletin, 32*, 1165–1176.

Flom, R., Gentile, D. A., & Pick, A. D. (2008). Infants' discrimination of happy and sad music. *Infant Behavior and Development, 31*, 716–728.

Fried, R., & Berkowitz, L. (1979). Music that charms . . . and can influence helpfulness. *Journal of Applied Social Psychology, 9*, 199–208.

Frisby, C. M., & Aubrey, J. S. (2012). Race and genre in the use of sexual objectification in female artists' music videos. *The Howard Journal of Communications, 23*, 66–87.

Garrido, S., & Schubert, E. (2011a). Negative emotion in music: What is the attraction? A qualitative study. *Empirical Musicology Review, 6*, 214–230.

Garrido, S., & Schubert, E. (2011b). Individual differences in the enjoyment of negative emotion in music: A literature review and experiment. *Music Perception: An Interdisciplinary Journal, 28*, 279–296.

Gentile, D. A., & Bushman, B. J. (2012). Reassessing media violence effects using a risk and resilience approach to understanding aggression. *Psychology of Popular Media Culture, 1*, 138–151.

Gentile, D. A., Linder, J. R., & Walsh, D. A. (2003, April). *Looking through time: A longitudinal study of children's media violence consumption at home and aggressive behaviors at school*. Paper presented at the 2003 Society for Research in Child Development Biennial Conference, Tampa, Florida.

Greenberg, B., Ku, L., & Li, H. (1989, June). *Young people and their orientation to the mass media: An international study, Study #2: United States*. East Lansing, MI: College of Communication Arts, Michigan State University.

Greenfield, P. M., Bruzzone, L., Koyamatsu, K., Satuloff, W., Nixon, K., Brodie, M., & Kinsgsdale, D. (1987). What is rock music doing to the minds of our youth? A first experimental look at the effects of rock music lyrics and music videos. *Journal of Early Adolescence, 7*, 315–329.

Greeson, L., & Williams, R. A. (1986). Social implications of music videos for youth: An analysis of the content and effects of MTV. *Youth and Society, 18*, 177–189.

Gregory, A. H. (1997). The roles of music in society: The ethnomusicological perspective. In D. J. Hargreaves & A. C. North (Eds.), *The social psychology of music* (pp. 123–140). New York, NY: Oxford University Press.

Greitemeyer, T. (2009a). Effects of songs with pro-social lyrics on pro-social thoughts, affect and behavior. *Journal of Experimental Social Psychology, 45*, 186–190.

Greitemeyer, T. (2009b). Effects of songs with prosocial lyrics on prosocial behavior: Further evidence and a mediating mechanism. *Personality and Social Psychology Bulletin, 35*, 1500–1511.

Greitemeyer, T. (2011). Exposure to music with pro-social lyrics reduces aggression: First evidence and test of underlying mechanism. *Journal of Experimental Social Psychology, 47*, 28–36.

Gruber, E. L., Thau, H. M., Hill, D. L., Fisher, D. A., & Grube, J. W. (2005). Alcohol, tobacco and illicit substances in music videos: A content analysis of prevalence and genre. *Journal of Adolescent Health, 37*, 81–83.

Gueguen, N., Jacob, C., Lamy, L. (2010). "Love is in the air": Effects of songs with romantic lyrics on compliance with a courtship request. *Psychology of Music, 38*, 303–307.

Hansen, C. H., & Hansen, R. D. (1990). Rock music videos and antisocial behaviour. *Basic and Applied Social Psychology, 11*, 357–369.

Hansen, C. H., & Hansen, R. D. (1991). Schematic information processing of heavy metal lyrics. *Communication Research, 18*, 373–411.

Hays, T. (2005). Well-being in later life through music. *Australasian Journal on Ageing, 24*, 28–32.

Hepper, P. G. (1991). An examination of fetal learning before and after birth. *Irish Journal of Psychology, 12*, 95–107.

Herd, D. (2009). Changing images of violence in rap music lyrics: 1979–1997. *Journal of Public Health Policy, 30*, 395–406.

Hunter, P. G., Schellenberg, G., & Griffith, A. T. (2011). Misery loves company: Mood-congruent emotional responding to music. *Emotion, 11*, 1068–1072.

Johnson, J. D., Adams, M. S., Ashburn, L., & Reed, W. (1995). Differential gender effects of exposure to rap music on African American adolescents' acceptance of teen dating violence. *Sex Roles, 33*, 597–605.

Johnson, J. D., Jackson, L. A., & Gatto, L. (1995). Violent attitudes and deferred academic aspirations: Deleterious effects of exposure to rap music. *Basic and Applied Social Psychology, 16*, 27–41.

Jones, K. (1997). Are rap videos more violent? Style differences and the prevalence of sex and violence in the age of MTV. *Howard Journal of Communications, 8*, 343–356.

Jorgenson, H. (1974). The contingent use of music activity to modify behaviors which interfere with learning. *Journal of Music Therapy, 11*, 41–46.

Kaestle, C. E., Tucker-Halpern, C., & Brown, J. D. (2007). Music videos, pro wrestling, and acceptance of date rape among middle school males and females: An exploratory analysis. *Journal of Adolescent Health, 40*, 185–187.

Kaiser Family Foundation. (2003). *Reaching the MTV Generation: Recent research on the impact of the Kaiser Family Foundation/MTV public education campaign on sexual health*. Retrieved from http://www.kff.org/entmedia/upload/Reaching-the -MTV-Generation-Recent-Research-on-the-Impact-of-the-Kaiser-Family -Foundation-MTV-Public-Education-Campaign-on-Sexual-Health.pdf

Kenealy, P. M. (1988). Validation of a music mood induction procedure: Some preliminary findings. *Cognition and Emotion, 2,* 41–48.

Kistler, M. E., & Lee, M. J. (2009). Does exposure to sexual hip-hop music videos influence the sexual attitudes of college students? *Mass Communication and Society, 13,* 67–86.

Klein, J. D., Brown, J. D., Childers, K. W., Oliveri, J., Porter, C., & Dykers, C. (1993). Adolescents' risky behavior and mass media use. *Pediatrics, 92,* 24–31.

Krahé, B., & Bieneck, S. (2012). The effect of music-induced mood on aggressive affect, cognition and behavior. *Journal of Applied Social Psychology, 42,* 271–290.

Kubrin, C. E. (2005a). Gangstas, thugs, and hustlas: Identity and the code of the street in rap music. *Social Problems, 52,* 360–378.

Kubrin, C. E. (2005b). "I see death around the corner": Nihilism in rap music. *Sociological Perspectives, 48,* 433–459.

Laiho, S. (2004). The psychological functions of music in adolescents. *Nordic Journal of Music Therapy, 13,* 47–63.

Lamont, A. (2001, August). *Infants' preferences for familiar and unfamiliar music: A sociocultural study*. Paper presented at the Meeting of the Society for Music Perception and Cognition, Queens University, Kingston, Ontario, Canada.

Larson, R. W. (1995). Secrets in the bedroom: Adolescents private use of media. *Journal of Youth and Adolescence, 24,* 535–550.

Larson, R., Kubey, R., & Colletti, J. (1989). Changing channels: Early adolescent media choices and shifting investments in family and friends. *Journal of Youth and Adolescence, 18*(6), 583–599.

Lima, C. F., & Castro, S. L. (2011). Emotion recognition in music changes across the adult lifespan. *Cognition and Emotion, 25,* 585–598.

Lonsdale, A. J., & North, A. C. (2011). Why do we listen to music? A uses and gratification analysis. *British Journal of Psychology, 102,* 108–134.

Magowen, F. (1994). The land is our märr (essence): It stays forever. The Yothu Yindi relationship in Australian Aboriginal traditional and popular musics. In M. Stokes (Ed.), *Ethnicity, identity and music: The musical construction of place*. Oxford, UK: Berg Publishers.

Markert, J. (2001). Sing a song of drug use-abuse: Four decades of drug lyrics in popular music—from the sixties through the nineties. *Sociological Inquiry, 71,* 194–220.

Martin, G., Clarke, M., & Pearce, C. (1993). Adolescent suicide: Music preference as an indicator of vulnerability. *Journal of the American Academy of Child and Adolescent Psychiatry, 32,* 530–535.

Martino, S. C., Collins, P. L., Elliott, M. N., Strachman, A., Kamouse, D. E., & Berry, S. H. (2006). Exposure to degrading versus non-degrading music lyrics and sexual behavior among youth. *Pediatrics, 118,* e430-e441.

Mast, J. F., & McAndrew, F. T. (2011). Violent lyrics in heavy metal music can increase aggression in males. *North American Journal of Psychology, 13,* 63–64.

Miranda, D., & Claes, M. (2004). Rap music genres and deviant behaviors in French-Canadian adolescents. *Journal of Youth and Adolescence, 33*, 113–122.

Miranda, D., & Claes, M. (2007). Musical preferences and depression in adolescence. *International Journal of Adolescence and Youth, 13*, 285–309.

Miranda, D., & Claes, M. (2009). Music coping, peer affiliation and depression in adolescence. *Psychology of Music, 37*, 215–233.

Miranda, D., & Gaudreau, P. (2011). Écoute de la musique et bien-être émotionnel à l'adolescence: Une étude centrée sur les personnes et sur les variables. [Music listening and emotional well-being in adolescence: A person- and variable-oriented study.] *Revue Européenne de Psychologie Appliquée, 61*, 1–11.

Mula, M., & Trimble, M. R. (2009). Music and madness: Neuropsychiatric aspects of music. *Clinical Medicine, 9*, 83–86.

Mulder, J., ter Bogt, T., Raaijmakers, Q., Gabhainn, S. N., Monshouwer, K., & Vollebergh, W. A. M. (2009). The soundtrack of substance use: Music preference and adolescent smoking and drinking. *Substance Use and Misuse, 44*, 514–531.

Mulder, J., ter Bogt, T., Raaijmakers, Q., Gabhainn, S. N., Monshouwer, K., & Vollebergh, W. A. M. (2010). Is it the music? Peer substance use as a mediator of the link between music preferences and adolescent substance use. *Journal of Adolescence, 33*, 387–394.

Mulder, J., ter Bogt, T., Raaijmakers, Q., & Vollebergh, W. (2007). Music taste groups and problem behavior. *Journal of Youth and Adolescence, 36*, 313–324.

Nater, U. M., Abbruzzese, E., Krebs, M., & Ehlert, U. (2006). Sex differences in emotional and psychophysiological responses to musical stimuli. *International Journal of Psychophysiology, 62*, 300–308.

National Television Violence Study (NTVS). (1998). *National Television Violence Study (Vol. 3)*. Santa Barbara: University of California, Santa Barbara, Center for Communication and Social Policy.

North, A. C., & Hargreaves, D. J. (2006). Problem music and self-harming. *Suicide and Life-Threatening Behavior, 36*, 582–590.

North, A. C., Tarrant, M., & Hargreaves, D. J. (2004). The effects of music on helping behavior: A field study. *Environment and Behaviour, 36*, 266–275.

Pareles, J. (1990, June 17). Rap: Slick, violent, nasty, and, maybe, hopeful. *New York Times*, p. 19.

Perry, I. (1995). It's my thang and I'll swing it the way that I feel! In J. G. Dines & J. M. Humes (Eds.), *Gender, race, and class in media: A test reader* (pp. 524–530). Thousand Oaks, CA: Sage.

Peterson, D. L., & Pfost, K. S. (1989). Influence of rock videos on attitudes of violence against women. *Psychological Reports, 64*, 319–322.

Peterson, S. H., Wingood, G. M., DiClemente, R. J., Harrington, K., & Davies, S. (2007). Images of sexual stereotypes in rap videos and the health of African American female adolescents. *Journal of Women's Health, 16*, 1157–1164.

Pignatiello, M., Camp, C. J., Elder, S. T., & Rasar, L. A. (1989). A psychophysiological comparison of the Velten and musical mood induction techniques. *Journal of Music Therapy, 26*, 140–154.

Pignatiello, M. F., Camp, C. J., & Rasar, L. A. (1986). Musical mood induction: An alternative to the Velten technique. *Journal of Abnormal Psychology, 95*, 295–297.

Primack, B. A., Dalton M. A., Carroll M. V., Agarwal A. A., & Fine M. J. (2008). Content analysis of tobacco, alcohol, and other drugs in popular music. *Archives of Pediatrics and Adolescent Medicine, 162*, 169–175.

Primack, B. A., Douglas, E. L., & Kraemer, K. L. (2009). Exposure to cannabis in popular music and cannabis use among adolescents. *Addiction, 105*, 515–523.

Prinsky, L. E., & Rosenbaum, J. L. (1987). "Lee-rics" or lyrics: Teenage impressions of rock 'n' roll. *Youth and Society, 18*, 384–397.

Rafalovich, A. (2006). Broken and becoming god-sized: Contemporary metal music and masculine individualism. *Symobolic Interaction, 29*, 19–32.

Rana, S. A., Tanveer, S., & North, A. C. (2009). Peak experiences of music & subjective well-being (a qualitative approach). *Journal of Behavioral Sciences, 19*, 41–57.

Recours, R., Aussaguel, F., & Trujillo, N. (2009). Metal music and mental health in France. *Culture, Media and Psychiatry, 33*, 473–488.

Rentfrow, P. J., & Gosling, S. D. (2003). The do re mi's of everyday life: The structure and personality correlates of music preferences. *Journal of Personality and Social Psychology, 84*, 1236–1256.

Rideout, V. J., Foehr, U. G., & Roberts, D. F. (2010). *Generation M2: Media in the lives of 8–18 year olds.* Merlo Park, CA: Henry J. Kaiser Foundation.

Roberts, D. F., & Foehr, U. G. (2008). Trends in media use. *The Future of Children, 18*, 11–37.

Roberts, D. F., Foehr, U. G., & Rideout, V. (2005). *Generation M: Media in the lives of 8–18 year-olds.* Washington, DC: Henry J. Kaiser Family Foundation.

Roberts, D. F., Foehr, U. G., Rideout, V. J., & Brodie, M. (1999). *Kids & media @ the new millennium.* Menlo Park, CA: Kaiser Family Foundation.

Roberts, D. F., & Henriksen, L. (1990, June). *Music listening vs. television viewing among older adolescents.* Paper presented at the annual meetings of the International Communication Association, Dublin, Ireland.

Roe, K. (1985). Swedish youth and music: Listening patterns and motivations. *Communication Research, 12*(3), 353–362.

Roe, K. (1996). Music and identity among European youth: Music as communication. In P. Rutten (Ed.), *Music in Europe* (pp. 85–97). Brussels, BE: European Music Office.

Roskam, K. (1979). Music therapy as an aid for improving auditory awareness and improving reading skill. *Journal of Music Therapy, 16*, 31–42.

Rouner, D. (1990). "Rock music use as a socializing function." *Popular Music and Society, 14*(1), 97–107.

Rubin, A. M., West, D. V., & Mitchell, W. S. (2001). Differences in aggression, attitudes towards women, and distrust as reflected in popular music preferences. *Media Psychology, 3*, 25–42.

Saarikallio, S., & Erkkila, J. (2007). The role of music in adolescents' mood regulation. *Psychology of Music, 35*, 88–109.

Salimpoor, V. N., Benovoy, M., Larcher, K., Dagher, A., & Zatorre, R. J. (2011). Anatomically distinct dopamine release during anticipation and experience of peak emotion to music. *Nature Neuroscience, 14*, 257–262.

Samuels, A., Croal, N., & Gates, D. (2000, October 9). Battle for the soul of hip-hop. *Newsweek*, 58–65. Retrieved from http://bechollashon.org/database/index.php?/article/990

Savarimuthu, D. (2004). When music heals. In J. P. Morgan (Ed.), *Focus on aggression research* (pp. 175–187). New York, NY: Nova Science Publishers.

Scheel, K., & Westefield, J. (1999). Heavy metal music and adolescent suicidality: An empirical investigation. *Adolescence, 34*, 253–73.

Selfhout, M. H. W., Branje, S. J. T., ter Bogt, T. F. M., & Meeus, W. H. J. (2009). The role of music preferences in early adolescents' friendship formation and stability. *Journal of Adolescence, 32*, 95–107.

Selfhout, M. H. W., Delsing, M. J. M. H., ter Bogt, T. F. M., & Meeus, W. H. J. (2008). Heavy metal and hip-hop style preferences and externalizing problem behavior: A two wave longitudinal study. *Youth and Society, 39*, 435–452.

Slater, M. D., & Henry, K. L. (2013). Prospective influence of music-related media exposure on adolescent substance-use initiation: A peer group mediation model. *Journal of Health Communication, 18*, 291–305.

Sloan, K., Wilson, N., & Gunasekara, F. I. (2013). A content analysis of the portrayal of alcohol in televised music videos in New Zealand: Changes over time. *Drug and Alcohol Review, 32*, 47–52.

Sprankle, E. L., & End, C. M. (2009). The effects of censored and uncensored sexually explicit music on sexual attitudes and perceptions of sexual activity. *Journal of Media Psychology, 21*, 60–68.

Stack, S., Gundlach, J., & Reeves, J. L. (1994). The heavy metal subculture and suicide. *Suicide and Life-Threatening Behaviour, 24*, 15–23.

Stack, S., Lester, D., & Rosenberg, J. S. (2012). Music and suicidiality: A quantitative review and extension. *Suicide and Life-Threatening Behavior, 42*, 654–671.

Standley, J. (1995). Music as a therapeutic intervention in medical and dental treatment: Research and clinical applications. In T. Wigram, B. Saperston, & R. West (Eds.), *The art and science of music therapy: A handbook*. Langhorne, PA: Harwood Academic.

St. Lawrence, J. S., & Joyner, D. J. (1991). The effects of sexually violent rock music on males' acceptance of violence against women. *Psychology of Women Quarterly, 15*, 49–63.

Strasburger, V. C., Wilson, B. J., & Jordan, A. B. (2009). *Children, adolescents, and the media* (2nd ed.). Thousand Oaks, CA: Sage.

Ter Bogt, T. F. M., Gabhainn, S. N., Simons-Morton, B. G., Ferreira, M., Hublet, A., Godeau, E., Kuntsche, E., Richter, M., & the HBSC Peer Culture Focus Groups. (2012). Dance is the new metal: Adolescent music preferences and substance use across Europe. *Substance Use & Misuse, 47*, 130–142.

Ter Bogt, T. F. M., Keijsers, L., & Meeus, W. H. J. (2013). Early adolescent music preferences and minor delinquency. *Pediatrics, 131*, 380–389.

Ter Bogt, T. F. M., Mulder, J., Raaijmakers, Q. A. W., & Gabhainn, S. N. (2010). Moved by music: A typology of music listeners. *Psychology of Music, 39*, 147–163.

Thoma, M. V., Scholz, U., Ehlert, U., & Nater, U. M. (2012). Listening to music and physiological and psychological functioning: The mediating role of emotion regulation and stress reactivity. *Psychology and Health, 27*, 227–241.

Trehub, S. E., Hill, D. S., & Kamenetsky, S. B. (1997). Parents' sung performances for infants. *Canadian Journal of Experimental Psychology, 51*, 385–396.

Van den Bulck, J., Beullens, K., & Mulder, J. (2006). Television and music video exposure and adolescent "alcopop" use. *International Journal of Adolescent Medicine and Health, 18,* 107–114.

Waite, B. M., Hillbrand, M., & Foster, H. G. (1992). Reduction of aggressive behavior after removal of Music Television. *Hospital and Community Psychiatry, 43,* 173–175.

Wanamaker, C. E., & Reznikoff, M. (1989). Effects of aggressive and nonaggressive rock songs on projective and structured tests. *The Journal of Psychology, 123,* 561–570.

Warburton, W. A. (2013). Aggression: Definition and measurement of. In M. Eastin (Ed.), *Encyclopedia of media violence* (pp. 10–14). Thousand Oaks, CA: Sage.

Warburton, W. A. (2014). Apples, oranges and the burden of proof: Putting media violence findings in context. *European Psychologist, 19*(1), 60–67. doi:10.1027 /1016–9040/a000166

Warburton, W. A. (2012a). Growing up fast and furious in a media saturated world. In W. A. Warburton & D. Braunstein (Eds.), *Growing up fast and furious: Reviewing the impacts of violent and sexualised media on children* (pp. 1–33). Sydney, AU: The Federation Press.

Warburton, W. A. (2012b). How does listening to Eminem do me any harm? What the research says about music and antisocial behavior. In W. A. Warburton & D. Braunstein (Eds.), *Growing up fast and furious: Reviewing the impacts of violent and sexualised media on children* (pp. 85–115). Sydney, AU: The Federation Press.

Warburton, W. A., Gilmour, L., & Laczkowski, P. (2008). Eminem v. Rambo: A comparison of media violence effects for auditory versus visual modalities. In S. Boag (Ed.), *Personality down under: Perspectives from Australia* (pp. 253–271). New York, NY: Nova Science Publishers.

Ward, L. M., Hansbrough, E., & Walker, E. (2008). Contributions of music video exposure to black adolescents' gender and sexual schemas. *Journal of Adolescent Research, 20,* 143–166.

Weitzer, R., & Kubrin, C. E. (2009). Misogyny in rap music: A content analysis of prevalence and meanings. *Men and Masculinities, 12,* 3–29.

Wells, A. (1990). Popular music: Emotional use and management. *Journal of Popular Culture, 24*(1), 105–117.

Whelan, A. M. (2010). *Free music and trash culture: The reconfiguration of musical value online.* In K. Zemke & S. D. Brunt (Eds.), *2009 IASPM Australia-New Zealand Conference: What's it worth?: "Value" and popular music* (pp. 67–71). Dunedin, NZ: IASPM-ANZ.

Wingood, G. M., DiClemente, R. J., Bernhardt J. M., Harrington, K., Davies, S. L., Robillard, A., & Hook, E. W. (2003). A prospective study of exposure to rap music videos and African American female adolescents' health. *American Journal of Public Health, 98,* 437–439.

Young, R., Sweeting, H., West, P. (2006). Prevalence of deliberate self harm and attempted suicide within contemporary Goth youth subculture: Longitudinal cohort study. *British Medical Journal, 332,* 1058–1061.

Zhang, Y., Miller, L. E., & Harrison, K. (2008). The relationship between exposure to sexual music videos and young adults' sexual attitudes. *Journal of Broadcasting and Electronic Media, 52,* 368–386.

Zillmann, D., & Gan, S. (1997). Musical taste in adolescence. In D. J. Hargreaves & A. North (Eds.), *The social psychology of music* (pp. 161–187). Oxford, UK: Oxford University Press.

Zillmann, D., & Mundorf, N. (1987). Image effects in the appreciation of video rock. *Communication Research, 14*, 316–334.

CHAPTER 11

Cognitive Neuroscience Approaches to the Study of Media Violence Effects

Bruce D. Bartholow and Tom A. Hummer

> *"Given that cognitive processes are implemented by the brain, it seems to make sense to explore the possibility that measures of brain activity can provide insights into their nature."*
>
> —Rugg and Coles (1995), p. 27

Although Rugg and Coles (1995) are not scholars of media effects, their sentiment points to an excellent and obvious reason for the use of various kinds of brain imaging techniques to study all manner of psychological phenomena, including media violence. The argument also can be extended to affect- and emotion-related processes. With the possible exception of strict behaviorists in the Watsonian (e.g., 1913) or Skinnerian (e.g., 1974) traditions, virtually all scientists who study human behavior and its causes and correlates ultimately ask questions about the brain and the psychological processes to which it gives rise. Even researchers who never use tools more complicated than pencil and paper essentially assume that the observations they measure have some basis in thoughts and feelings, and that the psychological conditions that influence those thoughts and feelings do so because they affect processes of the mind, which originate in the brain.

For most of the century and a half or so that psychology has existed as a formal discipline of scholarly inquiry, researchers have had to rely on measures that only very indirectly revealed information about the workings of the brain. Measures like self-report and interview-based questionnaires; measures of observable behaviors such as choices, judgments, and ratings of various kinds; and more advanced, computer-aided measures such as response time measures with millisecond-level accuracy all have revealed a great deal about the ways in which various psychological conditions influence thoughts, feelings, and actions. Still, such measures are limited in a number of ways, especially from the standpoint of advancing theoretical understanding of the specific underlying processes responsible for observable responses. Take response time (RT), for instance. RT is by far the most commonly used technique for studying cognitive processes (see Luce, 1986) and has been lauded by many as a relatively direct line to the workings of the cognitive mind (see Fazio & Towles-Schwen, 1999). In its most basic form, RT theory holds that a stimulus eliciting a faster response (e.g., button press on a key pad) was more easily or efficiently processed than a stimulus eliciting a slower response, particularly when task instructions compel respondents to make responses as quickly as possible. Although this principle is not controversial, careful consideration indicates that the RT is an *outcome* of a set of cognitive, affective, and motor processes rooted in the brain, the total number of which is unknown, and is not itself a direct measure of any of them. In contrast to using behavioral measures alone, augmenting such measures by directly examining brain structure and function permits scientists to understand the machinery driving psychological processes of interest. By integrating knowledge of both the biological mechanisms and pertinent psychological processes with behavioral outcome measurements (e.g., RT, questionnaires, etc.), we can better understand effects of environmental variables from start (i.e., initial perception) to finish (observable behavior).

With regard to media violence, behavioral observations can be combined with neuroimaging data to identify specific neural process affected by media violence exposure, and how these processes may result in changes to emotional processes, cognition, and social interaction. For instance, increases in aggressive thoughts, behaviors, and cognitions related to violent media exposure, as described elsewhere in this text, can be better understood by examining the brain mechanisms underlying aggression and control of behavior, and how activity in these regions are affected by media exposure.

NEUROIMAGING TECHNIQUES

Various neuroimaging techniques exist to characterize the brain's structure and function. These techniques rely on detecting signals emanating from the brain's naturally occurring electromagnetic or hemodynamic properties, or the interaction of the brain's biochemical and physiological properties with exogenous input (e.g., radioactive molecules). In this chapter, we will focus on two common imaging techniques: electroencephalography (EEG) and magnetic resonance imaging (MRI), both of which provide relatively direct, noninvasive windows into neural structure and function and, ultimately, the workings of the psychological mind.

In EEG, an array of electrodes is placed on the scalp to record ongoing voltage fluctuations that are due to synchronized oscillations of neuronal activity. These electrodes can measure spontaneous activity over an extended period of time or how brain activity changes in response to specific events (internal or external stimuli or responses). EEG activity associated with this latter approach is known as the event-related potential (ERP), since it quantifies the EEG activity time-locked to a specific event, such as an image or word shown to the participant (averaged over many trials). Measuring ERP changes can characterize both the speed and nature of the brain's response to discrete stimuli. Because ERP directly detects the electrical activity generated by the firing of groups of neurons, it provides high temporal resolution, on the order of milliseconds, which can help differentiate between direct sensory and higher-level cognitive processes. However, because each electrode measures potential changes that could arise from a relatively widespread structural area, spatial resolution is poorer than with other imaging techniques. In other words, we can know exactly *when* activity is occurring in the brain, although we can only approximately know *where*.

An MRI scanner—essentially a very powerful magnet moving rapidly within a closed field around a biological target, such as the brain—works by exciting atomic nuclei within a magnetic field. The scanner then detects the radio frequency signal given off as nuclei relax to their default equilibrium. Because different tissue types have distinct magnetic susceptibilities and relaxation rates, MRI can provide an in-depth three-dimensional map of the brain that distinguishes, for instance, gray matter, white matter, and cerebrospinal fluid. MRI can also measure signals due to blood flow, blood volume, and oxygen metabolism changes presumed to occur following neuronal activity. This so-called blood-oxygen level-dependent (BOLD) signal is utilized in functional MRI (fMRI) to quantify brain activity occurring spontaneously or in response to particular stimuli. In fMRI, repeated measurements of the BOLD signal, typically taken over 3 to 10 minutes, characterize activity in brain regions with a two- to three-millimeter spatial resolution. However, because the BOLD signal is only an indirect measurement of brain activity and depends upon the relatively sluggish time course of blood flow, it does not provide the high temporal resolution provided by EEG techniques (~two- to three-second resolution). That is, in contrast to EEG, fMRI can detect exactly *where* some processing is occurring in the brain, but can only approximately determine *when*.

STUDYING MEDIA VIOLENCE EFFECTS

The scientific study of media violence effects has undergone a number of changes over the past century. Most early research on media effects, like research on most psychological topics, relied primarily on self-reports of behavior, namely, television and movie watching habits and incidents of relevant behaviors, such as aggression (see Eron & Huesmann, 1980; Eron, Huesmann, Lefkowitz, & Walder, 1972; Huesmann, 1999; Huesmann & Miller, 1994). Such studies were extremely valuable in establishing empirical relations between media use habits, especially exposure to media violence, and psychologically important outcomes. However, many early studies in this tradition were limited by their correlational nature (i.e., establishing whether media violence exposure causes or is simply associated with outcomes such as aggression is quite difficult with such designs) and by their use of relatively indirect measures of cognitive, emotional, and behavioral measures of interest.

The importance of more directly investigating mental processes instantiated in brain activity evoked by media exposure was noted by the communication scholar Wilbur Schramm, who commented, "Most of the communication process is in the 'black box' of the central nervous system, the contents of which we understand only vaguely" (Schramm, 1971, p. 24). Thus, in addition to questionnaires and observation-based measures, this stage of media effects research was characterized by the use of various behavioral measures not only to gauge overt reactions to media but also as indices of presumed, underlying cognitive operations carried out during media exposure. For example, media scholars interested in observing variation in levels of attention engaged during media exposure turned to secondary task reaction time as well as time spent looking at the screen (Anderson & Burns, 1991; Basil, 1994).

The cognitive revolution in the 1970s, along with formal development of the psychophysiological approach, has been credited with changing the paradigm for media effects research by enabling researchers to explore mental processes that intervene in determining media effects (Lang, Potter, & Bolls, 2009). These developments essentially shifted the paradigm from one focused on stimulus/response relationships to one that investigates media effects as occurring in a more complex stimulus-intervening processes/response fashion (Potter & Bolls, 2012). In recent years, the cognitive revolution has been supplanted by another shift in focus, which we might call the "cognitive neuroscience revolution" (Sherry, 2004; Weber, Sherry, & Mathiak, 2009). This new age of media research is characterized by scholars from both media studies and psychology using various psychophysiological measures to understand not only the information processing operations engaged by media content but also the neural underpinnings of those operations and the bodily responses they instantiate. The value of this new approach was recognized in the introduction to a special issue of the journal *Media Psychology* dedicated to the use of brain imaging in media effects research, which highlighted the promise of this approach for discovering biological mechanisms for previously observed media effects (Anderson et al., 2006).

Broadly speaking, cognitive neuroscience is the study of the biologic substrates of complex cognition, with a particular emphasis on the neural structures and processes that give rise to mental processes (Gazzaniga, Ivry, & Mangun, 2002). The cognitive neuroscience approach to understanding media effects is grounded in a theoretical orientation that assumes that integrating responses to media derived from cognitive, neural, and peripheral physiological levels provides a more comprehensive understanding of responses to media than can be achieved by investigating any one or two of these levels alone (Ochsner & Lieberman, 2001). The focus of this chapter is on how neuroimaging techniques are integrated into this new theoretical and methodological approach on the study of media effects (Lang et al., 2009).

Brain imaging techniques are a relatively new addition to the field of media violence research, essentially emerging within the last decade. Despite the excitement that such research holds, it is important to note that neuroimaging is not meant to replace the rich history of valuable psychological and behavioral research on media violence effects, which continues today. Rather, neuroimaging should be used to complement more traditional measurement methods, to provide information that cannot be gathered via other means. For instance, neuroimaging can provide insight into how brain development may be altered by media exposure, knowledge that should be combined with cognitive and behavioral measurements throughout childhood. In addition, identifying how neural networks interact during psychological tasks, and how activity is related to media exposure, can help inform theory on how media violence influences thoughts, feelings, and behaviors.

NEUROIMAGING STUDIES OF MEDIA VIOLENCE EFFECTS

Investigating effects of media violence through the lens of neuroimaging techniques is more complex than, for example, simply scanning the brain of someone who is watching a violent film or playing a violent video game and seeing what "lights up." Instead, researchers seek to test psychological and neurobiological hypotheses, which guide the experimental paradigm and subsequent data analyses. There are three primary techniques employed by neuroimaging researchers in this area: (1) measuring brain activity during media exposure, focusing on how activity in specified brain regions changes with specific media events or characteristics; (2) examining brain activity following an experimental manipulation, such as playing one type of video game versus another type, during psychological tasks geared towards testing *a priori* hypotheses concerning effects of manipulated media content; and (3) quantifying how brain structure or activity is related to measures of prior media exposure.

Within this framework, researchers identify psychological processes and neurobiological changes that are hypothesized to be influenced by media violence exposure. Early psychophysiological research on media violence was focused on attempting to understand effects of media violence on "arousal" (Cantor, Zillmann, & Einsiedel, 1978; Donnerstein & Barrett, 1978; Zillmann & Bryant, 1974; Zillmann, Hoyt, & Day, 1974; Zillmann, Mody, & Cantor, 1974). In large part, such studies were designed to test aspects of various arousal theories of aggression, which posit that exposure to "exciting" media content (e.g., violence, sex) increases arousal, and that this arousal may lead one to misattribute the source of the arousal to another source, such as a provoking action by another person, prompting a retaliatory response (Zillmann, 1983). Unfortunately, as later theorists described in detail (Cacioppo & Tassinary, 1990), arousal is not a single or simple construct, and there is rarely—if ever—a one-to-one relationship between the psychological construct of arousal and physiological responses thought to represent it. Therefore, contemporary research has turned away from this early focus on simple arousal and focuses instead on understanding broader theories of media violence effects and the ways in which psychophysiological measures can contribute to them (Anderson & Carnagey, this volume; Carnagey, Anderson, & Bartholow, 2007).

To date, neuroimaging research into the effects of media violence has largely focused on two potential causal mechanisms that extend from the early focus on arousal: desensitization and inhibitory control. Relevant theory posits that effects of media violence exposure on social behaviors like aggression can be caused by media consumers becoming desensitized to violence and its outcomes, a relaxation of inhibitory processes that typically would be expected to restrain aggressive impulses, or both. These two proposed mechanisms are more directly tied to changes in social interactions, emotional processing and control, higher-level cognitions, and aggressive or impulsive behaviors potentially influenced by exposure to media violence. By investigating desensitization and inhibitory control with neuroimaging techniques, researchers attempt to clarify the timing and underlying mechanisms driving changes in these constructs, to provide a better understanding of media violence effects over both short- and long-term durations.

Desensitization is an idea that—somewhat ironically, given earlier research on arousal theory—posits a role for *reduced* arousal following media violence exposure as a causal factor in aggression-related responses. Research has shown that exposure to media violence initially produces fear, disgust, and other avoidance-related motivational states (Cantor, 1998). In the brain, emotionally arousing stimuli induce heightened activity in a network of regions often called the limbic system. Although the boundaries of this system are not strictly defined, this network includes the amygdala, hippocampus, thalamus, and cingulate gyrus. In particular, the amygdala is highly sensitive to emotionally evocative stimuli, including emotional faces or fear-inducing images (Whalen & Phelps, 2009), acting to alert higher-level cortical regions to attend to important environmental information. According to some models (see Ochsner & Gross, 2005; Ochsner, Silvers, & Buhle, 2012), prefrontal and cingulate cortical regions act to regulate (i.e., inhibit) automatic emotional responses generated by lower-level, primarily limbic structures in order to engage in more rational, less impulsive behavioral and cognitive responses.

According to desensitization theory, repeated exposure to violence, whether in the media or in life, results in habituation of the initially negative cognitive, emotional, and physiological responses people experience in the presence of blood and gore (see Funk, Bechtoldt-Baldacci, Pasold, & Baumgartner, 2004; Rule & Ferguson, 1986), which in theory can produce more calloused attitudes toward violence and, ultimately, increased aggression. Numerous studies have provided evidence for the basic premise that media violence can produce desensitization to violence. For example, individuals exposed to violent media content are less physiologically aroused by subsequent depictions of actual violence (Lazarus, Speisman, Mordkov, & Davison, 1962; Cline, Croft, & Courrier, 1973; Thomas, Horton, Lippincott, & Drabman, 1977; Thomas, 1982; Linz, Donnerstein, & Adams, 1989; Carnagey, Anderson, & Bushman, 2007) and are less empathic toward the pain and suffering of others (Bushman & Anderson, 2009; Fanti, Vanman, Henrich, & Avraamides, 2009) than are participants initially exposed to nonviolent media.

However, it was not until relatively recently that researchers directly addressed the question of whether neural desensitization as a result of media violence exposure could be a pathway to increased aggressiveness. In an initial study, Bartholow, Bushman, and Sestir (2006) recorded ERPs from a group of participants varying in their history of video game violence exposure (VVE) while they viewed a series of images that were neutral (e.g., a towel lying on a table), violent (e.g., a man holding a gun in another man's mouth), and negative but nonviolent (e.g., a rotting dog corpse). The researchers were primarily interested in recording the amplitude of the P3 or P300 component of the ERP elicited in response to the three picture types. The P3 has been strongly associated with motivational and attentional processes (see Nieuwenhuis, Aston-Jones, & Cohen, 2005), and its amplitude in response to emotionally evocative images has been linked to the extent to which the content of the images activates underlying motivational propensities (e.g., to approach or avoid). Based on the idea that repeated video game violence exposure (VVE) would lead to desensitization to depictions of real violence, Bartholow et al. (2006) hypothesized that high-VVE participants would show reduced P3 responses to violent images than would their low-VVE peers. Consistent with this prediction, the P3 response elicited by violent pictures was significantly smaller among high-VVE participants than low-VVE participants, but responses to negative nonviolent images did not differ between the groups (see Figure 11.1). These findings suggest that violence-related images elicit less avoidance/withdrawal motivation among high-VVE individuals, consistent with the tenets of desensitization theory (also see Bailey, West, & Anderson, 2011).

In the second half of the study, participants completed a competitive game in which they were given the chance to deliver blasts of noxious noise as a punishment to an ostensible opponent. The intensity of noise blasts set by

Figure 11.1
ERP Waveforms Elicited by More Frequent Neutral Images, Infrequent Violent Images (Panel A) and Infrequent Negative Nonviolent Images (Panel B) as a Function of Previous Video Game Violence Exposure (VVE)

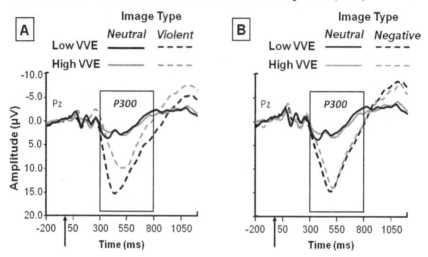

The amplitude of the P300 component (indicated by the dashed box) elicited by violent images was significantly attenuated as VVE increased. However, there was no effect of VVE on the P300 elicited by negative nonviolent images.
Source: As reported by Bartholow et al. (2006).

participants constitutes an often-used and externally valid laboratory measure of aggression (Carlson, Marcus-Newhall, & Miller, 1989; Bushman, 1995; Anderson & Bushman, 1997; Giancola & Chermack, 1998; Anderson, Lindsay, & Bushman, 1999; Bartholow & Anderson, 2002). Bartholow et al. (2006) found that high-VVE participants generally set louder noise blasts for their ostensible opponents than did low-VVE participants. Moreover, consistent with the desensitization hypothesis, there was a strong, negative correlation between the levels of noise punishment participants set for their opponents and the size of their brain responses to violent images measured in the first part of the study. That is, participants with smaller P3 responses to violence—a hypothesized neural indication of desensitization—tended to be more aggressive during the reaction-time task.

Although Bartholow et al.'s (2006) findings were generally consistent with desensitization theory, that study was limited by its correlational nature—participants were selected on the basis of their self-reported history of video game violence exposure, rather than being randomly assigned to violent or nonviolent game exposure conditions (Bailey et al., 2011). Therefore, despite research support from other correlational investigations indicating that past exposure to violent media is associated with abnormal neural activity in the prefrontal cortex (Mathews et al., 2005; Montag et al., 2012), the direct role of media violence as a causal influence on subsequent neural processes was not yet established. For instance, it could be that an extensive history of media violence exposure does not cause people to become desensitized, but that individuals with small brain responses to violence (caused by unknown factors) simply tend to play a lot of violent video games. To address this limitation, Engelhardt, Bartholow, Kerr, and Bushman (2011) recruited male and female participants varying in VVE and randomly assigned them to play either a violent or nonviolent video game in the lab for 25 minutes before completing the picture-viewing and aggression tasks used in Bartholow et al. (2006).

Consistent with what Bartholow et al. (2006) found, high-VVE individuals in Engelhardt et al. (2011) showed smaller P3 responses to violence compared with their low-VVE peers. However, of greater interest is that, among low-VVE participants, those who had just played a violent video game in the lab showed smaller P3 responses to violence than did their counterparts who had just played a nonviolent game (see Figure 11.2). This finding indicates that a brief exposure to video game violence caused acute desensitization to violence, which cannot be attributed to preexisting differences in brain responses. Also of interest is the finding that high-VVE participants showed reduced P3 amplitude to violence regardless of the game played in the lab, suggesting that these individuals had already been desensitized and another brief exposure to video game violence did not further desensitize them (i.e., a floor effect). Finally, Engelhardt et al. found that among those low in VVE, the size of the P3 elicited by violent pictures significantly mediated the effect of the video game exposure manipulation (violent or nonviolent) on aggressive behavior during the reaction-time task (intensity and duration of noise blasts). These data are the first to show that acute desensitization to violence can be a mechanism through which aggression can increase following exposure to video game violence.

A complementary approach aimed at understanding how media violence exposure could affect aggression has been to investigate the neural structures and circuits that are engaged when playing violent compared to nonviolent video games. One of the first such studies was conducted by Weber, Ritterfeld, and Mathiak (2006), who used fMRI to investigate neural structures that increase and decrease in activation during violent video game play. These authors measured participants' brain activations with fMRI while they played a violent video game and afterward coded each game scene in terms of its content. Of interest, Weber et al. (2006) found a negative linear relation between the potential for violence in a scene and the BOLD signal change in the rostral anterior cingulate cortex (rACC), amygdala, and orbitofrontal cortex, structures implicated in affect/emotion-related processing. More recently, Gentile, Swing, Anderson, Rinker, and Thomas (2014) compared

Figure 11.2
Panel A: ERP Waveforms Elicited by Violent Images as a Function of Chronic Video Game Violence Exposure (VVE) and the Type of Video Game Played in the Lab (Violent or Nonviolent)

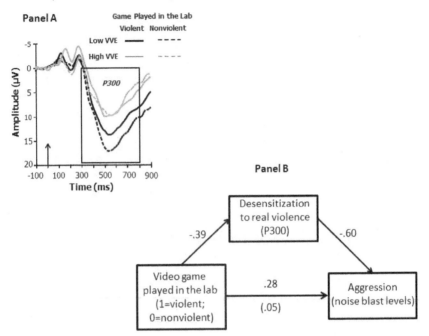

Among participants with a limited history of VVE, playing a violent game in the lab reduced the amplitude of the P300 elicited by violent images. Panel B: Structural equation model depicting the mediating role of P300 elicited by violent images (and indicator of desensitization) in the effect of acute violent game exposure on aggressive behavior.
Source: Adapted from Engelhardt et al. (2011).

neural activity during video game play between individuals with mostly violent or mostly nonviolent game experience. ACC and amygdala activity during violent games (compared to nonviolent games) was higher in individuals with predominantly nonviolent game experience, suggesting that these individuals were more emotionally reactive to the violence in the game than were individuals with considerable violent gaming experience, whose neural responses suggested desensitization to violence (see Bartholow et al., 2006).

Similar research has found that repeated exposure to violent movie clips, but not to equally arousing nonviolent movie clips (e.g., fearful scenes), produces diminished response in a network of neural areas, such as lateral orbitofrontal cortex and amygdala (Kelly, Grinband, & Hirsch, 2007; Strenziok et al., 2011), indicating desensitized neural responses within emotion-relevant regions with extended exposure to violence. Consistent with the ERP studies discussed previously (Bartholow et al., 2006; Engelhardt et al., 2011), Kelly et al. (2007) reported a significant association between the magnitude of this diminished neural response to violence and scores on a self-reported reactive aggression scale. Interestingly, higher levels of past media violence exposure were related to reduced orbitofrontal cortex density in male adolescents (Strenziok et al., 2010), suggesting changes to neural development may be a part of long-term effects on the brain's response to violent stimuli.

Additional fMRI evidence indicates that this desensitization is related to reductions in empathy. Guo et al. (2013) reported that, compared to individuals who viewed a nonviolent film clip, young adults who viewed a violent film clip showed reduced neural responses to subsequent images depicting pain in others, such as a finger being cut by a knife. The reduced neural responses were present in a well-known brain network related to evaluating pain in oneself and others, including sensorimotor regions and the insula. Furthermore, activity in these regions was correlated with pain intensity ratings, with participants in the nonviolent film group reporting that images depicting painful scenes to others were more intense, demonstrating greater empathy.

Although far from definitive, these findings suggest that violent media exposure can produce acute and chronic desensitization to violence by reducing the extent to which the emotional impact of violence is elaborated in the brain. A decreased neural response to violence can result in a decreased consideration of its negative impacts or inadequate cognitive/emotional resources deployed in the service of controlling responses that might cause pain in others, such as impulsive aggressive responses. This latter consequence overlaps with the second major area of research on the neuroimaging of media violence effects—namely, how inhibitory mechanisms to control emotional, cognitive, and behavioral responses are influenced by media violence exposure.

The prefrontal cortex is the primary driver of cognitive and emotional control mechanisms, providing inhibitory input to regions that directly respond to stimuli (see Aron, 2007; Ochsner & Gross, 2005). In particular, lateral regions of the prefrontal cortex are more involved in effortful control of behavior or conscious regulation of emotional output to perform a cognitive task. For instance, during a go/no-go task, participants must press a button to respond to repeatedly presented targets (such as letters) and withhold a response to less common non-targets (e.g., a specific letter, such as "X"). Lateral prefrontal cortex shows increased activity during inhibition of the button press (Konishi et al., 1999; Liddle, Kiehl, & Smith, 2000), which has been used to reflect neural control during more complex behavioral sequences. Medial prefrontal cortex, along with anterior cingulate, may be more important for automatic emotional control and stress regulation. These regions respond directly to emotionally relevant stimuli for appraisal of stimuli and emotional expression (Phan et al., 2003; Phan, Wager, Taylor, & Liberzon, 2002), and then regulate limbic region output when necessary (Amat et al., 2005; Etkin, Egner, & Kalisch, 2011).

The scientific interest in prefrontal control mechanisms is driven, in part, by the concept of skills transfer, the possibility that skills acquired during training in computer-based tasks or games could transfer to untrained behaviors (Fabiani et al., 1989; Frederickson & White, 1989; Gopher, Weil, & Bareket, 1994). Green and his colleagues have reported findings suggesting that long-term experience with so-called "action" video games, which are generally violent first-person shooter games, might lead to enhancement in certain cognitive skills, particularly those related to the scope of visual attention and spatial navigation (Green & Bavelier, 2003, 2006, 2007; Dye, Green, & Bavelier, 2009a, 2009b), and that some effects can occur after relatively short-term training (e.g., 30 hours over the course of 1 month) (Green & Bavelier, 2007). For example, in comparison to nongamers, action video game players have shown "improvements" in visual processing on a range of tasks (Green and Bavelier, 2003; Dye et al., 2009b) and an altered ERP response to peripheral targets.

Although such effects have been lauded as demonstrating the benefits of extended exposure to violent video games (as a counterpoint to the oft-cited harmful effects of such exposure; Anderson et al., 2010; see also Anderson & Gentile, this volume), an expanded scope of visual attention can be detrimental in some contexts. In fact, one prominent aspect of attention is inhibiting the effect of external distracters to divert focus away from the primary target of interest (for either visuospatial or cognitive foci). For example, if the goal of a particular task involves controlling attention so as to avoid the influence of peripheral distracters, then an expanded scope of visual attention can actually impede task performance. In the flanker task (Eriksen & Eriksen, 1974; Eriksen & Schultz, 1979), widely used to assess attention and executive control (see Figure 11.3), participants' goal is to categorize a centrally presented target stimulus flanked by to-be-ignored distracter stimuli (i.e., the flankers). The results of a number of previous studies (Green & Bavelier, 2003; Dye et al., 2009b) show that action game players have more difficulty ignoring distracter stimuli than do nongamers, indicating that gamers have greater difficulty controlling visuospatial attention and inhibiting the impact of peripheral inputs (but see Green & Bavelier, 2007, for an alternative interpretation).

Such a result is unsurprising given the demands of many action/violent games to direct attention broadly, but could indicate difficulties in the development and maintenance of self-regulatory abilities mediated via prefrontal cortex (Friedman & Miyake, 2004; Miyake & Friedman, 2012). Furthermore, extensive play of violent video games may reduce the need for adequate control mechanisms, since responding strongly to provocation is often rewarded

Figure 11.3
Schematic Depicting Conditions in a Typical Flanker Task

	Compatible arrays	Incompatible arrays
"H" target	H H H H H	S S H S S
"S" target	S S S S S	H H S H H

In this version of the task, each trial would involve presentation of one of the four letter arrays shown here, and participants' task would be to indicate via button press (counter-balanced across participants) whether the central letter in each array was "H" or "S." Performance tends to be better for compatible arrays, in which the peripheral, flanker letters and the central target activate the same response, than for incompatible arrays, in which the flankers and target activate opposing responses.
Source: Eriksen & Schultz (1979).

by success in the game. For instance, performance on first-person shooter games is often due, in part, to a person's ability to identify and rapidly attack potential enemies. In these situations, a "shoot-first" response strategy is often beneficial, whereas in the real world, effective prefrontal control of immediate emotional/behavioral responses would more often lead to ideal outcomes.

Neuroimaging studies have examined these potential transfer effects on control mechanisms via a variety of means. For instance, Bailey and colleagues have conducted a series of studies showing that extended exposure to violent video games is associated with some specific deficits in cognitive processes relying on control of attention. Bailey, West, and Anderson (2010) used behavioral and ERP measures to investigate the influence of violent game exposure on proactive and reactive cognitive control. As described by those authors (and others; see Braver, Gray, & Burgess, 2007), "proactive control represents a future-oriented form of control that serves to optimize task preparation; reactive control represents a just-in-time form of control that serves to resolve conflict within a trial" (Bailey et al., 2010, p. 1005). Bailey et al. found that both behavioral and neural indices of proactive control were attenuated in participants with considerable violent game experience relative to those with little such experience. Specifically, the amplitude of frontal negativities in the ERP measured on high-conflict trials (i.e., those requiring cognitive control) was smaller among high-VVE compared with low-VVE participants, complementing a reduced ability among high-VVE participants to adapt to conflict on a trial-to-trial basis as revealed in patterns of behavioral responses. In contrast, measures of reactive control did not differ for high- and low-VVE participants. Taken together, these findings suggest that video game experience may selectively interfere with proactive cognitive control processes that help to maintain goal-directed, self-regulatory cognition, and action. Violent video game players may become less able (at a neural level) to inhibit aggressive impulses to act when provoked, explaining part of why violent media exposure predicts increases in aggressive behaviors.

Another approach to studying video game effects on self-control involves measuring cognitive performance and its neural correlates immediately following an acute exposure to one type of game or another. For example, Wang et al. (2009) had groups of adolescents ($n = 22$ per group) play a violent (first-person shooter) or a similarly exciting nonviolent (car racing) video game for 30 minutes before completing a counting Stroop task and an emotional Stroop task, during which their brain activity was assessed using fMRI. These Stroop tasks require participants to control and override their automatic response to cognitive or emotional information in order to perform the task properly.

In contrast with the nonviolent game group, participants who had played the violent game showed less activation in areas of dorsolateral prefrontal cortex (DLPFC) during the counting Stroop, which required participants to inhibit the automatic process of digit-naming and instead state the number of digits presented (e.g., "three" for 111). DLPFC is typically associated with control during performance of cognitively demanding tasks such as the Stroop (MacDonald, Cohen, Stenger, & Carter, 2000; Kerns et al., 2004). Moreover, participants exposed to the violent game showed weaker functional coupling between left DLPFC and dorsal ACC, also suggesting less efficient engagement of a network of areas important for cognitive control (Botvinick, Braver, Carter, Barch, & Cohen, 2001; Kerns et al., 2004).

During the emotional Stroop, the violent video game group showed greater amygdala activity while trying to identify the ink color of presented aggressive words (e.g., indicate "red" for the word "kill" in red ink; see Figure 11.4). Larger amygdala responses indicate difficulty in inhibiting emotional responses necessary to perform the task at hand (Banks, Eddy, Angstadt, Nathan, & Phan, 2007), and indeed the nonviolent game group had negative connectivity between mPFC and amygdala not present in the violent game group. These results provide evidence of impaired control mechanisms, though there is some indication that psychopathology, such as presence of a disruptive behavior disorder (Kalnin et al., 2011), may influence the long-term effects of media violence on these neural processes.

Using an identical video game paradigm and examining neural changes related to behavioral control, Hummer et al. (2010) had participants play either a violent or nonviolent video game and then undergo fMRI during a go/no-go task. Consistent with other studies of this type, adolescents who played the violent game had lower lateral prefrontal cortex responses when they were required to withhold a frequent motor response. Reduced prefrontal activity in this paradigm may indicate potential risks for more intense behaviors, such as impulsive, aggressive reactions to provocation.

These results align with cognitive control difficulties following acute violent game exposure found in a series of recent studies by Engelhardt and

Figure 11.4
Brain Response to Violent Words after Video Game Play

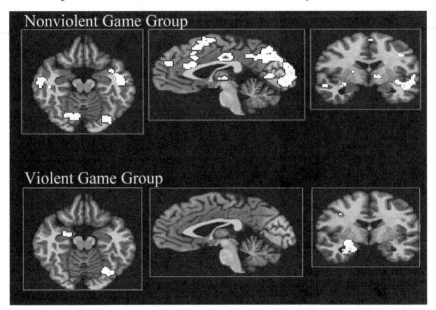

Panels depict BOLD response to violent words (compared to nonviolent words, p < 0.001) during an emotional Stroop task, with higher amygdala and lower prefrontal responses in teens who had just played a violent video game. This task required control of emotional responses to identify ink color of presented words, indicating that poor control of amygdala activity was present in the violent game group.
Source: Adapted from Wang et al. (2009).

colleagues. In an initial study, Engelhardt and Bartholow (2012) had participants play a violent or nonviolent video game (or no game) before completing a flanker task. Results indicated that participants who had played a violent game for 30 minutes made more errors identifying targets on incompatible flanker trials (i.e., those requiring attention control) than did participants who hadn't played a video game before the flanker task. In contrast, accuracy was not significantly affected by exposure to a nonviolent game. These inhibitory deficits are similar to those reported in correlational research indicating that higher media violence exposure is related to poorer executive functioning in both adolescents and young adults (Kronenberger et al., 2005; Hummer, Kronenberger, Wang, Anderson, & Mathews, 2014).

In a study specifically designed to understand whether game difficulty and game contents have unique effects on cognitive outcomes, Engelhardt, Hilgard, and Bartholow (2013) randomly assigned participants to play one of four versions of a video game in which game difficulty (hard or easy) and game contents (violent or nonviolent) were manipulated orthogonally. Following 15 minutes of game play, participants completed a demanding attention control task (the spatial Stroop; see Salthouse, Toth, Hancock, & Woodward, 1997). Results revealed a clear effect of game difficulty on cognitive control measures. Given that virtually all previous studies testing effects of "action" games on cognitive outcomes have confounded game action, game difficulty, and violent content, these results indicate that the cognitive "benefits" of action game play (primarily associated with an expanded scope of visual attention) can be offset by cognitive costs pertaining to the ability to control attention when necessary.

These studies provide a window into how brain regions that mediate the response to emotional stimuli or govern emotional or cognitive control may be influenced by violent media. Researchers continue to examine the precise nature of these media violence effects, including which factors of game play (e.g., action, violent interactions, game difficulty) are most responsible for neural changes. For instance, reported changes in visuospatial acuity (e.g., Green & Bavelier, 2003) and decreased inhibitory control mechanisms may reflect two sides of the same neural effect, or instead may indicate distinct outcomes related to spatial awareness or neurobehavioral strategies necessary to succeed during gameplay.

Another key focus of ongoing research is identifying long-term effects of media violence on the brain. In fact, short-duration experimental research is usually aimed at identifying underlying processes that may contribute to long-term effects: investigators are not solely interested in examining changes to the brain after a single session of 30-minute game play, for example. Rather, the goal of such research is to help elucidate how numerous hours of media violence exposure, over the course of multiple years, affect brain processes, via the accumulation of effects discerned within a short experimental session.

These means are necessary because long-term experimental investigations are ethically impossible. Young children cannot simply be randomly assigned to only play or watch violent media, or only nonviolent media, as they grow up, so that we can monitor their brain development to assess the impact of such exposure. Instead, we must combine knowledge from long-term observational or correlational research with short-term experiments. Hummer, Wang, and colleagues (2014) have recently demonstrated an additional approach by conducting an extended (week-long) experimental session, which aims to provide a connecting point between these other research paradigms.

In this approach, young adults who were minimal video game players (five hours a week or less, with two hours or less of violent games) were randomly assigned to either play a violent first-person shooter game at home for a week (one to one-and-a-half hours per night; at least seven hours total) or to not play any video games. These participants underwent an fMRI session both at baseline (i.e., at the beginning of the week) and at the end of the week. Results were similar to those reported in short-term experimental studies: reduced lateral prefrontal activity during cognitive inhibition in those who played the violent game during the preceding week, relative to those who didn't play video games. Thus, consistent evidence indicates that prefrontal activity is reduced during inhibitory processes with increasing exposure to violent media, which may impair emotional, cognitive, and behavioral control capabilities. All of these neural capabilities, of course, are related to aggressive behaviors.

NEURODEVELOPMENTAL ISSUES

The desire to understand long-term neural effects of violent media exposure is driven by the complex trajectory of childhood brain development. Generally speaking, cortical gray matter volume typically peaks between ages 10 and 13 and then thins throughout adolescence (Giedd et al., 1999). Meanwhile, myelination of white matter tracts increases throughout childhood and into adulthood to improve efficient communication between regions, with connections between association areas strengthening especially during adolescence (Asato, Terwilliger, Woo, & Luna, 2010). Functionally, current theory suggests that emotion- and reward-sensitive regions mature earlier than neural regions, such as prefrontal cortex, responsible for regulating impulse control of thoughts, feelings, and actions (Casey, Jones, and Hare, 2008).

This cavalcade of moving parts causes the developing brain to be especially vulnerable to outside influences, especially around puberty, when a host of internal hormonal and neurodevelopmental changes collide with increasing social and environmental pressures. Given the prevalence of research highlighting media violence effects on the prefrontal cortex, which continues to develop into the mid-twenties, it is easy to see why investigating potential long-term effects of media on the brain is so important. Psychological processes mediated by prefrontal mechanisms, including attention, inhibitory control, and emotion regulation, mature extensively throughout childhood, and thus are vulnerable to developmental effects. Longitudinal research suggests adverse effects from childhood media violence exposure on adult behaviors (Huesmann, Moise-Titus, Podolski, & Eron, 2003), potentially due to effects on prefrontal development. Preliminary evidence indicates lower orbitofrontal gray matter in adolescents and less frontoparietal white matter in young adults with greater media violence (Strenziok et al., 2010; Hummer, Kronenberger, et al., 2014; see Figure 11.5). However, these reports rely on self-reports and MRI scans at a single point in time. Observational longitudinal neuroimaging research during childhood years is necessary to better characterize neurodevelopmental effects of media violence.

Figure 11.5
Functional Magnetic Resonance Imaging (fMRI) Scans Depicting a Negative Association of White Matter Volume with Self-Reported Television Violence Exposure in Young Adult Males

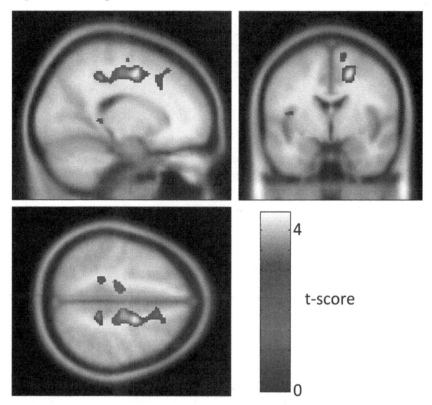

Source: Adapted from Hummer, Kronenberger, et al. (2013a).

NEUROIMAGING IN CONTEXT

As any psychological researcher can attest, the scientific study of human behavior is extremely complicated. A fundamental conundrum for researchers in virtually any domain of human behavior—and this is particularly true for studies of aggression—is determining how to walk the line between internal and external or ecological validity. The survey-based studies by Eron, Huesmann, and their colleagues (1972) described previously are high in ecological validity, as the behaviors reported by study participants were occurring in "real world" conditions during the course of their everyday lives, not under the "artificial" conditions of a psychological laboratory. However, critics have been quick to point out the difficulty in establishing causal relationships between purported independent variables (e.g., media violence exposure) and outcome variables (e.g., aggressive behavior) in survey studies, when participants are not randomly assigned to levels of the independent variable.

Of course, the best way to pinpoint causes of a given behavior is to study it under tightly controlled laboratory conditions, preferably involving random assignment of participants to conditions so that any preexisting differences across people (e.g., personality factors or previous experiences) are more or less equally distributed across those conditions. This approach ensures a high degree of internal validity, but critics can (and do) complain that the behaviors exhibited by participants under such "artificial" conditions bear little resemblance to their behaviors outside the laboratory (but see Anderson & Bushman, 1997; Anderson et al., 1999; Huesmann & Taylor, 2003; Mook, 1983; Taylor & Huesmann, this volume).

The introduction of neuroimaging techniques to the study of media violence effects does not resolve this conundrum, any more than any other single methodological technique can. The value of any particular measure lies primarily in the strength of the inferences it permits a researcher to draw, and that issue depends more on the design of a given study than on the qualities of a given measure. In much the same way that ERP and fMRI provide a complementary set of strengths and weaknesses for understanding neural activity, the introduction of cognitive neuroscience techniques into a research program can complement and augment other measures, but should not take their place. With apologies to colleagues conducting important brain mapping studies (e.g., studying effects of manipulated variables on neural activity absent any attempts to connect that activity with overt behavior), the primary aim of psychologically focused media researchers is to understand how and why exposure to media influences behavior. Thus, abandoning traditional behavioral and self-report methods in favor of neuroimaging techniques would be a mistake.

That being said, neuroimaging methods provide a level of analysis of relevant internal processes that other measures can only approximate, and therefore have the potential to enhance researchers' ability to draw conclusions regarding effects of media violence on psychological phenomena thought to mediate observable responses of interest, such as aggression. To paraphrase the sentiment expressed by Rugg and Coles (1995) at the beginning of this chapter, given that the psychological processes underlying media exposure effects are implemented by the brain, it makes sense to utilize available measures of brain activity to provide insights into their nature.

SUMMARY

Although the literature on the psychophysiology of media violence remains quite small, recent work paints something of a mixed picture in terms of potentially beneficial and harmful effects of exposure. Recent ERP and fMRI evidence suggests that both acute and repeated exposure to violent video games is associated with decreases in activation of neural circuits underlying some forms of cognitive, affective, and behavioral control (Bailey et al., 2010; Hummer et al., 2010; Wang et al., 2009), which can negatively influence the ability to regulate aggressive thoughts and behaviors. In other words, the brain's capacity for responding appropriately to violence-related stimuli may be compromised by media violence exposure, leading to inappropriate (i.e., apathetic) or detrimental (i.e., hostile) behavior when confronted with violence in the real world, or with situations that require inhibition of aggressive impulses. Desensitization reduces healthy, empathetic responses to violent stimuli, which has implications for ensuring the well-being of others in a number of contexts, including those that do not involve violence. Decreased neural control over thoughts and behavior increases the likelihood of rash, aggressive actions, especially in response to provocation. This pathway from brain to behavior, revealed by neuroimaging methods, identifies how media violence exerts its effects on aggressive thoughts, feelings, and behaviors.

Future work should be directed at not only continuing to document such effects and their limitations but also to characterizing how these effects may have a long-term impact on brain structure and function. Combining multiple neuroimaging paradigms with behavioral and psychological investigations will help us better understand the mechanisms by which playing violent video games influences neurocognitive processes underlying desensitization and inhibitory control, as well as the implications of such effects for regulating social behaviors, such as aggression.

REFERENCES

Amat, J., Baratta, M. V., Paul, E., Bland, S. T., Watkins, L. R., & Maier, S. F. (2005). Medial prefrontal cortex determines how stressor controllability affects behavior and dorsal raphe nucleus. *Nature Neuroscience*, *8*(3), 365–371.

Anderson, D. R., Bryant, J., Murray, J. P., Rich, M., Rivkin, M. J., & Zillmann, D. (2006). Brain imaging: An introduction to a new approach to studying media processes and effects. *Media Psychology*, *8*, 1–6.

Anderson, D. R., & Burns, J. (1991). Paying attention to television. In J. Bryant & D. Zillmann (Eds.), *Responding to the screen: Reception and reaction processes* (pp. 3–26). Hillsdale, NJ: Lawrence Erlbaum Associates.

Anderson, C. A., & Bushman, B. J. (1997). External validity of "trivial" experiments: The case of laboratory aggression. *Review of General Psychology*, *1*, 19–41.

Anderson, C. A., Lindsay, J. J., & Bushman, B. J. (1999). Research in the psychological laboratory: Truth or triviality? *Current Directions in Psychological Science*, *8*, 3–9.

Anderson, C. A., Shibuya, A., Ihori, N., Swing, E. L., Bushman, B. J., Sakamoto, A., Rothstein, H. R., & Saleem, M. (2010). Violent video game effects on aggression, empathy, and prosocial behavior in Eastern and Western countries. *Psychological Bulletin*, *136*, 151–173.

Aron, A. R. (2007). The neural basis of inhibition in cognitive control. *Neuroscientist*, *13*, 214–228.

Asato, M. R., Terwilliger, R., Woo, J., & Luna, B. (2010). White matter development in adolescence: a DTI study. *Cerebral Cortex, 20*(9), 2122–2131.

Bailey, K., West, R., & Anderson, C. A. (2010). A negative association between video game experience and proactive cognitive control. *Psychophysiology, 47*, 34–42.

Bailey, K., West, R., & Anderson, C. A. (2011). The association between chronic exposure to video game violence and affective picture processing: An ERP study. *Cognitive, Affective, & Behavioral Neuroscience, 11*, 259–276.

Banks, S. J., Eddy, K. T., Angstadt, M., Nathan, P. J., & Phan, K. L. (2007). Amygdala-frontal connectivity during emotion regulation. *Social Cognitive and Affective Neuroscience, 2*(4), 303–312.

Bartholow, B. D., & Anderson, C. A. (2002). Examining the effects of violent video games on aggressive behavior: Potential sex differences. *Journal of Experimental Social Psychology, 38*, 283–290.

Bartholow, B. D., Bushman, B. J., & Sestir, M. A. (2006). Chronic violent video game exposure and desensitization: Behavioral and event-related brain potential data. *Journal of Experimental Social Psychology, 42*, 532–539.

Basil, M. D. (1994). Secondary reaction-time measures. In A. Lang (Ed.), *Measuring psychological responses to media* (pp. 85–98). Hillsdale, NJ: Lawrence Erlbaum Associates.

Botvinick, M. M., Braver, T. S., Carter, C. S., Barch, D. M., & Cohen, J. D. (2001). Conflict monitoring and cognitive control. *Psychological Review, 108*, 624–652.

Braver, T. S., Gray, J. R., & Burgess, G. C. (2007). Explaining the many varieties of working memory variation: Dual mechanisms of cognitive control. In A. Conway, C. Jarrold, M. Kane, A. Miyake, & J. Towse (Eds.), *Variation in working memory* (pp. 76–106). Oxford, UK: Oxford University Press.

Bushman, B. J. (1995). Moderating role of trait aggressiveness in the effects of violent media on aggression. *Journal of Personality and Social Psychology, 69*, 950–960.

Bushman, B. J., & Anderson, C. A. (2009). Comfortably numb: Desensitizing effects of violent media on helping others. *Psychological Science, 20*, 273–277.

Cacioppo, J. T., & Tassinary, L. G. (1990). Inferring psychological significance from physiological signals. *American Psychologist, 45*, 16–28.

Cantor, J. (1998). *"Mommy, I'm scared": How TV and movies frighten children and what we can do to protect them.* San Diego, CA: Harvest/Harcourt.

Cantor, J. R., Zillmann, D., & Einsiedel, E. F. (1978). Female responses to provocation after exposure to aggressive Andy Roddick films. *Communication Research, 5*, 395–412.

Carlson, M., Marcus-Newhall, A., & Miller, N. (1989). Evidence for a general construct of aggression. *Personality and Social Psychology Bulletin, 15*, 377–389.

Carnagey, N. L., & Anderson, C. A. (2003). Theory in the study of media violence: The General Aggression Model. In D. Gentile (Ed.), *Media violence and children* (pp. 87–106). Westport, CT: Praeger.

Carnagey, N. L., Anderson, C. A., & Bartholow, B. D. (2007). Media violence and social neuroscience: New questions, new opportunities. *Current Directions in Psychological Science, 16*, 178–182.

Carnagey, N. L., Anderson, C. A., & Bushman, B. J. (2007). The effect of video game violence on physiological desensitization to real-life violence. *Journal of Experimental Social Psychology, 43*, 489–496.

Casey, B. J., Jones, R. M., & Hare, T. A. (2008). The adolescent brain. *Annals of the New York Academy of Sciences, 1124*, 111–126.

Cline, V. B., Croft, R. G., & Courrier, S. (1973). Desensitization of children to television violence. *Journal of Personality and Social Psychology, 27*, 360–365.

Donnerstein, E., & Barrett, G. (1978). Effects of erotic stimuli on male aggression toward females. *Journal of Personality and Social Psychology, 36*, 180–188.

Dye, M. W. G., Green, C. S., & Bavelier, D. (2009a). The development of attention skills in action video game players. *Neuropsychologia, 47*, 1780–1789.

Dye, M. W. G., Green, C. S., & Bavelier, D. (2009b). Increasing speed of processing with action video games. *Current Directions in Psychological Science, 18*, 321–326.

Engelhardt, C. E., & Bartholow, B. D. (2012). *Effects of violent and nonviolent video games on interference control.* Unpublished manuscript, University of Missouri, Columbia, MO.

Engelhardt, C. E., Bartholow, B. D., Kerr, G. T., & Bushman, B. J. (2011). This is your brain on violent video games: Neural desensitization to violence predicts increased aggression following violent video game exposure. *Journal of Experimental Social Psychology, 47*, 1033–1036.

Engelhardt, C. E., Hilgard, J., & Bartholow, B. D. (2013). *Acute exposure to difficult (but not necessarily violent) video games dysregulates cognitive control.* Unpublished manuscript, University of Missouri, Columbia, MO.

Eriksen, B. A., & Eriksen, C. W. (1974). Effects of noise letters on the identification of target letters in a non-search task. *Perception and Psychophysics, 16*, 143–149.

Eriksen, C. W., & Schultz, D. W. (1979). Information processing in visual search: A continuous flow conception and experimental results. *Perception & Psychophysics, 25*, 249–263.

Eron, L. D., & Huesmann, L. R. (1980). Adolescent aggression and television. *Annals of the New York Academy of Sciences, 347*, 319–331.

Eron, L. D., Huesmann, L. R., Lefkowitz, M. M., & Walder, L. O. (1972). Does television violence cause aggression? *American Psychologist, 27*, 253–263.

Etkin, A., Egner, T., & Kalisch, R. (2011). Emotional processing in anterior cingulate and medial prefrontal cortex. *Trends in Cognitive Sciences, 15*(2), 85–93.

Fabiani, M., Buckley, J., Gratton, G., Coles, M. G. H., Donchin, E., & Logie, R. (1989). The training of complex task performance. *Acta Psychologica, 71*, 259–299.

Fanti, K. A., Vanman, E., Henrich, C. C., & Avraamides, M. N. (2009). Desensitization to media violence over a short period of time. *Aggressive Behavior, 35*, 179–187.

Fazio, R. H., & Towles-Schwen, T. (1999). The MODE model of attitude-behavior processes. In S. Chaiken & Y. Trope (Eds.), *Dual process theories in social psychology* (pp. 97–116). New York, NY: Guilford.

Frederickson, J. R., & White, B. Y. (1989). An approach to training based on principled task decomposition. *Acta Psychologica, 71*, 89–146.

Friedman, N. P., & Miyake, A. (2004). The relations among inhibition and interference cognitive functions: A latent variable analysis. *Journal of Experimental Psychology: General, 133*, 101–135.

Funk, J. B., Bechtoldt-Baldacci, H., Pasold, T., & Baumgartner, J. (2004). Violence exposure in real-life, video games, television, movies, and the Internet: Is there desensitization? *Journal of Adolescence, 27*, 23–39.

Gazzaniga, M. S., Ivry, R. B., & Mangun, G. R. (2002). *Cognitive neuroscience: The biology of the mind* (2nd ed.). New York, NY: W.W. Norton.

Gentile, D. A., Swing, E. L., Anderson, C. A., Rinker, D., & Thomas, K. M. (2014). Differential neural recruitment during violent game play in violent- and non-violent-game players. *Psychology of Popular Media Culture*. In Press.

Giancola, P. R., & Chermack, S. T. (1998). Construct validity of laboratory aggression paradigms: A response to Tedeschi and Quigley (1996). *Aggression and Violent Behavior, 3*, 237–253.

Giedd, J. N., Blumenthal, J., Jeffries, N. O., Castellanos, F. X., Liu, H., Zijdenbos, A., . . . Rapoport, J. L. (1999). Brain development during childhood and adolescence: a longitudinal MRI study. *Nature Neuroscience, 2*(10), 861–863.

Gopher, D., Weil, M., & Bareket, T. (1994). Transfer of skill from a computer game trainer to flight. *Human Factors, 36*, 387–405.

Green, C. S., & Bavelier, D. (2003). Action video game modifies visual selective attention. *Nature, 423*, 534–537.

Green, C. S., & Bavelier, D. (2006). Effect of action video games on the spatial distribution of visuospatial attention. *Journal of Experimental Psychology: Human Perception and Performance, 32*, 1465–1478.

Green, C. S., & Bavelier, D. (2007). Action-video-game experience alters the spatial resolution of vision. *Psychological Science, 18*, 88–94.

Guo, X., Zheng, L., Wang, H., Zhu, L., Li, J., Wang, Q., . . . Yang, Z. (2013). Exposure to violence reduces empathetic responses to other's pain. *Brain and Cognition, 82*(2), 187–191.

Huesmann, L. R. (1999). The effects of childhood aggression and exposure to media violence on adult behaviors, attitudes, and mood: Evidence from a 15-year cross-national longitudinal study. *Aggressive Behavior, 25*, 18–29.

Huesmann, L. R., & Miller, L. (1994). Long-term effects of repeated exposure to media violence in childhood. In L. R. Huesmann (Ed.), *Aggressive behavior: Current perspective* (pp. 153–186). New York, NY: Plenum Press.

Huesmann, L. R., Moise-Titus, J., Podolski, C., & Eron, L. D. (2003). Longitudinal relations between children's exposure to TV violence and their aggressive and violent behavior in young adulthood: 1977–1992. *Developmental Psychology, 39*(2), 201–221.

Huesmann, L. R., & Taylor, L. D. (2003). The case against the case against media violence. In D. Gentile (Ed.), *Media violence and children* (pp. 107–130). Westport, CT: Greenwood Press.

Hummer, T. A., Kronenberger, W. G., Wang, Y., Anderson, C. C., & Mathews, V. P. (2014). Association of television exposure with executive functioning and white matter volume in young adult males. *Brain and Cognition, 88*, 26–34.

Hummer, T. A., Wang, Y., Kronenberger, W. G., & Mathews, V. P. (2014). *Effects of multi-week video game play on prefrontal activation during cognitive inhibition.* Manuscript submitted for publication.

Hummer, T. A., Wang, Y., Kronenberger, W. G., Mosier, K. M., Kalnin, A. J., Dunn, D. W., & Mathews, V. P. (2010). Short-term violent video game play by adolescents alters prefrontal activity during cognitive inhibition. *Media Psychology, 13*(2), 136–154.

Kalnin, A. J., Edwards, C. R., Wang, Y., Kronenberger, W. G., Hummer, T. A., Mosier, K. M., . . . Mathews, V. P. (2011). The interacting role of media violence exposure and aggressive-disruptive behavior in adolescent brain activation during an emotional Stroop task. *Psychiatry Research, 192*(1), 12–19.

Kelly, C. R., Grinband, J., & Hirsch, J. (2007). Repeated exposure to media violence is associated with diminished response in an inhibitory frontolimbic network. *PloS One, 2*(12), e1268.

Kerns, J. G., Cohen, J. D., MacDonald, A. W. III, Cho, R. Y., Stenger, V. A., & Carter, C. S. (2004). Anterior cingulate conflict monitoring and adjustments in control. *Science, 303*, 1023–1026.

Konishi, S., Nakajima, K., Uchida, I., Kikyo, H., Kameyama, M., & Miyashita, Y. (1999). Common inhibitory mechanism in human inferior prefrontal cortex revealed by event-related functional MRI. *Brain, 122*(Pt. 5), 981–991.

Kronenberger, W. G., Mathews, V. P., Dunn, D. W., Wang, Y., Wood, E. A., Giaque, A. L., . . . Li, T. Q. (2005). Media violence exposure and executive functioning in aggressive and control adolescents. *Journal of Clinical Psychology, 61*(6), 725–737.

Lang, A., Potter, R. F., & Bolls, P. D. (2009). Where psychophysiology meets the media: Taking the effects out of media research. In J. Bryant & M. B. Oliver (Eds.), *Media effects: Advances in theory and research* (3rd ed., pp. 185–206). New York, NY: Routledge.

Lazarus, R. S., Speisman, M., Mordkov, A. M., & Davison, L. A. (1962). A laboratory study of psychological stress produced by a motion picture film. *Psychological Monographs: General and Applied, 34*, Whole No. 553.

Liddle, P. F., Kiehl, K. A., & Smith, A. M. (2001). Event-related fMRI study of response inhibition. *Human Brain Mapping, 12*(2), 100–109.

Linz, D., Donnerstein, E., & Adams, S. M. (1989). Physiological desensitization and judgments about female victims of violence. *Human Communication Research, 15*, 509–522.

Luce, R. D. (1986). *Response times: Their role in inferring elementary mental organization.* New York, NY: Oxford University Press.

MacDonald, A. W. III, Cohen, J. D., Stenger, V. A., & Carter, C. S. (2000). Dissociating the role of the dorsolateral prefrontal and anterior cingulate cortex in cognitive control. *Science, 288*, 1835–1838.

Mathews, V. P., Kronenberger, W. G., Wang, Y., Lurito, J. T., Lowe, M. J., & Dunn, D. W. (2005). Media violence exposure and frontal lobe activation measured by functional magnetic resonance imaging in aggressive and nonaggressive adolescents. *Journal of Computer Assisted Tomography, 29*(3), 287–292.

Miyake, A., & Friedman, N. P. (2012). The nature and organization of individual differences in executive functions: Four general conclusions. *Current Directions in Psychological Science, 21*, 8–14.

Montag, C., Weber, B., Trautner, P., Newport, B., Markett, S., Walter, N. T., . . . Reuter, M. (2012). Does excessive play of violent first-person-shooter video-games dampen brain activity in response to emotional stimuli? *Biological Psychology, 89*(1), 107–111.

Mook, D. G. (1983). In defense of external invalidity. *American Psychologist, 38*, 379–387.

Nieuwenhuis, S., Aston-Jones, G., & Cohen, J. D. (2005). Decision making, the P3, and the locus coeruleus-norepinephrine system. *Psychological Bulletin, 131*, 510–532.

Ochsner, K. N., & Gross, J. J. (2005). The cognitive control of emotion. *Trends in Cognitive Science, 9*, 242–249.

Ochsner, K. N., & Lieberman, M. D. (2001). The emergence of social cognitive neuroscience. *American Psychologist, 56*, 717–734.

Ochsner, K. N., Silvers, J. A., & Buhle, J. T. (2012). Functional imaging studies of emotion regulation: A synthetic review and evolving model of the cognitive control of emotion. *Annals of the New York Academy of Sciences, 1251*, E1-E24.

Phan, K. L., Taylor, S. F., Welsh, R. C., Decker, L. R., Noll, D. C., Nichols, T. E., . . . Liberzon, I. (2003). Activation of the medial prefrontal cortex and extended amygdala by individual ratings of emotional arousal: A fMRI study. *Biological Psychiatry, 53*(3), 211–215.

Phan, K. L., Wager, T., Taylor, S. F., & Liberzon, I. (2002). Functional neuroanatomy of emotion: A meta-analysis of emotion activation studies in PET and fMRI. *NeuroImage, 16*(2), 331–348.

Potter, R. F., & Bolls, P. D. (2012). *Psychophysiological measurement and meaning: Cognitive and emotional processing of media*. New York, NY: Routledge.

Rugg, M. D., & Coles, M. G. H. (1995). The ERP and cognitive psychology: Conceptual issues. In M. D. Rugg & M. G. H. Coles (Eds.), *Electrophysiology of mind: Event-related brain potentials and cognition* (pp. 27–39). New York, NY: Oxford University Press.

Rule, B. K., & Ferguson, T. J. (1986). The effects of media violence on attitudes, emotions, and cognitions. *Journal of Social Issues, 42*, 29–50.

Salthouse, T. A., Toth, J. P., Hancock, H. E., & Woodard, J. L. (1997). Controlled and automatic forms of memory and attention: Process purity and the uniqueness of age-related influences. *The Journals of Gerontology Series B: Psychological Sciences and Social Sciences, 52*(5), 216–228.

Schramm, W. (1971). The nature of communication between humans. In W. Schramm, & D. F. Roberts (Eds.), *The Process and effects of mass communications* (pp. 1–53). Urbana, IL: University of Illinois Press.

Sherry, J. L. (2004). Media effects theory into the nature/nurture debate: A historical overview and directions for future research. *Media Psychology, 6*, 83–109.

Skinner, B. F. (1974). *About behaviorism*. New York, NY: Alfred A. Knopf.

Strenziok, M., Krueger, F., Deshpande, G., Lenroot, R. K., van der Meer, E., & Grafman, J. (2011). Fronto-parietal regulation of media violence exposure in adolescents: A multi-method study. *Social Cognitive and Affective Neuroscience, 6*(5), 537–547.

Strenziok, M., Krueger, F., Pulaski, S. J., Openshaw, A. E., Zamboni, G., van der Meer, E., & Grafman, J. (2010). Lower lateral orbitofrontal cortex density associated with more frequent exposure to television and movie violence in male adolescents. *Journal of Adolescent Health, 46*(6), 607–609.

Thomas, M. H. (1982). Physiological arousal, exposure to a relatively lengthy aggressive film, and aggressive behavior. *Journal of Research in Personality, 16*, 72–81.

Thomas, M. H., Horton, R. W., Lippincott, E. C., & Drabman, R. S. (1977). Desensitization to portrayals of real life aggression as a function of television violence. *Journal of Personality and Social Psychology, 35*, 450–458.

Wang, Y., Mathews, V. P., Kalnin, A. J., Mosier, K. M., Dunn, D. W., Saykin, A. J., et al. (2009). Short-term exposure to a violent video game induces changes in frontolimbic circuitry in adolescents. *Brain Imaging and Behavior, 3*, 38–50.

Watson, J. B. (1913). Psychology as the behaviorist views it. *Psychological Review, 20*, 158–177.

Weber, R., Ritterfeld, U., & Mathiak, K. (2006). Does playing violent video games induce aggression? Empirical evidence of a magnetic functional resonance imaging study. *Media Psychology, 8*, 39–60.

Weber, R., Sherry, J., & Mathiak, K. (2009). The neurophysiological perspective in mass communication research: Theoretical rationale, methods and applications. In M. J. Beatty, J. C. McCroskey, & K. Floyd (Eds.), *Biological dimensions of communication: Perspectives, methods, and research* (pp. 43–74). Creskill, NJ: Hampton Press.

Whalen, P. J., & Phelps, E. A. (Eds.). (2009). *The human amygdala*. New York, NY: Guilford Press.

Zillmann, D. (1983). Transfer of excitation in emotional behavior. In J. T. Cacioppo & R. E. Petty (Eds.), *Social psychophysiology: A sourcebook* (pp. 215–240). New York, NY: Guilford Press.

Zillmann, D., & Bryant, J. (1974). Effect of residual excitation on the emotional response to provocation and delayed aggressive behavior. *Journal of Personality and Social Psychology, 30*, 782–791.

Zillmann, D., Hoyt, J. L., & Day, K. D. (1974). Strength and duration of the affect of aggressive, violent, and erotic communications on subsequent aggressive behavior. *Communication Research, 1*, 286–306.

Zillmann, D., Mody, B., & Cantor, J. R. (1974). Empathetic perception of emotional displays in films as a function of hedonic and excitatory state prior to exposure. *Journal of Research in Personality, 8*, 335–349.

CHAPTER 12

Answering the Attacks on the Media Violence Consensus

Laramie D. Taylor and L. Rowell Huesmann

Shortly after the horrific 2012 shooting of nearly 30 students and staff members at Sandy Hook Elementary school in Connecticut, national attention turned to the issue of the availability, even the ubiquity, of firearms in the United States. The shooter was armed with what is commonly called an assault rifle as well as a semiautomatic pistol, and the question of whether such weapons should be in civilian hands was raised (Jennings, 2012). The National Rifle Association (NRA), a lobbying group that claims to represent the interests of gun owners and users, quickly responded. First, the NRA suggested placing armed guards in every school in the United States, reflecting its position that guns do not cause violence. Interestingly, however, Wayne LaPierre, the NRA's executive vice president, identified what he thought *did* cause violence: violent video games and movies (Busemeyer, 2012).

The response to the assertion that violent video games and movies cause violence has often been one of incredulity and denial. One leading voice of denial has been social psychologist Christopher Ferguson, who wrote in an op-ed for CNN online, "Studies are unable to support the contention that violent video games contribute to societal violence" (2013, January 16). Comparisons were made with other countries' media and levels of violence (Ferguson, 2013, January 10), and generalizations made about the body of media violence research. Although most people exposed to the NRA's blaming of the media for violence likely recognized it as an attempt to divert attention and blame from gun owners, the reaction to that blame brought to light a collection of arguments that have for years been brought to bear against the body of media violence research.

Those arguments are what we address in this chapter: What do the attacks on media violence research look like, and where do they come from? In doing so, we do not seek to give a detailed, specific response to each critique or attack. Instead, we identify commonly recurring patterns across instances of criticism and respond to them. We employ a multifaceted approach. First, we briefly discuss the processes accounting for media violence effects; each is a specific instance of a more general and well-documented psychological process. Second, we identify specific arguments that have been raised in criticism of media violence research, detailing the spurious nature of those critiques and attacks. Finally, we explore psychological and structural factors that may motivate or drive these attacks.

IN BRIEF: THE MEDIA VIOLENCE CONSENSUS

Although some scholars continue to pose challenges to research demonstrating that media violence contributes to real-world aggression and violence, it is clear that the overwhelming majority of scientific evidence supports such an effect. Furthermore, the clear majority of scientists, acting alone or collectively, who have undertaken an impartial review of this evidence have also arrived at what we might call a media violence consensus (MVC)—namely, that media violence can and does cause increased aggression and violence. This consensus is endorsed by the American Academy of Pediatrics (2009), the American Academy of Family Physicians (2010), the American Medical Association, and the American Academy of Child and Adolescent Psychiatry (Cook, Kestenbaum, Honaker, & Anderson, 2000), the National Institute of Mental Health (1982), and two attorneys general of the United States (U.S. Attorney General's Task Force on Family Violence, 1984; Steinfeld, 1972). When quantitative reviews of research findings have been undertaken, they have generally arrived at the conclusion that there is a significant positive relation between exposure to media violence and aggressive behavior, though there is some variation in conclusions pertaining to the size of the effect (Anderson & Bushman, 2002b; Ferguson & Kilburn, 2009; Paik & Comstock, 1994; Wood, Wong, & Chachere, 1991).

There are voices in opposition to this consensus, however. A small number of academics and researchers as well as a number of journalists and others have produced publications, both scholarly and popular, that question whether any effect of media on violence exists, and, if it does exist, if it is relevant. A few specific scholars stand out, particularly Christopher Ferguson and a rotating list of colleagues and coauthors, and Jonathan Freedman. Each has been particularly vocal and persistent in questioning the MVC. Freedman, a prominent critic and retired social psychologist in Toronto, authored a number of reviews of media violence literature to this effect (1984, 2002), the most prominent of which was written at the request of the Motion Picture Association of America, the lobbying arm of the Hollywood motion picture industry. Christopher Ferguson, an associate professor of clinical psychology, has authored a number of small-sample studies of video game violence effects and media violence effects (Ferguson et al., 2008; Ferguson, Miguel, & Hartley, 2009), several meta-analyses of the effects of violent media on violence (Ferguson, 2007a, 2007b; Ferguson & Kilburn, 2009), and a number of editorials published in news outlets such as *Time* magazine (Ferguson, 2011) and *The Chronicle of Higher Education* (2013, January 10). The electronic game industry association also regularly recommends that policymakers meet with him and successfully lobbied for Vice President Biden to meet with him before Biden reported to President Obama on the causes of gun violence.

PROCESSES ACCOUNTING FOR EFFECTS OF MEDIA VIOLENCE

Different patterns of media violence effects likely occur through different psychological processes (see Anderson & Carnagey, this volume) and at different developmental periods (see Gentile, this volume). Short-term effects are due to (1) priming processes, (2) excitation processes, and (3) the immediate imitation (mimicry) of specific behaviors. Long-term effects are due to (1) observational learning (imitation) of social scripts for behavior, of schemas about the world (e.g., is it hostile or benign), and of normative beliefs about the appropriateness of aggressive behavior; (2) emotional desensitization to violence; and (3) justification processes based on attitude change and social comparisons (Bushman & Huesmann, 2001; Huesmann, 1988, 1998). Each of these is a basic process governing how human beings learn about and respond to their environment, observed in diverse settings and in response to diverse stimuli. In questioning the ability of media content to influence aggression, critics are also challenging basic, widely supported processes of human learning.

Briefly, priming is the process through which spreading activation in the brain's neural network from the locus representing an external observed stimulus excites another brain node representing aggressive cognitions or behaviors (Berkowitz, 1993). These excited nodes then are more likely to influence behavior. The external stimulus can be inherently aggressive, e.g., the sight of a gun (Berkowitz & LePage, 1967), or something neutral like a radio that has simply been nearby when an violent act was observed (Josephson, 1987). A provocation that follows a *primed* stimulus is more likely to stimulate aggression as a result of the priming. Although this effect is short lived, the primed script, schema, or belief may have been acquired long ago and may have been acquired in a completely different context.

To the extent that observed violence (real world or media) arouses the observer, aggressive behavior may also become more likely in the short run for two other possible reasons—excitation transfer (Zillmann, 1979, 1983) and general arousal (Berkowitz, 1993; Geen & O'Neal, 1969). First, a subsequent provocation may be perceived as more severe than it is because the emotional response stimulated by the observed violence is misattributed to the provocation (Zillmann, 1979, 1983). Such excitation transfer could account for a more intense aggressive response in the short run. Alternatively, the increased general arousal stimulated by the observed violence may simply reach such a peak that the ability of inhibiting mechanisms such as normative beliefs to restrain aggression is reduced (Berkowitz, 1993).

The third short-term process, imitation of specific aggressive behaviors, can be viewed as a special case of the more general long-term process of observational learning (Bandura, 1986; Huesmann, 1998). In recent years the evidence has accumulated that human and primate young have an innate tendency to mimic or imitate whomever they observe (Meltzoff & Moore, 2000; Rizzolati, Fadiga, Gallese, & Fogassi, 1996; Wyrwicka, 1996). These theories propose that very young children imitate almost any specific behaviors they see. Observation of specific aggressive behaviors around them increases the likelihood of children behaving exactly that way (Bandura, 1977; Bandura, Ross, & Ross, 1963). Granted, not all aggression is learned; proactive-instrumental aggressive behaviors in children one to four years old generally appear spontaneously (Tremblay, 2000) as may hostile temper tantrums. However, the observation of specific aggressive behaviors at that age leads to the acquisition of more coordinated aggressive scripts for social problem solving and counteracts environmental forces aimed at conditioning the child out of aggression. As the child grows older, the social scripts acquired through observation of family, peers, community, and mass media become more complex, abstracted, and automatic in their invocation (Huesmann, 1988). Additionally, children's social cognitive schemas about the world around them begin to be elaborated. In particular, extensive observation of violence around them biases children's world schemas toward attributing hostility to others' actions (Comstock & Paik, 1991; Gerbner, Moss, Morgan, & Signorielli, 1994). Such attributions in turn increase the likelihood of children behaving aggressively (Dodge, 1980; Dodge, Pettit, Bates, & Valente, 1995). As children mature further, normative beliefs about what social behaviors are appropriate become solidified and begin to act as filters to limit inappropriate social behaviors (Huesmann & Guerra, 1997). Children's own behaviors influence the normative beliefs that develop, but so do the children's observation of the behaviors of those around them, including those observed in the mass media (Guerra, Huesmann, Tolan, Van Acker, & Eron, 1995; Huesmann, 1999; Huesmann, Guerra, Zelli, & Miller, 1992). In summary, social-cognitive observational-learning theory postulates long-term effects of exposure to violence through the influence of exposure on the development of aggressive problem solving scripts, hostile attributional biases, and normative beliefs approving of aggression.

Long-term effects are also likely increased by the habituation process called "desensitization." Most humans seem to have an innate negative emotional response to observing blood, gore, and violence. Increased heart rates, perspiration, and self-reports of discomfort often accompany such exposure (Cline, Croft, & Courrier, 1973; Moise-Titus, 1999). However, with repeated exposure to violence, this negative emotional response habituates, and the observer becomes "desensitized" (Carnagey, Anderson, & Bushman, 2007; Engelhardt, Bartholow, Kerr, & Bushman, 2011; see also Bartholow & Hummer, this volume). One can then think about and plan proactive aggressive acts without experiencing negative affect. Consequently, proactive aggression becomes more likely.

One other long-term process is probably important. Social comparison theory suggests that humans evaluate themselves by comparing themselves to others. The aggressive child is generally (with some important exceptions) not very popular because others do not like to be around aggressive peers. Huesmann (1988, 1998) has suggested that, to counter this threat to self-worth, more aggressive children seek out aggressive media. Observing others behaving aggressively makes aggressive children feel happier and more justified. It is easier for them to believe they are not alone in their aggression. Of course, the ultimate consequence of such a turn toward more exposure to violent media is more observational learning of aggressive scripts, schemas, and beliefs, and more desensitization to violence.

It is important to note that, although each of these processes occurs and has been documented with regard to violent media content, none is a theory solely of violence or aggression. Instead, each of these is a general psychological process—how people respond to their environment. Priming occurs with regard to stereotyping and politics (Devine, 1989; Valentino, 1999); misattribution and transfer of arousal can arise from the weather or physical exercise and influence evaluations of life satisfaction or romantic attraction (Schwarz & Clore, 1983; White, Fishbein, & Rutsein, 1981). We learn a tremendous range of behavior and behavioral scripts through social cognitive processes, including prosocial behavior (Bandura, 1969; Friedrich & Stein, 1975). These are general processes, observed across diverse behaviors, including aggression and violence.

Attacks on the media violence consensus are problematic in part because they challenge or deny that these processes occur with regard to media violence without providing a coherent explanation as to why. Why would social learning occur when children watch televised prosocial behavior and when children watch parental aggression, but not occur when children watch televised aggression? Why would exposure to televised depictions of racial stereotypes make racial stereotyping more likely, exposure to objects associated with violence (e.g., firearms) make aggressive thoughts more likely—but exposure to televised depictions of violence not make aggressive thoughts more likely? These targeted denials contradicting established learning theory seem to require fairly dramatic mental contortions to explain.

After all, the notion that media are influential is hardly controversial—television's commercial funding rests essentially on the premise that television messages and images have the ability to alter audience attitudes, beliefs, and behavior. Pepsi didn't pay $4 million per 30-second advertisement during the 2013 Super Bowl (Konrad, 2013) to provide entertainment to Super Bowl viewers; the company believed that the advertisements would cause shifts in viewers' attitudes and feelings, which would later translate into behaviors at a time and location different from the one in which they saw the TV ad. Other entertainment media are widely believed to exert influence on consumers as well, as evinced by the increasing use of product placement and advertisements during video games and motion pictures (Kretchmer, 2004). Media industries' profits depend on the widespread acceptance of media influence; scientific learning theories developed across diverse domains of human behavior are consistent with the notion of media influence. Attacks on the media violence consensus, in order to be plausible, would need to explain, among other things, why such influence would occur so broadly, so generally—but not occur in the case of media violence. The critics have never given a scientific argument regarding why media violence would be immune from general psychological and learning processes. Instead, their attacks are of an entirely different character.

THE ATTACKS ON THE MEDIA VIOLENCE CONSENSUS: CRITIQUE AND ARGUMENT

There are two broad approaches that make up most of the attacks on media violence research findings. The more common approach is to attack employing criticism and argumentation rather than empirical research data. This is the approach that has been employed by critics such as Freedman (1984, 2002), whose critiques have focused on elements of research design, and Jones (2002) and Fowles (1999), whose subjective critiques emphasized what they have described as positive contributions of media violence—and, to a lesser extent, by Ferguson and various colleagues (2008, 2009). Attacks on media violence research in the popular press and by lay critics tend to consist of opinion rather than evidence as well. The second approach is to present research findings that seem to call research documenting an effect of media violence on aggression into question; such is the approach favored predominantly by early media violence researchers Howitt and Cumberbatch (1975) and, more recently, by Ferguson and colleagues (2008, 2009). Although some authors engage in both types of critique, these really constitute fundamentally different challenges to the media violence effect and will be addressed separately.

A number of overlapping approaches have been taken to criticize the media violence consensus. Many of these criticisms, at least in the way they are applied to attack the media violence consensus, are deceptive, are used deceptively, or represent flaws in logic and reasoning. One type of argument that most people recognize as representing flawed logic or reasoning conflates correlation or relatedness with causality; most people are familiar with the (correct) assertion that "correlation does not equal causation." Below, we will enumerate a number of common logical fallacies and how they have been employed to attack the media violence consensus.

Setting Up a Straw Man

One approach to dismissing research on media violence effects involves setting up a "straw man." The straw man is a logical fallacy, or an error of reasoning and logic. Specifically, a straw man is a weaker or flawed version of the position against which one is arguing. This weaker position is then shown to be flawed or incorrect (knocking down the straw man), and the claim is made that the original, authentic argument has been shown to be incorrect. The name of this fallacy likely has reference to the practice dummy used for martial drills—new recruits may have honed their bayonet skills by skewering dummies filled with straw rather than trying them out against a real enemy (with an equally sharp bayonet).

An example of a straw man would be if, in order to attack the claim that media violence contributes to aggression, a critic misrepresented that claim as "all aggression is caused by media violence," or "media violence is a sole and sufficient cause of aggression," each of which misrepresents the original claim and is erroneous. Clearly, disproving a claim that has never been made does nothing to disprove claims that *have* been made; one must knock down the real man, not a straw man one has erected for the sole purpose of knocking down.

One straw man argument misrepresents claims that research has demonstrated that violent media increase aggression; the distorted version of this claim is that research has shown that violent media are *the* cause of violence. Freedman (2002) takes this approach when he asserts in the opening pages of his book, "There . . . is not the slightest possibility that [television violence] is the major cause of violence in our society" (p. 2). The straw man is evident—it is the position that television violence is *the* major cause of societal violence. Freedman dismisses this position, knocking down the straw man. What makes it a straw man is that this is not a position that media violence researchers have advanced. Instead, media violence has been shown to be one of many factors that contribute to aggression and violence (Gentile & Bushman, 2012). Such a statement, however, is harder to tilt against; hence, the straw man.

Another closely related straw man argument involves inappropriately conflating the words "aggression" and "violence." Generally speaking, aggression refers to any behavior intended to do harm, whereas violence is an extreme physical subtype of aggression that can cause serious injury or death

(Gentile & Bushman, 2012). Most research on media violence effects has examined its impact on aggression, yet when critics attack that body of work, they focus on extreme examples or use the term "violence." Thus, the straw man argument "video games make people commit murder," is easily dismissed, but then is used to dismiss the broader issue that "violent video games can cause aggression."

Variations on this straw man exist, and often take the form of a belief in simple, powerful, universal effects. First, critics claim that media violence researchers argue the effects should be universal and uniform, unaffected by predispositions toward aggression, for example. Then, any moderating effect, any null finding, is held out as proof that no universal, uniform effect exists. Finally, the absence of such a universal effect is used as evidence that no effect exists or as justification for the dismissal of research documenting effects. Ferguson and colleagues (2008) employ a similar, if distinct, approach in their attacks on the media violence consensus. They have argued that because the General Aggression Model (GAM; Anderson & Bushman, 2002a) focuses on learning aggressive scripts that it is a "tabula rasa" theory, requiring that all aggression be learned and dismissing the possibility of inherent tendencies toward aggression that lie at the heart of Ferguson's theorizing about violence. In fact, the scholars who have demonstrated media influence on aggressive behavior acknowledge a wide range of moderating factors, including personality traits, familial and other environmental factors, and genetic predispositions (Huesmann & Miller, 1994; Huesmann, Moise, & Podolski, 1997; Paik & Comstock, 1994; Strasburger & Wilson, 2003). In fact, a substantial body of media violence research has emphasized the identification of moderators of the effects of media violence on aggression (for a meta-analysis, see Hogben, 1998).

This same pattern of setting up and knocking down straw men can be observed in criticisms that appeal to population-level data to dismiss the media violence consensus. These appeals, seemingly common in both academic and popular press attacks on the media violence consensus, make sweeping comparisons between violence or crime rates in areas or time periods with similar or different media access, and draw conclusions therefrom. A number of examples are illustrative. First, in a 2012 blog post for the *Washington Post*, Max Fisher produced a graph that charted 10 developed nations' gun-related murder rates against per capita video game spending. The graph is characterized by relatively low murder rates for all countries, with the exception of the United States as an outlier. Fisher then displays a bright red line on the graph, representing a linear relationship that, visually, seems to suggest a perfect correlation, and asserts that that line represents the way the data would look "if there were a correlation between video game consumption and gun-related murders." Data do not fall along that line; therefore, Fisher concludes, "video game consumption . . . does not seem to correlate at all with an increase in gun violence." Fisher's red line is, in essence, a straw man. No reasonable media violence researcher has, to our knowledge, ever asserted that all (or even most) gun-related murders are attributable to video game play, or that all video games are violent, for that matter. But rather than address the real evidence for the media violence consensus, Fisher sets up the straw man of simple, uniform, powerful effects, and then knocks it down.

Jib Fowles's (1999) attack on the media violence consensus rests largely on a straw man, which he raises in the form of a recitation of evidence, primarily historical and anthropological, that violence and violent entertainment did not begin with television. Fowles points out that interpersonal violence and warfare have been common among people belonging to what he refers to as primitive hunter-gatherer cultures such as the Bushmen of the Kalahari, American Plains Indians, Aborigines of Australia, and Inuit. Violence, according to Fowles, is the natural state of human existence. Fowles also observes that cultures throughout history have had public displays of state-controlled violence, including the human sacrifices of the Aztecs and Incas, the gladiatorial games of ancient Rome, and the violent sporting contests that arose in nineteenth-century Europe and North America, and presents media violence as their modern equivalent. This history of violence, both spontaneous and personal and staged and public, demonstrates a human violent streak that precedes the existence of television violence. Although this is certainly true, that history does not speak to what is learned from witnessing such violence.

Ferguson (2013b) engages in a similar appeal to population-level data, setting up the straw man of simple, uniform effects. First, he notes that youth violence has declined over the last 40 years, and that video games have been part of popular culture for roughly that same period. This, Ferguson concludes, demonstrates that violent video games do not cause violence. The fallaciousness of this argument is apparent; violence, even on an individual level, is a function of a complex web of biological, familial, and societal factors (for a review, see Berkowitz, 1993). In order for the concurrent decline in violence and rise in video game play to signify the lack of an impact of games on aggression, we would either have to accept that all of these other factors (as well as causes of aggression as-yet unidentified) remained somehow constant over the same 40-year period, or believe that the media violence consensus is that violent media are an overwhelming, unmoderated, irresistible cause of violence. Ferguson (2013a) continues his argument by noting that other countries with similar media diets have lower levels of violence than the United States, concluding again that this demonstrates that media do not cause violence. This is a close echo of Freedman's (2002) assertion that if media violence causes aggression, then all countries with television would have experienced a simultaneous increase in societal violence. These represent a reasonable critique of the media violence consensus only if media are so powerful that they constitute an overwhelming determinant of violence in a society, which is not what researchers have been saying (another straw man). Never mind that the countries with which Ferguson would compare the United States (i.e., Canada, the Netherlands, and South Korea) have entirely different histories, legal and judicial systems, access to guns, rates of incarceration, mental health-care systems, economies, and cultural values. According to Ferguson, if media causes violence, none of these can matter. This is particularly odd given Ferguson's assertions elsewhere that depression, a lack of empathy, parental aggression, and peer influence all contribute to violence by young people (Ferguson, Miguel, & Hartley, 2009; Negy, Ferguson, Galvanovskis, & Smither, 2013).

The Texas Sharpshooter

This colorfully named fallacy references a story about a man driving along a country road in Texas; as he travels, he periodically comes across barns with a number of bulls-eye targets drawn on the wall, each with a bullet hole in the very center. Eventually, he chances upon the marksman at his task, examining a barn riddled with new bullet holes and carefully painting a target around each one. The term Texas Sharpshooter, therefore, refers to the careful selection of evidence or examples for inclusion and exclusion in such a way as to support a particular argument or point of view. Just such cherry-picking seems to be at work in attacks on the media violence consensus. Take, for example, Freedman's early (1984) approach: he argued that media violence research did not show causal relationships while excluding all experimental research as ecologically invalid. This same dismissal is seen in critiques from industry representatives. An online article quoted game designer Cliff Bleszinski as dismissing research findings linking violent video games with aggression as spurious correlations (Makuch, 2013), an assertion that can only be made if one ignores the large body of controlled experimental evidence.

Freedman's (2002) more recent work does not dismiss all experiments out of hand, but it still adopts a Texas Sharpshooter approach. Studies that seem to contradict the media violence consensus (e.g., Feshbach & Singer, 1971) Freedman lauds as landmark, high-quality studies, whereas studies with similar methods that support the consensus are dismissed as fundamentally, hopelessly flawed. By applying different criteria and standards to evaluate different studies based, apparently, on whether or not their outcomes agree with Freedman's position, a favorable outcome is assured.

The Texas Sharpshooter approach is particularly clear in an interesting meta-analysis of the effects of media violence on aggression conducted by Ferguson and Kilburn (2009). The target was drawn carefully as studies for inclusion were selected. First, they narrowed the temporal window of the studies to include only a 10-year period, one that occurred after the question of *whether* media violence contributed to aggression was generally considered an answered question. Second, they only included behavioral aggression measures. Even at that, their analysis indicated a significant relation between media violence and aggression, so the target was drawn even smaller as the authors adopted a dismissive tone toward those studies that employed measures described as invalid or illegitimate in previous articles published by vocal critics of media violence research—namely, Ferguson himself and Freedman.

Public intellectuals who rely on anecdotes rather than quantitative empirical evidence to attack the media violence consensus are prone to the Texas Sharpshooter fallacy as well. Take, for example, the work of Gerard Jones, an author of comic books and nonfiction. In writing about media and violence, Jones endorses the radical position that media violence actually reduces aggression among children, and he does so with anecdotal evidence. For the most part, Jones (2002) recounts anecdotes about the children he has known best—himself as a child and his own son, as well as a few of his son's friends. He also recounts anecdotes shared with him by other parents in which they express relief after relenting to their children's demands for access to violent media and toys. Typical of these is the tale told by Emily's mother; Emily obsessed about guns for years, but her mother refused to buy her a toy gun or allow her to play with one. Finally, when Mom gave in and bought Emily a toy gun, Emily became much more well adjusted and much less gun obsessed, and everything was wonderful. Similar stories are related by adults who reflect on how much violent media content helped them to become healthy, functioning adults. Finally, the effects of continued restriction are presented when Jones describes the case of Kip Kinkel, the Oregon teenager who murdered his father before opening fire in a school cafeteria. Though Kip expressed an avid interest in guns from a very early age, his parents strictly forbade him from using violent toys or media until he was a teenager, when his father relented and bought him his first real gun. If only his parents hadn't forbidden him access to violent television programming and toy guns, Jones muses, things would have been different; Kip clearly needed violent television. Jones's handful of anecdotes are each precisely on target, of course.

Red Herrings

The logical fallacy known as a red herring is a distraction, a misdirection, an irrelevant bit of information meant to distract from the main argument. Critics of the media violence consensus have employed a number of such red herrings. For example, when the assertion is made that parents should control their children's use of violent media or teach their children good values, this is a red herring. They may be true statements, but the question of whether media violence contributes to real world aggression is independent of their truthfulness. Bushman, Rothstein, and Anderson (2011) label as a red herring the argument by Ferguson and Kilburn (2010) that media violence scholars are engaged in an attempt to instigate a "moral panic." Such allegations have nothing to do with the actual evidence regarding the impact of media violence on violence and aggression. Similarly, the fact that not all perpetrators of mass shootings are heavy video game players (Ferguson, 2013, January 10) is no more than a distraction. It is like arguing that being bitten by a rattlesnake must not be deadly because people who have not been bitten by rattlesnakes have died.

The red herring most commonly employed by critics of the media violence consensus is a focus on alleged flaws in individual studies' design. When reviewing empirical literature that identifies an effect of media violence on aggression or violence, critics such as Freedman (1984, 2002) and Ferguson (2013a) identify what they describe as flaws with the research. At times, they use these flaws to dismiss broad areas of published research, as when Freedman (1984) argued that laboratory experiments had the capacity to produce demand effects and were therefore unreliable, or when Ferguson (2013a) dismissed all research that employs laboratory measures of behavioral aggression because, according to him, they are not reliable and valid. At other times, individual studies are singled out for particular attention; for example, Ferguson (2013a) argues that the findings of Lefkowitz, Eron, Walder, and Huesmann (1977) are invalid because their peer-nominated aggression measure included items that were reflective not only of physical violence but also of relational and indirect aggression, which Ferguson characterizes as "naughtiness" or "poor social skills (p. 109). Ferguson seems unaware that Bandura, in one of his earliest experiments, showed that media violence stimulates aggression that is quite different from the aggression portrayed in the film—in other words, response generalization operates as it does with most learned behaviors. It is interesting to note that different studies are criticized for different elements of their design. This focus on variation among study designs, along with the labeling of such variation as flaws, is meant to distract from the remarkable consistency among the actual findings of these studies. Employing widely diverse methods, conceptualizing and operationalizing both media violence and aggression in widely diverse ways, and with widely diverse samples, most studies find that media violence exposure leads to an increase in aggression (Anderson & Bushman, 2002b). In fact, this variability is a great strength of scientific research. If the effect could only be demonstrated in one way or in one context, it wouldn't be a robust finding worth much attention. Multiple studies employing diverse methods help to counter flaws in any one particular study or method.

Another red herring deals with the putative benefits of video game play. Ferguson (2010), for example, in reviewing research on violent video game effects, dismisses violence effects in part by focusing on research suggesting that some types of video game play likely lead to improvements in certain cognitive skills. This research is valuable, and such benefits likely occur, though they are probably attributable to characteristics of the games other than the violent content. However, the question of whether the games also have beneficial effects has no bearing on the question of whether the games increase aggression among those who play them. The description of benefits, when presented in conjunction with a discussion of the research on aggression effects, is calculated to take the reader away from weighing scientific evidence in a more general evaluation, colored by thoughts of benefits rather than harm.

A final red herring is the question of banning or censoring violent content. By raising the specter of censorship, critics attempt to distract media consumers from research findings linking violent media and real-world aggression. The approach taken by James Alan Fox (2013), a commentator in the *New York Daily News*, is typical: after citing public opinion research that found a majority of Americans believed entertainment media contributed to school violence, and that a greater majority endorsed some form of restriction on sales of violent media to minors, he ignores both the question of causality and the question of reasonable restriction of sales. Instead, he concludes, "Banning violent video games . . . would do little to avert the next mass murder." The specter of a ban is the red herring—it is a distraction from the core issue of whether violent media causes aggression. We are not aware of any researchers in the field of media violence who advocate a "ban" on violent media, and indeed such a ban is impossible under the U.S. Constitution; when critics suggest or assume that their research calls for a ban, they are trying to distract the audience from the very real—and very consistent—finding that violent media contributes to real aggression.

Personal Incredulity

Another common logical fallacy is personal incredulity—the inability to accept or believe something. The argument is, at its core, that if I cannot believe or accept an argument, that argument cannot be true. This is, perhaps, the most obviously fallacious argument. One individual may very well find it difficult to believe a great many things that are perfectly believable to another. When Copernicus articulated his heliocentric model of the solar system, it seemed to many to be too difficult to believe; it was, nevertheless, true (North, 1994).

Regardless, personal incredulity has been employed to attack the media violence consensus. In Freedman's work, for example, in addition to applying varying standards for judging different studies and dismissing research evidence, when faced with a result inconsistent with his attack and difficult to ignore, he relies on personal expressions of incredulity, such as, "It is a complicated study with very complicated results. I am confident that, overall, these results do not show that exposure to media violence increases aggression" (Freedman, 2002, p. 29). Or in response to a published assertion Freedman does not like, he may simply exclaim: "This is incredible," or "Scandalous," or, "It is junk science." None of these represents a legitimate, logical argument.

Instead, Freedman simply expresses that, to him, the findings are not believable (i.e., incredible) and expects readers to adopt that incredulity.

Nature

Another common fallacy employed in attacks against the media violence consensus has been an appeal to nature, which rests on the assumption that if something is natural then it must be justified, valid, or inevitable. Arguments in this vein rest on two basic tenets: (1) violence existed before violent media, and (2) violent thoughts and behaviors are natural human tendencies. The arguments are often glib, as when game designer Tommy Tallarico asserted, "Violence unfortunately is a part of human nature. And last time I checked, Cain didn't bludgeon Abel with a Game Boy; Genghis Khan didn't have an Xbox Live account; and Hitler didn't play Crash Bandicoot" (Makuch, 2013). Generally, critics argue that the social sciences in general have few parallels in the natural sciences, creating a resistance to evolutionary and biological influences on behavior (Pinker, 2002). These critics assert that genetics play a large role in violent behavior (Ferguson, 2008; Rhee & Waldman, 2002) and that the mechanisms between genes and environment need to be further evaluated rather than focusing on media. When applying this perspective, media violence is viewed as a result, not a cause; media violence is simply a reflection of violent human nature (Ferguson, 2013a). Of course, exposure to violent media is not a "necessary or sufficient cause of aggressive behavior, let alone both necessary and sufficient" (Anderson et al., 2003, p. 83). Also, asserting that violence is natural in no way suggests that media cannot contribute to violence. Cancer is natural, but exposure to tobacco smoke, asbestos, and radioactive material clearly contribute to it nevertheless.

This notion that violence is natural and therefore inevitable is linked to the idea that violent media has beneficial effects on aggressive individuals. Some researchers have argued that exposure to violent media has positive effects as it lowers violent crime rates by providing inherently violent individuals with a nonviolent outlet (Fowles, 1999; Savage & Ferguson, 2012). For example, these critics contend that mediated violence helps children cope with fears and deal with the violence they see and experience in real life (Jones, 2002). This line of reasoning has spurred the idea that limiting violence on television would be detrimental, as children would lose the "right to pick the content of which they are of psychological need" (Fowles, 1999, p. 17).

This catharsis hypothesis is as old as Aristotle, who taught in *Poetics* that people could find emotional release from viewing tragic plays where heroes often suffer a violent demise (Bushman & Anderson, 2001). As the characters experience tragic events, the viewer's own negative feelings are purged, benefiting both the viewer and society. This notion was revived by Freudian psychoanalytic techniques that proposed using prizefights and violent plays and media as a measure for reducing pent up aggression through release (Feshbach

& Price, 1984). More recent proponents of this stance point to a set of experiments (Feshbach, 1961; Feshbach & Singer, 1971) that was interpreted as a catharsis effect. Importantly, however, research that has explicitly tested the catharsis hypothesis has found that rehearsing or acting out aggression leads to an increase, rather than a decrease, in aggression. This is true when such rehearsal consists of watching violence (Doob & Wood, 1972) and when it is more actively carried out through physical behavior such as punching a punching bag (Bushman, 2002; for a more complete discussion of the history of and research on the catharsis hypothesis, see Gentile, 2013).

Fallacious Arguments as Propaganda

Employing fallacious arguments is not new; clever names exist for many fallacies because they are commonly employed. What is the function of such a consistent body of fallacious reasoning being brought to bear on this topic? Insight may be gained from Ross's (2002) epistemic merit model of propaganda. Ross has argued that two of the basic traits of propaganda are that it has a persuasive intent and that it employs defective epistemology, or ways of knowing. Attacks on the media violence consensus certainly have a persuasive intent, but do they employ defective epistemology? Ross, in defining defective epistemology, includes both false statements and bad arguments. The fallacious reasoning employed so often in attacks on the media violence consensus can therefore best be conceptualized as part of a propaganda effort rather than part of the legitimate scientific conversation about the existence and nature of violent media content's effects on audiences.

Attacks on the Media Violence Consensus: The Null Findings

A more relevant challenge to the media violence consensus takes the form of null findings in scientific investigations of media violence effects. Several surveys that have included media measures among other predictors of violence and aggression have found media to not be a statistically significant predictor (Ferguson, Miguel, & Hartley, 2009; Ferguson & Rueda, 2010; Ferguson et al., 2008).

The temptation, both on the part of the popular press and on the part of the authors of studies with null results, is to take these null results as proof that no effect exists. In fact, to do so represents a misunderstanding of the purpose of scientific research, the logic of hypothesis testing, and, more generally, the philosophy of modern science. In the sort of hypothesis testing common to the social sciences, including both disciplines in which media violence research most often appears—communication and psychology—the statistical test is a comparison of the results found against the effects expected under a "null" hypothesis of no effects whatsoever. Typically, if you show mathematically that the chances of getting the relation between media violence and aggression that you got are less than 0.05 under the null hypothesis of no media violence effects, you reject the null hypothesis of no effects and conclude that there is an effect. However, what do you conclude if you show mathematically that the chances of getting the relation between media violence and aggression that you got are *more* than 0.05 under the null hypothesis of no media violence effects? You conclude that you "can't conclude anything" from this study. You don't conclude that media violence has no effects! This is because in general you cannot statistically compute the probability that you would get the relation you observed between media violence and aggression if there really *is* an effect. It may be very high—particularly if the sample size is small—which means you are more likely to be wrong than if you conclude there is "no effect." A result that is not statistically significant at the 5 percent level does not indicate a 95 percent certainty that there is no relationship; instead, it only shows that you would be wrong more than 5 percent of the time if you concluded, each time this happened, that there really was an effect. Ferguson (2009) does not seem to grasp this point when he refers to a study that reports significant evidence of a "link between video game violence exposure and aggressive behavior," but suggests that an additional statistical test would have resulted in a null finding which therefore would "indicate quite the opposite" (p. 110). But a null finding does not indicate "the opposite." It just indicates that the study did not prove anything!

EXPLAINING THE ATTACKS: POSSIBLE DRIVERS

What, then, drives these attacks, both academic and popular, against the media violence consensus? Why do so many see the evidence as ambiguous when it is actually not very ambiguous by normal scientific standards? Why do so many intelligent writers use fallacious reasoning in arguing against the effects when in other situations they would recognize the arguments as fallacious? We see three plausible explanations for the discrepancy, which are all grounded in established psychological theory: (1) the need for cognitive consistency, (2) reactance against control, and (3) susceptibility to the "third person effect" of human behavior. However, all of these psychological processes depend on two underlying facts—one based on economics and one based on political principle, American history, and constitutional law. The economic fact is that violence in entertainment attracts audiences and makes large amounts of money for its purveyors (see Hamilton, 1998; Mustonen, 1997). The political principle is the sanctity of freedom of expression in American society and law.

Cognitive Consistency

We propose that individuals involved in any way in the production, marketing, or extensive use of violent media will find it difficult to believe that viewing violence could be damaging to audiences because that belief would be cognitively inconsistent with their behaviors. Striving for cognitive consistency can shape perceptions of media violence and media violence research for audiences as well as producers, including academics. Violent media are often enjoyable. For some individuals, it is likely that the violence itself is a source of enjoyment (Hoffner & Levine, 2005), though it is also likely that the presence of violence serves as a signal of mature subject matter, or is a characteristic of content that is enjoyable for other reasons (Bushman & Stack, 1996; Weaver, 2011). Violence is a common element of mainstream media content—a great many of the television series and movies that have received critical acclaim in recent years are violent. In the 10 years preceding the publication of this volume, the Emmy for best dramatic series has been awarded to *The West Wing* (2003), *The Sopranos* (2004, 2007), *Lost* (2005), *24* (2006), *Mad Men* (2008–2011), and *Homeland* (2012). Of these, only *The West Wing* and *Mad Men* are not demonstrably and consistently violent. Oscar winners for best picture fare somewhat worse, as violence is, again, commonplace, including in *The Return of the King* (2003), *Million Dollar Baby* (2004), *Crash* (2005), *The Departed* (2006), *No Country for Old Men* (2007), the intermittently violent *Slumdog Millionaire* (2008), *The Hurt Locker* (2009), and *Argo* (2012). In 10 years of winners, only *The King's Speech* (2010) and *The Artist* (2011) were arguably nonviolent.

Audiences who enjoy violent media content may also have a difficult time accepting that such content is harmful. Having given lectures, talks, and interviews on media violence effects, each of the authors has had the experience of being asked some version of the same "gotcha" questions: "Do you watch violent television?" and, "Do you let your children watch violent programs?" The core assumption underlying such questions is that consuming violent media content and believing such content to be harmful are fundamentally inconsistent with each other. If this is, in fact, a source of dissonance for audiences, then resolving it would likely involve either turning off the violent media content, a decision that would shape a substantial portion of many viewers' leisure time, or rejecting the notion that media violence is harmful.

Similarly, the cognitive consistency process can lead to a denial of effects for those who believe strongly in free expression in the mass media. Many individuals with strong beliefs about such free expression also have strong beliefs about society having a duty to protect children. If they accepted the fact that media violence harms children, they might have to rethink their beliefs about balancing freedom of expression with protecting children. It is easier for them to avoid this cognitive dissonance by denying that media violence has effects than it would be for them to resolve the dissonance.

Psychological Reactance

The second psychological process we see as relevant, namely reactance, applies principally to the producers of violent media. Most humans at a young age develop an aversion to being controlled and respond with reactance or counter-control to attempts to control them (Brehm & Brehm, 1981). We suggest that artists, writers, and producers are susceptible to displaying such reactance when attempts are made to control their creative products. Statements that programs or films harm viewers are likely to be linked in the artists' minds with the threat of control. The general statement that violent media can produce harm may be perceived by the artist as an assertion that a particular work or product produces harm; furthermore, the artist may perceive an implied call for censorship of that work. The artist, rightly or wrongly, consciously or unconsciously, may then interpret this statement as a threat of control. Therefore, a plausible response of the artist according to reactance theory would be to attack the researcher's thesis that the program is harmful. Ferguson has accused researchers who report that media violence causes aggression of being influenced by a "moral panic." Paraphrasing his own words, we would suggest that Ferguson (who is an author of violent fiction and a lifelong player of violent games) and others who deny the effects are displaying a "regulatory panic."

Audiences may also respond with reactance when facing the assertion that exposure to violent media is harmful. Such an assertion is likely perceived as an attempt to control viewing behavior and therefore to produce some measure of reassertion of independence. Evidence of this process can be found in Bushman and Stack's (1996) study of what they call the "forbidden fruit" effect. In an experimental setting, television content that was labeled as appropriate only for older audiences was preferred by children over the same content without restrictive labeling. This effect was particularly pronounced among children who had scored high in measures of reactance. In other words, when children who tended to respond to perceived attempts at control were told, "This is not for you," it became more appealing. What happens when audiences are told, "Violent media content is not for you"? They may reassert their independence by rejecting the research that supports it.

Third-Person Effects

The third psychological process we offer is intended more to explain a frequent opinion one hears from violence viewers who believe that viewing violence cannot be bad. The opinion is that "media violence may affect some 'susceptible' people, but it will not affect 'me' or 'my children'" because we are impervious to such influences. It is common in opinion surveys to find people reporting that a media message or personal communication might affect some people, but not the respondent. This phenomena has been labeled the "third-person effect" in the literature (Davison, 1983). Of course, as the research reported elsewhere in this book shows, media violence can affect any child. The third-person effect is probably driven at least partly by self-enhancement motivations.

We offer these three psychological processes only as suggestions that may help explain how many informed and intelligent people can read the reports of the studies and still deny that media violence has real effects on viewers. We certainly cannot offer any empirical evidence that they do operate among the academics, journalists, and producers who are the most vocal critics of the media violence consensus. However, they are well-established psychological processes that are likely to operate among any of us.

News Values and Practices

A final consideration may go a long way toward explaining why attacks on the media violence consensus achieve the visibility they do in the popular press. Fairness or balance is an important value driving the shape of news coverage in the United States (see Entman, 1989; Gans, 1979). This value requires that, when a controversial issue is covered, "both" sides of the issue must be presented, either within a single story or in related stories. In fact, it may also require the journalist to seek out perspectives that have been neglected by other journalists and report on them. When the issue is media violence, that has meant that when journalists report on assertions regarding the harmful effects of media violence, either in the form of scientific re-search (e.g., a new research study) or assertions by public figures (e.g., the NRA's executive vice president), they have tended to seek to offer a balanced perspective by giving voice to critics of that research—such as Ferguson. It seems likely, however, that this norm of fairness actually results in biased coverage—that is, coverage that systematically favors one side through mis-representation of actual evidence (for an analysis of a similar issue, see Boykoff & Boykoff, 2004). If most studies find (as most researchers believe) that media violence contributes to aggression, is it fair or balanced reporting to devote equivalent time or column inches to both perspectives or bodies of evidence? The skewed nature of this is illustrated in the preponderance of a small handful of scholars quoted arguing against the media violence consensus; when seeking such an opinion, there are relatively few from which to choose. Therefore those few are given a voice that becomes disproportionately loud. Ultimately, the data should speak for themselves, and this is where meta-analyses are so beneficial—they allow for examination of the total record of data, including contradictory results (see chapter 13 in this volume). This empirical approach can help us to bypass the rhetoric. Given the psychological and structural factors likely to motivate attacks on the media violence consensus, it is not surprising that such attacks occur. These attacks, however, are often based on faulty logic or basic misunderstandings about the conduct of science. The best approach to responding to them is to consider them in light of the overwhelming weight of evidence and theory showing that violent media content can and does increase aggression in viewers.

REFERENCES

American Academy of Family Physicians. (2010). *Violence, media*. Retrieved from http://www.aafp.org/online/en/home/policy/policies/v/violencemedia.html

American Academy of Pediatrics. (2009). Media violence. *Pediatrics, 124*, 1495–1503.

Anderson, C. A., Berkowitz, L., Donnerstein, E., Huesmann, L. R., Johnson, J. D., . . . & Wartella, E. (2003). The influence of media violence on youth. *Psychological Science in the Public Interest, 4*(3), 81–110. doi:10.1111/j.1529-1006.2003. pspi_1433.x

Anderson, C. A., & Bushman, B. J. (2002a). Human aggression. *Annual Review of Psychology, 53*, 27–51.

Anderson, C. A., & Bushman, B. J. (2002b). The effects of media violence on society. *Science, 295*, 2377–2379. doi:10.1126/science.1070765

Bandura, A. (1969). Social-learning theory of identificatory processes. In D. A. Goslin (Ed.), *Handbook of socialization theory and research* (pp. 213–262). New York, NY: Rand McNally.

Bandura, A. (1977). *Social learning theory*. Englewood Cliffs, NJ: Prentice Hall.

Bandura, A. (1986). *Social foundations of thought and action: A social-cognitive theory*. Englewood Cliffs, NJ: Prentice Hall.

Bandura, A., Ross, D., & Ross, S. A. (1963). Imitation of aggression through imitation of film-mediated aggressive models. *Journal of Abnormal and Social Psychology, 66*, 3–11.

Berkowitz, L. (1993). *Aggression: Its causes, consequences, and control*. New York, NY: McGraw-Hill.

Berkowitz, L., & LePage, A. (1967). Weapons as aggression-eliciting stimuli. *Journal of Personality and Social Psychology, 7*, 202–207.

Boykoff, M. T., & Boykoff, J. M. (2004). Balance as bias: Global warming and the U.S. prestige press. *Global Environmental Change, 14*, 125–136. doi:10.1016/j. gloenvcha.2003.10.001

Brehm, S. S., & Brehm, J. W. (1981). *Psychological reactance: A theory of freedom and control*. New York, NY: Academic Press.

Busemeyer, S. (2012, December 21). NRA calls for more armed security in schools. *The Hartford Courant*. Retrieved from articles.courant.com

Bushman, B. J. (2002). Does venting anger feed or extinguish the flame? Catharsis, rumination, distraction, anger, and aggressive responding. *Personality and Social Psychology Bulletin, 28*, 724–731. doi:10.1177/0146167202289002

Bushman, B. J., & Anderson, C. A. (2001). Media violence and the American public: Scientific facts versus media misinformation. *American Psychologist, 56*(6/7), 477–489. doi:10.1037/0003-066X.56.6-7.477

Bushman, B. J., & Huesmann, L. R. (2001). Effects of televised violence on aggression. In D. Singer & J. Singer (Eds.), *Handbook of children and the media*. Thousand Oaks, CA: Sage.

Bushman, B. J., Rothstein, H. R., & Anderson, C. A. (2011). Much ado about something: Violent video game effects and a school of red herring; Reply to Ferguson and Kilburn (2010). *Psychological Bulletin, 136*, 182–187. doi:10.1037/a0018718

Bushman, B. J., & Stack, A. D. (1996). Forbidden fruit versus tainted fruit: Effects of warning labels on attraction to television violence. *Journal of Experimental Psychology: Applied, 2*, 207–226. doi:10.1037/1076-898X.2.3.207

Carnagey, N. L., Anderson, C. A., & Bushman, B. J. (2007). The effect of video game violence on physiological desensitization to real-life violence. *Journal of Experimental Social Psychology, 43*, 489–496. doi:10.1016/j.jesp.2006.05.003

Cline, V. B., Croft, R. G., & Courrier, S. (1973). Desensitization of children to television violence. *Journal of Personality & Social Psychology, 27*, 360–365.

Comstock, G., & Paik, H. (1991). *Television and the American child.* San Diego, CA: Academic Press.

Cook, D. E., Kestenbaum, C., Honaker, L. M., & Anderson, E. R. (2000). *Joint statement on the impact of entertainment violence on children: Congressional public health summit.* American Academy of Pediatrics, Washington, D.C. Retrieved from http://www2.aap.org/advocacy/releases/jstmtevc.htm.

Davison, W. P. (1983). The third-person effect in communication. *Public Opinion Quarterly, 47*, 1–15.

Devine, P. G. (1989). Stereotypes and prejudice: Their automatic and controlled components. *Journal of Personality and Social Psychology, 56*, 5–18. doi:10.1037/0022-3514.56.1.5

Dodge, K. A. (1980). Social cognition and children's aggressive behavior. *Child Development, 51*, 620–635.

Dodge, K. A., Pettit, G. S., Bates, J. E., & Valente, E. (1995). Social information-processing patterns partially mediate the effect of early physical abuse on later conduct problems. *Journal of Abnormal Psychology, 104*, 632–643.

Doob, A. N., & Wood, L. E. (1972). Catharsis and aggression: Effects of annoyance and retaliation on aggressive behavior. *Journal of Personality and Social Psychology, 22*, 156–162.

Engelhardt, C. R., Bartholow, B. D., Kerr, G. T., & Bushman, B. J. (2011). This is your brain on violent video games: Neural desensitization to violence predicts increased aggression following violent video game exposure. *Journal of Experimental Social Psychology, 47*, 1033–1036. doi:10.1016/j.jesp.2011.03.027

Entman, R. (1989). *Democracy without citizens: Media and the decay of American politics.* New York, NY: Oxford University Press.

Ferguson, C. J. (2007a). Evidence for publication bias in video game violence effects literature: A meta-analytic review. *Aggression and Violent Behavior, 12*, 470–482. doi:10.1016/j.avb.2007.01.001

Ferguson, C. J. (2007b). The good, the bad and the ugly: A meta-analytic review of positive and negative effects of violent video games. *Psychiatric Quarterly, 78*, 309–316. doi:10.1007/s11126-007-9056-9

Ferguson, C. J. (2008). An evolutionary approach to understanding violent antisocial behavior: Diagnostic implications for dual-process etiology. *Journal of Forensic Psychology Practice, 8*(4), 321–343. doi:10.1080/15228930802199168

Ferguson, C. J. (2010). Blazing angels or resident evil? Can violent video games be a force for good? *Review of General Psychology, 14*, 68–81. doi:10.1037/a0018941

Ferguson, C. J. (2011, December 7). Video games don't make kids violent. Time online. Retrieved from HYPERLINK "http://ideas.time.com/" \t "_blank"ideas .Time.com.

Ferguson, C. J. (2013a). Media violence effects: Confirmed truth or just another x-file? *Journal of Forensic Psychology Practice, 9*, 103–126. doi:10.1080/15228930802572059

Ferguson, C. J. (2013b). *Adolescents, crime, and the media: A critical analysis.* New York, NY: Springer.

Ferguson, C. J. (2013, January 10). Don't blame video games for real world violence. *The Chronicle of Higher Education.* [Blog post]. Retrieved from chronicle.com

Ferguson, C. J. (2013, January 16). NRA's video game smacks of hypocrisy. *CNNOpinion.* [Blog post]. Retrieved from CNN.com

Ferguson, C. J., & Kilburn, J. (2009). The public health risks of media violence: A meta-analytic review. *The Journal of Pediatrics, 154,* 759–763. doi:10.1016/j.peds.2008.11.033

Ferguson, C. J., & Kilburn, J. (2010). Much ado about nothing: The misestimation and overinterpretation of violent video game effects in Eastern and Western nations: Comment on Anderson et al. (2010). *Psychological Bulletin, 136,* 174–178. doi:10.1037/a0018566

Ferguson, C. J., Miguel, C. S., & Hartley, R. D. (2009). A multivariate analysis of youth violence and aggression: The influence of family, peers, depression, and media violence. *The Journal of Pediatrics, 155*(6), 904–908. doi:10.1016/j.jpeds.2009.06.021

Ferguson, C. J., & Rueda, S. M. (2010). The hitman study: Violent video game exposure effects on aggressive behavior, hostile feelings, and depression. *European Psychologist, 15,* 99–108. doi:10.1027/1016-9040/a000010

Ferguson, C. J., Rueda, S. M., Cruz, A. M., Ferguson, D. E., Fritz, S., & Smith, S. M. (2008). Video games and aggression: Causal relationship or byproduct of family violence and intrinsic violence motivation? *Criminal Justice and Behavior, 35,* 311–332. doi:10.1177/0093854807311719

Feshbach, S. (1961). The stimulating versus cathartic effects of a vicarious aggressive activity. *Journal of Abnormal and Social Psychology, 63,* 381–385.

Feshbach, S., & Price, J. (1984). Cognitive competencies and aggressive behavior: A developmental study. *Aggressive Behavior, 10,* 185–200. doi:10.1002/1098-2337(1984)

Feshbach, S., & Singer, R. D. (1971). *Television and aggression.* San Francisco, CA: Jossey-Bass.

Fisher, M. (2012, December 17). Ten-country comparison suggests there's little or no link between video games and gun murders. *The Washington Post.* Retrieved from www.washingtonpost.com

Fowles, J. (1999). *The case for television violence.* Thousand Oaks, CA: Sage.

Fox, J. A. (2013, March 24). Expert: Banning violent video games would do little to avert the next mass murder. *New York Daily News online.*

Freedman, J. L. (1984). Effect of television violence on aggressiveness. *Psychological Bulletin, 96,* 227–246. doi:10.1037//0033-2909.96.2.227

Freedman, J. L. (2002). *Media violence and its effect on aggression: Assessing the scientific evidence.* Toronto, ON: University of Toronto Press.

Friedrich, L. K., & Stein, A. H. (1975). Prosocial television and young children: The effects of verbal labeling and role playing on learning and behavior. *Child Development, 46,* 27–38. doi:10.2307/1128830

Gans, H. (1979). *Deciding what's news.* New York, NY: Pantheon.

Geen, R. G., & O'Neal, E. C. (1969). Activation of cue-elicited aggression by general arousal. *Journal of Personality and Social Psychology, 11,* 289–292.

Gentile, D. A. (2013). Catharsis and media violence: A conceptual analysis. *Societies, 3,* 491–510. doi:10.3390/soc3040491

Gentile, D. A., & Bushman, B. J. (2012). Reassessing media violence effects using a risk and resilience approach to understanding aggression. *Psychology of Popular Media Culture, 1*, 138–151. doi:10.1037/a0028481

Gerbner, G., Gross, L., Morgan, M., & Signorielli, N. (1994). Growing up with television: The cultivation perspective. In J. Bryant & D. Zillmann (Eds.), *Media effects* (pp. 17–41). Hillsdale, NJ: Erlbaum.

Guerra, N. G., Huesmann, L. R., Tolan, P., Van Acker, R., & Eron, L. D. (1995). Stressful events and individual beliefs as correlates of economic disadvantage and aggression among urban children. *Journal of Consulting and Clinical Psychology, 63*, 518–528.

Hamilton, J. T. (1998). *Channeling violence: The economic market for violent television programming*. Princeton, NJ: Princeton University Press.

Hogben, M. (1998). Factors moderating the effect of televised aggression on viewer behavior. *Communication Research, 25*, 220–247. doi:10.1177/009365098 025002005

Hoffner, C. A., & Levine, K. J. (2005). Enjoyment of mediated fright and violence: A meta-analysis. *Media Psychology, 7*, 207–237. doi:10.1207/S1532785XMEPO702_5

Howitt, D., & Cumberbatch, G. (1975). *Mass media violence and society*. New York, NY: John Wiley & Sons.

Huesmann, L. R. (1988). An information processing model for the development of aggression. *Aggressive Behavior, 14*, 13–24.

Huesmann, L. R. (1998). The role of social information processing and cognitive schemas in the acquisition and maintenance of habitual aggressive behavior. In R. G. Geen & E. Donnerstein (Eds.), *Human aggression: Theories research, and implications for policy* (pp. 73–109). New York, NY: Academic Press.

Huesmann, L. R. (1999). The effects of childhood aggression and exposure to media violence on adult behaviors, attitudes, and mood: Evidence from a 15-year cross-national longitudinal study. *Aggressive Behavior, 25*, 18–29.

Huesmann, L. R., & Guerra, N. G. (1997). Normative beliefs about aggression and aggressive behavior. *Journal of Personality and Social Psychology, 72*, 408–419.

Huesmann, L. R., Guerra, N. G., Zelli, A., & Miller, L. (1992). Differing normative beliefs about aggression for boys and girls. In K. Bjorkqvist & P. Niemala (Eds.), *Of mice and women: Aspects of female aggression*. Orlando, FL: Academic Press.

Huesmann, L. R., & Miller, L. S. (1994). Long-term effects of repeated exposure to media violence in childhood. In L. R. Huesmann (Ed.), *Aggressive behavior: Current perspectives* (pp. 153–186). New York, NY: Plenum Press.

Huesmann, L. R., Moise, J. F., & Podolski, C.-L. (1997). The effects of media violence on the development of antisocial behavior. In D. Stoff, J. Breiling, & J. D. Maser (Eds.), *Handbook of antisocial behavior* (pp. 181–193). New York, NY: John Wiley & Sons.

Jennings, N. (2012, December 14). White House petition for gun control gaining traction. *Washington Post*. Retrieved from www.washingtonpost.com/blogs

Jones, G. (2002). *Killing monsters: Why children need fantasy, super heroes, and make-believe violence*. New York, NY: Basic Books.

Josephson, W. L. (1987). Television violence and children's aggression: Testing the priming, social script, and disinhibition predictions. *Journal of Personality and Social Psychology, 32*, 346–360.

Konrad, A. (2013, February 2). Even with record prices, expect $10 million Super Bowl ad soon. *Forbes Online*. Retrieved from www.Forbes.com

Kretchmer, S. B. (2004). Advertainment: The evolution of product placement as a mass media marketing strategy. *Journal of Promotion Management, 10*, 37–54. doi:10.1300/J057v10n01_04

Lefkowitz, M. M., Eron, L. D., Walder, L. O., & Huesmann, L. R. (1977). *Growing up to be violent*. New York, NY: Pergamon Press.

Makuch, E. (2013, May 29). *Industry sounds off on violent games debate*. Retrieved from www.gamespot.com

Meltzoff, A. N., & Moore, K. M. (2000). Resolving the debate about early imitation. In D. Muir (Ed.), *Infant development: The essential readings* (pp. 167–181). Malden, MA: Blackwell.

Moise-Titus, J. (1999). *The role of negative emotions in the media violence-aggression relation*. (Unpublished doctoral dissertation). University of Michigan, Ann Arbor, MI.

Mustonen, A. (1997). Nature of screen violence and its relation to program popularity. *Aggressive Behavior, 23*, 281–292. doi:10.1002/(SICI)109-2337(1997)

National Institute of Mental Health. (1982). *Television and behavior: Ten years of scientific progress for the eighties* (Vol. 1: Summary report). Washington, DC: U.S. Government Printing Office.

Negy, C., Ferguson, C. J., Galvanovskis, A., & Smither, R. (2013). Predicting violence: A cross-national study of United States and Mexican young adults. *Journal of Social and Clinical Psychology, 32*(1), 54–70. doi:10.1521/jscp.2013 .32.1.54

North, J. (1994). *The Fontana history of astronomy and cosmology*. London, UK: Fontana.

Paik, H., & Comstock, G. (1994). The effects of television violence on antisocial behavior: A meta-analysis. *Communication Research, 21*, 516–546. doi:10.1177 /009365094021004004

Pinker, S. (2002). *The blank slate: The modern denial of human nature*. New York, NY: Penguin.

Rhee, S. H., & Waldman, I. D. (2002). Genetic and environmental influences on antisocial behavior: A meta-analysis of twin and adoption studies. *Psychological Bulletin, 128*, 490–529. doi:10.1037/0033-2909.128.3.490

Rizzolati, G., Fadiga, L., Gallese, V., & Fogassi, L. (1996). Premotor cortex and the recognition of motor actions. *Cognitive Brain Research, 3*, 131–141.

Ross, S. T. (2002). Understanding propaganda: The epistemic merit model and its application to art. *Journal of Aesthetic Education, 36*, 16–30. doi:10.2307/3333623

Savage, J., & Ferguson, C. J. (2012). Media violence. In *Encyclopedia of adolescence* (pp. 1685–1691). New York, NY: Springer.

Schwarz, N., & Clore, G. L. (1983). Mood, misattribution, and judgments of well-being: Informative and directive functions of affective states. *Journal of Personality and Social Psychology, 45*, 513–523. doi:10.1037//0022-3514.45.3.513

Steinfeld, J. (1972). *Statement in hearings before Subcommittee on Communications of Committee on Commerce* (United States Senate, Serial #92 - 52, pp. 25–27). Washington, DC: U.S. Government Printing Office.

Strasburger, V. C., & Wilson, B. J. (2003). Television violence. In D. A. Gentile (Ed.), *Media violence and children: A complete guide for parents and professionals* (pp. 57–86). Westport, CT: Praeger.

Tremblay, R. E. (2000). The development of aggressive behavior during childhood: What have we learned in the past century? *International Journal of Behavioral Development, 24*, 129–141.

U.S. Attorney General's Task Force on Family Violence. (1984). *The attorney general's task force on family violence: Final report*. Washington, DC: Author.

Valentino, N. A. (1999). Crime news and the priming of racial attitudes during evaluations of the president. *The Public Opinion Quarterly, 63*, 293–320. doi:10.1086/297722

Weaver, A. J. (2011). A meta-analytical review of selective exposure to and the enjoyment of media violence. *Journal of Broadcasting and Electronic Media, 55*, 232–250. doi:10.1080/08838151.2011.570826

White, G. L., Fishbein, S., & Rutsein, J. (1981). Passionate love and the misattribution of arousal. *Journal of Personality and Social Psychology, 41*, 56–62. doi:10.1037/0022-3514.41.1.56

Wood, W., Wong, F. Y., & Chachere, J. G. (1991). Effects of media violence on viewers' aggression in unconstrained social interaction. *Psychological Bulletin, 109*, 371–383. doi:10.1037/0033-2909.109.3.371

Wyrwicka, W. (1996). *Imitation in human and animal behavior*. New Brunswick, NJ: Transaction Publishers.

Zillmann, D. (1979). *Hostility and aggression*. Hillsdale, NJ: Erlbaum.

Zillmann, D. (1983). Arousal and aggression. In R. Geen & E. Donnerstein (Eds.), *Aggression: Theoretical and empirical review* (Vol. 1, pp. 75–102). New York, NY: Academic Press.

CHAPTER 13

The Contribution of Meta-Analysis to the Controversy over Television Violence and Aggression

George Comstock, Erica Scharrer, and Jack Powers

The meaningfulness of scientific inquiry rests on two factors. The first is the quality and veracity of evidence, which is assessed by the various applications of the concepts of reliability and validity (Cook & Campbell, 1979). The second is the inevitably somewhat subjective interpretation of these findings. Both are well served by meta-analysis, which provides estimates of relationships among variables based on all retrievable studies and can confine inferences to data from studies of the highest quality and greatest conformity to real life circumstances (Hunt, 1997).[1]

In the case of television and film violence and aggressive and antisocial behavior, there is a substantial array of data; 10 meta-analyses have studied outcomes that often overlap in their coverage but are far from identical. In addition, there have been eight meta-analyses of violent video game effects, which will be discussed (more briefly) later. Meta-analysis, because it provides estimates of the magnitude of the relationships among variables that are more reliable and more valid than those produced by a single study, assists enormously in addressing five important questions:

1. Is there a statistically significant relationship between the independent and dependent variables of primary interest (in this case, exposure to television or film violence and aggressive or antisocial behavior)?

2. Does the pattern of outcomes favor a causal inference (the explanation for any significant relationship)?

3. What are the circumstances that facilitate or inhibit a relationship (the attributes of the portrayal, viewer, or situation that make a difference)?

4. How robust is the relationship in the face of methodological challenges (the stability of outcomes when criteria such as ecological validity and study quality are applied)?[2]

5. What is the magnitude of the relationship (in meta-analytic jargon, the "effect size")?

IN THE LAP OF THE ANALYST

The strength of meta-analysis is that it addresses these questions by pooling all retrievable data, thereby ordinarily surpassing the informativeness of any single study. Any single study has particular strengths and weaknesses. These might reside in the measures, procedures, or samples. Other studies have different strengths and weaknesses. Multiple studies in effect compensate for each other's weaknesses. Thus, a strength of meta-analysis is that by combining studies, the weaknesses of specific individual studies are overcome. Nevertheless, meta-analysis is no substitute for interpretation.

Interpretation occurs on two levels. At the first, the very outcomes that are quantitatively aggregated must be assigned some meaning. Experimental findings that clearly document causation within the circumstances of experimental data collection may not generalize to other circumstances. Positive correlation coefficients within a survey may or may not imply causation. Adjudication is required. At the second level, individual studies may produce data that challenge or lead to the qualification of an explanation offered for the outcomes aggregated by meta-analysis. Adjustment of perspective may be necessary. Thus, meta-analysis is a nifty machine that supplies superior data but stubbornly leaves scientific meaning in the lap of the analyst.

There are surprisingly few meta-analyses of television and film violence and its ability to shape aggression, despite the perennial presence of the topic among popular concerns. In a pioneering effort, Andison (1977) simply categorized the outcomes of 67 experiments and surveys as to the direction and size of the relationship between violence viewing and aggressive or antisocial behavior. He was followed by Hearold (1986), who was the first to apply the now widely accepted meta-analytic practice of using the statistical measure of variance, the standard deviation, as a criterion of effect size to the literature on media and behavior. She was a student of Eugene Glass at the University of Colorado, who is credited with developing meta-analysis in the 1970s in an attempt to quantitatively discredit H. J. Eysenck's claims that psychotherapy was ineffective.[3] In an ambitiously comprehensive undertaking, she examined more than 1,000 relationships drawn from 168 studies between exposure to anti- and prosocial portrayals and anti- and prosocial behavior. In stark contrast, Wood, Wong, and Chachere (1991) focused only on manipulations that clearly permitted causal inference and spontaneous antisocial behavior, examining 23 experiments in and out of the laboratory in which the dependent variable was "unconstrained interpersonal aggression" among children and teenagers, thereby strengthening ecological validity. Allen, D'Alessio, and Brezgel (1995) were similarly focused, aggregating the data from 33 laboratory-type experiments in which the independent variable was exposure to video or film erotica and the dependent variable was aggression. Hogben (1998) chose a very different focus, assessing only studies measuring everyday viewing. He also chose to include outcomes that varied widely, including aggressive behavior, hostile attitudes, personality variables, and in one instance (Cairns, Hunter, & Herring, 1980) the inventing by children of imagined news stories. Paik and Comstock (1994), in a comprehensive updating of Hearold's assessment of the relationship between exposure to television violence and aggressive and antisocial behavior, included 82 new studies for a total of 217, which produced 1,142 coefficients between the independent and dependent variables.[4] Bushman and Anderson (2001) produced a time series representing the correlations between exposure to violent portrayals and aggressive behavior by five-year intervals over 25 years beginning in 1975. Bushman and Huesmann (2006) included 264 studies of media violence and its role in predicting aggressive outcomes among children, as well as 167 studies examining the same among adults, and examined a multitude of media forms including TV, film, video games, music, and comic books. Savage and Yancey (2008) confined the dependent variable in question to violent behavior that is criminal in nature or, among children, those physical forms of violence that would be analogous to illegal actions if they were perpetrated by older individuals, which yielded 26 independent samples for their analysis. Most recently, Ferguson and Kilburn (2009) limited their analysis to later studies (those published between 1998 and 2008); although they examine a host of differing media types and their statistical relationships with aggressive behavior, we'll focus the majority of our observations on the eight studies within the sample that examined television.

This is a vast accumulation of data representing the behavior of many thousands of persons of all ages, a wide range of independent and dependent variables, and an array of methods. These are all typically positive features of meta-analyses, which reflect the characteristics of their topic areas in contrast to the narrow profile of a single study.

ASSOCIATION AND CAUSATION

The analyses listed above—despite the recent addition of the Savage and Yancey (2008) and Ferguson and Kilburn (2009) analyses that make claims otherwise—make it irrefutably clear that children and teenagers who view greater amounts of violent television and movie portrayals are more likely to behave in an aggressive manner (Table 13.1). Across meta-analyses, this holds for the data from both of the basic designs, experiments (where the effects of a treatment are assessed and causality can be inferred), and surveys (where everyday behavior is reflected). Interpretation nevertheless is important.

Table 13.1
Selected Effects Sizes from Ten Meta-Analyses of Screen Violence and Aggression

Author	Independent Variable	Dependent Variable	N* (r =)	Effect Size
Andison, 1977	Television violence	Aggressive behavior	67	.28**
Hearold, 1986	Antisocial portrayals	Antisocial behavior	528	.30
Wood, Wong & Chachere, 1991	Aggressive portrayals	Unconstrained interpersonal aggression	12	.20
Paik & Comstock, 1994	Television violence	Aggressive behavior	1142	.31
Allen, D'Alessio & Brezgel, 1995	Pornography	Aggressive behavior	7	.13
Hogben, 1998	Violent programming	Aggression-related responses	56	.11
Bushman & Anderson, 2001	Television violence	Aggressive behavior	202	.15**
Bushman & Huesmann, 2006	Media violence	Aggressive behavior	262	.19
Savage & Yancey, 2008	Television/film violence	Criminal or analogous behavior	26	.10***
Ferguson & Kilburn, 2009	Television violence	Aggressive behavior	7	.12****

* Number of coefficients represented by effect size.
** Calculated from the distribution of coefficients by size of effect.
*** Calculated by averaging across the overall effect sizes for each of four categories of studies reported by the authors: aggregate comparisons, experimental and quasi-experimental studies, cross-sectional simple correlations, and multivariate longitudinal comparisons. In the latter case (multivariate longitudinal comparisons), we utilize the combined coefficient that includes original hypothesis tests and post hoc analyses.
**** We report the uncorrected rather than the corrected coefficient since Ferguson and Kilburn's test for publication bias among the studies on television was inconclusive. NB: Their analysis was confined to research published between 1998 and 2008. In some cases, Cohen's $\underline{d}$ converted to $\underline{r}$ by Table 2.3 (p. 16, Rosenthal, Rosnow, and Rubin (2000).
All $\underline{r}$'s statistically significant; for example, the Paik and Comstock $\underline{p}$ is less than .0000.

What should be made of this association? The case for causation rests on (1) the relative consistency of the outcomes for the experimental designs and (2) the general confirmation by the outcomes of the survey designs that the condition indicative of real-life causation exists—an everyday positive correlation between violence viewing and aggressive or antisocial behavior. Across the experimental designs, exposure to violent portrayals is typically followed by increases in aggressive outcomes. Across the survey designs, there is consistently an association between violence viewing and behavior (as well as cognitions and affect) not readily explainable without some contribution by exposure to violent portrayals.

In our views, the newer findings of Savage and Yancey (2008) and Ferguson and Kilburn (2009) do not compellingly challenge this. Despite the confinement of dependent variables to behavior that meets the definition of, or would be analogous to, violent crime, Savage and Yancey report significant and positive relationships among the cross-sectional correlations generated by surveys ($r = 0.16$) and the multivariate longitudinal comparisons ($r = 0.12$) in their sample. Indeed, the failure of the experimental group of studies to support a television effect seems readily understandable from the point of view of both ethics and practicality. Can we rightly expect a study to trigger a behavior in the lab that would be classified as criminally violent in nature? In the case of Ferguson and Kilburn (2009), their decision to exclude studies conducted before 1998 eliminated much of the evidence for the purposes of the central focus of this chapter, as the preponderance of the more recent studies of media violence have focused on video games rather than television and film. The effect sizes that Ferguson and Kilburn report for their small number of studies on television violence, in particular, vary widely between a corrected ($r = 0.04$) and an uncorrected ($r = 0.12$) statistic. The correction is used to account for publication bias and the authors argue that it provides the more trustworthy result, and yet in the case of those studies pertaining to television—our primary concern here—the authors' test for publication bias is inconclusive, as are a number of other tests for subtypes of data they report. The claim for publication bias is also questionable given that they excluded most of the research on violent television.

The fact that coefficients can vary widely and interpretation of the size and strength of an association can diverge accordingly stems from a number of decisions that meta-analysts must make regarding how to handle the data. Indeed, there have been a series of critiques and rejoinders among Ferguson and colleagues and Bushman and Anderson and colleagues—as well as others (Huesmann, 2010; Zimmerman & Strasburger, 2010)—on such points (Bushman, Rothstein, & Anderson, 2010; Rothstein & Bushman, 2012; as well as Ferguson & Brannick, 2012; Ferguson & Kilburn, 2010a, 2010b). The researchers differ, for instance, in their view of whether the inclusion of unpublished studies in meta-analysis is likely to increase or decrease the presence of publication bias (or bias of any other sort). They take issue as well with which studies were included (or failed to be included) in one another's analyses, with the accuracy of measures of aggression, and with the social significance of the effects observed (are small effects trivial?). Our own over-all conclusion is that even with these sources of disagreement, many of the results produced in the existing meta-analyses, particularly in those con-ducted most recently, are relatively similar in size, as seen in the bottom half of Table 13.1, and therefore we feel confident in discussing them as a collective.

The "reverse hypothesis" (Belson, 1978), which holds that the association in everyday life is attributable to the seeking out of violent entertainment by those particularly likely to engage in such behavior, fares particularly badly. The most striking evidence comes from Kang's (1990) reanalysis of the NBC panel data (Milavsky, Kessler, Stipp, & Rubens, 1982) on elementary school children.[5] Most survey data must be confined to claims of association (and thus fail to decidedly rule out the reverse hypothesis) rather than causation because variables are measured at only one point in time, thereby obscuring the issue of which variable caused a change in the other. Kang (1990) over-came this methodological obstacle by using data from a survey design in which questionnaires were administered at multiple points in time, allowing for the establishment of time order that is necessary to claim causation. He found twice as many significant coefficients, eight versus four, for a viewing-to-behavior effect than for a behavior-to-viewing outcome out of a total of 15 waves of earlier and later measurement, with only one instance of reciprocal association. Belson (1978) similarly found in his survey of about 1,600 London teenage males that the data did not support the reverse hypothesis as the explanation for a positive association between violence viewing and the committing of seriously harmful acts (such as attempted rape; use of a tire iron, razor, knife, or gun in a fight; falsely reporting a bomb threat) among a subpopulation with a high likelihood of delinquent behavior (violence view-ing predicted a substantial difference in antisocial behavior, while aggressive propensity predicted only a minute difference in violence viewing). There is also the very widely cited finding of Lefkowitz, Eron, Walder, and Huesmann (1977) in an upstate New York sample of about 200 males that the amount of violent television viewing at age 8 predicted aggressive behavior at age 19 ($r = 0.31$), but aggressive behavior at age 8 did not predict the viewing of vio-lent television at age 19 ($r = 0.01$). More recently, Slater, Henry, Swaim, and Anderson (2003) utilized hierarchical linear modeling in data derived from over 2,500 middle school students from across the United States and found evidence of a mutually reinforcing relationship between violent media use (including television, movies, video games, and Internet) and aggressiveness over time. Yet their "downward spiral" model was asymmetrical, and ulti-mately more robust for media effects than the reverse hypothesis. Specifically, the growth curves supported associations between media violence exposure and aggression that were both concurrent (both measured at once) and prospective in nature (in which violent media use predated aggression), whereas prospective paths between earlier aggression and later violent media use were non-significant.

CIRCUMSTANCES AND ROBUSTNESS

Gender

Both females and males are affected by media violence. In the meta-analysis of Paik and Comstock, effect sizes are similar for the two genders in surveys (females, $r = 0.19$; males, $r = 0.18$), the method that most closely represents real-life, everyday associations, and it is only in the experiments that effect sizes are somewhat greater for males (females, $r = 0.39$; males, $r = 0.44$). This is a pattern whose recognition is owed to meta-analysis and is quite different from the impression given (and often repeated in textbooks) by the early experiments with nursery school children of Bandura and colleagues (Bandura, Ross, & Ross, 1963a, 1963b) in which effects appeared greater among males. Savage and Yancey (2008) report effect sizes of 0.14 for males and 0.19 for females among the 16 (for males) and 13 (for females) cross-sectional surveys with relevant data by gender, respectively. They found further that for multivariate, longitudinal studies, effects sizes differed substantially in analyses of gender according to whether authors of the studies confined themselves to their original hypotheses or engaged in some sort of post hoc statistical analyses. Among the post hoc models, effects sizes are reported at 0.19 for males and 0.25 for females—even when controlling for trait aggression as well in the model (apropos of the former section of this chapter on the reverse hypothesis)—although it should be noted the number of studies included in the analysis varies from just four for females to six for males and, as Savage and Yancey report, the post hoc data may be an overestimation since, in some cases, the authors of the original studies report only that original analyses were nonsignificant rather than also including the coefficients necessary to include those original analyses in the meta-analysis.

Age

Somewhat surprisingly, age fails to offer the mitigation that one might expect from enhanced ability to comprehend, analyze, and react critically to what is seen on the television screen. In the Paik and Comstock meta-analysis, effect sizes in experiments are nonlinear: they do decrease between the preschool and adult years, but they increase among those of college age. Furthermore, in surveys that most accurately reflect everyday events, the effect size for adults is greater than for any other age group except those of preschool age. Our conclusion is that television violence effects cannot be said to disappear as people grow older, although they are particularly pronounced among the very young. When we expand the lens to include a variety of media forms rather than solely focusing on television, the Bushman and Huesmann (2006) meta-analytic data show an interaction effect between study type (experiments compared to surveys) and age group of research participants (children compared to adults). In those data—encompassing television, film, video games, music, and comic books—effect sizes are larger for adults in the studies that use experimental design and for children in the studies that use survey design. The pattern is convincingly explained by the application of theory: short-term effects as measured in the laboratory (experiments) typically rest on the participant's ability to associate a new violent media stimulus with a network of similar mental models, an ability logically more developed among adults. Conversely, children appear to be more susceptible to long-term influence through observational learning. For children, repeated exposure to media violence over time may both develop their scripts for aggressive behavior and send the cultural message that aggression is acceptable.

Time

The likelihood of an effect among children and adolescents increases with the passage of time presumably due to cumulative exposure. In addition to the Bushman and Huesmann (2006) data showing larger effects for young research participants among surveys that associate longer-term media exposures with aggressive outcomes, this conclusion rests, as well, on four different aspects of the NBC panel data.

In the original analysis by Milavsky, Kessler, Stipp, and Rubens (1982), the coefficients among the elementary school sample became larger as the span of time between measurements grew longer. In the same analysis, the coefficients among the same sample are somewhat larger when there are no statistical controls to eliminate the influence of earlier viewing. In the further reanalysis of the NBC panel data by Cook, Kendzierski, and Thomas (1983), there is evidence throughout of increasing coefficients among both the elementary and teenage samples with the passage of time, and for a variety of alternate measures of aggression. And finally, Kang (1990) found among his eight significant viewing-to-behavior coefficients that five were clustered among the longest time spans (while among his four significant behavior-to-viewing coefficients, three were clustered among the shortest time spans), thereby providing additional evidence that effects on behavior increase with the passage of time and any behavior-to-viewing effects are largely confined to the short term.

Taken together, these studies show an important pattern of results. The Milavsky et al. (1982) study above suggests a longitudinal effect. It also shows a cumulative effect. The Cook et al. (1983) analysis shows either a longitudinal or cumulative effect. And the Kang (1990) study shows the apparently decisive role of the passage of time in behavioral effects. Earlier viewing appears to affect later behavior, presumably because the young viewer becomes better prepared or more motivated to emulate in some fashion what has been observed, and this phenomenon is enhanced when greater amounts of violence viewing continue between the dates when earlier viewing and later behavior are measured. Again, the longitudinal analyses included in the Savage and Yancey (2008) meta-analysis also show significant effects sizes when including post hoc statistical analyses, a result that implies a link between television violence and behaviors that would be classified as criminal (although the post hoc nature of the analyses may well inflate the link).

Severity of Aggressive Expression

The evidence is mounting that the size of the relationship between television and film violence exposure and an aggressive effect is larger for less severe forms of aggression. Paik and Comstock (1994) found an effect size of 0.10 when examining only those studies in which the dependent measure of aggressive behavior would be criminal in nature, in comparison with an effect of 0.31 for more minor aggressive behavior. Savage and Yancey's (2008) small and nonsignificant effect sizes in their analysis of the small subset of studies for which the outcome variable would be illegal or criminal in nature among aggregate studies (those that examine macro-level associations such as between the advent of television and crime rates in communities) and experiments and quasi-experiments supports the point. Ferguson and Kilburn (2009) also report higher effects sizes for "proxy" measures of aggression, in which aggressive behavior is not directly measured (such as through teacher or peer nominations; $r = 0.25$, $r^{\text{corrected}} = 0.25$), compared to more direct measures of aggressive behavior (physical assaults, fighting, or arguing [$r = 0.10$, $r^{\text{corrected}} = 0.08$] and violent crime [$r = 0.07$, $r^{\text{corrected}} = 0.02$]).

Exacerbating Conditions

Of course, media are not the sole source of aggression, nor are they the largest influence (see Figure 13.1). The effects of media violence exposure are likely to be exacerbated by such causal contributors to aggression as low socioeconomic status, poor or neglectful parenting, unsatisfactory social relationships, low psychological well-being, and a predisposition toward aggressive and antisocial behavior. These factors function either through increasing the frequency of exposure to violent portrayals or as direct (and often times stronger, compared to media) predictors of engaging in antisocial behavior (Comstock & Scharrer, 1999; U.S. Department of Health and Human Services, 2001). Socioeconomic status is inversely associated with exposure to television and television violence (i.e., lower SES groups tend to be exposed to higher amounts of TV violence; Comstock & Scharrer, 1999), although the

Figure 13.1
Effect Sizes of Factors Constituting Early Risks (Ages 6–11) for Serious Violence at Ages 15–18

General offenses	.38 ////////////////////////
Substance use	.30 /////////////////
Being male	.26 //////////////
Low SES/poverty	.24 /////////////
Antisocial parents	.23 ////////////
Male aggression	.22 ///////////
Psychological condition	.15 ////////
Hyperactivity	.13 //////
Poor parent-child relations	.15 ////////
Harsh, lax, or inconsistent discipline	.13 //////
Weak social ties	.15 ////////
Problem behavior (antisocial)	.13 //////
Exposure to television violence	.13 //////
Poor attitude toward performance in school	.13 //////
Low IQ	.12 /////
Other family conditions	.12 /////
Broken home	.09 ////
Separation from parents	.09 ////
Antisocial attitudes, beliefs	
Dishonesty (Males only)	.12 /////
Abusive parents	.07 ///
Neglect	.07 ///
Antisocial peers	.04 //

-02 -01 0 0.1   0.2   0.3   0.4

Meta-analysis by Hawkins et al. (1998); Lipsey and Derzon (1998); and Paik and Comstock (1994); or, pooling of outcomes from two or more longitudinal studies of general population samples. Specific factors listed when data permits.
Source: Adapted from U.S. Department of Health and Human Services (p. 60, Table 4–1, 2001).

role of socioeconomic status is certainly not powerful enough to account fully for the relationship between exposure to television violence and aggression. An emphasis within the family on constructive, open communication among parents and children also is inversely associated with exposure to television programming in general as well as to violent television entertainment (Chaffee, McLeod, & Atkin, 1971; McLeod, Atkin, & Chaffee, 1972). Parental interest in children's whereabouts is inversely associated with a wide range of delinquent behavior (Thornton & Voigt, 1984). Social conflicts and psychological stress similarly increase the likelihood of viewing greater amounts of television, and thereby greater amounts of violence (Comstock & Scharrer, 1999).

There is certainly plenty of evidence that those with a predisposition for aggressive or antisocial behavior are particularly likely to be affected. By predisposition, we mean higher levels of antisocial behavior or attributes that are correlates of antisocial behavior. For example, in two survey designs, correlations with violence are particularly pronounced or limited to those already committing delinquent acts or earlier displaying aggression (Belson, 1978; Robinson & Bachman, 1972). In experiments, effects sometimes have been limited to those scoring higher in earlier aggressiveness (Josephson, 1987; Celozzi, Kazelskis, & Gutsch, 1981). And Paik (1991), in her meta-analytic dissertation, found a larger effect size for those scoring higher on measures of aggressive predisposition. We are somewhat hesitant, however, to conclude that predisposition is a necessary condition. Our basis is the consistency of results for surveys of samples with no known biases and for experiments with subjects randomly assigned to conditions. This consistency indicates that the association between exposure and behavior is common among the general population. If prior aggression is necessary, then it is also relatively common (and thereby no reason to expect that effects will be rare). The issue is further complicated by the Savage and Yancey (2008) data about criminal behavior, in which they report three studies in favor of a stronger television effect among those with high trait aggression and another three that provide data contradicting such a relationship. For a discussion of risk factors, see chapter 2 by Gentile, in this volume.

Sex versus Violence

Two of the meta-analyses produced effect sizes for exposure to explicitly sexual treatments. Both Allen, D'Alessio, and Brezgel (1985), who examined only sexually explicit portrayals, and Paik and Comstock (1994), who examined sexually explicit as well as violent portrayals, report effect sizes for violent erotica that are among the largest they recorded. Allen and colleagues reported an overall effect size for exposure to all types of pornography (with nudity, nonviolent sexual behavior, and violent sexual behavior pooled) that was modest ($r = 0.13$), although it achieved statistical significance. However, the picture changed somewhat when they confined the analyses to erotica without violence ($r = 0.17$) and violent erotica ($r = 0.22$). Paik and Comstock reported an effect size for violent erotica (vs. all other treatments with which violent erotica was compared) that was substantial ($r = 0.60$). Their comparable effect size for erotica without violence was smaller but still substantial ($r = 0.46$). Both well exceed the Paik and Comstock overall effect size for exposure to television and film violence ($r = 0.31$).

There has been considerable debate over whether "sex" is a major factor contributing to aggressive or antisocial outcomes (Weaver, 1991) or whether the contributing factor is primarily the "violence" (Donnerstein, Linz, & Penrod, 1987). The answer appears to be "both." Effect sizes for erotica with violence are consistently higher than they are for erotica without violence. However, coefficients for the latter are consistently positive. In both cases, exposure to the sexually explicit portrayals can be considered the cause of the aggressive or antisocial behavior because all the studies employed experimental designs.

Thus, a strong claim can be made for an effect on aggressive and antisocial behavior of erotica without violence, and a recent meta-analysis extends the dependent variable in question into attitudes toward violence against women. Hald, Malamuth, and Yuen (2010) meta-analyzed nine studies with just over 2,300 males who participated in nonexperimental research. They found attitudes supportive of violence against women were more strongly associated with exposure to violent pornography ($r = 0.24$) compared to nonviolent, but even nonviolent pornography exposure produced significant effect sizes ($r = 0.13$). The results reveal considerable heterogeneity across studies, however, indicating the presence of unmeasured moderating variables. Among 46 published studies encompassing a number of research methods, Oddone-Paolucci, Genuis, and Violato (2000) found even larger associations between use of pornography and support of rape myths.

Allen and colleagues (1995) provide additional important data. They followed the schema developed by the 1986 Attorney General's Commission on Pornography and divided their independent variables into an ascending scale representing the treatment of females as objects of sexual domination. There were three categories: portrayals of nudity without sex, erotica without violence, and violent erotica. For portrayals of nudity, they found an inverse effect size (i.e., greater exposure was associated with lower levels of aggressive or antisocial behavior; $r = -0.14$). For erotica without violence and violent erotica, effect sizes, as just discussed, were positive, and increased with the shift from the former to the latter. Violent portrayals alone, as the evidence clearly attests, can have an effect without an erotica element. Erotica can have an effect without violence. The two in combination, however, apparently become a powerful joint stimulus.

Our interpretation is that the inverse effect size in the data of Allen and colleagues for nudity and the weaker effect size for erotica are attributable to the comparative absence of cues that would encourage aggression, including the depiction of the female participants as meriting abuse, derision, or contempt. This factor would be at a maximum for violent erotica, reduced for erotica, and largely absent for nudity. We are constrained from invoking a logical alternative, lower levels of induced arousal, by Allen and colleagues' finding that self-reported arousal was inversely associated to a modest degree with aggressive and antisocial outcomes.

Ecological Validity and Study Quality

One of the features of meta-analysis is that it permits objectively testing whether confining the analysis to studies that were particularly high in ecological validity or methodological quality would alter the conclusions (e.g., better sampling, better controls, etc.). The sole requirement is that the studies be rated on these two characteristics. Neither Hearold nor Paik and Comstock, who both rated the studies they collected on both dimensions, found any evidence that the conclusion that exposure to violent portrayals predicts aggressive and antisocial behavior would be altered by focusing only on studies high either in ecological validity or methodological quality. However, Hearold, who examined prosocial as well as antisocial portrayals and outcomes did uncover an interesting symmetry when examining only the studies higher in methodological quality. Exposure to antisocial portrayals predicted heightened aggressive or antisocial behavior and lowered prosocial behavior. Exposure to prosocial portrayals predicted lowered aggressive or antisocial behavior and heightened prosocial behavior. Hearold (1986) concluded, "When the analysis is confined to studies of higher quality, antisocial and prosocial treatments are symmetrical in their association with behavior, and the data become entirely consistent with the view that the former encourages antisocial and inhibits pro-social behavior and the latter encourages pro-social and inhibits antisocial behavior" (p. 99). Conversely, Ferguson and Kilburn (2009) found weaker effect sizes in their much narrower sample among the studies that provided evidence of the validity and reliability of measures of aggression, as well as among those studies that employed control variables—although only seven of the studies Ferguson and Kilburn included in their meta-analysis pertained to television.

EVIDENCE AND MEDIA COVERAGE

Two parallel analyses were conducted by Bushman and Anderson (2001). In one, they examined the correlations between exposure to violent portrayals and aggressive behavior in both experimental and nonexperimental designs by five-year intervals beginning in 1975. In the other, they examined news coverage of the television violence and aggression controversy beginning in 1950.

In the first, they found statistically significant positive associations for experimental designs that were essentially stable across the 25 years and statistically significant positive associations for nonexperimental designs that increased in magnitude over the same period. The net result was an increase in the estimated size of the relation between exposure to violent portrayals and aggressive behavior. In the second, the dependent variable was the scientifically accurate report that exposure to media violence is positively correlated with aggressive behavior. They found that the scientific evidence and media coverage diverged (see Figure 13.2). The former had become stronger since 1975, while the accurate representation of the scientific record since 1950, after increasing in frequency between 1950 and 1980, had actually become less frequent. Thus, the curve representing the correlations sweeps upward while the curve representing the accuracy of coverage languishes

Figure 13.2
Comparison of News Reports with Scientific Studies on the Topic of the Effects of Media Violence on Aggression

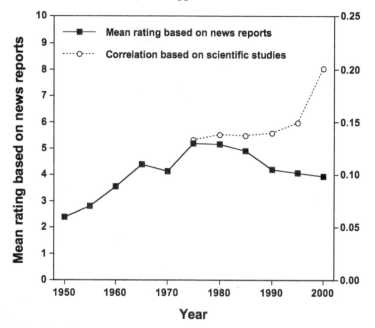

Note: Ratings based on news reports are positive if the article said that exposure to media violence is positively related to aggression. Correlations based on scientific studies are positive if media violence was positively related to aggression.
Source: B. J. Bushman & C. A. Anderson (2001), Media violence and the American public, *American Psychologist, 56*, 477–489.

with a visible (if less dramatic) decline. In fact, for the six data points since 1975, they record a large negative correlation of $r = -0.68$ between effect sizes and the accuracy ratings of news stories.

More recently, Martins et al. (2013) examined 540 news articles about the effects of media violence among the 25 top-circulating newspapers in the United States between 1982 and 2012. Overall, a greater proportion of news coverage did indicate a statistical link between media exposure and aggression (53%) compared to those that were either neutral on the subject of a statistical link (38%) or suggested there was no such link (9%). However, of the *studies* examined in the news coverage, the vast majority—80 percent—did find an association between media exposure and aggression, thereby showing that the news coverage underestimated the strength of the research evidence. The conclusiveness of the news coverage changes significantly over time. Beginning in the year 2000, Martins and colleagues found a precipitous drop in the number of news items that concluded there is an association, with the most recent period examined (2007–2011) exhibiting the smallest number of stories across each of five time periods that claim a statistical link between media violence and aggression (just 39%). The authors suggest the drop may be attributed to the increase in news coverage of the effects of video games (for which the news coverage of a media effect is considerably less decisive).

The conclusions of Bushman and Anderson (2001) at the close of their own content analysis seem enduringly apt. The behavior of the news media "is disheartening at best" and they observe that "it has been decades since one could reasonably claim that there is little reason for concern about media violence effects" (p. 485). Yet, if one were to rely on the news media alone for this information, particularly most recently, one would get an entirely different impression.

INTERPRETING EFFECT SIZES

There are four ways to interpret meta-analytic effect sizes. The first essentially employs the kind of labeling that we use so frequently in everyday life—established criteria for what should be considered large, medium, small, or null. The second introduces the seriousness of the purported outcome to weight the size of the effect (the analogy is fear, with fear increasing not only with the probability of an undesirable event but also with the direness of its consequences). The third is a comparison with effect sizes in other realms to provide some context as to what might be expected and what should be judged as substantial. The fourth is the predictability of the fate of the individual implied by the effect size.

Established Criteria

The most widely employed guidelines are those developed by Cohen (1988). By his criteria, $r = 0.10$ should be considered "small," $r = 0.30$ "medium," and $r = 0.50$ "large" (Rosenthal, Rosnow, & Rubin, 2000). His grounds were essentially pragmatic. The frequency of statistically significant correlation coefficients, an accepted measure of effect size, in the social and behavioral sciences is inversely related to their size. As size increases, coefficients become increasingly scarce. More recently, Hemphill (2003) used an empirical approach and found that Cohen's labels should be revised, where $r = 0.10$ should be considered "small," $r = 0.20$ "medium," and $r = 0.30$ "large." Nonetheless, the thresholds at which null crosses into small territory, or other borders are violated, remain open to judgment.

By these criteria, the effect sizes for interpersonal aggression in the Paik and Comstock meta-analysis, the most comprehensive in regard to violent television portrayals and a wide range of aggressive behavior, would be considered small or medium ($r. = 0.24$ for physical aggression and $r. = 0.27$ for verbal aggression). We use the plural, "effect sizes," because they differ for each category of aggression, and within each category of aggression vary depending on method, program characteristics, and age and gender of respondents or subjects. The approach of the medium range in this instance is quite important. Interpersonal aggression is the real-life (and thereby, ecologically valid) outcome that has been studied most often, and it clearly possesses an unpleasant and definitely-to-be-avoided experience for the victim—for example, stealing, hitting, name-calling. Thus, it combines extensive data with personal discomfort and thus social significance. In the same Paik and Comstock meta-analysis, coefficients for both simulated aggression (such as aggressive inclination measured by questionnaire or performance on an aggression machine) and minor aggression (such as violence done to an object or aggression against a person that ordinarily would not come to the attention of a law enforcement agency)[6] usually approach or achieve the medium range by Cohen's criteria, although sometimes are in the large range.

While Savage and Yancey (2008) insist that their data are an exception to the positive relationships found in other meta-analyses examining television violence and aggression, they too report significant positive correlations for both cross-sectional surveys ($r = 0.16$) and longitudinal comparison data ($r = 0.12$). Since they limited their dependent variable to violent crime, even these small effect sizes can have major societal implications. They are also in range with the effect size found by Bushman and Huesmann (2006) for aggressive behavior in general ($r = 0.19$). Ferguson and Kilburn (2009), meanwhile, argue forcefully that the existing literature offers no evidence of a relationship between exposure to media violence (including TV violence—our main concern) and real-life aggression. We respectfully disagree. Even they report positive effect sizes for the few studies that examine the effects of television violence. These correlations range between a corrected statistic where $r = 0.04$ and an uncorrected statistic where $r = 0.12$, smaller than many of those found by Paik and Comstock, but again, representing far fewer studies (and again, in the case of the studies on television violence in particular, there does not appear to be a convincing reason to accept the corrected statistic as the better approximation, since the test for publication bias was inconclusive).

Seriousness

If a focus on more perilous or decidedly illegal behavior is demanded, the Paik and Comstock meta-analysis produces effect sizes that are decidedly smaller than for interpersonal aggression but are statistically significant, represent greater harm than stealing, hitting, or name-calling, and almost always achieve the small and sometimes achieve the medium range in magnitude. For seriously hurtful or illegal activities, the omnibus effect for all observations is $r = 0.17$. As the seriousness of the offense increases, effect sizes become smaller. Even so, violence against a person registers an effect size of $r = 0.10$, achieves statistical significance, and produces a fail-safe number of almost 3,000.[7] Again, Savage and Yancey (2008) insist that their data are an exception here, yet their summary coefficient for longitudinal data is also positive and statistically significant.

Examples from individual studies certainly support the view that sizable effects are not limited to interpersonal aggression. In his large London probability sample of teenage males, Belson (1978) found that among delinquents, the very low rate of committing seriously hurtful (and decidedly criminal) acts increased by 50 percent among those who viewed greater amounts of violent television entertainment, and he presents a good case for attributing this difference to the contribution of viewing violence. In a second noteworthy instance, a group led by the methodologist Thomas Cook (Hennigan et al., 1982) took advantage of the Federal Communication Commission's (FCC) freeze on television station licenses in the late 1940s to conduct a quasi-experimental time series with switching replications (Cook & Campbell, 1979). They found that at two points in time (the early and late introduction of television) and in two samples (cities and states, with the frequency of set ownership used to distinguish those that were early and late adoption sites) that the arrival of the medium was accompanied by a significant increase in larceny theft. This outcome has been variously attributed to relative deprivation traceable to the materialistic emphasis of the medium (Hennigan et al., 1982) and the emulation of television's antisocial portrayals at a level where apprehension would be unlikely and sanctions minimal (Comstock, 1991). Whatever the underlying dynamics, the increases of about 6 to about 17 percent across the four coefficients represented a sizable change. One can imagine the huge headlines that would follow similar percentage increases in national crime rates or the prevalence nationally of a serious disease such as cancer. These increases constitute a socially substantial effect. And in their widely publicized longitudinal study of 707 individuals that appeared in *Science*, Johnson, Cohen, Smailes, Kasen, and Brook (2002) found that "assault or physical fights resulting in injury" as well as "any aggressive act against another person" were more frequent among males at ages 16 or 22 who viewed greater amounts of television (and presumably, therefore, greater amounts of violence) at the age of 14. The fact that the statistically significant results remain after controlling for five important co-variates (or predictors) of both television viewing and aggression—childhood neglect, growing up in an unsafe neighborhood, low family income, low parental education, and psychiatric disorder (p. 2469)—suggest that television contributed causally as well as possibly reinforcing the effects of these enemies of well-being.

Finally, drawing on Paik and Comstock, the Surgeon General's recent report on youth violence (U.S. Department of Health and Human Services, 2001) identifies exposure to television violence as 1 of about 20 early (between the ages of 6 and 11) risk factors (including individual, family, school, and peer variables) for the committing of seriously harmful criminal violence between the ages of 15 and 18. The effect size of $r = 0.13$ was classified as small. However, effects are similarly small for three-fourths of the variables identified as early risk factors (again, see Figure 13.1).

Other Effect Sizes

Bushman and Anderson (2001) supply a catalogue of effect sizes from other realms (see Figure 13.3). There exist, of course, effect sizes that are much grander than those presented. For example, the effect sizes for gender on height or for a year of additional school on the ability of a child to read are far larger (Hearold, 1986). However, these represent substantial associations occurring in the natural order of things—physical differences between males and females, and the consequences among children of study and maturation for the acquisition of a cognitive skill. When we confine ourselves to interventions that are outside such basic human phenomena, the effect sizes for exposure to television or film violence and aggressive or antisocial behavior are respectable. Quite a few effect sizes whose importance socially or statistically are hard to deny fall into the small range: exposure to lead and IQ scores among children, nicotine patch adoption and smoking cessation, calcium intake and bone mass, homework and academic achievement, exposure to asbestos and laryngeal cancer, and self-examination and extent of breast cancer. All of these match the range of effects sizes found in the most recent meta-analyses pertaining to television violence (see Table 13.1).

Predictability

The criterion of predictability extends the comparison of effect sizes as a means of estimating the importance that should be attached to a particular size of effect to a narrower focus on what an effect size implies for the individual. We step from the effect size as our outcome of interest to its informativeness about what would be expected, given a particular effect size, once a score or standing on the independent variable is known.

Rosenthal and colleagues have been at the forefront in the development of this approach, offering both an analysis of the behavioral research on media violence and aggression (Rosenthal, 1986) and a more general treatment of effect sizes in social research (Rosenthal, Rosnow, & Rubin, 2000). The key in these analyses is the "binomial effect size display" (BESD), initially introduced as a way of displaying the magnitude of effects demonstrated experimentally (Rosenthal & Rubin, 1982). The question asked is, "What should we expect in regard to an individual's standing on the dependent variable given a particular effect size and exposure to the treatment?" In practice in our case, the predictor becomes belonging to the treatment or control group in an experiment or falling above or below the median in exposure in a survey. The BESD is a crude measure but has two important properties: (1) it conveys a

Figure 13.3
Selected Effect Sizes vs. the Paik and Comstock Meta-Analytic Television
Violence Effect Size of r = 0.31

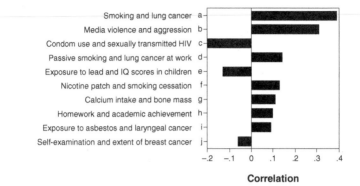

Correlation

Note: A correlation coefficient can range from −1 (a perfect negative linear relation) to +1 (a perfect positive linear relation), with 0 indicating no linear relation.

Sources: (a) The effect of smoking tobacco on lung cancer was estimated by pooling the data from Figures 1 and 3 in Wynder and Graham's (1950) classic article. The remaining effects were estimated from meta-analyses: (b) Paik and Comstock (1994); (c) Weller (1993); (d) Wells (1998); (e) Needleman and Gatsonis (1990); (f) Fiore, Smith, Jorenby, and Baker (1994); (g) Welten, Kemper, Post, and van Staveren (1995); (h) Cooper (1989); (i) Smith, Handley, and Wood (1990); (j) Hill, White, Jolley, and Mapperson (1988). Adapted from Bushman and Anderson (2001).

sense of how much an effect size improves knowledge about the outcome, and (2) it permits an estimate of how many persons will be affected.

This is a matter in this case of translating the "*r*" into a contingency table with the rows representing the independent variable and the columns the dependent variable, with both treated as dichotomous. Rosenthal, Rosnow, and Rubin (2000) present a general example using *r* = 0.32 as an effect size with equal Ns, with interesting results (Table 13.2). The effect size was chosen because it was one reported by Glass (1976) for psychotherapy in what was the public unveiling of what has become known as meta-analysis. The effect size ensures a success rate—modestly represented in this case by some degree of improvement—of 66 percent for those experiencing the treatment (in this case, some form of psychotherapy), in contrast with a rate of 34 percent for those not experiencing the treatment. In other words, a more desirable state of affairs is achieved for two-thirds instead of one-third of the population. Construed in this way, an effect size of this magnitude has important social implications if the dependent variable has social importance.

The reader undoubtedly will have noticed that the Paik and Comstock effect size of *r* = 0.31 for media exposure and aggression in general is almost identical. Bushman and Huesmann (2001) performed the necessary calculations:

Table 13.2
Binomial Effect Size Display

$r = .32$
OUTCOME

Condition	Improved	Not Improved	Totals
Treatment (Psychotherapy)	66	34	100
Control	34	66	100
Totals	100	100	200

Source: Adapted from Rosenthal, Rosnow, & Rubin (2000).

The .31 correlation is equivalent to aggressive behavior being exhibited by 65.5 percent of those above the median in exposure . . . but only by 34.4 percent of those below the median. . . . (p. 234)

In symmetry with the outcome for psychotherapy, the peril rate (those who behaved more aggressively) was increased from slightly more than one-third to two-thirds of the population by the treatment of exposure to television or film violence.

Rosenthal, Rosnow, and Rubin present three examples from biomedical research that compellingly identify very small effect sizes as important when the effect is of consequence. Effect sizes of small ($r = 0.03$, 0.04, and 0.07) obtained from large samples (22,071 male physicians, 2,108 heart patients, and 4,462 army veterans, respectively) produced BESDs indicating that 3.4 percent fewer of the physicians would have suffered from a heart attack, 4 percent fewer of the patients would have suffered from a new attack, and 7 percent more veterans suffered from alcohol abuse or dependence if they had served in Vietnam rather than some other place. In the first two instances, the results were judged so important that the placebo trials were halted on the grounds that it was unethical to deprive the control population (and everyone else) of the benefits; in the second, Rosenthal, Rosnow, and Rubin (p. 27) remark with glee (because of the dramatic support for their advocacy of the importance of small effect sizes) that the r^2 began with a double zero (which means that less than 1 percent of the variance in total attacks was explained by or associated with the independent variable despite the undeniable social—and personal—benefit of reducing attacks by 4 percent).

We are led to three conclusions. First, effect sizes in the realm of media violence and aggressive or antisocial behavior handily satisfy each of the four criteria. Second, they are not trivial, and in each case represent a socially substantial impact. Third, size inevitably must be weighted by the risk or benefit implied. Thus, ascription of substantial social impact rests on the unwelcome and undesirable character of the outcome—minor aggressive behavior, with a medium effect size, and hurtful and illegal acts, with a smaller effect size (in the Paik and Comstock meta-analysis, $r = 0.31$ and 0.17, respectively).

RELATED META-ANALYSES AND BEYOND

The preponderance of more recent media violence studies have abandoned traditional TV and film for video games and pornography (the latter accessed mostly via the Internet). These, too, have been subjected to meta-analysis.

Specifically, eight meta-analyses examining the relationship between violent video game use and aggressive thoughts, attitudes, and behaviors have been published (Anderson, 2004; Anderson & Bushman, 2001; Anderson et al., 2004; Anderson et al., 2010; Ferguson, 2007a, 2007b; Greitemeyer & Mügge, 2014; Sherry, 2001). What is most striking across all eight analyses is the remarkable consistency of the results with aggressive behavior as a dependent variable, for which effects sizes range from a low of 0.14 to a high of 0.23, with an average of 0.18. Similar consistent results are reported in regard to violent video game use being inversely related to prosocial behavior, as evidenced in Table 13.3.

Even so, there is disagreement among the authors of the video game meta-analyses as to whether the *significant* results are *meaningful*. Whereas Anderson, Bushman, and their colleagues believe the empirical findings are indeed important in the real-world connection between media use and violence, Ferguson and Sherry largely do not. The point here is that even though there is disagreement about how to interpret the data, there is very little difference in the empirical findings themselves. The bottom line is that there appears to be a small to moderate effect size between the use of violent video games and aggression, and a small to moderate inverse relationship between violent video game use and prosocial behavior. The essence of the disagreement, therefore, once again has to do with whether the results are meaningful in a real-world context. Indeed, since the enactment of aggression in day-to-day life has many risk factors, including genetics (nature) and circumstances (nurture), it is important to remember that the contribution of media—whether television or video games or other forms—should be understood as one of many potentially facilitating factors.

In the most comprehensive study, Anderson et al. (2010) conducted a meta-analysis on exposure to violent video games and the effects of such exposure on six outcome variables: physically aggressive behavior, aggressive cognition, aggressive affect, physiological arousal, prosocial behavior, and a combined empathy/desensitization variable. They report results similar to those found in the meta-analyses examining exposure to television violence and aggression.

Table 13.3
Effect Size Findings from Eight Meta-Analyses of Violent Video Game Effects on Aggressive and Prosocial Behaviors

Dependent variable	Anderson & Bushman (2004)	Sherry (2001)	Anderson (2004)	Anderson et al. (2010)	Ferguson (2007a)	Ferguson (2007b)	Anderson et al. (2001)	Greitemeyer & Mügge (2014)
Aggressive Behaviors	0.18	0.16	0.20	0.23	0.15	0.14	0.19	0.19
Prosocial Behaviors	-0.16	x	-0.21	-0.25	0.30	x	-.010	-0.11

Note: x = not provided.
Sources: Anderson, 2004; Anderson & Bushman, 2001; Anderson et al., 2004; Anderson et al., 2010; Ferguson, 2007a, 2007b; Greitemeyer & Mügge, 2014; Sherry, 2001.

Specifically, they report that—regardless of research design—exposure to violent video games was positively correlated in the best raw samples to higher levels of aggressive behavior (overall $r = 0.24$); aggressive cognition ($r = 0.18$); aggressive affect ($r = 0.12$); and physiological arousal ($r = 0.18$). Further, they found that exposure to violent video games leads to lower levels of prosocial behavior ($r = -0.11$) and empathy ($r = -0.19$). In summary, Anderson et al. calculate an overall effect size estimate of $r = 0.15$ for exposure to violent video games and the outcome variables.

What should strike the attentive reader here is the remarkable consistency across myriad meta-analyses of television violence, video game violence, and pornography violence. In each case, overall significant positive correlations between exposure to violent content and attitudes/behaviors that facilitate or indicate aggression have been reported.

Despite the authors who find the statistically significant relationships between violent video game use and aggression to be unimportant, most scholarly reviews—often a broader range of evidence—have concluded that the media violence debate has been effectively answered and that exposure to media violence primarily through television and video game forms is one significant risk factor (among many) for aggressive and violent behavior (Anderson et al., 2003). We agree, on the basis of evidence, at the same time that we call upon scholars to engage with some of the ecological criticisms that have been levied against the literature—such as how well any study's measure of aggression actually corresponds to the expression of violent behavior on a day-to-day, "real life" basis, or how studies of the media's contribution can be understood in the context of declining violent behavior statistics in the United States and other locations—in future research. Such engagement would further strengthen the research record and perhaps help to bridge diverging interpretations.

Meta-analysis, as should now be apparent, does not substitute for individual studies but complements them. Meta-analysis has the benefit of determining whether there is an effect and estimating its strength. Sometimes, however, individual studies are particularly useful for indicating how an effect occurs or whether a particular independent or dependent variable is involved. Often, individual studies will provide information not found in a meta-analysis because that particular issue has not been investigated often enough to appear in a meta-analysis or because a particular study has unusual strengths. An example of the latter occurs with Belson's (1978) sample of about 1,600 male teenagers in London. The sample was extremely large, and is a probability sample (and thus the only survey that statistically can be said to represent a larger population). Procedures were high in quality, with respondents personally interviewed for three-and-a-half hours in a physician-like clinical setting by a conservatively attired male. Thus, the data appear to us as highly credible in representing real-world patterns of behavior.

EVALUATING THE META-ANALYSES

The meta-analyses provide a strong and impressive body of data linking exposure to violent television portrayals with subsequent aggressive or anti-social behavior. Regardless of the vagaries and variety in the independent and dependent variables, each of the meta-analyses produces positive and statistically significant effect sizes among its findings. Even the meta-analyses by Ferguson and Kilburn (2009) and Savage and Yancey (2008) that claim no meaningful association between violent media exposure and aggression report some (but not all) significant positive correlations in the realm of television and film media. This means that many types of violent portrayals are implicated in any effects on behavior. Those who view greater amounts of violent television and film portrayals of many kinds tend to engage in higher levels of aggressive behavior. This is an outcome that holds for all ages and both genders (except for experiments employing sexually explicit treatments, where subjects usually are males), and occurs across both experimental designs, where causation can be inferred, and nonexperimental survey designs that produce data describing everyday occurrences. Thus, the meta-analyses not only confirm a correlation between exposure to portrayals and behavior, but also point to the portrayals as a causal factor (because of the data from the experimental designs), and one that operates in real life (because of the evidence from the nonexperimental designs). Four criteria were advanced to evaluate the meta-analytic effect sizes: accepted scientific guidelines for assessing magnitude, social seriousness of the outcomes, comparisons with effect sizes in other areas where health and safety are of concern, and the degree to which the likelihood of an individual engaging in the behavior is increased and can be predicted. In each case, the effect sizes met the criteria.

The overall effect size in the Paik and Comstock meta-analysis ($r = 0.31$) is of medium magnitude by Cohen's guidelines and large by Hemphill's. Similar effect sizes were registered by two (out of three) other meta-analyses that were comprehensive in the measures of exposure and behavior included (Andison, 1977; Hearold, 1986). This implies that television violence in general—again, a wide range of types of violent portrayals—is implicated in any effects. Many of the analyses report effect sizes for portions of the data that are larger, sometimes substantially so, than their overall effect size. For example, Allen, D'Alessio, and Brezgel (1995) report $r = 0.22$ for violent erotica (compared to their overall effect size of $r = 0.13$, which was depressed by the negative association for portrayals of nudity); Hearold reports $r = 0.62$ for human or real versus cartoon violence and $r = 0.44$ for justified versus unjustified violence (compared to her overall $r = 0.30$); and Paik and Comstock report $r = 0.60$ for violent erotica and $r = 0.46$ for erotica without violence (compared to their overall $r = 0.31$). This means that some types of portrayals are particularly problematic. Of course, by the very nature of arithmetic, effect sizes for some types of portrayals would be smaller than average, but the overall effect sizes of medium magnitude indicate a substantial social impact for television and film violence in general.

The criterion of sufficient seriousness also is met. Wood, Wong, and Chachere (1991) examined only experimental designs, so causation could be inferred, and unconstrained interpersonal aggression, so that their outcome represents real, observable conflict. Their effect size was $r = 0.20$. Paik and Comstock reported $r = 0.17$ for illegal activities, although the figure for violent illegal activities was much smaller. These effect sizes, which fall between small and medium by Cohen's guidelines, are buttressed by the outcomes of several individual studies that document an association between exposure to television violence and criminal behavior. For example, Belson (1978), the group led by Cook (Hennigan et al., 1982), and Johnson et al., (2002) all present such data ranging from larceny theft to rape and physical injury, and each presents an analysis that makes a good case for causation. In addition, the Surgeon General's report on youth violence (U.S. Department of Health and Human Services, 2001) specifies television violence viewing between the ages of 6 and 11 as a risk factor for criminal violence between the ages of 15 and 18, with an effect size that is about the same as that for 15 of the 20 conditions identified as risk factors (Figure 13.2). Thus, the outcomes of exposure to television and film violence cannot be dismissed as inconsequential.

Comparison with effect sizes for other threats to health and safety document that the media effect sizes are comparable and often larger in size. These other effect sizes include the effects of passive smoking, exposure to asbestos, and exposure to lead (Figure 13.3). Conversely, the (social and individual) positive effect sizes for homework and scholastic achievement, calcium intake and bone mass, and self-examination and extent of breast cancer are actually *smaller* than the effect size for the adverse association of aggressive and antisocial behavior with exposure to violent television and film portrayals. Thus, the media effect sizes stand up quite well when compared with those for other effects whether the focus is on undesired or desirable outcomes.

The criterion of predictive power also is handily met. The effect sizes for media violence lead to the conclusion that in the absence of violence viewing, substantially greater numbers of people would fall below the median currently observed for aggressive and antisocial behavior. Comparable effect sizes, and for that matter much smaller ones, from the field of public health indicate that the differences for individual welfare are substantial. This criterion also leads to an important observation. Effect size must be weighted by the risk or benefit implied. A large effect size is of scant importance if the outcome involved is of no significance. Conversely, even a very small effect size is of great social and individual significance, as exemplified by the data represented by Rosenthal, Rosnow, and Rubin (2000) indicating that a minute correlation between a remedy and the arrest of a disorder means that its application can save hundreds of thousands of lives. Thus, the evaluation of the meta-analyses in the end rests on a judgment about the seriousness of the behavior represented—hitting, fighting, and engaging in illegal activities.

Meta-analyses have made it clear to the scientific and public health communities that the effects of media violence on aggressive and antisocial behavior are real and important. Two apparent puzzles have made it difficult for the public to accept this. One is the indisputable fact that violent crime rates in the United States have been going down at the same time that violent media content has either stayed the same or increased in its prominence in the culture. Our response is that given the likelihood that other variables may overshadow the potential role of television or other media forms when an aggressive act is severe in nature, this is not entirely surprising. It reminds us to always consider the potential contribution of the media in context with other factors that produce violence, some much more systemic in nature, such as poverty and the feeling of hopelessness that may accompany it. The second puzzle is when the enormity of a violent act seems to exceed any imaginable contribution of the media. Our response is, once again, that the role of the media in the complex processes governing behavior may be comparatively modest when the act is severe and dramatic. It may be confined to gatekeeping, in the sense that the media contribute to the options that individuals perceive as open to them. In that respect, the modest contribution may be crucial by increasing the likelihood of behavior made more prominent and often seemingly endorsed by the media. Thus, violent television and film portrayals may contribute indirectly to acts of extreme violence as well as more directly to the comparatively minor but nonetheless frequently socially disruptive behavior represented by interpersonal aggression.

NOTES

1. Meta-analysis estimates the size of the relationship between two variables using all retrievable data. An attempt is made to gather all existing studies on a particular topic for the purpose of making inferences about them in the collective. It addresses the "file drawer problem" (publication bias favoring statistically significant relationships) by including all locatable unpublished studies, although some have called into question the validity of non-peer-reviewed studies among those in the file drawer, or raised concerns about the interests of the researcher herself/himself in providing studies when presented with a file drawer request (Cook et al., 1993). The key concept is effect size. The prototypic calculation is represented by the ratio of the difference between treatment and control means and an estimate of the standard deviation:

$$\text{Effect Size} = \frac{\text{Mean}_t - \text{Mean}_c}{\text{ESD}}$$

where t = treatment, c = control, and ESD = estimate of the standard deviation. Because the standard deviation bears the same relationship to all normal distributions regardless of the particular metric, the resulting effect sizes can be averaged. This calculation obviously fits the data offered by experimental designs. However, over the years, statistical maneuvers have made it possible to estimate comparable effect sizes for surveys and other designs. In addition, it has become possible to calculate statistical significance for the average effect size and fail-safe numbers (the quantity of nonsignificant findings necessary to reduce an effect size to the null range). In this process, studies are treated as if they were respondents in a survey with every conceivable attribute open to coding. A single study with multiple measures can generate more than one effect size; this has become the preferred practice in order to extract as much information as possible about the performance of different variables. Thus, analyses can be as narrow and theoretically focused as the investigator wishes, although most meta-analyses begin with a broad and inclusive treatment of the independent and dependent variables. The three strengths of meta-analysis are: (1) the unrelenting search for all available data; (2) estimates using the total number of cases studied; and, (3) the ability to focus on questions of theoretical interest or data possessing particular qualities.

2. Ecological validity refers to the degree to which the conditions of a study match the everyday circumstances in which the phenomenon under observation occurs. Generally speaking, the greater the ecological validity, the more generalizable the results to everyday life. The exception is when a study, by whatever means, induces a response that also would influence behavior in everyday life; generalizability here is advanced regardless of the degree of ecological validity. For example, we need ecological validity to understand the conditions that lead to frustration, but we don't need ecological validity to conclude that frustration, however induced, enhances the likelihood of aggression. Study quality refers to attributes that facilitate valid inference. These include (depending on the analyst) a corroborating measure for a dependent variable, random assignment of subjects in an experiment, or high scores on scales of internal or external (ecological) validity.

3. Glass is foremost among the pioneers of the meta-analytic paradigm because its public unveiling occurred in 1976 in his presidential address at the annual meeting of the American Educational Research Association in San Francisco (Glass, 1976). However, Robert Rosenthal at Harvard was working on a similar scheme (Rosenthal & Rubin, 1978), and neither Glass nor Rosenthal knew of the other's work.

4. Although aggressive portrayals and aggressive behavior comprised the largest number of independent and dependent variables examined by Hearold (1986), she included all possible combinations of antisocial and prosocial portrayals and behavior. Among the antisocial outcomes, she included such putatively undesirable responses as stereotyping, passivity, reduced social interaction, and feelings of powerlessness. However, she did not include erotica with or without violence as an independent variable. Paik and Comstock (1994) took a narrower approach in regard to their dependent variables. They confined themselves to aggressive outcomes but included erotica with and without violence among their independent variables.

5. NBC collected the data over a three-and-half-year period from panels of elementary and high school students in a Midwestern and a Southwestern city. Measures of viewing and behavior were collected at six points in time, leading to 15 wave pairs (I-II, I-III, etc.) of earlier and later measurement. The time lags varied from three months to three-and-a-half years. The Ns varied from 497 for the shortest period to 112 for the longest period and progressively declined as time lags grew longer because of attrition.

6. Please note that "minor aggression" may still be quite serious from the perspective of the victim, especially if the victim is a child.

7. As pointed out in an earlier footnote, fail-safe numbers are the quantity of nonsignificant findings necessary to reduce an effect size to the null range. A small fail-safe number indicates that only a few new studies with null results would be necessary to do so. A large fail-safe number, as is the case in the present instance, indicates that a very great many such studies would be necessary to do so.

REFERENCES

Allen, M., D'Alessio, D., & Brezgel, K. (1995). A meta-analysis summarizing the effects of pornography II: Aggression after exposure. *Human Communication Research*, *22*(2), 258–283.

Anderson, C. A. (2004). An update on the effects of playing violent video games. *Journal of Adolescence*, *27*(1), 113–122.

Anderson, C. A., Berkowitz, L., Donnerstein, E., Huesmann, L. R., Johnson, J. D., Linz, D., Malamuth, N. M., & Wartella, E. (2003). The influence of media violence on youth. *Psychological Science in the Public Interest*, *4*(3), 81–110.

Anderson, C. A., & Bushman, B. J. (2001). Effects of violent video games on aggressive behavior, aggressive affect, physiological arousal, and prosocial behavior: A meta-analytic review of the scientific literature. *Psychological Science*, *12*(5), 353–359.

Anderson, C. A., Carnagey, N. L., Flanagan, M., Benjamin, Jr., A. J., Eubanks, J., & Valentine, J. C. (2004). Violent video games: Specific effects of violent content on aggressive thoughts and behavior. *Advances in Experimental Social Psychology*, *36*, 199–249.

Anderson, C. A., Shibuya, A., Ihori, N., Swing, E. L., Bushman, B. J., Sakamoto, A., Rothstein, H. R., & Saleem, M. (2010). Violent video game effects on aggression, empathy, and prosocial behavior in Eastern and Western countries: A meta-analytic review. *Psychological Bulletin*, *136*(2), 151.

Andison, F. S. (1977). TV violence and viewer aggression: A cumulation of study results. *Public Opinion Quarterly*, *41*(3), 314–331.

Attorney General's Commission on Pornography. (1986). *Final report*. Washington, DC: U.S. Government Printing Office.

Bandura, A., Ross, D., & Ross, S. A. (1963a). Imitation of film-mediated aggressive models. *Journal of Abnormal and Social Psychology*, *66*(1), 3–11.

Bandura, A., Ross, D., & Ross, S. A. (1963b). Vicarious reinforcement and imitative learning. *Journal of Abnormal and Social Psychology*, *67*(6), 601–607.

Belson, W. A. (1978). *Television violence and the adolescent boy*. Westmead, UK: Saxon House, Teakfield.

Bushman, B. J., & Anderson, C. A. (2001). Media violence and the American public: Scientific facts versus media misinformation. *American Psychologist*, *56*(6–7), 477–489.

Bushman, B. J., & Huesmann, L. R. (2001). Effects of television violence on aggression. In D. G. Singer & J. L. Singer (Eds.), *Handbook of children and the media* (pp. 223–254). Thousand Oaks, CA: Sage.

Bushman, B. J., & Huesmann, L. R. (2006). Short-term and long-term effects of violent media on aggression in children and adults. *Archives of Pediatrics and Adolescent Medicine*, *160*, 348–352.

Bushman, B. J., Rothstein, H., & Anderson, C. A. (2010). Much ado about something: Violent video game effects and a school of red herring: Reply to Ferguson and Kilburn (2010). *Psychological Bulletin, 136*, 182–187.

Cairns, E., Hunter, D., & Herring, L. (1980). Young children's awareness of violence in Northern Ireland: The influence of Northern Irish television in Scotland and Northern Ireland. *British Journal of Social and Clinical Psychology, 19*, 3–6.

Celozzi, M. J. II, Kazelskis, R., & Gutsch, K. U. (1981). The relationship between viewing televised violence in ice hockey and subsequent levels of personal aggression. *Journal of Sport Behavior, 4*(4), 157–162.

Chaffee, S. H., McLeod, J. M., & Atkin, D. K. (1971). Parental influences on adolescent media use. *American Behavioral Scientist, 14*, 323–340.

Cohen, E. E. (1988). *Children's television commercialization survey.* Washington, DC: National Association of Broadcasters.

Comstock, G. (1991). *Television and the American child.* San Diego, CA: Academic Press.

Comstock, G., & Scharrer, E. (1999). *Television: What's on, who's watching, and what it means.* San Diego, CA: Academic Press.

Cook, D., Guyatt, G., Ryan, G., Clifton, J., Buckingham, I., William, A., et al. (1993). Should unpublished data be included in meta-analyses? *JAMA, 269,* 2749–2753.

Cook, T. D., & Campbell, D. T. (1979). *Quasi-experimentation: Design and analysis issues for field settings.* Chicago, IL: Houghton Mifflin.

Cook, T. D., Kendzierski, D. A., & Thomas, S. A. (1983). The implicit assumptions of television research: An analysis of the 1982 NIMH report on television and behavior. *Public Opinion Quarterly, 47*(2), 161–201.

Cooper, H. (1989). *Homework.* New York, NY: Longman.

Donnerstein, E., Linz, D., & Penrod, S. (1987). *The question of pornography: Research findings and policy implications.* New York, NY: Free Press.

Ferguson, C. J. (2007a). The good, the bad and the ugly: A meta-analytic review of positive and negative effects of violent video games. *Psychiatric Quarterly, 78*(4), 309–316.

Ferguson, C. J. (2007b). Evidence for publication bias in video game violence effects literature: A meta-analytic review. *Aggression and Violent Behavior, 12*(4), 470–482.

Ferguson, C. J., & Brannick, M. T. (2012). Publication bias in psychological science: Prevalence, methods for identifying and controlling, and implications for the use of meta-analyses. *Psychological Methods, 17,* 120–128. doi:10.1037/a0024445

Ferguson, C. J., & Kilburn, J. (2009). The public health risks of media violence: A meta-analytic review. *The Journal of Pediatrics, 154*(5), 759–763.

Ferguson, C. J., & Kilburn, J. (2010a). "Violence in media research": Reply. *The Journal of Pediatrics, 156,* 169–170.

Ferguson, C. J., & Kilburn, J. (2010b). Much ado about nothing: The misestimation and overinterpretation of violent video game effects in Eastern and Western nations: Comment on Anderson et al. (2010). *Psychological Bulletin, 136,* 174–178.

Fiore, M. C., Smith, S. S., Jorenby, D. E., & Baker, T. B. (1994). The effectiveness of the nicotine patch for smoking cessation. *Journal of the American Medical Association, 271,* 1940–1947.

Glass, G. V. (1976). Primary, secondary, and meta-analysis of research. *Educational Researcher, 5*, 3–8.

Greitemeyer, T., & Mügge, D. O. (2014). Video games do affect social outcomes: A meta-analytic review of the effects of violent and prosocial video game-play. *Personality and Social Psychology Bulletin*, 1–12. doi:10.1177/01461672 13520459.

Hald, G. M., Malamuth, N. M., & Yuen, C. (2010). Pornography and attitudes supporting violence against women: Revising the relationship in non-experimental studies. *Aggressive Behavior, 36*, 14–20.

Hawkins, J. D., Herrenkohl, T. L., Farrington, D. P., Brewer, D., Catalano, R. F., & Harachi, T. W. (1998). A review of predictors of youth violence. In R. Loeber & D. P. Farrington (Eds.), *Serious and violent juvenile offenders: Risk factors and successful interventions* (pp. 106–146). Thousand Oaks, CA: Sage.

Hearold, S. (1986). A synthesis of 1043 effects of television on social behavior. In G. Comstock (Ed.), *Public communication and behavior* (Vol. 1, pp. 65–133). New York, NY: Academic Press.

Hemphill, J. F. (2003). Interpreting the magnitudes of correlation coefficients. *American Psychologist, 58*, 78–79.

Hennigan, K. M., Heath, L., Wharton, J. D., Del Rosario, M. L., Cook, T. D., & Calder, B. J. (1982). Impact of the introduction of television on crime in the United States: Empirical findings and theoretical implications. *Journal of Personality and Social Psychology, 42*(3), 461–477.

Hill, D., White, V., Jolley, D., & Mapperson, K. (1988). Self-examination of the breast: Is it beneficial? Meta-analysis of studies investigating breast self-examination and extent of disease in patients with breast cancer. *British Medical Journal, 297*, 271–275.

Hogben, M. (1998). Factors moderating the effect of television aggression on viewer behavior. *Communication Research, 25*, 220–247.

Huesmann, L. R. (2010). Nailing the coffin shut on doubts that violent video games stimulate aggression: Comment on Anderson et al. (2010). *Psychological Bulletin, 136*, 179–181.

Hunt, M. (1997). *How science takes stock*. New York, NY: Russell Sage.

Johnson, J. G., Cohen, P., Smailes, E. M., Kasen, S., & Brook, J. S. (2002). Television viewing and aggressive behavior during adolescence and adulthood. *Science, 295*, 2468–2471.

Josephson, W. L. (1987). Television violence and children's aggression: Testing the priming, social script, and disinhibition predictions. *Journal of Personality and Social Psychology, 53*(95), 882–890.

Kang, N. (1990). *A critique and secondary analysis of the NBC study on television and aggression*. (Unpublished dissertation). Syracuse University, Syracuse, NY.

Lefkowitz, M. M., Eron, L. D., Walder, L. O., & Huesmann, L. R. (1977). *Growing up to be violent: A longitudinal study of the development of aggression*. Elmsford, NY: Pergamon.

Lipsey, M. W., & Derzon, J. H. (1998). Predictors of violent and serious delinquency in adolescence and early adulthood: A synthesis of longitudinal research. In R. Loeber & D. P. Farrington (Eds.), *Serious and violent juvenile offenders: Risk factors and successful interventions* (pp. 86–105). Thousand Oaks, CA: Sage.

Martins, N., Weaver, A. J., Yeshua-Katz, D., Lewis, N. H., Tyree, N. E., & Jensen, J. D. (2013). A content analysis of print news coverage of media violence and aggression research. *Journal of Communication, 63*(6), 1070–1087.

McLeod, J. M., Atkin, C. K., & Chaffee, S. H. (1972). Adolescents, parents, and television use: Self-report and other-report measures from the Wisconsin sample. In G. A. Comstock & E. A. Rubinstein (Eds.), *Television and social behavior: Television and adolescent aggressiveness* (Vol. 3, pp. 239–313). Washington, DC: U.S. Government Printing Office.

Milavsky, J. R., Kessler, R., Stipp, H. H., & Rubens, W. S. (1982). *Television and aggression: A panel study.* New York, NY: Academic Press.

Needleman, H. L., & Gatsonis, C. A. (1990). Low-level lead exposure and the IQ of children. *Journal of the American Medical Association, 263,* 673–678.

Oddone-Paolucci, E., Genuis, M., & Violato, C. (2000). A meta-analysis of the published research on the effects of pornography. In C. Violato, E. Oddone-Paolucci, & M. Genuis, (Eds.), *The changing family and child environment* (pp. 48–59). Aldershot, UK: Ashgate.

Paik, H. (1991). *The effects of television violence on aggressive behavior: A meta-analysis.* (Unpublished doctoral dissertation). Syracuse University, Syracuse, NY.

Paik, H., & Comstock, G. (1994). The effects of television violence on antisocial behavior: A meta-analysis. *Communication Research, 21*(4), 516–546.

Robinson, J. P., & Bachman, J. G. (1972). Television viewing habits and aggression. In G. A. Comstock & E. A. Rubinstein (Eds.), *Television and social behavior: Television and adolescent aggressiveness.* (Vol. 3, pp. 372–382). Washington, DC: U.S. Government Printing Office.

Rosenthal, R. (1986). Media violence, antisocial behavior, and the social consequences of small effects. *Journal of Social Issues, 42*(3), 141–154.

Rosenthal, R., Rosnow, R. L., & Rubin, D. B. (2000). *Contrasts and effect sizes in behavioral research: A correlational approach.* New York, NY: Cambridge University Press.

Rosenthal, R., & Rubin, D. B. (1978). Interpersonal expectancy effects: The first 345 studies. *Behavioral and Brain Sciences, 3,* 377–415.

Rosenthal, R., & Rubin, D. B. (1982). A simple general purpose display of magnitude of experimental effect. *Journal of Educational Psychology, 74,* 166–169.

Rothstein, H. R., & Bushman, B. J. (2012). Publication bias in psychological science: Comment on Ferguson and Brannick (2012). *Psychological Methods, 17,* 129–136.

Savage, J., & Yancey, C. (2008). The effects of media violence exposure on criminal aggression: A meta-analysis. *Criminal Justice and Behavior, 35,* 772–791.

Sherry, J. L. (2001). The effects of violent video games on aggression. *Human Communication Research, 27*(3), 409–431.

Slater, M. D., Henry, K. L., Swaim, R. C., & Anderson, L. L. (2003). Violent media content and aggressiveness in adolescents: A downward spiral model. *Communication Research, 30*(6), 713–736.

Smith, A. H., Handley, M. A., & Wood, R. (1990). Epidemiological evidence indicates asbestos causes laryngeal cancer. *Journal of Occupational Medicine, 32,* 499–507.

Thornton, W., & Voigt, L. (1984). Television and delinquency. *Youth and Society, 15*(4), 445–468.

U.S. Department of Health & Human Services. (2001). *Youth violence: A report of the Surgeon General.* Rockville, MD: U.S. Department of Health and Human Services. Centers for Disease Control and Prevention, National Center for Injury Prevention and Control; Substance Abuse and Mental Health Services Administration, Center for Mental Health Services; and National Institutes of Health, National Institute of Mental Health.

Weaver, J. (1991). Responding to erotica: Perceptual processes and dispositional implications. In J. Bryant & D. Zillmann (Eds.), *Responding to the screen: Reception and reaction processes* (pp. 329–354). Mahwah, NJ: Erlbaum.

Weller, S. C. (1993). A meta-analysis of condom effectiveness in reducing sexually transmitted HIV. *Social Science and Medicine, 36,* 1635–1644.

Wells, A. J. (1998). Lung cancer from passive smoking at work. *American Journal of Public Health, 88,* 1025–1029.

Welten, D. C., Kemper, H. C. G., Post, G. B., & van Staveren, W. A. (1995). A meta-analysis of the effect of calcium intake on bone mass in young and middle aged females and males. *Journal of Nutrition, 125,* 2802–2813.

Wood, W., Wong, F., & Chachere, J. (1991). Effects of media violence on viewers' aggression in unconstrained social interaction. *Psychological Bulletin, 109*(3), 371–383.

Wynder, E. L, & Graham, E. A. (1950). Tobacco smoking as a possible etiological factor in bronchiogenic carcinoma. *Journal of the American Medical Association, 143,* 329–336.

Zimmerman, F. J., & Strasburger, V. C. (2010). Violence in media research. *The Journal of Pediatrics, 156,* 168–169.

CHAPTER 14

Media Violence and Public Policy: Where We Have Been and Where We Should Go Next

Douglas A. Gentile and John P. Murray

As noted across the chapters of this book, the research findings that media violence is a risk factor for aggression have been generally robust and consistent. Given this consistency and the public attention that is paid to violence, it may be surprising that very few useful policies have been proposed or implemented over the past half century (Gentile & Walsh, 2002; Pecora, Murray, & Wartella, 2007). This chapter outlines the history of the public policy debate in the United States and proposes new directions for the future.

A BRIEF HISTORY OF PUBLIC CONCERN

Although there have been expressions of concern about violence in radio programs, movies, and comic books since the 1920s and 1930s, it was not until the advent of television broadcasting, in the late 1940s, that wide public concern was expressed in the United States. Indeed, the early indications of legislative concern about television violence occurred in the early 1950s (U.S. Congress, 1952, 1955)—only about five years after television broadcasting had become established. Teachers and parents were the first to raise concerns about the effects of TV, but they were quickly joined by social scientists, both in the United States and abroad (e.g., Maccoby, 1954; Lazarsfeld, 1955; Himmelweit, Oppenheim, & Vince, 1958; Schramm, Lyle, & Parker, 1961).

By the 1960s social scientists began to demonstrate experimentally that television and film violence can have significant causal effects on children's aggressive behaviors. The work of Albert Bandura (e.g., Bandura, Ross, & Ross, 1963), working with young children at Stanford University, and the research of Leonard Berkowitz (1962), studying teens and young adults at the University of Wisconsin, were early landmarks in media violence research.

The 1960s also saw a rise in broad public concern about violence in American society. The assassinations of President John Kennedy, Martin Luther King Jr., and Robert Kennedy served to intensify public scrutiny of factors that might influence violence. As a result, President Lyndon Johnson established the National Commission on the Causes and Prevention of Violence in the mid-1960s. In 1969 the violence commission released a bookshelf of reports, including *Mass Media and Violence* (Baker & Ball, 1969), with the research demonstrating a strong role for exposure to violence as a stimulus for aggression in society.

Several parallel developments had an influence on both the public perceptions of media violence and the directions for continuing research. For a start, President Kennedy had appointed a new chair of the FCC (Federal Communications Commission—the government agency that monitors broadcasting licenses for television, among other things). The new chair, Newton Minow, gave a speech to the National Association of Broadcasters (NAB) at their annual convention in Las Vegas in which he described commercial television as a "vast wasteland" of crime, violence, and advertising directed to children (a claim that he repeated in his book, *Abandoned in the Wasteland: Children, Television, and the First Amendment*, Minow & LaMay, 1995). The NAB was not amused by the harsh criticism of commercial television, but responded by professing support for a public broadcasting system that might provide alternative programming for children (the thinking was that endorsing a noncommercial, public system would take the heat off the commercial system and allow it to continue business as usual). And so PBS (the Public Broadcasting System) and CPB (Corporation for Public Broadcasting) were born in the late 1960s.

At the same time, the public became involved. Peggy Charren, a mother who spent time watching TV with her children, did not like what she saw: cheap, advertising-supported programming designed to encourage children to harass their parents to buy high-sugar cereal and candy and clothes—the "Snickers and Sneakers" approach. She created the grassroots organization Action for Children's Television (ACT) and began to lobby the FCC and Congress to ensure more educational and less commercial programming for children. Others added their voices to the call and included an emphasis on lowering violence.

By the end of the 1960s, the stage was set for a robust debate about children and television. It began with the release of the National Commission on Causes and Prevention of Violence report in 1969. This triggered a congressional hearing in 1969, which focused on the impact of media violence on children. The hearing, headed by Senator John Pastore (D-RI), asked U.S. Secretary of Health, Education and Welfare Robert Finch to direct the Surgeon General of the United States, William H. Stewart, to appoint a committee to review the evidence on the harmful effects of violent television programs. On March 12, 1969,

Surgeon General Stewart announced that he would appoint an appropriate panel and on April 16, 1969, the secretary of the department of Health, Education and Welfare (HEW) authorized the establishment of the "Surgeon General's Scientific Advisory Committee on Television and Social Behavior" and asked the National Institute of Mental Health (NIMH) to administer the program.

The Surgeon General's committee began by accumulating the prior research on children and media and publishing an annotated bibliography on "Television and Social Behavior" (Atkin, Murray, & Nayman, 1971). Concurrent with this survey of existing research, the 12 committee members and the NIMH staff members began contacting various researchers and consultants around the United States and overseas to encourage them to develop research projects for possible funding through NIMH via a 1 million dollar appropriation (a transfer of funds from the NIMH Community Mental Health Centers funding program). In the end, about 60 projects were funded, involving over 100 researchers. The final report by the committee was published in 1972 under the title of "Television and Growing Up: The Impact of Televised Violence." This summary report was accompanied by five volumes of research reports submitted by the individual researchers and research teams, and assembled and edited by the NIMH staff (the summary report and five research volumes can be accessed online at the National Library of Medicine, e.g., http://profiles.nlm.nih.gov/ps/access/NNBCGX.pdf).

Controversy began, however, even at the beginning of the Surgeon General's committee development. Questions were raised about the membership of the committee; 5 of the 12 members had connections with the commercial television industry (one of these was a vice president of NBC; another was the director of social research at CBS; and the other three held academic positions but conducted research and consulting activities for ABC, CBS, and NBC). Also, the secretary of HEW took the questionable step of sending the names of potential committee members to the three commercial television networks and the NAB for prior review and commentary on the suitability of the nominees (the secretary's rationale for this action was that a similar procedure had been followed with the tobacco industry in appointments to the Surgeon General's review committee on smoking and health, which, in retrospect, also seems to have been a bad decision). The CBS network declined to comment on the nominees, but ABC, NBC, and the NAB were allowed to veto seven distinguished social scientists whose research was most relevant, including Albert Bandura (Stanford University), Leonard Berkowitz (University of Wisconsin), and Percy Tannenbaum (University of California–Berkeley) (Cater & Strickland, 1972). The interested reader can learn more about the history of this committee in the book *TV Violence and the Child: The Evolution and Fate of the Surgeon General's Report* (Cater & Strickland, 1975). Nevertheless, when the Surgeon General's report was released, there was an optimistic view that this ambitious program of research would resolve the questions about TV violence. Even with the deck potentially stacked in the industry's favor, the scientific results and the final report did show that TV violence is one factor in the development of aggressive behavior in children. The report summarized the research as follows:

Thus, there is a convergence of the fairly substantial experimental evidence for *short-run* causation of aggression among some children by viewing violence on the screen and the much less certain evidence from field studies that extensive violence viewing precedes some *long-run* manifestations of aggressive behavior. (1972, p. 10)

A summary article in the flagship journal of the American Psychological Association, the *American Psychologist* (Murray, 1973), supported that opinion. Prior to the official release, however, the *New York Times* leaked a summary under the erroneous headline "TV Violence Held Unharmful to Youth," which led the public to believe the opposite of what the report actually found!

The NBC television network also commissioned its own research, which was conducted in the late 1960s and early 1970s but was not published until 1982, attempting to contradict some of the Surgeon General's findings (Milavsky, Kessler, Stipp, & Rubens, 1982). It was a complex panel study with several waves of interviews and observations of youth. The researchers, employed by NBC, reported that there was little evidence of significant effects of viewing violence. The report attracted considerable public attention when it was released. David Kenny (1984), a distinguished statistician, re-analyzed the NBC data and concluded that the results had been misrepresented: there were important and significant demonstrations of media violence effects in the NBC data and that the effects had been minimized or distorted by the NBC researchers. It is worth noting that one of the original NBC authors, Ronald Kessler, was asked 30 years later to participate in a committee at the National Academy of Sciences–Institute of Medicine (2013) (Leshner, Altevogt, Lee, McCoy, & Kelly, 2013), where he again asserted his disbelief in the effects of media violence.

In 1983 the National Institute of Mental Health (NIMH) published a 10-year follow-up review of the Surgeon General's report, which concluded that the Surgeon General was correct in the initial report and that a decade of further research confirms that

violence on television does lead to aggressive behavior by children and teenagers who watch the programs. . . . In magnitude, television violence is as strongly correlated with aggressive behavior as any other behavioral variable that has been measured. The research question has moved from asking whether or not there is an effect to seeking explanations for that effect. (p. 6)

Ten years later, the American Psychological Association (APA) published another follow-up review, conducted by a panel of nine psychologists (Huston et al., 1992). After examining all the evidence that had accumulated since the 1960s, they also concluded that viewing TV violence is causally related to increases in aggressive behavior.

The APA report was followed by numerous public policy statements by the American Academy of Pediatrics (AAP) and other organizations expressing concern about the harmful effects of media violence (e.g., American Academy of Pediatrics, 2001, 2009). In fact, in 2000, six major public health organizations released a joint statement at a ceremony on the White House lawn. The signing organizations of this summary statement included the American Medical Association, the American Academy of Pediatrics, the American Psychological Association, the American Academy of Child and Adolescent Psychiatry, the American Academy of Family Physicians, and the American Psychiatric Association. Their statement reported:

Although a wide variety of viewpoints on the import and impact of entertainment violence on children may exist outside the public health community, within it, there is a strong consensus on many of the effects on children's health, well-being and development. . . . [The combined studies] point overwhelmingly to a causal connection between media violence and aggressive behavior in some children. The conclusion of the public health community, based on over 30 years of research, is that viewing entertainment violence can lead to increases in aggressive attitudes, values and behavior, particularly in children.

Its effects are measurable and long-lasting. Moreover, prolonged viewing of media violence can lead to emotional desensitization toward violence in real life.

The effect of entertainment violence on children is complex and variable. Some children will be affected more than others. But while duration, intensity, and extent of the impact may vary, there are several measurable negative effects of children's exposure to violent entertainment. These effects take several forms.

- Children who see a lot of violence are more likely to view violence as an effective way of settling conflicts. Children exposed to violence are more likely to assume that acts of violence are acceptable behavior.

- Viewing violence can lead to emotional desensitization towards violence in real life. It can decrease the likelihood that one will take action on behalf of a victim when violence occurs.

- Entertainment violence feeds a perception that the world is a violent and mean place. Viewing violence increases fear of becoming a victim of violence, with a resultant increase in self-protective behaviors and a mistrust of others.

- Viewing violence may lead to real life violence. Children exposed to violent programming at a young age have a higher tendency for violent and aggressive behavior later in life than children who are not so exposed.

We in no way mean to imply that entertainment violence is the sole, or even necessarily the most important factor contributing to youth aggression, antisocial attitudes, and violence.

About 10 years later, the International Society for Research on Aggression gathered a group of 12 internationally known aggression researchers to review and summarize the evidence on the link between media violence and aggression. Again, after examining the data, including 15 published meta-analyses, they concluded:

No single risk factor causes a child or adolescent to act aggressively. Instead, it is the accumulation of risk factors that leads to an aggressive act (Berkowitz, 1993). After taking into consideration numerous characteristics of the child and the environment, including protective factors, research suggests that media violence consumption increases the relative risk of aggression, defined as intentional harm to another person which could be verbal, relational, or physical.

... Exposure to media violence can influence not only aggressive behavior in a variety of forms, but also aggressive cognition, aggressive feelings, physiological arousal, and pro-social behavior. The effects of media violence can be different for different people, and can be very subtle, especially when examined over the course of a person's lifetime.

It is important to note, however, that these conclusions are about *aggressive* behavior, not *violent* behavior. That is, media violence increases the risk of unkind and hurtful behaviors, such as verbal, relational, and sometimes physical aggression, especially when provoked (e.g., Coyne et al., 2008). Very few studies have looked at the effects on serious violent behavior, and the existing evidence (and theory) suggests that the effect is much smaller as the type of aggression becomes more severe (Savage & Yancey, 2008). Criminal violence, which is relatively rare and difficult to predict, is typically the result of multiple risk factors.

Three aspects of these decades of reviews are worth noting. First, the organizations that are on record as stating that the evidence is clear that media violence can play a causal role in the development of aggression are not crazy fringe organizations with some Luddite agenda. They are the major scientific and public health organizations on which the public rely to evaluate and summarize the research, and on whom they rely for recommendations to maintain optimal health. Second, it should be noted that these summaries all appear thoughtful and measured. None claim that media violence causes school shootings, or even that media violence exposure is a primary cause for serious violence. Indeed, some go out of their way to clarify that media violence is just one risk factor among many. Third, the conclusions they have drawn are remarkably similar. This might be surprising, given that the research literature is constantly changing, and new challenges to the conventional wisdom are always being tested. This is, of course, exactly what science should do. Nonetheless, each challenge needs to be examined on its own merits and also in the context of other studies, and it is on this basis that all of the major public health and scientific organizations have found such consensus.

THE PUBLIC DIALOGUE

One might imagine that this scientific and public health consensus has created unity in the public discussion about media violence, including some direction about what policy actions should be taken. In the past 25 years, however, the "debate" has consistently been derailed by forces inherent to the mass media and also by organizations and people who likely have an agenda beyond simply describing the scientific data.

The primary problem is that members of the public get almost all of their information from the mass media. The media, however, do not typically discuss science in the detail that is needed to make it comprehensible and accurate. News reporters are not usually scientists, and may have difficulty interpreting the results or translating them into the words and images that will help the public understand the research correctly. Most journalists aren't trained as statisticians and don't want to try to communicate to readers what a correlation means, much less what a structural equation model shows. Journalists don't want to write about statistical effects; they want to write about how many more people have been killed by those who watched media violence than by those who did not watch media violence. In addition, most news outlets are for-profit ventures, so there is pressure to report in ways that seem more shocking, extreme, or dangerous than the research may actually show in order to attract more readers or viewers.

It also seems that the standard of proof in public discourse for a scientific finding on a controversial topic is surprisingly inappropriate. For a scientific finding to be accepted does not require 100 percent agreement among scientists, but the public often believes that if there is any dissension, the jury must still be out. This seems particularly strange because actual juries do not require this level of proof when deciding legal cases that can destroy lives. In a civil case, juries simply need to achieve the standard of 50 percent plus a "grain of sand." In a criminal case, juries simply need to achieve the standard of "beyond a reasonable doubt." That is, the public seem more willing to send someone to jail when not everyone agrees than they are to accept the findings of a preponderance of scientific evidence if a minority of scientists disagree with it.

In our opinion, the primary problem with the public understanding of the media violence research is driven by the circumstances under which it gets discussed. It seems that the only time the public engages in a discussion of media violence and public policy options is after there has been some terrible tragedy such as a school shooting. In the highly charged atmosphere after a national tragedy, the dialogue becomes dominated by what could be called a "culprit mentality," in which we ask the question, "What was the cause of this violence?" (Gentile & Bushman, 2012). This is an inappropriate question because aggression and violence are *never* caused by any single factor. Nonetheless, it is usually only in this atmosphere that media violence gets discussed, which diminishes the value of the research in two ways. First, the inappropriately simplistic question about whether media violence caused a given school shooting is absurd and inaccurate. No media violence researcher would claim such a thing. This is not, however, the same as asking the more appropriate question about *the multiple risk factors* that came together to cause the violent act and whether media violence was one of them.

Second, by continually focusing the question on extreme criminal violence, the media continually frame the research at an inappropriate level. Almost all of the research on media violence focuses on what we might call playground-level aggression, not serious lethal violence. The public discussion of media violence research tends to only be discussed in the context of criminal-level violence, however, and this misleads the public into believing that scientists must be making extreme claims about how violent video games will turn their children into mass murderers—a statement that, again, no researcher has made.

Once the discussion about media violence effects has been framed within the context of a highly rare and devastating violent criminal act, it polarizes the debate, with some people wanting to find something to blame and others wanting to protect their personal favorite issue from being blamed.

Following the killing of 20 six- to eight-year-old children at Sandy Hook Elementary School in Newtown, Connecticut, in December 2012, and the assertion that the shooter trained on violent video games, there was renewed concern about media violence. Much of that concern was driven by the National Rifle Association, which wanted to direct attention away from gun control. The NRA stated,

Here's another dirty little truth that the media try their best to conceal: There exists in this country a callous, corrupt and corrupting shadow industry that sells, and sows, violence against its own people. Through vicious, violent video games with names like *Bulletstorm*, *Grand Theft Auto*, *Mortal Kombat* and *Splatterhouse*. . . . Then there's the blood-soaked slasher films like *American Psycho* and *Natural Born Killers* that are aired like propaganda loops on "Splatterdays" and every day, and a thousand music videos that portray life as a joke and murder as a way of life. And then they have the nerve to call it "entertainment." (National Rifle Association, 2012)

Senator Jay Rockefeller (D-WV) proposed legislation to conduct studies of violent video games. The video game industry in turn claimed, "The search for meaningful solutions must consider the broad range of actual factors that may have contributed to this tragedy. Any such study needs to include the years of extensive research that has shown no connection between entertainment and real-life violence" (Gamepolitics.com, 2012).

On January 12, 2013, Vice President Biden convened a meeting to discuss the potential impact of violent video games on real-world violence. The attendees at the meeting were carefully chosen by the video game industry to represent only their point of view. They included seven executives from the video game industry (e.g., Electronic Arts CEO John Riccitiello) and two researchers who have made their careers by attacking the violent video game research, Christopher Ferguson and Cheryl Olson (Nunneley, 2013).

After these meetings, on January 16, 2013, the White House released a report titled, "Now Is the Time: The President's Plan to Protect Our Children and Our Communities by Reducing Gun Violence." At the same time there was a request that the Institute of Medicine (IOM) at the National Academy of Sciences (NAS)/National Research Council (NRC) convene a panel to develop research strategies to study and reduce firearm violence. One of the panel topics was "the influence of video games and other media." Discussions and reviews were undertaken in April and the committee released its report on June 5, 2013. The report, titled "Priorities for Research to Reduce the Threat of Firearm-Related Violence" (Leshner et al., 2013) identified a key research topic: "Examine the relationship between exposure to media violence and real-life violence." The chair of the media violence section of the committee was Ronald Kessler, the former NBC employee who 30 years previously authored the misleading NBC study casting doubt on the effects of TV violence (Milvasky et al., 1982). And so, we have the National Academy of Sciences report that only tangentially deals with media violence and the debate continues with a dispute in the *Mayo Clinic Proceedings* (Murray et al., 2011; Ferguson, 2011; Hall, Day, & Hall, 2011) and continuing research (Whitaker & Bushman, 2012) and commentary (Strasburger & Donnerstein, 2013).

It seems clear to us that it is almost impossible to come to a good understanding of the scientific evidence in the political and polarized atmospheres in which media violence research typically gets discussed. It is perhaps not surprising, then, that the public policy response has been so uniformly ineffective.

FAILED PUBLIC POLICY INITIATIVES

For the past 20 years, the U.S. public policy discussion has been surprisingly focused almost entirely on one medium—video games—and the policy options have been focused primarily on one approach—access restriction. Numerous municipalities and states have attempted to pass laws that restrict children's ability to play, rent, or purchase violent video games. The first such law to pass was in Indianapolis, which required video game arcade owners to forbid minors to play games that included graphic violence (Smith, Fallow, Pozza, & Hellman, 2006). This was followed by similar laws focusing on the sale of violent video games to minors. These types of laws were passed in St. Louis County, the state of Illinois, Washington State, California, Michigan, Minnesota, and Louisiana. The video game industry immediately sued to have these laws struck down. All of them were struck down by the courts as unconstitutional, saying such measures violated the protection for free speech.

These types of cases could serve to help educate the public about the science, but it seems that they have just increased the polarization around the media violence dialogue. This is partly because inappropriate language often gets used in the public discussion, such as the use of the word "ban" when describing legislative policy initiatives. The laws actually have *never* sought to ban violent video games. They have sought only to restrict the sale of violent games directly to children without parental consent. These seem to us to be basically common-sense laws. The store can't sell a violent game to a child unless a parent agrees (or buys it for the child). This kind of law actually puts parents in control and is not a ban. But by using extreme words like "banning" games, this makes the legislators (and the media violence researchers by extension) look extreme, even though that is not what they were advocating.

So if the laws were not advocating a ban, in what way did they violate the constitutional right to free speech? The California case that was appealed to the U.S. Supreme Court is particularly instructive.

The California law (AB 1179), which prohibited the sale or rental of violent video games to minors without parental consent, was passed in 2005. Violent games were defined carefully as those in which the player actions included: "killing, maiming, dismembering, or sexually assaulting an image of a human being, if those acts are depicted in the game" in a manner that "appeals to a deviant or morbid interest," is "patently offensive . . . as to what is suitable for minors," and lacks "serious literary, artistic, political, or scientific value for minors," or "enables the player to virtually inflict serious injury upon images of human beings or characters with substantially human characteristics in a manner which is especially heinous, cruel, or depraved in that it involves torture or serious physical abuse to the victim." If a store was found to have sold such a game to a child without parental consent, the store was subject to a $1,000 fine. Notice again that this is not a "ban" on violent games, although newspaper reports continued to use that term (e.g., "Lawmaker defends law banning sale of violent video games to minors," Fritz, 2010). Even before the law had been enacted, the Entertainment Software Association (ESA), the video game industry association, was planning a lawsuit to have the bill ruled unconstitutional (Thorson, 2005).

The case went to U.S. district court, where the bill was overturned in 2007. It was overturned because there is legal precedent that any restrictions on free speech based on content are presumed to be invalid and must pass "strict scrutiny." Strict scrutiny is the most rigorous form of judicial review, and once the court has determined that it should be applied, the law under consideration is *assumed to be unconstitutional.* The burden then rests with the state to demonstrate (1) a compelling governmental interest that is necessary rather than preferred, (2) that the law is narrowly defined to affect only that issue and not others, and (3) that the law uses the least restrictive means to achieve its goal and that there wouldn't be another way to achieve the same ends (such as a rating system). The court found that the law, as written, was not narrowly defined enough and that it was not the least restrictive approach.

The court was also not convinced that the state had demonstrated a compelling interest. Judge Ronald Whyte stated, "At this point, there has been no showing that violent video games as defined in the Act, *in the absence of other violent media*, cause injury to children" (*Video Software Dealers Association and Entertainment Software Association v. Schwarzenegger*, 2007, p. 15). Governor Schwarzenegger appealed, and the case went to Ninth Circuit Court of Appeals.

In 2009 the court noted again that strict scrutiny was the appropriate level of judicial review. Historically, only obscene content restrictions for children have passed strict scrutiny (e.g., the 1968 case *Ginsberg v. New York*, 390 U.S. 629). Obscenity was limited to mean sexual content, and the courts "have resisted attempts to broaden obscenity to cover violent material as well as sexually-explicit material" (*Video Software Dealers Association v. Schwarzenegger*, 556 F.3d 950, 2009, p. 1954). The court in this case also declined to consider violence as obscene and therefore did not believe that the law could pass strict scrutiny. It argued again that less restrictive means were available, such as public education about the ratings. The court also was unconvinced that the state had met the burden demonstrating a compelling interest to limit First Amendment protections.

In the court's summary, Judge Callahan stated, "None of the research establishes or suggests a causal link between minors playing violent video games and actual psychological or neurological harm, and inferences to that effect would not be reasonable" (*Video Software Dealers Association v. Schwarzenegger*, 556 F.3d 950, 2009, p. 1963). In reaching this conclusion, however, it is instructive to examine carefully how the judges understood (or actually misunderstood) the research. They noted that the state relied heavily on Dr. Craig Anderson's work, which made sense because at the time, Anderson was the researcher who had conducted most of the quality violent game research. Nonetheless, they then examined the statements where Dr. Anderson appropriately identifies the limitations of his and other research and misconstrue them: "Dr. Anderson's research has readily admitted flaws that undermine its support of the State's interest in regulating video games sales and rentals to minors. . . . We note that other courts have either rejected Dr. Anderson's research or found it insufficient" (p. 1961). The justices then examined another study (by the current chapter's first author) and concluded:

the extent to which this study supports the State's position is suspect for similar reasons as Dr. Anderson's work. First, this study states that due to its "correlational nature" it could not directly answer the following question: "Are young adolescents more hostile and aggressive because they expose themselves to media violence, or do previously hostile adolescents prefer violent media?" Second, this study largely relates to the player's violent or aggressive behavior toward others—which, as noted above, is not the interest relied on by the State here—rather than the psychological or neurological harm to the player. Moreover, the study glaringly states that "[i]t is important to note . . . that this study is limited by its correlational nature. *Inferences about causal direction should be viewed with caution*" [emphasis added]. Finally, Dr. Gentile's study suggests that "[a]dditional experimental and longitudinal research is needed. (pp. 1961–1962)

From this, the justices concluded, "most of the studies suffer from significant, admitted flaws in methodology" (p. 1963). This is not an accurate conclusion. It demonstrates instead that judges are experts in the law, not in science. It is an ethical and scientific necessity that researchers state any limitations of their studies. No study is perfect. Every study has strengths and weaknesses, and it is incumbent on researchers to state them clearly in published peer-reviewed scientific journals. Furthermore, researchers also usually try to describe what studies remain to be done to help answer questions more fully. The judges seem to misunderstand proper ethical scientific reporting as meaning that the studies themselves have serious flaws. In fact, if the studies truly had had "significant, admitted flaws in methodology," they would not have been accepted for publication in good peer-reviewed journals.

In addition, two additional aspects of the courts' approach to understanding the science are observed here. First, courts rely heavily on precedent from other courts. Therefore, if one court has misunderstood the scientific evidence, future court cases are likely to misunderstand it similarly. Second, and more important, the ruling states clearly that the court is looking for a very different type of evidence than the research provides. As quoted above, the court is expecting studies to demonstrate that playing a violent video game will necessarily and immediately cause "psychological or neurological harm to the player." The courts can only uphold a law restricting speech if there is a clear and compelling case that the speech causes *immediate harm*. This is why freedom of speech does not apply to yelling "Fire!" in a crowded room or to inciting others to violence. Note that these examples fit a causal model that lawyers call proximal cause: taking an action will cause an immediate result with a high likelihood of serious harm, and without which that harm would not have occurred. Media violence does not meet this standard. The studies demonstrate that playing violent games or watching violent TV or movies increases the odds that the viewer will behave aggressively if provoked. Although this conclusion has important public health implications (for increasing or decreasing the risk of aggression in society), this is not what the courts are looking for. Therefore, most of the scientific research seems largely irrelevant to the courts.

This disconnect between what the science says and what the courts expect it should say became even more apparent once the case reached the U.S. Supreme Court. The 2011 ruling, which again struck down the 2005 law, also confirmed that the law had to pass strict scrutiny because video games are a form of speech and children have First Amendment rights to access them. In its ruling, the Court focused primarily on the question of whether video games were so different from other media that they deserved a lower level of legal protection. They concluded that there seems to be no reason to believe that they are different from other media, and we would agree that the current literature seems to support that. Therefore, if video games are speech and are deserving of the same First Amendment protections as other speech, then there is no legal precedent on which to restrict violent content, as this "country has no tradition of specially restricting children's access to depictions of violence" (*Brown v. Entertainment Merchants Association*, p. 2). Once this decision had been reached, the case was basically over. Nonetheless, the judges then went on to make claims about the research, with some justices being unconvinced and others being highly convinced by the research. In his dissent from majority opinion, for example, Justice Breyer observed:

But what sense does it make to forbid the selling to a 13-year old boy a magazine with a picture of a nude woman [as the Supreme Court did in *Ginsberg v. New York*] while protecting a sale to that 13-year old of an interactive video game in which he actively, but virtually, binds and gags the woman, then tortures and kills her. (p. 19)

Regardless of their personal interpretations of the data, be aware that the justices' mission was to judge whether laws fit within the current interpretation of the Constitution, not to judge the quality of research (which they're not necessarily qualified to do). Therefore, one cannot interpret this ruling to suggest that the psychological research literature on violent video game effects is of poor quality or that it shows no effects. Nonetheless, once the ruling was known, this is what many on the video game industry's side of the debate claimed, further polarizing and politicizing the issue.

Regardless of the details of these court cases, however, there is a bigger picture that often gets missed. The country has been captivated and traumatized by tragic events, but in seeking a policy response, we have suffered from a serious lack of imagination. The only public policy initiatives that have been attempted or even discussed seriously have all been about access restriction. As should be apparent by now, restricting access to violent media based on content is never likely to work. Because the courts' rulings are strongly influenced by precedent, it is unlikely that any law limiting the sale of violent media to children will ever be considered to be constitutional. So why have we put so many resources into this approach while ignoring all others?

WHAT SHOULD WE BE DOING?

First, we should accept the preponderance of evidence and the general public health consensus that media violence does cause an increase in the risk of later aggression. Accepting this, however, does not necessarily require any particular policy response. There is an approach that has been found to be valuable based on the scientific evidence, but it has largely been ignored by the public, the media industries, and policymakers.

There is now a substantial body of research demonstrating that parents are in a much more powerful role than they may realize. Setting limits on the amount and content of media is a powerful protective factor for children (Anderson, Gentile, & Buckley, 2007; Gentile, Lynch, Linder, & Walsh, 2004; Gentile, Nathanson, Rasmussen, Reimer, & Walsh, 2012; Nathanson, 2001). Children whose parents set such limits get better grades in school, get more sleep, and are less aggressive and more prosocial in their behaviors (Gentile, Coyne, & Walsh, 2011; Gentile, Reimer, Nathanson, Walsh, & Eisenmann, 2014). Knowing this, however, does not necessarily help parents to *do* it. Setting appropriate limits on media content requires that parents have some knowledge of the content, and it is for this reason that media ratings matter so much.

All of the media industries have a voluntary rating system that they each administer. That is, each TV network rates its own programs, the movie industry rates movies, the video game industry rates video games, and music producers rate their own CDs. Each rating system was created only after congressional pressure; none is legally required (Gentile, 2008). If the rating systems provide valuable information for parents, then parents are able to use it to set limits appropriate for each child based on their individual family's values. Unfortunately, the research on the reliability and validity of the rating systems documents that each of the rating systems is not very useful for parents.

When asked what they would like in a rating system, parents overwhelmingly state that they would prefer ratings to be content-based rather than age-based (Bushman & Cantor, 2003; Cantor, 1998; Cantor, Stutman, & Duran, 1996; Gentile, Maier, Hasson, & de Bonetti, 2011). Over three-quarters of parents say that it is "very important" to have information about the amount of violence, offensive language, and sexual content present in media (Gentile, 1996). The music system provides no information about content at all. The television and movie systems provide content information only for certain rating categories, and what they provide is vague. For example, the movie *Hunger Games: Catching Fire* was rated PG-13 for "thematic elements," and *Best Man Down* was rated PG-13 for "brief language." It is completely unclear what is meant by these content descriptors. Does *Best Man Down* only use short words? What are the themes alluded to in *Hunger Games*? In national surveys of parents, only 6 percent of parents said that the TV, movie, or video game ratings were "always accurate" (Gentile, Maier, et al., 2011).

Parents' perceptions of ratings inaccuracy, however, are accurate. The rating systems all have serious problems. In a study of 2,757 television shows, 79 percent contained violence but no V (violence) descriptor rating, 91 percent of programs with offensive language lacked an L (offensive language) rating, and 92 percent of programs with sexual content had no S (sexual scenes) rating (Kunkel et al., 2001). Unfortunately, the video game, movie, and music ratings also suffer from similar problems (Gentile, 2008; Haninger & Thompson, 2004; Thompson & Haninger, 2001; Thompson, Tepichin, &

Haninger, 2006). Ratings also have been criticized for what is called "ratings creep"; that is, becoming more lenient over time (Gentile, 2008). One content analysis of about 2,000 films found that a film rated PG-13 in 2003 included approximately the same amount of violence, offensive language, and nudity as an R-rated film of 10 years before (Thompson & Yokota, 2004).

Studies have also demonstrated that rating systems lack validity, as measured by accurately labeling content known to be harmful or being congruent with parents' perceptions (Kunkel et al., 2001; Thompson & Yokota, 2004; Walsh & Gentile, 2001). A content analysis of 1,332 TV shows measured the dimensions of shows posing the highest degree of risk for harmful effects on youth and then compared these with their assigned TV ratings (Kunkel et al., 2001). The industry ratings did not match the content of the shows. For example, over two-thirds of children's shows with high-risk violent content were rated as TV-Y (the youngest rating) without the V (violence) descriptor (in fact, the youngest ratings are designed to not include content descriptors). Parents generally do not agree with the industry ratings, which shows a serious lack of validity (Gentile, Maier, et al., 2011; Walsh & Gentile, 2001). In addition, because parents do not agree which types of content are appropriate for children of a given age, the current age-based ratings are necessarily invalid (Gentile, Maier, et al., 2011). In sum, the research documents serious problems with each rating system, and these problems hamper their value for parents.

When discussing public policy options, we feel that the conversation has been unreasonably limited to considering only legislative efforts. There are many more policy options available than legislation. For example, public health organizations such as the American Medical Association or the American Academy of Pediatrics could set a policy that requires all medical students to complete four hours of training on the effects of media on children as part of their pediatrics rotation. This would allow family physicians and pediatricians to be able to know when to ask questions about the media, to be better at spotting potential problems due to media, and to discuss the research in some detail with their clients rather than merely giving simplistic statements such as to reduce screen time. Community or regional health care organizations could include a training session on media effects as part of their hospitals' birth classes for new parents. Our experience has been that parents are most receptive to the science when their children are very young (or not yet born!). Businesses who conduct wellness programs for their employees could give seminars on media effects to their employees. Notice that all of these types of "public policy" do not need any government intervention but would still serve the goal of creating a healthier society by getting the information to people who can use it most.

If, however, government-level intervention is desired, there are much more potentially effective policies that could be pursued than the failed attempts at access restriction. Given the research demonstrating that parents setting limits on media is a powerful protective factor, improving the media ratings might be the single most effective policy we could enact. There is some legal precedent that it would pass constitutional muster as well. The 1996 Telecommunications Act mandated that a TV rating system be created to be used by the V-chip (a computer chip in televisions that can be set by parents to filter out shows with certain ratings). This is likely constitutional because the government is not the agency creating the ratings, and therefore it cannot be government censorship. Given the multiple problems with the existing rating systems (Cantor, 1997; Kaiser Family Foundation, 1999; Gentile, Humphrey, & Walsh, 2005; Gentile, Maier, et al., 2011; Haninger & Thompson, 2004; Jenkins, Webb, Brown, Afifi, & Kraus, 2004; Kaiser Family Foundation, 1998; Kunkel et al., 1998; Kunkel et al., 2001; Leone, 2002; Linder & Gentile, 2009; Nalkur, Jamieson, & Romer, 2010; Thompson et al., 2006; Thompson & Yokota, 2004; Walsh & Gentile, 2001), federal legislation could be enacted to create a new rating system. Instead of each industry having its own idiosyncratic rating system, one universal rating system could be created based on the decades of research now available demonstrating what would work best as well as what parents want. Parents support the idea of having one universal rating system (Gentile, Maier, et al., 2011). Instead of each industry rating its own products (leaving the children in charge of the candy store), the legislation could require that the ratings board be independent of the media industries, although it would be valuable for each industry to have representatives on the board. The legislation could require that the ratings be content based, rather than age based. The legislation could require that the ratings maintain some minimum standard of scientific reliability and validity. The law could require that research be conducted annually to ensure that the reliability and validity are being maintained, and that the ratings are not shifting due to ratings creep. All of these aspects would not only be constitutional but they would also likely have a much larger benefit than the earlier approaches toward access restriction would have because they serve to improve the information parents have at their disposal. Ultimately, this would give parents more power to maximize the benefits and minimize the potential harms of media, without the government trying to impose any particular values on all families. With reliable and valid content information, each family can establish limits that fit their individual values.

After so many decades of research, high public interest, and multiple public policy attempts, it is disappointing that so little has been accomplished. Nevertheless, it is not particularly surprising when one considers that the media organizations have constitutional rights, that they largely control the public's access to information, that the discussion of media violence is generally only discussed in inappropriate contexts (e.g., school shootings), and that we as a society have had a failure of imagination about what types of policy responses would actually be legal and effective. We believe that anything that gives better information to parents will be the most effective approach.

REFERENCES

American Academy of Pediatrics. (2001). Policy statement: Children, adolescents and television. *Pediatrics, 107*, 423–426.

American Academy of Pediatrics. (2009). Policy statement: Media violence. *Pediatrics, 124*, 1495–1503.

Anderson, C. A., Gentile, D. A., & Buckley, K. E. (2007). *Violent video game effects on children and adolescents: Theory, research, and public policy.* New York, NY: Oxford University Press.

Atkin, C. K., Murray, J. P., & Nayman, O. B. (1971). Television and social behavior: An annotated bibliography of research focusing on television's impact on children. Washington, DC: U.S. Public Health Service.

Baker, R. K., & Ball, S. J. (1969). *Mass media and violence: A staff report to the National Commission on the Causes and Prevention of violence, Vol. XI.* Washington, DC: U.S. Government Printing Office.

Bandura, A., Ross, D., & Ross, S. A. (1963). Imitation of film-mediated aggressive models. *Journal of Abnormal and Social Psychology, 66*, 3–11.

Berkowitz, L. (1962). *Aggression: A social psychological analysis.* New York, NY: McGraw-Hill.

Brown, Governor of California, et al. v. Entertainment Merchants Association et al. (2011). Docket No. 08–1448. Argued November 2, 2010. Decided June 27, 2011. http://www.supremecourt.gov/opinions/10pdf/08-1448.pdf

Bushman, B. J., & Cantor, J. (2003). Media ratings for violence and sex: Implications for policymakers and parents. *American Psychologist, 58*, 130–141.

Cantor, J. (1997). Critique of the new rating system for United States television. *News on Children and Violence on the Screen: A Newsletter from the UNESCO International Clearinghouse on Children and Violence on the Screen, 1*, 26–27.

Cantor, J. (1998). Ratings for program content: The role of research findings. *The Annals of the American Academy of Political and Social Science, 557*, 54–69.

Cantor, J., Stutman, S., & Duran, V. (1996). *What parents want in a television rating system: Results of a national survey.* Chicago, IL: National PTA.

Cater, D., & Strickland, S. (1972). *A first hard look at the Surgeon General's report on television and violence.* Palo Alto, CA: Aspen Program on Communications and Society.

Cater, D., & Strickland, S. (1975). *TV violence and the child: The evolution and fate of the Surgeon General's report.* New York, NY: Russell Sage Foundation.

Ferguson, C. J. (2011). A further plea for caution against medical professionals overstating video game violence effects. *Mayo Clinic Proceedings, 86*(8), 820–821.

Fritz, B. (2010, April 29). Lawmaker defends law banning sale of violent video games to minors. *Los Angeles Times.* http://articles.latimes.com/2010/apr/29/business/la-fi-ct-facetime-20100429

GamePolitics.com. (2012, December 20). ESA issues brief statement on Sandy Hook Elementary School shooting. Retrieved from http://www.gamepolitics.com/2012/12/20/esa-issues-brief-statement-sandy-hook-elementary-school-shooting#.UpYOWMRDuSo

Gentile, D. A. (1996). *National survey of parent media attitudes, behaviors, and opinions.* Minneapolis, MN: National Institute on Media and the Family.

Gentile, D. A. (2008). The rating systems for media products. In S. Calvert & B. Wilson (Eds.), *Handbook of children, media, and development* (pp. 527–551). Oxford, UK: Blackwell.

Gentile, D. A., & Bushman, B. J. (2012). Reassessing media violence effects using a risk and resilience approach to understanding aggression. *Psychology of Popular Media Culture, 1*, 138–151.

Gentile, D. A., Coyne, S. M., & Walsh, D. A. (2011). Media violence, physical aggression and relational aggression in school age children: A short-term longitudinal study. *Aggressive Behavior, 37*, 193–206.

Gentile, D. A., Humphrey, J., & Walsh, D. A. (2005). Media ratings for movies, music, video games, and television: A review of the research and recomendations for improvements. *Adolescent Medicine Clinics, 16*, 427–446.

Gentile, D. A., Lynch, P. J., Linder, J. R., & Walsh, D. A. (2004). The effects of violent video game habits on adolescent hostility, aggressive behaviors, and school performance. *Journal of Adolescence, 27*(1), 5–22.

Gentile, D. A., Maier, J. A., Hasson, M. R., & de Bonetti, B. L. (2011). Parents' evaluation of media ratings a decade after the television ratings were introduced. *Pediatrics, 128*, 36–44.

Gentile, D. A., Nathanson, A. I., Rasmussen, E. E., Reimer, R. A., & Walsh, D. A. (2012). Do you see what I see? Parent and child reports of parental monitoring of media. *Family Relations, 61*, 470–487.

Gentile, D. A., Reimer, R. A., Nathanson, A. I., Walsh, D. A., & Eisenmann, J. C. (2014). Protective effects of parental monitoring of children's media use: A prospective study. *JAMA-Pediatrics, 168*, 479–484.

Gentile, D. A., & Walsh, D. A. (2002). A normative study of family media habits. *Journal of Applied Developmental Psychology, 23*, 157–178.

Hall, R. C. W., Day, T., & Hall, R. C. W. (2011). In Reply. *Mayo Clinic Proceedings, 86*(8), 821–823.

Haninger, K., & Thompson, K. M. (2004). Content and ratings of teen-rated video games. *Journal of American Medical Association, 291*(7), 856–865.

Himmelweit, H. T., Oppenheim, A. N., & Vince, P. (1958). *Television and the child: An empirical study of the effect of television on the young.* London, UK: Published for the Nuffield Foundation by Oxford University Press.

Huston, A. C., Donnerstein, E., Fairchild, H., Feshbach, N. D., Katz, P. A., Murray, J. P., Rubinstein, E. A. Wilcox, B. L., & Zuckerman, D. (1992). *Big world, small screen: The role of television in American society.* Lincoln, NE: University of Nebraska Press.

Jenkins, L., Webb, T., Brown, N., Afifi, A. A., & Kraus, J. (2004). An evaluation of the Motion Picture Association of America's treatment of violence in PG, PG-13 and R rated films. *Pediatrics, Manuscript 2004–1977.*

Kaiser Family Foundation. (1998). New national survey of parents and children on TV ratings system: Half of parents use the new TV ratings, but many say changes could make them more helpful. Menlo Park, CA: Kaiser Family Foundation.

Kaiser Family Foundation. (1999). *Parents and the V-chip: A Kaiser Family Foundation Survey.* Menlo Park, CA: Henry J. Kaiser Family Foundation.

Kenny, D. A. (1984). The NBC study and television violence. *Journal of Communication, 34*(1), 176–182.

Kunkel, D., Farinola, W. J. M., Cope, K. M., Donnerstein, E., Biely, E., & Zwarun, L. (1998). *Rating the TV ratings: One year out; An assessment of the television industry's use of V-chip ratings*. Menlo Park, CA: Kaiser Family Foundation.

Kunkel, D., Farinola, W. J. M., Cope, K. M., Donnerstein, E., Biely, E., Zwarun, L., & Rollin, E. (2001). Assessing the validity of V-chip rating judgments: The labeling of high-risk programs. In B. Greenberg (Ed.), *The alphabet soup of television program ratings* (pp. 51–68). Cresskill, NJ: Hampton Press.

Lazarsfeld, P. F. (1955). Why is so little known about the effects of television and what can be done? *Public Opinion Quarterly, 19*, 243–251.

Leone, R. (2002). Contemplating ratings: An examination of what the MPAA considers "too far for R" and why. *Journal of Communication, 52*(4), 938–954.

Leshner, A. I., Altevogt, B. M., Lee, A. F., McCoy, M. A., & Kelley, P. W. (Eds.). (2013). *Priorities for research to reduce the threat of firearm-related violence*. Washington, DC: National Academies Press.

Linder, J. R., & Gentile, D. A. (2009). Is the television rating system valid? Indirect, verbal, and physical aggression in programs viewed by fifth-grade girls and associations with behavior. *Journal of Applied Developmental Psychology, 30*, 286–297.

Maccoby, E. E. (1954). Why do children watch television? *Public Opinion Quarterly, 18*, 239–244.

Milavsky, J. R., Kessler, R. C., Stipp, H. H., & Rubens, W. S. (1982). *Television and aggression: A panel study*. New York, NY: Academic Press.

Minow, N. N., & LaMay, C. L. (1995). *Abandoned in the wasteland: Children, television, and the First Amendment*. New York, NY: Hill & Wang.

Murray, J. P. (1973). Television and violence: Implications of the Surgeon General's research program. *American Psychologist, 28*(6), 472–478.

Murray, J. P., Biggins, B., Donnerstein, E., Kunkel, D., Menninger, R. W., Rich, M., & Strasburger, V. (2011). A plea for concern regarding violent video games. *Mayo Clinic Proceedings, 86*(8), 818–820.

Nalkur, P. G., Jamieson, P. E., & Romer, D. (2010). The effectiveness of the Motion Picture Association of America's rating system in screening explicit violence and sex in top-ranked movies from 1950 to 2006. *Journal of Adolescent Health, 47*, 40–47.

Nathanson, A. I. (2001). Mediation of children's television viewing: Working toward conceptual clarity and common understanding. In W. Gudykunst (Ed.), *Communication Yearbook* (Vol. 25, pp. 115–151). Mahwah, NJ: Lawrence Erlbaum.

National Institute of Mental Health (NIMH). (1982). *Television and behavior: Ten years of scientific progress and implications for the eighties* (Vol. 1. Summary report). Washington, DC: U.S. Government Printing Office.

National Rifle Association. (2012, December 21). Statement from press conference. Retrieved from http://articles.courant.com/2012-12-21/news/hc-full-text-nra -statement-from-dec-21-press-conference-20121221_1_insane-killer-press -conference-prosecutions

Nunneley, S. (2013, January 12). Video game researcher "cautiously optimistic" over Biden meeting. *VG24/7.com*. Retrieved from http://www.vg247.com/2013/01 /12/video-game-researcher-%E2%80%9Ccautiously-optimistic%E2%80% 9D-over-meeting-with-biden/

Pecora, N., Murray, J. P., & Wartella, E. A. (2007). *Children and television: Fifty years of research*. Mahwah, NJ: Erlbaum Publishers.

Schramm, W., Lyle, V., & Parker, E. B. (1961). *Television in the lives or our children*. Stanford, CA: Stanford University Press.

Smith, P. M., Fallow, K. A., Pozza, D. C., & Hellman, M. S. (2006). Attack on violent video games. *Communications Lawyer, 24*, No. 1.

Strasburger, V. C., & Donnerstein, E. (2013). The new media of violent video games: Yet same old media problems. *Clinical Pediatrics, 53*, 721–725.

Surgeon General's Scientific Advisory Committee on Television and Social Behavior. (1972). *Television and growing up: The impact of televised violence*. Washington, DC: U.S. Government Printing Office.

Thompson, K. M., & Haninger, K. (2001). Violence in E-rated video games. *Journal of the American Medical Association, 286*, 591–598.

Thompson, K. M., Tepichin, K., & Haninger, K. (2006). Content and ratings of mature-rated video games. *Archives of Pediatrics and Adolescent Medicine, 160*, 402–410.

Thompson, K. M., & Yokota, F. (2004). Violence, sex, and profanity in films: Correlation of movie ratings with content. *Medscape General Medicine, 6*(3), 1–19.

Thorson, T. (2005, October 7). Schwarzenegger signs game-restriction bill. *Gamespot.com*. Retrieved from http://www.gamespot.com/articles/schwarzenegger-signs -game-restriction-bill/1100-6135332/

U.S. Congress. (1952). House Committee on Interstate and Foreign Commerce. Investigation of Radio and Television Programs. Hearings and Report, 82nd Congress, 2nd session, June 3–December 5, 1952. Washington, DC: U.S. Government Printing Office.

U.S. Congress. (1955). Senate Committee on the Judiciary. Subcommittee to Investigate Juvenile Delinquency. Juvenile Delinquency (Television Programs). Hearings, 84th Congress, 1st Session, April 6–7, 1955. Washington, DC: U.S. Government Printing Office.

Video Software Dealers Association and Entertainment Software Association v. Schwarzenegger, 5:05-cv-04188-RMW. (2007).

Video Software Dealers Association v. Schwarzenegger, 556 F.3d 950 (9th Circuit). (2009).

Walsh, D. A., & Gentile, D. A. (2001). A validity test of movie, television, and video-game ratings. *Pediatrics, 107*, 1302–1308.

Whitaker, J. L., & Bushman, B. J. (2012). "Boom, headshot!": Effect of video game play and controller type on firing aim and accuracy. *Communication Research, 39*, 1–13.

White House. (2013). Now is the time. The president's plan to protect our children and our communities by reducing gun violence. Wh.gov/now-is-the-time

CHAPTER 15

The Frontiers of Media Violence Research

W. James Potter

The purpose of all media violence research is, in essence, to contribute to our understanding of the risks or benefits of exposure to such content. In moving us toward this goal, each media violence study can be categorized as advancing our understanding along one of three paths. One path advances with findings from studies seeking to determine which effects could occur as a result of exposure to violence in the media; this is the "effects" path. A second path advances with findings from studies seeking to determine which factors—in the portrayals, in the viewers, and in the exposure environments—are associated with which effects; this is the "influence" path. The third path advances with findings from studies seeking to determine how much violence is being presented, where it is being displayed, and the nature of those portrayals; this is the "content" path. The more progress we make along each of these three paths, the more we construct a useful understanding of the size and nature of the media violence problem.

In this chapter, I will briefly show how far we have come along each of these three paths, thus defining the frontier of our understanding. My thesis is that media violence scholars have made much progress along all three paths, but that our rate of progress has slowed as our challenge has evolved much faster than our response to it. Up until this point, most of our research has been rather explanatory; we have been searching for evidence for all kinds of effects and have been hunting for indications that many different kinds of factors may be contributing to those effects. Now our challenge lies much more in developing systems of explanation that can build from the findings in this very large literature. Also, the profound changes in the media environment (especially in the last decade) have altered our challenge. Throughout this chapter, I present a series of recommendations about how we can move toward meeting these new challenges.

EFFECTS PATH

For almost a century, social critics have been speculating on the variety of changes the media have been bringing about in our lives, and social scientists have been conducting studies to document which of those effects actually do occur. This formal research began in the 1920s with a set of a dozen investigations—called the Payne Studies—of the effect of movies on children (Charters, 1933). By 2000 it was estimated that there were already more than 1,000 studies and reports published examining the effects of exposure to media violence (American Academy of Pediatrics, 2000).

With such a large literature, we should expect that we now have a clear idea about what those effects are, but this is not the case. There are still some critics who question the validity of the entire literature (see chapter 12 of this volume). And although almost all social scientists who are familiar with this literature agree that exposure to media violence leads to effects, they are far from agreeing on how many effects there are.

Validity of Effects Research

By the early 1970s the media violence research had grown large enough to attract the attention of scholars who analyzed the literature to determine if it was strong enough to draw any conclusions (Baker & Ball, 1969; Chaffee, 1972; Comstock, Chaffee, Katzman, McCombs, & Roberts, 1978; Goranson, 1970; Liebert, 1972; Liebert, Neale, & Davidson, 1973; Liebert & Poulos, 1975; Liebert & Schwartzberg, 1977; Maccoby, 1964; Roberts & Schramm, 1971; Stein & Friedrich, 1972; Tannenbaum & Zillmann, 1975). All of those reviewers concluded that exposure to violent portrayals in the media increases subsequent viewer aggression largely through a process of disinhibition. This conclusion was featured in both the 1972 and 1982 reports on the effects of media violence presented to the U.S. Surgeon General. The later report said, "Most of the researchers look at the totality of evidence and conclude, as did the Surgeon General's Advisory Committee, that the convergence of findings supports the conclusion of a causal relationship between televised violence and later aggressive behavior" (National Institute of Mental Health, 1982, p. 37).

This conclusion, however, had its critics (Jones, 1971; Howitt & Cumberbatch, 1975; Kniveton, 1976; Kaplan & Singer, 1976; Lesser, 1977). For example, Lesser's position highlighted five criticisms: (1) lack of distinction between filmed and TV violence, (2) the restriction to an immediate effect, (3) the inadequate exploration in the observational learning experiments of the developmental function of imitation in children's play, (4) the questionable definitions and operationalizations of aggression, and (5) the artificial nature of laboratory experiments that limits the ecological validity of the findings.

In the decades since this early disagreement, a great deal more empirical research has served to overcome these shortcomings so that most (but not all) of these critics have been convinced of the general finding that exposure to media violence can lead to an immediate disinhibition effect. Narrative reviews since 1980 have all concluded that there is a consistent relationship between viewing violence and subsequent aggressiveness. This finding holds in surveys, lab experiments, and naturalistic experiments (Comstock, 1985; Comstock & Strasburger, 1990; Friedrich-Cofer & Huston, 1986; Geen, 1994; Heath, Bresolin, & Rinaldi, 1989; National Institute of Mental Health, 1982; Roberts & Maccoby, 1985; Rule & Ferguson, 1986). For example, Roberts and Maccoby (1985) concluded that "the overwhelming proportion of results point to a causal relationship between exposure to mass communication portrayals of violence and an increased probability that viewers will behave violently at some subsequent time" (p. 576). And Friedrich-Cofer and Huston (1986) concluded that "the weight of the evidence from different methods of investigation supports the hypothesis that television violence affects aggression" (p. 368).

Meta-analytical studies that have re-examined the data quantitatively across sets of studies have also consistently concluded that viewing of aggression is likely to lead to antisocial behavior (see chapter 13, this volume; Anderson & Bushman, 2002b; Andison, 1977; Carlson, Marcus-Newhall, & Miller, 1990; Hearold, 1986; Paik & Comstock, 1994; Wood, Wong, & Chachere, 1991). For example, Paik and Comstock (1994) conducted a meta-analysis of 217 studies of the effects of television violence on antisocial behavior and report a positive and significant correlation. They concluded that "regardless of age—whether nursery school, elementary school, college, or adult—results remain positive at a high significance level" (p. 537). Anderson and Bushman's meta-analysis (2002b) examined the results of about 300 studies conducted on a total of 50,000 participants in all kinds of research designs, including laboratory experiments, field experiments, cross-sectional studies, and even longitudinal studies. They concluded that there was consistent evidence of an aggressor effect throughout this literature.

There are still some critics (Ferguson & Kilburn, 2009; Freedman, 1984, 2002; Grixti, 1985; Guantlett, 2005; McGuire, 1986; Olson, 2004; Savage, 2004; Stipp & Milavsky, 1988) who continue to question the validity of the research that supports this conclusion. These critics argue that the entire literature of media effects is faulty because of three characteristics. First, these critics point out that the media effects literature that is generated by laboratory experiments produces findings that may not be generalizable from the artificial conditions in the laboratory to real-world situations. Critics argue that those findings do not reflect what happens to people in their everyday lives when they make their own choices regarding media exposures and responses to those exposures. Therefore, they claim, the literature lacks ecological validity, so the results cannot be generalized from these artificial experiments to real world patterns.

Second, critics argue that the media effects literature that has been generated by surveys does not allow for causal claims. They point out that surveys report correlations, which only provide evidence of associations, not of causation. Critics also argue that many studies fail to account for "third variables" that could better account for findings than the independent variables built into the experimental designs. Third, critics point to the weak effect sizes, ranging from predicting between 1 percent and 9 percent of variance in aggression, and much less variation for other types of effects of media violence.

In responding to these criticisms, social scientists (e.g., Cantor, 2003; Huesmann & Taylor, 2003; see also Taylor & Huesmann, chapter 12 of this volume) point out that although any individual experiment may have flaws, the big picture that emerges across all these studies is that media violence does exert an influence on people exposed to it—that the media influence is so robust that it emerges in the literature by consistently showing a difference between those participants who were exposed to some form of media violence compared to participants who were not. They also point out that the literature includes some longitudinal studies that clearly show patterns of influence that can be regarded as causal. And although the effect size reported in these studies might appear small, it is similar to other health-related risks such as smoking and lung cancer or condom use and transmission of STDs (Bushman & Huesmann, 2001).

Despite the critics' claims, however, support for the conclusion that exposure to media violence can lead to effects is much more widespread than the criticism. In 2000 six leading health organizations issued a joint statement (American Academy of Pediatrics, 2000) that had a blue-ribbon panel of social scientists review the more than 1,000 studies conducted on the effects of media violence over a 30-year period; the panel concluded that there was overwhelming evidence of a "causal connection between media violence and aggressive behavior in some children." Furthermore, "The effect of entertainment violence on children is complex and variable. Some children will be affected more than others. But although duration, intensity, and extent of the impact may vary, there are several measurable negative effects of children's exposure to violent entertainment."

The controversy essentially is one of "whether the glass is half full or half empty," or in this case, whether the glass is full enough or not. Given the size of the literature and the length of time scholars have been studying this issue, it may seem disappointing that the high-water mark is around predicting only 9 percent of the variance. But as Bushman and Huesmann (2001) point out, this is the standard across many fields of inquiry (see also chapter 2, this volume).

There are at least two ways to view this controversy. The pessimistic view is to focus on the 91 percent of the variance we have yet to explain and conclude that we have not accomplished much—or anything. The optimistic view is to treasure whatever knowledge we have developed. In addition, there is also a third way to view this controversy; a practical way, which regards what we have accomplished thus far as providing valuable suggestions for what media effects likely occur, then move forward with a commitment to greater precision in documenting the full set of outcomes in the constellation of media effects, calibrating the relative importance of each effect, and estimating the prevalence of each effect occurring in the course of everyday lives.

What Are the Effects of Exposure to Media Violence?

Despite the continuing criticism of the media effects literature, there is a very high level of agreement among media effects scholars that exposure to violence in the media can lead to negative effects. However, there appears to be a good deal of confusion about what those effects are. To illustrate this point, look at Table 15.1 to see how different reviewers of this same literature display considerable variation in what they regard as the effects of exposure to media violence. Although all these reviewers conclude that there is more than one effect, they differ substantially in their views about what those effects are. Even more confusing is the fact that reviewers seem to use different names for the same effects, and also use the same term to label what appear to be different effects. For example, the term "learning" seems to be an umbrella term for very different kinds of effects. The National Television Violence Study (NTVS) (1996, 1997) used the term "learning" to apply to a range of effects including what some reviewers split into disinhibition and imitation (Comstock et al., 1978; Condry, 1989; Gunter, 1994; Liebert & Schwartzberg, 1977) or into observational learning and disinhibition (Signorielli, 1990). Also, some reviewers (Gunter, 1994; Sparks, Sparks, & Sparks, 2009) separate arousal and desensitization, while Condry (1989) lumps them together as one effect. Donnerstein, Slaby, and Eron (1994) refer to an "aggressor effect," but what they seem to be doing is including the effects of observational learning, imitation, triggering, and disinhibition into one effect.

We need to be careful that we do not equate different terminology across reviewers with doubt. These reviewers show no indication that they doubt exposure to media violence leads to effects. Instead, the confusion is an indication of a need for greater precision in naming those effects and organizing them in a more coherent manner, such as what is illustrated in Table 15.2. By using just two analytical dimensions (time and type of effect), it is possible to organize these effects in such a way as to reveal that there are at least 17 effects that differ from one another in nontrivial ways. This table is not intended to be the definitive statement on the number or types of effects that currently exist in the media literature; instead, it is presented as an illustration of the importance of organizing the findings from this large literature.

Table 15.1
How Many Effects of Media Violence Are There?

- Liebert and Schwartzberg (1977) see two primary effects: direct imitation and disinhibition.

- Comstock, Chaffee, Katzman, McCombs, and Roberts (1978) see four major effects: imitation, disinhibition, desensitization, and catharsis.

- Hearold (1986) sees three: learning, incitement of violent acts, and catharsis.

- Condry (1989) observes four: cultivation, imitation, disinhibition, and arousal/desensitization. He says he considers arousal and desensitization together because they are part of the same process or mechanism, and aggression is positively related to both.

- Signorielli (1991) sees five: catharsis, observational learning, disinhibition, arousal, and cultivation.

- Donnerstein, Slaby, and Eron (1994) claim there are four: aggressor effect, victim effect, bystander effect, and appetite effect.

- Gunter (1994) lists seven: catharsis, arousal, disinhibition, imitation, desensitization, cultivation, and fear.

- Josephson (1995) lists four for children: imitation, disinhibition, triggering, and "displacing of activities, such as socializing with other children and interacting with adults, that would teach children non-violent ways to solve conflicts" (p. 9) although she says that none of the effects is specific to a certain age.

- The NTVS (1996, 1997) perceives three: learning, desensitization, and fear.

- Bushman & Huesmann (2001) see six effects mechanisms leading to aggression: observational learning of behaviors and scripts, observational learning of beliefs and attitudes, emotional desensitization, cognitive cueing and priming, arousal, and excitation transfer.

- Sparks, Sparks, & Sparks (2009) see five effects mechanisms: social learning, priming, arousal, desensitization, and neurophysiological.

- Bushman, Huesmann, & Whitaker (2009) see three: the aggressor effect, the fear of victimization effect, and the conscious numbing effect.

Recommendations

The key to making progress from this point onward has less to do with conducting yet another empirical test and more to do with organizing the underutilized findings in our existing literature. That is, we need to focus more on the task of conceptualizing what a media effect is and organizing the scattering of effects that appear under various names in our literature. Then we can design the kinds of studies that will move us beyond our current stage of exploration and into a more challenging stage of explanation. To help guide that shift, I present three recommendations: increase precision, expand on time, and expand on units.

Table 15.2
Overview of Media Effects

Type	Immediate	Long Term
Physiological	Fight/Flight Reaction	Physiological Habituation
Emotional	Temporary Fear	Emotional Habituation
Cognitive	Learning Specific Acts and Lessons	Generalizing Patterns (Cultivation of Estimates)
		Acquiring Social Norms (Prosocial & Antisocial)
Attitudinal	Opinion creation/change	Reinforcement
		Cultivation of Beliefs
Behavioral	Imitation/Copying	Generalizing Novel Behaviors
	Disinhibition	
	Triggering/Activation	
	Attraction (Avoidance)	
Societal		Shifting Norms
		Changing Institutions

Increase precision

Most fundamental and pressing is the need to increase our precision in conceptualizing the effects of exposure to media violence. Unless we can do this, the continuing growth of this literature will generate more confusion from the fragmentation of findings than it will generate useful knowledge about media effects. To guide this task of increasing precision, I suggest the following procedure. First, we need to think about what constitutes a media effect of any kind. This is a huge task that I cannot fully lay out here, but I have done so elsewhere (see Potter, 2011).

Once we have clear criteria for what constitutes an effect, the second step is to search through the literature to identify all examples of effects. Notice in Table 15.1 that some reviewers label effects as outcomes, while others label effects as processes. We need to increase our precision in separating effects and processes; both are important, but they are not the same thing, and theories should be careful in how they describe and test them.

Third, we need to organize those effects according to some meaningful analytical dimensions. Table 15.2 used the analytical dimensions of time and type; there are likely to be other analytical dimensions that would be useful.

This step is important for several reasons. First, we need to analyze the meaning that researchers have applied to the effects they have documented to determine which are using the same name to label different effects and which are using different names to label the same effect. Also, arranging all the different effects documented in the existing literature would help us create a better assessment of which kinds of effects may have been overlooked in the past, and thus orient us to where additional research is most needed. The use of analytical dimensions to organize effects would also open the door for thinking much more about systems of explanation. Until we can do a better job of organizing all the findings we have already generated, we will have little coherent direction in moving forward, and any additional empirical studies may contribute more to clutter than to knowledge.

Expand on time

A second recommendation is that we need to think more about time when we consider the various effects of media violence. Almost all of the media effects literature is composed of studies that generate outcome data at a single point in time—therefore, we have little idea about how long any of these effects last. Designing studies that would be able to identify long-term effects is a very difficult task. This is one of the major reasons why we do not have more tests of long-term effects. However, the difficulty of the task should not continue to be a barrier for us in exploring long-term effects now that we have a good deal of guidance from the current research. For example, cultivation is claimed to be a long-term effect, but very few cultivation studies gather data at more than one point in time. There is a fair-sized body of cross-sectional research studies that give us indications that people who watch more television on average are more likely to hold real-world beliefs that are associated with the television world. This type of finding had value in the past to suggest that television might be cultivating long-term beliefs, but until researchers begin testing cultivation over time, we cannot know if the evidence we have is a misleading artifact, or if there is in fact a long-term cultivation effect.

There have been very few longitudinal studies of long-term effects. Perhaps the best example of such a study was conducted by Huesmann and Eron (1986), in which they followed the behavior of their participants over a 10-year period. They were able to find that degree of exposure to violent media messages early in life was associated with increased aggressive activity later.

Until we consider time much more carefully when thinking about media effects and designing our studies, we will be limiting our conception of effects. Some effects might only be short-term blips—flaring up during exposure and decaying in a matter of seconds. Other effects may suddenly occur and manifest themselves throughout a person's life. Other effects may slowly build (either increasing or decreasing) in a linear way or exponentially.

Expand on units

A third recommendation is that effects researchers need to move beyond the limitation of looking for effects on individuals and also look for effects on more macro units, such as society or its institutions. Because there are many documented effects on individuals, it is likely that those changes in individuals manifest themselves on a broader scale in society. For example, if many more people are behaving aggressively, the criminal justice system will be affected. If some of that aggression is physically violent in nature, the medical community will be affected. Many public schools now have metal detectors at the doors and a lowering of students' privacy as a result of massacres in a handful of schools.

In chapter 3 of this volume, Tannis MacBeth displays a key study that examined effects on the macro level. As will be clear from reading her chapter, there is reason to believe that society has been affected by media violence. But the number of studies examining those macro effects is much smaller than the number of studies on individuals. This is a serious shortcoming, especially considering the importance of these macro effects.

In summary, we now have a very large literature suggesting that there are many effects from exposure to violence in the media. However, that literature does not present a clear picture about what those effects are and how they are organized. Instead, it is fragmented by conflicting conceptualizations about what constitutes an effect and how to label them. The literature is also highly concentrated in the areas of short-term effects from laboratory experiments, and very sparse in terms of useful evidence of long-term effects and what naturally occurs in people's everyday lives when they make their own decisions about media exposure and following through on effects. In order to continue making progress down this effects path, we need to increase our precision in conceptualizing effects, and shift much or our research effort into examinations that are more naturalistic, more longitudinal, and more oriented toward macro units.

INFLUENCE PATH

The studies contributing to the influence path are largely the same as the studies in the effects path. Typically, researchers will conduct a study that seeks to determine if a particular effect will occur, and at the same time identify the factors that contribute to that effect. This is a very large literature and includes evidence of influence by a great many factors.

Although we have identified many factors, we are far from understanding *the process* of that influence. To illustrate this point, imagine yourself trying to understand the process of playing the game of baseball. A scholar of the game shows you a bat, a ball, a base, a dugout, a chalked line, an umpire, a patch of green grass, a ballpark frank, and the words to the national anthem. All of these are relevant to the game of baseball, some more centrally than others, but studying each of these elements does not help you much to understand the process of playing the game. Even if the scholar worked hard to add additional elements to this pile of things, the bigger pile would not do much to increase your understanding of the game of baseball. What we need is an explanation of how all these things work together—that is, how the game is played and how the game attracts fans. Thus we need less a description of individual elements and more an explanation about how the elements work together.

With the process of influence leading up to the manifestation of media effects, scholars have been showing us a great many factors that seem to play a role (see Table 15.3). But few scholars have taken on the task of explaining how these factors work together. One example of scholars who have begun this task is the General Aggression Model (GAM), in which Anderson and Bushman (2002a) have attempted to explain one effect—aggression—and arranged some factors of influence into three categories: cognition, affect, and arousal. They then argued that these three factors mediate the effects of situational and personal variables on aggression. The GAM also shows promise to extend its explanation beyond experimental situations created in psychological laboratories and into more naturalistic settings in the everyday world (DeWall, Anderson, & Bushman, 2011; Gentile & Bushman, 2012).

The work of Anderson and Bushman defines the frontier of work on the influence path. There is, however, a lot more work that needs to be done to move the field forward into explanation across the wide range of media effects documented by the literature. To move forward, we need to shift some of our effort away from identifying yet another possible factor in the process of influence and instead put that effort into meeting a sequence of three challenges that now face us on the frontier. These challenges, which are presented from the least difficult to the most difficult, are: calibration, factor linkage, and structures of explanation.

Calibration

Although we have developed a fairly extensive list of factors that look promising for building useful explanations of the process of media influence, we have not done much to calibrate the relative importance among those factors. The literature is rich with studies that examine a small set of factors of influence, but there is a paucity of analyses that serve to sort out the relative importance of these many factors. One notable example is Figure 13.1 in chapter 13 of this volume (Comstock, Scharrer, & Powers), in which it is clear that although exposure to television violence is not the major factor in predicting aggressive behavior, it does make a contribution at a fairly important level—much more important than having abusive parents or antisocial peers.

As we work through this calibration process, we are likely to notice that active variables have a larger effect than grouping variables. As an illustration

Table 15.3
Factors Associated with Negative Effects from Exposure to Media Violence

Factors about the Media Portrayals of Violence
    Consequences in plot
        Rewards and punishments for perpetrators of violence
        Pain and harm to victims of violence
    Justification for the violent action
    Realism
        Animation or real action
        Settings and characters resembling viewer's life
        Potential applicability of actions in one's own life
    Presences of weapons as cue value
    Production techniques
        Graphicness and explicitness to elicit arousal
        Enhancing comprehension
    Humor
    Eroticism
    Frequency of violent actions
        Rates per hour
        Time on screen
    Consistency across portrayals over time

Factors about People Exposed to the Portrayals of Violence
    Demographics
        Age
        Gender
        Socio-Economic Status
        Ethnicity
    Traits
        Developmental level (cognitive, emotional, moral)
        Socialization against behaving aggressively
        Intelligence
        Personality
        Depression
        Cognitive Processing Style
        Ability to use coping strategies
    States
        Arousal
        Emotions (especially anger and frustration)
        Identification with characters and situations
    Prior experience
        Abused as child
        Witness to violence and aggression in real life
        History of use of violence and aggression
    Motivations for exposure

Factors about the Environment
    Presence of cues in the real life situation
    Absence of sanctions against antisocial behavior

of the difference, a person's age is a grouping variable, while a person's level of cognitive development is an active variable. Grouping variables have utility when a research field is new and scholars conduct exploratory research. In the early days of research that tried to explain why exposure to media led to certain effects, it was useful to test grouping variables such as age and gender because researchers were looking for indicators of which paths to prediction were most promising. The results from studies that use grouping variables can only be suggestive, not explanatory, because grouping variables require us to make assumptions that often cannot be supported. For example, when we use age as a surrogate for cognitive development level, we must make the assumption that all people of a certain age have the same cognitive abilities and that those abilities are different from all people of another age. This, of course, is a foolish assumption to make; its use introduces error into the measurement, and this error creates a low ceiling on the potential strength of such variables as predictors of effects. However, it is useful in exploratory research because it can indicate the presence of something robust enough to emerge from all the error.

Given the size and nature of our literature, we have many (almost too many) candidates for factors that might play a major explanatory role in the process of influence. At this point, we have little need to identify additional candidates compared to the need we have to test the relative importance among the candidates we have already identified.

Factor Linkage

After we have sorted through all the factors in the literature to determine which are the most influential and active in the process of influence, we need to turn our attention toward assembling them into a system of explanation. The first step in such an assembly task is to think about how a factor of influence may be related to an outcome variable. The media violence literature is filled with findings that display relations among pairs of variables using the Pearson Product Moment Correlation (or its many downstream statistical procedures such as multiple regression, factor analysis, etc.), which is essentially a test of linear, symmetrical relationships. If the Pearson r is large, we can conclude that there is a strong linear, symmetrical relationship between the two variables tested. However, when the Pearson r is small (which is frequently the case), we cannot conclude that there is a weak relation; there may be a strong relation that is neither linear nor symmetrical. Yet almost all the analyses reported in the literature stop at this point and fail to take additional steps to determine the nature of the relation between the pair of variables being examined. This is a serious shortcoming in analytical practices.

When we think of the process of influence in our everyday lives—a process that is ongoing over our entire lifetime—it is likely that the influence is neither linear nor symmetric. Media influence is more likely to follow a nonlinear pattern, of which there are many. One nonlinear pattern is the learning curve, which is the expression that one unit of effort delivers only a small fraction of a unit of learning until a person has invested a certain amount of effort at which point the units of learning start increasing at a more rapid rate. Media influence might also follow a curvilinear relationship where, as input increases, output also increases up to a point then begins to decrease after that point. Or perhaps the relation is an inverse curvilinear, where someone experiences an effect after one exposure to media violence because of its shock value, but that effect evaporates until the person reaches a very high level of exposure, in which case the effect starts to manifest itself once again.

Some relations are nonlinear because of a threshold. Two variables may show a relation that can be assessed by Pearson r, but only after the values of one of the variables passes beyond a certain threshold. For example, paper will not burst into flame until it reaches about 451 degrees Fahrenheit. Let's say Harry conducts an experiment where he increases the temperature from 100 to 200 degrees. Then he conducts another experiment where he doubles the temperature again—from 200 to 400 degrees. Harry concludes that temperature increases are not related to fire. Next, let's say that Harriet conducts an experiment where she increases the temperature from 440 to 460 and concludes that paper is sensitive to small increases in temperature. Although both conclusions are accurate inferences from their findings, both are wrong because the phenomenon being studied requires the researchers to consider thresholds if they are to understand the relationship between heat and fire.

Media effects researchers rarely take thresholds into consideration in their analysis, and this shortcoming keeps a low ceiling on our understanding of the effects process. There are some effects that do not show up until media exposure exceeds a certain point. For example, viewing television generally does not have a negative influence on a child's academic performance until it reaches a point of about 30 hours per week, when it really begins cutting into study time (Potter, 1987). So a student who increases her television viewing time from 10 hours to 15 hours per week is not likely to show a serious decrease in academic performance. But a student who increases his viewing from 30 to 35 hours per week is very likely to show a drop in grades. With media violence, it is possible that exposure does not begin to have an observable influence until a person has reached a certain threshold, but this type of research has not yet been conducted. For example, with the testing of immediate effects, researchers could vary the amount, duration, and/or intensity of violence across their experimental treatments to document the point at which disinhibition effects begin to become prevalent. Until this type of research is conducted, we cannot know if the existing experimental literature has relied on treatments with violence below the threshold—in which case this set of research reflects an underestimation of the disinhibition influence of media violence.

As for the assumption of symmetry, the Pearson coefficient indicates that the way variable A influences variable B is the same as the way variable B influences variable A. Once again, it appears risky to make this assumption about media effects. It seems safer to assume that most things in life are asymmetrical, where certain people have more influence on others than others have on them. For example, some variables may be necessary but not sufficient, such that B cannot occur unless A is present, but when A is present, B does not always occur. This type of relationship has been found with cultivation (Potter, 1991).

Although the media influence literature is large, it is severely limited by the assumption that media influence is only linear and only symmetrical. Until we broaden our conception of types of relationships among variables and test for a wider range of relationships, we will continue to labor under a self-imposed limitation on our ability to understand how media exposures act in concert with many other factors to exert influence in the long-term process that leads to manifestations of effects.

Structures of Explanation

Our ultimate challenge is to explain the structure in the process of media influence—that is, we need to consider how all the factors work together to exert their influence. The simplest thing to do would be to weight each factor of influence by its relative importance then sum across factors. The resulting number would be degree of risk, with the higher the number the greater the degree of risk. Although this would be a simple solution, it is likely to be too simple because the world is more complex than that (see also chapter 2, this volume).

Among these "complexities" is the idea of interaction. We may have evidence that two factors each exert a relatively strong influence in a process but that when they exist together, they cancel each other out, such that their independent contributions greatly overestimate their actual contributions when they occur together. To explain this rather complex idea, I'll use a real word type of example. Let's say you have two friends whom you like to spend time with. When you are alone with Harry, you always have a good time, and when you are alone with Joan you always have a good time. Does it then follow that you will have a truly great time if you spend time with Harry and Joan together? Of course, it is possible that the chemistry among the three of you is even better than it is between any pair of you, so that the best times are had when all three of you are together (a positive interactive effect). But what if Harry and Joan hate each other? If so, then bringing the three of you together would destroy the chance for a good time that you would have with either of them alone.

Factors interact like friends in the example above. However, researchers have little idea at this time which of the factors interact in a positive way, which interact in a negative way, and which do not interact at all. Gentile and Bushman (2012) did find evidence that as the number of risk factors increases, the risk increases in a nonlinear fashion. They did not, however, identify which factors were interacting with which others to cause the interaction.

If we are to move beyond our currently stagnant position along the influence path, we need to shift our focus onto active variables and select those that have been found to exert greater influence. This change will serve to simplify the literature by serving to move to the background all those studies that are more exploratory and place more emphasis on the findings that lend themselves more to explanation. However, complexity is then reintroduced with the need to look more analytically at the nature of relationships and to assemble the most viable factors into a structure of explanation. This is a huge conceptual and methodological challenge. But if we are to take significant steps toward explaining the process of influence, we need to recognize this challenge; ignoring it will keep us in stagnation.

When we consider all of these issues, the resulting model is likely to be very complex. But the influence process itself is very complex. This is a huge challenge methodologically. We need to design effects studies that take into account large numbers of these factors simultaneously. We need to see how the factors work together in altering levels of risk. Until we have, such research will be limited to providing simple additive formulas (NTVS, 1997). But such formulas have no scientific basis; science has told us some of the factors to include but not all of them, and an even more serious shortcoming is that we have not conducted the scientific tests to determine the calculus needed to assemble all the factors into a single formula of risk. It matters how we do this. For example, I took the same factors and used them in four formulas to predict which television network presented programs that would present the greatest degree of risk of a disinhibition effect (Potter, 1996). The rank orders of those networks were different across all four models.

One final note. The recommendations I laid out in this section might lead some readers to believe that I think that humans are machines, albeit complex machines, such that we as media effects scholars need to continually increase our scientific precision until we fully capture the process of influence in a powerful system of explanation. Such an attribution would be faulty. Instead, my approach is that the way human beings encounter the world involves a combination of mechanisms as well as creative flights. See my development of this distinction between meaning matching and meaning construction (Potter, 2004, 2009). Scientific methods offer great value in analyzing those more mechanistic processes. The large literature on media influence is built largely on scientifically based investigations. My point here is that although we will never be able to provide a 100 percent prediction of human reactions or explanation of processes of influence, we can do a much better job of prediction and explanation if we recognize the shift in our challenge and get past the limitations we have now institutionalized in our literature.

CONTENT PATH

By the late 1990s, there were more than 60 published studies documenting the amount of violence in the media, particularly television, which was the dominant medium up until that time (Potter, 1999). Almost all of these studies generated samples of television programs that purported to reflect the entire television landscape. Most notable among these studies were the annual analyses of prime-time and Saturday morning programming on three big commercial networks conducted by Gerbner and his cultivation team from 1967 to 1993 (e.g., Gerbner, Gross, Morgan, & Signorielli, 1980). Then in the mid-1990s NTVS (1997) conducted a content analysis of violence with an expanded sample (23 TV channels from 6:00 a.m. to 11:00 p.m.) in order to capture the expanding television landscape.

The results of these studies repeatedly showed that violence was pervasive throughout the television landscape, with over 60 percent of all programs analyzed containing at least one act of physical violence. Some of these studies also sought to profile the context of that violence, and those studies typically reported that most of the violence was sanitized (with little blood and gore or even much harm being depicted to the victims), trivialized (much of the violence is camouflaged by humor or fantasy such as in cartoons), and glamorized (perpetrators are often attractive in some way, successful with much of their violent acts, and as likely to be a hero as a villain).

In the two decades since the NTVS, the television landscape has continued to expand with more channels, more platforms, and more genres. Although people keep increasing their exposure time with video, that increased time is fragmented over many different outlets. The highest-rated television series now draws less than 4 percent of the population. Also, viewers have been shifting away from traditional television services to alternative forms where the messages are produced by nonmedia programmers. One of these video services is YouTube, which was started in 2007, and by 2011, was attracting 1 trillion users each year—or 140 views for every person on earth. Users upload more than 100,000 hours of video content *each day*, and over 130 million hours of video are watched *each day* (YouTube, 2013).

This new media environment makes it foolhardy to try to construct a sample of television shows that would represent the entire television landscape. And even if a researcher could construct a sample that would be representative of all the many genres across all the broadcast, cable, video on demand, and interactive video platforms, it is not clear how the profiling of such a diverse range would be useful. We are far beyond the point where any individual—much less the majority of the population—can experience the entire television landscape.

These changes in the media environment require us to set aside our old practices of trying to profile the entire television landscape with regard to violence and instead profile smaller units within that landscape. As we make this shift, it becomes important that we think more about different kinds of violence that might appear in different types of niche programming—that is, there is less need to construct a single definition that would fit all kinds of programming. For example, the nature of violence is likely to be significantly different on the History Channel, the Weather Channel, *Jackass*, the sci-fi channel, and an after-school special on cyberbullying, and so on.

The way media violence is defined has enormous implications for determining how it is measured. It also makes a difference to effects research that must build a treatment of violence into its designs. What counts as violence determines the treatment and hence what is examined.

The term "media violence" is treated by the public and in the scholarly literature as if it has one definition that is shared by everyone. However, when we carefully examine the content analysis literature, we can see that there is a considerable difference of meaning across different scholars in published work, thus making it tricky to compare the results of different content analyses. Furthermore, it appears that the definitions used by content researchers are very different than the definitions used by the public, which raises questions about the ecological validity of those scholarly definitions. It is also important to note that most content analyses focus on counting "acts of violence," while almost all experiments on this topic focus on "aggression" as their dependent variable. Although the two are related, they are not the same.

Scholarly definitions

Let's examine the differences in scholarly definitions of media violence first. Researchers who want to conduct a content analysis to determine how much violence appears in the media must first decide what should qualify as an act of violence, and this task involves at least eight criteria (see Table 15.4). Although there is a fairly high degree of agreement on some of these criteria, there is little agreement on others (see Table 15.5).

To avoid a problem of nondefinitional agreement, I recommend that content analysts answer yes to all eight issues listed in Table 15.5 and thus craft a broad definition. This would allow them to make a more complete count of the incidence of violence and its various types. Another advantage of using a broad definition that catalogs types of violence is that it provides effects researchers with some guidance. For example, if serious acts of violence (such as killings) are disappearing and lesser forms of violence (such as insults) are increasing, then stimulus materials in experiments should feature insults. This pattern appears to be the case (Potter & Vaughan, 1997). We found that although the number of serious violent acts decreased from the mid-1970s to the mid-1990s, the number of verbally violent acts increased dramatically. Therefore, studies focusing only on murder and rape would conclude that television became less violent over those two decades; however, studies taking a broader definition would conclude that television had become much more violent and that the type of violence that increased the most was the type that was most easily imitatable.

Table 15.4
Key Elements in Definitions of Violence

1. Does the act have to be directed toward a person? Gang members swing baseball bats at a car and totally destroy it. Is this violence?

2. Does the act have to be committed by a person? A mudslide levels a town and kills 20 people. Do acts of nature count? Remember that nature does not write the scripts or produce the programming.

3. Does the act have to be intentional? A bank robber drives a fast car in a getaway chase. As he speeds around a corner he hits a pedestrian (or destroys a mailbox). Do accidents count?

4. Does the act result in harm? Tom shoots a gun at Jerry, but the bullet misses. Is this violence? Or what if Tom and Jerry are cartoon characters and Tom drops an anvil on Jerry, who is momentarily flattened like a pancake. A second later Jerry pops back to his original shape and appears fine.

5. What about violence we don't see? If a bad guy fires a gun at a character off-screen and we hear a scream and a body fall, is this violence even though we do not see it?

6. Does the act have to be physical (such as assaults) or can it be verbal (such as insults)? What if Tom viciously insults Jerry, who is shown through the rest of the program experiencing deep psychological and emotional pain as a result? What if Tom embarrasses Jerry who then runs from the room, trips, and breaks his arm?

7. What about fantasy? If 100 fighting men "morph" into a giant creature the size of a 10-story building which then stomps out their enemies, does this count as violence?

8. What about humorous portrayals? When the three stooges hit each other with hammers, is this violence?

Also, more recent research has found that verbal aggression and social/relational aggression is frequent (see Coyne & Stockdale, this volume). Martins and Wilson (2012) conducted a content analysis of the portrayal of social aggression in the 50 most popular television programs among 2- to 11-year-old children. Results revealed that 92 percent of the programs in the sample contained some social aggression. On average, there were 14 different incidents of social aggression per hour in these shows, or one every four minutes.

The ignoring of verbal and relational aggression in many content analyses of television is also puzzling because experiments in the effects path of research have not ignored them. Verbal aggression is often a prominent part of the media shown in studies (Geen, 1975; Thomas & Drabman, 1978; Thomas & Tell, 1974). Some studies show arguments with insults and intimidation leading up to a fistfight. In one study, viewers were shown a brief film showing a businessman and his secretary in a hostile verbal interaction (Carver, Ganellan, Froming, & Chambers, 1983). Also, Berkowitz (1970) had women listen to a tape recording of either a hostile comedy routine by Don Rickles or a nonaggressive routine by George Carlin.

Table 15.5
Comparing Definitions of Violence/Aggression

Study	Acts of Nature	Non-Intentional Accidents	No Harm	Non-Phys	Off Screen	Non-Human Target	Fantasy	Humor
			Are These Elements Included in the Counting?					
Gerbner & colleagues	Yes	Yes	Yes	No	No	Yes	Some	Some
Gunter & Harrison	No	Some	Yes	No	No	Yes	?	?
Center for M. & P. A.	No	No	Yes	No	No	No	?	?
NTVS	Some	Some	Yes	No	Yes	Yes	Yes	Yes
NCTV	No	No	?	No	?	No	?	?
ABC	Yes	Yes	Yes	No	?	Yes	?	?
Mustonen & Pulkkinen	Yes	Yes	Yes	Yes	?	Yes	?	?
Williams, Zabrack, & Joy	?	?	No	Yes	?	?	?	?
Potter, Vaughan, Warren, Howley, Land & Hagemeyer	Yes	Yes	Yes	Yes	Yes	Yes	Yes	Yes
Oliver	No	Yes	Yes	Yes	No	Yes	?	?
Sommers-Flanagan	No	No	Yes	Yes	Yes	No	?	?
Potter & Ware	Yes	Yes	Yes	Yes	No	Yes	Yes	Yes
Greenberg & colleagues	No	Yes	Yes	Yes	No	Yes	?	?

The definition used by ABC is included in this analysis for purposes of comparison. No results of content analyses have been published by ABC; instead, this commercial broadcast network uses this definition for internal monitoring of prospective programs and episodes by its Broadcast Standards and Practices Department.

Sometimes verbal aggression appears as a treatment variable (serving to anger participants) in addition to the media exposure treatment. Although most of these studies used electric shocks to produce anger in their participants, some had an experimenter insult the participants to make them angry (Baron, 1977; Berkowitz, 1974; Berkowitz & Rawlings, 1963; Donnerstein & Berkowitz, 1981; Goranson, 1969; Turner & Berkowitz, 1972).

And finally, verbal aggression is sometimes included as a dependent variable. Hapkiewicz and Stone (1974) used a variety of measures of aggression of their experimental participants, and one of these was their verbal aggression. Berkowitz & Alioto (1973) had their participants evaluate another participant in the study, and this retaliation was not physical (such as administering electric shocks) but symbolic (ratings on a form).

To date, the reporting of results from these studies does not make it possible to draw conclusions about the degree to which different kinds of violence lead to different effects. It is time for experimental researchers to bring the type of violence more prominently into their designs so that they can assess the relative influence of different kinds of violence. Perhaps it is the less serious forms of violence that pose the greatest risk to viewers. Perhaps because the inhibitions preventing viewers from imitating insults, lies, and other relationally aggressive behaviors are much lower than the inhibitions that prevent them from imitating assaults, a small reduction in a person's inhibition would be more likely to show up as a behavioral effect with the less serious forms of violence. This is an important issue that needs to be addressed by experimenters before we can make an accurate assessment of viewer risk.

Public conception

The definitions that scholars use seem to be at variance with how the public conceptualizes violence in the media. The public seems to be most concerned about whether an act offends them or not; in contrast, social scientists count the number of acts that meet their definition to determine whether the show is violent or not. Social scientists then examine context to judge harm to viewers. From a scholarly point of view, cartoons such as the *Road Runner* and *Bugs Bunny* are very violent—in fact, cartoons are consistently rated as the most violent of all programs on television. The characters in these shows are continuously getting stabbed, shot, hit with heavy objects, blown up, rocketed into the sky, and flattened into the ground. Social scientists who make strong statements about the harmfulness of viewing *Tom and Jerry*, *Road Runner*, *Three Stooges*, and *America's Home Videos* put themselves in danger of being regarded as being fuzzy-headed academics wasting their time with silly research. Most viewers would not regard any of these programs as violent. Critics (such as Morrison, 1993) look at this situation and conclude that social scientists must use poor definitions of violence.

It is not that scientific content analyses use "poor" definitions. Instead, the definitions used by scientists and the public are based on different concerns. The public is primarily concerned with being shocked by graphic depictions of harm to victims. Social scientists are primarily concerned with harm to viewers.

Viewers' judgments of the degree of violence are not based on the actual number of violent acts in the program. Also, children have been found to rate the frequency of violence in particular programs as lower than the frequency found in content analysis (Van der Voort, 1986). Instead, the public focuses on context. In the public's judgment, the degree of violence is associated with graphicness, realism, harm, and degree of justification. If a great deal of shooting, stabbings, hitting, and the like takes place in a humorous fantasy context where the perpetrators are justified and the victims show no real harm—such as in children's cartoons—then viewers will not be likely to "see" violence. Therefore, the most important element in their conceptualization of violence is graphicness. Potter and Berry (1999) conducted a study to determine which characteristics in portrayals of violence are most associated with participants' ratings of the violence in those portrayals. They found that ratings of graphicness were by far the most important predictor of ratings of violence consistently across all the stimulus tapes. This finding did not vary by gender, weekly amount of TV viewing, experience as a victim of violence, religiosity, or political conservatism. We concluded that when people watch shows with high rates of sanitized violence, they are not shocked and therefore not concerned with the violence.

The difference in definitions is traceable to the focus of concern. The public wants formulaic action—that is, safe, sanitized violence (no graphicness, low harm) that does not threaten them (not shocking, low reality), and where the good guys are strong and prevail (high revenge, high justification). When the public sees this formula in action, there is no violence and there is no need to complain. When social scientists see this pattern, they see no reason to discount the actions. On the contrary, they see a high potential of viewer harm, and there are strong reasons to be concerned. As an illustration of this point, Kunkel and colleagues (2001) conducted a content analysis of 1,147 randomly selected entertainment programs representing the entire television landscape of programming and found that 10 percent of those programs presented violence with a high risk to children, yet 73 percent of those programs were given a rating of TV-PG, indicating only moderate violence. Only 27 percent of those programs received a rating of TV-14 (viewing should be restricted to people 14 or older), and none received a rating of TV-MA (suitable for mature audiences only).

The differences in definitions lead to an apparent problem of ecological validity. The definitions used by social scientists appear too abstract and out of touch with real people. We could close the definitional gap by simply accepting the public's definition of violence. But given what we know about effects, that would be unethical. We would then become part of this public health problem rather than using our knowledge to effect a solution. The definitional gap, of course, needs to be closed. But it is the public that needs to move its conception. The problem is not with our definition; instead, the problem is with our failure to educate the public better.

Nonetheless, as social scientists, we need to be more sensitive to how individuals interpret violence. Several critics of social science have been bothered by researchers' focus on their scientific definitions instead of on how viewers interpret violence. For example, Buckingham (1993) observes that "much of the research takes 'violence' as a homogeneous category, and tends to ignore crucial distinctions between different types of violence" (p. 12). He continues, "While there have been attempts to classify types of television violence ... these have typically been based, not on the judgments of viewers who are actually exposed to the programmes, but on the supposedly objective judgments of researchers" (p. 12).

Van der Voort (1986) also sees this lack of attention to viewer interpretations as a problem. He found that the judgments of 9- to 12-year-olds about the amount of violence contained in a program differ little from that of adults. However, their estimates do differ from those found in content analyses. He says, "Programs that are extremely violent according to 'objective' content analysis can be seen by children as hardly containing any violence. This, for example, is the case with violent cartoons of the *Tom and Jerry* type" (p. 329). He argues that content analysts might find only one act of violence in a program, but for children this one act might be enough for them to regard the entire program as very violent. He suggests that "a 'subjective' determination of the violence-content of a program based on children's mean violence ratings is preferable to an 'objective' content-analytical assessment" (p. 330). However, Van der Voort's language reveals an assumption that content analysis is objective in some sense and free of individual interpretations. Clearly, this is not the case. Even if coders could be fully trained to follow all the coding rules systematically, they would still have to make many difficult interpretations. And even if they encountered a program that did not require any difficult interpretations, the coding rules themselves are really indicators of a person or persons' subjective interpretations codified into a coding manual. As seen earlier in this chapter, there are many judgments a scholar must make in constructing a definition of violence, and each of these judgments is subjective. The results of scientific content analyses are never perfectly objective—they can't be. However, good content analyses are systematic counts using a consistently applied definition of violence. In order for the results of content analyses to be useful for the public, the definition of violence must be understood and accepted.

Unless scholars consider the received view, their definitions will not have resonance with the viewing public. I am not recommending that scholars throw out their definitions and accept the public's definition. But what I am suggesting is that scholars (1) need to do a better job educating the public about elements of risk and (2) need to focus more in their effects research on those elements that the public is ignoring in their conceptions of violence.

On this definitional issue, both sides need more education. Social scientists need to attend more to receiver definitions of violence and focus on how the salient and interruptive characteristics of violence contribute to or reduce the risk for a negative effect. The public needs to attend more to the case being made by social scientists who show that certain types of violent portrayals about which the public is not concerned do in fact lead to negative effects.

CONCLUSIONS

Researchers have generated a great deal of insight into the risks we incur from exposure to violence in the media. This research has proceeded down three paths: documenting effects, determining which factors influence risk, and examining media content for evidence of violence.

Once researchers can move beyond the current frontiers and provide a better understanding of the variety of effects and a better conceptualization of what violence is, they can test the influence of various forms of violence and how those content influences interact with factors in a person's life. This will put scholars in a position to braid the findings from the three lines of research together in a more systematic, complete manner and thus generate the insight we need to understand risk well enough to manage it.

REFERENCES

American Academy of Pediatrics. (2000). *Joint statement on the impact of entertainment violence on children.* Retrieved from http://www2.aap.org/advocacy/releases /jstmtevc.htm

Anderson, C. A., & Bushman, B. J. (2002a). Human aggression. *Annual Review of Psychology, 53,* 27–51.

Anderson, C. A., & Bushman, B. J. (2002b). Media violence and societal violence. *Science, 295,* 2377–2378.

Andison, F. S. (1977). TV violence and viewer aggression: A cumulation of study results. *Public Opinion Quarterly, 41,* 314–331.

Baker, R. K., & Ball, S. J. (1969). *Violence and the media.* Washington, DC: U.S. Government Printing Office.

Baron, R. A. (1977). *Human aggression.* New York, NY: Plenum.

Berkowitz, L. (1970). Aggressive humors as a stimulus to aggressive responses. *Journal of Personality and Social Psychology, 16,* 710–717.

Berkowitz, L. (1974). Some determinants of impulsive aggression: The role of mediated associations with reinforcements for aggression. *Psychological Review, 81,* 165–176.

Berkowitz, L., & Alioto, J. T. (1973). The meaning of an observed event as a determinant of its aggressive consequences. *Journal of Personality and Social Psychology, 28*(2), 206–217.

Berkowitz, L., & Rawlings, E. (1963). Effects of film violence on inhibitions against subsequent aggression. *Journal of Abnormal and Social Psychology, 66*(5), 405–412.

Buckingham, D. (1993). *Children talking television: The making of television literacy.* London, UK: The Falmer Press.

Bushman, B. J., & Huesmann, L. R. (2001). Effects of televised violence on aggression. In D. G. Singer & J. L. Singer (Eds.), *Handbook of children and the media* (pp. 223–254). Thousand Oaks, CA: Sage.

Bushman, B. J., Huesmann, L. R., & Whitaker, J. L. (2009). Violent media effects. In R. L. Nabi & M. B. Oliver (Eds.), *Media processes and effects* (pp. 361–376). Los Angeles, CA: Sage.

Cantor, J. (2003). Review of the book *Media violence and its effect on aggression: Assessing the scientific evidence. Journalism and Mass Communication Quarterly, 80*, 468–470.

Carlson, M., Marcus-Newhall, A., & Miller, N. (1990). Effects of situational aggression cues: A quantitative review. *Journal of Personality and Social Psychology, 58,* 622–633.

Carver, C., Ganellen, R., Fromming, W., & Chambers, W. (1983). Modeling: An analysis in terms of category assessibility. *Journal of Experimental Social Psychology, 19*, 403–421.

Chaffee, S. H. (1972). Television and adolescent aggressiveness (overview). In G. A. Comstock & E. A. Rubinstein (Eds.), *Television and social behavior: Television and adolescent aggressiveness* (Vol. 3, pp. 1–34). Washington, DC: U.S. Government Printing Office.

Charters, W. W. (1933). *Motion pictures and youth: A summary.* New York, NY: Macmillan.

Comstock, G. A. (1985). Television and film violence. In S. Apter & A. Goldstein (Eds.), *Youth violence: Programs and prospects.* New York, NY: Pergamon.

Comstock, G., Chaffee, S., Katzman, N., McCombs, M., & Roberts, D. (1978). *Television and human behavior.* New York, NY: Columbia University Press.

Comstock, G., & Scharrer, E. (2003). The contribution of meta-analysis to the controversy over television violence and aggression. In Gentile, D. A. (Ed.), *Media violence and children.* Westport, CT: Ablex.

Comstock, G., & Strasburger, C. C. (1990). Deceptive appearances: Television violence and aggressive behavior. *Journal of Adolescent Health Care, 11*(1), 31–44.

Condry, J. (1989). *The psychology of television.* Hillsdale, NJ: Erlbaum.

DeWall, C. N., Anderson, C. A., & Bushman, B. J. (2011). The General Aggression Model: Theoretical extensions to violence. *Psychology of Violence, 1*(3), 245–258. doi:http://dx.doi.org/10.1037/a0023842

Donnerstein, E., & Berkowitz, L. (1981). Victim reactions in aggressive erotic films as a factor in violence against women. *Journal of Personality and Social Psychology, 41*(4), 710–724.

Donnerstein, E., Slaby, R. G., & Eron, L. D. (1994). The mass media and youth aggression. In L. D. Eron, J. H. Gentry, & P. Schlegel (Eds.), *Reason to hope: A psychological perspective on violence and youth* (pp. 219–250). Washington, DC: American Psychological Association.

Ferguson, C. J., & Kilburn, J. (2009). The public health risks of media violence: A meta-analytic review. *The Journal of Pediatrics, 154*(5), 759–763.

Freedman, J. L. (1984). Effect of television violence on aggressiveness. *Psychological Bulletin, 96*(2), 227–246.

Freedman, J. L. (2002). *Media violence and its effect on aggression: Assessing the scientific evidence.* Toronto, ON: University of Toronto Press.

Friedrich-Cofer, L., & Huston, A. C. (1986). Television violence and aggression: The debate continues. *Psychological Bulletin, 100*, 364–371.

Geen, R. G. (1975). The meaning of observed violence: Real vs. fictional violence and consequent effects on aggression and emotional arousal. *Journal of Research in Personality, 9*, 270–281.

Geen, R. G. (1994). Television and aggression: Recent developments in research and theory. In D. Zillmann, J. Bryant, & A. C. Huston (Eds.), *Media, children, and the family* (pp. 151–162). Hillsdale, NJ: Lawrence Erlbaum.

Gentile, D. A., & Bushman, B. J. (2012). Reassessing media violence effects using a risk and resilience approach to understanding aggression. *Psychology of Popular Media Culture*, 1–14.

Gerbner, G., Gross, L., Morgan, M., & Signorielli, N. (1980). The "mainstreaming" of America: Violence profile no. 11. *Journal of Communication*, *30*(3), 10–29.

Goranson, R. (1969). *Observed violence and aggressive behavior: The effects of negative outcomes to the observed violence*. (Unpublished doctoral dissertation). University of Wisconsin, Madison, WI.

Goranson, R. E. (1970). Media violence and aggressive behavior: A review of the experimental research. In L. Berkowitz (Ed.), *Advances in experimental social psychology* (Vol. 5, pp. 1–31). New York, NY: Academic Press.

Greenberg, B. S., Edison, N., Korzenny, F., Fernandez-Collado, C., & Atkin, C. K. (1980). In B. S. Greenberg (Ed.), *Life on television: Content analysis of U.S. TV drama* (pp. 99–128). Norwood, NJ: Ablex.

Grixti, J. (1985). The controversy over "mass media violence" and the study of behavior. *Educational Studies*, *11*, 61–76.

Guantlett, D. (2005). *Moving experiences: Media effects and beyond*. Luton, UK: John Libbey.

Gunter, B. (1994). The question of media violence. In J. Bryant & D. Zillmann (Eds.), *Media effects: Advances in theory and research* (pp. 163–211). Hillsdale, NJ: Erlbaum.

Hapkiewicz, W. G., & Stone, R. D. (1974). The effect of realistic versus imaginary aggressive models on children's interpersonal play. *Child Study Journal*, *4*(2), 47–58.

Hearold, S. (1986). A synthesis of 1043 effects of television on social behavior. In G. Comstock (Ed.), *Public communication and behavior* (Vol. 1, pp. 65–133). San Diego, CA: Academic Press.

Heath, L., Bresolin, L. B., & Rinaldi, R. C. (1989). Effects of media violence on children. *Arch Gen Psychiatry*, *46*, 376–379.

Howitt, D., & Cumberbatch, G. (1975). *Mass media violence and society*. New York, NY: Wiley.

Huesmann, L. R., & Eron, L. D. (1986). *Television and the aggressive child: A cross national comparison*. Hillsdale, NJ: Erlbaum.

Huesmann, L. R., & Taylor, L. D. (2003). The case against the case against media violence. In D. A. Gentile (Ed.), *Media violence and children: A complete guide for parents and professionals* (pp. 107–130). Westport, CT: Praeger.

Jones, G. W., Jr. (1971). *The relationship of screen-mediated violence to antisocial behavior*. (Unpublished doctoral dissertation). Syracuse University, Syracuse, NY. University Microfilms No. 72–60,592.

Kaplan, R. M., & Singer, R. D. (1976). Psychological effects of television violence: A review and methodological critique. *Journal of Social Issues*, *34*(1), 176–188.

Kniveton, B. H. (1976). Social learning and imitation in relation to TV. In R. Brown (Ed.), *Children and television* (pp. 237–266). Beverly Hills, CA: Sage.

Kunkel, D., Farinola, W. J. M., Cope, D. M., Donnerstein, E., Biely, E., Zwarun, L., & Rollin, E. (2001). Assessing the validity of V-chip rating judgments: The labeling of high-risk programs. In B. S. Greenberg (Ed.), *The alphabet soup of television program ratings* (pp. 51–68). Cresskill, NJ: Hampton Press.

Lesser, H. (1977). *Television and the preschool child.* New York, NY: Academic Press.

Liebert, R. M. (1972). Television and social learning: Some relationships between viewing violence and behaving aggressively (overview). In J. P. Murray, E. A. Rubinstein, & G. A. Comstock (Eds.), *Television and social behavior: Television and social learning* (Vol. 2, pp. 1–42). Washington, DC: U.S. Government Printing Office.

Liebert, R. M., Neale, J. M., & Davidson, E. A. (1973). *The early window: Effects of television on children and youth.* Elmsford, NY: Pergamon.

Liebert, R. M., & Poulos, R. W. (1975). Television and personality development: The socializing effects of an entertainment medium. In A. Davids (Ed.), *Child personality and psychopathology: Current topics* (Vol. 2, pp. 61–97). New York, NY: Wiley.

Liebert, R. M., & Schwartzberg, N. S. (1977). Effects of mass media. *Annual Review of Psychology, 28,* 141–173.

Maccoby, E. E. (1964). Effects of the mass media. In M. L. Hoffman & L. W. Hoffman (Eds.), *Review of child development research* (pp. 323–348). New York, NY: Russell Sage Foundation.

Martins, N., & Wilson, B. J. (2012). Mean on the screen: Social aggression in programs popular with children. *Journal of Communication, 62,* 991–1009.

McGuire, W. J. (1986). The myth of massive media impact: Savagings and salvagings. In G. Comstock (Ed.), *Public communication and behavior* (Vol. 1, pp. 173–257). San Diego, CA: Academic Press.

Morrison, E. E. (1993). The idea of violence. In A. M. Hargrave (Ed.), *Violence in factual television, annual review 1993* (pp. 124–129). London, UK: John Libbey.

National Institute of Mental Health. (1982). *Television and behavior: Ten years of scientific progress and implications for the eighties.* Washington, DC: U.S. Government Printing Office.

National Television Violence Study (NTVS). (1996). *Technical Report, Vol 1.* Thousand Oaks, CA: Sage.

National Television Violence Study (NTVS). (1997). *Technical Report, Vol 2.* Thousand Oaks, CA: Sage.

Olson C. (2004). Media violence research and youth violence data: Why do they conflict? *Academy of Psychiatry, 28,* 144–150.

Paik, H., & Comstock, G. (1994). The effects of television violence on antisocial behavior: A meta-analysis. *Communication Research, 21,* 516–546.

Potter, W. J. (1987). Does television viewing hinder academic achievement among adolescents? *Human Communication Research, 14*(1), 27–46.

Potter, W. J. (1991). The relationships between first and second order measures of cultivation. *Human Communication Research, 18,* 92–113.

Potter, W. J. (1996). *An analysis of qualitative thinking and research.* Englewood, NJ: Erlbaum.

Potter, W. J. (1999). *On media violence.* Thousand Oaks, CA: Sage.

Potter, W. J. (2004). *Theory of media literacy: A cognitive approach.* Thousand Oaks, CA: Sage.

Potter, W. J. (2009). *Arguing for a general framework for mass media scholarship.* Thousand Oaks, CA: Sage.

Potter, W. J. (2011). Conceptualizing mass media effect. *Journal of Communication, 61*, 896–915.

Potter, W. J., & Berry, M. (1999, May). *A schema explanation for viewers' judgments of television violence*. Paper presented at the Annual Meeting of the International Communication Association, San Francisco, CA.

Potter, W. J., & Vaughan, M. (1997). Aggression in television entertainment: Profiles and trends. *Communication Research Reports, 14*, 116–124.

Roberts, D. F., & Maccoby, N. (1985). Effects of mass communication. In G. Lindzey & E. Aronson (Eds.), *Handbook of social psychology: Vol. 2, Special fields and applications* (3rd ed., pp. 539–598). New York, NY: Random House.

Roberts, D. F., & Schramm, W. (1971). Children's learning from the mass media. In W. Schramm & D. F. Roberts (Eds.), *The process and effects of mass communication* (Rev. ed., pp. 596–611). Urbana, IL: University of Illinois Press.

Rule, B. G., & Ferguson, T. J. (1986). The effects of media violence on attitudes, emotions, and cognitions. *Journal of Social Issues, 42*, 29–50.

Savage, J. (2004). Does viewing violent media really cause criminal violence? A methodological review. *Aggression and Violent Behaviour, 10*, 99–128.

Signorielli, N. (1990). Television's mean and dangerous world: A continuation of the cultural indicators perspective. In N. Signorielli & M. Morgan (Eds.), *Cultivation analysis: New directions in media effects research* (pp. 85–106). Newbury Park, CA: Sage.

Sparks, G. G., Sparks, C. W., & Sparks, E. A. (2009). Media violence. In J. Bryant & M. B. Oliver (Eds.), *Media effects: Advances in theory and research* (3rd ed., pp. 269–286). New York, NY: Routledge.

Stein, A. H., & Friedrich, L. K. (1972). Television content and young children's behavior. In J. P. Murray, E. A. Rubinstein, & G. A. Comstock (Eds.), *Television and social behavior: Reports and papers; Vol. 2: Television and social learning* (pp. 202–317). Washington, DC: U.S. Government Printing Office.

Stipp, H., & Milavsky, J. R. (1988). U.S. television programming's effects on aggressive behavior of children and adolescents. *Current Psychology: Research and Reviews, 7*(1), 76–92.

Surgeon General's Scientific Advisory Committee on Television and Social Behavior. (1971). *Television and growing up: The impact of televised violence*. Report to the Surgeon General, United States Public Health Service. Washington, DC: U.S. Government Printing Office.

Tannenbaum, P. H., & Zillmann, D. (1975). Emotional arousal in the facilitation of aggression through communication. In L. Berkowitz (Ed.), *Advances in experimental social psychology* (Vol. 8, pp. 149–192). New York, NY: Academic Press.

Thomas, M. H., & Drabman, R. S. (1978). Effects of television violence on expectations of other's aggression. *Personality and Social Psychology Bulletin, 4*, 73–76.

Thomas, M. H., & Tell, P. M. (1974). Effects of viewing real versus fantasy violence upon interpersonal aggression. *Journal of Research in Personality, 8*, 153–160.

Turner, C. W., & Berkowitz, L. (1972). Identification with film aggressor (covert role taking) and reactions to film violence. *Journal of Personality and Social Psychology, 21*, 256–264.

Van der Voort, T. H. A. (1986). *Television violence: A child's-eye view*. Amsterdam, NL: North-Holland.

Wood, W., Wong, F. Y., & Chachere, J. G. (1991). Effects of media violence on viewers' aggression in unconstrained social interaction. *Psychological Bulletin, 109*, 371–383.

YouTube. (2013). Statistics. Retrieved from http://www.youtube.com/t/press_statistics

About the Editor and Contributors

DOUGLAS A. GENTILE, PhD, is an award-winning research scientist, educator, author, and an associate professor of psychology at Iowa State University. His experience includes over 25 years conducting research with children and adults. He is the editor of the book *Media Violence and Children* (Praeger, 2003) and coauthor of the book *Violent Video Game Effects on Children and Adolescents: Theory, Research, and Public Policy* (Oxford University Press, 2007). He has authored scores of peer-reviewed scientific journal articles, including studies on the positive and negative effects of video games on children in several countries, the validity of the American media ratings, how screen time contributes to youth obesity, and what is being called video game and Internet "addiction." He is the creator and host of the radio show *The Science of Parenting* (and also has a nationally syndicated comedy music radio show, *The Tom & Doug Show*). His work has been featured on National Public Radio, the BBC World Service, CNN, *Good Morning America*, and *The Today Show*, as well as the *New York Times*, *Washington Post*, *Los Angeles Times*, and hundreds of other newspapers and television stations internationally. In 2010 he was honored with the Distinguished Scientific Contributions to Media Psychology Award from the American Psychological Association (Division 46). He was named one of the top 300 professors in the United States by *Princeton Review*. Gentile earned his doctorate in child psychology at the University of Minnesota.

PATRICIA W. AGATSTON, PhD, is coauthor of the book *Cyberbullying: Bullying in the Digital Age* with Robin Kowalski, PhD, and Susan Limber, PhD, and coauthored a chapter for the book, "Expert Perspectives in

Cyberbullying." She is also coauthor of the *Cyberbullying Curriculum for Grades 6–12* and the *Cyberbullying Prevention Curriculum for Grades 3–5*. Dr. Agatston is a certified trainer and technical assistance consultant for the Olweus Bullying Prevention Program. She has been quoted in articles on cyberbullying in the *Washington Post, CNET News, Time Magazine*, and the *Christian Science Monitor*. She has appeared on CNN as well as other local and national radio and television programs to discuss cyberbullying and other youth online risky behavior. She was a participant in the CDC's Expert Panel on Electronic Media and Youth Violence, and the CDC's Expert Panel on Youth Involvement in Bullying and Suicide-Related Behaviors. She has presented nationally and internationally on bullying, cyberbullying, and digital citizenship. Agatston is a licensed professional counselor and prevention specialist with the Cobb County School District's Prevention/Intervention Center in Marietta, Georgia. She serves on the board of directors for the International Bullying Prevention Association and Connect Safely.

CRAIG A. ANDERSON, PhD, is Distinguished Professor of Liberal Arts and Sciences in the Department of Psychology at Iowa State University. He is currently the director of Iowa State University's Center for the Study of Violence and is past president of the International Society for Research on Aggression. He also serves as an associate editor for the journals *Aggressive Behavior* and *Personality and Social Psychology Bulletin*. He received his PhD from Stanford University in 1980 and has served on the faculties of Rice University, Ohio State University, and the University of Missouri–Columbia. He has been awarded Fellow status by the Association for Psychological Science and the American Psychological Association, among others. Anderson's 160-plus publications span a wide range of areas, including judgment and decision making; depression, loneliness, and shyness; personality theory and measurement; attribution theory; and human aggression. Professor Anderson is one of the most widely cited scholars in social psychology, in textbooks and in the psychological science literature in general. Since the 1990s, most of his work has focused on the development of a General Aggression Model, designed to integrate insights from cognitive, developmental, personality, and social psychology. This model is now widely used by scholars in psychology, communications, and criminology. His pioneering work on video game violence has led to consultations with educators, government officials, child advocates, and news organizations worldwide. His 2007 book on *Violent Video Game Effects on Children and Adolescents* (with Douglas A. Gentile and Katherine Buckley) describes the effects of playing violent video games, explains how these effects occur, and explores possible actions that parents, educators, and public policy creators can take to deal with this important social issue. His 2010 meta-analysis article published in *Psychological Bulletin*, psychology's top review journal, combined the results of all relevant empirical studies (over 130,000 participants) and conclusively demonstrated the harmful effects of violent video games. His current work with his talented graduate students and collaborators has addressed issues such as global climate change effects on violence and war; media effects on stereotyping of Arabs/Muslims; media effects on impulsivity, attention deficits, brain function, and aggression; and reappraisal training as a tool to reduce aggression.

KATHRYN B. ANDERSON, PhD, is a social psychologist at Our Lady of the Lake University in San Antonio, Texas. She has conducted research on the causes of aggression for over 20 years. She is particularly interested in the intersection of current feminist and multicultural theories with research on aggression and community violence prevention. She serves on the executive committee of the Society for the Psychology of Women (Division 35 of the American Psychological Association) and writes a blog on aggression and violence for *In-Mind Magazine* at www.in-mind.org.

BRUCE D. BARTHOLOW, PhD, received his doctorate in psychology from the University of Missouri in 2000, where he is currently professor of psychological sciences. Bartholow's research uses a psychophysiological approach to understand phenomena in social and cognitive psychology, including stereotyping, aggression, and media effects on thoughts, feelings, and behavior, as well as the cognitive and emotional processes involved in these phenomena. He also studies effects of alcohol on social and cognitive processes. Bartholow's research has been funded by the National Institute on Alcohol Abuse and Alcoholism, the National Science Foundation, the Foundation for Alcohol Research, and by several smaller awards. In 2007 he received the award for Distinguished Early Career Contribution to Psychophysiology from the Society for Psychophysiological Research and in 2013 received the Outstanding Graduate Faculty Award from the University of Missouri Graduate Student Association. His teaching interests include courses in social psychological theory, social cognitive neuroscience, psychophysiology, and research methods.

JOANNE CANTOR, PhD, is professor emerita and outreach director of the Center for Communication Research at the University of Wisconsin–Madison, where she was a professor for 26 years. She is most widely known for her research on children's fears from the mass media, the effects of media ratings and advisories, and media violence effects and interventions. Her books include *"Mommy, I'm Scared": How TV and Movies Frighten Children and What We Can Do to Protect Them, Teddy's TV Troubles*, and *Conquer CyberOverload: Get More Done, Boost Your Creativity, and Reduce Stress*. She has published more than 90 articles in academic publications. Dr. Cantor has testified on numerous occasions before U.S. congressional committees as well as the Federal Communications Commission, and she frequently talks about her research and gives advice for parents in national media outlets. She received her PhD in Communication from Indiana University.

NICHOLAS L. CARNAGEY, PhD, earned his doctorate in social psychology from Iowa State University in 2006. After receiving his doctorate, he served as a visiting assistant professor at Wake Forest University. During his academic career, his research interests included aggressive priming, attitudes toward violence, and effects of media violence on aggression-related variables.

PETER G. CHRISTENSON, PhD, is professor of rhetoric and media studies at Lewis and Clark College in Portland, Oregon. His primary areas of research are health communication and the impact of media on children and adolescents, and he has published a number of books, book chapters, and articles on those subjects. He is coauthor of *It's Not **Only** Rock & Roll—Popular Music in the Lives of Adolescents* (1998, with Donald Roberts), *Substance Use in Popular Movies and Music* (1999, with Donald Roberts and Lisa Henriksen), *Substance Use in Popular Prime Time Television* (2000, also with Roberts and Henriksen), and "Popular Music: The Soundtrack of Adolescence" (*Sage Handbook of Children and the Media*, 2012). Christenson earned his BA from Dartmouth College and his PhD from Stanford University.

GEORGE COMSTOCK, PhD, is professor emeritus at the S. I. Newhouse School of Public Communications, Syracuse University, where he was the S. I. Newhouse Professor. He was science advisor to the Surgeon General's Scientific Advisory Committee on Television and Social Behavior that issued the federal report, *Television and Growing Up: The Impact of Televised Violence*, and has previously served as the chair of the Department of Journalism and Communication, Chinese University, Hong Kong. His more recent books (coauthored with Erica Scharrer) include: *Television: What's On, Who's Watching, and What It Means* (1999); *Media and the American Child* (2007); and *The Psychology of Media and Politics* (2005). He earned his doctorate from Stanford University.

SARAH M. COYNE, PhD, is an associate professor of human development in the School of Family Life at Brigham Young University. She received her BSc degree in psychology from Utah State University and her PhD in psychology from the University of Central Lancashire in Preston, England. Her research interests involve media, aggression, gender, and child development. Dr. Coyne has over 60 publications on these and other topics. She recently completed a study examining the effects of viewing princesses and superheroes on preschool children. She has four young children and currently lives in Spanish Fork, Utah.

KAREN E. DILL-SHACKLEFORD, PhD, earned her doctorate in social psychology from the University of Missouri–Columbia, under the supervision of Craig Anderson. Her dissertation on video game violence effects has been cited 1,300 times. She has testified twice before the U.S. Congress on issues related to media effects. Her current research interests include using media to improve well-being and to promote social justice, especially as related to women's issues and racial issues. For example, Dr. Dill-Shackleford has used mediated guided meditation to improve women's self-compassion and body satisfaction; she has demonstrated how to use live theater and print media as vehicles for entertainment-education, such as to dispel myths about intimate partner violence. Her research interests also include fandom, narrative persuasion, and how mediated stories engage us and change us. Dr. Dill-Shackleford is the author of *How Fantasy Becomes Reality* and the editor of the *Oxford Handbook of Media Psychology*.

L. ROWELL HUESMANN, PhD, is Amos N. Tversky Collegiate Professor of Psychology and Communication Studies at the University of Michigan and Director of the Aggression Research Program in the Research Center for Group Dynamics at Michigan's Institute for Social Research. Huesmann's research focuses on understanding the psychological foundations of aggressive behavior and in particular on understanding how the observations of others behaving violently influences the development of a youth's aggressive and violent behavior and produces a contagion of violence. Over the past 45 years, Huesmann has authored over 100 widely cited scientific articles and books, including *Growing Up to Be Violent* (1977), *Television and the Aggressive Child* (1986), and *Aggressive Behavior* (1994). He has been editor of the international journal *Aggressive Behavior* and was the 2005 recipient of the American Psychological Association's award for *Distinguished Lifetime Contributions to Media Psychology*. He has testified frequently before Congress and directed several national committees examining the causes of violence. He is a member of the USA National Academy of Science's Institute of Medicine's *Forum on Global Violence Prevention*. He is a past president of the *International Society for Research on Aggression* and a life member of Clare Hall College, Cambridge. While on the faculty at Michigan he has been director of the Research Center for Group Dynamics (2006–2012) and chair of the Communication Studies Department (1994). He received his BS from the University of Michigan in 1964 and his PhD from Carnegie-Mellon University in 1969. Prior to joining the faculty at Michigan, he was an assistant and associate professor of psychology at Yale University and professor of psychology and chair of the psychology department at the University of Illinois at Chicago.

TOM A. HUMMER, PhD, is an assistant research professor in the Department of Psychiatry at Indiana University School of Medicine. Before coming to Indianapolis, he received his undergraduate degree in psychology from the Ohio State University and a PhD in computational neuroscience from the University of Chicago. He is primarily interested in modeling how child and adolescent brain development is shaped by biological and environmental factors, using a variety of brain imaging techniques. He has employed magnetic resonance imaging (MRI) to examine short- and long-term effects of violent video-game play or television violence on brain structure and function. He continues to conduct research that helps us understand how the characteristics of childhood media exposure influence brain development during this time and specifies how changes to brain circuitry can have potential life-long impacts on behavioral control and emotion regulation.

ROBIN M. KOWALSKI, PhD, is a professor of psychology at Clemson University. She earned her PhD in social psychology from the University of North Carolina at Greensboro. Her research interests focus primarily on aversive interpersonal behaviors, most notably complaining, teasing and bullying, with a particular focus on cyber bullying. She is the author or coauthor of several books including *Complaining, Teasing, and Other Annoying Behaviors*, *Social Anxiety*, *Aversive Interpersonal Behaviors*, *Behaving Badly*, *The Social Psychology of Emotional and Behavioral Problems*, and *Cyberbullying: Bullying in the Digital Age*. Her research on complaining brought her international attention, including an appearance on NBC's *Today Show*. Kowalski has received several awards including Clemson University's Award of Distinction, Clemson University's College of Business and Behavioral Science Award for Excellence in Undergraduate Teaching, the Phil Prince Award for Excellence and Innovation in the Classroom, Clemson University's College of Business and Behavioral Science Senior Research Award, and the Clemson Board of Trustees Award for Faculty Excellence. She was also recently named by *Princeton Review* as one of the best 300 professors in the nation, and was selected as a finalist for the 2013 and 2014 South Carolina Governor's Professor of the Year Awards.

SUSAN P. LIMBER, PhD, MLS, is the Dan Olweus Distinguished Professor at the Institute on Family and Neighborhood Life at Clemson University. She is a developmental psychologist with a PhD from the University of Nebraska–Lincoln and also holds a master's in legal studies. Dr. Limber's research and writing have focused on youth participation, children's rights, and legal and psychological issues related to bullying among children. Since 2001, she has provided consultation to bullying prevention efforts supported Health Resources and Services Administration (U.S. Department of Health and Human Services). She oversees dissemination of the Olweus Bullying Prevention Program in the United States. Dr. Limber has published numerous articles and chapters on the topic of bullying and coauthored the book, *Cyberbullying: Bullying in the Digital Age*. She is the recipient of a number of awards for her work, including the Early Career Award for Distinguished Contributions to Psychology in the Public Interest, awarded by the American Psychological Association (APA); the Distinguished Career Award for

Outstanding Contributions to Public Service Psychology, awarded by the APA's Division of Psychologists in Public Service; and the Nicholas Hobbs Award, awarded by the Society for Child and Family Policy and Practice (Division 37 of the APA). She is a Fellow of the American Psychological Association.

JAMES J. LINDSAY, PhD, is a senior researcher with American Institutes for Research, where he specializes in educational research. His current work focuses on three broad subjects: literacy, the process of implementing school-wide interventions, and teacher effectiveness. Lindsay is primary investigator on several large randomized control trials of education interventions and also serves as lead methodologist for the *What Works Clearinghouse*'s teacher quality topic area. Prior to his current position, he served as an evaluator of publicly funded volunteer programs, health care delivery systems, and child abuse prevention programs. He earned his PhD in social psychology from the University of Missouri.

TANNIS M. MACBETH, PhD (also known as and published as Tannis MacBeth Williams), was a professor at the University of British Columbia for 42 years. She earned her doctorate at Purdue University in 1969. Her primary areas of research are human development, gender, and the influences of media on socialization. She coauthored and edited the book *The Impact of Television: A Natural Experiment in Three Communities*, which is based on her remarkable research exploring television's influences on socialization and development. As well, she is the editor of and a contributor to the book *Tuning In to Young Viewers: Social Science Perspectives on Television*. Her many other contributions to research on the effects of television include chapters in *Violence in Television, Films, and News (Report of the Royal Commission on Violence in the Communication Industry)*; *Telecommunications in Transcultural Perspective* (edited by Steinbring & Granzberg); *National Workshop on Television and Youth* (edited by Corder-Bolz); *Television as a Teacher: A Research Monograph* (edited by Coelho); *Communications in Canadian Society* (edited by Singer); *Research Paradigms, Television, and Social Behavior* (edited by Assamen & Berry); *Media Violence and Children* (edited by Gentile); *The Handbook of Media Studies* (edited by McQuail, Schlesinger, & Wartella); *Mass Media and Mental Health: Their Influence on Each Other* (edited by Jakab); and the *Encyclopedia of Children, Adolescents, and the Media* (edited by Arnett). Her television research was also highlighted as unique in Robert Putnam's bestseller *Bowling Alone*.

JOHN P. MURRAY, PhD, is a research fellow in the Department of Psychology at Washington College; an emeritus professor of developmental psychology in the School of Family Studies and Human Services at Kansas State University; and a visiting scholar in the Center on Media and Child Health at Children's Hospital Boston, Harvard Medical School. He has conducted research on children's social development for almost 40 years—starting in 1969 as a research coordinator for the Surgeon General's Scientific Advisory Committee on Television and Social Behavior at the National Institute of Mental Health, in Washington, DC. Dr Murray was the "last-standing scientist" at the Surgeon General's program when the dust settled in 1972 (the 5 other scientists had been fired, retired, or simply disappeared), so he "turned out the lights" on the project and fled to Australia for the cover of political safety in Sydney. Subsequent appointments included teaching and re-search at the University of North Carolina–Chapel Hill; Macquarie University in Sydney, Australia; the University of Michigan; the Boys Town Center for the Study of Youth Development; and Kansas State University. His recent research projects are focused on children and violence and include studies mapping children's brain activations—using functional Magnetic Resonance Imaging (fMRI)—while the youngsters view violent and nonviolent videos. Murray has published 14 books and about 90 articles on the social develop-ment of children and youth. His recent book *Children and Television: Fifty Years of Research* (edited with Norma O. Pecora and Ellen A. Wartella) was pub-lished by Erlbaum Publishers in 2007. His most recent article is "Thoughtless Vigilantes: Media Violence and Brain Activation Patterns in Young Viewers," published in the *International Handbook of Media Studies* in 2013.

W. JAMES POTTER, PhD, is professor of communication at the University of California–Santa Barbara. With doctorates in communication theory and instructional systems, he has also taught at Western Michigan University, Florida State University, Indiana University, UCLA, and Stanford University. He is a former editor of the *Journal of Broadcasting & Electronic Media*. He has published numerous scholarly articles and book chapters, as well as 20 books, including *Media Literacy, Media Effects, The 11 Myths of Media Violence, Cognitive Theory of Media Literacy*, and *Arguing for a General Framework for Mass Media Scholarship*.

JACK POWERS, PhD, is associate professor in the Television-Radio Program at the Roy H. Park School of Communications at Ithaca College. He holds a PhD in mass communications from the S. I. Newhouse School of Public Communications at Syracuse University, an MA in journalism from Ohio State University, and a BA in communications and French from the University of Mount Union. He teaches mass media research methods and mass media and behavior courses. His research interests include the influence of entertainment media on the socialization of children, behavior of information users, and entertainment media processes.

MICHAEL RICH, MD, MPH, FAAP, FSAHM, an associate professor at Harvard Medical School and Harvard School of Public Health, came to medicine after a 12-year career as a filmmaker (including serving as assistant director to Akira Kurosawa on *Kagemusha*). As Director of the Center on Media and Child Health (www.cmch.tv) at Boston Children's Hospital, Dr. Rich combines his creative experience with rigorous scientific evidence about the powerful positive and negative effects of media to advise pediatricians and parents how to use media in ways that optimize child development at www.askthemediatrician.org. Recipient of the AAP's Holroyd-Sherry Award and the SAHM New Investigator Award, Dr. Rich has developed media-based research methodologies and authored numerous papers and AAP policy statements, testified to the U.S. Congress, and makes regular national press appearances.

KARYN RIDDLE, PhD, is an assistant professor in the School of Journalism and Mass Communication, University of Wisconsin–Madison. Her research focuses on the psychology of media effects with an emphasis on the effects of exposure to media violence. Most recently, she has explored media violence vividness, the degree to which a violent portrayal is graphic, explicit, and memorable. She also studies children's fear responses to media violence, with a focus on violence in the news. Riddle earned her doctorate in communication at the University of California–Santa Barbara.

DONALD F. ROBERTS, PhD, is the Thomas More Storke Professor Emeritus in the Department of Communication at Stanford University, where he served on the faculty from 1968 to 2009, including stints as department chair and as director of the Institute for Communication Research. Roberts's research examines how children and adolescents use and respond to the mass media, a topic on which he has written extensively (e.g., chapters in the *Handbook of Communication*; the *International Encyclopedia of Communications*; *Learning from Television: Psychological and Education Research*; *Trends in the Well-Being of Children and Youth*; *At the Threshold: The Developing Adolescent*; and *The Handbook of Children and the Media*). He has also authored comprehensive reviews of the research literature on the effects of mass communication for the *Annual Review of Psychology*, for the third edition of the *Handbook of Social Psychology*, and for the *Handbook of Adolescent Psychology*. Roberts's books include *The Process and Effects of Mass Communication*; *Television and Human Behavior*; *It's Not **Only** Rock & Roll: Popular Music in the Lives of Adolescents*; and *Kids and Media in America*. Over the past decade, Roberts has been a co-principal investigator on a series of national surveys of young people's media use, conducted under the auspices of the Kaiser Family Foundation. These studies were the first to examine young people's use of all media (i.e., print, audio, TV, computers, mobile phones), and to document/explore the media-multitasking phenomenon. Roberts helped design a parental advisory system for the computer game industry that was adapted by the International Content Rating Association for use with Internet content. In 1995 he served as a planner and panelist for then Vice President Al Gore's

Conference on Families and Media. Roberts began advising on the development of children's television content in the 1980s and over the years has worked with such children's entertainment companies as Filmation, Nickelodeon, ABC-Disney, Kids WB!, Fox Family, MGM, Nelvana, Sunbow Entertainment, DIC Entertainment, Planet Nemo, and A² Entertainment.

ERICA SCHARRER, PhD, is professor and chair of the Department of Communication at the University of Massachusetts–Amherst. She studies media violence and media and gender, in terms of content patterns, opinions of media influence, media effects, and media literacy. Her recent work includes editing the *Media Effects/Media Psychology* volume of the *International Encyclopedia of Media Studies* (2013) and publishing studies of early adolescents' responses to media literacy curricula in the *Journal of Children and Media*. Her other work has appeared in the journals *Media Psychology*, *Communication Research*, and *Human Communication Research* (among others), and she is coauthor of three books with first author George Comstock, including *Media and the American Child* (2007). She is currently chair of the Children, Adolescents, and Media division of the International Communication Association. Scharrer earned her doctorate from Syracuse University in 1998.

LAURA STOCKDALE is a PhD candidate in developmental psychology at Loyola University in Chicago. Her research focuses on the influence of media violence exposure on relational and physical aggression, empathy, and prosocial behavior.

VICTOR C. STRASBURGER, MD, is Distinguished Professor of Pediatrics and founding chief, Division of Adolescent Medicine in the Department of Pediatrics at the University of New Mexico School of Medicine. He has published 13 books and nearly 200 journal articles and book chapters on the subjects of children, adolescents, and the media and adolescent medicine. His current textbook is *Children, Adolescents, and the Media* (3rd. ed., 2014), written with Barbara Wilson and Amy Jordan. He has lectured in 47 of 50 states and on five continents, and been featured on *Oprah*, *The Today Show*, *CBS This Morning*, and National Public Radio, and appeared frequently in the national print media. He has also authored or coauthored most of the American Academy of Pediatrics' policy statements on children, adolescents, and the media, including the 2009 statement on media violence.

LARAMIE D. TAYLOR, PhD, is an associate professor of communication at the University of California–Davis. Taylor's research investigates how people use media to feel socially connected and how media use can shape social interactions. This interest in questions of media influence can be traced back to his experiences teaching composition, American literature, and media literacy to high school students in Minnesota. Taylor also sees public outreach as an important part of his work. In addition to giving talks to civic and educational groups, he recently offered expert testimony on media and violence before the California State Senate. Taylor received his PhD from the University of Michigan in 2005.

WAYNE A. WARBURTON, PhD, is a senior lecturer in developmental psychology and deputy director of the Children and Families Research Centre at Macquarie University. He is also a registered psychologist and has a strong research interest in the fields of aggressive behavior, media psychology, and parenting. He has received a number of awards for his scholarship, including the Macquarie Foundation Science Prize and two awards from the Australian Psychological Society. He has several dozen publications in scientific journals and books, primarily on topics around aggressive behavior and the impact of violent and prosocial media. He is coauthor of the International Society for Research on Aggression's *Statement on Media Violence*, the Society for Psychological Study of Social Issues' *Research Summary on Media Violence*, and the testimony of world experts on violent video game effects in the Gruel Amicus Curiae Brief for the U.S. Supreme Court case of *California vs. Entertainment Merchants*. His most recent book (edited with Danya Braunstein) is *Growing Up Fast and Furious: Reviewing the Impacts of Violent and Sexualized Media on Children*.

BARBARA J. WILSON, PhD, is the Executive Vice Provost of Academic Affairs at the University of Illinois at Urbana–Champaign and also the Kathryn Lee Baynes Dallenbach Professor in the Department of Communication. Her research focuses on the social and psychological effects of the media on youth. She is coauthor of three book volumes of the National Television Violence Study (1997–1998). She also coedited the *Handbook of Children, Media, and Development* (2008) and has published over 100 articles, chapters, and technical reports on media effects and their implications for media policy. Professor Wilson currently serves on the editorial boards of five academic journals, including *Journal of Communication*, *Media Psychology*, and the *Journal of Media and Children*. In 2008 she was elected as fellow of the International Communication Association. She has served as a research consultant for Nickelodeon, the National Association of Television Program Executives, Discovery Channel Pictures, and the Centers for Disease Control and Prevention.

Index